Cybersecurity Thre Malware Trends, and Strategies

Second Edition

Discover risk mitigation strategies for modern threats to your organization

Tim Rains

BIRMINGHAM—MUMBAI

Cybersecurity Threats, Malware Trends, and Strategies
Second Edition

Senior Publishing Product Manager: Aaron Tanna
Acquisition Editor – Peer Reviews: Gaurav Gavas
Project Editor: Meenakshi Vijay
Content Development Editor: Liam Thomas Draper
Copy Editor: Safis Editing
Technical Editor: Aneri Patel
Proofreader: Safis Editing
Indexer: Sejal Dsilva
Presentation Designer: Rajesh Shirsath
Developer Relations Marketing Executive: Meghal Patel

First published: May 2020
Second edition: January 2023

Production reference: 1170123

Published by Packt Publishing Ltd.
Livery Place
35 Livery Street
Birmingham
B3 2PB, UK.

ISBN 978-1-80461-367-2

www.packt.com

Foreword

Being a security leader in this day and age is a bit like putting on the comedy and tragedy masks you see in theaters. Some incidents that come across security leaders' desks are comedies of entirely avoidable errors. Others are tragedies that are completely out of the control of victimized companies, and there is no hope but to react to such things. Unpatched vulnerabilities and supply chain security issues come to mind. There are two things, one being very preventable with the right processes or technology, and the other where you have no choice but to respond to the downstream effects. With the volume of commodity attacks hitting infrastructures every second, CISOs have little to no room for error. Knowing there is no such thing as 100% secure anything, a security program must address the most likely and most impactful risks.

With that in mind, it's critical to find the most significant source of vulnerability and protect against it repeatedly. As a CISO that has run security operations for four major brands, each company will have unique challenges that influence your ability to respond, such as its culture, industry limitations, or just plain resistance to change. Security leadership's job is to fight through these areas of resistance to get to aligned outcomes that achieve the primary mission of keeping the company, customers, and employees safe from harm from a cyber incident.

There are many tools at the disposal of leaders in dealing with these challenges. I've found that my best source of knowledge is connecting with peers who have been through the challenges and problems I've faced. The tactile knowledge of a round table is unmatched in my experience of what you can get from any conference session or training room. That is one reason I'm so excited to see *Cybersecurity Threats, Malware Trends, and Strategies* revised by Tim Rains. Tim has been at the table at more of this type of discussion than anyone.

I've known Tim Rains for over 12 years. The only person that knows as many CISOs as I do is Tim. Tim's career has been driven by hearing complex problems from leaders and centering them on rational solutions. Tim has had the advantage of sitting at round tables with some of the best security leadership in the industry. Combining that with leadership positions in some of the largest fortune 500 companies, he has a unique, informed perspective. I've had the pleasure of being a part of many of these round tables as my peers battle with some of the most challenging problems in the industry. In several cases, there are no good answers, and it's a best-effort situation because of limitations in technology or industry forces.

Tim has provided some of his best lessons in this book. He brings forward all his years of industry knowledge and in-depth research on topics security leaders care about. CISOs need help with aligning their operational intent with strategic objectives. Starting with a good set of fundamentals is critical to having a sound, dependable approach to cyber threats. As outlined in the book, the fundamentals are continuously attacked by the usual suspects: unpatched systems, misconfigurations, social engineering, insider threat, and weak passwords. My experience has taught me that these challenges transcend industries, budgets, and organizational talent. CISOs must ask themselves what parts of their programs address these baseline challenges and how effective those programs are. From there, CISOs must connect the dots of how those fundamental programs support the more significant strategic initiatives. No magic solution or consultative service can do it for you. It's putting in the time to understand the supporting data and connecting with leaders across your enterprise. Tim provides an excellent guide on accessing the data and making it relevant to every leader.

This is an important and timely book on how leaders can get a handle on the comedy and tragedy of cybersecurity. What is crucial for leaders is to have a definable approach to understanding their risk, know the most common security shortcomings, and understand the strategies to mitigate impacts. *Cybersecurity Threats, Malware Trends, and Strategies* will give you the guardrails that a CISO, CTO, CIO, or senior leader in an organization will need to get started. For that novice in the language of cyber security, an education on what matters when it comes to protecting your company is within each chapter, and those seasoned vets will see a framework for testing theories on addressing threats. The forces at play multiply for leaders as malware doubles year over year, regulatory issues require greater constraint, and the ease of automated attacks grows. Leaders must ask themselves serious questions, such as do I know the threats facing my organization? Do I have appropriate responses to those threats? Is there an approach to staying knowledgeable of impactful industry trends? Do I have a cybersecurity strategy that aligns with my risk profile? If you don't know the answers to these questions, this book will get you started on the pathway to being confident in your future responses.

Timothy Youngblood, CISSP

Contributors

About the author

Tim Rains is an internationally recognized cybersecurity executive, strategist, advisor, and author. He has held the most senior cybersecurity advisor roles at both Microsoft and Amazon Web Services. Tim has experience across multiple cybersecurity and business disciplines including incident response, crisis communications, vulnerability management, threat intelligence, among others. Tim is currently Vice President, Trust & Cyber Risk at T-Mobile. Tim is the author of the popular book, *Cybersecurity Threats, Malware Trends, and Strategies*, published by Packt Publishing

I'd like to thank my wife, Brenda, for encouraging me to write a second edition of this book and for her assistance and patience. Thank you Karen Scarfone for being our Technical Reviewer extraordinaire. I'd also like to thank Liam Draper, our Development Editor, and the entire team at Packt Publishing for making this book a reality.

About the reviewer

Karen Scarfone is the Principal Consultant for Scarfone Cybersecurity. She develops cybersecurity publications for federal agencies and other organizations. She was formerly a Senior Computer Scientist at the National Institute of Standards and Technology (NIST). Since 2003, Karen has co-authored over 100 NIST publications on a wide variety of cybersecurity topics. In addition, she has co-authored or contributed to 18 books and published over 200 articles on cybersecurity topics. Karen holds master's degrees in computer science and technical writing.

Thanks to my husband, John—for everything.

Join our community on Discord

Join our community's Discord space for discussions with the author and other readers:

`https://packt.link/SecNet`

Table of Contents

Preface

Imagine you are in a submarine submerged hundreds of feet below the surface surrounded by dark, freezing water. The hull of the submarine is under constant immense pressure from all directions. A single mistake in the design, construction, or operation of the submarine spells disaster for it and its entire crew.

This is analogous to the challenge that **Chief Information Security Officers (CISOs)** and their teams face today. Their organizations are surrounded on the Internet by badness that is constantly probing for ways to penetrate and compromise their IT infrastructures. The people in their organizations receive wave after wave of social engineering attacks designed to trick them into making poor trust decisions that will undermine the controls that their security teams have implemented. The specters of ransomware and data breaches continue to haunt CISOs, **Chief Information Officers (CIOs)**, and **Chief Technology Officers (CTOs)** of the most sophisticated organizations in the world.

After conducting hundreds of incident response investigations for Microsoft's enterprise customers, publishing thousands of pages of threat intelligence, and assisting some of **Amazon Web Services' (AWS)** largest customers, I have had the opportunity to learn from and advise literally thousands of businesses and public sector organizations in almost every country around the world. I wrote this book to share some of the insights and lessons I've learned during this extraordinary journey.

The views and opinions expressed in this book are my own personal opinions and not those of my current or past employers.

Who this book is for

Chief Information Security Officers (CISOs) and aspiring CISOs, **Chief Security Officers (CSOs)**, **Chief Technology Officers (CTOs)**, **Chief Information Officers (CIOs)**, cybersecurity professionals, compliance and audit professionals, senior IT management with cybersecurity responsibilities, vendors' cybersecurity professional services consultants and salespeople, computer hobbyists with an interest in cybersecurity, and university level students aspiring to become cybersecurity professionals would all benefit from reading this book.

Readers should have basic knowledge of **Information Technology (IT)**, with some insight into IT challenges in large-scale, complex enterprise IT environments. Intermediate knowledge of networking (TCP/IP networks) and software development principles, people management experience and insights into how enterprise scale organizations generally operate, and knowledge of basic cybersecurity concepts would all be useful as well.

What this book covers

Chapter 1, *Introduction*, discusses the most common ways that enterprise IT environments get initially compromised and how to mitigate them. This will prepare you to evaluate cybersecurity strategies that are designed to mitigate intrusion attempts (covered in later chapters).

Chapter 2, *What to Know about Threat Intelligence*, explains what threat intelligence is, how to determine good intelligence from bad, and how enterprise cybersecurity teams use it.

Chapter 3, *Using Vulnerability Trends to Reduce Risk and Costs*, covers what security vulnerabilities are, how they are scored, and the long-term industry disclosure trends across major vendors, operating systems, and browsers. This chapter also provides tips and tricks for running an enterprise vulnerability management program and how threat intelligence (covered in *Chapter 2*, *What to Know about Threat Intelligence*) can be integrated.

Chapter 4, *The Evolution of Malware*, provides a unique data-driven perspective of how malware has evolved around the world over the past 10+ years. This will help you understand the types of malware threats you face, and which malware threats are most and least prevalent.

This chapter also provides a deep dive into the evolution of ransomware – the most feared threat for security teams.

Chapter 5, Internet-Based Threats, examines some of the ways that attackers have been using the Internet and how these methods have evolved over time. Several types of threats are examined including phishing attacks, drive-by download attacks, malware hosting sites, and Distributed Denial of Service (DDoS) attacks.

Chapter 6, The Roles Governments Play in Cybersecurity, explains that many CISOs rely on governments to help them achieve their objectives by setting and regulating industry security standards, while others look to governments as a source of threat intelligence and guidance, while yet other CISOs view governments as threats to their organizations. What role do governments really play in cybersecurity? This chapter explores this question and help you decide whether to treat governments as threats.

Chapter 7, Government Access to Data, many CISOs and security teams view governments as threats to their organizations' data. This is especially true of organizations based outside of the United States. Why is this and what do they know that you don't? This chapter will examine the threat of government access to data and how to mitigate it.

Chapter 8, Ingredients for a Successful Cybersecurity Strategy, discusses developing a cybersecurity strategy, which is necessary, but not a guarantee of success by itself. There are several other ingredients that are necessary for a successful cybersecurity program. This chapter describes each of these ingredients in detail. This will give you the best chance of success for their own cybersecurity strategy.

Chapter 9, Cybersecurity Strategies, critically evaluates the major cybersecurity strategies that have been employed in the industry over the past 20 years, including Zero Trust. This chapter shows you how to evaluate the effectiveness of cybersecurity strategies.

Chapter 10, Strategy Implementation, provides an example of how to implement one of the best cybersecurity strategies. This chapter illustrates how an attack-centric strategy that leverages the intrusion kill chain and MITRE ATT&CK® can be implemented.

Chapter 11, Measuring Performance and Effectiveness, examines one of the challenges that CISOs and security teams have always had: how to measure the effectiveness of their cybersecurity programs. It's hard to prove that something bad didn't happen because of the work of the cybersecurity team - this chapter provides guidance on how to measure the performance and effectiveness of cybersecurity strategies.

Chapter 12, Modern Approaches to Security and Compliance, provides insights into how the cloud is the great cybersecurity talent amplifier. This chapter describes how Application Programming Interfaces (APIs) and automation can be leveraged to support a highly effective cybersecurity strategy.

To get the most out of this book

- You'll already understand basic IT concepts and have some experience of using, implementing, and/or operating IT systems and applications.

- Possessing some knowledge of basic cybersecurity concepts will make this book an easier read.

- Experience of managing enterprise IT, compliance, and/or cybersecurity teams will be helpful, but is not strictly required.

- You'll bring curiosity and the desire to learn about key aspects of cybersecurity that CISOs and CSOs of large organizations manage in the course of doing their jobs.

Download the color images

We also provide a PDF file that has color images of the screenshots/diagrams used in this book. You can download it here: `https://packt.link/INq4w`.

Conventions used

There are a number of text conventions used throughout this book.

`CodeInText`: Indicates code words in text, database table names, folder names, filenames, file extensions, pathnames, dummy URLs, user input, and Twitter handles. For example: "Attackers could be registering and using domain names in this ccTLD to catch web browser users that type `.om` instead of `.com`."

Any code snippet is written as follows:

```
void func(int index, int value)
{
    char buf[4];
    buf[index] = value;
}
```

Bold: Indicates a new term, an important word, or words that you see on the screen. For instance, words in menus or dialog boxes appear in the text like this. For example: "DevOps typically includes concepts like continuous testing, **Continuous Integration (CI)**, **Continuous Delivery (CD)**, continuous deployment, and continuous performance monitoring."

 Warnings or important notes appear like this.

 Tips and tricks appear like this.

Get in touch

Feedback from our readers is always welcome.

General feedback: Email feedback@packtpub.com and mention the book's title in the subject of your message. If you have questions about any aspect of this book, please email us at questions@packtpub.com.

Errata: Although we have taken every care to ensure the accuracy of our content, mistakes do happen. If you have found a mistake in this book, we would be grateful if you reported this to us. Please visit http://www.packtpub.com/submit-errata, click **Submit Errata**, and fill in the form.

Piracy: If you come across any illegal copies of our works in any form on the internet, we would be grateful if you would provide us with the location address or website name. Please contact us at copyright@packtpub.com with a link to the material.

If you are interested in becoming an author: If there is a topic that you have expertise in and you are interested in either writing or contributing to a book, please visit http://authors.packtpub.com.

Share your thoughts

Once you've read *Cybersecurity Threats, Malware Trends, and Strategies, Second Edition*, we'd love to hear your thoughts! Scan the QR code below to go straight to the Amazon review page for this book and share your feedback.

https://packt.link/r/1804613673

Your review is important to us and the tech community and will help us make sure we're delivering excellent quality content.

Download a free PDF copy of this book

Thanks for purchasing this book!

Do you like to read on the go but are unable to carry your print books everywhere? Is your eBook purchase not compatible with the device of your choice?

Don't worry, now with every Packt book you get a DRM-free PDF version of that book at no cost.

Read anywhere, any place, on any device. Search, copy, and paste code from your favorite technical books directly into your application.

The perks don't stop there, you can get exclusive access to discounts, newsletters, and great free content in your inbox daily

Follow these simple steps to get the benefits:

1. Scan the QR code or visit the link below

https://packt.link/free-ebook/9781804613672

2. Submit your proof of purchase
3. That's it! We'll send your free PDF and other benefits to your email directly

1

Introduction

After advising thousands of commercial sector and public sector organizations all over the world while working as a security advisor at Microsoft and then **Amazon Web Services (AWS)**, I concluded that most organizations do not have a cybersecurity strategy that their security executives or security teams can articulate. In fact, thinking about all the security briefings I provided and meetings I had with executives and their teams over the last couple of decades, I recall meeting fewer than 10 organizations that had a written cybersecurity strategy that the **Chief Information Security Officers (CISOs)** could describe and that security team members could repeat. Instead of discussing cybersecurity domains such as Risk Management and Identity and Access Management, I found myself advising CISOs on cybersecurity strategies almost exclusively. This isn't surprising given that there are plenty of sources of information on all the cybersecurity domains described in various industry frameworks and certifications, but strategy typically isn't among them.

Given this, I decided to write a book about cybersecurity strategies for CISOs, **Chief Information Officers (CIOs)**, **Chief Technology Officers (CTOs)**, aspiring cybersecurity executives, cybersecurity teams, and **Information Technology (IT)** professionals that have significant cybersecurity responsibilities. *Cybersecurity Threats, Malware Trends, and Strategies* (Rains) was published by Packt in May, 2020. The response to the book in the industry was very positive; cybersecurity strategies continue to garner overwhelming interest. This is an updated, second edition of that book.

Why does the topic of cybersecurity strategies garner so much interest? Cybersecurity has never been more important to commercial enterprises and public sector organizations. As the world has become more and more dependent on technology and the internet, threat actors have flourished.

The world's economies literally depend on technology constantly operating, without disruption. No industry or geography is immune to cyber-attacks.

In 2021, the global cybersecurity industry was estimated to be valued at around $140 billion. Combine that with an estimated **Compound Annual Growth Rate (CAGR)** of 12% to 15% and this results in an estimated industry market size of around $375 billion before the end of this decade. More and more cybersecurity vendors join the chorus in using the specter of the "ever-changing threat landscape" to market and sell their wares to anxious and sometimes punch-drunk organizations across every industry. What started out as a relatively simple concept to use computers to make faster and potentially better business decisions has led to a proliferation of technologies, regulations, and standards that require an ever-expanding set of people, processes, and technologies to protect them.

For example, when I started working at Microsoft in the late 90s, they had little to no material revenue from developing and selling cybersecurity products. In 2021, revenue from Microsoft's cybersecurity business exceeded $10 billion (Jakkal, 2021). In 2016, I could walk customers through Microsoft's relatively large and complicated security reference model crammed into a single PowerPoint slide. Over the following five years, this evolved into what they now call "Microsoft Cybersecurity Reference Architectures," which includes no less than nine different reference models (Microsoft Corporation, 2021).

When I started working at AWS in 2017, they had around 40 cloud services in their portfolio. When I left AWS almost four and a half years later, they offered over 300 cloud services and had a growing portfolio of security services. Besides the introduction of new services, existing services were constantly improved, and their functionality expanded. Many IT teams that took the time to evaluate AWS' services before they adopted them would have to re-evaluate them annually to ensure they still fully understood them.

Combine the growth from just these two vendors with the growth of other major IT and cloud vendors (Oracle, IBM, Google, etc) that enterprises typically also leverage, and *thousands* of cybersecurity vendors all vying for their business, and you have a *lot* of options, complexity, noise, and confusion.

Of course, the backdrop to all this technology proliferation, industry growth, and complexity is the constant drumbeat of successful cybersecurity attacks. New technologies have also enabled attackers to increase the speed and impact of their attacks. New ways of performing large international financial transactions have enabled attackers to build sophisticated business models based on extortion and human-operated ransomware.

If you skipped reading the preface in this book (the submarine analogy), please read it as it captures the pressurized environment that all enterprises operate in today.

Subsequently, many of the organizations that I advised would often ask very basic questions. *Which cybersecurity capabilities are most important? What do we do first? How do you prioritize requirements and capabilities? What are other organizations in our industry doing? Do you have any threat intelligence from other organizations in our industry? Is there an algorithm that helps us determine the right priorities?* After having thousands of these discussions, and reading between the lines, what they were really asking me about was a cybersecurity strategy. The fundamental question they were asking me was: *which cybersecurity strategy or combination of strategies will be most effective for our organization given the industry we are in, the locations where we do business, our regulatory compliance requirements, and the appetite for risk our business has?*

I wrote this book with this question in mind; I hope it contains some insights that help you answer this question for your organization. I mentioned that I wrote this book for CISOs, aspiring CISOs, and other professionals that work with CISOs. Did you know that there are different types of CISOs? Whether you are a CISO yourself, a security team member supporting a CISO, a salesperson trying to sell to a CISO, or a member of a Board of Directors that a CISO reports to, understanding the type of CISO you are working with can help make communicating with them a lot more predictable, efficient, and perhaps even enjoyable.

Different types of CISOs: "The CISO Spectrum"

After spending so much time with CISO over the past two decades, I can tell you with confidence that there are different types of CISOs. Different types of CISOs can have different approaches to cybersecurity that dictate, or at least strongly influence, the focus of their security programs.

I call this list of types of CISOs the "CISO Spectrum." This list isn't exhaustive; it simply contains the types of CISOs I have encountered over the past 20 years of my career:

- **Type 1**: The IT Director with cybersecurity responsibility. They were perhaps the most technical of all the types of CISOs I encountered, typically having had more IT expertise than cybersecurity expertise. They knew all about the IT infrastructure that they supported and were trusted members of the IT leadership team. They were assigned cybersecurity as part of their job function. They had the aptitude and the desire to learn about security and compliance, sometimes purely out of a sense of self-preservation. Their comfort zone was IT systems, and they were keen for insights and help with cybersecurity.

- **Type 2**: The Incident Responder. Some of the CISOs I met became CISOs because they were the go-to person for responding to incidents for their organization. They became incident response and remediation experts. Their organizations trust them during crises and look to them to help the organization avoid crisis situations in the future. They tended to be threat intelligence geeks and focused on making it harder for attackers to succeed using their technical knowledge. They had a deep knowledge of IT systems as they were typically involved in building and administrating them earlier in their career.

- **Type 3**: The Compliance or Audit Expert. These folks tended to focus on control sets that helped meet regulated and industry standards. Their experience in managing compliance or audit programs gave them deep expertise in managing large control sets in large complex IT environments that were required to comply with multiple standards, such as PCI, CMMC, NIST SP 800-53, ISO 27000, etc. They'd rather discuss control sets and compliance challenges than threats or threat actors.

- **Type 4**: The Policy Wonk. I met two different types of CISOs that rely on their strong policy backgrounds:

  - **Governance, Risk, and Compliance (GRC)** policy experts: These CISOs typically had lots of experience writing and enforcing GRC-related policies. To get things done, they relied on policies the same way police rely on laws.

  - Cybersecurity Public Policy experts: These CISOs typically weren't IT experts or enterprise cybersecurity experts. Rather, they tended to be attorneys with deep public policy and privacy expertise. They had experience with national cybersecurity policies, that is, cybersecurity policies that national or federal governments implement to protect citizens, and private sector and public sector organizations within their borders.

- **Type 5**: The Strategist. These CISOs tended to focus on aligning resources around frameworks. To do this, they required some cybersecurity expertise along with some business acumen. Many of these folks had experience in at least a couple of different cybersecurity domains, like Incident Response and Risk Management. They were always on the lookout for technologies or processes that would help them address known gaps in their capabilities and improve the effectiveness of their strategies.

- **Type 6**: The Risk Expert. In my experience, this type of CISO was rarer than the rest. Their area of expertise was **risk**. They approached cybersecurity like an actuary using quantitative risk calculations to determine areas of investment for their cybersecurity program.

If I remember correctly, I met this type of CISO almost exclusively when advising insurance companies. They always seemed to report to the **Chief Risk Officer (CRO)**.

- **Type 7**: The Cybersecurity Advisor. These CISOs saw themselves as advisors to the businesses they supported. Typically, their position was that they didn't actually "own" anything – the business did. They advised the business to make cybersecurity investments but didn't necessarily design and operate cybersecurity capabilities themselves – the IT team would instead. This type of CISO was typically able to avoid the conflict that naturally occurs when there is tension between the freedom the business wants and the control necessary to defend the business' assets. Many CISOs of this ilk didn't believe their role was to provide oversight, just advice.

- **Type 8**: The Trusted Business Executive. These CISOs weren't cybersecurity experts and sometimes weren't IT experts either. They were executives that had proven themselves to business leadership by managing different parts of the business or particularly difficult or important projects or initiatives. Leadership trusted them because of their track record of success at the company. Since they had proven they could manage challenging assignments, they were given cybersecurity to manage. These businesses believed that these CISOs would succeed given their ability to lead and manage, and that cybersecurity expertise was not a prerequisite for success. Many of the CISOs that I met in this category were attorneys.

That is the CISO Spectrum. The types of CISOs I discussed probably describe 90% of the thousands of CISOs I have met. I don't view any of them as better than the others; they simply have different backgrounds and approaches to cybersecurity. However, frequently, factors within the organizations that CISOs support dictate the approach to cybersecurity they take, regardless of their backgrounds or personal preferences. Many CISOs I met were frustrated because they wanted to be a specific type of CISO while their organizations demanded a different type. Proving once again that even at the top of a business discipline, you can't always get what you want.

I learned to identify the type of CISO I was advising as quickly as possible in order to make the conversation more meaningful for us both. For example, if a CISO was really interested in discussing how a new exploit worked, it would be a short and annoying conversation trying to discuss Risk Management with them. For this reason, many of the sales teams that I supported at Microsoft and AWS were intimidated by the CISOs of their accounts. Once they learned about the CISO Spectrum, it made it easier for them to understand the CISOs they supported and connect them with the people and resources that could really address the things they were most interested in.

In most cases, this would earn some trust with CISOs because the salespeople became perceived as helpful and not just interested in sales transactions. Recognizing the type of CISO you support can help you become a trusted advisor to them.

Next, let's examine how enterprise IT environments get compromised in the first place. This is key to understanding, developing, and evaluating the effectiveness of cybersecurity strategies for enterprise IT environments.

How organizations get initially compromised and the cybersecurity fundamentals

The foundation of an effective cybersecurity strategy is what I call the "cybersecurity fundamentals." A solid foundation is required for a successful strategy. The cybersecurity fundamentals are based on decades of threat intelligence that I discuss in detail later in this book. After performing hundreds of incident response investigations and studying Microsoft's and other vendors' threat intelligence for over a decade, I can tell you with confidence that there are only five ways that organizations get *initially* compromised. After the initial compromise, there are many, many **Tactics, Techniques, and Procedures (TTPs)** that attackers can use to move laterally, steal credentials, compromise infrastructure, remain persistent, gain illicit access to information, destroy data and infrastructure, etc. Some of these have been around for decades and some are newer and novel.

The five ways that organizations get initially compromised are what I call the "Cybersecurity Usual Suspects":

1. Unpatched vulnerabilities
2. Security misconfigurations
3. Weak, leaked, and stolen credentials
4. Social engineering
5. Insider threats

The cybersecurity fundamentals are part of a strategy that focuses on mitigating the Cybersecurity Usual Suspects. Let's look at each one of these in more detail, starting with the exploitation of unpatched vulnerabilities.

Unpatched vulnerabilities

A vulnerability is a flaw in software or hardware design and/or the underlying programming code that allows an attacker to make the affected system do something that wasn't intended.

The most severe vulnerabilities allow attackers to take complete control of the affected system, running arbitrary code of their choice. Less severe vulnerabilities lead to systems disclosing data in ways that weren't intended or denying service to legitimate users. In *Chapter 3, Using Vulnerability Trends to Reduce Risk and Costs*, I provide a deep dive into vulnerability management and some of the key vulnerability disclosure trends over the past 20+ years. I'll save that in-depth discussion for that chapter, but I will provide some more context here.

Attackers have been using vulnerabilities to compromise systems at scale since at least the days of Code Red and Nimda in 2001. In 2003, SQL Slammer and Blaster successfully disrupted the internet and compromised hundreds of thousands of systems worldwide by exploiting unpatched vulnerabilities in Microsoft Windows operating systems. In the years following these attacks, a cottage industry developed an ongoing effort to help enterprise organizations, those with the most complex environments, inventory their IT systems, identify vulnerabilities in them, deploy mitigations for vulnerabilities, and patch them. By the end of 2022, there were over 192,000 vulnerabilities disclosed in software and hardware products from across the industry, on record, in the National Vulnerability Database (National Vulnerability Database, n.d.). As you'll read in a later chapter, the number of vulnerabilities disclosed across the industry surged 128% between 2016 and 2017, reaching levels never seen before. The number of vulnerability disclosures has increased year over year, every year since, reaching over 25,000 disclosures in 2022.

An economy has evolved around the supply and demand for vulnerabilities and exploits, with a varied list of participants including vendors, attackers, defenders, various commercial entities, governments, and others. The number of participants in this economy and their relative sophistication makes it harder for organizations to protect themselves from the exploitation of vulnerabilities in their IT environments by pressurizing the associated risks. Using unpatched vulnerabilities is a mainstay of attackers' toolkits.

Organizations that are highly efficient and competent at vulnerability management make it much harder for attackers to successfully attack them. A well-run vulnerability management program is a fundamental component and a critical requirement of an effective cybersecurity strategy. Without it, organizations' cybersecurity efforts will fail regardless of the other investments they make. This point is important enough that we should reiterate it. Unpatched vulnerabilities in operating systems, and the underlying platform components that advanced cybersecurity capabilities rely on, enable attackers to completely undermine the effectiveness of these investments. Failing to efficiently address ongoing vulnerability disclosures in the "trusted computing base" that your systems rely on renders it untrustworthy.

An accurate inventory of all IT assets is critical for a vulnerability management program. Organizations that can't perform accurate and timely inventories of all their IT assets, scan all IT assets for vulnerabilities, and efficiently mitigate and/or patch those vulnerabilities shouldn't bother making other investments until this is addressed. If your organization falls into this category, please reread the *Preface* section of this book and recall the submarine analogy I introduced. If the CISO and vulnerability management program managers rely on their organization's IT group or other internal partners to provide IT asset inventories, those inventories need to be complete – not just inventories of systems they want to comply with.

Assets that don't show up in inventories won't get scanned or patched and will become the weak link in the security chain you are trying to create. Very often, this is at odds with the uptime objectives that IT organizations are measured against, because patching vulnerabilities increases the number of system reboots and, subsequently, decreases uptime even if everything goes smoothly. My advice in scenarios where asset inventories are provided by parties other than the vulnerability management program itself is to trust but verify. Spend the extra effort and budget to continually check asset inventories against reality. This includes those official and unofficial development and test environments that have been responsible for so many breaches in the industry over the years. Shadow IT and unofficial cloud accounts also fall into this category.

If the sources of asset inventories resist this requirement or fail to provide accurate, timely inventories, this represents the type of risk that the board of directors should be informed of. Providing them with a view of the estimated percentage of total asset inventory currently not managed by your vulnerability management program should result in the sources of asset inventories reprioritizing their work and the disruption of a dangerous status quo.

 Tip: **Cloud Access Security Brokers (CASB)** and Attack Surface Management products can help identify unknown and rogue assets. Today, most Attack Surface Management tools focus on external (internet-facing) assets, but the industry is poised to include internal assets in the scope of the tools on offer.

I'll discuss vulnerability management in more detail in *Chapter 3, Using Vulnerability Trends to Reduce Risk and Costs*. I'll also discuss vulnerability management in *Chapter 13, Modern Approaches to Security and Compliance*, on cloud computing and containers. The cloud can render the old-fashioned methods of inventorying, scanning, and patching security vulnerabilities obsolete.

Of course, one challenge with the approach I just described is environments that have embraced **Bring Your Own Device (BYOD)** policies that allow information workers to use their personal mobile devices to access and process enterprise data. The underlying question is whether enterprise vulnerability management teams should inventory and manage personal devices.

This debate is one reason why many security professionals originally dubbed BYOD "Bring Your Own Disaster." Different organizations take different approaches when answering this question. Some organizations give employees corporate-owned and fully managed mobile devices, while others require personal devices to enroll in enterprise mobile device management programs. I've also seen a more passive management model, where users are required to have an access PIN on their devices and aren't allowed to connect to their employers' networks if the latest mobile operating system version isn't installed on their devices. Some organizations use **Network Access Control (NAC)** or **Network Access Protection (NAP)** technologies to help enforce policies related to the health of systems connecting to their network. Some vendors have made this model a cornerstone for the "Zero Trust" architectures they offer to their customers. They won't trust endpoints unless their health has been verified to meet the organization's mobile device security policies. This typically includes running the latest operating system version, being patched for known vulnerabilities including the latest vulnerabilities, and having up-to-date anti-malware signatures installed. These characteristics make endpoints more trustworthy because they meet minimum security standards, thus reducing the likelihood that they are compromised and could provide attackers with entry into the corporate network. If an endpoint doesn't meet these minimum standards, remote connection requests from it are refused until it complies with the policy and has a "clean bill of health."

Minimizing the number of unpatched systems allowed to connect to enterprise networks is a best practice but can be challenging to accomplish depending on corporate cultures and mobile device policies. For example, who wants to wait for security updates to install and reboot their system when they were simply trying to get access to a document on the corporate network before their flight? Many "road warriors" tend to avoid connecting to their corporate networks for this reason, thus leading to worse, not better, endpoint security. Collecting data that helps security teams understand the risk that mobile devices pose to their environments is very helpful for a rationalized risk-based approach.

Next, we'll consider security misconfigurations. Like unpatched vulnerabilities, security misconfigurations can potentially enable attackers to take a range of actions on a system including disrupting its operation, stealing information, lowering security settings, disabling security features, seizing control of it, and using it to attack other systems.

Security misconfigurations

Security misconfigurations can be present in a system as a default setting, like a pre-set key or password that is the same on every system manufactured by a vendor. Security misconfigurations can also be introduced gradually as a system's configuration changes incrementally as it's managed over time. After performing hundreds of incident response investigations while I was on the customer-facing incident response team at Microsoft, I can tell you that a significant percentage of systems get initially compromised through security misconfigurations.

This is especially true of internet-facing systems such as web servers, firewalls, and other systems found in enterprise **Demilitarized Zones (DMZs)**. Once a misconfiguration enables an attacker to control a system in a DMZ or use it to send authenticated commands on the attacker's behalf (such as a server-side request forgery attack), the attacker aspires to use the system to gain access to other systems in the DMZ and ultimately get access to systems inside the internal firewall of the organization. This has been a common pattern in attackers' playbooks for 20 years or more.

Security misconfigurations have also plagued endpoint devices, such as PCs, smartphones, and **Internet of Things (IoT)** devices. The infrastructures that these endpoints connect to, such as wireless access points, are also frequently probed by attackers for common misconfigurations. Security misconfigurations have also been an issue in **Industrial Control Systems (ICS)**. For example, one scenario with ICS that has burned security teams in the past is "fall back to last known status," which can override more recent security configuration changes in favor of former, less secure settings. Hardcoded credentials and vulnerable default configurations have long haunted manufacturers of all sorts of software and hardware across the industry.

A well-run vulnerability management program typically includes identifying security misconfigurations as part of its scope. Many of the same vulnerability scanners and tools that are used to identify and patch security vulnerabilities are also capable of identifying security misconfigurations and providing guidance on how to address them. Some vulnerability scanners can determine if systems' configurations meet industry standards, like **Center for Internet Security (CIS)** Benchmarks (Center for Internet Security, n.d.) or an organization's own internal security standards. Again, organizations should forego big investments in advanced cybersecurity capabilities if they aren't already very proficient at identifying and mitigating security misconfigurations in their environment. There's no point in spending a lot of money and effort looking for the **Advanced Persistent Threat (APT)** in an environment if attackers can use decades-old lists of hardcoded passwords, which are available on the internet, to successfully compromise and move around the environment. Even if CISOs found such attackers in their IT environment, they would be powerless to exorcise them with unmanaged common security misconfigurations present.

Some of the biggest breaches in history were a result of an initial compromise through a combination of unpatched vulnerabilities and security misconfigurations. Both can be managed through a well-run vulnerability management program.

This is a non-optional discipline in any cybersecurity strategy, that should be resourced accordingly. Don't forget, it is easier to manage things you can measure; complete, accurate, and timely IT asset inventories are critical for vulnerability management programs. Trust but verify asset inventories, always. It's worth keeping in mind that the cloud provides several advantages over the old on-premises IT world. I'll discuss this in detail in *Chapter 13, Modern Approaches to Security and Compliance*, in this book.

Security misconfigurations can be present by default with new hardware and software or can creep in over time. Another ongoing threat that requires constant attention is that of compromised credentials. Organizations must constantly and proactively work to mitigate this threat vector.

Weak, leaked, and stolen credentials

Compromised IT environments due to weak, leaked, or stolen credentials are common. There are several ways that credentials get leaked and stolen, including social engineering such as phishing, malware that does keystroke logging or steals credentials from operating systems and browsers, and compromised systems that cache, store, and/or process credentials. Sometimes, developers put projects on publicly available code-sharing sites but forget that their code contains secrets such as keys and passwords. Old development and test environments that are abandoned but still running will ultimately yield credentials to attackers after not being patched over time.

Massive lists of stolen and leaked credentials have been discovered on the internet over the years. In addition to these lists, the availability of **High-Performance Computing Clusters** (HPC) and GPU-based password cracking tools have rendered passwords, by themselves, ineffective to protect resources and accounts. Once passwords have been leaked or stolen, they can be potentially leveraged for unauthorized access to systems, in "reuse" attacks, and for privilege escalation. The usefulness of passwords by themselves to protect enterprise resources has long passed. Subsequently, using **Multi-Factor Authentication** (MFA) is a requirement for enterprises and consumers alike. Using MFA can mitigate stolen and leaked credentials in many, but not all, scenarios. Using MFA, even if attackers possess a valid username and password for an account, they won't get access to the account if attackers don't also possess the other factor required for authentication. Other factors that can be used for authentication include digital certificates, one-time passwords and PINs generated on dedicated hardware or a smartphone app, a call to a preregistered landline or mobile phone, and more.

MFA isn't a silver bullet for weak, leaked, or stolen passwords, but it's super helpful in many scenarios. There have been some successful attacks on some MFA methods. For example, SIM-swapping attacks to intercept PIN codes sent to preregistered mobile phones via SMS. Another real limitation of MFA is that it isn't ubiquitous in enterprise IT environments. Organizations with decades of legacy applications that use old-fashioned authentication and authorization methods are less likely to fully mitigate the risk with MFA. Even if the latest systems and cloud-based services require MFA, chances are there are more legacy applications that cannot utilize it easily.

A picture of an iceberg comes to mind here. Several CISOs that I've talked to have experienced this limitation firsthand during penetration tests that exposed the limitations of MFA in their environments. Still, MFA should be widely adopted as it successfully mitigates many attack scenarios where weak, leaked, and stolen passwords are involved. It should be required for new systems being adopted and the risks posed by the old systems without it should be carefully considered and mitigated where possible. There are several vendors that specialize in such mitigations.

When an on-premises enterprise environment is initially compromised, attackers use leaked or stolen credentials to perform reconnaissance and to look for other credentials that have been cached or stored in the environment. They are especially on the lookout for administrator credentials that could give them unlimited access to resources in the compromised environment. Typically, within seconds of the initial compromise, attackers try to access the victim organization's user account directory service, such as **Microsoft Active Directory (AD)**, to dump all the credentials in the directory. The more credentials they can use to move and stay persistent, the harder it will be to expel them from the environment – they can persist indefinitely. Attackers will try to steal user account databases. If attackers successfully get all the credentials from their victim's directory service, then recovery really is aspirational.

Once attackers have stolen hashed credentials, the weakest of these credentials can be cracked in offline attacks in a matter of hours. The longer, uncommon, and truly complex passwords will get cracked last. There have been raging debates for decades about the efficacy of passwords versus passphrases, as well as appropriate character lengths, character sets, password lockout policies, password expiration policies, and the like. Guidance for passwords has changed over the years as threats and risks have changed and new data has become available. Some of the people I worked with on Microsoft's Identity Protection team published password guidance based on the data from 10 million credential attacks per day that they see on their enterprise and consumer identity systems. *Microsoft Password Guidance* (Hicock, 2016) is recommended reading.

When credentials are leaked or stolen from an organization, it doesn't take attackers long to run them through scripts that try to log in to financial institutions, e-commerce sites, social networking sites, and other sites in the hopes that the credentials were reused somewhere.

Reusing passwords across accounts is a terrible practice. Simply put, credentials that provide access to more than one account have a higher ROI for attackers than those that don't. Sets of compromised credentials that can provide access to corporate resources and information, as well as social networks that can also serve as a rich source of information and potential victims, are valuable.

Using unique passwords for every account and using MFA everywhere can mitigate this risk. If you have too many accounts to assign unique passwords to, then use a password vault to make life easier. There are numerous commercially available products for consumers and enterprises.

Identity has always been the hardest part of cybersecurity. Identity governance and management deserve their own book. I offer a very incomplete list of recommendations to help manage the risk of weak, leaked, and stolen credentials:

- MFA can be very effective – use it everywhere you can. Microsoft published a great blog post about the effectiveness of MFA called *Your Pa$$word Doesn't Matter* (Weinert, 2019), which is recommended reading.
- You should know if your organization is leaking credentials and how old those leaked credentials are. Using a service that collects leaked and stolen credentials and looks for your organization's credentials being sold and traded online can give you a little peace of mind that you aren't missing something obvious. Getting some idea as to the age of these credentials can help decide if password resets are necessary and the number of people potentially impacted.
- Privileged Access Management solutions can detect pass-the-hash, pass-the-ticket, and Golden Ticket attacks, as well as attackers' lateral movement and reconnaissance in your infrastructure:
  - Many of these solutions also offer password vaulting, credential brokering, and specialized analytics. Some of these solutions can be noisy and prone to false positives, but still, they can help you to manage and detect weak, leaked, and stolen credentials.

- In cloud-based environments, **Identity and Access Management (IAM)** controls are the most powerful controls you have. Taking advantage of all the power that IAM controls offer can help you to protect and detect threats to resources in the cloud. But this is one control set area that can proliferate into an unmanageable mess quickly. Extra thoughtful planning around your organization's IAM strategy will pay huge security dividends.

I will discuss identity a little more in *Chapter 9, Cybersecurity Strategies*, of this book.

An important aspect of protecting credentials involves educating information workers to be aware of social engineering attacks in which attackers may attempt to steal credentials through methods such as phishing. This is not the only way in which social engineering is used to compromise systems, however. I'll cover social engineering in a little more detail next.

Social engineering

Of the Cybersecurity Usual Suspects, social engineering is the most widely used method. Simply put, social engineering is tricking users into making poor trust decisions. Examples of poor trust decisions include lowering the security posture of a system by changing its settings without understanding the possible outcomes of doing so or unknowingly installing malware on a system. Attackers rely on the naivety of their victims in social engineering attacks.

The volume of social engineering attacks is orders of magnitude larger than other types of attacks. For example, the volume of email phishing attacks Microsoft reported for July 2019 was 0.85% of the more than 470 billion email messages that flowed through Office 365 that month (Microsoft Corporation, n.d.). That's 4 billion phishing emails that all relied on social engineering detected in a single month. Similarly, Trojans, a category of malware that relies on social engineering to be successful, has been the most prevalent category of malware in the world continuously for many years. I'll discuss this category of malware and many others in detail in *Chapter 4, The Evolution of Malware*.

Given the massive volume of social engineering attacks, and their historical record of success, mitigating these attacks really isn't optional for enterprises. A fundamental component of an enterprise cybersecurity strategy is a mitigation strategy for social engineering attacks. Put another way, not including social engineering attacks in your cybersecurity strategy would mean ignoring the top way that organizations get initially compromised by volume.

Social engineering attacks are typically perpetrated by attackers external to organizations, to which users must be prepared through appropriate education and training. Another challenging threat to defend against is one from within.

The final potential route of compromise, which we'll discuss next, is that of the insider threat.

Insider threats

When discussing insider threats with CISOs and security teams, I find it useful to break them down into three different categories, listed here from most likely to least likely:

1. Users and administrators that make mistakes or poor trust decisions that lead to bad security outcomes.

2. The lone wolf insider or a very small group of individuals that use their privileged access to steal information or otherwise negatively impact the confidentiality, integrity, or availability of the organization's information technology and/or data.

3. The mass conspiracy, where multiple insiders work together to overcome the separation of duties that distributes the span of security control. I've found that enterprises typically bring this category up in discussions about risks in managed service provider environments and the cloud.

Mitigating insider threats is an important aspect of cybersecurity and is something that should be fundamental to any enterprise-wide strategy. Enforcing meaningful separation of duties and embracing the principle of least privilege are helpful, as are automation, monitoring and auditing.

I became a big fan of deception technology after seeing how it can be used to mitigate insider threats. There are a few different approaches to deception technology, but the basic concept is to present attackers with a system, potentially with publicly known vulnerabilities or common security misconfigurations that, when interacted with, alert defenders to the presence of attackers. This approach can help alert defenders to the presence of external attackers and insider threats. I've heard some security professionals refer to it as a "canary in the coal mine" for IT environments. Implementing deception technology with as few people involved as possible and keeping the program confidential can be helpful in exposing at least two of the three categories of insider threats that I have outlined. However, it is important to be transparent with the right people in the organization, so that there is appropriate oversight and visibility.

Tip: the revelation of a clandestine insider threat program is one of the easiest ways to create lasting distrust within an organization. Revealing the program's existence only when you need other people's help can lead to trust issues. Setting up an insider threat program steering committee composed of senior representatives from the office of the CISO (OCISO), Legal, HR, Fraud, and IT departments will help you avoid or minimize issues later if the program identifies malicious insiders and action is warranted.

A steering committee that sets the program's charter and scope and approves its playbooks can help avoid alienating your partners and allow you to manage the program more effectively.

Those are the five ways organizations get initially compromised. Defending against these five vectors of attack is fundamental to effective cybersecurity.

Focus on the cybersecurity fundamentals

In order to achieve a successful cybersecurity program, organizations need to get very good at continuously mitigating all five of the Cybersecurity Usual Suspects. This competency forms the foundation of a sound cybersecurity strategy. Other cybersecurity-related investments will potentially have diminishing returns if the foundation of the strategy is not solid.

After an attacker uses one or more of these five ways to initially compromise an organization, then they might employ a plethora of novel and advanced TTPs. Organizations that focus on the cybersecurity fundamentals make it much harder for attackers to be successful; that is, by focusing on the inside 85% of the bell curve below which the cybersecurity fundamentals sit, instead of the activities in the outlying 7.5% on either end of the curve, security teams will be much more successful. Unfortunately, the allure of hunting advanced persistent threats can take resources away from the less sexy, but critical work in the middle of the curve.

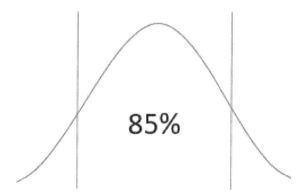

Figure 1.1: A bell curve illustrating that most security teams should spend their time on the cybersecurity fundamentals

If there really are only five ways that organizations get initially compromised, why does there seem to be so much confusion in the industry on proper priorities for cybersecurity programs? I think there are a bunch of factors contributing to the confusion. One reason for the confusion is the way that attacks, security incidents, and data breaches have been reported in popular media outlets sometimes confuses attackers' tactics with their motivations.

This can lead organizations to make the wrong security prioritization decisions.

Understanding the difference between attackers' motivations and tactics

One of the reasons I've found so many organizations lack focus and competency around the cybersecurity fundamentals is the way big data breaches have been reported in the news over the last decade. Stories that claim an attack was the "most advanced attack seen to date" or the work of "a nation state" seem to be common. But when you take a closer look at these attacks, the victim organization was always initially compromised by attackers using one or more of the Cybersecurity Usual Suspects that I outlined in this chapter.

There are attackers that operate in the open because they don't believe there are consequences for their illicit activities, based on their location, legal jurisdiction, or who sponsors their work. This used to be the exception to the rule that they will obfuscate their true affiliations and identities. However, there has been a proliferation of nation-state threat groups and some threat intelligence providers are now tracking many such groups (more than 30 groups) that they identify as bona fide nation states.

Attributing an attack to an individual or group can be extremely hard. This is because the internet is based on a suite of protocols that were developed over 40 years ago. The engineers that developed these immensely scalable and sophisticated protocols never envisioned a future world where an entire 100 billion+-dollar-a-year industry would be based on the discoveries of new security vulnerabilities, malware research, social engineering protection, and the proliferation of sophisticated criminal organizations and nation-state actors. The TCP/IP (version 4) protocol suite, the basis of the internet, was never designed to help investigators perform attribution for cyber-attacks that leverage vast networks of compromised distributed systems around the world. Comparing code fragments from two malware samples to determine if the same attackers developed both is not a reliable way to perform attribution, especially when the attackers know this is a common technique. Finding "patient zero," where the compromise started, in large environments that have been compromised for months or years, using data from compromised systems, can't be done with complete confidence.

However, attackers that have embraced the modern ransomware business model have made it easier to do attribution with much more confidence. They essentially identify themselves, or at least their ransomware gang affiliation, when they demand a ransom from their victims. Having a known ransomware gang designation can help strike fear in the minds of victims, especially when the gang has a history of successful attacks.

Victims take them seriously when they have a record of keeping their promises – both good and bad.

Attribution is relatively easy when a known ransomware gang posts a Dark Web blog post in the same way they have in the past, publishing some of their latest victim's data. It proves they have possession of stolen data and are demanding one or more ransoms from the victim. I examine some of the ways that ransomware has evolved in *Chapter 4, The Evolution of Malware.*

When security teams find **Indicators of Compromise (IOCs)** that precisely match the "rat droppings" of a known threat actor, it's hard not to conclude that the associated threat actor is involved in an attack. I discuss IOCs in more detail in *Chapter 2, What to Know about Threat Intelligence.* But I still think it's important to keep in mind that even if you were able to identify an attacker and capture them, they likely would never tell you their true motivations – criminals rarely do. This is especially true of organized crime and nation states – you will be left with a lot of assumptions about their motivations. I discuss governments and the myriad of motivations they have in *Chapter 6, The Roles Governments Play in Cybersecurity.*

In the case of ransomware, it would seem like the motivation is quite straightforward – profit. However, Microsoft threat research suggests that attackers used "fake" ransomware against Ukraine government targets during the Russian invasion in 2022. The motivation of these "fake" ransomware attacks wasn't profit; it was really the destruction of Ukrainian assets. Microsoft reported, "MSTIC assesses that the malware, which is designed to look like ransomware but lacking a ransom recovery mechanism, is intended to be destructive and designed to render targeted devices inoperable rather than to obtain a ransom" (Microsoft Corporation, January 15, 2022). Apparently, wiper malware was disguised as ransomware. The difference is that this wiper malware wasn't designed to encrypt data in a way that is reversible using a decryption key; the data is instead destroyed. This wasn't the first time, nor will it be the last time that attackers try to make their motivations opaque.

Still, many cybersecurity professionals use this type of data to surmise the attackers' motivations, affiliations, and identities. Attacker motivations can include:

- **Notoriety**: The attacker wants to prove they are smarter than the big high-tech companies and their victims.
- **Profit**: As I discuss in *Chapter 4, The Evolution of Malware,* after the successful global worm attacks in 2003, malware began to evolve to support a profit motive that continues to the present day.
- **Economic espionage**: For example, alleged activities by groups in China to steal valuable intellectual property from western nations to give their own industries a competitive and economic advantage.

- **Military espionage**: A motivation as old as governments themselves, where governments want to understand the military capabilities of their adversaries and allies.

- **Hacktivism**: Attacks against organizations and institutions based on disagreements on political or philosophical issues.

- **Foreign policy objectives**: Governments run sophisticated cyber-influence operations using cultural manipulation and information warfare tactics, amplifying false narratives to influence and manipulate target populations. Examples include influencing elections and lowering the morale of enemy civilian populations during wartime.

- **Many others**: Watch any James Bond movie where the **Special Executive for Counterintelligence, Terrorism, Revenge, and Extortion (SPECTRE)** is part of the plot, and you'll see some creative motivations.

I think it's fair to say that most organizations won't really understand what an attacker's motivation is. If attackers' motivations are unclear, how are CISOs supposed to know what a proportional response is? Who should help the victim organization with the response to the attack – local authorities, the military, or an international coalition?

Still, I have talked to organizations whose cybersecurity strategies rely heavily on attribution. After performing hundreds of incident response investigations for Microsoft's customers and publishing threat intelligence for almost a decade, I find the assumption that timely attribution can be done with any confidence to be overly optimistic. Certainly, the advances that purveyors of threat intelligence and cybersecurity tool makers have made in the last several years have made the playing field a little more level. Security teams armed with the knowledge of attackers' TTPs, catalogs of IOCs, and improved detection and response automation, can defend against known threat actors much more effectively and efficiently than ever before. As successful and promising as these new capabilities are, and even when attackers identify their affiliations with ransom demands and data leak blog posts, attacks continue unabated, and arguably, attackers have never been more successful.

Fortunately, understanding who the attackers are is not a prerequisite for a successful cybersecurity strategy. Regardless of who sponsors their work or how sophisticated attackers are, they all use the Cybersecurity Usual Suspects for initial compromise: "the tools used by nation states to compromise victim networks are most frequently the same tools used by other malicious actors" (Microsoft Corporation, October 2021). I believe we can, with 99.9% certainty, predict the tactics the attackers will use when they try to initially compromise an enterprise IT environment. This is what organizations should invest in – the cybersecurity fundamentals to mitigate the Cybersecurity Usual Suspects.

A large and thriving Threat Intelligence industry has grown out of the insatiable desire for attribution, TTPs, and IOCs. In the next chapter, we'll dive deep into threat intelligence. You'll learn what threat intelligence is, how to determine good intelligence from bad, and how enterprise cybersecurity teams use it. This will help prepare you to evaluate the cybersecurity strategies that are designed to mitigate intrusion attempts, which are discussed in later chapters of this book.

Summary

The context I provided in this chapter will be helpful for readers throughout the rest of this book. In this chapter, I introduced the cybersecurity fundamentals and the Cybersecurity Usual Suspects; I will relentlessly refer to these concepts throughout the rest of this book.

Organizations that are very proficient at managing the cybersecurity fundamentals make it much harder for attackers to be successful. A solid foundation, focused on the fundamentals, is required for a successful strategy.

Don't confuse an attacker's motivations with their tactics. Since accurate attribution for attacks can be difficult or impossible to accomplish, it's unlikely most organizations will be able to determine who is attacking them and what attackers' motivations really are. Whether the attacker is a purveyor of commodity malware or a nation state, the ways they will try to initially compromise their victims' IT environments are limited to the Cybersecurity Usual Suspects. Being very proficient at the cybersecurity fundamentals makes it much harder for attackers, whether they are a nation state trying to steal intellectual property or an extortionist using ransomware.

References

- Rains, T. (2020). *Cybersecurity Threats, Malware Trends, and Strategies*. Packt Publishing. Retrieved from https://www.packtpub.com/product/cybersecurity-threats-malware-trends-and-strategies/9781800206014.

- Jakkal, V. (2021). "Microsoft surpasses $10 billion in security business revenue, more than 40 percent year-over-year growth". Microsoft.com. Retrieved from https://www.microsoft.com/security/blog/2021/01/27/microsoft-surpasses-10-billion-in-security-business-revenue-more-than-40-percent-year-over-year-growth/.

- Microsoft. (2021). "Microsoft Cybersecurity Reference Architectures". Microsoft Corporation. Retrieved from https://docs.microsoft.com/en-us/security/cybersecumrity-reference-architecture/mcra.

- Khalid Kark, Taryn Aguas (July 26, 2016). "The new CISO: Leading the strategic security organization," Deloitte Review issue 19. Retrieved from `https://www2.deloitte.com/us/en/insights/deloitte-review/issue-19/ciso-next-generation-strategic-security-organization.html`.

- National Vulnerability Database. (n.d.). Retrieved from `https://nvd.nist.gov/vuln`.

- Center for Internet Security. (n.d.). Retrieved from `https://www.cisecurity.org/cis-benchmarks/`.

- Hicock, R. (2016). "Microsoft Password Guidance". Microsoft Corporation. Retrieved from: `https://www.microsoft.com/en-us/research/wp-content/uploads/2016/06/Microsoft_Password_Guidance-1.pdf`.

- Weinert, A. (July 9, 2019). "Your Pa$$word doesn't matter". Microsoft Corporation. Retrieved from `https://techcommunity.microsoft.com/t5/azure-active-directoryidentity/your-pa-word-doesn-t-matter/ba-p/73198`.

- Microsoft Corporation. (n.d.). "Microsoft Digital Defense Report". Microsoft Corporation. Retrieved from `https://www.microsoft.com/securityinsights/Phishing`.

- Microsoft Corporation. (January 15, 2022). "Destructive malware targeting Ukrainian organizations". Microsoft Corporation. Retrieved from `https://www.microsoft.com/security/blog/2022/01/15/destructive-malware-targeting-ukrainian-organizations/`.

- Microsoft Corporation. (October 2021). "Microsoft Digital Defense Report - October 2021". Microsoft Corporation. Retrieved from `https://query.prod.cms.rt.microsoft.com/cms/api/am/binary/RWMFIi`.

Join our community on Discord

Join our community's Discord space for discussions with the author and other readers:

`https://packt.link/SecNet`

2

What to Know about Threat Intelligence

I admit it, I'm a threat intelligence data geek. I really enjoy studying threat intelligence. It helps me understand the tactics and techniques that are in vogue with attackers and how the threat landscape is evolving. One of the best jobs I had at Microsoft was working as a Director of Trust-worthy Computing. In this role I was the executive editor and a contributor to the Microsoft Security Intelligence Report, which we called "the SIR." During the 8 or 9 years I helped produce the SIR, we published more than 20 volumes and special editions of this report, spanning thousands of pages. I gave literally thousands of threat intelligence briefings for customers around the world, as well as press and analyst interviews. I can tell you from experience, interviews on live television in front of millions of people, discussing threat intelligence, are nerve-wracking! (BBC News, 2013).

Building and publishing the SIR was a *lot* of work, but very rewarding. In this role, I had the opportunity to work with so many smart people in the **Microsoft Security Response Center (MSRC)**, the **Microsoft Malware Protection Center (MMPC)**, the **Microsoft Digital Crimes Unit (DCU)**, the **Security Development Lifecycle (SDL)** team, Microsoft IT, and many others. Doing this work gave me a deep appreciation for the value of good threat intelligence and some of the ways it is produced. Microsoft has continued to invest in threat intelligence and they now have a center dedicated to it called the **Microsoft Threat Intelligence Center (MSTIC)**, in which a few of my former colleagues work.

I provide a deep dive into data from the SIR in *Chapter 4, The Evolution of Malware*. I also provide a deep dive into security vulnerabilities in *Chapter 3, Using Vulnerability Trends to Reduce Risk and Costs*.

But before I get to this data, let me provide some useful context to help you consume the data in those chapters and other threat intelligence you encounter in your career.

What is threat intelligence?

Threat Intelligence (**TI**) is sometimes referred to as **Cyber Threat Intelligence** (**CTI**) to make it clear that the intelligence focuses on cybersecurity threats as opposed to other types of threats. The concept is ancient: the more you know about your enemies and how they plan and execute their attacks, the more prepared you can be for those attacks.

Simply put, CTI provides organizations with data and information on how attackers have been leveraging the *Cybersecurity Usual Suspects*, what they have been doing in IT environments post-initial compromise, and sometimes attribution for attacks to specific threat actors. Threats can also include various categories of malware, exploitation of vulnerabilities, web-based attacks, **Distributed Denial of Service** (**DDoS**) attacks, social engineering attacks, and others. Of course, as I wrote in *Chapter 1, Introduction*, there is also high interest in information about the attackers themselves – who they are, where they are located, whether they are state-sponsored or an independent criminal organization, and details on their modus operandi from their past attacks. An entire industry has grown around the demand for attribution and information on threat actors.

Where does CTI data come from?

Purveyors of CTI collect and analyze data from data sources. There are many potential sources of data that CTI providers can use. For example, data on malware threats can come from anti-malware products and services running on endpoints, networks, email servers, web browsers, cloud services, honey pots, etc. Data on weak, leaked, and stolen credentials can come not only from identity providers like Microsoft Azure Active Directory, Google's identity offerings, and Okta, but also from monitoring illicit forums where such credentials are bought and sold. Data on social engineering attacks can come from phishing and spam filtering services, as well as social networking services.

There is also **Open Source Threat Intelligence** (**OSINT**) that leverages publicly available data sources such as social media, news feeds, court filings and arrest records, attackers' disclosed information on their victims, activity in illicit forums, and many others. OSINT can help defenders in at least a couple of ways. First, it can help notify you that your IT environment has been compromised. Observing attackers offering your data for sale or chattering about illicit access to your network can be leading indicators of a breach that has gone undetected. Another way many organizations use OSINT is for researching attackers and the tactics they use.

Of course, attackers can use OSINT to research and perform reconnaissance on their potential targets. There are a plethora of tools to help find OSINT including Maltego, Shodan, theHarvester, and many others.

Purveyors of CTI can use data sources that they own and operate, CTI data procured from third parties, and OSINT data sources. For example, anti-malware vendors that operate their own research and response labs collect malware for analysis and operate various anti-malware offerings. Their customers agree to submit malware samples that they encounter, and the vendors' products and services generate data from detections, installation blocking, and disinfections in the course of operating. All this data can be collected, aggregated, and analyzed to provide the vendor insight into how their products and services are operating and steer future research and response activities and investments.

Many vendors also publish threat intelligence reports and provide CTI to their customers via web portals and emails, but also integrate it into APIs, products, and services. Examples of vendors that do this include CrowdStrike, Google, Mandiant, McAfee, Microsoft, Recorded Future, Sophos, Symantec, and many others. They do this to share their CTI and help organizations understand what is happening in the threat landscape. But they also do this to generate new business by demonstrating the breadth and depth of their CTI. Many vendors like to claim they provide better visibility than their competitors, and thus better protection from threats. This is where scale can be a differentiator.

When I worked at Microsoft, some anti-malware vendors would make claims like this. However, *hundreds of millions* of Windows users around the world agreed to share threat data with Microsoft. Layer in data from web browsers, the Bing internet search engine, the world's most popular productivity suite, and enterprise identity products and services, and the CTI generated is impressive. This massive reach enabled Microsoft to develop an excellent understanding of the global threat landscape and share it with their customers via the SIR, blogs, whitepapers, products, services, and APIs. I demonstrate the reach of such data sources, in detail, in *Chapter 4, The Evolution of Malware.*

Some CTI vendors differentiate themselves not necessarily by scale, but by the quality of their data and analysis. They are able to correlate data they have to specific industries and to specific customers within those industries and provide more actionable insights than high-level, anonymized, global trends will typically enable.

For example, if I'm a CISO of an organization in the healthcare industry, I am likely interested in CTI from a vendor that really understands my industry and its unique challenges and has data on attackers and their attacks in the healthcare industry, and in the geographic locations my organization does business. This combination will help me understand the threats specifically impacting my industry and better prepare for them in a healthcare context that potentially includes heavy regulation, a big focus on patient privacy, expensive equipment certification requirements, and risk to human life. I'm always looking for insights into what other organizations similar to mine are doing to protect, detect, and respond to these threats. This information will inform some of my efforts and make it easier to convince the business I support to provide the budget and resources I need.

Some CTI vendors tout their abilities to perform attribution and their knowledge of nation-state attackers. They have coined sometimes fun, but always intriguing names for such attack groups. Examples include Lazarus Group, Sandworm Team, PHOSPHORUS, and many others. It can be very interesting to get some insight into how well-funded attackers operate. It doesn't take long for other attackers to try to mimic the tactics and techniques that the professionals use once they are revealed via CTI. In this way, nation-state threat actors have been lowering the barrier to entry for criminals for decades. However, in my experience advising many organizations over the years, the threat of nation-state actors can skew the approach security teams take in a way that isn't helpful. Focusing on threat actors that potentially have unlimited resources (governments can print money) can distract CISOs and security teams from focusing on the cybersecurity fundamentals. After all, no matter how well funded attackers are, they will use one or more of the Cybersecurity Usual Suspects to initially compromise their target's IT environment, just like common criminals will. CISOs need to ask themselves, "Do we really need to be concerned with these nation-state threat actors now or do we have more fundamental challenges to address first?" After all, becoming excellent at the cybersecurity fundamentals will drive down the ROI for all potential threat actors that target your organization.

Don't get me wrong, I have talked with plenty of security teams at public sector and private sector organizations where paying attention to nation-state threat actors is not optional due to their organizations' own charters or the intellectual property they possess. But even in these cases, focusing on the cybersecurity fundamentals can pay big dividends.

Using threat intelligence

Cybersecurity programs can make use of CTI in several ways. Here are some examples (this list is not exhaustive):

- **Security Operations Centers (SOCs)** are only as good as the CTI they have
- Inform **Cybersecurity Incident Response Teams' (CIRT)** investigations
- Inform threat hunting, Red, Blue, and Purple teams' efforts
- Profiling attackers in order to be better prepared for them
- Inform executive protection programs designed to protect executives and their families
- Inform risk management

Let's dig into that last example a bit more, inform risk management. CTI can inform the risks that organizations pay attention to. Recall that risk is composed of probability and impact. CTI can help quantify both the probability side and the impact side of risk calculations. For example, let's say you are a CISO and the business leaders you support are very concerned about ransomware because they keep seeing news stories about attacks. CTI can help provide some idea of the probability of encountering ransomware. I'll discuss ransomware in detail in *Chapter 4, The Evolution of Malware*, but it turns out that ransomware (the category of malware) is typically one of the least prevalent categories of malware. There are some logical reasons why this is the case that I'll cover in *Chapter 4, The Evolution of Malware*. However, if you were to stack-rank risks by priority based on probability alone, ransomware would likely show up near the bottom of the list. But once we quantify the potential impact of ransomware to reflect that encountering it could be an extinction event for your business, it likely bumps it way up in the ranking on the list of risks.

Another use for CTI is to help security teams mitigate risks by providing details about specific threats and how they operate. Understanding the **Tactics, Techniques, and Procedures (TTPs)** that attackers employ can provide some concrete ideas on how they can be mitigated. NIST defines TTPs as,

> *The behavior of an actor. A tactic is the highest-level description of this behavior, while techniques give a more detailed description of behavior in the context of a tactic, and procedures an even lower-level, highly detailed description in the context of a technique." (Badger et al 2016)*

A tactic is the reason the attacker performs a particular action. Why do they decide to take a specific action? It was a tactical goal. For example, once an attacker is inside their victim's network, they typically need to move laterally to explore the network and find sensitive data. The tactic in this example is lateral movement. Other examples of tactics include reconnaissance, persistence, and exfiltration.

Techniques are how the attacker tries to accomplish the tactic – the specific actions they take. For example, the attacker needed to move laterally (the tactic) on the victim's network, so they used Pass the Hash and stolen web authentication cookies (these are techniques) to do this.

Using this combination of tactics and techniques enables security teams to take a structured approach to planning for attacks. Knowing the tactics and techniques that attackers use allows defenders to put people, processes, and technologies in place that will detect or mitigate the techniques when they are employed. In our example where Pass the Hash was employed, we could plan to mitigate this technique using some guidance from Microsoft or procuring a security product designed to detect it.

Using TTPs this way might seem like a daunting task because there must be many combinations and permutations of attacker tactics and techniques. A great resource to help security teams is the MITRE ATT&CK® knowledge base (found at `https://attack.mitre.org/`). This knowledge base contains tactics and techniques that have been seen in use during attacks. It maps techniques to tactics and provides ways that each technique can potentially be mitigated and detected. The popularity of this approach with security teams has skyrocketed in recent years.

Many security teams also use **Indicators of Compromise (IOCs)** to help determine if their enterprise IT environments have been compromised. Where TTPs can help protect, detect, and respond to attacks, IOCs can help post-compromise to try to determine when and how the initial compromise happened, and what the attackers did with their illicit access afterward. IOCs are described this way in *NIST Special Publication 800-53 Revision 5*:

> *Indicators of compromise (IOC) are forensic artifacts from intrusions that are identified on organizational systems at the host or network level. IOCs provide valuable information on systems that have been compromised. IOCs can include the creation of registry key values. IOCs for network traffic include Universal Resource Locator or protocol elements that indicate malicious code command and control servers. The rapid distribution and adoption of IOCs can improve information security by reducing the time that systems and organizations are vulnerable to the same exploit or attack. Threat indicators, signatures, tactics, techniques, procedures, and other indicators of compromise may be available via government and non-government cooperatives, including the Forum of Incident Response and Security Teams, the United States Computer Emergency Readiness Team, the Defense Industrial Base Cybersecurity Information Sharing Program, and the CERT Coordination Center."* (NIST Special Publication 800-53 Revision 5, September 2020).

Examples of IOCs include unusual network traffic (destination, origin, or volume), network traffic to or from known malicious domain names or IP addresses, unusual volumes of authentication failures, the presence of specific tools, files, or registry entries, recently added unrecognized accounts, and many others. Incident response and forensics teams can use IOCs to help them identify compromised systems. To do this, they typically need **MD5**, **SHA1**, or **SHA256** hashes for files, scripts, and tools that attackers leave behind. File hashes can help identify the presence of files that were potentially used during attacks among the mountains of legitimate files on systems.

IP addresses for command-and-control servers, data exfiltration locations, and other attacker-controlled resources can also be helpful to investigators as they comb through network flow data logs on firewalls, proxy servers, and other devices on a network.

PowerShell Scripts	
File Name	MD5 Hash
bad-file1.ps1	600738dd15eb7fc50568f0e39a69f510
bad-file2.ps1	0e40dd752e7692f2f5c758de4eab3f5f

Additional PowerShell File Names	
psexec.ps1	cmd.ps1
rundll32.ps1	

Batch Scripts	
File name	MD5 Hash
os-checker.bat	9e2874169fdfb20846fe7ffe34635acc
download-libs.bat	ff37a6eeb9f836215954dae03459720e
disable-av.bat	2f5309285e8a8471fce7320fcade188c

Executables and DLLs	
File name	MD5 Hash
rpcdump.exe	91625f7f5d590534949ebe08cc728380
gmode.exe	79db4c04f5dcea3bfcd75357adf98465
gmode.dll	5a2874160fdfb20846fe7ffe34635e44

File name	SHA1 Hash
my-encoder.exe	4e7ac1b113df21360ef68c450b5fca278d08fff1
my-mimikatz.exe	e371df7b9d2ec0b8194751cd5ce153e27cc40ce6

Command & Control IP Addresses	
169.254.66.22	169.254.66.25
169.254.66.23	169.254.66.26
169.254.66.24	169.254.66.27

Figure 2.1: An example of IOCs with fictional filenames, hashes, and IP addresses

I learned so much about the tricks that attackers like to use when I worked on Microsoft's customer-facing Incident Response team. We built tools to collect system data on live-running Windows systems that were suspected of being compromised. We'd compare the data on system configurations and running states with known good and known bad datasets – essentially looking for IOCs. This was as much art as it was science because attackers were using all sorts of creative tricks to try to avoid detection, stay persistent, and perform data exfil.

Some memorable tricks include attackers using IP addresses in Base-8 instead of Base-10 format to bypass proxy server rules, taking advantage of bugs in browsers and proxy servers when domain names in Cyrillic were used, running processes using the same name as well-known legitimate Windows system processes, but from slightly different directories to avoid detection, and so many more. Fun stuff!

Security teams can leverage TTPs and IOCs with a variety of security tools, products, and services. Examples include, **Security Information and Event Management (SIEM)** systems, behavioral analytics tools, data visualization tools, email filtering services, web browsing filtering services, endpoint protection products, **Extended Detection and Response (XDR)** products, **Security Orchestration, Automation, and Response (SOAR)** products, and many others. There are a vast number of ways to leverage CTI to protect, detect, and respond to modern threats.

Different roles on security teams can leverage CTI in slightly different ways. For example, as I mentioned earlier, **Cyber Incident Response Teams (CIRT)** will use IOCs when performing intrusion investigations. Meanwhile, IT analysts are using CTI to ensure protection and detection capabilities are optimized. CTI has the potential to inform the efforts of many different roles and stakeholders.

The key to using threat intelligence

I've provided a few examples of some of the ways that security teams use CTI. Whatever ways security teams choose to leverage CTI, it's important to recognize that although CTI is a product offered by many vendors and organizations, it's also a process – a process that is used to collect data, process that data, analyze the processed data, and then share the results with those stakeholders that need them. This typically takes time, budget, and resources to accomplish. I haven't met a security team yet that has unlimited resources and does not need to make trade-offs. The combination of so many potential sources of CTI, so many uses for it, and limited resources, can lead to security teams drowning in CTI. In many cases, the CTI wouldn't be helpful to them even if they could consume it.

The most common reason I have seen for this is that teams didn't take the time to develop a set of requirements for their CTI program. In this context, "requirements" are statements about the specific problems the CTI program is trying to solve. These requirements help the CTI program rationalize the CTI they use by tying the specific CTI collected and analyzed to the specific needs of the program's stakeholders. If some CTI source has some interesting data, but the data it provides doesn't help fulfill a requirement defined by a program stakeholder, then that source likely should not be leveraged.

This approach helps the CTI program optimize the resources it has and prevents it from drowning in CTI.

Outcome	Requirement Statement	Priority	Data Sources	Stakeholders	Reporting Speed	CTI Shared
Detection	CTI program will collect and analyze data that enables early detection of attacks on our firm's internet-facing systems.	High	OSINT; Palo Alto Networks; X-Force Exchange	CISO; CIRT; Digital Marketing Team; Server Operations	Immediate	Stakeholder alert email; CIRT incident tool
Respond	CTI program will support CIRT team before, during, and after security incidents to enable fast and effective response to failed, partially successful, and fully successful attacks.	Medium	Internal sources; OSINT; Law Enforcement	CIRT; CISO; SLT; BoD; Compliance team; Legal; Fraud team	As scenario warrants	CIRT incident tool; SLT alert email; BoD incident review deck
...						

Figure 2.2: An example of CTI requirements

I've seen a few different approaches to documenting requirements. *Figure 2.2* provides an example. If your CTI program doesn't have a set of documented requirements, I recommend working with the program's stakeholders to develop them, as they are the key to an optimized approach.

It's also worth mentioning that **Artificial Intelligence (AI)** and machine learning capabilities have matured a lot over the last several years. Services that leverage these capabilities can churn through massive amounts of CTI very quickly compared to human analysts. This can help your organization manage large volumes of CTI on an ongoing basis. Of course, like many aspects of computer science and cybersecurity, the value derived here is a function of the effort that is put into it.

Threat intelligence sharing

Security teams can find themselves in situations where they want to share CTI they possess with security teams at other organizations or vice versa. There are lots of different scenarios where this happens. For example, a parent company wants all the security teams at its subsidiaries to share CTI with each other. Another example is an industry-specific **Information Sharing and Analysis Center (ISAC)** that facilitates CTI sharing among its member organizations. Sharing CTI across organizations in the same industry could make it more challenging for attackers to victimize individual members, because they all have the TTPs that threat actors use when targeting the industry. For this reason, the financial services industry and the healthcare industry both have ISACs, as examples.

NIST published Special Publication 800-150, Guide to Cyber Threat Information Sharing, which provides some guidelines for sharing CTI, as well as a good list of scenarios where sharing CTI can be helpful.

The benefits of sharing CTI that the authors cite are numerous, including shared situational awareness, improved security posture, knowledge maturation, and greater defensive agility. (NIST Special Publication 800-150 Badger et al, October 2016).

However, sharing CTI can be more complicated than it sounds. Sharing CTI is not without risk. Sensitive information, like **Personally Identifiable Information** (**PII**), can be swept up as part of an investigation into an intrusion. If its context and sensitivity are lost and the CTI is shared without the proper safeguards, it could be used as an example of how the organization failed to keep its regulatory compliance obligations to standards like PCI DSS, SOX, GDPR, and a host of others. For public sector organizations that possess classified information that requires security clearances to access, information sharing programs can be fraught with challenges that make sharing information hard or impossible. Because of all the sensitivities and potential land mines, many organizations that decide to share CTI do so anonymously. However, CTI that isn't attributed to a credible source might not inspire the requisite confidence in its quality among the security teams that receive it, and go unused.

If your security team is considering sharing CTI with other organizations, I suggest they leverage NIST Special Publication 800-150 to inform their deliberations.

CTI sharing protocols

I can't discuss sharing CTI without at least mentioning some of the protocols for doing so. Recall that protocols are used to set rules for effective communication. Some protocols are optimized for human-to-human communication, while others are optimized for machine-to-machine (automated) communication, machine-to-human communication, and so on. The three protocols I'll discuss in this section include **Traffic Light Protocol** (**TLP**), **Structured Threat Information eXpression** (**STIX**), and **Trusted Automated eXchange of Indicator Information** (**TAXII**).

Traffic Light Protocol

The **Traffic Light Protocol** (**TLP**) has become a popular protocol for sharing CTI and other types of information. TLP can help communicate the expected treatment of CTI shared between people. I don't think it is especially optimized for automated CTI sharing between systems – it's really a protocol for humans to use when sharing potentially sensitive information with each other. For example, if a CTI team decides to share some CTI with another CTI team or a CIRT via email or in a document, they could use TLP.

TLP helps set expectations between the sender of the information and the receiver of the information on how the information should be handled. The sender is responsible for communicating these expectations to the receiver. The receiver could choose to ignore the sender's instructions. Therefore, trust between sharing parties is very important. The receiver is trusted by the sender to honor the sender's specified information sharing boundaries. If the sender doesn't trust the receiver to honor their expectations, they shouldn't share the CTI with the receiver.

As its name suggests, TLP uses a traffic light analogy to make it easy for people to understand information senders' expectations and their intended information sharing boundaries. The "traffic light" analogy in this case has four colors: red, amber, green, and clear (*FIRST*, n.d.). The colors are used to communicate different information sharing boundaries, as specified by the sender. The rule the protocol sets is that the color be specified as follows, when the CTI is being communicated in writing (in an email or document): TLP:COLOR. "TLP:" is followed by one of the color names in caps – for example, TLP:AMBER.

TLP:RED specifies that the shared information is "not for disclosure, restricted to participants only" (*FIRST*, n.d.). Red tells the receiver that the sender's expectation is that the information shared is not to be shared with other people. The information is limited to only the people the sender shared it with directly and is typically communicated verbally as a further step to limit how the information can be shared, and to make it harder to attribute the information to a particular sender, thus protecting their privacy. Senders use this color when they want to limit the potential impact on their reputation or privacy and when other parties cannot effectively act on the information shared.

TLP:AMBER specifies "limited disclosure, restricted to participants' organizations" (*FIRST*, n.d.). Receivers are only permitted to share TLP:AMBER information within their own organization and with customers with a need to know. The sender can also specify more restrictions and limitations that it expects the receivers to honor.

TLP:GREEN permits "limited disclosure, restricted to the community" (*FIRST*, n.d.). Senders that specify TLP:GREEN are allowing receivers to share the information with organizations within their community or industry, but not by using channels that are open to the general public. Senders do not want the information shared outside of the receiver's industry or community. This is used when information can be used to protect the broader community or industry.

Lastly, using TLP:CLEAR means the "disclosure is not limited" (*FIRST*, n.d.). In other words, there are no sharing restrictions on information that is disclosed using TLP:CLEAR. Receivers are free to share this information as broadly as they like.

This is meant to be used when sharing information has minimal risk.

The TLP designation should be used when sharing CTI via email or documents. Convention dictates that emails should have the TLP designation in the subject line and at the top of the email, while the designation should appear in the page headers and footers in documents (*CISA*, n.d.). This makes it clear to the receiver what the sender's expectations are before they read the CTI. Again, the sender trusts the receiver to honor the TLP designation and any sharing boundaries they have specified.

If you are doing research on the internet on threats, you'll likely come across documents marked with TLP:CLEAR. For example, both the **Federal Bureau of Investigation (FBI)** and **Cybersecurity and Infrastructure Security Agency (CISA)** publish threat reports for public consumption labeled TLP:CLEAR. If you weren't aware of TLP before, these markings will make more sense to you now.

STIX and TAXII

Now that we've covered a protocol for use among humans, let's look at two complementary protocols that enable automated CTI sharing, **Structured Threat Information eXpression (STIX)** and **Trusted Automated eXchange of Indicator Information (TAXII)**. Employing protocols that are optimized to be processed by machines can help dramatically accelerate the dissemination of CTI to organizations that can benefit from it and operationalize it, as well as across different types of technologies that know how to consume it.

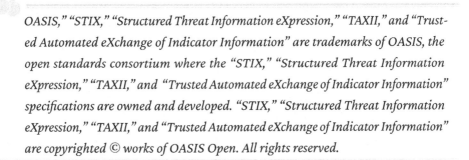

OASIS," "STIX," "Structured Threat Information eXpression," "TAXII," and "Trusted Automated eXchange of Indicator Information" are trademarks of OASIS, the open standards consortium where the "STIX," "Structured Threat Information eXpression," "TAXII," and "Trusted Automated eXchange of Indicator Information" specifications are owned and developed. "STIX," "Structured Threat Information eXpression," "TAXII," and "Trusted Automated eXchange of Indicator Information" are copyrighted © works of OASIS Open. All rights reserved.

STIX is a structured language or schema that helps describe threats in a standard way. The schema defined by STIX includes core objects and meta-objects that are used to describe threats. The specification for STIX version 2.1 is 313 pages. (STIX-v2.1) Needless to say, it's very comprehensive and can be used to describe a broad range of threats. To give you an idea of what STIX looks like, below you'll find an example of a campaign described using STIX.

All the data in this example is random and fictional – it's provided so you can see an example of the format.

```
{
  "type": "campaign",
  "spec_version": "2.1",
  "id": "campaign-3a3b4a4b-16a3-0fea-543e-10fa55c3cc2c",
  "created_by_ref": "identity-e552e362-722c-33f1-bb4a-7c4455ace3ef",
  "created": "2022-07-09T15:02:00.000Z",
  "modified": "2022-07-09T15:02:00.000Z",
  "name": "Attacker1 Attacks on Retail Industry",
  "description": "Campaign by Attacker1 on the retail industry."
}
```

While STIX is used to describe threats in a standard way, TAXII is an application layer protocol used to communicate that information between systems that can consume it. TAXII standardizes how computers share CTI with each other. Stated another way, TAXII is a protocol designed to exchange CTI between the sender and receiver(s) and enables automated machine-to-machine sharing of CTI over HTTPS. TAXII supports various sharing models, including hub and spoke, source and subscriber, and peer-to-peer. To do this, TAXII specifies two mechanisms: collections and channels. These enable CTI producers to support both push and pull communications models. Collections are sets of CTI data that CTI producers can provide to their customers when requested to do so. Channels enable CTI producers to push data to their customers – whether it's a single customer or many customers. This same mechanism also enables customers to receive data from many producers (TAXII-v2.1). The TAXII version 2.1 specification is 79 pages and contains all the details needed to implement client and server participants in the CTI sharing models I mentioned earlier.

Threats described using STIX are not required to be shared via TAXII – any protocol can be used to do this as long as the sender and receiver both understand and support it.

A key benefit of using STIX and TAXII is standardization. When CTI producers publish CTI using a standardized schema like STIX, it makes it easier for organizations to consume it, even when they are using technologies from different vendors. If everyone uses the same standard way to describe threats versus proprietary protocols, CTI consumers get the benefit regardless of the vendors they procure cybersecurity capabilities from. In other words, cybersecurity vendors and teams can focus on innovation using CTI, instead of spending time devising ways to model and share it. These protocols help scale CTI sharing to organizations and technologies around the world.

Reasons not to share CTI

Many of the security teams I have talked to opt not to share CTI with other organizations, even when they have good relationships with them. This might seem counterintuitive. Why wouldn't a security team want to help other organizations detect threats they have already discovered in their own IT environment?

There are at least a couple of good reasons for this behavior. First, depending on the exposure, disclosing CTI could be interpreted as an admission or even an announcement that the organization has suffered a data breach. Keeping such matters close to the chest minimizes potential legal risks and PR risks, or at least gives the organization some time to complete their investigation if one is ongoing. If the organization has suffered a breach, they'll want to manage it on their own terms and on their own timeline if possible. In such scenarios, many organizations simply won't share CTI because it could end up disrupting their incident response processes and crisis communication plans, potentially leading to litigation and class action lawsuits.

A second reason some security teams opt not to share CTI is that they don't want to signal to the attackers that they know that their IT environment is compromised. For example, when they'd find a file suspected of being malware on one of their systems, instead of uploading a copy of it to VirusTotal or their anti-malware vendor for analysis, they'd prefer to do their own analysis behind closed doors so as not to tip off the attackers. Their reasoning is that once they upload the malware sample to an anti-malware vendor, that vendor will develop signatures to detect, block, and clean that malware and distribute those signatures to their customers and samples of the malware to other anti-malware vendors. The malware will also appear in anti-malware vendors' online threat encyclopedias.

A "best practice" that many malware purveyors use is to scan the malware they develop offline with multiple anti-malware products to ensure their new malware is not detected by any of them. This gives them a measure of confidence that they are still undetected in their victims' IT environments. However, if at some point they see that their malware is being detected by the anti-malware products they test, they will know that one or more of their victims has found their malware, submitted it to an anti-malware vendor, and are likely investigating further to determine the extent of the intrusion. This is a signal to attackers that their victims can now detect one of the tools they have been using (the malware) and might be on the hunt for them in the compromised environment. As the detection signatures for the malware are distributed to more and more systems around the world, the chances of detection increase dramatically.

Subsequently, many security teams do their own in-house malware reverse engineering and will not share CTI with other organizations, even the security vendors they procure products and services from, until they believe there is no opportunity cost to doing so. This approach gives them the best chance to find and exorcize the attackers before they decide to perform actions on objectives, such as deploying ransomware or destructive wiper malware.

How to identify credible cyber threat intelligence

I'm going to give you some guidance on how to identify good CTI versus the questionable threat intelligence I see so often in the industry today. After publishing one of the industry's best threat intelligence reports for the better part of a decade (OK, I admit I'm biased), I learned a few things along the way that I'll share with you here. The theme of this guidance is to understand the methodology that your threat intelligence vendors use. If they don't tell you what their methodology is, then you can't trust their data, period. Additionally, the only way you'll be able to truly understand if or how specific threat intelligence can help your organization is to understand its data sources, as well as the methodology used to collect and report the data; without this context, threat intelligence can be distracting and the opposite of helpful.

Data sources

Always understand the sources of CTI data that you are using and how the vendors involved are interpreting the data. If the source of data is unknown or the vendors won't share the source of the data, then you simply cannot trust it and the interpretations based on it. For example, a vendor claims that 85% of all systems have been successfully infected by a particular family of malware. But when you dig into the source of the data used to make this claim, it turns out that 85% of systems that used the vendor's online malware cleaner website were infected with the malware referenced. Notice that "85% of all systems" is a dramatic extrapolation from "85% of all systems that used their online tool."

Additionally, the online tool is only offered in US English, meaning it's less likely that consumers who don't speak English will use it, even if they know it exists. Finally, you discover that the vendor's desktop anti-virus detection tool refers users to the online tool to get disinfected when it finds systems to be infected with the threat. The vendor does this to drive awareness that their super-great online tool is available to their customers. This skews the data as 100% of users referred to the online tool from the desktop anti-virus tool were already known to be infected with that threat. I can't count how many times I've seen stunts like this over the years.

Always dive deep into the data sources to understand what the data actually means to you. The more familiar you are with the data sources, the easier it will be for you to determine the true value of that data to your organization. In *Chapter 4, The Evolution of Malware*, I spend a lot of time describing the intricacies of the sources of data used in that chapter. This is the only way to understand the picture the data is providing, relative to your organization and the risks it cares about.

For example, if you work at a public sector organization in Japan, how valuable is CTI to you that focuses on a specific industry vertical in the private sector in the United States? The answer is you don't know until you understand the sources of data and what they might mean to your organization.

Specificity is your friend in this context. Understanding where the data was collected from and how, the limitations of the data sources, and the underlying assumptions and biases present while processing the data are all key to understanding how the resulting CTI might help your organization. CTI is a lot less credible without the context that allows you to understand it. Purveyors of credible CTI are happy to provide this context to you. However, they might not volunteer this information and you might need to request it. Providing such information tends to highlight the limitations of the CTI and the CTI provider's capabilities. Also, I've found that not everyone is a connoisseur of the finer points of CTI; being prepared to ask your own questions is typically the best way to get the context you need to truly understand CTI.

Time periods

When consuming threat intelligence, understanding the time scale and time periods of the data is super important. Are the data and insights provided from a period of days, weeks, months, quarters, or years? The answer to this question will help provide the context required to understand the intelligence. The events of a few days will potentially have a much different meaning to your organization than a long-term trend over a period of years.

Anomalies will typically warrant a different risk treatment than established patterns. Additionally, the conclusions that can be made from CTI data can be dramatically altered based on the time periods the vendor uses in their report.

Let me provide you with an example scenario. Let's say a vendor is reporting on how many vulnerabilities were exploited in their products for a given period. If the data is reported in regular sequential periods of time, such as quarterly, the trend looks really bad as large increases are evident.

But instead of reporting the trend using sequential quarterly periods, the trend looks much better when comparing the current quarter to the same quarter last year; there could actually be a decrease in the exploitation of vulnerabilities in the current quarter versus the same quarter last year. This puts a positive light on the vendor, despite an increase in the exploitation of vulnerabilities in their products quarter over quarter.

Another potential red flag is when you see a vendor report data that isn't for a normal period of time, such as monthly, quarterly, or annually. Instead, they use a period of months that seems a little random. If the time period is irregular or the reason it's used isn't obvious, the rationale should be documented with the CTI. If it's not, ask the vendor why they picked the time periods they picked. Sometimes, you'll find vendors use a specific time period because it makes their story more dramatic, garnering more attention, if that's their agenda. Alternatively, the period selected might help downplay bad news by minimizing changes in the data.

Understanding why the data is being reported in specific time scales and periods will give you some idea about the credibility of the data, as well as the agenda of the vendor providing it to you.

Recognizing hype

One of the biggest mistakes I've seen organizations make when consuming CTI is accepting their vendor's claims about the scope, applicability, and relevance of their data. For example, a CTI vendor publishes data that claims 100% of attacks in a specific time period involved social engineering or exploited a specific vulnerability. The problem with such claims is that no one in the world can see 100% of all attacks, period.

They'd have to be omniscient to see all attacks occurring everywhere in the world simultaneously, on all operating systems and cloud platforms, in all browsers and applications. Similarly, claims such as 60% of all attacks were perpetrated by a specific APT group are not helpful. Unless they have knowledge of 100% of attacks, they can't credibly make claims about the characteristics of 60% of them. A claim about the characteristics of all attacks or a subset that requires knowledge of all attacks, even when referencing specific time periods, specific locations, and specific attack vectors, simply isn't possible or credible. A good litmus test for CTI is to ask yourself, does the vendor have to be omniscient to make this claim? This is where understanding the data sources and the time periods will help you cut through the hype and derive any value the intelligence might have.

Many times, the vendor publishing the data doesn't make such claims directly in their threat intelligence reports, but the way new intelligence is reported in the headlines is generalized or made more dramatic in order to draw attention to it. Don't blame CTI vendors for the way the news is reported, as this is typically beyond their control. But if they make such claims directly, recognize them and adjust the context in your mind appropriately. For many years, I made headlines around the world regularly speaking and writing about threats, but we were always very careful not to overstep the mark from conclusions supported by the data. To make bolder claims would have required omniscience and omnipotence.

Predictions about the future

I'm sure you've seen some vendors make predictions about what's going to happen in the threat landscape in the future. One trick that some CTI vendors have used is again related to time periods. Let's say I'm publishing a threat intelligence report about the last 6-month period covering January through June. By the time the data for this period is collected and the report is written and published, a month or two might have gone by. Now we are in September. If I make a prediction about the future in this report, I have two months of data from July and August that tell me what's been happening since the end of the reporting period.

If my prediction is based on what the data tells us already happened in July and August, readers of the report will be led to believe that I actually predicted the future accurately, thus reinforcing the idea that we know more about the threat landscape than anyone else. Understanding when the prediction was made relative to the time period it was focused on will help you decide how credible the prediction and results are, and how trustworthy the vendor making the prediction is. Remember, predictions about the future are guesses – what happened in the past does not define what can happen in the future.

Vendors' motives

Trust is a combination of credibility and character. You can use both to decide how trustworthy your vendors are. Transparency around CTI data sources, time scales, time periods, and predictions about the future can help vendors prove they are credible. Their motives communicate something about their character. Do they want to build a relationship with your organization as a trusted advisor or is their interest limited to a financial transaction? There's a place for both types of vendors when building a cybersecurity program, but knowing which vendors fall into each category can be helpful, especially during incident response-related activities, when the pressure is on. Knowing who you can rely on for real help when you need it is important.

Those are some of the insights I can offer you from 10 years of publishing threat intelligence reports. Again, the big takeaway here is understanding the methodology and data sources of the CTI you consume - this context is not optional. One final word of advice: do not consume threat intelligence that doesn't meet this criterion. There is too much fear, uncertainty, doubt, and complexity in the IT industry. You need to be selective about who you take advice from.

I hope you enjoyed this chapter. Over the last few years, the CTI industry has exploded. Finding credible sources of CTI shouldn't be a challenge for well-funded cybersecurity programs. CTI is being integrated into cybersecurity products and services more and more, which means protecting, detecting, and responding to threats should be easier and faster than ever. However, I have to wonder if this is true, how are attackers being more successful now than ever before? There are many historical examples that teach us that threat intelligence isn't sufficient by itself to mitigate attacks - defenders need to be willing to act on the intelligence they have and need the capabilities to do so effectively. Despite the proliferation of CTI, organizations still need effective cybersecurity strategies to be successful. In order to develop an effective strategy for your organization, it is helpful to first understand the types of threats you face and how they operate. This is the theme of the next three chapters of this book.

Summary

Cyber Threat Intelligence (CTI) provides organizations with data and information on potential cyber threats. Those threats can include various categories of malware, exploitation of vulnerabilities, web-based attacks, **Distributed Denial of Service (DDoS)** attacks, social engineering attacks, and others. **Open Source Threat Intelligence (OSINT)** leverages publicly available data sources such as social media, news feeds, court filings and arrest records, attackers' disclosed information on their victims, activity in illicit forums, and many others.

Cybersecurity programs can make use of CTI in several ways including in **Security Operations Centers (SOCs)**, to inform **Cybersecurity Incident Response Teams' (CIRT)** investigations, to inform threat hunting, Red, Blue, and Purple teams' efforts, and many others. Understanding the **tactics, techniques, and procedures (TTPs)** that attackers employ can provide some concrete ideas on how they can be mitigated. A tactic is the reason the attacker performs a particular action. Many security teams also use **Indicators of Compromise (IOCs)** to help determine if their enterprise IT environments have been compromised. Where TTPs can help protect, detect, and respond to attacks, IOCs can help post-compromise to try to determine when and how the initial compromise happened, and what the attackers did with their illicit access afterward.

The **Traffic Light Protocol (TLP)** has become a popular protocol for sharing CTI and other types of information. The "traffic light" analogy in this case has four colors: red, amber, green, and clear. The colors are used to communicate different information-sharing boundaries, as specified by the sender.

This chapter provided some context to help you understand the analysis of various threats in the next three chapters: *Chapter 3, Using Vulnerability Trends to Reduce Risk and Costs, Chapter 4, The Evolution of Malware,* and *Chapter 5, Internet-Based Threats.*

References

- BBC News. (2013). "Microsoft sees rise in net attacks". BBC News. Retrieved from https://www.bbc.com/news/av/business-22348290.

- Badger, L.; Johnson, C.; Skorupka, C.; Snyder, J.; Watermire, D. (October 2016). "NIST Special Publication 800-150". NIST. Retrieved from https://nvlpubs.nist.gov/nistpubs/SpecialPublications/NIST.SP.800-150.pdf.

- MITRE ATT&CK® (n.d.). Retrieved from https://attack.mitre.org/.

- "NIST Special Publication 800-53 Revision 5". (September 2020). NIST. Retrieved from https://nvlpubs.nist.gov/nistpubs/SpecialPublications/NIST.SP.800-53r5.pdf.

- FIRST. (n.d.). Retrieved from https://www.first.org/tlp/.

- CISA. (n.d.). Retrieved from https://www.cisa.gov/tlp.

- STIX Version 2.1. (10 June 2021). *OASIS Standard.* https://docs.oasis-open.org/cti/stix/v2.1/os/stix-v2.1-os.html. Latest stage: https://docs.oasis-open.org/cti/stix/v2.1/stix-v2.1.html.

- TAXII™ Version 2.1. (10 June 2021). *OASIS Standard.* https://docs.oasis-open.org/cti/taxii/v2.1/os/taxii-v2.1-os.html. Latest stage: https://docs.oasisopen.org/cti/taxii/v2.1/taxii-v2.1.html.

Join our community on Discord

Join our community's Discord space for discussions with the author and other readers:

https://packt.link/SecNet

3

Using Vulnerability Trends to Reduce Risk and Costs

Vulnerabilities represent risk and expense to all organizations. Vendors who are serious about reducing both risk and costs for their customers focus on reducing the number of vulnerabilities in their products and work on ways to make it hard and expensive for attackers to exploit their customers, thereby driving down attackers' return on investment. Identifying the vendors and the products that have been successful in doing this can be time-consuming and difficult.

In this chapter, I will provide you with valuable background information and an in-depth analysis of how some of the industry's leaders have managed vulnerabilities in their products over the last two decades, focusing on operating systems and web browsers. I introduce a vulnerability improvement framework that can help you to identify vendors and products that have been reducing risks and costs for their customers. This data and analysis can inform your organization's vulnerability management strategy.

In this chapter, we'll cover the following topics:

- A primer on vulnerability management
- Introducing a vulnerability management improvement framework
- Examining vulnerability disclosure trends for select vendors, operating systems, and web browsers
- Guidance on vulnerability management programs

Let's begin by looking at what vulnerability management is.

Introduction

Over the past 20 years, organizations have been challenged to manage a continual volume of new vulnerabilities in software and hardware. Attackers and malware constantly attempt to exploit unpatched vulnerabilities on systems in every industry and every part of the world. Vulnerabilities are a currency for many interested groups, including security researchers, the vulnerability management industry, governments, various commercial organizations, and, of course, attackers and purveyors of malware. These groups have different motivations and goals, but they all value new vulnerabilities, with some willing to pay handsomely for them. I had a front-row seat at ground zero for the tumultuous period where worms and other malware first started exploiting vulnerabilities in Microsoft software at scale. After working on the enterprise network support team at Microsoft for a few years, I was asked to help build a new customer-facing security incident response team. I accepted that job on Thursday, January 23, 2003. Two days later, on Saturday, January 25th, SQL Slammer hit the internet, disrupting networks worldwide. That Saturday morning, I got into my car to drive to the office but had to stop for gas. Both the cash machine and the pumps at the gas station were offline due to "network issues." At that point, I realized just how widespread and serious that attack was. Then, one day in August 2003, Blaster disrupted the internet to an even greater extent than SQL Slammer had. Then, over the course of the following year, Blaster variants followed, as well as MyDoom, Sasser, and other widespread malware attacks. It turns out that millions of people were willing to double-click on an email attachment labeled "MyDoom." Most of these attacks used unpatched vulnerabilities in Microsoft products to infect systems and propagate. This all happened before Windows Update existed, or any of the tools that are available today for servicing software. Because Microsoft had to release multiple security updates to address the underlying vulnerabilities in the components that Blaster used, many IT departments began a long-term pattern of behavior, delaying patching systems to avoid patching the same components repeatedly and rebooting systems repeatedly. Most internet-connected Windows-based systems were not running anti-virus software in those days either, and many of them that did, didn't have the latest signatures installed. Working on a customer-facing security incident response team, supporting security updates, and helping enterprise customers with malware infections and hackers was a very tough job in those days—you needed a thick skin. Subsequently, I had the opportunity to learn a lot about malware, vulnerabilities, and exploits in this role.

Later in my career at Microsoft, I managed marketing communications for the **Microsoft Security Response Center (MSRC)**, the **Microsoft Security Development Lifecycle (SDL)**, and the **Microsoft Malware Protection Center (MMPC)**.

The MSRC is the group at Microsoft that manages the incoming vulnerability reports and attack reports. The MMPC is what they called Microsoft's anti-virus research and response lab back then. The SDL is a software development methodology that was instituted at Microsoft in the years that followed these devastating worm attacks. I learned a lot about vulnerabilities, exploits, malware, and attackers in the 8 or 9 years I worked at this organization, called Trustworthy Computing. I often get asked if things are better today than they were 5 or 10 years ago. This chapter is dedicated to answering this question and providing some insights into how things have changed from a vulnerability management perspective. I also want to provide you with a way to identify vendors and products that have been reducing risk and costs for their customers.

Vulnerability Management Primer

Before we dive into the vulnerability disclosure trends for the past couple of decades, let me provide you with a quick primer on vulnerability management so that it's easier to understand the data and analysis I provide, and how some vulnerability management teams use such data.

There are many different definitions of what a vulnerability is. Since I provide a lot of data in this chapter based on MITRE **Common Vulnerabilities and Exposures (CVEs)** as reported by CVE Numbering Authorities, here is how they define a vulnerability in that context:

> *A weakness in the computational logic (e.g., code) found in software and hardware components that, when exploited, results in a negative impact on confidentiality, integrity, or availability. Mitigation of the vulnerabilities in this context typically involves coding changes, but could also include specification changes or even specification deprecations (e.g., the removal of affected protocols or functionality in their entirety)." (CVE, 2020)*

If you are wondering what a vulnerability actually looks like, this little code snippet is a good example, as its author explains below. Vulnerabilities, like this example, can be obvious bugs that are identified by developers reviewing code, the development tools they use, or **Static Application Security Testing (SAST)** and **Dynamic Application Security Testing (DAST)**. Other vulnerabilities can be very subtle and hard to find.

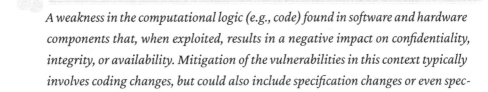

```
void func(int index, int value)
{
    char buf[4];
    buf[index] = value;
}
```

Let's assume the arguments index and value come from a call to recv() which reads a packet from the Internet. Is this a security bug? Heck yeah. The attacker controls everything about that poor old buffer. Even with /GS and ASLR in place, this would be a serious bug and would be fixed at the earliest." (Howard, May 9, 2021)

When a vulnerability is discovered in a released software or hardware product and reported to the vendor that owns the vulnerable product or service, the vulnerability will ultimately be assigned a CVE identifier at some point. MITRE Corporation started a catalog of all CVEs, called the CVE List, in 1999. The CVE List can be accessed at `https://cve.mitre.org/cve/search_cve_list.html`.

The U.S. **National Vulnerability Database (NVD)** was established in 2005 by the **National Institute of Standards and Technology (NIST)**. The NVD imports data from the CVE List and adds metadata to it (including metrics and scoring information) (CVE, 2020). The NVD can be used to track publicly disclosed vulnerabilities in all sorts of software and hardware products across the entire industry. The NVD is a publicly available database that can be accessed at `https://nvd.nist.gov`.

The exact date when a CVE identifier is assigned to a vulnerability is a function of many different factors, to which an entire chapter in this book could be dedicated. In fact, I co-wrote a Microsoft white paper on this topic called Software Vulnerability Management at Microsoft, which described why it could take a relatively long time to release security updates for Microsoft products. It appears that this paper has disappeared from the Microsoft Download Center with the sands of time. However, the following are some of the factors explaining why it can be a long time between a vendor receiving a report of a vulnerability and releasing a security update for it:

- **Identifying the bug**: Some bugs only show up under special conditions or in the largest IT environments. It can take time for the vendor to reproduce the bug and triage it. Additionally, the reported vulnerability might exist in other products and services that use the same or similar components. All of these products and services need to be fixed simultaneously so that the vendor doesn't inadvertently produce a zero-day vulnerability in its own product line. I'll discuss zero-day vulnerabilities later in this chapter.

- **Identifying all variants**: Fixing the reported bug might be straightforward and easy. However, finding all the variations of the issue and fixing them too is important as it will prevent the need to re-release security updates or release multiple updates to address vulnerabilities in the same component. This can be the activity that takes the most time when fixing vulnerabilities.

- **Code reviews and testing**: Ensuring the updated code actually fixes the vulnerability and doesn't introduce more bugs and vulnerabilities is important and sometimes time-consuming.

- **Functional testing**: This ensures that the fix doesn't impact the functionality of the product—customers don't appreciate it when this happens.

- **Application compatibility testing**: In the case of an operating system or web browser, vendors might need to test thousands of applications, drivers, and other components to ensure they don't break their ecosystem when they release the security update. For example, the integration testing matrix for Windows is huge, including thousands of the most common applications that run on the platform.

- **Release testing**: Ensuring the distribution and installation of the security update works as expected and doesn't make systems unbootable or unstable.

It is important to realize that the date that a CVE identifier is assigned to a vulnerability isn't necessarily related to the date that the vendor releases an update that addresses the underlying vulnerability; that is, these dates can be different. The allure of notoriety that comes with announcing the discovery of a new major vulnerability leads some security researchers to release details publicly before vendors can fix the flaws. The typical best-case scenario is when the public disclosure of a vulnerability occurs on the same date that the vendor releases a security update that addresses the vulnerability. This reduces the window of opportunity for attackers to exploit the vulnerability to the time it takes for each organization to test and deploy the update in their IT environments.

An example of a CVE identifier is CVE-2018-8653. As you can tell from the CVE identifier, the number 8653 was assigned to the vulnerability it was associated with in 2018. When we look up this CVE identifier in the CVE List, we can get access to some basic information including a short description, references, and the date the CVE was added to the list. Here is the description of the CVE:

> *A remote code execution vulnerability exists in the way that the scripting engine handles objects in memory in Internet Explorer, aka "Scripting Engine Memory Corruption Vulnerability." This affects Internet Explorer 9, Internet Explorer 10, and Internet Explorer 11." (CVE)*

By looking up the same CVE ID in the NVD we can get access to more detail about the vulnerability it is associated with. Examples include the severity score for the vulnerability, whether the vulnerability can be accessed remotely, and its potential impact on confidentiality, integrity, and availability.

What is this additional information that the NVD provides used for? Risk is the combination of probability and impact. In the context of vulnerabilities, risk is the combination of the probability that a vulnerability can be successfully exploited and the impact on the system if it is exploited. A score is assigned to each CVE in the NVD that represents this risk calculation for the vulnerability. The **Common Vulnerability Scoring System (CVSS)** is used to estimate the risk for each vulnerability in the NVD. The **Forum of Incident Response and Security Teams (FIRST)** CVSS **Special Interest Group (SIG)** is the custodian of the CVSS with the goal of improving it over time. You can find more information on this SIG at `https://www.first.org/cvss/`.

To calculate the risk, the CVSS uses "exploitability metrics," such as the attack vector, attack complexity, privileges required, and user interaction (FIRST, 2019). To calculate an estimate of the impact on a system if a vulnerability is successfully exploited, the CVSS uses "impact metrics," such as the expected impact on confidentiality, integrity, and availability (FIRST, 2019).

The exploitability metrics and impact metrics are provided in the NVD's details on each CVE. The CVSS uses these details in some simple mathematical calculations to produce a base score for each vulnerability (NIST, n.d.).

Vulnerability management professionals can further refine the base scores for vulnerabilities by using metrics in a temporal metric group and an environmental group. The temporal metric group reflects the fact that the base score can change over time as new information becomes available – for example, when proof of concept code for a vulnerability becomes publicly available. Environmental metrics can be used to reduce the score of a CVE because of the existence of mitigating factors or controls in a specific IT environment. For example, the impact of a vulnerability might be blunted because a mitigation for the vulnerability had already been deployed by the organization in their previous efforts to harden their IT environment. The vulnerability disclosure trends that I discuss in this chapter are all based on the base scores for CVEs.

The CVSS has evolved over time—there have been some different versions released over time, such as v2, v3, and v3.1. The ratings for the current version, version 3.1, are represented in the following diagram (FIRST, 2019). NVD CVSS calculators for CVSS v3 and v3.1 are available to help organizations calculate vulnerability scores using temporal and environmental metrics (NIST, n.d.).

The scores can be converted into ratings such as low, medium, high, and critical to make it easier to manage than using granular numeric scores (FIRST, 2019).

Rating	CVSS Score
Low	0.1 - 3.9
Medium	4.0 - 6.9
High	7.0 - 8.9
Critical	9.0 - 10.0

Figure 3.1: Rating descriptions for ranges of CVSS version 3.1 scores

Vulnerabilities with higher scores have higher probabilities of exploitation and/or greater impacts on systems when exploited. Put another way, the higher the score, the higher the risk. This is why many vulnerability management teams use these scores and ratings to determine how quickly to test and deploy security updates and/or mitigations for vulnerabilities in their environments, once the vulnerabilities have been publicly disclosed.

Another important term to understand is "zero-day" vulnerability. A zero-day vulnerability is a vulnerability that has been publicly disclosed before the vendor that is responsible for it has released a security update to address it. These vulnerabilities are the most valuable of all vulnerabilities, with attackers and governments willing to pay relatively large sums for them (potentially a million dollars or more for a working exploit).

A scenario that vulnerability management teams dread is when a critical-rated zero-day vulnerability in software or hardware they have in their environment has been publicly disclosed. This means the risk of exploitation could be super high and that a security update that could prevent exploitation of the vulnerability is not publicly available. Sometimes in these scenarios, there are "workarounds" that can be implemented to help make exploitation of the vulnerability harder or impossible. Workarounds like specific system configurations that prevent exploitation are typically meant to be temporary. After all, if the only thing preventing exploitation is a configuration setting, what happens if that setting gets changed inadvertently? Oftentimes, changing a configuration setting as a workaround also disables functionality that was previously available. The one way to address the vulnerability with the highest confidence and least impact is to install an update that fixes it.

An even worse scenario is when a vendor releases a security update for an exploitable, critical rated vulnerability, but the update doesn't fix the vulnerability completely. In this scenario, the existence of the vulnerability is public knowledge, and the publicly available security update that isn't 100% effective essentially draws a map to the vulnerability for attackers to use. Typically, in such scenarios, exploit code for such a vulnerability becomes publicly available and widely circulated on the internet, very quickly.

This scenario might sound theoretical, but unfortunately, it has occurred numerous times over the past two decades. Perhaps the latest and best example is the dreaded "Log4j" vulnerabilities (CVE-2021-44228 and CVE-2021-45046). This vulnerability was in the ubiquitous Java logging library Apache Log4j2. CVE-2021-44228 has a "perfect" 10 CVSS score, meaning it is easy to exploit and can result in attackers taking complete control of impacted systems. It is so easy to exploit that some cybersecurity professionals nicknamed it "Log4Shell" – a tongue-in-cheek reference to the ability to remotely run any command on systems compromised using this vulnerability. The Software Engineering Institute CERT Coordination Center at Carnegie Mellon University described it this way:

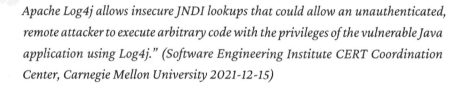

> *Apache Log4j allows insecure JNDI lookups that could allow an unauthenticated, remote attacker to execute arbitrary code with the privileges of the vulnerable Java application using Log4j." (Software Engineering Institute CERT Coordination Center, Carnegie Mellon University 2021-12-15)*

Because this vulnerability was in a very popular software library, it impacted literally thousands of products that leveraged that library across operating systems like Windows, Linux, and macOS. For many security teams, the ubiquity of Log4j and the wide variety of places it could be present in enterprise IT environments made it challenging to find and remediate. Organizations that had immature asset management practices or imperfect asset inventories (almost everyone) were left with a ticking time bomb on their hands. Subsequently, many of the customers I advised managed the remediation of this vulnerability the same way they would manage an active cybersecurity incident. Using incident response processes instead of their vulnerability management processes enabled these teams to deem remediation as a top priority for their organizations and get access to resources commensurate with this declaration.

However, to make matters worse, more than one security update had to be released to fully address this critical-rated vulnerability, which was already in active use by attackers at the time.

CVE-2021-45046 stated, "It was found that the fix to address CVE-2021-44228 in Apache Log4j 2.15.0 was incomplete in certain non-default configurations" (CVE, 12/14/2021).

These factors resulted in much more work for cybersecurity and IT teams than remediating a typical critical rated vulnerability. This scenario occurred at Christmas time in 2021 and spilled over into the new year, forcing many security teams to work through the holiday season on remediation. All these factors conspired to exhaust many cybersecurity and IT professionals. Months later, vulnerable versions of Log4j continued to endear themselves to cybersecurity and IT teams around the world, by continuing to "pop up" unexpectedly in many enterprise IT environments, seeping back in from a variety of sources such as vulnerable systems restored from backups, spinning up virtual machines from unpatched images, vendors continuing to deploy unpatched applications and appliances, and many others. This fun will continue for years.

If you are interested in reading all the details about how the Log4j vulnerabilities were reported and the crisis unfolded, the newly formed United States Cyber Safety Review Board investigated and published a report on their findings. I saw the board's chair from the Department of Homeland Security and the deputy chair from Google discuss the report and their findings at Black Hat 2022. It was interesting to hear about the **People's Republic of China (PRC)** government's reaction to the security researcher from Alibaba who found the vulnerability and initially reported it to the Apache Software Foundation, instead of to the PRC's **Ministry of Industry and Information Technology (MIIT).**

> *Independent of a possible sanction against Alibaba, the Board noted troubling elements of MIIT's regulations governing disclosure of security vulnerabilities. The requirement for network product providers to report vulnerabilities in their products to MIIT within two days of discovery could give the PRC government early knowledge of vulnerabilities before vendor fixes are made available to the community. The Board is concerned this will afford the PRC government a window in which to exploit vulnerabilities before network defenders can patch them. This is a disturbing prospect given the PRC government's known track record of intellectual property theft, intelligence collection, surveillance of human rights activists and dissidents, and military cyber operations." (Cyber Safety Review Board. July 11, 2022).*

This quote lays bare how globally important and politically charged vulnerability disclosures can get! I'll discuss this tension in *Chapter 6, The Roles Governments Play in Cybersecurity*. If you are interested in reading the report, it can be downloaded from `https://www.cisa.gov/sites/default/files/publications/CSRB-Report-on-Log4-July-11-2022_508.pdf`.

Zero-day vulnerabilities aren't as rare as you might think. Data that Microsoft published indicates that of the CVEs that were known to be exploited in Microsoft products in 2017, the first time they were exploited, 100% were zero-day vulnerabilities and, in 2018, 83% were zero-day vulnerabilities (Matt Miller, 2019).

Here is a fun fact for you. I created a large, sensational news cycle in 2013 when I coined the term "zero day forever" in a blog post I wrote on Microsoft's official security blog. I was referring to any vulnerability found in Windows XP after official support for it ended. In this scenario, any vulnerability found in Windows XP after the end of support would be a zero day forever, as Microsoft would not provide ongoing security updates for it.

Let me explain this in a little more detail. Attackers can wait for new security updates to be released for currently supported versions of Windows, like Windows 11. Then, they reverse-engineer these updates to find the vulnerability that each update addresses. Then, they check whether those vulnerabilities are also present in Windows XP. If they are, and Microsoft won't release security updates for them, then attackers have zero-day vulnerabilities for Windows XP forever. To this day, you can search for the term "zero day forever" and find many news articles quoting me. I became the poster boy for the end of the life of Windows XP because of that news cycle.

Over the years, I have talked to thousands of CISOs and vulnerability managers about the practices they use to manage vulnerabilities for their organizations. Historically, the four most common groups of thought on the best way to manage vulnerabilities in large, complex enterprise environments are as follows:

- **Prioritize critical rated vulnerabilities**: When updates or mitigations for critical rated vulnerabilities become available, they are tested and deployed immediately. Lower-rated vulnerabilities are tested and deployed during regularly scheduled IT maintenance in order to minimize system reboots and disruption to business. These organizations are mitigating the highest risk vulnerabilities as quickly as possible and are willing to accept significant risk in order to avoid constantly disrupting their environments with security update deployments.

- **Prioritize high- and critical-rated vulnerabilities**: When high and critical rated vulnerabilities are publicly disclosed, their policy dictates that they will patch critical vulnerabilities or deploy available mitigations within 24 hours and high rated vulnerabilities within a month. Vulnerabilities with lower scores will be patched as part of their regular IT maintenance cycle to minimize system reboots and disruption to business.

- **No prioritization** – just patch everything: Some organizations have come to the conclusion that given the continuous and growing volume of vulnerability disclosures that they are forced to manage, the effort they put into analyzing CVSS scores and prioritizing updates isn't worthwhile. Instead, they simply test and deploy all updates on essentially the same schedule. This schedule might be monthly, quarterly, or, for those organizations with inflated risk appetites, semi-annually. These organizations focus on being really efficient at deploying security updates regardless of their severity ratings.

- **Delay deployment**: For organizations that are acutely sensitive to IT disruptions and have been disrupted by poor-quality security updates in the past, delaying the deployment of security updates has become an unfortunate practice. In other words, these organizations accept the risk related to all publicly known, unpatched vulnerabilities in the products they use for a period of months to ensure that security updates from their vendors aren't re-released due to quality issues. These organizations have decided that the cure is potentially worse than the disease; that is, disruption from poor quality security updates poses the same or higher risk to them than all potential attackers in the world. The organizations that subscribe to this school of thought tend to bundle and deploy months' worth of updates. The appetite for risk among these organizations is high, to say the least.

A newer approach to managing vulnerabilities in large enterprise IT environments that focuses even further on prioritizing specific vulnerabilities for remediation has become very popular among security teams. As I wrote in *Chapter 2, What to Know about Threat Intelligence*, **Cyber Threat Intelligence (CTI)** has many uses. One of those uses is to inform the priority of vulnerability remediation. Most of the organizations I have advised in the last few years now use CTI to identify the vulnerabilities that are being used in active attacks on the internet. They view these vulnerabilities as the highest risk because their exploitation isn't just theoretical, which is what a CVSS score represents. Given that someone has figured out how to exploit a vulnerability, has exploit code or a tool to do this, and they are actively out there attacking systems with it, the probability side of the risk equation is as high as it gets. Subsequently, they prioritize patching these vulnerabilities before all others. This approach provides remediation teams with more time to address vulnerabilities where there is no CTI indicating that they are actively being exploited.

Arguably, organizations that use this approach accept more risk, at least until all critical and high-severity vulnerabilities in their IT estates are addressed. Essentially, they are gambling on the quality and timeliness of the CTI they use to inform their vulnerability remediation priorities. However, for organizations that struggle with vulnerability management and remediation, this approach helps them maintain a manageable scope for their remediation efforts while genuinely reducing risk. The key though is to address the other critical and high severity vulnerabilities that weren't being actively exploited when they were initially evaluated, in a reasonable period of time. Allowing these vulnerabilities to sit in inventory and accumulate over time is foolhardy. Remember what I wrote in *Chapter 2* – no one is omniscient, and subsequently, no one can see 100% of all attacks. Understanding the sources of data and the limitations of the CTI used to inform vulnerability management is critical when using this approach.

Leveraging CTI to prioritize vulnerability remediation has become so popular that major vulnerability scanner vendors offer CTI integrations into their vulnerability scanner products, and the NVD now integrates exploitation information into the details of each CVE.

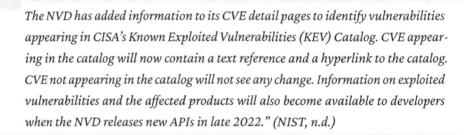

The NVD has added information to its CVE detail pages to identify vulnerabilities appearing in CISA's Known Exploited Vulnerabilities (KEV) Catalog. CVE appearing in the catalog will now contain a text reference and a hyperlink to the catalog. CVE not appearing in the catalog will not see any change. Information on exploited vulnerabilities and the affected products will also become available to developers when the NVD releases new APIs in late 2022." (NIST, n.d.)

To the uninitiated, these approaches and the trade-offs might not make much sense. The primary pain point that deploying vulnerabilities creates, besides the expense, is disruption to the business. For example, historically, most updates for Windows operating systems required reboots. When systems get rebooted, the downtime incurred is counted against the uptime goals that most IT organizations are committed to. Rebooting a single server might not seem material, but the time it takes to reboot hundreds or thousands of servers starts to add up. Keep in mind that organizations trying to maintain 99.999% (5 "9s") uptime can only afford to have 5 minutes and 15 seconds of downtime per year. That's 26.3 seconds of downtime per month. Servers in enterprise data centers, especially database and storage servers, can easily take more than 5 minutes to reboot when they are healthy. Additionally, when a server is rebooted, life is like a box of chocolates; this is a prime time for issues to surface that require troubleshooting, thereby exacerbating downtime. The worst-case scenario is when a security update itself causes a problem.

The time it takes to uninstall the update and reboot yet again, on hundreds or thousands of systems, leaving them in a vulnerable state, also negatively impacts uptime.

Patching and rebooting systems can be expensive, especially for organizations that perform supervised patching in off-hours, which can require overtime and weekend wages. The concept of the conventional maintenance window is no longer valid, as many businesses are global and operate across borders, 24 hours per day, 7 days per week. A thoughtful approach to scheduled and layered patching, keeping the majority of infrastructure available while patching and rebooting a minority, has become common.

Reboots are the top reason that many organizations decide to accept some risk by patching quarterly or semi-annually, so much so that the MSRC that I worked closely with for over a decade used to try to minimize the number of security updates that required system reboots to every second month. To do this, when possible, they would try to release all the updates that required a reboot one month and then release updates that didn't require reboots the next month. When this plan worked, organizations that were patching systems every month could at least avoid rebooting systems every second month. But the "out of band" updates, which were unplanned updates, seemed to spoil these plans frequently.

When you see how vulnerability disclosures have trended over time, the trade-offs that organizations make between the risk of exploitation and uptime might make more sense. Running servers in the cloud can dramatically change this equation—I'll cover this in more detail in *Chapter 12, Modern Approaches to Security and Compliance*. There are many other aspects and details of the NVD, CVE, and CVSS that I didn't cover here, but I've provided enough of a primer that you'll be able to appreciate the vulnerability disclosure trends that I provide next.

The bulk of the rest of this chapter is devoted to data and analysis with more than 50 graphs and tables. If you aren't interested in seeing the data and analysis, you can skip it and go right to the section called *Vulnerability Improvement Framework Summary*.

Vulnerability Disclosure Data Sources

Before we dig into the vulnerability disclosure data, let me tell you where the data comes from and provide some caveats regarding the validity and reliability of the data. There are three primary sources of data that I used for this chapter:

- The CVE List: https://www.cve.org/
- The NVD: https://nvd.nist.gov/vuln/search
- CVE Details: https://www.cvedetails.com/

The CVE List is the de facto authoritative source of vulnerability disclosures for the industry. The NVD imports data from the CVE List and adds metadata to it (including metrics and scoring information) (CVE, 2020). The CVSS is used to calculate severity scores for each CVE imported into the NVD. However, this doesn't mean the data in the CVE or the NVD is perfect, nor is the CVSS. I attended a session at the Black Hat USA conference in 2013 called "Buying into the Bias: Why Vulnerability Statistics Suck" (Brian Martin, 2013).

This session covered numerous biases in CVE data. This talk is still available online and I recommend watching it so that you understand some of the limitations of the CVE data that I discuss in this chapter. CVE Details is a great website that saved me a lot of time collecting and analyzing CVE data. CVE Details inherits the limitations of the NVD because it uses data from the NVD. It's worth reading how CVE Details works and its limitations (CVE Details, n.d.). Since the data and analysis that I provide in this chapter are based on the NVD and CVE Details, they inherit these limitations and biases.

Given that the two primary sources of data that I used for the analysis in this chapter have stated limitations, I can state with confidence that my analysis is not entirely accurate or complete. Also, vulnerability data changes over time as the NVD is updated constantly. My analysis is based on a snapshot of the CVE data taken months ago that is no longer up to date or accurate. I'm providing this analysis to illustrate how vulnerability disclosures were trending over time, but I make no warranty about this data – use it at your own risk.

Industry Vulnerability Disclosure Trends

First, let's look at the vulnerability disclosures each year since the CVE List was started in 1999. It is interesting to note that I can find vulnerabilities with publication dates going back to January 1989 (CVE-1999-1471) in the NVD. Vulnerabilities published prior to 1999 appear to have been assigned CVE IDs starting with "1999" because that's when the first CVE List was collected and published by MITRE. An archived bulletin published by the **Computer Security Division Information Technology Laboratory (ITL)** at NIST in July 2000 provides some historical insight into the early days of the NVD. NIST's original CVE search service was called ICAT.

> *The Computer Security Division at NIST's Information Technology Laboratory has created a searchable index containing 700 of the most important publicly known computer security vulnerabilities. This index, called ICAT (pronounced eye-cat), helps the user to search for specific vulnerabilities and identify those vulnerabilities that are applicable to their organizations... The vulnerability information indexed by ICAT pertains to those vulnerabilities included in a standard vulnerability naming scheme called CVE (Common Vulnerabilities and Exposures)... Since the current list of 700 vulnerabilities is too large for system administrators to manually review, we created ICAT to allow one to search for vulnerabilities applicable to a particular organization's hosts." (Mell, Peter. NIST. 2000).*

The reviewer for this book, Cybersecurity Threats, Malware Trends, and Strategies, Karen Scarfone, worked closely with Peter Mell and others at NIST to develop the NVD as the successor to ICAT. The NVD was launched in mid-2005. Analysts at NIST performed CVSS (v1) scoring for all the existing ICAT vulnerabilities. They then used that body of scoring data to inform improvements for CVSS v2 (Scarfone, Karen. personal communication, September 4, 2022).

The total number of vulnerabilities assigned a CVE identifier between 1999 and 2021 was over 167,000 (CVE Details, n.d.). As *Figure 3.2* illustrates, there was a large increase in disclosures in 2017 that has not receded to historically typical volumes since. A new era in vulnerability disclosures started in 2017.

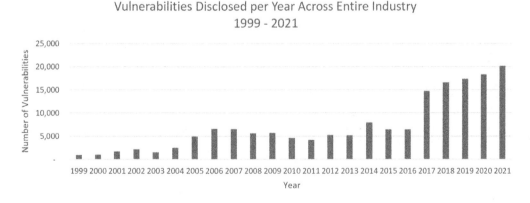

Figure 3.2: Vulnerabilities disclosed across the industry per year (1999–2021)

There was a 128% increase in disclosures between 2016 and 2017, and a 157% increase between 2016 and 2018. Put another way, in 2016, vulnerability management teams were managing 18 new vulnerabilities per day on average. That number increased to 40 vulnerabilities per day in 2017 and 45 per day in 2018, on average. As *Figure 3.3* illustrates, vulnerability management teams were managing 55 new vulnerabilities per day on average in 2021, a 206% increase from 2016 levels. In 2022, there were 25,213 vulnerabilities disclosed. That was an average of 69 vulnerability disclosures per day for security teams to cope with.

Many of the organizations I advised during these years had not increased the staffing levels or budget for their vulnerability management teams and remediation teams commensurate with these increases. This is one factor that helps explain why so many enterprises carry large inventories of unpatched vulnerabilities, dramatically increasing the risk to them. For example, in 2021, if their remediation teams were not keeping up 55 or more new vulnerability disclosures every day (including weekends and holidays), that's potentially 385 vulnerabilities per week, 1,650 per month, 20,075 in a year, multiplied by the number of instances, systems, and IoT devices that these vulnerabilities impact in their IT estates – a backlog that they need to remediate while simultaneously dealing with the continuous volume of new disclosures every day, all the while facing dramatically higher risk for their organization. Not a fun position to be in. For large enterprises that have not invested in developing excellent vulnerability management capabilities, this can easily translate into inventories of hundreds of thousands or millions of unpatched vulnerabilities that they carry for months at a time.

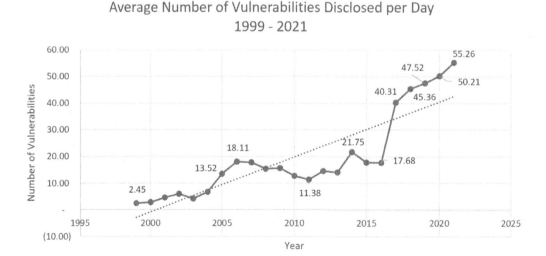

Figure 3.3: Average number of vulnerabilities disclosed per day between 1999 and 2021

Remember that a single unpatched vulnerability can be all the opportunity attackers need to initially compromise an enterprise IT environment. There are many examples of a single unpatched vulnerability leading to data breaches of major corporations that made headlines. Attackers can take advantage of unpatched vulnerabilities in many different ways, including using purpose-built tools, malware, email attachments, and drive-by download attacks, among other methods. Unpatched vulnerabilities are also used by attackers to move laterally and get access to systems post-compromise. Unpatched vulnerabilities are also used in dreaded mass ransomware attacks – remember the WannaCry "crypto-worm" ransomware attack that impacted hundreds of thousands of systems around the world?

Subsequently, carrying massive inventories of unpatched vulnerabilities is like setting sail in a submarine that you know has holes in the hull. I'd often ask executives that I advised, who were a little cavalier about the state of vulnerability management in their IT environments, whether they would put their families and retirement savings in such a submarine and set sail, knowing the state of the hull. To date, I haven't found one executive that said they would do such a thing.

A risk-based approach informed by the **Cyber Threat Intelligence** (CTI) that I discussed in *Chapter 2* and that makes heavy use of automation can help manage this new normal. Alternatively, as I have pleaded with so many enterprises to do, moving to modern compute environments like the cloud can dramatically change this calculus. I'll share more on this approach in *Chapter 12, Modern Approaches to Security and Compliance*.

You might be wondering what factors contributed to such a large increase in vulnerability disclosures. The primary factor was likely a change made to how CVE identifiers are assigned to vulnerabilities in the CVE List. During this time, the CVE anointed and authorized what they call "**CVE Numbering Authorities (CNAs)**" to assign CVE identifiers to new vulnerabilities (Common Vulnerabilities and Exposures, n.d.). According to MITRE, who manages the CVE process that populates the NVD with data:

> *CNAs are software vendors, open source projects, coordination centers, bug bounty service providers, hosted services, and research groups authorized by the CVE Program to assign CVE IDs to vulnerabilities and publish CVE Records within their own specific scopes of coverage. CNAs join the program from a variety of business sectors; there are minimal requirements, and there is no monetary fee or contract to sign." (Common Vulnerabilities and Exposures. (n.d.))*

> *CVE Usage: MITRE hereby grants you a perpetual, worldwide, non-exclusive, no-charge, royalty-free, irrevocable copyright license to reproduce, prepare derivative works of, publicly display, publicly perform, sublicense, and distribute Common Vulnerabilities and Exposures (CVE®). Any copy you make for such purposes is authorized provided that you reproduce MITRE's copyright designation and this license in any such copy.*

The advent of CNAs means that there are many more organizations assigning CVE identifiers after 2016. On January 1, 2020, there were 110 organizations in 21 countries participating as CNAs. By July 2022, the number of CNAs had grown to 232 organizations in 35 countries (Common Vulnerabilities and Exposures, n.d.). That's a 111% increase in the number of organizations entering CVEs into the NVD, in less than two years. The names and locations of the CNAs are available at `https://www.cve.org/PartnerInformation/ListofPartners`. Clearly, this change has made the process of assigning CVE identifiers more efficient, thus leading to a large increase in vulnerability disclosures in 2017 and every year since.

There are other factors that have led to higher volumes of vulnerability disclosures. For example, there are more people and organizations doing vulnerability research than ever before and they have better tools than in the past. Finding new vulnerabilities is big business and a lot of people are eager to get a piece of that pie. However, most of the focus has been on critical and high severity vulnerabilities. This is where the money is, and many security researchers are only interested in finding the most valuable vulnerabilities to maximize the return on their investments in time, expertise, and expenses. This leaves reporting of lower severity vulnerabilities largely to the vendors themselves. Stated another way, vendors largely engage in the honor system to self-report low-rated vulnerabilities. This has likely led to the under-reporting of low-rated vulnerabilities. After all, it is easier to simply fix low risk bugs that likely aren't exploitable, for the next product update, than go through the vulnerability-reporting process and patch them individually.

Another factor in the dramatic increase in vulnerability disclosures is that new types of hardware and software are rapidly joining the computer ecosystem in the form of **Internet of Things (IoT)** devices. The great gold rush to get meaningful market share in this massive new market space has led the industry to make all the same mistakes that software and hardware manufacturers made over the past quarter century.

I talked to some manufacturers about the security development plans for their IoT product lines several years ago, and it was evident they planned to do very little. Developing IoT devices that lack updating mechanisms takes the industry back in time to when personal computers couldn't update themselves, but on a much, much larger scale. Consumers simply are not willing to pay more for better security and manufacturers are unwilling to invest the time, budget, and effort into aspects of development that do not drive demand. After 5 years of significantly increased volumes of disclosures, which continue to grow every year, this appears to be the new normal for the industry, leading to much more risk and more work to manage for enterprises. And with the specter of ransomware, which could be an extinction event for a business, the pressure on security teams has never been higher.

The distribution of the severity of these CVEs is illustrated in *Figure 3.4* (CVE Details, n.d.). The period covered here is 1999 to July 2022 (the latest data available at the time of writing). There are almost three times more CVEs rated medium severity (104,223 CVEs with CVSS scores between 4 and 6.9) than high severity (36,894 CVEs with CVSS scores between 7 and 8.9). The number of critical and high severity vulnerabilities combined is little more than half (55%) the number of medium-rated vulnerabilities. 31.4% of all vulnerabilities, 56,872 of 180,979, are rated critical or high. This is a 4.3% decrease in critical and high - rated vulnerability disclosures since 2019. The biggest changes in the distribution between 2019 and mid-2022 are a 2.2% decrease in high severity vulnerabilities and a 2% decrease in critical severity vulnerabilities. The weighted average CVSS score of the CVEs that are reported is 6.5, a 0.1 decrease compared to 2019. Could these decreases represent progress toward reducing the severity of vulnerabilities disclosed across the industry? Time will tell. Keep in mind that since low severity vulnerabilities are likely under-reported, the weighted average of all vulnerabilities, including those not reported, is almost certainly lower than that of reported vulnerabilities.

For organizations that have vulnerability management policies dictating the emergency deployment of all critical rated vulnerabilities and the monthly deployment of CVEs rated high, that's potentially close to 20,000 emergency deployments and almost 28,000 monthly patch deployments over a 20-year period.

This is one reason why some organizations decide not to prioritize security updates based on severity—there are too many high - and critical-severity vulnerabilities to make managing them differently than lower-rated vulnerabilities an effective use of time. Many of these organizations focus on becoming really efficient at testing and deploying security updates in their environment so that they can deploy all updates as quickly as possible without disrupting the business, regardless of their severity.

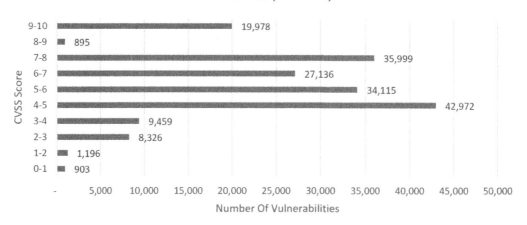

Figure 3.4: CVSS scores by severity (1999–2022 (Jan–Jul))

Let's dive a little deeper into the long-term trends of critical and high severity vulnerabilities that have CVSS scores of 7 and higher. As I mentioned previously, most security teams focus on remediating these vulnerabilities first because they are the highest risk. As *Figure 3.5* illustrates, although the number of critical and high severity vulnerabilities did increase in 2017 as the total number of vulnerabilities dramatically increased, the trend has been relatively flat since (CVE Details, n.d.).

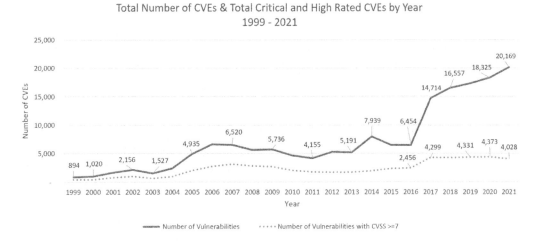

Figure 3.5: Total number of CVEs by year and the total number of critical- and high-severity
CVEs by year

When the number of vulnerability disclosures across the industry increased 128% between 2016 and 2017, the number of critical and high-rated CVEs did not increase proportionately, growing by only 75%, meaning the number of critical and high severity vulnerabilities as a percentage of the total declined. *Figure 3.6* illustrates how the percentage of CVEs with a CVSS score of 7 and higher has been declining relative to the total since 2016. The figure also shows us that the number of critical and high-rated vulnerabilities relative to the total is lower in recent years than it ever has been in the history of the NVD. This is positive news because the last thing the industry needs is ever-increasing volumes of critical and high severity vulnerabilities to deal with.

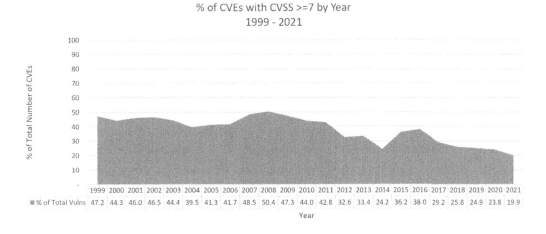

Figure 3.6: CVEs rated critical or high severity as a percentage of the total of all CVEs, by year

However, don't open the champagne just yet. The aforementioned 75% increase between 2016 and 2017 is plain as day in *Figure 3.7*. When translated into potential work for vulnerability management teams and remediation teams, *Figure 3.7* reveals that the average number of vulnerability disclosures per day that have CVSS scores of 7 or higher has never been higher. With an average of 11 or 12 new critical - or high-rated CVEs disclosed every day, vulnerability management teams and remediation teams need highly efficient people, processes, and technologies to keep up. Left untended, that volume is potentially 77 CVEs per week, 330 CVEs per month, and 4,015 CVEs per year, all of which have the highest probability of exploitation. The number of vulnerabilities multiplied by the number of instances, systems, and IoT devices that these vulnerabilities impact means the inventory of unpatched vulnerabilities can get very large, very quickly.

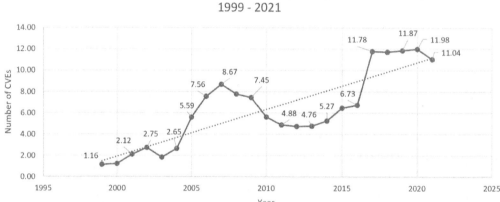

Figure 3.7: Average number of vulnerabilities disclosed per day that are rated critical or high severity, by year

Remember my story about all the successful worm attacks in 2003? The daily average volume of critical- and high-severity vulnerability disclosures back then was only 17% of what it was in 2021. How times have changed. Fortunately, the volume of vulnerability disclosures isn't the only thing that has changed; capabilities to detect, block, contain, and respond to exploitation have as well.

Using vulnerability severity to prioritize near-term remediation, security teams would have been able to reduce the potential maximum average number of new vulnerabilities to investigate every day from 55.26 to 11.04 in 2021. That's potentially 80% fewer vulnerabilities to triage every day.

Security teams that use CTI on active exploitation can potentially reduce that number even further. For example, let's use the **Cybersecurity and Infrastructure Security Agency's (CISA's)** Known **Exploited Vulnerabilities (KEV)** Catalog, which is available for download from `https://www.cisa.gov/known-exploited-vulnerabilities-catalog`, to determine how many CVEs disclosed in 2021 are known to be actively exploited. Of course, this data is subject to change anytime without warning. At the time of writing, I counted 163 CVEs disclosed in 2021 that are listed in KEV. However, 43 of these were added to the catalog in 2022, which likely would have been too late to help security teams initially triage vulnerabilities disclosed during 2021. That leaves 120 CVEs that were disclosed in 2021 and were added to the KEV Catalog in 2021. Security teams would have triaged, on average, 0.33 vulnerability disclosures per day in 2021. That's potentially 97% fewer vulnerabilities to triage every day versus using vulnerability severity to prioritize efforts. This is why using CTI to inform vulnerability management and remediation is so popular with security teams – they can actually keep up with the volume and measurably reduce risk at the same time.

As I mentioned, in this example 43 CVEs from 2021 were added to KEV in 2022. Is it possible that those CVEs were being exploited back in 2021, but it took time for this to be discovered and then reflected in the CTI? This is why security teams can't simply focus exclusively on vulnerabilities that are known to be actively exploited, without accepting a lot more risk on behalf of their organizations. There is time between when attackers can start exploiting a vulnerability, when they are observed doing so, and when up-to-date CTI that reflects this is distributed. Some exploitations might never be observed.

Today, many security teams use CTI to identify and remediate the CVEs that are actively being exploited, as quickly as possible. Then they work to meet the **Service Level Agreements (SLAs)** that their organization has put in place for critical and high severity vulnerabilities. A 30-day SLA for critical- severity vulnerabilities and a 60-day SLA for high severity vulnerabilities seems to be fairly common among the organizations that I have advised. I have also seen much more aggressive SLAs and much less aggressive SLAs – theoretically, these depend on the risk appetite of the organization. However, I have met very few executives that really understand just how much risk their remediation SLAs represent to their organizations; these SLAs and compliance with them are typically a function of how fast their remediation teams can work based on target resourcing levels.

Finally, those teams address their inventories of lower severity vulnerabilities to meet defined SLAs. Simply not patching medium - and low-severity vulnerabilities is riskier than it seems.

Since many security teams focus on mitigating critical and high severity vulnerabilities first, attackers have been using combinations of lower-severity vulnerabilities to compromise systems for many years. Failing to address such vulnerabilities in a timely fashion and allowing large inventories to accumulate is not a best practice of a well-run vulnerability management program. Remember, critical- and high-severity vulnerabilities combined only comprise roughly a third of all CVEs in any given year.

Vendor and Product Vulnerability Trends

At this point, you might be wondering what type of products these vulnerabilities are in. By categorizing the top 25 products with the most CVEs into operating systems, web browsers, and applications, *Figure 3.8* illustrates the breakdown (CVE Details, retrieved July 2022). Operating systems dominate this list, making up 90.75% of the total, meaning there are more CVEs impacting operating systems than browsers and applications combined in the top 25 products with the most CVEs.

In a big departure from past time periods, no applications made it onto the top 25 list. Typically, 15% to 20% of this list would be composed of applications like Acrobat, Acrobat Reader, and Flash Player. Predictably, as the number of products is expanded from 25 to 50, this distribution starts to shift quickly. There are 10 applications (20%) in the top 50 products with the most CVEs. I suspect that as the number of products included in this analysis increases, applications would eventually have more CVEs than the other categories, if for no other reason than the fact that there are many, many more applications than operating systems or browsers, despite all the focus operating systems have received over the years. Also keep in mind that the impact of a vulnerability in a popular development library, such as JRE or Microsoft .NET, can be magnified because of the millions of applications that use it.

There are 3 web browsers in the top 25 products with the most CVEs, composing just under 10% of the list, and 7 in the top 50, composing less than 15%.

Top 25 Product Vulnerability Distribution
1999 - 2022 (Jan - Jul)

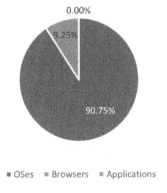

0.00%

9.25%

90.75%

■ OSes ■ Browsers ■ Applications

Figure 3.8: Top 25 products with the most CVEs broken down by product type (1999–2022 (Jan–July))

The specific products that these vulnerabilities were reported in are illustrated in the following list (CVE Details. Retrieved July 2022). This list will give you an idea of the number of vulnerabilities that many popular software products have and how much effort vulnerability management teams might spend managing them.

Rank	Product	Vendor	Product Type	Number of CVEs
1	Debian Linux	Debian	OS	6,603
2	Android	Google	OS	4,406
3	Ubuntu Linux	Canonical	OS	3,413
4	Fedora	Fedoralproject	OS	3,394
5	Mac Os X	Apple	OS	3,017
6	Linux Kernel	Linux	OS	2,856
7	Windows 10	Microsoft	OS	2,806
8	Iphone Os	Apple	OS	2,680
9	Windows Server 2016	Microsoft	OS	2,592
10	Chrome	Google	Browser	2,387
11	Windows Server 2008	Microsoft	OS	2,303
12	Windows 7	Microsoft	OS	2,156
13	Windows Server 2012	Microsoft	OS	2,146
14	Windows Server 2019	Microsoft	OS	2,041
15	Windows 8.1	Microsoft	OS	2,002
16	Firefox	Mozilla	Browser	1,993
17	Windows Rt 8.1	Microsoft	OS	1,830
18	Enterprise Linux Desktop	Redhat	OS	1,642
19	Enterprise Linux Server	Redhat	OS	1,596
20	Enterprise Linux Workstation	Redhat	OS	1,557
21	Leap	Openuse	OS	1,544
22	Tvos	Apple	OS	1,363
23	Opensuse	Opensuse	OS	1,328
24	Enterprise Linux	Redhat	OS	1,169
25	Internet Explorer	Microsoft	Browser	1,168

Figure 3.9: The top 25 products with the most CVEs, 1999–2022 (January–July) (CVE Details. Retrieved July 2022)

The vendors and Linux distributions that had the most CVEs according to CVE Details' Top 50 Vendor List (CVE Details, retrieved July 2022) are listed in *Figure 3.9*. This list shouldn't be all that surprising as some vendors in this list are also the top vendors when it comes to the number of products they have had in the market over the last 20+ years. The more code you write, the more potential for vulnerabilities there is, especially in the years prior to 2003 when the big worm attacks (SQL Slammer, Blaster, and suchlike) were perpetrated. After 2004, industry leaders like the ones on this list started paying more attention to security vulnerabilities in the wake of those attacks. I'll discuss malware more in *Chapter 4*, *The Evolution of Malware*. Additionally, operating systems and web browser vendors have had a disproportionate amount of attention and focus on their products because of their ubiquity. A new critical - or high-rated vulnerability in an operating system or browser is worth considerably more than a vulnerability in an obscure application.

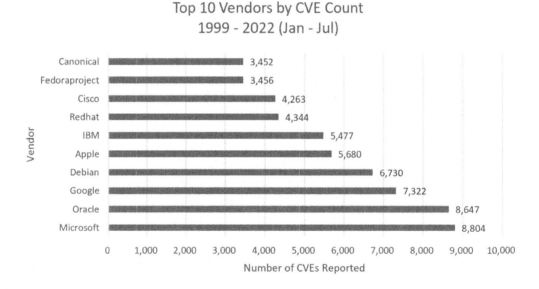

Figure 3.10: Top 10 vendors/distributions with the most CVE counts, 1999–2022 (Jan–Jul) (CVE Details. Retrieved July 2022)

Back in 2003, when the big worm attacks on Microsoft Windows happened, many of the organizations I talked to at the time believed that only Microsoft software had vulnerabilities, and other vendors' software was perfect. Even though, thousands of CVEs were being assigned each year before and after 2003 for software from many vendors.

Two decades later, I haven't talked to any security teams recently that still believe this myth, as they are dealing with vulnerabilities in all software and hardware. This data is not perfect and counting the total number of vulnerabilities in this manner does not necessarily tell us which of these vendors and products have improved over the years or whether the industry has improved its security development practices as a whole. Let's explore these aspects more next.

In the next few sections of this chapter, I provide a deep dive analysis of the top five vendors with the most vulnerability disclosures. Then you'll see a similar analysis for two mobile operating systems, two desktop operating systems, two server operating systems, and two web browsers. All these numbers and graphs will provide you with insight into how some of the most popular products in these categories have been trending with regard to CVEs, showing you how to do this analysis yourself on the hardware and software products you are interested in.

Reducing Risk and Costs — Measuring Vendor and Product Improvement

How can you reduce the risk and costs associated with security vulnerabilities? By using vendors that have been successful at reducing the number of vulnerabilities in their products, you are potentially reducing the time, effort, and costs related to your vulnerability management program and remediation efforts. Additionally, if you choose vendors that have also invested in reducing attackers' return on investment by making exploitation of vulnerabilities in their products hard or impossible, you'll also be reducing your risk and costs. I'll now provide you with a framework that you can use to identify such vendors and products.

In the wake of the big worm attacks in 2003, Microsoft started developing the Microsoft SDL (Microsoft, n.d.). Microsoft continues to use the SDL to this day. I managed marketing communications for the SDL for several years, so I had the opportunity to learn a lot about this approach to development. The stated goals of the SDL are to decrease the number and severity of vulnerabilities in Microsoft software.

The SDL also seeks to make vulnerabilities that are found in software after development harder or impossible to exploit. It became clear that even if Microsoft was somehow able to produce vulnerability-free products, the applications, drivers, and third-party components running on Windows or in web browsers would still render systems vulnerable. Subsequently, Microsoft shared some versions of the SDL and some SDL tools with the broader industry for free. It also baked some aspects of the SDL into some of their publicly available development tools.

I'm going to use the goals of the SDL as an informal "vulnerability improvement framework" to get an idea of whether the risk (probability and impact) of using a vendor or a specific product has increased or decreased over time. This framework has three criteria:

- Is the total number of vulnerabilities trending up or down?
- Is the severity of those vulnerabilities trending up or down?
- Is the access complexity of those vulnerabilities trending up or down?

Why does this seemingly simple framework make sense? Let's walk through it. Is the total number of vulnerabilities trending up or down? Vendors should be working to reduce the number of vulnerabilities in their products over time. An aspirational goal for all vendors should be to have zero vulnerabilities in their products. But this isn't realistic as humans write code, and they make mistakes that lead to vulnerabilities. However, over time, vendors should be able to show their customers that they have found ways to reduce vulnerabilities in their products to reduce risk for their customers.

Is the severity of those vulnerabilities trending up or down? Given that there will be some security vulnerabilities in products, vendors should work to reduce the severity of those vulnerabilities. Reducing the severity of vulnerabilities reduces the number of those emergency security update deployments I mentioned earlier in the chapter. It also gives vulnerability management teams more time to test and deploy vulnerabilities, which reduces disruptions to the businesses they support. More specifically, the number of critical and high severity CVEs should be minimized as these pose the greatest risk to systems.

Is the access complexity of those vulnerabilities trending up or down? Again, if there are vulnerabilities in products, making those vulnerabilities as hard as possible or impossible to exploit should be something vendors focus on. Access complexity or attack complexity (depending on the version of CVSS being used) is a measure of how easy or hard it is to exploit a vulnerability. CVSS v2 provides an estimate of access complexity as low, medium, or high, while CVSS v3 uses attack complexity as either high or low. The concept is the same—the higher the access complexity or attack complexity, the harder it is for the attacker to exploit the vulnerability.

Using these measures, we want to see vendors making the vulnerabilities in their products consistently hard to exploit. We want to see the number of high-complexity CVEs (those with the lowest risk) remaining high or trending up over time, and low-complexity vulnerabilities (those with the highest risk) trending down or zero. Put another way, we want the share of high-complexity CVEs to increase toward 100% of CVEs.

To summarize this vulnerability improvement framework, I'm going to measure:

- CVE count per year
- The number of critical-rated and high-rated CVEs per year; these are CVEs with scores of between 7 and 10
- The number of CVEs per year with low-access complexity or attack complexity

When I apply this framework to vendors, who can have hundreds or thousands of products, I'll use the last five years' worth of CVE data. I think 5 years is a long enough period to determine whether a vendor's efforts to manage vulnerabilities for their products have been successful. When I apply this framework to an individual product, such as an operating system or web browser, I'll use the last full 3 years of available CVE data so that we see the most recent trend.

Note that one limitation of this approach is that it won't be helpful in cases where vendors and/or their products are new and there isn't enough data to evaluate. Another limitation is the "mergers and acquisitions scenario" where vendors acquire new companies and their products. For example, Oracle acquired numerous technology companies and new technologies along with their vulnerabilities, including MySQL and Sun Microsystems. Acquisitions of new technologies can lead to significant changes in CVE numbers for vendors. It can take time for acquiring vendors to get the products they obtain into shape to meet or exceed their standards.

Now that we have a framework to measure whether vulnerability disclosures are improving over time, I'll apply this framework to years of historical CVE data for some select vendors, operating systems, and web browsers to get a better idea of the state of popular software in the industry. We'll start by looking at trends for Microsoft, since they lead the industry in the total number of CVEs over time, as illustrated in *Figure 3.10*.

Let me make one more important point before we dive into the data. As I mentioned earlier, I've done literally thousands of threat intelligence briefings around the world. I've given enough briefings to enough people to recognize behavior curiosities among the audiences I've briefed. There were typically one or two people in every audience who, upon seeing vulnerability disclosure trends, even for vendors they said they weren't fans of, suddenly became "vendor apologists." The typical refrain was that we can't really see how vendors are performing by counting CVEs unless we examine specific products, or even a subset of distributions of products. After all, they could be developed by different development teams, and we really want to measure how those specific development teams improve over time.

After working at Microsoft and **Amazon Web Services (AWS)** for many years, I have a different point of view, however. Every product and every distribution are the outputs of the people, processes, and technologies that each vendor uses to develop them. The vendors we will examine in this chapter are some of the biggest software vendors in the world. They all have **Software Development Lifecycles (SDLCs)** and **Security Development Lifecycles (SDLs)** of some sort that they use to meet their own requirements for minimum viable products, while improving security and controlling development costs.

Some smaller vendors might suffer from inconsistent quality across the products they develop because they lack these things, but these big vendors have people, processes, and technologies that help them meet their minimum requirements to ship their products. This is what we are measuring in this chapter – the effectiveness of their people, processes, and technologies, to continuously develop better quality products measured by the number of security disclosures they had. Once a product or distribution is released to their customers, the customers bear the brunt of the volume of security updates that follow, in the form of dramatically increased risk, disruptions to their operations, and associated expenses.

Five years is a long enough period to measure changes to entire national economies, so it should be enough time for any of these well-resourced vendors to measure their own performance and course-correct if they wanted to. Three years is plenty of time to make performance course corrections to individual products, especially in an industry where Agile, continuous integrations, and continuous deployments are the mantra. They all take security seriously, so let's take an objective, quantitative approach to examining their performance. Now let's dive into the data.

Microsoft Vulnerability Trends

Let's look at how Microsoft has been managing vulnerabilities in its products over the past 22 years. They top the list of vendors with the most CVEs, with 8,804 between 1999 and mid-July 2022 (CVE Details, n.d.). Of the aforementioned 8,804 CVEs, 4,118 were rated critical or high. That's 47% of all CVEs assigned to Microsoft with CVSS scores of 7 or higher. *Figure 3.11* provides a very long-term view of the volume of vulnerability disclosures as well as those CVEs with critical or high severity ratings.

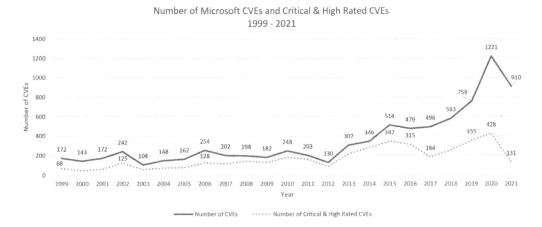

Figure 3.11: The number of CVEs and the number of CVEs rated critical or high in Microsoft products per year (1999–2021) (CVE Details, n.d.)

Of those critical and high severity CVEs, 1,775 CVEs had low access/attack complexity, or about 43% of them (CVE Details, n.d.). These represent the highest risk CVEs because they are rated with the highest severities along with low-complexity (easy to exploit). *Figure 3.12* illustrates the percentage of all Microsoft vulnerabilities that were rated critical or high severity. It also shows us the percentage of Microsoft CVEs that were rated critical or high severity and had low-complexity. In 2001 for example, 33.72% of all Microsoft CVEs published that year were rated critical or high severity. Of those critical and high severity CVEs, 100% of them had low-complexity. This helps explain why mass worm attacks were so successful in the early 2000s.

Figure 3.12 also suggests that shortly after Microsoft started focusing on the SDL in earnest in 2004 after the big worm attacks in 2003, the percentage of critical and high severity CVEs with low access complexity dropped significantly. Microsoft managed to keep this measure relatively low during the "Trustworthy Computing" years, through the end of 2014 when the Trustworthy Computing group was shut down. (Kovacs, Eduard. Security Week. September 23, 2014). This meant that corporate governance for security, privacy, and reliability went from a centralized model managed by the Trustworthy Computing group at Microsoft to a decentralized model managed by individual product teams. Since then, there have been significant increases in the total number of CVEs assigned to Microsoft products.

Of course, changes in Microsoft's governance model are not the only factors that potentially contribute to this increase in vulnerability disclosures; as I mentioned earlier, there are several.

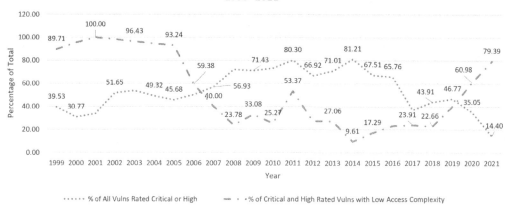

Figure 3.12: Critical- and high-severity CVEs, and critical- and high-severity CVEs with low Access Complexity in Microsoft products as percentages of total (1999–2021)

Focusing on the 5 years between the start of 2017 and the end of 2021, *Figure 3.13* illustrates an 84% increase in CVEs assigned to Microsoft products (CVE Details, n.d.). There was a total of 3,969 CVEs assigned to Microsoft during these years. There was a 29% decrease in critical- and high-severity vulnerabilities after an elevated period and a 420% increase in low access complexity CVEs. The silver lining here is the big decrease in critical and high severity CVEs during this period, specifically between 2020 and 2021 when there was a 69% decrease. Microsoft has made significant investments in making it harder to exploit vulnerabilities. They released compelling data on the exploitability of their products that is worth a look to get a more complete picture (Matt Miller, 2019).

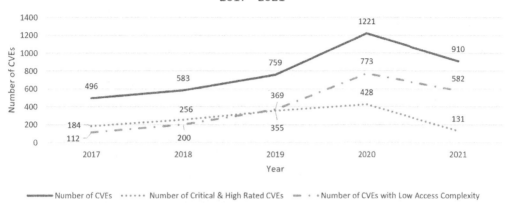

Figure 3.13: Number of CVEs, critical and high severity CVEs, and low Access Complexity CVEs in Microsoft products (2017–2021) (CVE Details, n.d.)

As *Figure 3.14* illustrates, between 2017 and 2021, the number of low complexity vulnerabilities, as a percentage of all Microsoft vulnerabilities in each year, increased, while the percentage of critical- and high rated vulnerabilities decreased. The 29% decrease in critical and high severity vulnerabilities during this period is impressive; during a time of historically high vulnerability disclosures for Microsoft, they were able to keep the CVSS scores for the majority of their CVEs below 7. In 2021, the CVSS score ranges with the most Microsoft CVEs were 4–5 and 6–7.

Figure 3.14: Critical- and high-severity-rated CVEs and low-complexity CVEs in Microsoft products, as a percentage of the total (2017–2021)

The products that contributed the most to Microsoft's overall CVE count include Windows 10, Windows Server 2016, Windows Server 2008, Windows 7, Windows Server 2012, Windows Server 2019, and Windows 8.1 (CVE Details, n.d.). Did you notice anything missing from that list of products? There were no Microsoft web browsers (Internet Explorer or Microsoft Edge) in the top 20 products with the most CVEs across the industry. I'll discuss vulnerability disclosure trends for operating systems and web browsers later in this chapter.

Now let's apply the vulnerability improvement framework that I introduced earlier in this chapter to the Microsoft CVE data from 2017 to 2021. The three measures of the framework are:

- Did they reduce the number of CVEs during this five-year period? No.
- Did they reduce the number of critical- and high-severity CVEs? Yes.
- Did they reduce the number of CVEs with low access complexity? No.

As you can see, they only accomplished one of the goals defined by the framework. Let's see how some other vendors performed across these same three measures.

Oracle Vulnerability Trends

Since Oracle is #2 in the top 10 list of vendors with the most CVEs since 1999, let's examine their CVE trends next (CVE Details, n.d.). There are CVEs in the NVD for Oracle products dating back to 1999. *Figure 3.15* illustrates the number of CVEs published each year for Oracle products between 2017 and 2021, as well as the number of CVEs with critical and high severity ratings, and the number of CVEs with low access complexity.

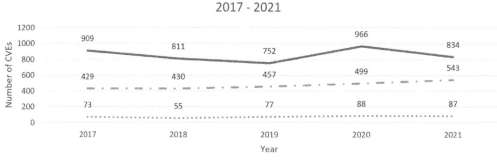

Figure 3.15: Number of CVEs, critical and high CVEs, and low-complexity CVEs in Oracle products (2017–2021) (CVE Details, n.d.)

There were more CVEs assigned to Oracle (4,272) during these five years than those assigned to Microsoft (3,969). However, Oracle had a fraction of the number of critical- and high-rated CVEs compared to Microsoft during this period; Oracle was assigned 380 versus Microsoft's 1,354 (CVE Details, n.d.).

After years of steady increases in the number of CVEs each year starting in 2014, Oracle appears to have flattened that curve between 2017 and 2021, as *Figure 3.15* illustrates. Oracle ended this five-year period with fewer annual CVE disclosures than when it started. However, there was a 26% increase in CVEs with low access complexity and a 19% increase in critical and high rated CVEs during this same period. This means they will not meet the criteria set for our vulnerability improvement framework for this five-year period.

Figure 3.16 shows us that Oracle has kept the number of critical- and high-severity CVEs, as a percentage of all Oracle vulnerabilities in each year, relatively low and stable.

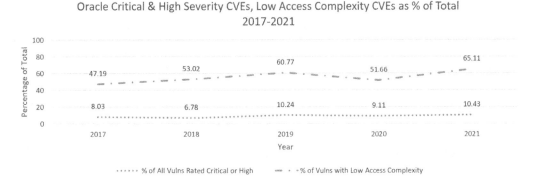

Figure 3.16: Critical- and high-severity-rated CVEs, and low-complexity CVEs in Oracle products, as a percentage of the total (2017–2021)

According to CVE Details, the Oracle products that contributed the most to the total number of CVEs during this period included MySQL, JRE, and JDK.

Google Vulnerability Trends

The #3 vendor on CVE Details' Top Vendor list with the most CVEs is Google. Let's examine their CVE trends. Between 2017 and 2021, there were 4,777 CVEs assigned to Google, compared to 3,969 Microsoft CVEs and 4,272 Oracle CVEs (CVE Details, n.d.). Of those CVEs in Google products, 1,253 or 26% were rated critical or high severity, and 2,447 or 51% had low access complexity.

All three measures are illustrated in *Figure 3.17*.

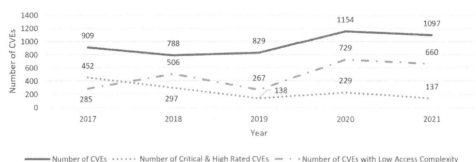

Figure 3.17: Number of CVEs, critical and high CVEs, and low complexity CVEs in Google products (2017–2021) (CVE Details, n.d.)

Looking at the trend in the five years between 2014 and the end of 2018, there was a 398% increase in CVEs assigned to Google products. After this dramatic increase in Google CVEs, they receded slightly in 2018 and 2019 before rising to a new all-time high in 2020, then receding slightly in 2021. The annual number of CVEs and the annual number of low access complexity CVEs both increased between the start and end of the five-year period, with the number of CVEs increasing 20% and low access complexity CVEs increasing 132%. This means Google will not meet the criteria set for our vulnerability improvement framework for this five-year period. However, Google did reduce critical and high severity CVEs by 69% during this time – a great accomplishment. *Figure 3.18* illustrates both the increase in low access complexity vulnerabilities and the decrease in critical and high severity CVEs over the five-year period.

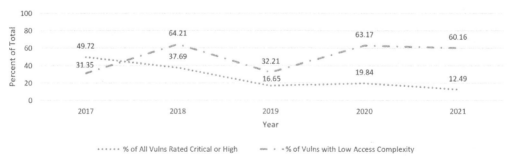

Figure 3.18: Critical and high severity rated CVEs and low-complexity CVEs in Google products, as a percentage of the total (2017–2021)

According to CVE Details, the products contributing the most CVEs to Google's totals included Android, Chrome, and TensorFlow.

Google and Microsoft are fierce competitors, both offering consumers and enterprises operating systems, web browsers, and cloud services among other products. They are under similar competitive pressures, as well as legal and regulatory pressures, they are both based on the west coast of the United States and have global operations, and they compete for the same pool of technical talent for their workforces. So, you might wonder how they compare when it comes to vulnerability disclosures? *Figures 3.19* and *3.20* reveal the answer to this question. There are some differences, but it is interesting how similar these tech titans' CVE data points are at the end of the five-year period.

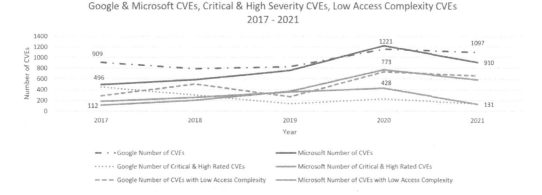

Figure 3.19: Number of CVEs, critical and high CVEs, and low-complexity CVEs in Google and Microsoft products (2017–2021) (CVE Details, n.d.)

Figure 3.20 Illustrates the highest risk vulnerabilities from both Google and Microsoft between 2017 and 2021 – those with critical and high severity and low access complexity. It looks like Microsoft did a better job managing these high-risk CVEs in each of the five years, especially in 2018. However, this difference was all but gone by 2021.

Unfortunately, neither of these vendors met the criteria for our vulnerability improvement framework during this five-year period.

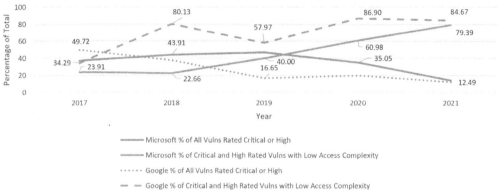

Figure 3.20: Critical and high severity CVEs, and critical and high severity CVEs with low Access Complexity in Google and Microsoft products as percentages of total (2017–2021)

Debian Vulnerability Trends

Next, let's examine CVEs in Debian as it appears in the #4 spot in CVE Details Top Vendors list (CVE Details, n.d.). Between 2017 and 2021, there were 4,814 CVEs assigned to Debian of which 824 or 17% were critical or high severity, and 2,324 or 48% were low access complexity. You might recall there were 4,777 CVEs assigned to Google, 3,969 assigned to Microsoft, and 4,272 assigned to Oracle during the same period of time (CVE Details, n.d.). The annual number of CVEs and the annual number of CVEs with low access complexity were both higher at the end of the five-year period than they were at the beginning of it. CVEs saw a 26% increase while CVEs with low access complexity climbed 14%. Subsequently, Debian won't meet the criteria for our vulnerability improvement framework for this time period.

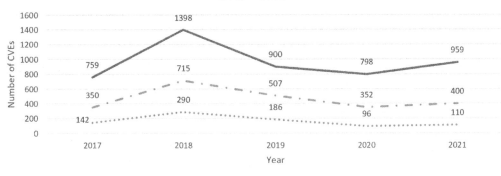

Figure 3.21: Number of CVEs, critical and high CVEs, and low complexity CVEs in Debian products (2017–2021) (CVE Details, n.d.)

Both *Figures 3.21* and *3.22* illustrate the same reduction in critical and high severity CVEs during the five years examined, ending the period with 22% fewer than at the start.

Figure 3.22: Critical and high severity rated CVEs and low complexity CVEs in Debian products, as a percentage of the total (2017–2021)

Debian Linux was the largest contributor to CVEs for Debian during this period.

Apple Vulnerability Trends

The final vendor I'll examine is Apple, which is ranked as the #5 Top Vendor in CVE Details' Top Vendor list (CVE Details, n.d.). Apple had 2,404 CVEs assigned to it during the five years between 2017 and 2021. That's significantly fewer CVEs than any of the other four vendors I examined.

Apple had half the CVEs that Debian had during the same period. As *Figure 3.23* illustrates, Apple started the five-year period with 598 CVEs in 2017 and ended the period with 592 in 2021, a 1% decrease. The number of CVEs rated critical or high decreased by 24% and the number of low access complexity CVEs decreased by 56%.

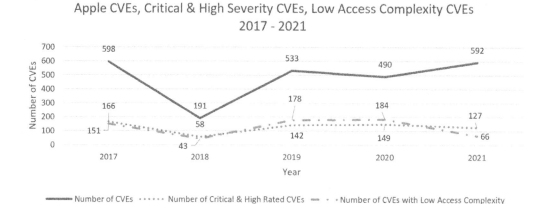

Figure 3.23: Number of CVEs, critical and high CVEs, and low complexity CVEs in Apple products
(2017–2021) (CVE Details, n.d.)

While the percentage of low access complexity CVEs ending the period in 2021 was relatively high in Microsoft and Google CVEs, at 65% and 60% respectively, Apple only had 11%. This is illustrated in *Figure 3.24*.

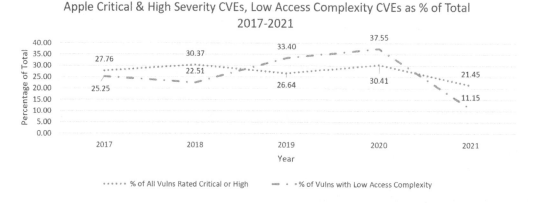

Figure 3.24: Critical and high severity CVEs and low complexity CVEs in Apple products, as a
percentage of the total (2017–2021)

The products that contributed the most to Apple's CVE count included macOS, iPhone OS, tvOS, Safari, and watchOS (CVE Details, n.d.).

As we did with the other four vendors, let's apply the vulnerability improvement framework to the Apple CVE data from 2017 to 2021. The three measures of the framework are:

- Did they reduce the number of CVEs during this five-year period? Yes.
- Did they reduce the number of critical and high severity CVEs? Yes.
- Did they reduce the number of CVEs with low access complexity? Yes.

Congratulations Apple, you did it! You met all the criteria in the vulnerability improvement framework. In fact, Apple also succeeded in meeting the same criteria when I applied it to the five-year period between 2014 and 2018, which I discussed in the first edition of this book. They were the only vendor in the top five vendors to accomplish this, back then too. Clearly Apple has the people, processes, and technologies tuned to make continuous, meaningful improvement in the security of their products. This is something that the other vendors haven't been able to do in the two five year periods. I've examined in the first and second editions of this book.

Vendor Vulnerability Trend Summary

A new era in vulnerability disclosures started in 2017 – an era of historically high volumes. All of the vendors we examined in this chapter saw increases in the number of vulnerability disclosures in their products between 2016 and 2017. Since then, these vendors have struggled to reduce CVE volumes to pre-2017 levels. The volume of vulnerability disclosures in the years of the big worm attacks of the 2003–2004 timeframe seems quaint compared to the volumes we have seen over the past five years.

Figure 3.25 plots the CVE counts for the top 5 vendors from 2016 to 2021.

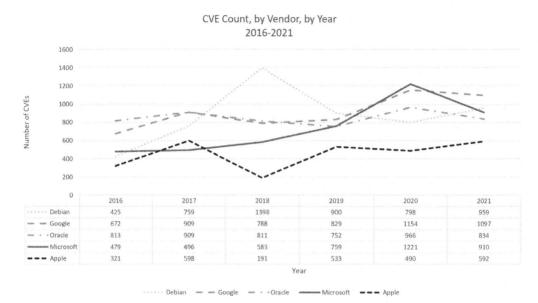

Figure 3.25: Number of CVEs in vendor products (2016–2021) (CVE Details, n.d.)

Figure 3.26 shows how the number of critical and high rated CVEs has trended for each of the five vendors between 2017 and 2021. Oracle deserves an honorable mention for maintaining the lowest number of critical and high CVEs across all five years. Debian, Google, and Microsoft all had big reductions in critical and high severity vulnerabilities during this period.

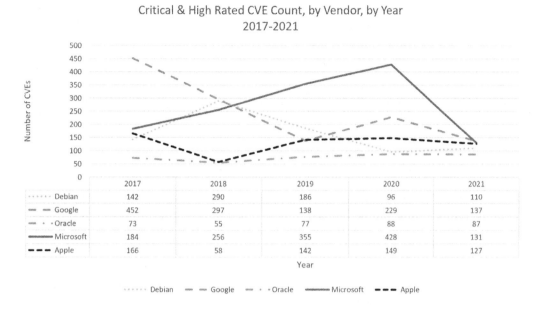

Figure 3.26: Number of critical and high severity CVEs in vendor products (2017–2021) (CVE
Details, n.d.)

Figure 3.27 shows the raw number of CVEs, critical and high severity CVEs, and low access complexity CVEs for each vendor. This graph makes it easy to see Apple's relatively low numbers compared to the other vendors.

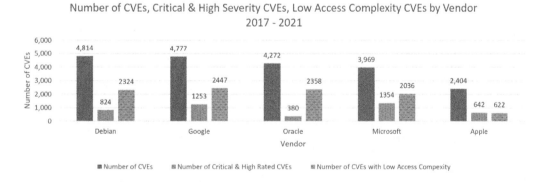

Figure 3.27: Number of CVEs, critical and high severity rated CVEs, and low complexity CVEs
in vendor products (2017–2021) (CVE Details, n.d.)

Finally, the overall results of the vulnerability improvement framework are contained in *Figure 3.28*.

Vendor	Fewer CVEs?	Fewer CVEs with CVSS Score 7-10?	Fewer Low Access Complexity CVEs?
Apple	Yes	Yes	Yes
Debian	No	Yes	No
Google	No	Yes	No
Microsoft	No	Yes	No
Oracle	Yes	No	No

Figure 3.28: Vulnerability Improvement Framework Results for 2017–2021

Simply put, our vulnerability improvement framework measures how these vendors have or have not reduced risk for their customers. Fewer CVEs, fewer severe CVEs, and fewer easy-to-exploit CVEs translate into less complexity, less expense, and less risk for enterprises. Apple clearly understands this and is able to achieve it for its customers.

Now that we have examined vulnerability disclosure trends for the aggregated CVEs for the top five vendors with the most CVEs, let's dive a little deeper and look at vulnerability disclosure trends for some popular operating systems and web browsers.

Operating System Vulnerability Trends

Operating systems have garnered a lot of attention from security researchers over the past couple of decades. A working exploit for a zero-day vulnerability in a popular desktop or mobile operating system can be potentially worth hundreds of thousands of dollars or more. Let's look at the vulnerability disclosure trends for operating systems and look closely at a few of the products that have the highest vulnerability counts. *Figure 3.29* illustrates the operating systems that had the most unique vulnerabilities between 1999 and July of 2022, according to CVE Details (CVE Details, n.d.). The list contains desktop, server, and mobile operating systems from an array of vendors, including Apple, Google, Linux, Microsoft, and others.

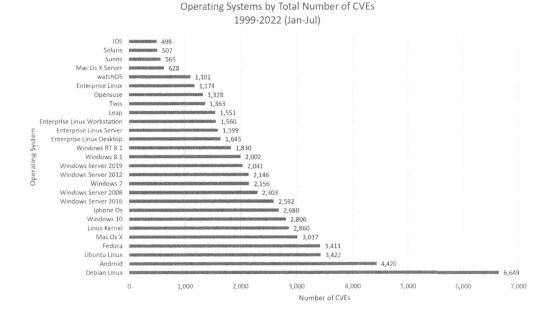

Figure 3.29: Operating systems with the most unique vulnerabilities by total number of CVE counts (1999 to 2022 (Jan–Jul)) (CVE Details, n.d.)

In this section I'll select a few operating systems (OS) and examine their last three full years of vulnerability disclosure measures, as I did with vendors in the last section. The OSes I select will be based on their popularity with the enterprise customers I've advised in the past. Since I largely covered Debian in the vendor section and Debian Linux is almost the only source of CVEs for Debian, let's start with the next OS with the most CVEs, Android.

Google Android Vulnerability Trends

Let's look at Android, a mobile operating system manufactured by Google. Android's initial release date was in September 2008 and CVEs for Android started showing up in 2009. Android only had 38 CVEs in the 6 years spanning 2009 and 2014 (CVE Details, n.d.). The volume of CVEs in Android started to increase significantly in 2016, increasing 426% from the previous year. During the three years between 2019 and 2021, on average there were 641 CVEs filed for Android per year. On average, there were 158 CVEs per year rated critical or high severity and 459 CVEs with low access complexity. The three-year trend is illustrated in *Figure 3.30*.

During this time, the annual number of CVE disclosures increased by 16% and the annual number of vulnerability disclosures with low access complexity increased by 81%. Critical and high rated vulnerabilities ended the period with a modest 6% increase. Together, these increases mean that Android will not meet the criteria of our vulnerability improvement framework for this time period.

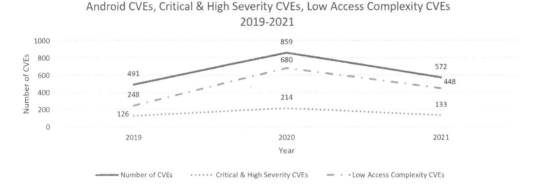

Figure 3.30: The number of CVEs, critical and high rated severity CVEs, and low complexity CVEs in Google Android per year (2019–2021) (CVE Details, n.d.)

Figure 3.30 shows us that there was a large increase in Android vulnerabilities that are easy to exploit, between 2019 and 2020. In the last two years, upward of 80% of all Android CVEs had low access complexity. Google has kept the level of critical and high severity vulnerabilities in Android stable across these three years, at nearly a quarter of all CVEs.

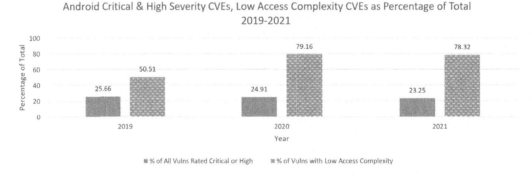

Figure 3.31: Critical and high severity rated CVEs and low complexity CVEs in Google Android as a percentage of all Google Android CVEs during 2019-2021

Let's look at how Google has managed the highest risk CVEs in Android, those with critical and high severity that also have low access complexity. During these three years, 385 CVEs or 20% of all Android CVEs fell into this category.

Figure 3.32 reveals that there was a large increase in the percentage of CVEs in this category between 2019 and 2020, resulting in 93% of critical and high rated CVEs with low access complexity in 2020 and 87% in 2021. This is likely the result of the increase in low access complexity CVEs during the same period that is illustrated in *Figure 3.31*. The conclusion is that 93% of the most severe vulnerabilities in Android were relatively easy to exploit in 2020 and 87% in 2021.

Figure 3.32: Critical and high severity CVEs that have low access complexity, as a percentage of all critical and high rated CVEs in Google Android during 2019–2021

During this three-year period, Android saw increases in all three of our vulnerability improvement framework measures and an increase in the percentage of the highest risk CVEs. You might be wondering if these trends are typical for mobile operating systems that are so popular with so many people around the world? Is the hypercompetitive world of vulnerability research putting pressure on all such mobile OS vendors? To try to answer these questions, let's compare these trends for Android to another hugely popular OS, Apple iPhone OS, also known as iOS.

Apple iOS Vulnerability Trends

Apple started releasing iPhone OS in June 2007 and later it was renamed iOS. Only 34 CVEs were assigned in the first four years after release. Big incremental increases in CVEs happened in 2011 and 2015, with 315% and 219% increases respectively. iOS had 1,052 CVEs between 2019 and 2021. That's an average of 351 CVEs per year. iOS had 248 critical and high rated CVEs, equivalent to 24% of the total, and an average 83 CVEs per year. Low access complexity CVEs had a total count of 290 in those three years, or 97 per year on average. These CVEs were 28% of all Android CVEs during this three-year period.

Figure 3.33 illustrates how the CVEs, critical and high severity CVEs, and CVEs with low access complexity trended between 2019 and 2021.

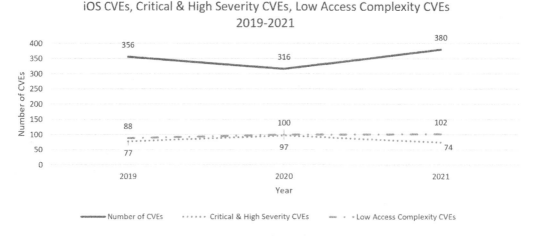

Figure 3.33: The number of CVEs, critical and high severity CVEs, and low-complexity CVEs in Apple iOS (2019–2021)

Figure 3.34 shows the percentages of critical and high rated CVEs as a percentage of all iOS CVEs. It also shows the percentages of CVEs with low access complexity relative to the total.

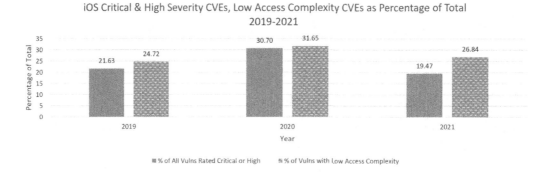

Figure 3.34: Critical and high severity CVEs and low complexity CVEs in Apple iOS as a percentage of all Apple iOS CVEs during 2019–2021

Mobile Operating System Summary

So how did Apple iOS compare to Android? *Figure 3.35* provides a summary. Fewer vulnerabilities, fewer severe vulnerabilities, and fewer easier-to-exploit vulnerabilities means less risk and less expense.

	Total Number of CVEs	Total Number of Critical & High Severity CVEs	Total Number of Low Access Complexity CVEs	Total Number of CVEs with Critical & High Severity and Low Access Complexity
Apple iOS	1052	248	290	64
Google Android	1922	473	1376	385
% Difference	59%	62%	130%	143%

Figure 3.35: Apple iOS & Google Android Comparison 2019–2021

Although Apple had a better record with iOS versus Android during this time period, it did not meet the criteria for our vulnerability improvement framework because both the annual number of CVEs and the low severity CVEs were higher in 2021 than they were in 2019. Apple did reduce the number of critical and high severity CVEs during this time, by a modest 4%.

Next, let's look at a couple of OSes that run on desktop computing platforms.

Microsoft Windows 10 Vulnerability Trends

Windows 10 was called "the most secure version of Windows ever" (err...by me (Ribeiro, n.d.)). Windows 10 was released in July 2015. In the seven years since it was released, there have been 2,806 vulnerability disclosures in this OS. To add a little perspective, in the 20 years and 9 months since its release date, Windows XP has had 685 CVEs assigned to it (CVE Details, n.d.). To make the difference easier to understand, Windows XP had 0.15 vulnerabilities disclosed per day, on average, between its release date and end of support date. Windows 10 has had 1.1 CVEs disclosed per day since its release date. As I have previously mentioned, there are many factors that can help explain this difference, including a massive hypercompetitive cybersecurity industry that continues to grow.

Focusing on the last three years for which we have full years' worth of data, Windows 10 had 1,740 CVEs, of which 34% were critical or high severity and 68% had low access complexity. Raw figures for each of these measures are presented in *Figure 3.36*.

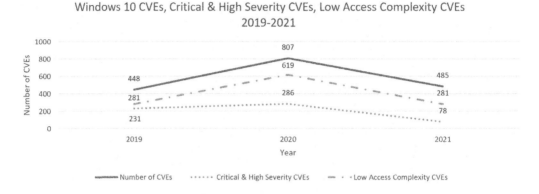

Figure 3.36: The number of CVEs, critical and high rated severity CVEs, and low complexity CVEs in Microsoft Windows 10 (2019–2021) (CVE Details, n.d.)

As *Figure 3.36* illustrates, the number of CVEs per year was higher at the end of the three years than at the start, while the number of CVEs per year with low access complexity was the same. The number of CVEs rated critical or high severity decreased 66% during this period – a major accomplishment. This decrease can also be seen in *Figure 3.37* where the percentage of critical and high severity vulnerabilities relative to all Windows 10 CVEs steadily decreased across all three years, starting at 51.56% in 2019, decreasing to 35.44% in 2020, and ending the period with 16.08%.

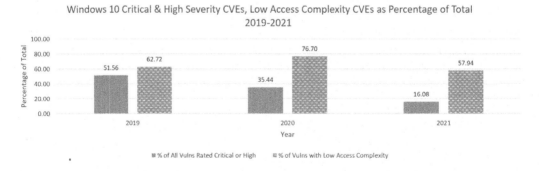

Figure 3.37: Critical and high severity rated CVEs and low complexity CVEs in Microsoft Windows 10 as a percentage of all Microsoft Windows 10 CVEs during 2019–2021

But as Microsoft decreased the number of the most severe vulnerabilities in Windows 10, the proportion of severe vulnerabilities that also had low access complexity increased.

Figure 3.38 shows us that the percentage of critical and high severity vulnerabilities that also had low access complexity, as a percentage of all critical and high severity vulnerabilities, increased during the three-year period. As a result, in 2021, 89% of all critical and high rated CVEs were easy to exploit. Note that it is possible to reduce the percentage of CVEs that have both high severity and low access complexity, as the number of high severity vulnerabilities decreases – check out this same chart for macOS.

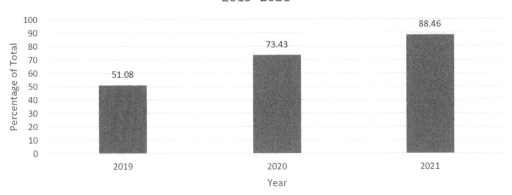

Figure 3.38: Critical and high severity CVEs that have low access complexity, as a percentage of all critical and high rated CVEs in Microsoft Windows 10 during 2019-2021

Despite this, Windows 10 was very close to meeting our vulnerability improvement framework criteria. Just 38 fewer CVEs in 2021, and Windows 10 would have likely met the criteria. Next let's look at another desktop OS, but from a different vendor.

Apple macOS Vulnerability Trends

Now I'll examine Apple's macOS X. There are CVEs dating back to 2001 for this OS – it was initially released in March of that year. To date, 3,016 CVEs have been entered into the NVD for macOS (CVE Details, n.d.). On average that's 0.38 CVEs per day. You'll recall that Windows 10 has had 1.1 CVEs per day, on average, since its release.

Between 2019 and 2021, macOS had 929 vulnerability disclosures, of which 31% were critical or high rated, and 35% had low access complexity. This is illustrated by *Figure 3.39*, where the annual number of CVEs increased by 7 or 2.3% over three years.

During this time, low complexity CVEs decreased by 33.3% and critical and high severity vulnerabilities decreased by 27%. macOS failed to meet the criteria of our vulnerability improvement framework by a paltry 8 CVEs over 3 years. So close!

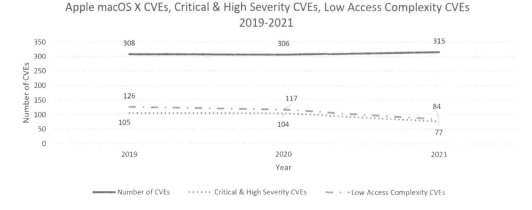

Figure 3.39: The number of CVEs, critical and high rated severity CVEs, and low complexity CVEs in Apple macOS per year (2019–2021)

This reduction in severe vulnerabilities and low access complexity vulnerabilities can also be seen in *Figure 3.40*, where the percentage of both decreased each year relative to the total number of CVEs in macOS.

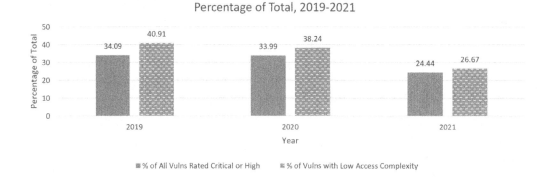

Figure 3.40: Critical and high severity rated CVEs and low complexity CVEs in Apple macOS as a percentage of all Apple macOS CVEs during 2019–2021

While Apple was able to decrease high severity vulnerabilities by 27% between the start and end of the three-year period, they also managed to reduce the percentage of CVEs that were critical and high severity that also had low access complexity, meaning they reduced the highest risk category of CVEs in macOS during this time, as reflected in *Figure 3.41.* Bravo Apple!

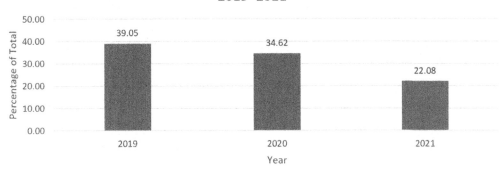

Figure 3.41: Critical and high severity CVEs that have low access complexity, as a percentage
of all critical and high rated CVEs in Apple macOS during 2019–2021

Desktop Operating System Summary

You might be wondering how Apple macOS compares to Microsoft Windows 10? *Figure 3.42* provides a summary. Fewer vulnerabilities, fewer severe vulnerabilities, and fewer easy-to-exploit vulnerabilities means less risk and less expense.

	Total Number of CVEs	Total Number of Critical & High Severity CVEs	Total Number of Low Access Complexity CVEs	Total Number of CVEs with Critical & High Severity and Low Access Complexity
Apple macOS	929	286	327	94
Microsoft Windows 10	1740	595	1181	397
% Difference	61%	70%	113%	123%

Figure 3.42: Apple macOS & Microsoft Windows 10 Comparison 2019–2021

Next let's examine some server OSes that are run in enterprise data centers. I've already examined Debian CVEs in the vendor section of this chapter, which are heavily based on CVEs in Debian Linux. Let's examine Ubuntu Linux next.

Ubuntu Linux Vulnerability Trends

Did you know there are hundreds of active Linux distros? Canonical Ubuntu Linux is one of the most popular. Canonical provides a web page that can be used for CVE research at `https://ubuntu.com/security/cves`. There are CVEs with publication dates going back to 2005 for Ubuntu. Between then and the time of writing, 3,423 CVEs have been assigned to Ubuntu Linux.

Figure 3.43 illustrates the CVE trend over the last three years for which we have a full year's data. As the figure shows, there was a huge (94%) drop in CVEs between 2020 and 2021. Whenever I see big changes in data like this, without more context, I'm highly skeptical of the quality of the data. If accurate, the volume of CVEs in 2021 is similar to the volume Ubuntu had in 2011 and 2006. I'm skeptical because it's hard for companies to change, in a single year, the people, processes, and technologies they use to develop software as complex as an operating system, in a way that leads to a 94% reduction in vulnerability disclosures. I haven't seen an OS vendor do that in the 20 years I've been studying vulnerability disclosures. There have been many cases where a version is retired because the end of its life arrives, and users migrate off it in droves. This tends to shift the attention of development teams and security researchers to currently supported versions. Subsequently the volume of CVEs can drop quickly if old code that is a perennial source of vulnerabilities is finally exorcised. That could be what happened in 2021. Canonical provides life cycle information at `https://wiki.ubuntu.com/Releases`. This page indicates that three versions of Ubuntu hit their end-of-life dates in 2020 and 2021, including Disco Dingo (version 19.04), Eoan Ermine (version 19.10), and Groovy Gorilla (version 20.10). Additionally, the number of CVEs midway through 2022 is in the same ballpark (21 CVEs) as in 2021. We'll see if these numbers stand the test of time and if a new low volume trend emerges. For this analysis, I will assume this data is accurate, because I want to believe!

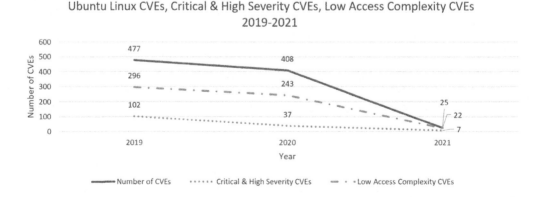

Figure 3.43: The number of CVEs, critical and high severity CVEs, and low complexity CVEs in Canonical Ubuntu Linux per year (2019–2021)

Figure 3.43 clearly indicates that Canonical Ubuntu Linux satisfies the criteria of our vulnerability improvement framework – a feat that neither Apple nor Microsoft achieved during the same time period. Bravo Ubuntu!

Figure 3.44 shows us that as the number of CVEs was dramatically reduced in 2021, the percentage of those CVEs with low access complexity increased to 88%, and there was a big increase in the percentage of critical and high severity vulnerabilities between 2020 and 2021. However, 25 CVEs in 2021 is much easier for vulnerability management and remediation teams to manage than 408 or 477 as seen in previous years.

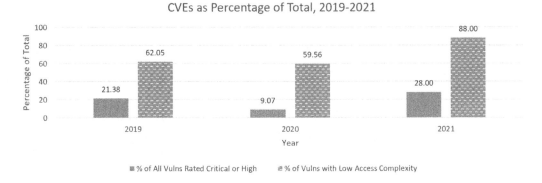

Figure 3.44: Critical and high severity CVEs and low complexity CVEs in Canonical Ubuntu Linux as a percentage of all Canonical Ubuntu Linux CVEs during 2019–2021

Because my Ubuntu data is a little suspect, I thought I'd provide analysis into another Linux OS where the data I have looks a little more reliable. Next, I examine CVE trends for Linux Kernel, an open source OS kernel.

Linux Kernel Vulnerability Trends

In the three years between 2019 and 2021, there were 576 CVEs assigned to Linux Kernel. Of these CVEs, 25% were critical and high severity and 77% were low access complexity. *Figure 3.45* reveals that all three measures in our vulnerability improvement framework were reduced in this three-year period. Congratulations Linux Kernel for meeting the criteria!

The number of CVEs was reduced by 44%, the most severe vulnerabilities were reduced by 69%, and the low access complexity CVEs were reduced by 40%.

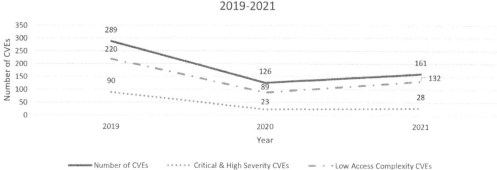

Figure 3.45: The number of CVEs, critical and high severity CVEs, and low complexity CVEs in Linux Kernel per year (2019–2021)

Figure 3.46 shows us that although the critical and high severity CVEs as a percentage of the total went down over the three years, the percentage of low access complexity CVEs increased, meaning, as the number of CVEs was reduced each year, there were fewer severe vulnerabilities but a higher proportion of easy-to-exploit vulnerabilities.

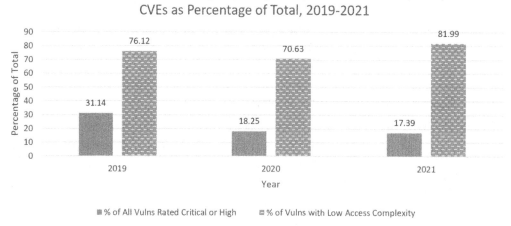

Figure 3.46: Critical and high severity CVEs and low complexity CVEs in Linux Kernel as a percentage of all Linux Kernel CVEs during 2019–2021

Next, let's examine one of Microsoft's popular server OSes, Windows Server 2016.

Microsoft Windows Server 2016 Vulnerability Trends

Windows Server 2016 is a very popular server OS. It was released near the end of 2016, meaning, at the time of writing, we have more than three full years of CVE data for it to examine. This isn't true for more recent versions of Microsoft's server products, like Windows Server 2019 or Windows Server 2022.

During 2019 to 2021, Windows Server 2016 had 1,739 CVEs assigned to it. Of these, 34% were critical and high severity, while 76% were low access complexity. The raw numbers of CVEs for each of these categories are displayed in *Figure 3.47*.

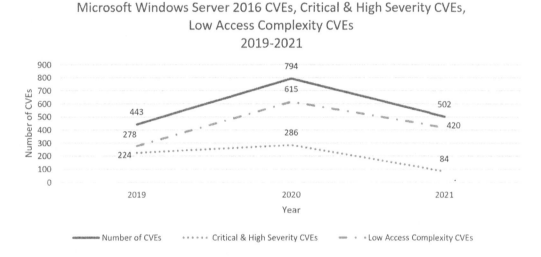

Figure 3.47: The number of CVEs, critical and high severity CVEs, and low complexity CVEs in Windows Server 2016 per year (2019–2021)

Since the annual number of CVEs increased 13% and the number of low access complexity CVEs increased 51% during these three years, Windows Server 2016 does not meet the criteria for our vulnerability improvement framework. The silver lining is that Microsoft reduced the annual number of critical and high severity vulnerabilities by 63% during this period. This is a major accomplishment and very positive for Microsoft's customers.

Figure 3.48 reveals that as Microsoft reduced the proportion of the most severe vulnerabilities in Windows Server 2016, the proportion of low access complexity vulnerabilities increased. In 2021, according to the data from CVE Details, 84% of CVEs in this OS were low access complexity; this is significantly higher than the percentage in Windows 10 (58%) during the same period, but in the same range as other server OSes, such as Ubuntu and Linux Kernel.

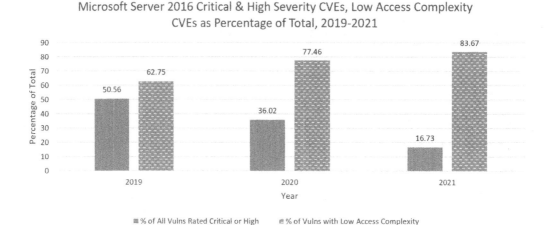

Figure 3.48: Critical and high severity CVEs and low complexity CVEs in Microsoft Windows Server 2016 as a percentage of all Microsoft Windows Server 2016 CVEs during 2019–2021

I could write an entire book dedicated to examining server OSes because there are so many of them – we've barely scratched the surface here. I promised to provide analysis for two server OSes and I provided analysis for three! Using the examples that I have provided here, I think I've given those readers that want to do their own analysis on other server OSes a good framework. Let's finish our examination of server OSes by comparing the three we looked at.

Server Operating System Summary

Figure 3.49 provides a summary of the key metrics we examined for server OSes. Fewer vulnerabilities, fewer severe vulnerabilities, and fewer easy-to-exploit vulnerabilities means less risk and less expense.

	Total Number of CVEs	Total Number of Critical & High Severity CVEs	Total Number of Low Access Complexity CVEs	Total Number of CVEs with Critical & High Severity and Low Access Complexity
Ubuntu Linux	910	146	561	131
Linux Kernel	576	141	441	127
Windows Server 2016	1,739	594	1,313	401

Figure 3.49: Ubuntu Linux, Linux Kernel, and Windows Server 2016 Comparison 2019-2021

Now let's shift gears and finish this deep dive into vulnerability trends by examining two of the world's most popular web browsers.

Web Browser Vulnerability Trends

Web browsers attract a lot of attention from security researchers and attackers alike. This is because they are hard to live without. Everyone uses at least one browser on desktops, mobile devices, and on many types of servers. Operating systems' development teams can bake layers of security features into their products, but web browsers tend to bring threats right through all those host-based firewalls and other security layers. Web browsers have been notoriously difficult to secure but have improved over the years.

I'll examine two popular web browsers in this section: Apple Safari and Google Chrome. Everyone tends to have a favorite browser and some people I've briefed in the past became emotional when their favorite browser had more vulnerabilities than they thought possible. Please keep in mind that all of this CVE data is imperfect and is a snapshot in time that can change rapidly. Please don't let this data put you in a bad mood.

Apple Safari Vulnerability Trends

Apple Safari was introduced in 2003 and runs on a range of devices including those powered by Apple OSes, macOS, and iOS. There have been 1,137 CVEs assigned to Safari between 2003 and the end of 2021. This is equivalent to, on average, 60 CVEs per year. *Figure 3.50* illustrates the three-year trend for the three measures in our vulnerability improvement framework. There was an 85% decrease in CVEs, an 84% decrease in severe vulnerabilities, and a 57% decrease in low access complexity CVEs during this time. Apple has done it again – they have met the criteria for our vulnerability improvement framework!

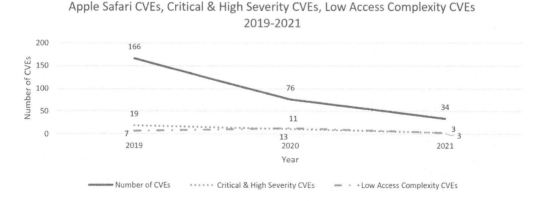

Figure 3.50: The number of CVEs, critical and high severity CVEs, and low complexity CVEs in Apple Safari per year (2019–2021)

Figure 3.51 reveals that Apple was able to maintain relatively low percentages of severe vulnerabilities and low complexity CVEs as the number of CVEs trended down over the three years.

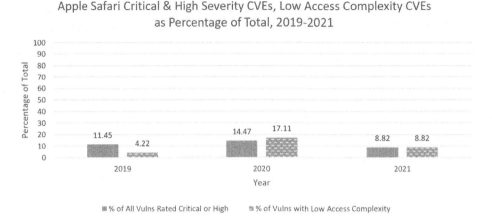

Figure 3.51: Critical and high severity CVEs and low complexity CVEs in Apple Safari as a percentage of all Apple Safari CVEs during 2019–2021

Congratulations Apple! Next let's look at another very popular web browser, Google Chrome.

Google Chrome Vulnerability Trends

The Google Chrome browser was released in 2008, first on Windows and then later on other operating systems. There were 2,296 CVEs for Chrome between 2008 and the end of 2021, an average of 164 vulnerabilities per year (CVE Details, n.d.). As illustrated in *Figure 3.52*, all three measures in our vulnerability improvement framework decreased between 2019 and 2021. Wow, congratulations Google!

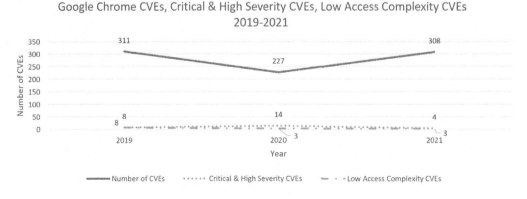

Figure 3.52: The number of CVEs, critical and high severity CVEs, and low complexity CVEs in Google Chrome per year (2019–2021)

Figure 3.53 reveals that Google was also able to reduce the percentages of severe and low access complexity CVEs, while the total number of CVEs was reduced. The volume of critical and high severity vulnerabilities and low complexity vulnerabilities were so low in 2021, it's hard not to be impressed with Google Chrome.

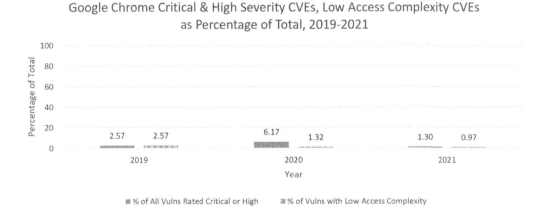

Figure 3.53: Critical and high severity CVEs and low complexity CVEs in Google Chrome as a
percentage of all Google Chrome CVEs during 2019–2021

Web Browser Summary

It is really cool and reassuring to see that the volumes of vulnerability disclosures on such widely used web browsers are managed so well.

Apple Safari appears to have an advantage in that it had significantly fewer CVEs during the same period as Google Chrome. However, for vulnerability management and remediation teams that focus on critical and high severity CVEs, both browsers had relatively few severe vulnerability disclosures. They had an identical number of critical and high severity CVEs that also had low access complexity.

I know what some readers are thinking at this point – what about Mozilla Firefox? The data on CVE Details reveals a modest 7% increase in the annual number of CVEs over the three-year period. This means Firefox would not meet the criteria for our vulnerability improvement framework for this period. However, the annual number of critical and high severity CVEs and low access complexity CVEs were reduced in Firefox during this time.

This is very positive. Firefox was assigned 377 CVEs during the three years.

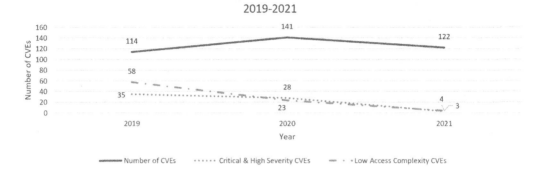

Figure 3.54: The number of CVEs, critical and high severity CVEs, and low complexity CVEs in
Mozilla Firefox per year (2019–2021)

Now I've opened Pandora's box – I know someone is wondering, what about Microsoft Edge? Microsoft released their new version of Microsoft Edge based on the Chromium open source project on January 15, 2020 (Microsoft, January 15, 2020). At the time of writing, Edge Chromium did not have three full years of CVE data. An analysis will have to wait until we have more data.

Figure 3.55 provides a summary of the measures we examined for these web browsers over three years.

	Total Number of CVEs	Total Number of Critical & High Severity CVEs	Total Number of Low Access Complexity CVEs	Total Number of CVEs with Critical & High Severity and Low Access Complexity
Apple Safari	276	33	23	4
Google Chrome	846	26	14	4
Mozilla Firefox	377	66	85	48

Figure 3.55: Web Browser Comparison 2019–2021

That wraps up my web browser analysis. That was a lot of data – let me summarize it for you now.

Vulnerability Improvement Framework Summary

Let's finish this section on vendor and product vulnerability trends with a summary of how the vendors, operating systems, and web browsers we examined fared with regard to our vulnerability improvement framework.

Figure 3.56 summarizes how each vendor, operating system, and web browser that we examined did across the three measures of the vulnerability improvement framework.

Vendor	Fewer CVEs?	Fewer CVEs with CVSS Score 7-10?	Fewer Low Access Complexity CVEs?
Apple	Yes	Yes	Yes
Debian	No	Yes	No
Google	No	Yes	No
Microsoft	No	Yes	No
Oracle	Yes	No	No
Mobile OS	Fewer CVEs?	Fewer CVEs with CVSS Score 7-10?	Fewer Low Access Complexity CVEs?
Apple iOS	No	Yes	No
Google Android	No	No	No
Desktop OS	Fewer CVEs?	Fewer CVEs with CVSS Score 7-10?	Fewer Low Access Complexity CVEs?
Microsoft Windows 10	No	Yes	No
Apple macOS	No	Yes	Yes
Server OS	Fewer CVEs?	Fewer CVEs with CVSS Score 7-10?	Fewer Low Access Complexity CVEs?
Canonical Ubuntu	Yes	Yes	Yes
Linux Kernel	Yes	Yes	Yes
Microsoft Server 2016	No	Yes	No
Web Browser	Fewer CVEs?	Fewer CVEs with CVSS Score 7-10?	Fewer Low Access Complexity CVEs?
Apple Safari	Yes	Yes	Yes
Google Chrome	Yes	Yes	Yes
Mozilla Firefox	No	Yes	Yes

Figure 3.56: Summary of whether the vendors, operating systems, and web browsers examined in this chapter met the criteria of the vulnerability improvement framework

The data suggests that the combination of Safari on macOS during the time period we examined had fewer CVEs and fewer low complexity vulnerabilities than other non-server OS combinations. macOS didn't have the fewest severe CVEs of any client OS (iOS did) but was among the OSes with the lowest count. Based on the data, the combination of Google Chrome on macOS or iOS also appears to be a great choice for client systems. On servers, the Linux-based OSes we examined would have helped reduce risk.

The data also tells us that the vendors we examined have been making efforts to reduce the number of critical and high severity vulnerabilities in their products, even as the volume of CVEs increased for many of them. Enterprise IT organizations should prefer those vendors that demonstrate they are willing and able to make positive progress on reducing risk for their customers over time. Congratulations to all the vendors that cracked this code and those that came close. Each of them is setting an example for the entire industry to follow.

Let me finish this chapter by providing some general guidance on vulnerability management.

Vulnerability Management Guidance

A well-run vulnerability management program is critical for all organizations. As you've seen from the data and analysis in this chapter, there have been lots of vulnerabilities disclosed across the industry and the volumes have been increasing, not decreasing. At the end of 2022, there were over 192,000 CVEs in the NVD. Attackers know this and understand how challenging it is for organizations to keep up with the volume and complexity of patching the various hardware and software products they have in their environments. Defenders have to be perfect while attackers just have to be good or lucky once. Let me provide you with some recommendations regarding vulnerability management programs.

First, I cannot overstate the importance of asset management and its role enabling effective vulnerability management, incident response, and many other aspects of IT management. If an organization doesn't maintain an accurate inventory of IT assets, it is very difficult, indeed nearly impossible, to effectively manage vulnerabilities and security misconfigurations. For example, let's say a vulnerability management team can scan a system for unpatched vulnerabilities. In this example, they discover numerous unpatched critical and high severity vulnerabilities present on the system that exceed remediation time service level agreements. The next step would be to quickly remediate these findings. Who should the vulnerability management team or remediation team contact to perform application compatibility testing for the security updates and perform the updates on the system? Without an accurate asset inventory, finding the owner of that system might be a daunting task in a large enterprise environment. The same problem is pressurized during an active cybersecurity incident when a system has been compromised, but there isn't an accurate asset inventory in which to find the owner and get other vital details on the system being investigated.

Organizations that are really good at managing their assets' life cycles and maintaining accurate, detailed inventories have a much easier time in such scenarios. For example, imagine if a vulnerability management team didn't have to scan hundreds of thousands of systems looking for the dreaded Log4j vulnerability during the Christmas holiday period. What if, instead, they could simply query their asset management database and find a list of assets with the vulnerable component? What if the asset management database could provide the name and contact information of the owner of every system where the vulnerable component exists? Remediation could be a lot faster and with less drama than scanning hundreds of thousands of systems looking for the vulnerable component, while active attacks are underway on the internet, and scrambling to try to find system owners to start testing and remediation efforts.

There are some powerful integrations between enterprise asset management products and many enterprise vulnerability scanners that make vulnerability management and incident response easier.

The key to efficient vulnerability management, including vulnerability reporting, is good asset management. Investing in asset management will pay dividends in many ways in large enterprise environments. That said, asset management is neither easy nor inexpensive for large enterprises that have complex, diverse computing environments. I have talked to some CISOs recently who have taken ownership of asset management for their enterprises because it is too critical to the success of their cybersecurity programs to leave to other teams to manage. In my experience this is the exception, not the rule. However, I can see some wisdom in this approach. Asset management can be an immense amount of work, especially for organizations that are just starting or resuming that journey after many years without focusing on asset management. But since it's on the critical path for some key cybersecurity functions, I can understand why some CISOs would want to manage it themselves. However, asset management can be resource-intensive and could consume resources on a cybersecurity team that should be used for cybersecurity instead. In such scenarios, a carefully weighted balance between the two needs to be maintained.

A second thing to keep in mind about vulnerability management is that one objective of a vulnerability management program is to understand the risk that vulnerabilities present in your IT environment. This is not static or slow-moving in large IT environments. Vulnerabilities are constantly being disclosed in all hardware and software. Because of this, data on the vulnerabilities in your environment can get stale quickly. The organizations that I have met that decided they would deploy security updates once per quarter, or every six months, have an unusually high appetite for risk; although, paradoxically, some of these same organizations tell me they have no appetite for risk. It is always interesting to meet people that believe their highest priority risks are their vendors, instead of the cadre of attackers who are actively looking for ways to take advantage of them – attackers who, given the chance, will gladly encrypt all their data and demand a ransom for the decryption keys.

When I meet an organization with this type of policy, I wonder whether they really do have a data-driven view of the risk and whether the most senior layer of management really understands the risk that they are accepting on behalf of the entire organization.

Do they know that on average in 2019, 33.4 new vulnerabilities were disclosed per day, and in 2018, there were 45.4 disclosures per day? If they are patching quarterly, that is equivalent to 4,082 vulnerabilities potentially unpatched for up to 90 days in 2018 and 3,006 in 2019. Double those figures for organizations that patch semi-annually.

On average, more than a third of those vulnerabilities are rated critical or high. Attackers only require one exploitable vulnerability in the right system to successfully initially compromise an environment. Instead of avoiding patching and rebooting systems to minimize disruption to their business, most of these organizations need to focus on building very efficient vulnerability management programs with the goal of reducing risk in a more reasonable amount of time. Attackers have a huge advantage in environments that are both brittle and unpatched for long periods.

For most organizations, my recommendation is that vulnerability management teams scan everything, every day. Read that line again if you have to. Remember the submarine analogy I used in the preface section of this book. Your vulnerability management program is one of the ways in which you look for defects in the hull of your submarine. Scanning every asset you have in your environment for vulnerabilities every day will help identify cracks and imperfections in the hull that, if exploited, would sink the boat. Scanning everything every day for vulnerabilities and misconfigurations provides the organization with important data that will inform its risk decisions. Remember the Cybersecurity Usual Suspects – finding and addressing security misconfigurations is just as important as vulnerabilities. Without up-to-date data, they are managing risk in an uninformed way. For example, scanning everything every day will help identify when the most severe vulnerabilities, like Log4j, show up in an environment months or years after it was thought to be remediated. Scanning every day provides the organization with the visibility required to identify and mitigate high and critical risk vulnerabilities before they can become problematic.

Note that I'm not recommending patching every day, just scanning to get a daily snapshot of the risk. Remediation time service level agreements should be based on the risk appetite of the organization. Remember what I recommended earlier in the chapter: use CTI to inform remediation priorities. This will help your organization reduce the highest risk vulnerabilities first and provide the prescriptive priorities that remediation teams so often want. The combination of CTI and effective asset management can simplify and reduce costs related to your vulnerability management and remediation efforts.

For organizations that can accomplish it, using MITRE ATT&CK® to also inform vulnerability remediation priorities, can reduce the number of high priority vulnerabilities while reducing risk of exploitation. I discuss this framework in detail, in *Chapter 9, Cybersecurity Strategies*. By prioritizing patching the vulnerabilities that can support the techniques and procedures that attackers are known to use, it makes it harder for attackers to be successful.

It's important to note that mobile devices, especially of the BYOD variety, pose a significant challenge to vulnerability management teams.

The data on mobile OS vulnerabilities provided earlier in this chapter indicates that there are hundreds of CVEs in popular mobile OSes every year. Most organizations simply can't scan these devices for vulnerabilities the same way they scan other assets. This is one reason why many cybersecurity professionals refer to BYOD as "bring your own disaster." Instead, limiting mobile devices' access to sensitive information and high value assets is more common. Requiring newer operating system versions and minimum patch levels in order to connect to corporate networks is also common. To this end, most of the enterprises I've met with over the years leverage **Mobile Device Management (MDM)** or **Mobile Application Management (MAM)** solutions.

For some organizations, scanning everything every day will require more resources than they currently have. For example, they might require more vulnerability scanning engines than they currently have in order to scan 100% of their IT assets every day. They might also want to do this scanning during off hours to reduce network traffic generated by all this scanning during regular work hours. This might mean that they have to scan everything, every night, for a defined number of hours. To accomplish this, they'll need a sufficient number of vulnerability scanning engines and staff to manage them. Once they have up-to-date data on the state of the environment, then that data can be used to make risk-based decisions – for example, when newly discovered vulnerabilities and misconfigurations should be addressed. Without up-to-date data on the state of the environment, hope will play a continual and central role in their vulnerability management strategy.

The data generated by all this vulnerability scanning is gold dust for CISOs, especially for security programs that are relatively immature. Providing the C-suite and Board of Directors with data from this program can help CISOs get the resources they need and communicate the progress they are making with their security program. Providing a breakdown of the number of assets in inventory, how many of them they can actually manage vulnerabilities on, the number of critical and high severity vulnerabilities present, and an estimate of how long it will take to address all these vulnerabilities can help build an effective business case for more investment in the vulnerability management program. Providing senior management with quantitative data like this helps them understand reality versus opinion. Without this data, it can be much more difficult to make a compelling business case and communicate progress against goals for the security program.

Of course, there are more modern approaches to vulnerability management that can reduce the number of assets that vulnerability management teams need to scan every day. Using more modern "Zero Trust" approaches that verify systems are fully patched before they are allowed to connect to corporate networks is a popular approach.

Requiring systems that are missing security updates to self-remediate prior to being trusted enough to connect to a corporate network can dramatically reduce the amount of vulnerability scanning and patching that vulnerability management and remediation teams must do. However, most large organizations have complex IT estates that were built over a period of decades and that typically rely on significant amounts of legacy technologies. Unfortunately, there's no shortcut to get from massive legacy IT environments to modern Zero Trust architectures. Most organizations modernize parts of their IT estates over years, never really being able to modernize everything at once. These environments very often require legacy approaches, like scanning everything every day, to manage effectively. The cloud can change the costs and effort related to vulnerability management in a dramatically positive way. I'll discuss this in *Chapter 12, Modern Approaches to Security and Compliance.*

Summary

Hopefully, I didn't blind you with too much science in this chapter—there were a lot of numbers to digest! Allow me to recap some of the key takeaways for this chapter.

Risk is a combination of probability and impact. The **Common Vulnerability Scoring System (CVSS)** is used to estimate the risk for each vulnerability (CVE) in the **National Vulnerability Database (NVD)**. This freely available data should be used to inform your vulnerability management program. Using vendors who have been successful at reducing the number of vulnerabilities in their products can potentially reduce the time, effort, and costs related to your vulnerability management program. If you choose vendors who have also invested in reducing attackers' return on investment by making the exploitation of vulnerabilities in their products hard or impossible, you'll also be reducing your risk and costs.

Of the vendors examined in this chapter, only Apple met the criteria of our vulnerability improvement framework by reducing the number of vulnerabilities in their products, reducing the severity of vulnerabilities in their products, and reducing the number of low access complexity vulnerabilities (those with the highest risk) over the 5 years studied. The operating systems that I examined that achieved the objectives of our vulnerability improvement framework over a 3-year period were Linux Kernel and Canonical Ubuntu Linux. The web browsers I examined with the best vulnerability management track record between 2019 and 2021 included Apple Safari and Google Chrome. The way vulnerabilities were managed in these browsers during these 3 years reduced the risk to their users.

Please keep in mind that the data used for these comparisons has many biases and is not complete or completely accurate. But you can do your own CVE research and use the informal vulnerability improvement framework I've provided.

Vulnerability management teams that scan everything, every day, provide the best visibility for their organizations to manage risk. Data from vulnerability management programs provide CISOs with some of the data they need to manage the performance of their security programs and steer future investments into the programs.

In the next chapter, we are going to dive into malware infection data from hundreds of millions of systems around the world to examine how the threat landscape has evolved over the years. Did you know that socioeconomic factors, such as **Gross Domestic Product** (**GDP**), are related to regional malware infection rates? We are going to look at this as well.

References

- NIST. (n.d.). Retrieved from National Vulnerability Database: `https://nvd.nist.gov/vuln`

- CVE. (March 5, 2020). CVE Numbering Authority (CNA) Rules. Retrieved from `https://www.cve.org/ResourcesSupport/AllResources/CNARules`

- Howard, M. (May 9, 2021). "The Best Security Advice I Can Give…". Retrieved from `https://michaelhowardsecure.blog/2021/05/09/the-best-security-advice-i-can-give/`.

- CVE. (n.d.). CVE-2018-8653 Detail. Retrieved from `https://cve.mitre.org/cgi-bin/cvename.cgi?name=CVE-2018-8653`

- FIRST. (June, 2019). Common Vulnerability Scoring System version 3.1: Specification Document. Retrieved from `https://www.first.org/cvss/specification-document`

- NIST. (n.d.). Common Vulnerability Scoring System Calculator. Retrieved from `https://nvd.nist.gov/vuln-metrics/cvss/v3-calculator`

- CVE. (December 11, 2020). CVE and NVD Relationship. Retrieved from `https://cve.mitre.org/about/cve_and_nvd_relationship.html`

- Mell, Peter. (July, 2000). Computer Security Division Information Technology Laboratory, National Institute of Standards and Technology, ITL Bulletin. Retrieved from `https://csrc.nist.gov/csrc/media/Publications/Shared/documents/itl-bulletin/itlbul2000-07.pdf`

- Cybersecurity & Infrastructure Security Agency (CISA). (n.d.). Known Exploited Vulnerabilities Catalog. Retrieved from `https://www.cisa.gov/known-exploited-vulnerabilities-catalog`

- Cyber Safety Review Board. July 11, 2022. Review of the December 2021 Log4j Event. Retrieved from https://www.cisa.gov/sites/default/files/publications/CSRB-Report-on-Log4-July-11-2022_508.pdf

- Brian Martin, S. C. (December 3, 2013). Black Hat USA 2013 - Buying into the Bias: Why Vulnerability Statistics Suck. Retrieved from YouTube: https://www.youtube.com/watch?time_continue=20&v=3Sx0uJGRQ4s CVE Details. (n.d.). How does it work? Retrieved from CVE Details: https://www.cvedetails.com/how-does-it-work.php

- Tripwire. (2020). The History of Common Vulnerabilities and Exposures (CVE). Retrieved from https://www.tripwire.com/state-of-security/featured/history-common-vulnerabilities-exposures-cve/

- CVE Details. (n.d.). Current CVSS Score Distribution For All Vulnerabilities. Retrieved from CVE Details: https://www.cvedetails.com/index.php

- Common Vulnerabilities and Exposures. (n.d.). CVE Numbering Authorities. Retrieved from Common Vulnerabilities and Exposures: https://www.cve.org/ProgramOrganization/CNAs

- CVE Details. (n.d.). Current CVSS Score Distribution For All Vulnerabilities. Retrieved from CVE Details: https://www.cvedetails.com/index.php

- CVE Details. (Retrieved July, 2022). Top 50 List of Products with the most CVEs. Retrieved from CVE Details: https://www.cvedetails.com/top-50-products.php

- CVE Details. (Retrieved July, 2022). Top 50 List of Vendors with the most CVEs. Retrieved from CVE Details: https://www.cvedetails.com/top-50-vendors.php

- Microsoft. (n.d.). Security Engineering. Retrieved from Microsoft: https://www.microsoft.com/en-us/securityengineering/sdl

- Software Engineering Institute CERT Coordination Center, Carnegie Mellon University (December 15, 2021). "Apache Log4j allows insecure JNDI lookups, Vulnerability Note VU#930724". Retrieved from https://www.kb.cert.org/vuls/id/930724

- CVE. (12/14/2021). "CVE-2021-45046 Detail". Retrieved from https://cve.mitre.org/cgi-bin/cvename.cgi?name=CVE-2021-45046

- NIST. (n.d.). "Known Exploited Vulnerabilities". Retrieved from https://nvd.nist.gov/General/News/cisa-exploit-catalog

- CVE Details. (n.d.). Microsoft Vulnerability Statistics. Retrieved from CVE Details: https://www.cvedetails.com/vendor/26/Microsoft.html

- Kovacs, Eduard. Security Week (September 23, 2014). "Microsoft Shutting Down Trustworthy Computing Unit". Retrieved from `https://www.securityweek.com/microsoft-shutting-down-trustworthy-computing-unit`

- Matt Miller, M. (February 14, 2019). BlueHat IL 2019 – Matt Miller. Retrieved from YouTube: `https://www.youtube.com/watch?v=PjbGojjnBZQ`

- CVE Details. (n.d.). Microsoft List of Products. Retrieved from CVE Details: `https://www.cvedetails.com/top-50-products.php`

- CVE Details. (n.d.). Top 50 List of Vendors with the most CVEs. Retrieved from CVE Details: `https://www.cvedetails.com/top-50-vendors.php`

- CVE Details. (n.d.). Oracle Vulnerability Statistics. Retrieved from CVE Details: `https://www.cvedetails.com/vendor/93/Oracle.html`

- CVE Details. (n.d.). Google Chrome vulnerability details. Retrieved from CVE Details: `https://www.cvedetails.com/product/15031/GoogleChrome.html?vendor_id=122`

- CVE Details. (n.d.). Debian vulnerability details. Retrieved from CVE Details: `https://www.cvedetails.com/vendor/23/Debian.html`

- CVE Details. (n.d.). Apple vulnerability details. Retrieved from CVE Details: `https://www.cvedetails.com/vendor/49/Apple.html`

- CVE Details. (n.d.). Apple list of products. Retrieved from CVE Details: `https://www.cvedetails.com/product-list/vendor_id-49/Apple.html`

- CVE Details. (n.d.). Apple iOS vulnerability details. Retrieved from CVE Details: `https://www.cvedetails.com/product/15556/Apple-Iphone-Os.html?vendor_id=49`

- CVE Details. (n.d.). Apple Mac OS X vulnerability details. Retrieved from CVE Details: `https://www.cvedetails.com/product/156/Apple-MacOs-X.html?vendor_id=49`

- CVE Details. (n.d.). Apple Safari vulnerability statistics. Retrieved from CVE Details: `https://www.cvedetails.com/product/2935/AppleSafari.html?vendor_id=49`

- CVE Details. (n.d.). Apple Vulnerability Statistics. Retrieved from CVE Details: `https://www.cvedetails.com/vendor/49/Apple.html`

- CVE Details. (n.d.). Google Android vulnerability statistics. Retrieved from CVE Details: `https://www.cvedetails.com/product/19997/GoogleAndroid.html?vendor_id=1224`

- CVE Details. (n.d.). Google Chrome vulnerability details. Retrieved from CVE Details: `https://www.cvedetails.com/product/15031/GoogleChrome.html?vendor_id=1224`

- CVE Details. (n.d.). Google List of Products. Retrieved from CVE Details: `https://www.cvedetails.com/product-list/vendor_id-1224/Google.html`

- CVE Details. (n.d.). Linux Kernel vulnerability statistics. Retrieved from CVE Details: https://www.cvedetails.com/product/47/Linux-LinuxKernel.html?vendor_id=33

- CVE Details. (n.d.). Microsoft List of Products. Retrieved from CVE Details: https://www.cvedetails.com/product-list/product_type-/ firstchar-/vendor_id-26/page-1/products-by-name.html?sha=4b975b df63b781745f458928790e4c8fd6a77f94&order=3&trc=525

- CVE Details. (n.d.). Windows 10 Vulnerability Details. Retrieved from CVE Details: https://www.cvedetails.com/product/32238/Microsoft-Windows-10.html?vendor_id=26

- CVE Details. (n.d.). Windows Server 2016 Vulnerability Details. Retrieved from CVE Details: https://www.cvedetails.com/product/34965/ Microsoft-Windows-Server-2016.html?vendor_id=26

- CVE Details. (n.d.). Microsoft Edge vulnerability statistics. Retrieved from CVE Details: https://www.cvedetails.com/product/32367/Microsoft-Edge.html?vendor_id=26

- Ribeiro, R. (n.d.). Understanding the Security Benefits of Windows 10. Retrieved from BizTech: https://biztechmagazine.com/article/2016/04/understanding-security-benefits-windows-10

- CVE Details. (n.d.). Canonical Ubuntu Linux vulnerability statistics. Retrieved from CVE Details: https://www.cvedetails.com/product/20550/Canonical-Ubuntu-Linux.html?vendor_id=4781

- CVE Details. (n.d.). Mozilla Firefox vulnerability details. Retrieved from CVE Details: https://www.cvedetails.com/product/3264/MozillaFirefox.html?vendor_id=452

- CVE Details. (n.d.). Mozilla Firefox vulnerability statistics. Retrieved from CVE Details: https://www.cvedetails.com/product/3264/MozillaFirefox.html?vendor_id=452

- Microsoft. (n.d.). New year, new browser – The new Microsoft Edge is out of preview and now available for download. Retrieved from Microsoft: https://blogs.windows.com/windowsexperience/2020/01/15/new-year-new-browser-the-new-microsoft-edge-is-out-of-preview-and-now-available-for-download/

Join our community on Discord

Join our community's Discord space for discussions with the author and other readers:

https://packt.link/SecNet

4

The Evolution of Malware

I have always thought of malware as a synonym for "attackers' automation." Purveyors of malware seek to compromise systems for a range of motivations, as I described in *Chapter 1*. Any system that sends and receives email, is used to surf the web, has applications that connect to a network, or takes other forms of input can be attacked, regardless of whether it was manufactured in Redmond, Raleigh, Cupertino, Helsinki, or anywhere else. The AV-TEST Institute, one of the world's premier independent anti-virus testing labs, based in Germany, has one of the world's largest malware collections (AV-Test Institute, 2020). They have accumulated this collection over 15 years. "Every day, the AV-TEST Institute registers over 450,000 new malicious programs (malware) and **potentially unwanted applications (PUA)**" (AV-Test Institute, n.d.). The statistics that they have published indicate that the volume of total malware has increased every year; for example, in 2013 they detected 182.9 million malware samples, compared to the current time (July 2022) with 1.4 billion malware samples, a 646% increase. (AV-Test Institute, July 10, 2020). According to the data that AV-Test has published in their annual security reports, the share of malware developed for Windows operating systems was 69.96% in 2016 (AV-Test Institute, 2017), 67.07% in 2017 (AV-Test Institute, 2018), 51.08% in 2018 (AV-Test Institute, 2019), and 78.64% in 2019 (AV-Test Institute, 2020).

The operating system with the next highest share of malware samples in these years was Google Android, with less than 7% of the share in every year reported (AV-Test Institute, 2020). The number of new malware samples detected for Linux operating systems was 41,161 in March of 2019, while number of malware samples for Windows during the same time was 6,767,397 (AV-Test Institute, 2019). Malware samples for macOS during this month surged to 11,461 from 8,057 the month before (AV-Test Institute, 2019).

This data clearly suggests that the platform of choice for malware authors is the Windows operating system. That is, more unique malware is developed to attack Windows-based systems than any other platform. Once Windows systems are compromised, attackers will typically harvest software and game keys, financial information such as credit card numbers, and other confidential information they can use to steal identities, sometimes taking control of the system and its data for ransom. Many attackers will use compromised systems as platforms to perpetrate attacks from, using the anonymity that the compromised systems provide to them.

Given that attackers have been targeting and leveraging Windows-based systems more than any other platform, and given the ubiquity of Windows, security experts need to understand how and where attackers have been using these systems. CISOs, aspiring CISOs, security teams, and cybersecurity experts can benefit from understanding how Windows-based systems are attacked in at least a few ways:

- CISOs and security teams that are responsible for Windows systems in their environment should understand how attackers have been attacking Windows-based systems with malware, as well as how this has evolved over time.

- Being knowledgeable about malware will help security teams do their jobs better.

- This knowledge can be useful to help recognize the fear, uncertainty, and doubt that some security vendors use to sell their products and services; understanding how attackers have been using malware will help CISOs make better security-related investments and decisions.

- CISOs and security teams that are responsible for Linux-based systems, and other non-Microsoft operating systems, should have some insight into how their adversaries are compromising and using Windows systems to attack them. We can take lessons from the Windows ecosystem and apply them to Linux-based systems and other platforms. Very often, the methods that malware authors use on the Windows platform will be adapted to attack other platforms, albeit usually on a smaller scale. Understanding malware authors' methods is important for security teams, regardless of the types of systems they protect. Unfortunately, CISOs don't get to tune out of Windows-based threats, even if they don't use Windows in their environments.

- Finally, in my opinion, it's hard for cybersecurity subject matter experts to use that moniker if they are blissfully unaware of malware trends in an online ecosystem consisting of over a billion systems that supports, at times, more than three-quarters of all the new malware in the world. It doesn't matter if there are more mobile devices, more IoT devices, or more secure operating systems.

It is undeniable that Windows is everywhere. Subsequently, all cybersecurity experts should know a little about the largest participant in the global threat landscape.

This chapter will provide a unique, detailed, data-driven historical perspective of how malware has evolved around the world. There are some very interesting differences in regional malware encounter rates and infection rates that I'll also dive into in this chapter. This view of the threat landscape will help CISOs and security teams understand how attackers change their malware ambitions over time. Not only is this data super interesting, but it can help take some of the **fear, uncertainty, and doubt (FUD)** out of conversations about malware and how to manage the risks it poses.

Speaking of FUD, I'll also provide a deep dive into how ransomware has changed over time to demystify this term, as it has largely been hijacked and overloaded in recent years. I'll explain how ransomware has always been one of the least prevalent categories of malware but continues to strike fear into CISOs and security teams and has become a fixture in the news.

In this chapter, we'll cover the following topics:

- Some of the sources of data that threat intelligence for Windows comes from
- Defining malware categories and how their prevalence is measured
- Global malware evolution and trends
- Regional malware trends for the Middle East, the European Union, Eastern Europe and Russia, Asia and Oceania, and North and South America
- The evolution of ransomware

Introduction

In 2003, when I worked on Microsoft's customer-facing incident response team, we began finding user mode rootkits on compromised systems with some regularity, so much so that one of our best engineers built a tool that could find user mode rootkits that were hiding from Windows. A user mode rootkit runs like any other application that a normal user would run, but it hides itself. Then, one day, we received a call from a Microsoft support engineer who was helping troubleshoot an issue that a customer had on an Exchange email server. The symptom of the problem was that once every few days, the server would blue screen. The support engineer couldn't figure out why and was doing a remote debug session, trying to find the code that caused the server to blue screen. It took weeks, but once he found the code responsible for the blue screen, he couldn't explain what the code was, nor how it was installed on the server. This is when he called us for help.

When the server blue-screened and rebooted, this enabled us to look at a partial memory dump from the system. After a few days of analysis, we determined that the server was compromised in a way we had never seen before. A device driver on the system was hiding itself and other components. We had found the first kernel mode rootkit that we had ever seen in the wild.

This was a big deal. Unlike a user mode rootkit, developing and installing a kernel mode rootkit required incredible expertise. This is because this type of rootkit runs in the most privileged part of the operating system, which few people really understand. At the time, although the concept of kernel mode rootkits was discussed among security experts, finding one installed on a server running in an enterprise's production environment signaled that attackers were becoming far more sophisticated than they had been in the past. Graduating from user mode rootkits to kernel mode rootkits was a major leap forward in the evolution of malware.

To our incident response team, this was a call to action. We had to let the Windows kernel developers at Microsoft know that the thing that makes Windows a trusted computing base, its kernel, was being directly attacked by sophisticated authors of malware. Until then, a kernel mode rootkit running in the wild was mythical. But now, we had evidence that these rootkits were real and were being used to attack enterprise customers. We scheduled a meeting with the lead developers, testers, and program managers on the Windows kernel development team. We gathered in a room used for training, with an overhead projector, so that we could walk the developers through the memory dump we had from the compromised server to show them how the rootkit worked. We provided them with some context about the server, such as where it was running, the operating system version, the service pack level, a list of all the applications running on the server, and so on. We answered numerous questions about how we debugged the source of the blue screen, found the hidden driver, and discovered how it worked.

At first, the Windows kernel team was completely skeptical that we had found a kernel mode rootkit running on a Windows server. But after we presented all the evidence and showed them the debug details, they gradually came to accept the fact that it was a kernel mode rootkit. Our team expected adulation and respect for all the very technical work we had done, as well as our expertise on Windows kernel internals that allowed us to make this discovery. Instead, the kernel developers told us that our tools and our methods were as bad as the malware authors'. They warned us to stop using our tools to find rootkits as the tools could make the Windows systems they ran on unstable unless rebooted. Finally, they offered to do nothing to harden the kernel to prevent such attacks in the future. It was a disappointing meeting for us, but you can't win them all!

After the successful large-scale worm attacks of 2003 and 2004, this tune changed. The entire Windows team stopped the development work they were doing on what would later become Windows Vista. Instead, they worked on improving the security of Windows XP and Server 2003, releasing Windows XP Service Pack 2 and Windows Server 2003 Service Pack 1. There was even talk of a new version of Windows, code-named Palladium, that had a security kernel to help mitigate rootkits like the one we discovered, but it never came to pass (Wikipedia, n.d.). Ultimately, our work on detecting kernel mode rootkits did help drive positive change as future 64-bit versions of Windows would not allow kernel mode drivers, like the one we discovered, to be installed unless they had a valid digital signature.

Later in my career at Microsoft, I had the chance to work with world-class malware researchers and analysts in Microsoft's anti-malware research and response lab, who were protecting a billion systems from millions of new malware threats. Malware like the kernel mode rootkit we had discovered 4 or 5 years earlier was now a commodity. Attackers were using large-scale automation and server-side polymorphism to create millions of unique pieces of malware every week. To win this war, the anti-virus industry was going to have to have bigger and better automation than large-scale purveyors of commodity malware, which has proven to be surprisingly difficult to accomplish.

Why is there so much malware on Windows compared to other platforms?

There are certainly more mobile internet-connected devices today than there are Windows-based systems. Mobile device adoption exploded as Apple, Google, Samsung, and others brought very popular products to the global marketplace. But if there are far more mobile devices, shouldn't there be far more families of malware developed for those platforms?

The answer to this question lies in how applications get distributed in these ecosystems. Apple's App Store was a game-changer for the industry. Not only did it make it easy for iPhone users to find and install applications, but it almost completely eliminated malware for iOS-based devices.

Apple was able to accomplish this by making the App Store the one and only place consumers could install applications from (jailbreaking aside). **Independent Software Vendors (ISVs)** who want to get their apps onto consumers' iOS-based devices, such as iPhones and iPads, need to get their apps into Apple's App Store. To do this, those apps need to meet Apple's security requirements, which they verify behind the scenes. This makes the App Store a perfect choke point that prevents malware from getting onto Apple devices.

By contrast, Microsoft Windows was developed in more naive times, when no one could predict that, one day, there would be more malicious files in the Windows ecosystem than legitimate files. One of the big advantages of Windows, for developers, was that they could develop their software for Windows and sell it directly to consumers and businesses. This model was the predominant software distribution model for PCs for decades. Since software can be installed without regard for its provenance, and with limited ability to determine its trustworthiness, malware flourished in this ecosystem and continues to do so. Microsoft has taken numerous steps over the decades to combat this "side effect" of this software distribution model, with limited success.

Some would argue that the Android ecosystem has ended up somewhere in between these two extremes. Google also has an app store, called Google Play. Google has also taken steps to minimize malware in this app store. However, third-party app stores for Android-based devices didn't all maintain Google's high security standards, subsequently allowing malware for these devices to get into the ecosystem. But, as I mentioned earlier, the number of malware samples detected for Android-based devices is many times smaller than that of Windows-based devices.

These differences in software distribution models, at least partially, help to explain why there is so much more malware developed for Windows than for other platforms. Cybersecurity professionals can take some lessons from this into their own IT environments. Controlling how software is introduced to an enterprise IT environment can also help minimize the amount of malware in it. This is one advantage of leveraging **Continuous Integration (CI)/Continuous Deployment (CD)** pipelines. CI/CD pipelines can help enterprises build their own app store and restrict how software is introduced into their environments.

Now that we've briefly discussed how software distribution models can impact the distribution of malware, let's dive deep into malware. Security teams can learn a lot from studying malware developed for Windows operating systems, even if they don't use Windows themselves. The methods that malware authors employ on Windows can be and are used for malware developed for many different platforms, including Linux. Studying how malware works in the largest malware ecosystem can help us defend against it almost everywhere else. But before I dive right into the historical malware trend data, it's important for you to understand the sources of the data that I'm going to show you. As I discussed in *Chapter 2, What to Know about Threat Intelligence*, threat intelligence, also known as **Cyber Threat Intelligence (CTI)**, is only as good as its source, so let's start there.

Data sources

The primary source for the historical data in this chapter is the Microsoft Security Intelligence Report (Microsoft Corporation, n.d.). During my time working with the researchers and analysts in the **Microsoft Malware Protection Center** (**MMPC**), I was the executive editor and a contributor to the Microsoft Security Intelligence Report, which we called "the SIR." During the 8 or 9 years I helped produce the SIR, we published more than 20 volumes and special editions of this report, spanning thousands of pages. I gave literally thousands of threat intelligence briefings to customers around the world, as well as press and analyst interviews. I have read, re-read, and re-re-read every page of these reports—I know the ins and outs of this data very well.

The data in these reports comes from Microsoft's anti-malware products, including the Malicious Software Removal Tool, Microsoft Safety Scanner, Microsoft Security Essentials, Microsoft System Center Endpoint Protection, Windows Defender, Windows Defender Advanced Threat Protection, Windows Defender Offline, Azure Security Center, and the SmartScreen filter built into Microsoft web browsers. Other non-security products and services that provide valuable data for volumes of this report include Exchange Online, Office 365, and Bing. Note that some of the names of these products and tools have changed since these reports were published. Let me explain in more detail how this eclectic group of data sources helps paint a well-rounded picture of the threat landscape.

The Malicious Software Removal Tool

The Malicious Software Removal Tool (**MSRT**) is an interesting tool that provides valuable data. In the wake of the Blaster worm attacks (there were variants) (Microsoft Corporation, n.d.) in the summer of 2003, Microsoft developed a free "Blaster Removal Tool" designed to help customers detect and remove the Blaster worm and its variants. Remember that, at this time, relatively few systems ran up-to-date, real-time anti-virus software. The Blaster Removal Tool was free. This tool made a huge difference as tens of millions of systems ran it. Because of the tool's success and the constant barrage of malware attacks that followed it in history, such as Sasser, MyDoom, and many others, and the fact that so few systems had anti-virus software running, Microsoft decided to release a "malicious software removal tool" every month. The MSRT was born.

It was meant to be a way to detect infected systems and clean the most prevalent or serious malware threats from the entire Windows ecosystem. Microsoft's anti-malware lab decides what new detections to add to the MSRT every month. A list of all the malware it detects is published on Microsoft's website (Microsoft Corporation, n.d.). Between January 2005 and July 2022, 427 malware families were added to the detections for the MSRT.

Keep in mind that there are at least hundreds of thousands, if not millions, of known malware families, so this is a very small subset of the total that real-time anti-malware software packages detect. The MSRT has been released monthly (more or less) with security updates on "Patch Tuesday," the second Tuesday of every month. It gets automatically downloaded from Windows Update or Microsoft Update to every Windows system in the world that has opted to run it. During the time I was publishing data from the MSRT in the SIR, the MSRT was running on hundreds of millions of systems per month on average.

Once the EULA is agreed to, the MSRT runs silently without a user interface as it's a command-line tool. If it doesn't find any malware infections, it stops execution and is unloaded from memory. No data is sent to Microsoft in this case. But if malware is detected by the MSRT, then it will try to remove the malware from the system and report the infection to the user and to Microsoft. In this case, data is sent to Microsoft.

Microsoft publishes the specific list of data fields that the MSRT sends back for analysis, including the version of Windows that the malware was detected on, the operating system locale, and an MD5 hash of the malicious files removed from the system, among others (Microsoft Corporation, n.d.). Administrators can download the MSRT and run it manually; the MSRT can also be configured not to send data back to Microsoft. Most enterprises that I talked to that ran the MSRT typically blocked data sent to Microsoft at their firewall. Subsequently, my educated guess is that 95% or more of the hundreds of millions of systems returning MSRT data to Microsoft are likely consumers' systems.

The MSRT provides a great post-malware exposure snapshot of a small list of known, prevalent malware that is infecting consumers' systems around the world. When Microsoft's anti-malware lab adds a detection to the MSRT for a threat that's very prevalent, we should expect to see a spike in detections for that malware family in the data. This happens from time to time, as you'll see in the data. Keep in mind that the infected systems might have been infected for weeks, months, or years prior to the detection being added to the MSRT. Since the MSRT runs on systems all over the world and it returns the Windows locale and country location of infected systems, it provides us with a way to see regional differences in malware infections. I will discuss this in detail later in this chapter.

Real-time anti-malware tools

Unlike the MSRT, which cleans Windows-based systems that have already been successfully infected with prevalent malware, the primary purpose of real-time, anti-malware software is to block the installation of malware.

It does this by scanning incoming files, monitoring systems for tell-tale signs of infection, scanning files when they are accessed, and periodically scanning storage. Real-time anti-malware software can also find pre-existing infections on systems when the real-time anti-malware package is initially installed. Real-time anti-malware software typically gets signature and engine updates periodically (daily, weekly, monthly, and so on). This helps it block new and emerging threats but also old threats it wasn't previously able to detect.

For example, if detection is added for a malware threat, but that malware threat has already successfully infected systems that are running the real-time anti-malware software, the update enables the anti-malware software to detect, and hopefully remove, the existing infection.

My point is that data from real-time anti-malware software provides us with a different view of the threat landscape compared to MSRT. Microsoft Security Essentials, Microsoft System Center Endpoint Protection, Windows Defender (now called Microsoft Defender), and Windows Defender Advanced Threat Protection are all examples of real-time anti-malware software that are data sources. Windows Defender is the default anti-malware package for Windows 10-based systems, which now runs on over half of all personal computers in the world (Keizer, Windows by the numbers: Windows 10 resumes march toward endless dominance). Microsoft Defender Antivirus is installed on Windows 11 systems by default. This means that Windows Defender could be potentially running on hundreds of millions of systems around the world, making it a great source of threat intelligence data.

During some of the threat intelligence briefings I've done, some attendees asserted that this approach only provides a view of malware that Microsoft knows about. But this isn't quite true. The major anti-malware vendors share information with each other, including malware samples. So, while the first anti-malware lab that discovers a threat will have detections for that threat before anyone else, over time, all anti-malware vendors will have detections for it. Microsoft manages several security information-sharing programs, with the goal of helping all vendors better protect their shared customers (Microsoft Corporation, 2019). Additionally, in recent years Microsoft has expanded support for Microsoft Defender to non-Microsoft operating systems, like Android, iOS, and macOS, that will give them even more data on threats across these platforms (Microsoft Corporation, n.d.).

Although Microsoft's Internet Explorer and Edge web browsers haven't had as large a market share as some of the other web browsers available, the SmartScreen filter built into these browsers gives us a view of malware hosted on the web (Microsoft Corporation, n.d.). SmartScreen is like anti-malware software for the browser. As users browse the web, SmartScreen will warn them about known malicious websites they try to visit and scan files that are downloaded in the browser looking for malware.

The data on sites hosting malicious software, and the malicious files themselves, can give us a view of the most common threats hosted on the web, as well as where in the world threats are hosted most and the regions that the victim populations are in.

Non-security data sources

Sources of data, such as email services and internet search services, can provide an additional dimension to threat intelligence. For example, data from Office 365 (now called Microsoft 365) and Outlook.com provides visibility of the threats that flow through email, including the sources and destinations of these threats and their volumes. The volume of data that Microsoft has from Office 365 is mind-boggling, with hundreds of billions of email messages from customers all over the world flowing through it every month (Microsoft Corporation, 2018).

Bing, Microsoft's internet search engine service, is also a rich source of threat intelligence data. As Bing indexes billions of web pages so that its users can get quick, relevant search results, it's also looking for drive-by download sites, malware-hosting sites, and phishing sites. This data can help us better understand where in the world malware is being hosted, where it moves to over time, and where the victims are.

When data from some select non-security data sources is combined with data from some of the security sources of data I discussed previously, we can get a more rounded view of the threat landscape. Office 365 and Outlook.com receive emails sent from all sorts of non-Microsoft clients and email servers, and Bing indexes content hosted on all types of platforms. Certainly, the combination of this data does not provide us with perfect visibility, but the scale of these data sources gives us the potential for good insights.

Now that you know where I retrieved the historical malware-related data from that I'm going to share with you, let's take a quick look at the different categories of malware that are included in the data and analysis. These categories of malware have been fixtures in the global threat landscape for decades, meaning that CISOs and security teams should be very knowledgeable about these categories. I'm going to show you how attackers change the malware categories they use over time when those categories become less effective. Some people call this "evolution," but I call it old wine in new bottles because the data clearly shows us attackers moving from one known malware category to another known malware category. It's not very often that a novel category of malware is discovered – more often, attackers use variations on themes invented decades ago. This isn't to say that nothing has changed; as an example, we will examine the ways that ransomware has changed over time later in this chapter.

About malware

Before we dive into the historical threat data, I need to provide you with some definitions for terms I'll use throughout the rest of this chapter.

Malicious software, also known as malware, is software whose author's intent is malicious. The developers of malware are trying to impede the confidentiality, integrity, and/or availability of data and/or the systems that process, transmit, and store it.

As I discussed in *Chapter 1*, malware authors can be motivated by many different things, including hubris, notoriety, military espionage, economic espionage, and hacktivism.

Most malware families today are blended threats. What I mean by this is that many years ago, threats were discrete—they were either a worm or a backdoor, but not both. Today, most malware has characteristics of multiple categories of malware. Analysts in anti-malware labs that reverse-engineer malware samples typically classify malware by the primary or most prominent way each sample behaves.

For example, a piece of malware might exhibit characteristics of a worm, a Trojan, and ransomware. An analyst might classify it as ransomware because that's its dominant behavior or characteristic. The volume of threats has grown dramatically over the years. Malware researchers in major anti-malware labs generally don't have time to spend weeks or months researching one malware threat, as they might have done 20 years ago. However, I have seen analysts in CERTs or boutique research labs do this for specific sophisticated threats found in their customers' environments. Protecting vast numbers of systems from an ever-growing volume of serious threats means that some major anti-virus labs are spending less time researching and publishing detailed findings on every threat they discover. Also, most enterprise customers are more interested in blocking infections or recovering from infections as quickly as possible and moving on with business than diving into the inner workings of malware du jour.

Generally speaking, malware research and response is more about automation and science now than the art it once was. Don't get me wrong; if you can understand how a piece of malware spreads and what its payload is, then you can effectively mitigate it. But the volume and complexity of threats seen today will challenge any organization to do this at any scale. Instead, security teams typically must spend time and resources mitigating as many malware threats as possible, not just one popular category or family. As you'll see from the historical data I provide in this chapter, some attackers even use old-school file infectors (viruses).

How malware infections spread

Malware isn't magic. It must get into an IT environment somehow. Hopefully, you'll remember the Cybersecurity Usual Suspects, that is, the five ways that organizations are initially compromised, which I wrote about in detail in *Chapter 1*. To refresh your memory, the Cybersecurity Usual Suspects are:

- Unpatched vulnerabilities
- Security misconfigurations
- Weak, leaked, and stolen credentials
- Social engineering
- Insider threats

Malware threats can use all the Cybersecurity Usual Suspects to compromise systems. Some malware is used to initially compromise systems so that threat actors achieve their objectives. Some malware is used in IT environments after the environment has already been compromised. For example, after attackers use one or more of the Cybersecurity Usual Suspects to initially compromise a network, then they can use malware that will encrypt sensitive data and/or find cached administrator credentials and upload them to a remote server. Some malware is sophisticated enough to be used for both initial compromise and post-compromise objectives. As I mentioned earlier, I have always thought of malware as a synonym for **"attackers' automation."** Instead of the attacker manually typing commands or running scripts, malware is a program that performs illicit activities for the attacker, autonomously or in a semiautonomous fashion. Malware helps attackers achieve their objectives, whether their objective is destruction and anarchy, or economic espionage.

The categories of malware I'll discuss in this chapter include different types of Trojans, browser modifiers, exploits, exploit kits, potentially unwanted software, ransomware, viruses, and worms. Microsoft provides definitions for these categories of malware and others (Microsoft Corporation, n.d.). Your favorite anti-malware provider or threat intelligence provider might have different definitions than these. That's perfectly OK, but just keep in mind that there might be some minor nuanced differences between definitions. I'll provide you with my own, less formal, definitions to make this chapter easier to read and understand.

Trojans

I'll start with Trojans since, worldwide, they have been the most prevalent category of malware for the last decade or more. A Trojan is a program or file that represents itself as one thing when really it is another, just like the Trojan horse story that it's based on. The user is tricked into downloading it and opening or running it. Trojans don't spread themselves using unpatched vulnerabilities or weak passwords like worms do; they must rely on social engineering.

A backdoor Trojan is a variation of this. Once the user is tricked into running the malicious program (scripts and macros can be malicious too), a backdoor Trojan gives attackers remote access to the infected system. Once they have remote access, they can potentially steal identities and data, steal software and game keys, install software and more malware of their choice, enlist the infected system into botnets so that they can do "project work" for attackers, and so on. Project work can include extortion, **Distributed Denial of Service (DDoS)** attacks, storing and distributing illicit and questionable content, or anything else the attackers are willing to trade or sell access to their network of compromised systems for.

Trojan downloaders and droppers are yet another variation on this theme. Once the user is tricked into running the malicious program, the Trojan then unpacks more malware from itself or downloads more malicious software from remote servers. The result is typically the same—malicious servitude and harvesting the system for all that it is worth. Trojan downloaders and droppers were all the rage among attackers in 2006 and 2007 but have made dramatic appearances in limited time periods since then. A great example of a Trojan downloader and dropper is the notorious threat called **Zlob**. Users were tricked into installing it on their systems when visiting malicious websites that had video content they wanted to view. When they clicked on the video file to watch it, the website told them they didn't have the correct video codec installed to watch the video. Helpfully, the website offered the video codec for download so that the user could watch the video. The user was really downloading and installing Zlob (Microsoft Corporation, n.d.). Once installed, it would then expose the user to pop-up advertisements for free "security software" that would help them secure their system. Users that clicked on the ads to download and install the security software were giving the attackers more and more control over their systems.

Potentially unwanted software

While I am discussing threats that use social engineering, another near-ubiquitous threat category is called **potentially unwanted software**, also known as potentially unwanted applications, potentially unwanted programs, and a few other names. Why does this category have so many seemingly unassuming names? This is a category of threats that lawyers invented.

That's not necessarily a bad thing—it really is an interesting threat category. There are some shades of gray in malware research, and this category exposes this.

Let me give you a hypothetical example of potentially unwanted software that isn't based on any real-world company or organization. What would happen if a legitimate company offered consumers a free game in exchange for monitoring their internet browsing habits, all so that they could be targeted more accurately with online advertising? I think most people I know would think that's creepy and not give up their privacy in exchange for access to a free game. But if this privacy trade-off was only listed in the free game's **End User License Agreement (EULA)**, where very few people would read it, how many people would simply download the free game and play it? In this case, let's say the free game ended up as a malware sample in an anti-malware company's threat collection. The analysts in the anti-malware lab could decide that the game company wasn't being transparent enough with the game's users and categorize the game as a Trojan. The anti-malware company would then update the signatures for their anti-malware products to detect this new threat. The anti-malware company's anti-malware solution would then detect and remove the game from every system where it was running. Did the anti-malware company help its customers by removing the game and its ability to track their internet browsing habits? Or did it damage a legitimate company's business by deeming their product as malware and removing it from their customers' systems without permission?

The answer that the anti-malware industry came up with was to call it "Potentially Unwanted Software" (or a similar name), flag it for users when it's detected, and ask the users to explicitly approve or disapprove its removal. This way, the game company's customer decides whether they want to remove the game company's product, not the anti-malware company. This helps mitigate the predictable damage claims and litigation that the anti-malware industry faces with potentially unwanted software.

Many, many variations of the example I described here are being offered on the internet today and are installed on systems all over the world. Some of them are legitimate companies with legitimate businesses, while others are threat actors pretending to be legitimate companies with legitimate products. Some families of this threat category start off as legitimate programs but later turn malicious when their supply chain is compromised, or their operators turn malevolent. Other examples of this category include fake anti-virus software, fake browser protector software, software bundles that contain a bunch of different software offerings and components, and so on. My advice and mantra for many years has been don't trust the software if you don't trust the people who wrote it. You'll see potentially unwanted software appear prominently in the threat data I share in this chapter.

Exploits and exploit kits

Next, let's look at exploits and exploit kits. *Chapter 3, Using Vulnerability Trends to Reduce Risk and Costs*, was dedicated to the topic of vulnerabilities. Remember that a vulnerability can allow an attacker to compromise the confidentiality, integrity, or availability of hardware or software. Exploits are malware that takes advantage of vulnerabilities. You might also remember from my discussion of vulnerabilities in *Chapter 3* that not all vulnerabilities are the same. Some vulnerabilities, if exploited, have a higher potential impact on the system than others. Exploits for critical-rated vulnerabilities are highly sought after by attackers. This is because they give attackers the best chance to take full control of the vulnerable system and run arbitrary code of their choice. That arbitrary code can do anything that the user context it is running in can do. For example, it can download more malware from servers on the internet that will enable attackers to remotely control the system, steal identities and data, enlist the system into a botnet, and so on.

Working exploits for vulnerabilities in web browsers, operating systems, and file parsers (for file formats like .pdf, .doc, .xlsx, and so on) can be worth a lot of money because of the ubiquity of these products. Subsequently, a sophisticated marketplace has developed over the last two decades around the supply and demand for exploits.

Exploits must be delivered to their target. They can be delivered in several different ways, some of which rely on social engineering to succeed. For example, an attacker might deliver an exploit by developing a malformed .pdf file designed to exploit a specific unpatched vulnerability in a parser like Adobe Acrobat Reader or Microsoft Word.

When a victim opens the .pdf file with a parser that isn't patched for the vulnerability that the attacker is using, and if no other mitigations are in place, then the vulnerability is exploited on the system, potentially running arbitrary code of the attacker's choice. But how does the attacker get the victim to run the exploit? One way is social engineering. The malformed .pdf file can be sent to the victim via an email, with the sender masquerading as a co-worker or friend of the victim. Since the victim trusts their co-worker or friend, they open the email attachment and the exploit is executed. Exploits can be hosted on web pages as downloads for victims, sent via social networks, and distributed on USB drives and other removable media.

An exploit kit is a library of exploits with some management software that makes it easier for attackers to manage attacks that use exploits. A kit's exploit library can contain any number of exploits for any number of products. An exploit kit might also provide attackers with web pages that make it easy to deliver the exploits in its exploit library to victims.

Some level of management software built into the kit helps attackers understand which exploits are successfully exploiting vulnerabilities on victims' systems and which are not. This helps attackers make better decisions about which exploits to use and where to maximize their return on investment. This management software might also help attackers identify and replace exploits on their web pages that are no longer effective with new exploits. Examples of exploit kits include Angler (also known as Axpergle), Neutrino, and the notorious Blackhole exploit kit. This approach underpins a business model and has led to the coining of a new phrase, **Malware as a Service (MaaS)**.

Worms

A **worm** provides its own delivery mechanism so that it can automatically spread from system to system. Worms can use unpatched vulnerabilities, security misconfigurations, weak passwords, and social engineering to propagate themselves from system to system. A great example of a worm is Conficker. There were at least a few variants of this worm. It used unpatched vulnerabilities, like MS08-067, a hardcoded list of weak passwords, and Autorun feature abuse (a feature in Windows) to spread from Windows system to Windows system (Rains, 2011). It could spread via removable drives, like USB drives, as well as across networks. Successful worms can be very difficult to get out of an IT environment once they get into the environment. This is because they can "hide" in online and offline storage media and operating system images.

Other examples of successful worms include SQL Slammer and Microsoft Blaster, which both spread like wildfire around the world using unpatched vulnerabilities. There are also worms like MyDoom that spread via email. It's interesting that millions of people were willing to double-click on an email attachment called MyDoom when it arrived in their inbox. Opening this attachment ran the worm that then sent a copy of itself to all the email addresses in the user's contact list. Worms are not a threat from the distant past. Since the days of Conficker (2007), there have been a few wormable vulnerabilities in Windows that were accessible through default exceptions in Windows Firewall. In most of these cases, Microsoft was able to patch hundreds of millions of systems on the internet quickly enough so that large-scale worm attacks were avoided. But this is as dangerous a scenario as it can get for a world that relies so heavily on technology.

Let me paint you a picture of a worst-case worm scenario, based on past successful global worm attacks. An attacker discovers a new zero-day vulnerability in a Windows service. The service runs by default on the vast majority of Windows systems in the world.

The vulnerable service uses a well-known TCP port to listen on the network for connection attempts to it. There is a default rule in Windows Firewall on every system that allows network connections directly to the vulnerable service. The attacker designs a worm capable of exploiting this zero-day vulnerability and releases it on the internet.

The worm uses the vulnerability to spread before Microsoft is aware of the vulnerability and before a security update is available to patch the vulnerability. With a default rule in Windows Firewall that allows the worm to talk directly to the TCP port that the vulnerable service is listening on, there is nothing preventing the worm from exploiting the vulnerability on virtually every consumer system running Windows that is directly connected to the internet and does not have an additional firewall protecting it. But vulnerable Windows systems behind professionally managed enterprise firewalls wouldn't be safe either, as infected laptops would introduce the worm into corporate IT environments when they connect via VPN or on their wireless networks (Microsoft Corporation, n.d.). The worm propagates from system to system around the world in a matter of minutes.

The public internet and most private networks would be disrupted and rendered unusable. First, the network traffic generated by the worm as it attempts to propagate and re-propagate over and over again, from system to system, would significantly disrupt legitimate network traffic on the internet, as well as the private networks it found its way into. After a system gets infected, the worm tries to infect all the systems it has network connectivity with. It simply tries to connect to the vulnerable service via the TCP port it is listening on, on every system the infected system can reach. Hundreds of millions of systems doing this at the same time would disrupt the global internet and private networks. When the worm exploits the unpatched vulnerability, it causes the target system to destabilize, causing a "Blue Screen of Death," a memory dump, and a system reboot. This exacerbates the problem because it's hard to disinfect and patch systems that are constantly rebooting.

All the systems rebooting generate even more network traffic. When each system comes back up, they generate **Address Resolution Protocol (ARP)** traffic and ask their DHCP servers for IP addresses. When the network segments with DHCP servers get saturated with requests for IP addresses, the DHCP servers are prevented from giving rebooting systems IP addresses. Subsequently, rebooting systems start using automatic private IP addresses that are typically non-routable (169.254.x.x). Subsequently, in some cases, these systems can no longer be reached by management software used to patch them, update anti-malware signatures, or deploy possible mitigations or workarounds to them.

The damage such an attack could do shouldn't be underestimated. The United States government has identified 16 critical infrastructure sectors (US Department of Homeland Security, n.d.). These sectors are deemed critical because if their network or systems are disrupted, it would have dire consequences on the security, economy, and public health and safety of the country. These sectors include the chemical sector, the commercial facilities sector, the communications sector, the critical manufacturing sector, the dams sector, the defense industrial base sector, the emergency services sector, the energy sector, the financial services sector, the food and agriculture sector, the government facilities sector, the healthcare and public health sector, the information technology sector, the nuclear reactors, materials, and waste sector, the transportation systems sector, and the water and wastewater systems sector (US Department of Homeland Security, n.d.).

When the worm exploits the zero-day vulnerability on vulnerable systems in these sectors, the economy, energy, water, communications, transportation, hospitals, and many other critical functions for society are disrupted and potentially taken offline. If the attacker included a malicious payload with the worm, such as encrypting data or destroying storage media, recovery would be slow in most cases. Recovering from such an attack would require lots of manual intervention as management software tools and automation systems would be disrupted, as would the networks they are connected to. If underlying storage media on infected systems also had to be replaced, the damage from such an attack would linger for years.

Of course, I've painted a picture of a worst-case scenario. What are the chances that such a worm attack could actually be perpetrated? There were three wormable vulnerabilities in Windows operating systems in 2019 alone. On May 14, 2019, Microsoft announced the existence of a critical-rated vulnerability (CVE-2019-0708) in Windows Remote Desktop Services that was wormable (NIST, n.d.). In their announcement, the Microsoft Security Response Center (MSRC) wrote the following:

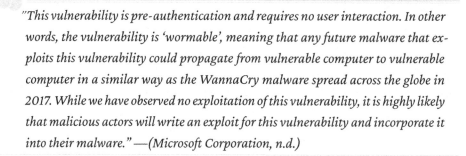

> *"This vulnerability is pre-authentication and requires no user interaction. In other words, the vulnerability is 'wormable', meaning that any future malware that exploits this vulnerability could propagate from vulnerable computer to vulnerable computer in a similar way as the WannaCry malware spread across the globe in 2017. While we have observed no exploitation of this vulnerability, it is highly likely that malicious actors will write an exploit for this vulnerability and incorporate it into their malware."* —(Microsoft Corporation, n.d.)

CVE-2019-0708, the so-called BlueKeep vulnerability, applied to Windows 7, Windows Server 2008, and Windows Server 2008 R2; a third of all Windows systems were still running Windows 7 in 2019 (Keizer, 2020). This vulnerability was so serious that Microsoft released security updates for old, unsupported operating systems like Windows XP and Windows Server 2003. They did this to protect the large number of systems that had never been upgraded from old operating systems that were out of support. Protecting these old systems, which no longer get regular security updates, from a highly probable worm attack leaves less "fuel" on the internet for a worm to use to attack supported systems. Large numbers of systems that lack security updates for critical-rated vulnerabilities are a recipe for disaster as they can be used for all sorts of attacks after they are compromised, including DDoS attacks.

Then, on August 13, 2019, Microsoft announced the existence of two more wormable vulnerabilities (CVE-2019-1181 and CVE-2019-1182). More Windows versions contained these vulnerabilities, including Windows 7, Windows Server 2008 R2, Windows Server 2012, Windows Server 2012 R2, Windows 8.1, and all versions of Windows 10 (including Server versions). In the announcement, the MSRC wrote:

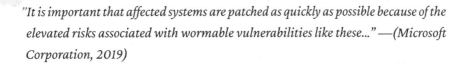

> *"It is important that affected systems are patched as quickly as possible because of the elevated risks associated with wormable vulnerabilities like these..." —(Microsoft Corporation, 2019)*

In each of these three cases in 2019, Microsoft was able to find and fix these critical, wormable vulnerabilities before would-be attackers discovered them and perpetrated worm attacks that would have had crippling effects like the ones I painted here. Unfortunately, there have been other wormable CVEs since 2019, including CVE-2022-21907, published January 11, 2022 (Microsoft Corporation. January 11, 2022).

Ransomware

Another classic category of malware that can have potentially devastating consequences is **ransomware**. Once ransomware gets onto a system using one or more of the Cybersecurity Usual Suspects, it will then encrypt data and/or lock the user out of the desktop of the system. The locked desktop can show a message that demands a ransom to be paid and instructions on how to pay it. Successful ransomware attacks have made headlines around the world. Examples of ransomware families include Reveton (Microsoft Corporation, n.d.) and Petya (Microsoft Corporation, n.d.). Attackers that use ransomware are brazen in their attempts to extort all sorts of organizations, including hospitals and all levels of government.

Although ransomware gets headlines, as you'll see from the data in this chapter, it is actually one of the least prevalent threat categories, from a global perspective. Even old-fashioned viruses are typically more prevalent than ransomware. But remember that risk is composed of probability and impact. The thing that makes ransomware a high-risk threat isn't the probability of encountering it; it's the impact when it's encountered. Data that has been encrypted by ransomware that utilizes properly implemented strong encryption is gone forever without the decryption keys. Subsequently, many organizations decide to pay the ransom without any guarantee that they will be able to recover all of their data. Spending time and resources to implement a ransomware mitigation strategy is a good investment. Making offline backups of all datasets that are high-value assets is a good starting point. Backups are targets for attackers that use ransomware. Therefore, keeping backups offline is an effective and necessary practice.

Also, keep in mind that nothing stays the same for long, and ransomware is constantly evolving. There is nothing preventing authors of more prevalent and successful threats from incorporating ransomware tactics as the payloads in their malware. Ransomware has been used in targeted attacks for years. One thing that likely governs the use of ransomware tactics is just how criminal the attackers are; it's one thing to develop and anonymously release malware on the internet that disrupts people and organizations, but holding assets for ransom and collecting that ransom is a different proposition usually perpetrated by a different kind of criminal altogether. Regardless, organizations need to have a mitigation strategy in place for this threat.

In the past five years, the threat of ransomware has grown dramatically. This growth isn't because the classic category of malware suddenly became more prevalent. The taxonomy changed. That is, the way the industry started using the term "ransomware" has evolved. This has caused some confusion among consumers, governments, enterprise IT professionals, and security professionals alike. After you see the historic data on ransomware in this chapter, I will dive deeper into ransomware to demystify how this intensely high-profile threat has been evolving.

Viruses

Earlier, I mentioned viruses. **Viruses** have been around for decades. They are typically self-replicating file infectors. Viruses can spread when they are inadvertently copied between systems. Because they infect files and/or the **master boot record (MBR)** on systems, sometimes indiscriminately, they can be very "noisy" threats that are easy to detect, but hard to disinfect. In the last decade or so, viruses seem to have come back into fashion with some attackers. Modern attackers that develop viruses typically don't just infect files like their predecessors did decades ago; they can be more imaginative and malicious. Remember, most threats are blended.

Modern viruses have been known to download other malware once they infect a system, disable anti-malware software, steal cached credentials, turn on the microphone and/or video camera on a computer, collect audio and video data, open backdoors for attackers, and send stolen data to remote servers for attackers to pick up. In modern times, viruses have not been anywhere near as prevalent as Trojans or potentially unwanted software, but there always seems to be some volume of detections. A great example of a virus family that has been around for years is Sality (Microsoft Corporation, n.d.).

Browser modifiers

The final threat category I'll discuss here is browser modifiers. These threats are designed to modify browser settings without users' permission. Some browser modifiers also install browser add-ons without permission, change the default search provider, modify search results, inject ads, and change the home page and pop-up blocker settings.

Browser modifiers typically rely on social engineering for installation. The motivation for browser modifiers is typically profit; attackers use them to perpetrate click fraud. But like all threats, they can be blended with other categories and provide backdoor access and download command and control capabilities for attackers.

Measuring malware prevalence

In the next section, I provide a historical perspective on how malware infections evolved over a ten-year period. This will help you understand how attackers change their attacks over time.

Before diving into that data, you'll need to understand two of the ways that the prevalence of malware can be measured. The first one is called **computers cleaned per mille (CCM)** (Microsoft Corporation, n.d.). The term "per mille" is Latin for "in each thousand." We used this measure at Microsoft to measure how many Windows systems were infected with malware for every 1,000 systems that the MSRT scanned. You'll remember that the MSRT runs on hundreds of millions of systems when it's released on the second Tuesday of every month with the security updates for Microsoft products. CCM is calculated by taking the number of systems found to be infected by the MSRT in a country and dividing it by the total number of MSRT executions in that country. Then, multiply it by 1,000. For example, let's say the MSRT found 600 systems infected with malware after scanning 100,000 systems; the CCM would be $(600/100,000)*1,000 = 6$ (Microsoft Corporation, 2016).

The CCM is helpful because it allows us to compare malware infection rates of different countries by removing the Windows install base bias. For example, it's fair to say there are more Windows systems running in the US than in Spain. Spain is a smaller country with a smaller population than the US. If we compared the raw number of systems found infected in the US with the raw number of infected systems in Spain, the US would likely look many, many more times infected than Spain. In actual fact, the CCM exposes that for many time periods, the number of systems infected for every 1,000 scanned in Spain was much higher than the number in the US.

Before a system can get infected with malware, it must encounter it first. Once a system encounters malware, the malware will use one or more of the Cybersecurity Usual Suspects to try to infect the system. If the malware successfully infects the system, then the MSRT runs on the system, detects the infection, and cleans the system. This will be reflected in the CCM.

The **malware Encounter Rate (ER)** is the second definition you need to know about in order to understand the data I'm going to share with you. Microsoft defines the ER as:

> *"The percentage of computers running Microsoft real-time security software that report detecting malware or potentially unwanted software, or report detecting a specific threat or family, during a period." —(Microsoft Corporation, 2016)*

Put another way, of the systems running real-time anti-malware software from Microsoft that I described earlier in this chapter, the ER is the percentage of those systems where malware was blocked from being installed or where a malware infection was cleaned.

I'll use these two measures to show you how the threat landscape has changed over time. The only drawback to using this data is that Microsoft did not publish both of these measures for every time period. For example, they published CCM data from 2008 to 2016 and then stopped publishing CCM data. They started publishing ER data in 2013 and continued to publish some ER data into 2019. But as you'll see, they did not publish ER data for the second half of 2016, leaving a hole in the available data. Additionally, sometimes, data was published in half-year periods and other times in quarterly periods. I've done my best to compensate for these inconsistencies in the analysis I'll share with you next.

One of the things I hope you take away from this section is how being intimately familiar with the data sources helps you accurately interpret data. There are many ways this data could be interpreted, but really understanding how the data sources generate data is key to interpreting the data accurately.

Global Windows malware infection analysis

I have aggregated data from over 20 volumes and special editions of the SIR to provide a view of how the threat landscape evolved over a long period of time. The first measure we'll look at is the worldwide average CCM. This is the number of systems that the MSRT found to be infected with malware for every 1,000 systems it scanned around the world. *Figure 4.1* includes all the time periods that Microsoft published CCM data for in the SIR, each quarter between the third quarter of 2008 and the second quarter of 2016.

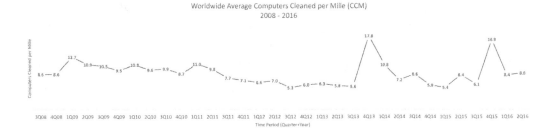

Figure 4.1: Worldwide average malware infection rate (CCM) 2008–2016 (Microsoft Corporation, n.d.)

The horizontal axis illustrates the time periods represented by the quarter and year. For example, 3Q08 is shorthand for the third quarter of 2008, while 4Q13 is the fourth quarter of 2013. The vertical axis represents the worldwide CCM for each time period. For example, in the 1st quarter of 2009 (1Q09), the worldwide average CCM was 12.7.

The worldwide average CCM for all 32 quarters illustrated in *Figure 4.1* is 8.82. To make this number clearer, let's convert it into a percentage: 8.82/1000*100 = 0.882%. For the 8-year period between the third quarter of 2008 and the end of the second quarter of 2016, the worldwide average infection rate, as measured by the MSRT, is less than 1 percent. This will likely surprise some of you who have long thought that the Windows install base has always had really high malware infection rates. This is why comparing the infection rates of different countries and regions is interesting. Some countries have much higher infection rates than the worldwide average, and some countries have much lower CCMs. I'll discuss this in detail later in this chapter. The other factor contributing to a lower malware infection rate than you might have been expecting is that the source of this data is the MSRT. Remember that the MSRT is a free ecosystem cleaner designed to clean largely unprotected systems from the most prevalent and serious threats. If you look at the dates when detections were added to the MSRT, you will see that it is really cleaning a tiny fraction of the known malware families.

For example, according to the list, at the end of 2005, the MSRT had detected 62 malware families (Microsoft Corporation, n.d.). But it's a certainty that there were orders of magnitude more malware in the wild in 2005.

While the MSRT is only capable of detecting a fraction of all malware families, it does run on hundreds of millions of systems around the world every month. This provides us with a limited, but valuable, snapshot of the relative state of computer populations around the world. When we cross-reference MSRT data with data from real-time anti-malware solutions and some of the other data sources I outlined, we get a more complete picture of the threat landscape.

Another aspect of the MSRT that's important to understand is that it is measuring which malware families have successfully infected systems at scale. Microsoft researchers add detections to the MSRT for malware families they think are highly prevalent. Then, when the MSRT is released with the new detections, the malware researchers can see whether they guessed correctly. If they did add detections for a family of malware that was really widespread, it will appear as a spike in the malware infection rate. Adding a single new detection to the MSRT can result in a large increase in the worldwide infection rate. For example, between the third and fourth quarters of 2015 (3Q15 and 4Q15 in *Figure 4.1*), the CCM increased from 6.1 to 16.9. This is a 177% change in the malware infection rate in a single quarter. Then, in the next quarter, the CCM went down to 8.4. What drove this dramatic increase and then decrease? Microsoft malware researchers added detections to the MSRT for a threat called Win32/Diplugem in October 2015 (Microsoft Corporation). This threat is a browser modifier that turned out to be installed on a lot of systems. When Microsoft added detection for it to the MSRT in October, it cleaned Diplugem from lots of systems in October, November, and December. Typically, when a new detection is added to the MSRT, it will clean lots of infected systems in the first month, fewer in the second month, and fewer yet in the third month. A lot of systems were cleaned of Diplugem in the three months of the fourth quarter of 2015. Once the swamp was mostly drained of Diplugem in 4Q15, the infection rate went down 50% in the first quarter of 2016.

This type of detection spike can also be seen between the third and fourth quarters of 2013 (3Q13 and 4Q13, in *Figure 4.1*) when the CCM increased from 5.6 to 17.8. This is a 218% change in the malware infection rate in a single quarter. Five new detections were added to the MSRT in the fourth quarter of 2013.

The detection rate spike in 4Q13 was a result of adding detection to the MSRT for a threat called Win32/Rotbrow (Microsoft Corporation, n.d.), which is a family of Trojans that can install other malware like Win32/ Sefnit (Microsoft Corporation, n.d.). After the big CCM increase that this detection produced, the CCM receded to lower levels over the next two quarters.

In order to see what's happening in a more recent time period, we'll have to use the malware ER instead of the CCM because Microsoft stopped publishing CCM data in 2016. *Figure 4.2* illustrates the ER for the period from the first quarter of 2013 (1Q13) to the fourth quarter of 2018 (4Q18). Microsoft didn't publish a worldwide average ER for the second half of 2016, so we are left without data for that period.

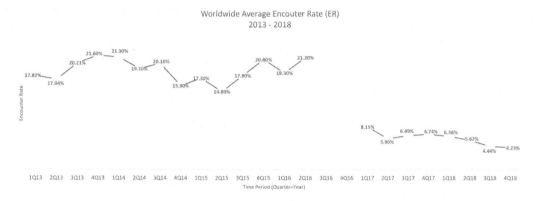

Figure 4.2: Worldwide average encounter rate (ER) 2013-2018

The average ER for the period between 2013 and the end of the first half of 2016 was 18.81%. This means that about 19% of Windows systems that were running Microsoft real-time anti-malware software encountered malware. Almost all of these encounters likely resulted in anti-malware software blocking the installation of the malware. Some smaller proportion of encounters likely resulted in disinfection.

The ER dropped 62% between the second quarter of 2016 (2Q16) and the first quarter of 2017 (1Q17) and didn't go back up to normal levels. In 2017 and 2018, the worldwide average ER was only 6%. I haven't seen a satisfactory explanation for this reduction and so its cause remains a mystery to me.

That has given you a long-term view of malware trends on Windows operating systems from a global perspective. Many of the CISOs and security teams that I've briefed using similar data expressed surprise at how low the global ER and CCM numbers are, given all the negative press malware on Windows has generated over the years. In fact, during some of my speaking engagements at conferences, I would ask the attendees what percentage of Windows systems in the world they thought were infected with malware at any given time. Attendees' guesses would typically start at 80% and work their way up from there. CISOs, security teams, and security experts need to be firmly grounded in reality if they want to lead their organizations and the industry in directions that truly make sense. That's what makes this data helpful and interesting.

That said, I find regional perspectives much more interesting and insightful than the global perspective. Next, let's look at how malware encounters and infections differ between geographic locations around the world.

Regional Windows malware infection analysis

I started studying regional malware infection rates back in 2007. At first, I studied a relatively small group of countries, probably six or seven. But over time, our work in the SIR was expanded to provide malware CCM and ER data for all countries (over 100) where there was enough data to report statistically significant findings. Over the years, three loosely coupled groups of locations emerged from the data:

- Locations that consistently had malware infection rates (CCMs) lower than the worldwide average

- Locations that typically had malware infection rates consistent with the worldwide average

- Locations that consistently had malware infection rates much higher than the worldwide average

Figure 4.3 illustrates some of the locations with the highest and lowest ERs in the world between 2015 and 2018. The dotted line represents the worldwide average ER so that you can see how much the other locations listed deviate from the average. Countries like Japan and Finland have had the lowest malware encounter rates and the lowest malware infection rates in the world since I started studying this data more than 10 years ago. Norway is also among the locations with low CCM and ER. Ireland is a new addition to the list of least impacted locations. The CCM and ER for Ireland were typically lower than the worldwide average, just not one of the five or six lowest. For example, in 2008, the worldwide average CCM was 8.6, while Japan had a CCM of 1.7 and Ireland's CCM was 4.2 (Microsoft Corporation, 2009). It might be tempting to think, duh, a lower encounter rate means a lower infection rate, right? Some locations have both low CCM and low ER. But that's not always the case.

Over time, I have seen plenty of examples of locations that have high ERs but still maintain low CCMs, and vice versa. One reason for this is that not all locations have the same adoption rate of anti-malware software. This is one reason Microsoft started giving real-time anti-malware software away as a free download and now offers it as part of the operating system. There were parts of the world with alarmingly low anti-malware adoption rates. If these locations became heavily infected, they could be used as platforms to attack the rest of the world.

Countries with high anti-malware protection adoption can have high ERs, but generally have much lower CCMs. This is because the real-time anti-malware software blocks malware from installing, thus increasing the ER and leaving less prevalent threats for the MSRT to clean, thereby lowering the CCM.

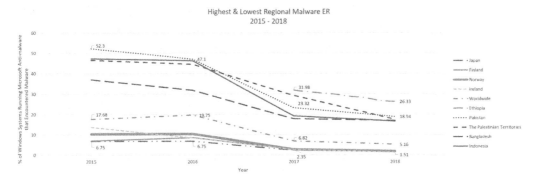

Figure 4.3: Highest and lowest regional malware ERs (Microsoft Corporation, n.d.)

Many years ago, locations like Pakistan, the Palestinian Territories, Bangladesh, and Indonesia all had much lower CCMs than the worldwide average (Microsoft Corporation, 2009). But over time, this changed, and these locations have had some of the highest ERs in the world in recent years. Unfortunately, we can't see whether the CCM for these regions has also increased because Microsoft stopped publishing CCM data in 2016. The last CCMs published for these locations in 2016 are shown in *Table 4.1.* (Microsoft, 2016). The CCMs for these locations are many times higher than the worldwide average, while Japan, Finland, and Norway are much lower.

Location	1Q16	2Q16
Bangladesh	29.2	24.9
Indonesia	45.1	34.4
Pakistan	42.6	37.3
The Palestinian Territories	48.0	47.9
Worldwide average	8.4	8.8
Norway	5.4	3.1
Finland	4.7	2.1
Japan	2.5	2.2

Table 4.1: Highest and lowest regional malware infection rates (CCM) in the first and second quarters of 2016 (Microsoft Corporation, n.d.)

At this point, you might be wondering why there are regional differences in malware encounter rates and infection rates. Why do places like Japan and Finland always have ultra-low infection rates, while places like Pakistan and the Palestinian Territories have very high infection rates? Is there something that the locations with low infection rates are doing that other locations can benefit from? When I first started studying these differences, I hypothesized that language could be the key difference between low and highly infected locations. For example, Japan has a hard language to learn as it's sufficiently different from English, Russian, and other languages, so it could be a barrier for would-be attackers. After all, it's hard to successfully attack victims using social engineering if they don't understand the language you are using in your attacks. But this is also true of South Korea, yet it had one of the highest CCMs in the world back in 2012, with a CCM that ranged between 70 and 93 (one of the highest CCMs ever published in the SIR) (Rains, 2013).

Ultimately, we tried to develop a model we could use to predict regional malware infection rates. If we could predict which locations would have high infection rates, then we were optimistic that we could help those locations develop public policy and public-private sector partnerships that could make a positive difference. Some colleagues of mine in Trustworthy Computing at Microsoft published a Microsoft Security Intelligence Report Special Edition focused on this work: The Cybersecurity Risk Paradox, Impact of Social, Economic, and Technological Factors on Rates of Malware (David Burt, 2014). They developed a model that used 11 socio-economic factors in 3 categories to predict regional malware infection rates. The categories and factors included (David Burt, 2014):

1. Digital access:

    - Internet users per capita
    - Secure network servers per million people
    - Facebook penetration

2. Institutional stability:

    - Government corruption
    - Rule of law
    - Literacy rate
    - Regime stability

3. Economic development:

    - Regulatory quality
    - Productivity

- Gross income per capita
- GDP per capita

The study found that as developing nations increased their citizens' access to technology, their CCM increased. But more mature nations that increased their citizens' access to technology saw decreases in their CCMs. This suggests that there is a tipping point for developing nations as they transition from developing to more mature across the aforementioned categories, where increasing access to technology no longer increases CCM; instead, it decreases it.

An example of a country that appeared to make this transition in 2011–2012 was Brazil. With some positive changes in some of the socio-economic factors in the digital access and institutional stability categories, Brazil's CCM decreased from 17.3 to 9.9 (a 42% reduction) between 2011 and 2012 (David Burt, 2014).

Another nuance from the study is that the locations that had some of the highest CCMs and worst-performing socio-economic factors tended to be war-torn countries, like Iraq. Another interesting insight is that in locations that don't have very good internet connectivity, whether it's because they are geographically isolated or perpetual military conflict has impacted the availability and quality of the internet, malware infects systems via USB drives and other types of removable storage media; that is, when the internet is not able to help attackers propagate their malware, malware that doesn't rely on network connectivity becomes prevalent. When internet connectivity and access improve, then CCMs tend to increase in these locations until socio-economic conditions improve to the point that the governments and public-private sector partnerships start to make a positive difference to cybersecurity in the region. Strife, and the poverty that can follow it, can slow down technology refresh rates, making it easier for attackers to take advantage of people. This is a super interesting area of research.

Looking at individual countries is interesting and helpful because it illuminates what's happening in the most and least impacted locations. We can learn from the failures and successes of these locations. But, very often, CISOs ask about the threat landscape in the groups of countries where their organizations do business or where they see attacks coming from. Examining malware trends for groups of locations makes it easy to identify anomalies in those groups. It also helps to identify which countries are maintaining low malware ERs and CCMs, despite their neighbors who are struggling with malware. What can we learn from these countries that we can apply in other locations to improve their ecosystems? In the next section, I'll show you the historical trends for the following groups of countries:

- The Middle East and Northern Africa: There's always high interest in what's happening in this region, especially in Iran, Iraq, and Syria. This data is super interesting.

- The **European Union** (**EU**): The EU prides itself on maintaining low malware infection rates. However, this hasn't always been the case and has not been consistent across all EU member states.

- Eastern Europe, including Russia: Many of the CISOs I've talked to believe this area of the world is the source of much of the world's malware. But what do these countries' own malware infection rates look like?

- Asia and Oceania: There is always high interest in malware trends in locations like China, Pakistan, and India. It's even more interesting looking at trends in East Asia, South Asia, Southeast Asia, and the countries of Oceania.

- North and South America: The US and Brazil are big markets that always garner high interest, but what about their neighbor's situations?

Some of these regions might not interest you. Please feel free to skip to the section on the region that interests you the most. Let's start by looking at perhaps the most interesting region in the world from a historical threat perspective, the Middle East and Northern Africa.

The threat landscape in the Middle East and Northern Africa

As a region, the Middle East and Northern Africa has had elevated malware ERs and CCMs for many years. I've had the opportunity to visit CISOs and security teams in a few of these locations over the years. The 14 locations I've included in my analysis had an average quarterly CCM of 23.9 across the 26 quarters between 2010 and 2016, while the worldwide average over the same period was 8.7 (Microsoft Corporation, n.d.). These locations as a group had nearly three times the average CCM as the rest of the world. The average quarterly ER of these locations for the 23 quarters between the last half of 2013 and 2019 was 21.9, while the worldwide average was 12.5. *Figure 4.4* illustrates the CCM for several locations in this region for the period, starting in the first quarter of 2010 and ending in the second quarter of 2016, when Microsoft stopped publishing CCM data (Microsoft Corporation, n.d.).

10-year regional report card for the Middle East and Northern Africa

This report card concerns the following data:

- **Region**: Middle East and Northern Africa

- **Locations included in analysis:** Algeria, Bahrain, Iran, Iraq, Israel, Jordan, Kuwait, Lebanon, Oman, Palestinian Authority, Qatar, Saudi Arabia, Syria, and United Arab Emirates

- **Average CCM (2010–2016):** 23.9 (93% higher than worldwide average)

- **Average ER (2013–2019):** 21.9% (55% higher than worldwide average)

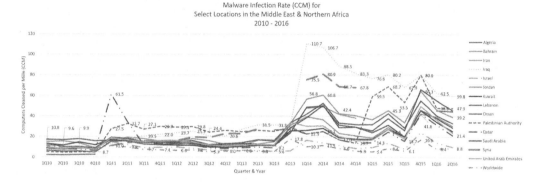

Figure 4.4: Malware infection rates for select locations in the Middle East and Africa 2010–2016
(Microsoft Corporation, n.d.)

Perhaps the most extreme example of malware infection rates climbing out of control as socio-economic factors turned very negative is Iraq. In the fourth quarter of 2013, the CCM in Iraq was 31.3, while the worldwide average was 17.8 (which, by the way, is the highest worldwide average recorded during this 5-year period). In the first quarter of 2014, the CCM in Iraq increased 254% to 110.7 (one of the highest CCMs ever recorded). During this time in Iraq, the Iraqi government lost control of Fallujah to Islamist militants (Al Jazeera, 2014). The first quarter of 2014 saw waves of violence in Iraq with multiple suicide and car bombings; police were being attacked and violence was ramping up in anticipation of parliamentary elections (Wikipedia, n.d.). As the country's economy suffered and its government and social underpinnings faded into the darkness of these extreme conditions, malware thrived.

Malware infection rates remained many times the worldwide average for at least the next 2 years, after which we no longer have CCM data. The malware encounter rate data does suggest that the ER in Iraq declined to points below the worldwide average in 2017, before normalizing at roughly three times the worldwide average in the last quarter of 2018 and in 2019.

The ER data also shows us that Iraq didn't have the highest ER in the region, with Algeria, the Palestinian Authority, and Egypt all having higher ERs at points between 2013 and 2019.

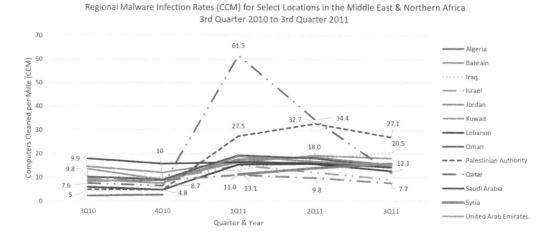

Figure 4.5: Close-up of the spike in regional malware infection rates in MENA in 2011 (Microsoft Corporation, n.d.)

Another more subtle example of regional changes in CCMs that could be linked to socio-economic changes can be seen between the fourth quarter of 2010 (4Q10) and the first quarter of 2011 (1Q11). The CCMs for locations in the region during this period are illustrated in *Figure 4.5*. The Arab Spring started in this region in December 2010, which led to a turbulent period in several locations (Wikipedia). One week earlier, I had just returned to the US from a business trip to Egypt, and it was unnerving to see a government building I had just visited burning on CNN. Civil unrest and mass protests led to changes in government leadership in several key locations in the region. During this same time, CCMs increased in all the locations I have data from in the region. Locations that typically had CCMs lower than the worldwide average, such as Lebanon, Palestinian Authority, and Qatar, suddenly had higher CCMs than the worldwide average. Since then, the CCMs for these locations haven't dropped below the worldwide average.

As mass protests impacted the economies of some key locations in the region, and reports of crime increased dramatically, government services were interrupted, and malware flourished. You might be also wondering about the big increase in the malware infection rate in Qatar in 1Q11. During this time, the prevalence of worms in Qatar was well above the worldwide average. Worms like Rimecud, Autorun, and Conficker were infecting systems with great success. All three of these worms use Autorun feature abuse to spread themselves. Once the infected systems in Qatar were disinfected, the infection rate returned to a more normal range.

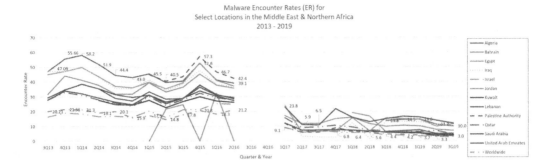

Figure 4.6: Malware encounter rates (ER) for select locations in MENA 2013–2019 (Microsoft Corporation, n.d.)

The Middle East and Northern Africa is a very interesting region. I could probably dedicate an entire chapter in this book to the things I've observed in the data from this region over the years. From a cybersecurity threat perspective, it continues to be one of the most active regions of the world, if not the most interesting.

We turn our gaze now to the threat landscape in Europe.

The threat landscape in the European Union and Eastern Europe

Prior to Brexit, there were 28 sovereign states in the **European Union (EU)**. I lived in the United Kingdom during the period when Brexit was happening. I was the Security and Compliance Leader for Worldwide Public Sector in **Europe, Middle East and Africa (EMEA)** at **Amazon Web Services (AWS)** at the time. In this role, I traveled to continental Europe to visit CISOs and security teams there almost every week. It was a very interesting experience being at the intersection of Brexit, the advent of the **General Data Protection Regulation (GDPR)**, the introduction of the CLOUD Act, the growing popularity of cloud computing, and heightened concern over cybersecurity. I learned a lot about European perspectives on so many topics, including data privacy and data sovereignty. I can highly recommend international experience for both personal and career growth.

From a malware perspective, in contrast to the Middle East and Northern Africa, the EU has typically had much lower infection rates. The 28 locations in the pre-Brexit EU had an average quarterly CCM of 7.9 for the 26 quarters between 2010 and 2016. The worldwide average CCM over the same period was 8.7. The average quarterly malware encounter rate for the EU for the 23 quarters between the last half of 2013 and 2019 was 11.7, while the worldwide average was 12.5. As a group, the pre-Brexit EU had lower CCM and ER than the worldwide average.

Figure 4.7 illustrates the CCM for the 28 locations in the EU for the period starting in the first quarter of 2010, and ending in the second quarter of 2016, when Microsoft stopped publishing CCM data.

10-year regional report card for the European Union

This report card concerns the following data:

- **Region**: European Union (pre-Brexit)
- **Locations included in analysis**: Austria, Belgium, Bulgaria, Croatia, Cyprus, Czech Republic, Denmark, Estonia, Finland, France, Germany, Greece, Hungary, Ireland, Italy, Latvia, Lithuania, Luxembourg, Malta, Netherlands, Poland, Portugal, Romania, Slovakia, Slovenia, Spain, Sweden, and the United Kingdom
- **Average CCM (2010–2016)**: 7.9 (10% lower than worldwide average)
- **Average ER (2013–2019)**: 11.7% (7% lower than worldwide average):

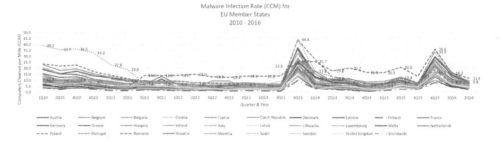

Figure 4.7: Malware infection rates (CCM) for EU member states 2010–2016 (Microsoft Corporation, n.d.)

The first thing you might notice about this data is that Spain had the highest, or one of the highest, infection rates in the EU for several quarters in 2010, 2011, 2013, and 2015. Spain's ER was above the worldwide average for 16 of the 23 quarters between 2013 and 2019. Spain has had a very active threat landscape; over the years, I've seen malware show up first at the local level in Spain before becoming growing global threats.

In 2010, worms like Conficker, Autorun, and Taterf (Microsoft Corporation, n.d.) drove infection rates up. Romania was also among the most active locations in the EU, at times having the highest CCM and ER in the region.

The spike in malware infection rates in the fourth quarter of 2013 (4Q13) was due to three threats that relied on social engineering, Trojan downloaders Rotbrow and Brantall, and a Trojan called Sefnit (Microsoft Corporation, n.d.).

The CCM spike in the fourth quarter of 2015 (4Q15) was due to the global rise in the prevalence of one browser modifier called Diplugem (Microsoft Corporation, n.d.).

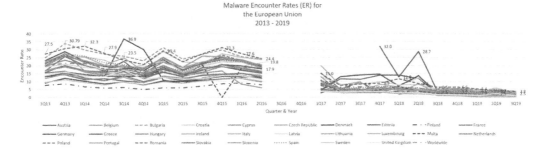

Figure 4.8: Malware encounter rates (ER) for select locations in the European Union 2013–2019
(Microsoft Corporation, n.d.)

The spike seen in Germany's ER in the third and fourth quarters of 2014 was due to some families of threats that were on the rise in Europe during that time, including EyeStye (also known as SpyEye), Zbot (also known as the Zeus botnet), Keygen, and the notorious BlackHole exploit kit (Rains, New Microsoft Malware Protection Center Threat Report Published: EyeStye).

The locations with the consistently lowest CCMs and ERs in the EU are Finland and Sweden. Neither Finland's CCM nor Sweden's CCM has gone above the worldwide average. Sweden's ER did not get above the worldwide average, while Finland's all-time high ER was a fraction of a point above the worldwide average. The positive socio-economic factors at work in the Nordics, including Norway, Denmark, and Iceland, seem to have inoculated them from malware compared to most of the rest of the world.

Location	1Q10 - 2Q16 Average CCM	Location	1Q10 - 2Q16 Average CCM
Spain	15.5	Finland	2.4
Romania	14.5	Denmark	3.7
Poland	13.2	Sweden	4.1
Greece	11.4	Austria	4.4
Croatia	11.3	Germany	5.0
Bulgaria	10.8	Luxembourg	5.2
Portugal	10.5	Estonia	5.3
Cyprus	9.9	Ireland	5.4
Lithuania	9.3	United Kingdom	5.7
Hungary	8.7	Czech Republic	5.9

Table 4.2: Left: EU locations with the highest average CCM, 1Q10–2Q16; right: EU locations
with the lowest average CCM, 1Q10–2Q16 (Microsoft Corporation, n.d.)

Location	3Q13 - 3Q19 Average ER	Location	3Q13 - 3Q19 Average ER
Bulgaria	20.5	Finland	5.2
Romania	17.9	Sweden	6.2
Croatia	15.9	Malta	6.5
Greece	15.4	Denmark	7.2
Spain	13.8	Ireland	8.0
Estonia	13.8	Luxembourg	8.1
Lithuania	13.7	United Kingdom	8.2
Latvia	13.7	Netherlands	8.2
Portugal	13.7	Austria	9.7
Italy	13.3	Belgium	10.5

Table 4.3: Left: EU locations with the highest average ER, 3Q13–3Q19; right: EU locations with the lowest average ER, 3Q19–3Q19 (Microsoft Corporation, n.d.)

Of course, when discussing malware, there's always high interest in Russia and their Eastern European neighbors. In my career, I've had the chance to visit CISOs and cybersecurity experts in Russia, Poland, and Turkey. I always learn something from cybersecurity experts in this region as there is always so much activity. My experience also suggests that there isn't a bad restaurant in Istanbul!

Russia's CCM has hovered around or below the worldwide average consistently over time. This is despite the ER in Russia being typically above the worldwide average. Russia did suffer the same malware infection spikes in 2013 and 2015 as the rest of Europe did.

The most active location in this region has been Turkey. The CCM and ER in Turkey have been consistently significantly higher than the worldwide average. It has had the highest CCM of these locations in all but one quarter, between 2010 and 2016. Turkey had the highest ER of these locations until the second half of 2016, when the ER of Ukraine started to surpass it. Turkey's threat landscape is as unique as its location at the point where Europe and Asia meet, driven by an eclectic mix of Trojans, worms, and viruses. There was a big increase in both the CCM and ER in Turkey in 2014. Interestingly, 2014 was a presidential election year in Turkey (Turkey's Premier Is Proclaimed Winner of Presidential Election, 2014), and saw large anti-government protests related to proposed new regulations of the internet there (Ece Toksabay, 2014). There were also significant spikes in CCM and ER in Turkey at the end of 2015 and into 2016. Again, it's interesting that a general election was held in June of 2015 and there were a series of ISIS-related bombings and attacks in Turkey during this time.

Estonia has had the lowest CCM and ER for much of the period I studied, both typically below the worldwide average.

But there are spikes in the ER data in the fourth quarter of 2017 and the second quarter of 2018. We can get some insights from the 2018 report (Republic of Estonia Information System Authority, 2018) and 2019 report (Authority, 2019) published by the Estonian Information System Authority, which seems to point the finger at the WannaCry and NotPetya ransomware campaigns and the exploitation of unpatched vulnerabilities.

10-year regional report card for select Eastern European locations

This report card concerns the following data:

- **Region**: Select Eastern European locations
- **Locations included in analysis**: Bulgaria, Estonia, Latvia, Slovakia, Russia, Turkey, and Ukraine
- **Average CCM (2010–2016)**: 10.5 (19% higher than worldwide average)
- **Average ER (2013–2019)**: 17.2% (32% higher than worldwide average)

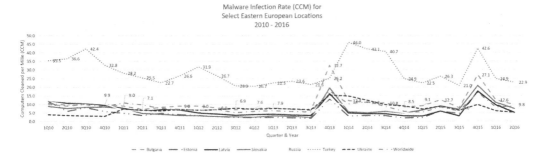

Figure 4.9: Malware infection rates for select locations in Eastern Europe 2010–2016 (Microsoft Corporation, n.d.

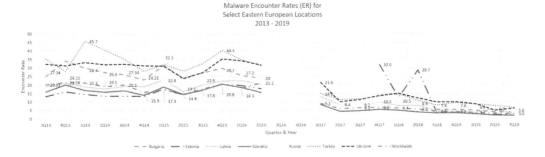

Figure 4.10: Malware encounter rates (ER) for select locations in Eastern Europe 2013–2019 (Microsoft Corporation, n.d.)

Location	1Q10 - 2Q16 Average CCM	Location	3Q13 - 3Q19 Average ER
Turkey	29.1	Turkey	23.0
Bulgaria	10.8	Ukraine	21.7
Worldwide	8.7	Bulgaria	20.5
Ukraine	7.6	Russia	17.2
Russia	7.3	Estonia	13.8
Latvia	6.9	Latvia	13.7
Slovakia	6.8	Worldwide	12.5
Estonia	5.3	Slovakia	10.9

Table 4.4: Left: Select Eastern European locations, average CCM, 1Q10–2Q16; right: Select Eastern European locations, average ER, 3Q19–3Q19 (Microsoft Corporation, n.d.)

Having looked at the landscape in Europe and Eastern Europe, let's shift gears and examine trends for some locations across Asia.

The threat landscape in select locations in Asia and Oceania

Did you know that about 60% of the world's population lives in Asia? I've been lucky enough to visit Asia and Oceania several times in my career, visiting CISOs and security teams in Japan, Korea, Singapore, Hong Kong, Malaysia, India, China, the Philippines, Australia, New Zealand, and so many other cool places there. Both continents have an interesting threat landscape where, as a whole, they have a significantly higher ER and CCM than the worldwide averages. Several locations in Asia have CCMs and ERs far above the worldwide average. Pakistan, Korea, Indonesia, the Philippines, Vietnam, India, Malaysia, and Cambodia all have much higher CCMs than the worldwide average. Asian countries like Japan and China and Oceanian countries like Australia and New Zealand have much lower infection rates than most Asian countries, and are well below the worldwide average.

Location	1Q10 - 2Q16 Average CCM
Pakistan	36.7
Korea	24.5
Indonesia	24.3
Philippines	22.2
Vietnam	21.9
India	20.4
Malaysia	15.9
Cambodia	15.6
Taiwan	12.3
Worldwide	8.7
Singapore	7.7
Hong Kong SAR	6.3
New Zealand	5.5
Australia	5.4
China	3.1
Japan	2.7

Table 4.5: Locations in Asia with the highest and lowest average CCM, 1Q10–2Q16
(Microsoft Corporation, n.d.)

Location	3Q13 - 3Q19 Average ER
Pakistan	35.9
Indonesia	32.7
Vietnam	29.2
India	25.4
Philippines	25.1
Cambodia	21.6
Malaysia	18.4
China	14.6
Worldwide	12.5
Taiwan	11.5
Korea	11.4
Singapore	9.5
Hong Kong SAR	8.7
Australia	8.6
New Zealand	7.4
Japan	5.3

Table 4.6: Locations in Asia with the highest and lowest average ER, 3Q13–3Q19
(Microsoft Corporation, n.d.)

10-year regional report card for Asia and Oceania

This report card concerns the following data:

- **Region**: Asia and Oceania

- **Locations included in analysis**: Australia, Cambodia, China, Hong Kong SAR, India, Indonesia, Japan, Korea, Malaysia, New Zealand, Pakistan, Philippines, Singapore, Taiwan, and Vietnam

- **Average CCM (2010–2016)**: 10.5 (19% higher than worldwide average)

- **Average ER (2013–2019)**: 17.2% (32% higher than worldwide average)

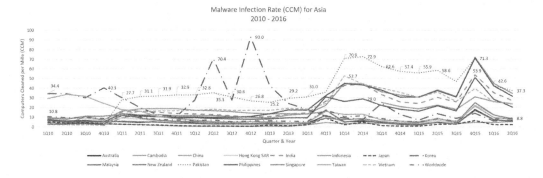

*Figure 4.11: Malware infection rates (CCM) for select locations in Asia and Oceania, 2010–2016
(Microsoft Corporation, n.d.)*

As *Figure 4.11* illustrates, there were big increases in the malware infection rate in South Korea in the second and fourth quarters of 2012. Korea had the highest malware infection rate in Asia during this time, even higher than Pakistan, which at times has had one of the most active threat landscapes in the world. These infection rate spikes were driven by just two families of threats that relied on social engineering to spread. One of these threats was fake anti-virus software that was found on a significant number of systems in Korea. Notice that this spike only happened in Korea. Social engineering typically relies on language to trick users to make poor trust decisions. Apparently, a Korean language version of this fake anti-virus software was very successful at the time. But that threat wouldn't trick very many non-Korean language speakers.

I remember visiting South Korea at the time to drive awareness among public sector and commercial sector organizations of the country's high malware infection rate. Many of the people I talked to in Seoul expressed surprise and even disbelief that the country had the highest infection rate in the world.

You might also notice the sharp increase in the malware infection rate in Pakistan in 2014. Pakistan also had one of the highest ERs in Asia during this time period, along with Indonesia. It's noteworthy that there was civil unrest and political instability in Pakistan during 2014 that led to multiple bombings, shootings, and military actions (Wikipedia, n.d.).

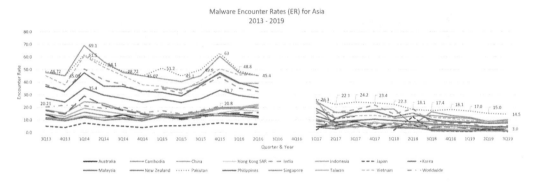

Figure 4.12: Malware encounter rates (ER) for select locations in Asia and Oceania, 2013–2019
(Microsoft Corporation, n.d.)

Asia is so large and diverse that we can get better visibility into the relative CCMs and ERs of these locations by breaking the data into sub-regions. My analysis doesn't include every country in every region, but the results are interesting, nonetheless. Oceania had a lower infection rate and encounter rate compared to any region in Asia; the CCM and ER of Oceania are below the worldwide average, while those in Asian regions are above the worldwide average. Without the aforementioned CCM spike in South Korea, East Asia's CCM likely would have also been below the worldwide average. This data clearly illustrates that South Asia has significantly higher levels of malware encounters and infections than anywhere else in Asia.

These are even higher than the average CCM and ER in the Middle East and Northern Africa, at 23.9 and 21.9%, respectively.

Figure 4.13: Asia and Oceania regional malware infection rates (2010–2016) and encounter rates (2013–2019) (Microsoft Corporation, n.d.)

Next, let's examine the situation in the Americas. I've had the opportunity to live in both the United States and Canada, where I have met with countless CISOs and security teams over the years. I have also had the opportunity to visit CISOs in different locations in South America.

The threat landscape in select locations in the Americas

When I examine CCM data from 2007 and 2008, I can find periods where the United States had a malware infection rate above the worldwide average. But for most of the period between 2010 and 2016, the CCM in the US hovered near or below the worldwide average. The ER in the US is also typically below the worldwide average.

It used to be that the US was a primary target for attackers because consumers' systems in the US had relatively good internet connectivity, relatively fast processors, and lots of available storage—all things that attackers could use for their illicit purposes. But over time, consumers in the US became more aware of attackers' tactics, and vendors started turning on security features in newer systems by default. Over time, the quality of the internet improved in other countries, as did consumers' computer systems. Attackers followed new populations as they came online and focus on attacking consumer systems in the US receded. In more recent periods, locations like Brazil, Argentina, Mexico, Venezuela, and Honduras have had the highest malware infection rates in the Americas.

10-year regional report card for the Americas

This report card concerns the following data:

- **Region:** The Americas
- **Locations included in analysis:** Argentina, Bolivia, Brazil, Canada, Chile, Colombia, Costa Rica, Ecuador, Guatemala, Honduras, Mexico, Nicaragua, Panama, Paraguay, Peru, the United States, Uruguay, and Venezuela
- **Average CCM (2010–2016):** 13.4 (43% higher than worldwide average)
- **Average ER (2013–2019):** 16.5% (26% higher than worldwide average)

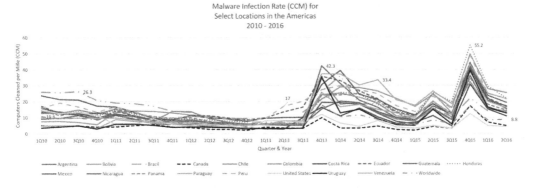

Figure 4.14: Malware infection rates for select locations in the Americas, 2010–2016 (Microsoft Corporation, n.d.)

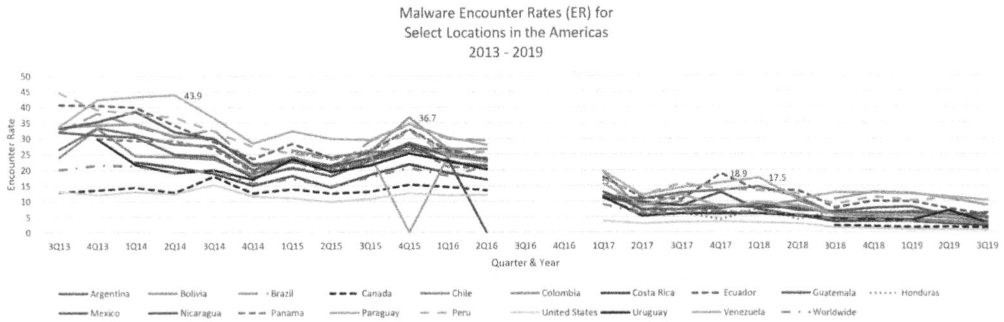

Figure 4.15: Malware encounter rates (ER) for select locations in the Americas 2013–2019 (Microsoft Corporation, n.d.)

Location	1Q10 - 2Q16 Average CCM
Peru	18.3
Bolivia	17.7
Mexico	17.4
Honduras	17.1
Ecuador	16.6
Venezuela	16.5
Brazil	16.3
Chile	13.7
Panama	13.5
Colombia	13.5
Argentina	13.1
Guatemala	13.1
Nicaragua	12.3
Paraguay	11.7
Costa Rica	10.0
Uruguay	9.1
Worldwide	8.7
United States	7.3
Canada	4.8

Table 4.7: Locations in the Americas with the highest and lowest average CCM, 1Q10–2Q16 (Microsoft Corporation, n.d.)

Location	3Q13 - 3Q19 Average ER
Venezuela	24.5
Brazil	22.2
Peru	22.1
Ecuador	21.6
Colombia	20.9
Guatemala	18.2
Mexico	18.1
Argentina	18.0
Bolivia	18.0
Chile	16.0
Panama	15.1
Uruguay	13.9
Honduras	13.7
Worldwide	12.5
Costa Rica	12.3
Paraguay	10.8
Canada	10.1
Nicaragua	8.2
United States	7.4

Table 4.8: Locations in the Americas with the highest average ER, 3Q13–3Q19 (Microsoft Corporation, n.d.)

As a whole, the Americas has a higher CCM and ER than the worldwide average. However, North America, Central America, and South America all have slightly different levels of malware encounters and infections. Although my analysis doesn't include all the locations in the Americas, breaking the data out by region makes it a little easier to compare them.

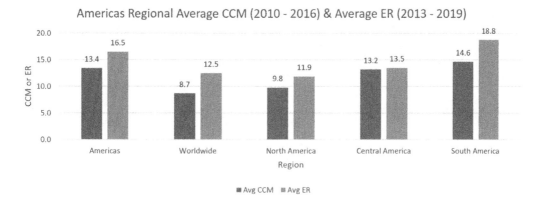

Figure 4.16: Americas average regional malware infection rates (2010–2016) and encounter rates (2013–2019) (Microsoft Corporation, n.d.)

I hope you enjoyed this tour around the world. It took me months to do this research and analysis, so obviously, I find regional malware trends really interesting. And for the security teams that live in these regions, especially outside of the United States, credible regional threat intelligence can be hard to find, while fear, uncertainty, and doubt always seems to be close by. Let me share some conclusions from this analysis with you.

Regional Windows malware infection analysis conclusions

Figure 4.17 illustrates the regional breakdown data on a single graph, which makes it easier to see the relative CCM and ER levels around the world. Over the 10-year period I examined, systems in South Asia, Southeast Asia, and the Middle East and Northern Africa have encountered more malware than anywhere else in the world. This is likely a primary contributing factor to these regions also having the highest malware infection rates in the world.

This is contrasted by the much lower ERs and CCMs of Oceania, East Asia, and the EU.

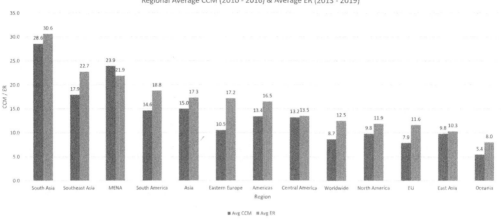

Figure 4.17: Average CCM and ER for regions worldwide, 2013–2019 (Microsoft Corporation, n.d.)

The top 10 locations with the highest average CCMs and ERs in the world are listed in *Table 4.9* here. The worldwide average CCM for the same period is 8.7, and the average ER is 12.5. All of these locations have at least twice the ER and CCM than the worldwide average.

Location	1Q10 - 2Q16 Average CCM	Location	3Q13 - 3Q19 Average ER
Iraq	43.6	Algeria	35.9
Pakistan	36.7	Pakistan	35.9
Syria	34.2	Indonesia	32.7
Palestinian Authority	30.3	Vietnam	29.2
Jordan	27.3	Egypt	27.7
Iran	25.0	Iraq	26.2
Korea	24.5	India	25.4
Oman	24.5	Philippines	25.1
Indonesia	24.3	Jordan	25.0
Lebanon	23.1	Venezuela	24.5

Table 4.9: Locations with the highest CCMs and ERs in the world 1Q10–2Q16 (Microsoft Corporation, n.d.)

What does this all mean for CISOs and enterprise security teams?

I've met many teams over the years that block all internet traffic originating from China, Iran, and Russia because of the attacks they see that originate from those country-level IP address ranges.

From what CISOs have told me, including attribution reports published by the US and UK governments and reports in the press, there certainly doesn't seem to be any doubt that many attacks originate from these locations. But of course, attackers are not limited to using IP address ranges from their home country or any particular country, so this isn't a silver bullet mitigation. And remember that the systems of the victims of such attacks are used to perpetrate attacks against other potential victims, so their IP addresses can be the sources of many attacks.

When systems are compromised by malware, some of them are used in attacks, including DDoS attacks, drive-by download attacks, watering hole attacks, malware hosting, and other "project work" for attackers. Therefore, some CISOs take the precautionary step of blocking internet traffic to/from the locations with the highest malware infection rates in the world. If your organization doesn't do business in these locations or have potential partners or customers in them, minimizing exposure to systems in these locations might work as an additional mitigation for malware infections. Many organizations use managed firewall, proxy, and WAF rules for this very reason. But given my analysis is for a full decade, in order to make it onto the list of most infected locations, these locations essentially must have consistently high infection rates. Limiting the places that Information workers can visit on the internet will reduce the number of potential threats they get exposed to.

For security teams that live in these locations or support operations in these locations, I hope you can use this data to get appropriate support for your cybersecurity strategy from your C-suite, local industry, and all levels of government. Using that submarine analogy I wrote about in the preface of this book, there's no place on Earth with more pressure on the hull of the submarine than in these locations.

This is a double-edged sword as it puts more pressure on security teams in these locations, but also provides them with the context and clarity that organizations in other parts of the world do not have. Use this data to drive awareness among your cybersecurity stakeholder communities and to get the support you need to be successful.

Some of the CISOs I know have used CCM and ER data as a baseline for their organizations. They use their anti-malware software to develop detection, blocked, and disinfection data for their IT environments. They compare the CCM and ER from their environments to the global figures published by Microsoft or other anti-malware vendors. They will also compare their CCM and ER datapoints to regional figures in the countries where they have IT operations. This allows them to see whether their organization is more, or less, impacted than the average consumer systems in their country or globally. Their goal is to always have lower CCM and ER figures than their country has and lower than the global averages.

They find global and regional malware data to be a useful baseline to determine whether they are doing a good job managing malware in their environment.

From a public policy perspective, it appears as though some of the governments in Oceania, East Asia, and the EU have something to teach the rest of the world about keeping the threat landscape under control. Specifically, governments in Australia, New Zealand, the Nordics, and Japan should help highly infected regions get on the right track. But this will be no easy task, as high levels of strife seem to be the underlying factor impacting the socio-economic factors that are linked to high regional malware infection rates. Addressing government corruption, embracing the rule of law, and improving literacy rates, regime stability, regulatory quality, productivity, gross income per capita, and GDP per capita are the first orders of business in order to reduce malware infection rates in many locations. Corporate CISOs and cybersecurity leaders in the public sector can contribute to a better future by educating their nations' public policy influencers.

Now that I've provided you with a deep dive into regional malware encounters and infections, let's look at how the use of different categories of malware has evolved over time globally, that is, how attackers have changed their tactics when they are no longer effective. At the risk of sounding like a cybersecurity data geek, this data is my favorite malware-related data! Social engineering is a mainstay technique for attackers, and this 10-year view of how attackers have used malware illustrates this clearly.

Global malware evolution

Understanding the evolution of malware will help CISOs and security teams put the hysteria they read in the news into context. Keep the Cybersecurity Usual Suspects in the back of your mind as you read this section.

In the wake of the successful large-scale worm attacks of 2003 and early 2004, Microsoft introduced Windows XP Service Pack 2 in August of 2004. Among other things, Windows XP Service Pack 2 turned on the Windows Firewall by default for the first time in a Windows operating system. Prior to this, it was an optional setting that was left to customers to turn on, configure, and test with their applications. This service pack also offered **Address Space Layout Randomization (ASLR)** and **Data Execution Prevention (DEP)** for the first time in a Windows operating system (David Ladd, 2011). These three features blunted the success of future mass worm attacks that sought to use the same tactics as SQL Slammer and MSBlaster.

A vulnerability in a service listening on a network port cannot be exploited if there's a host-based firewall blocking packets from getting to the port. The memory location of a vulnerability might not be the same on every system, making it harder to find and exploit.

18 months after Windows XP Service Pack 2 was released and its adoption was widespread, the data shows us that worms and backdoors fell out of favor with attackers. As shown in *Figure 4.18*, the number of detections of these categories of malware saw dramatic reductions in 2006, 2007, and 2008.

A different type of worm, one that didn't just use unpatched vulnerabilities, became popular with attackers in 2009, 5 years after Windows Firewall, ASLR, and DEP were turned on in Windows operating systems.

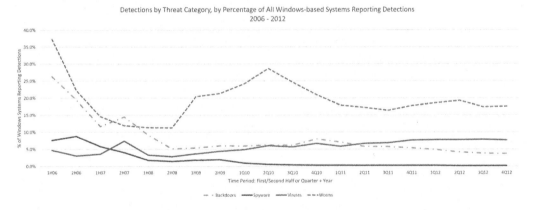

Figure 4.18: Detections by threat category, including backdoors, spyware, viruses, and worms by percentage of all Windows-based systems reporting detections, 2006–2012 (Microsoft Corporation, n.d.)

Once worms were no longer effective for mass attacks, the data shows us that miscellaneous potentially unwanted software became popular in 2006, 2007, and 2008. You can see this marked increase in *Figure 4.19*. As I described earlier in this chapter, this category of threat typically relies on social engineering to get onto systems.

Fake anti-virus software, fake spyware detection suites, and fake browser protectors were all the rage during this period.

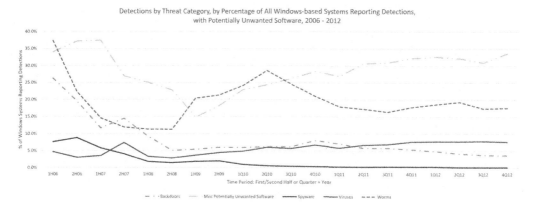

Figure 4.19: Detections by threat category, including backdoors, spyware, viruses, worms, and Miscellaneous Potentially Unwanted Software by percentage of all Windows-based systems reporting detections, 2006–2012 (Microsoft Corporation, n.d.)

As the use of potentially unwanted software peaked in 2006 and more people were getting wise to them, detections trended down in 2007 and 2008. During this time, the data shows us that Trojan downloaders and droppers came into fashion. This is clearly reflected in *Figure 4.20*. This category of threat also primarily relies on social engineering to initially compromise systems. They trick the user into installing them and then unpack or download more malware to the system to give attackers further control. During this time, it was not uncommon for Trojan downloaders and droppers to enlist their victims' systems into botnets for use in other types of attacks.

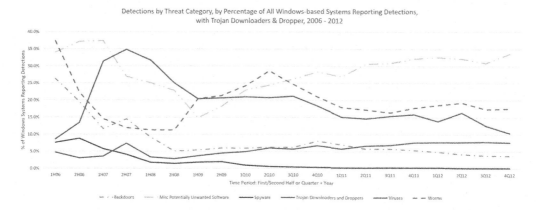

Figure 4.20: Detections by threat category, including backdoors, spyware, viruses, worms, Miscellaneous Potentially Unwanted Software, and Trojan downloaders and droppers by percentage of all Windows-based systems reporting detections, 2006–2012 (Microsoft Corporation, n.d.)

As people caught on to the dirty tricks that attackers were using with Trojan downloaders and droppers, and anti-virus companies focused on eradicating this popular category of malware, the data shows the popularity of droppers and downloaders receding, while detections of miscellaneous Trojans peaked in 2008 and again in 2009. This category of threat also relies primarily on social engineering to be successful. The data also shows us that there was a significant increase in the detection of password stealers and monitoring tools between 2007 and 2011.

There was a resurgence in the popularity of worms in 2008, when Conficker showed attackers what was possible by combining three of the Cybersecurity Usual Suspects into a single worm.

Since then, worms that rely on unpatched vulnerabilities, Autorun feature abuse (social engineering) and weak, leaked, and stolen passwords have remained popular. In *Figure 4.21*, notice the slow but steady rise of exploits starting in 2009. This trend peaked in 2012, when exploit kits were all the rage on the internet. Also, notice that there is no significant volume of ransomware throughout this entire period. As we leave this period at the end of 2012, the categories in the top-right corner of the graph, Trojans and potentially unwanted software, rely on social engineering to be successful.

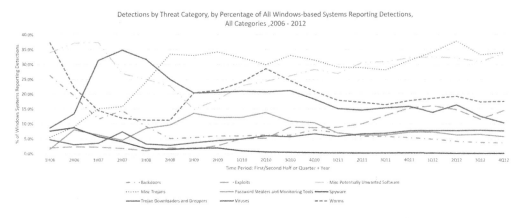

Figure 4.21: Detections by threat category, all categories, by percentage of all Windows-based systems reporting detections, 2006–2012 (Microsoft Corporation, n.d.)

Entering 2013, Microsoft started using the ER to measure threat detections. Note that the measure used between 2013 and 2017 is ER versus the detections measure used in the prior period. These are slightly different data points. Microsoft did not publish ER data in the third and fourth quarters of 2016, so there is a hole in the data for this period. The ER data confirms that miscellaneous Trojans was the most frequent threat category encountered in 2013. Unfortunately, I could not find a published data source for the ER of potentially unwanted software, so it's missing from *Figure 4.22*.

The ER spike for Trojan downloaders and droppers in the second half of 2013 was due to three threats: Rotbrow, Brantall, and Sefnit (Microsoft, 2014).

At the end of this period, in the fourth quarter of 2017, ransomware had an ER of 0.13%, while miscellaneous Trojans had an ER of 10.10%, meaning miscellaneous Trojans were encountered 78 times more often than ransomware. I'll discuss the reason for this difference later in the chapter when I dive deeper into ransomware. Note that although ransomware has a low ER, the impact of a ransomware infection can be devastating. Thus, don't forget to look at both parts of a risk calculation, that is, the probability and the impact of threats. This is a trend that continues into the last quarter of 2019. It appears that the investments Microsoft made in memory safety features and other mitigations in Windows operating systems have helped drive down the global ER, despite increasing numbers of vulnerability disclosures in Windows. If ER is an indicator, the one tactic that the purveyors of malware seem to get a solid **Return on Investment (ROI)** from is social engineering.

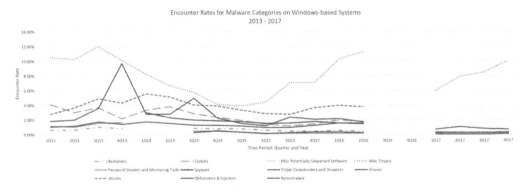

Figure 4.22: Encounter rates by threat category on Windows-based systems reporting detections, 2013–2017 (Microsoft Corporation, n.d.)

The vast majority of the data I just walked you through is from consumers' systems around the world that have reported data to Microsoft. There are some differences between the prevalence of threats on consumers' systems and in enterprises that security teams and cybersecurity experts should be aware of. After studying these differences for many years, I can summarize them for you. Three helpful insights from the data reported to Microsoft from enterprise environments are:

- **Worms**: This was typically the number one category of threat in enterprise environments that were reported to Microsoft over the years. This category of malware self-propagates, which means worms can spread quickly and be very difficult to get rid of once they are inside an enterprise environment. Worms can hide in enterprise IT environments and resurface quickly. For example, they can hide in storage area networks where no anti-virus software has been deployed.

- They can hide in old desktop and server images that, when used to build new systems, reintroduce worms into the environment. They can also be resurrected from backups when they are restored. Many CISOs I know battled worms like Conficker for years after their initial introduction into their environments. These worms typically spread in three ways: unpatched vulnerabilities, weak passwords, and social engineering. Sound familiar? They should because these are three of the five Cybersecurity Usual Suspects. Focusing on the cybersecurity fundamentals will help you keep worms out and contain those already inside your environment. Deploying up-to-date anti-malware everywhere is important to stop these threats.

- **USB drives and other removable storage media**: Many threats, such as worms and viruses, are introduced into enterprise environments on USB drives. Putting policies in place that block USB port access on desktops and servers will prevent Information workers from introducing such threats into your IT environment. Configuring anti-malware software to scan files on access, especially for removable media, will also help block these threats, many of which are old and well-known by anti-malware labs.

- **Malicious or compromised websites**: Drive-by download attacks and watering hole attacks expose Information Workers' systems to exploits and, if successful, malware. Carefully think about whether your organization really needs a policy that allows Information workers to surf the internet unfettered. Does everyone in the organization need to get to every domain on the internet, even IP addresses in the countries with, consistently, the highest malware infection rates in the world? Only permitting workers to get to trusted sites that have a business purpose might not be a popular policy with them, but it will dramatically reduce the number of potential threats they are exposed to.

This mitigation won't work for every organization because of the nature of their business, but I dare say that it will work for a lot more organizations than those that currently use it today. Think through whether unfettered access to the internet and visiting sites with content in foreign languages is really necessary for your staff, as well as whether the security team can make some changes that have high mitigation value and low or zero impact on productivity. Managed outbound proxy rules, IDS/IPS, and browser whitelists are all controls that can help.

And of course, patch, patch, patch! Drive-by download attacks don't work when the underlying vulnerabilities they rely on are patched. This is where those organizations that patch once a quarter or once per half really suffer; they allow their employees to go everywhere on the internet with systems they know have hundreds or thousands of publicly known vulnerabilities on them. What could possibly go wrong?

Now that you've seen the long-term historical trend and understand how attackers evolved their attacks over time, you might be wondering what has been happening with malware more recently. Microsoft offers a view of their anti-malware data from the last 30 days on this page: `https://www.microsoft.com/en-us/wdsi/threats`. It allows you to look at the top global threats as well as drill down into the top regional threats. It also gives you a view of how many systems have encountered malware worldwide and on a per-country basis. At the time of writing (mid-August 2022), the site indicated that there were 79,388,601 devices with encounters around the world in the past 30 days (Microsoft Corporation, n.d.). The top threats detected in these encounters included a few tools hackers and software pirates use as well as a Trojan (Microsoft Corporation, n.d.):

- HackTool:Win32/AutoKMS
- HackTool:Win64/AutoKMS
- HackTool:Win32/Keygen
- Trojan:Win32/Wacatac.B!ml
- HackTool:MSIL/AutoKms

Looking at the top threats in different countries you are interested in will show you just how different regional threats are and what threats they have in common. It's worthwhile looking at this data to ensure your security team is aware of the top threats present in the locations where your organization has a presence, as well as where you have customers and partners.

Global malware evolution conclusions

This malware category data shows us that purveyors of malware really are limited to only a few options when trying to initially compromise systems. Exploiting unpatched vulnerabilities is a reliable method for only limited periods of time, but this doesn't stop attackers from attempting to exploit old vulnerabilities for years after a security update has become available. Worms come in and out of fashion with attackers and require technical skills to develop. But the one tactic that is a mainstay tactic is social engineering. When the other four Cybersecurity Usual Suspects are not viable options, many attackers will attempt to use good old-fashioned social engineering.

Despite all the malware data that I just shared with you, some cybersecurity experts still assert that anti-malware software isn't worthwhile for enterprises. Let's dive into this argument to see whether it holds water. But first, let's take take a closer look at how ransomware has evolved.

The evolution of ransomware

Ransomware. The very word strikes fear into CISOs, security teams, and business leaders everywhere. An encounter with ransomware could be an extinction event for many organizations, particularly those that have not adequately prepared for such an encounter. The thought of critical data being encrypted or destroyed and the necessity of paying a lofty ransom to get access to the data again from criminals isn't how security teams or the businesses they support typically want to spend their time.

Figure 4.22 illustrates that the ER for ransomware was typically the lowest of any category of malware over a period of years. *Figure 4.23* shows us that the ER for ransomware was a fraction of 1% quarter after quarter between 2014 and 2016. Was it just a slow time for purveyors of ransomware? What about some of the headlines I've seen over the years, such as, "1,000% Increase in Ransomware"? This headline could be true because a 1,000% increase in a small number is still a relatively small number in this context. For example, a 1,000% increase of an ER of 0.1% is 1.1%.

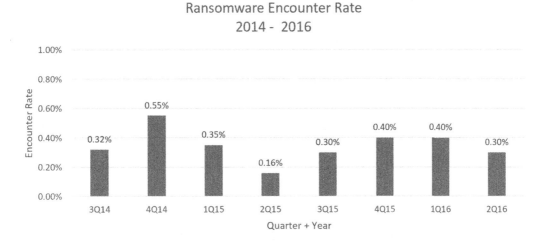

Figure 4.23: Ransomware ER between the 3rd quarter of 2014 and the fourth quarter of 2017 (Microsoft Corporation, n.d.)

Compared to other categories of malware, the classic ransomware category is detected on relatively few systems. *Figure 4.24* reveals this by comparing the ER for Trojans and worms to that of ransomware over eight quarters between 2014 and 2016.

During the quarter where ransomware had its highest ER during this period, the fourth quarter of 2014, the ER of Trojans and worms were 18 times and 17 times that of ransomware, respectively.

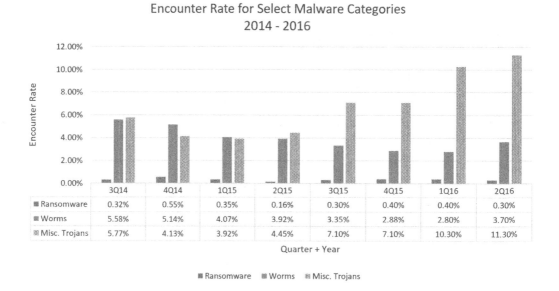

Figure 4.24: ER for ransomware, worms, and Trojans between the 3rd quarter of 2014 and the fourth quarter of 2017 (Microsoft Corporation, n.d.)

Could this trend have changed in more recent time periods, or would a different data source paint a different picture? Let's check. *Table 4.10* contains data from AV-Test Security Report 2018/19 (AV-Test Institute, April 2019) comparing the percentage of new Trojans developed for Windows to the percentage of new ransomware developed for Windows based on the samples that AV-Test collects. This data indicates that new ransomware collected in January 2018, August 2018, and March 2019 was a fraction of a percent, while new Trojans constituted the majority of new malware.

Period	Development of New Trojans % of Total	Development of New Ransomware % of Total
Jan-18	69.46	0.26
Aug-18	71.12	0.54
Mar-19	55.25	0.39

Table 4.10: New Trojans and new ransomware developed for Windows as a percentage of all new malware developed for Windows in January 2018, August 2018, and March 2019 (AV-Test Institute, April 2019)

If you are still skeptical, I don't blame you. Once ransomware stories started showing up on the evening news on major television networks and permeating online news outlets, it was easy to conclude that ransomware had become a very prevalent threat. Let's check one more credible data source and for a slightly different period of time.

The McAfee Labs Threat Report 06.21 provides the number of unique malware samples they collected during quarter-year periods. On average, in the seven quarters between the 3rd quarter of 2019 and the 1st quarter of 2021, McAfee collected over 71 million new malware samples per quarter. *Figure 4.25* reveals that of these tens of millions of malware samples, the highest proportion of new ransomware samples in any quarter was 6.03% in the 4th quarter of 2020 and each of the other quarters was below 4% (McAfee Labs, June 2021).

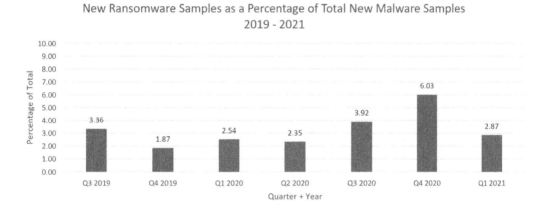

Figure 4.25: New ransomware samples as a percentage of total new malware samples between the 3rd quarter of 2019 and the 1st quarter of 2021 (McAfee Labs, June 2021)

We could examine even more data from other credible sources that supports the notion that the classic malware category called ransomware isn't anywhere near as prevalent as other malware categories. However, I think the explanation as to why this is the case is straightforward, and more data won't be necessary once that becomes clear.

Remember that ransomware is a category of malware that was first coined back in the mid-1980s. Besides a couple of malware categories that are capable of self-propagating like worms and viruses, other malware categories generally must rely on humans and other malware to spread. Ransomware is no exception. As I mentioned earlier, Trojans have been the highest volume malware category for a very long time. This is because Trojans are generally more successful at providing initial compromise for attackers than other threat categories.

Trojans rely on social engineering to spread and can be less technically challenging to develop than worms or viruses, with some exceptions. Once attackers have initially compromised a system using a Trojan, then they typically unpack or download more malware to the system that enables them to move forward with their objectives. If their objective is profit, destruction, or anarchy, deploying ransomware could be the second stage or payload of their attack.

What happens when the initial compromise attempt is unsuccessful? That is, when the Trojan isn't successful because it's detected and blocked by anti-malware software, the second stage of the attack involving ransomware doesn't have a chance to execute. When we use CTI data sources such as anti-malware software, the data will typically contain the malware encounters for the Trojans, but not the ransomware because the ransomware was never encountered. The attack was stopped before the ransomware was unpacked or downloaded to the system by the Trojan. This is another reason why first-stage malware like Trojans are so much more prevalent than second-stage malware, like ransomware.

The data from AV-Test, based on the number of ransomware malware samples they collect, provides some insight into how many unique Trojans are developed compared to other ransomware. Ransomware is typically a fraction of 1% of all the malware samples they collect, while Trojans constitute the majority in every quarter. This data suggests that attackers develop and employ Trojans consistently far more than ransomware.

If ransomware really is far less prevalent than other malware categories, why then is it viewed as such a severe threat? Recall that risk is the combination of probability and impact. I don't think I have seen extinction events announced for organizations after they've encountered Trojans, despite how prevalent they have been. On the other hand, the probability of encountering ransomware might be low, but the impact could be super high. High-risk threats like ransomware typically warrant some extra attention from security teams because their strategies to mitigate threats like this shouldn't be hope – playing the odds that their organizations simply won't encounter it.

Another reason security teams need to pay more attention to ransomware now than in the past is that in the last three to five years, the meaning of the term ransomware has changed. This has led to some confusion in the industry. The term "ransomware" still does refer to the classic category of malware first seen in the 1980s. This is ransomware with low prevalence relative to other malware categories. However, over the past few years, this term has been routinely used to describe any cyber attack where extortion is involved. This includes the same types of targeted attacks we've seen over the past 15 years, even when ransomware (the category of malware) isn't used at all. Ransomware is now the label used for DDoS attacks where attackers demand a ransom to prevent or stop an attack. There's no ransomware malware involved in these DDoS attacks.

Labeling all these different types of attacks as "ransomware" isn't helpful in my view. It confuses conversations among CISOs, security teams, their stakeholders, cybersecurity vendors, and even government agencies that provide cybersecurity guidance. I've been in so many meetings where one person is talking about the classic malware category while the others are discussing targeted attacks where sensitive data is stolen, and the attackers are threatening to release it publicly. Meanwhile, the ways they need to protect, detect, respond, and recover can be quite different depending on which of these things they really want to focus on. In such meetings, I have found it helpful to provide a definition of ransomware to the participants so that everyone in the meeting was referring to the same thing. Then the group could have a productive, single-threaded conversation about the specific threats they had in mind.

How did the concept behind a single unpopular malware category evolve to become so muddy and so pervasive at the same time? At least part of the answer to this question lies in the ways ransomware malware evolved. Let's examine some of the key ways that ransomware has evolved, to make sense of how this term is being used today. There are at least five different ways ransomware has evolved over time. Let's look at each one briefly.

Delivery mechanisms

For decades, the classic ransomware category of malware was largely spread by humans and other malware. Prior to the advent of the internet, floppy disks and Local Area Networks were really the only way to spread this type of malware. Luck played a role in which systems would get victimized and which would not because there wasn't really a targeted delivery system for malware. In the past decade, as ransomware became more popular with attackers, more blended malware was developed that enabled ransomware to spread more easily, such as worms that also encrypted data as they self-replicated from system to system. Today, ransomware is routinely leveraged in targeted attacks where humans, with hands on keyboards, are initially compromising their victims' IT environments (or buying access from an access broker), moving laterally, discovering valuable data and systems, and then using ransomware or other tools to deny access to the legitimate owners. Some vendors have called this type of attack "human-operated ransomware." Targeted attacks have been commonplace for at least 15 years, but instead of trying to stay persistent and exfiltrating data to sell or trade, attackers simply go for their victims' jugulars as quickly as possible. This has resulted in a shift in attacker dwell times from typically several months to just a few hours; as soon as they find data valuable enough to extort their victims, they exfiltrate it, encrypt it, delete it, etc., after which they aren't concerned if their presence is detected.

To facilitate this compressed "smash and grab" attack pattern, attackers have been using commercial threat emulation tools that accelerate their attacks, lower the barrier to entry for less technically sophisticated attackers, and act as a delivery mechanism for ransomware.

> *"Hacked Cobalt Strike suites have become the Saturday Night Specials of cybercrime: they are widely available on underground marketplaces and can be easily customized...As a result, most of the ransomware cases we've seen over the last year have involved the use of Cobalt Strike Beacons. While many malware operators use backdoors associated with the open source Metasploit framework, Cobalt Strike Beacons have become the favored tool of ransomware affiliates and access brokers who sell compromises to ransomware gangs and are often seen tied to ransomware execution."* – Sophos 2022 Threat Report

Of course, there are those that aspire to collect rich ransom demands and do not have the requisite technical skills to develop sophisticated ransomware tools and attack patterns. For these people, access brokers and **Ransomware-as-a-Service (RaaS)** are available. Access brokers are people that sell the details of compromised networks to other criminals. In other words, they have knowledge of organizations that have been compromised and are willing to sell the "keys" to attackers that will use them to pursue their own motivations, whether that's profit via ransomware or something else. Ransomware gangs develop and provide the tools required to perpetrate attacks and their affiliates use those tools to victimize organizations. Under this RaaS business model, these two groups share the profits from successful ransomware attacks. Not only does RaaS lower the barrier to entry for attackers, but it also makes it much harder for purveyors of **Cyber Threat Intelligence (CTI)** to perform strong attribution. If several groups of affiliates all use the same RaaS toolkit, attackers are much harder to distinguish from each other (SophosLabs, 2021). Ransomware gangs like Conti, Revil, Ryuk, and others have developed the RaaS model over time.

Execution mechanisms

Extortionists' modus operandi has evolved over time. Most of the ransomware families in the classic category of malware either encrypted data on the local system's attached storage or locked out the desktop, before making a ransom demand. Some malware developers failed to properly implement their encryption algorithms, which enabled security companies to help victims decrypt their data without paying the ransom in exchange for the decryption keys.

Sometimes attacker's decryption mechanisms failed, or only decrypted some of the data, or took inordinate amounts of time to decrypt. These failures made it less likely that future victims would pay ransoms. Over time, most purveyors of ransomware worked the bugs out of their encryption and decryption mechanisms.

As I mentioned earlier, today, human-operated ransomware has become commonplace. Human-operated ransomware attacks might or might not employ the classic ransomware category of malware. These attackers might not choose to encrypt data at all. Attackers have realized that victims are willing to pay for decryption keys, but many of them are also willing to pay to simply regain control of their data whether it's encrypted or not. For example, in the cloud the classic category of ransomware typically has a much harder time being successful because compute and mass storage devices are decoupled. That is, classic ransomware malware requires compute to run and typically encrypts the locally attached storage devices. In the cloud, compute can take many other forms, including serverless and AI/ML. Storage can also look and behave differently in the cloud compared to the traditional compute with locally attached storage. Subsequently, attackers had to devise other methods of getting leverage over their victims in the cloud. For example, after attackers initially compromise a cloud account and elevate their privileges (if necessary), they can change the cloud account's policies to deny the legitimate owner access to the account or limit their access to specific resources within the account. Then they demand a ransom to restore access to the account owner. The account owner knows that the attacker has control of their data in ways that will allow them to exfiltrate it, delete it, encrypt it, and so on. This creates a sense of extreme urgency for the victim and the willingness to pay a ransom to regain control of the account as quickly as possible. Notice there was no malware or encryption involved in this attack scenario; unauthorized access was the only execution mechanism used.

Many victims are willing to pay attackers to keep their stolen data confidential after exfiltration. The brand damage from a public revelation that they suffered a data breach motivates them to pay such ransom demands. Again, no encryption or decryption mechanisms were involved. Unauthorized access and data exfiltration were the execution mechanisms used.

Ransom payment methods

If there's any one area of advancement that has fueled the growth in attacks that involve extortion, it's payment methods. Payment methods used by the classic category of malware changed over time as new methods of transferring money or other valuables became available. Early on, schemes that required bank transfers typically employed "cash mules," people hired to physically walk into a bank to do a cash withdrawal.

This is risky business since the victim might decide against paying the ransom, instead partnering with law enforcement to arrest the person picking up the ransom. It's one thing to develop a program that encrypts disk drives and demands a ransom to decrypt them, but it's quite another to physically walk into a bank with the intention of committing fraud. These are two different types of criminals. Ransomware developers that didn't have the stomach to commit crime in the real world had to partner with those people that did to physically take possession of their ransom. The more people involved in a crime, the higher the risk of someone disclosing details or getting caught.

As other payment methods became available, ransomware developers had choices for payment methods. Premium SMS message scams and gift cards became the favorite payment methods of many purveyors of ransomware. The victim was forced to text a specific phone number at the rate of $20 per text until the ransom amount was met, or the victim was asked to mail a number of gift cards with equivalent value to the ransom demand. In both scenarios, the extortionists were able to collect their ransoms while maintaining their anonymity and without involving cash mules. However, the ransom demands were limited in size because of the relatively small amounts of cash these methods were capable of transferring.

The innovation that enabled ransomware gangs to dramatically increase their ransom demands into millions of dollars was cryptocurrencies. The proliferation of these financial tools enabled attackers to maintain their anonymity while collecting millions of dollars in illicit payments. Cryptocurrencies also helped foreign attackers target international victims across borders. For example, according to media reports, in the Colonial Pipeline attack, the attackers were paid 75 bitcoin, the equivalent of $4.4 million at the time (Bussewitz, 2021). Of course as the industry and governments develop effective methods to counter this trend, ransom payment methods will evolve yet again.

Ransom demands and communications

Ransom demands and communications with victims, media, and governments have evolved over time. With the classic category of malware, the malware itself communicated the ransom demand to the user on the screen of the system after it was infected and encrypted. But as ransom payment methods evolved to enable ever-increasing demand amounts, ransomware gangs' communications became more and more brazen. Quiet ransom demands directly to victims have been complemented by very public victim shaming exercises using blogs, web pages, and other public communications channels to persuade their victims to pay. Attackers are betting that large organizations that have strong brands and complicated regulatory compliance obligations are willing to pay millions of dollars to regain control of their sensitive data and avoid the financial, PR, legal, and regulatory fallout from the public revelation that they have had a data breach.

This has led the US federal government and industries themselves to try to standardize data breach reporting requirements and ransomware payment notifications specifically. If there is a regulation that requires disclosure of a data breach or ransom payment, this is a disincentive for victim organizations to participate. Sunlight is the best disinfectant.

In the Colonial Pipeline attack, the ransomware gang reportedly sent their victims a URL to a "personal leak page." This page contained the victim's stolen data, which was poised to be published if the ransom demand was not paid by the deadline (Russon, 2021).

Russia was seen by some as complicit in the attack because it was thought that the perpetrators, identified as the DarkSide ransomware gang, were in Russia. The DarkSide gang took the extraordinary step of publicly communicating directly with the US government via their website, to assure them that their motive for the attack was profit and not an attack on critical infrastructure as an act of war or political statement. They wrote on their website, "We do not participate in geopolitics, do not need to tie us with a defined government and look for... our motives...Our goal is to make money and not creating problems for society..." (Russon, 2021). Presumably they did this to deescalate the political tension between the US and Russia in order to reduce the likelihood that they would be pursued by law enforcement in Russia. What a tangled web indeed.

Not only have the ways in which extortionists deliver their ransom demands changed, but the number and nature of those demands have changed as well. Not content with victimizing organizations just once, it has become a popular approach for attackers to make multiple ransom demands once they have a victim on the hook. One demand for a ransom to return control of the data and infrastructure to the victim, another in exchange for promising not to publicly release the victim's sensitive data, another in exchange for promising to delete the victim's exfiltrated data, another in exchange not to sell access to the victim's compromised infrastructure to other attackers, and on and on. This is why so many security experts advise their clients not to pay ransoms; the only way to win this game is not to play – plan to be breached, prepare for it, and practice.

Business model

The evolution of delivery mechanisms, execution mechanisms, ransom payment methods, and ransom demands and communications has enabled attackers to change their business models over time. In decades past before the internet was pervasive, purveyors of classic ransomware relied on luck to support very small-scale attacks – typically one personal computer at a time. Once the internet was established and became wildly popular, attackers were able to leverage drive-by download attacks and worms to scale their attacks. However, the success of attacks still largely depended on luck as they did not have a precise targeting mechanism.

Once payment methods enabled illicit payments in the millions of dollars, the so-called **Advanced Persistent Threat (APT)** actors capable of perpetrating successful targeted attacks against enterprises changed their modus operandi. Instead of trying to maximize their dwell times in order to steal valuable information to sell or trade, now they could simply extort the victim directly and quickly. In other words, they could get a much bigger payday much quicker than ever before. Advances in attacker automation, like RaaS and commercial attack simulation tools, have lowered the bar to entry in this criminal industry and super-charged its growth.

In ransomware briefings I've done with CISOs and security teams, at this point someone typically asks, "what does this all mean?" What they are really asking is how does the evolution of ransomware change the work of cybersecurity strategists, architects, and operations teams? I think the answer to this question is straightforward. Clearly define ransomware for your organization. If your organization is mitigating ransomware as if it is just a category of malware, then you are going to have massive gaps in your strategy. Security teams that treat ransomware as if it is a category of malware typically employ a cybersecurity strategy that I call the "Protect and Recover" strategy that focuses on preventing ransomware from spreading in their IT environment and then restoring from backups when that fails. I will cover this strategy as well as many others in *Chapter 9, Cybersecurity Strategies*. There are better strategies to mitigate modern-day threats, like human-operated ransomware – targeted attacks where extortion is involved.

The key to devising an effective mitigation strategy for ransomware is to define it first so that any confusion about what this threat is to your organization is cleared up for the entire stakeholder community, including the CISO, the security team, IT leadership, IT professionals, business stakeholders, and all the vendors you procure IT and cybersecurity capabilities from. For example, this is how I defined ransomware in 2016 on the Microsoft Security blog:

> *"Ransomware is a type of malware that holds computers or files for ransom by encrypting files or locking the desktop or browser on systems that are infected with it, then demanding a ransom in order to regain access." – Tim Rains, 2016*

This definition is still accurate, but as I've discussed in this section, the term ransomware is also used a few different ways today, years later. To ensure everyone in your organization has a shared understanding of a high-risk threat you plan to spend budget and resources to mitigate, simply define it for everyone.

Today, after years of ransomware evolving in the ways I discussed, if I was going to rewrite that blog post I'd define ransomware as an extortionist business model that can employ a range of tactics, techniques, and procedures to deny victims access to their valuable data, IT infrastructure, or services until they fulfill the attackers' ransom demands. This might or might not involve the use of the classic ransomware category of malware or encryption more generally. Regardless of whether you plan to mitigate the ransomware category of malware, targeted attacks involving extortion more generally, or both, initial compromise will always use one or more of the Cybersecurity Usual Suspects that I discussed in detail in *Chapter 1*.

Once the threat has been defined, your strategy, architecture, CIRT, CSOC, and IT teams can approach it with the proper perspective in mind. For most organizations, a "ransomware strategy" is identical to an all-encompassing enterprise cybersecurity strategy. Put another way, a ransomware strategy is no narrower than a strategy that seeks to mitigate all targeted attacks. After all, in the modern lexicon, ransomware is any attack where extortion is involved. Don't approach it as if it is just malware because it can be much more sophisticated with many moving parts that anti-malware solutions and backups by themselves cannot stop.

The great debate — are anti-malware solutions really worthwhile?

Over the years, I've heard some cybersecurity experts at industry conferences ridicule the efficacy of anti-malware solutions and recommend that organizations don't bother using such solutions. They tend to justify this point of view by pointing out that anti-malware software cannot detect and clean all threats. This is true. They also point out that the anti-malware solutions can have vulnerabilities themselves that can increase the attack surface area instead of reducing it. This is also true. Since anti-malware software typically has access to sensitive parts of operating systems and the data they scan, they can be an effective target for attackers. Some anti-malware vendors have even been accused of using the privileged access to systems that their products have to provide illicit access to systems (Solon, 2017). Other vendors have been accused of improperly sharing information collected by their products (Krebs on Security, 2017).

But remember that malware purveyors are churning out *millions* of unique malware threats per week. As anti-malware labs around the world get samples of these threats, they inoculate their customers from them. So, while anti-malware solutions cannot protect organizations from all threats, especially new and emerging threats, they can protect them from hundreds of millions of known threats. On the other hand, if they don't run an anti-malware solution, they won't be protected from *any* of these threats.

Do the risk calculation using recent data and I think you'll see that running anti-malware software is a no-brainer. For enterprises, failing to run up-to-date anti-malware software from a trustworthy vendor is gross negligence.

Not all anti-malware products are equal. In my experience, anti-malware vendors are only as good as the researchers, analysts, and support staff in their research and response labs. Vendors that minimize false positives while providing the best response times and detections for real-world threats can be very helpful to security teams. To compare products on these measures, check out the third-party testing results from AV-Test and AV Comparatives. There's been discussion in the anti-malware lab community for decades about the best way to test their products.

In the past, the debate has focused on how test results can be skewed based on the collection of malware samples that products are tested against. For example, if a particular lab is really good at detecting rootkits, and the tests include more samples of rootkits, then that anti-malware product might score better than average, even if it's sub-par at detecting other categories of threats. The opposite is also true—if the test doesn't include rootkits or includes very few rootkits, the product could score lower than average. Since anti-malware tests can't include every known malware sample because of real-world resource constraints, whatever samples they do test will influence the score of the products tested. Some anti-malware labs have argued that this forces them to keep detections for older threats that are no longer prevalent in their products, rather than allowing them to focus on current and emerging threats that their customers are more likely to encounter. The counterargument is that anti-malware solutions should be able to detect all threats, regardless of their current prevalence. The tests and the industry continue to evolve with better tests, more competitors, and novel approaches to detecting, blocking, and disinfecting threats. Many vendors have evolved their products far beyond simple signature-based detection systems by leveraging heuristics, behavioral analysis, AI, ML, and cloud computing, among other methods. **Endpoint Detection and Response** (**EDR**) and **Extended Detection and Response** (**XDR**) tools promise to take anti-malware solutions to the next level.

Please remember, you don't want to be the one that has to explain to the C-suite, board of directors, and shareholders the reason a ransomware attack was successful is that you chose not to run an anti-malware solution because they aren't perfect.

This concludes my marathon discussion on malware, anti-malware solutions, the global Windows threat landscape, and ransomware. I feel like I have only scratched the surface here, but we have so many other interesting topics to discuss! Please remember the best practices and tips on what makes good CTI that I shared in *Chapter 2, What to Know about Threat Intelligence*, when consuming threat intelligence in the future.

Summary

This chapter required a lot of research. I tried to provide you with a unique long-term view of the threat landscape and some useful context. Now I'll try to summarize the key takeaways from this chapter.

Malware uses the Cybersecurity Usual Suspects to initially compromise systems; these usual suspects are unpatched vulnerabilities, security misconfigurations, weak, leaked, and stolen passwords, insider threat, and social engineering. Of these, social engineering is attackers' favorite tactic, as evidenced by the consistent prevalence of malware categories that leverage it. Malware can also be employed after the initial compromise to further attackers' objectives.

Some successful malware families impact systems around the world quickly after release, while others start as regional threats before growing into global threats. Some threats stay localized to a region because they rely on a specific non-English language to trick users into installing them. Regions have different malware encounter and infection rates. Research conducted by Microsoft indicates that some socio-economic factors, such as GDP, could be influencing these differences. Regions with unusually high levels of strife and the socio-economic conditions that accompany it typically have higher malware encounter and infection rates.

Focusing on the cybersecurity fundamentals, which address the Cybersecurity Usual Suspects, will help mitigate malware threats. In addition, running up-to-date anti-malware solutions from a trusted vendor will help block the installation of most malware and disinfect systems that get infected. Blocking Information workers' access to regions of the internet that do not have legitimate business purposes can help prevent exposure to malware and compromised systems in these regions.

Ransomware has evolved over time, and now this term means different things to different people. Ensuring your organization has a shared understanding of what modern ransomware is will help align strategies and resources required to mitigate it. An effective ransomware strategy is the same as an all-encompassing enterprise cybersecurity strategy designed to mitigate targeted attacks.

So far, we've examined the long-term trends for vulnerabilities and malware. In the next chapter, we'll explore the ways attackers have been using the internet and how these methods have evolved over time.

References

- Aljazeera (January 4, 2014). *Iraq government loses control of Fallujah*. Retrieved from Aljazeera.com: https://www.aljazeera.com/news/middleeast/2014/01/iraq-government-loses-controlfallujah-20141414625597514.html

- Authority, R. O. (2019). *Estonian Information System Authority Annual Cyber Security Assessment* 2019. Republic of Estonia Information System Authority.

- AV-Test Institute (2017). *The AV-TEST Security Report* 2016/2017. Magdeburg, Germany: AV-Test Institute

- AV-Test Institute (2018). *The AV-TEST Security Report* 2017/2018. Magdeburg, Germany: AV-Test Institute

- AV-Test Institute (April 2019). *The AV-TEST Security Report* 2018/2019. Magdeburg, Germany: AV-Test Institute. Retrieved from AV-Test: https://www.av-test.org/fileadmin/pdf/security_report/AV-TEST_Security_Report_2018-2019.pdf

- AV-Test Institute (April 2019). *The AV-TEST Security* Report 2019/2020. Magdeburg, Germany: AV-Test Institute. Retrieved from AV-Test: https://www.av-test.org/fileadmin/pdf/security_report/AV-TEST_Security_Report_2019-2020.pdf

- AV-Test Institute (April, 2020). *About the AV-TEST Institute*. Retrieved from AV-Test: https://www.av-test.org/en/about-the-institute/

- AV-Test Institute (n.d.). *AV-Test Malware Statistics*. Retrieved from AV-Test: https://www.av-test.org/en/statistics/malware/

- AV-Test Institute (July 2022). *AV-Test Total Malware*. Retrieved from AV-Test: https://www.av-test.org/en/statistics/malware/

- AV-Test Institute (April, 2020). *International Presence and Publications*. Retrieved from AV-Test Institute: https://www.av-test.org/en/about-the-institute/publications/

- David Burt, P. N. (2014). *The Cybersecurity Risk Paradox*, Microsoft Security Intelligence Report Special Edition. Microsoft. Retrieved from: https://query.prod.cms.rt.microsoft.com/cms/api/am/binary/REVroz

- David Ladd, F. S. (2011). *The SDL Progress Report*. Microsoft. Retrieved from: http://download.microsoft.com/download/c/e/f/cefb7bf3-de0c-4dcb-995a-c1c69659bf49/sdlprogressreport.pdf

- Ece Toksabay (February 22, 2014). *Police fire tear gas at Istanbul antigovernment protest*. Retrieved from Reuters: https://www.reuters.com/article/us-turkey-protest/police-fire-tear-gas-atistanbul-anti-government-protest-idUSBREA1L0UV20140222

- Keizer, G. (January 4, 2020). *Windows by the numbers: Windows 10 resumes march towards endless dominance.* Retrieved from Computerworld UK: `https://www.computerworld.com/article/3199373/windows-by-the-numbers-windows-10-continuesto-cannibalize-windows-7.html`

- Krebs on Security (August 17, 2017). *Carbon Emissions: Oversharing Bug Puts Security Vendor Back in Spotlight.* Retrieved from Krebs on Security: `https://krebsonsecurity.com/2017/08/carbon-emissionsoversharing-bug-puts-security-vendor-back-in-spotlight/`

- Leyden, J. (n.d.). *Microsoft releases Blaster clean-up tool.* Retrieved from The Register: `https://www.theregister.co.uk/2004/01/07/microsoft_releases_blaster_cleanup_tool/`

- Microsoft (2014). *Microsoft Security Intelligence Report Volume 16.* Retrieved from Microsoft Security Intelligence Report Volume 16: `https://go.microsoft.com/fwlink/p/?linkid=2036139&clcid=0x409&culture=en-us&country=us`

- Microsoft (December 14, 2016). *Microsoft Security Intelligence Report Volume 21.* Retrieved from Microsoft Security Intelligence Report Volume 21: `https://go.microsoft.com/fwlink/p/?linkid=2036108&clcid=0x409&culture=en-us&country=us`

- Microsoft Corporation (April 8, 2019). *Microsoft Security Intelligence Report Volume 6.* Retrieved from Microsoft Security Intelligence Report Volume 6: `https://go.microsoft.com/fwlink/p/?linkid=2036319&clcid=0x409&culture=en-us&country=us`

- Microsoft Corporation (July 7, 2016). *Microsoft Security Intelligence Report Volume 20.* Retrieved from Microsoft Security Intelligence Report Volume 20: `https://go.microsoft.com/fwlink/p/?linkid=2036113&clcid=0x409&culture=en-us&country=us`

- Microsoft Corporation (August 17, 2017). *Microsoft Security Intelligence Report Volume 22.* Retrieved from Microsoft Security Intelligence Report Volume 22: `https://go.microsoft.com/fwlink/p/?linkid=2045580&clcid=0x409&culture=en-us&country=us`

- Microsoft Corporation (2018). *Microsoft Security Intelligence Report Volume 23.* Retrieved from Microsoft Security Intelligence Report Volume 23: `https://go.microsoft.com/fwlink/p/?linkid=2073690&clcid=0x409&culture=en-us&country=us`

- Microsoft Corporation (August 10, 2019). *Industry collaboration programs.* Retrieved from Microsoft: `https://docs.microsoft.com/en-us/windows/security/threat-protection/intelligence/cybersecurity-industry-partners`

- Microsoft Corporation (August 13, 2019). *Patch new wormable vulnerabilities in Remote Desktop Services* (CVE-2019-1181/1182). Retrieved from Microsoft Security Response Center Blog: `https://msrc-blog.microsoft.com/2019/08/13/patch-new-wormable-vulnerabilities-in-remote-desktop-services-cve-2019-1181-1182/`

- Microsoft Corporation (n.d.). *Diplugem description.* Retrieved from Microsoft Security Intelligence: https://www.microsoft.com/en-us/wdsi/threats/malware-encyclopedia-description?Name=BrowserModifier%3aWin32%2fDiplugem

- Microsoft Corporation (January 11, 2022). *HTTP Protocol Stack Remote Code Execution Vulnerability* (CVE-2022-21907). Retrieved from Microsoft Security Response Center https://msrc.microsoft.com/update-guide/vulnerability/CVE-2022-21907

- Microsoft Corporation (n.d.). *DirectAccess.* Retrieved from Microsoft Corporation: https://docs.microsoft.com/en-us/windows-server/remote/remote-access/directaccess/directaccess

- Microsoft Corporation (n.d.). *How Microsoft identifies malware and potentially unwanted applications.* Retrieved from Microsoft Corporation: https://docs.microsoft.com/en-us/windows/security/threat-protection/intelligence/criteria

- Microsoft Corporation (n.d.). *Malware encounter rates.* Retrieved from Microsoft Security Intelligence Report: https://www.microsoft.com/securityinsights/Malware

- Microsoft Corporation (n.d.). *Microsoft Security Intelligence Report.* Retrieved from Microsoft Security: https://www.microsoft.com/en-us/security/business/security-intelligence-report

- Microsoft Corporation (n.d.). *Over a decade of reporting on the threat landscape.* Retrieved from Microsoft Corporation: https://www.microsoft.com/en-us/security/operations/security-intelligencereport

- Microsoft Corporation (n.d.). *Petya description.* Retrieved from Microsoft Security Intelligence: https://www.microsoft.com/en-us/wdsi/threats/malware-encyclopedia-description?Name=Ransom:DOS/Petya.A&threatId=-2147257025

- Microsoft Corporation (n.d.). *Prevent a worm by updating Remote Desktop Services* (CVE-2019-0708). Retrieved from Microsoft Security Response Center blog: https://msrc-blog.microsoft.com/2019/05/14/prevent-a-worm-by-updating-remote-desktop-services-cve-2019-0708/

- Microsoft Corporation (n.d.). *Remove specific prevalent malware with Windows Malicious Software Removal Tool.* Retrieved from Microsoft Corporation: https://support.microsoft.com/en-us/help/890830/remove-specific-prevalent-malware-with-windows-malicioussoftware-remo

- Microsoft Corporation (n.d.). *Microsoft Defender Online security, simplified.* Retrieved from https://www.microsoft.com/en-us/microsoft-365/microsoft-defender-for-individuals

- Microsoft Corporation (n.d.). *Zlob description*. Retrieved from Microsoft Security Intelligence: https://www.microsoft.com/en-us/wdsi/threats/malware-encyclopedia-description?Name=TrojanDownloader:Win32/Zlob&threatId=16998

- Microsoft Corporation (n.d.). *Reveton description*. Retrieved from Microsoft Security Intelligence: https://www.microsoft.com/en-us/wdsi/threats/malware-encyclopedia-description?Name=Ransom:Win32/Reveton.T!lnk&threatId=-2147285370

- Microsoft Corporation (n.d.). *Rotbrow description*. Retrieved from Microsoft Security Intelligence: https://www.microsoft.com/en-us/wdsi/threats/malware-encyclopedia description?name=win32%2frotbrow

- Microsoft Corporation (n.d.). *Sality description*. Retrieved from Microsoft Security Intelligence: https://www.microsoft.com/en-us/wdsi/threats/malware-encyclopedia-description?Name=Virus%3aWin32%2fSality

- Microsoft Corporation (n.d.). *Sefnit description*. Retrieved from Microsoft Security Intelligence: https://www.microsoft.com/en-us/wdsi/threats/malware-encyclopedia-description?Name=Win32/Sefnit

- Microsoft Corporation (n.d.). *SmartScreen: FAQ*. Retrieved from Microsoft Corporation: https://support.microsoft.com/en-gb/help/17443/windows-internet-explorer-smartscreen-faq

- Microsoft Corporation (n.d.). *Taterf description*. Retrieved from Microsoft Security Intelligence: https://www.microsoft.com/en-us/wdsi/threats/malware-encyclopedia-description?Name=Win32/Taterf

- Microsoft Corporation (n.d.). *Virus alert about the Blaster worm and its variants*. Retrieved from Microsoft Corporation: https://support.microsoft.com/en-us/help/826955/virus-alert-about-the-blasterworm-and-its-variants

- NIST (n.d.). CVE-2019-0708 Detail. Retrieved from National Vulnerability Database: https://nvd.nist.gov/vuln/detail/CVE2019-0708

- Rains, T. (June 27, 2011). *Defending Against Autorun Attacks*. Retrieved from Microsoft Official Security Blog: https://www.microsoft.com/security/blog/2011/06/27/defending-against-autorun-attacks/

- Rains, T. (September 24, 2013). *Examining Korea's Rollercoaster Threat Landscape*. Retrieved from Microsoft Official Security Blog: https://www.microsoft.com/security/blog/2013/09/24/examining-koreasrollercoaster-threat-landscape/

- Rains, T. (n.d.). *New Microsoft Malware Protection Center Threat Report Published: EyeStye.* Retrieved from Microsoft Official Security Blog: https://www.microsoft.com/en-us/security/blog/2012/07/20/new-microsoft-malware-protection-center-threat-report-published-eyestye/

- Republic of Estonia Information System Authority (2018). *Estonian Information System Authority: Annual Cyber Security Assessment 2018.* Republic of Estonia Information System Authority. Retrieved from: https://www.ria.ee/sites/default/files/content-editors/kuberturve/ria-csa-2018.pdf

- Solon, O. (September 13, 2017). *US government bans agencies from using Kaspersky software over spying fears.* Retrieved from The Guardian: https://www.theguardian.com/technology/2017/sep/13/us-government-bans-kaspersky-lab-russian-spying

- *Turkey's Premier Is Proclaimed Winner of Presidential Election* (August 10, 2014). Retrieved from The New York Times: https://www.nytimes.com/2014/08/11/world/europe/erdogan-turkeys-premier-wins-presidential-election.html?_r=0/

- US Department of Homeland Security (n.d.). *Critical Infrastructure Sectors.* Retrieved from CISA Cyber Infrastructure: https://www.cisa.gov/critical-infrastructure-sectors

- Wikipedia (n.d.). *2014 in Iraq.* Retrieved from Wikipedia.com: https://en.wikipedia.org/wiki/2014_in_Iraq

- Wikipedia (n.d.). *2014 in Pakistan.* Retrieved from Wikipedia.com: https://en.wikipedia.org/wiki/2014_in_Pakistan

- Wikipedia (n.d.). *Next-Generation Secure Computing Base.* Retrieved from Wikipedia.com: https://en.wikipedia.org/wiki/NextGeneration_Secure_Computing_Base

- Wikipedia (n.d.). *Timeline of the Arab Spring.* Retrieved from Wikipedia.com: https://en.wikipedia.org/wiki/Timeline_of_the_Arab_Spring

- Microsoft Corporation (n.d.). *Microsoft Security Intelligence.* Retrieved from https://www.microsoft.com/en-us/wdsi/threats

- McAfee Labs (June 2021). *McAfee Labs Threat Report 06.21.* Retrieved from https://www.mcafee.com/enterprise/en-us/assets/reports/rp-threats-jun-2021.pdf

- SophosLabs, November 2021. *Sophos 2022 Threat Report.* Retrieved from https://www.sophos.com/en-us/content/security-threat-report

- Popkin, G. (2020, August 12). *Global warming could unlock carbon from tropical soil.* The New York Times. https://www.nytimes.com/2020/08/12/climate/tropical-soils-climate-change.html

- Bussewitz, Cathy. (2021, May 19). *Colonial Pipeline confirms it paid $4.4 million to hackers*. Associated Press. `https://www.pbs.org/newshour/economy/colonial-pipeline-confirms-it-paid-4-4-million-to-hackers`

- Russon, Mary-Ann. (2021, May 10). *US fuel pipeline hackers 'didn't mean to create problems'*. BBC News. `https://www.bbc.com/news/business-57050690`

- Rains, Tim. (2016, April 22). *Ransomware: Understanding the Risk*. Microsoft Security blog. `https://www.microsoft.com/security/blog/2016/04/22/ransomware-understanding-the-risk/`

Join our community on Discord

Join our community's Discord space for discussions with the author and other readers:

`https://packt.link/SecNet`

5

Internet-Based Threats

Over the past quarter century, attackers have learned to leverage the internet to compromise the IT environments of their victims, achieve their illicit objectives, and satisfy their motivations. CISOs and security teams can inform their cybersecurity strategies by studying how attackers use the internet. In this chapter, we'll look at some of the ways attackers have been using the internet and how these methods have evolved over time. In this chapter, we'll look at the following topics:

- Phishing attacks
- Drive-by download attacks
- Malware hosting sites

Let's get started by looking at the anatomy of a typical attack pattern.

Introduction

In the last two chapters, I provided a deep examination of data and trends for vulnerability disclosures and malware. Both types of threats are constantly leveraged by attackers seeking to compromise organizations and consumers around the world. Subsequently, the risk that these threats represent are actively managed by enterprises. But the ways that attackers deliver their weapons, whether they are exploits for vulnerabilities or malware that provides illicit backdoors for attackers, are varied.

In this chapter, we'll look at some of the methods attackers use to attack their victims; understanding these are just as important as understanding how vulnerabilities and malware have evolved.

The threats we've examined so far have the potential to enable attackers to compromise applications, clients, servers, consumer and IoT devices, routing and switching equipment, and other systems that enterprises rely on. Whether these attacks are designed to victimize massive numbers of organizations and consumers or are targeted at specific organizations, attackers will use the Cybersecurity Usual Suspects to initially compromise IT systems. As a reminder, these include unpatched vulnerabilities, security misconfigurations, social engineering, insider threats, and weak, leaked, or stolen credentials.

It's rare that an attacker is physically sitting at the keyboard of the system they are attempting to compromise. The vast majority of attackers perpetrate their attacks remotely over networks, none more than the internet. In the same way that the internet has allowed small businesses to compete with large multinationals, it also enables individuals and small groups to attack a massive number of consumers and the world's largest organizations.

Now let's look at a typical attack pattern as an example of how attackers have learned to leverage the internet.

A typical attack

In this fictional example, the attacker is physically located in Australia and the intended victim of the attack is headquartered in the United States. The attacker's motivation is profit and they seek to steal valuable information from the organization they are targeting and sell it.

The intended victim has a CISO and a security team. The attacker's constant vulnerability scans of the victim's perimeter reveal that they are proficient at vulnerability management, as vulnerabilities on internet-facing systems are quickly and efficiently patched. After doing some research on the victim organization, the attacker decides to use a multi-pronged approach to initially compromise the organization.

The attacker has always been successful, one way or another, using social engineering to trick non-technical business people into making **poor trust decisions** that could be capitalized on. A poor trust decision in this context is where the victim decides to open an attachment or click on a URL in an email, lower their system's security settings, open host-based firewall ports, or take other such actions that enable the attacker to more easily victimize them. In this case, the attacker is going to use two different tactics to try to compromise a few information workers' laptops, with the goal of getting access to their email inboxes. Both tactics will leverage email as their delivery mechanism and rely on social engineering and sloppy security mitigation to succeed.

The first tactic is to send phishing emails to specific individuals the attacker has identified as working in the company's finance department using the company's public website as a source of information. It didn't take long to get a list of email addresses for the people the attacker wanted to target. The goal of the phishing emails is to trick one or more of the targeted information workers into sharing their Microsoft 365 credentials, which the attacker can then use to access their email inbox.

The second tactic is to send emails to the same information workers that contain a malicious link to a drive-by download site. If the information workers take the bait and click on the link, their web browser will take them to a malicious webpage that will expose them to several exploits for browser and operating system vulnerabilities. If their client isn't fully patched, there's a good chance that the attacker will be able to install a backdoor into their system that might allow them to get privileged access to the victim's laptop and, ultimately, to their email.

Of course, if the attacker does get privileged access to the victim's laptop, they might be able to harvest all sorts of other valuable information in addition to email. Examples include documents stored locally on the laptop, contact lists, access to social networking accounts, software license keys, expense and credit card information, banking information and credentials, as well as personal information that can be used for identity theft, and so on. If the laptop is passively managed by IT, it could be used to store illicit material, enrolled in a botnet, and used in attacks against other targets. For example, it could be used for spam and phishing campaigns, to host drive-by download attacks, malware, advertising click-fraud, DDoS attacks, or whatever "project work" the attacker decides to undertake.

Additionally, the attacker could sell or trade any of the information they pilfered, including account credentials. The criminals they give this information to could turn out to be located much closer to the victim and be much more aggressive at leveraging the information to maximize their profit and/or the damage to the victim.

This type of attack is all too typical. It involved three of the five Cybersecurity Usual Suspects, including social engineering, unpatched vulnerabilities, and stolen credentials. Let's now take a closer look at some of these methods, how they work, and how popular they really are. To do this, I'll draw on threat intelligence and data that has been published by industry leaders over the years. Let's start by looking at phishing.

Phishing attacks

Social engineering is a mainstay tactic for attackers around the world. **Phishing** is at the intersection of two of the Cybersecurity Usual Suspects: social engineering and weak, leaked, and stolen passwords. Many of the largest data breaches in history started with a phishing attack. In simple terms, phishing is a social engineering tactic where the attacker tries to trick their victim into sharing confidential information with them. Attackers use emails, websites, and advertising to entice people into disclosing account credentials, personal details, credit cards, and financial account information, among other things. The information that victims disclose might be used to illegally access online accounts, conduct illegal financial transactions, and steal the victims' identities, among other purposes.

Some attackers cast an indiscriminate wide net for their phishing attacks to snare as many people as possible in order to increase the odds of success. Some attackers focus their phishing activities on an industry or group of targets. Spear phishing is used to focus attacks on individuals, presumably because they have access to information or wealth that the attacker desires.

Very often, after attackers successfully compromise an information worker's system, the victims' own contact lists are used to attack their friends, family, co-workers, and business contacts. For example, once a victim's social networking account has been compromised, attackers can use the victim's account to communicate with the victim's social network. Since the communications are seemingly coming from a trusted source, others in the victim's social network are easily tricked by phishing emails and websites shared via the victim's account. Attackers do not limit themselves to attacking their target's corporate accounts and will seek to compromise the personal systems of information workers, knowing that these systems often have remote access to corporate assets. Installing keyloggers or other types of malware to automate the collection of data from victims' systems is common.

Phishing attacks can involve several technology components, including the victims' clients and the infrastructure used to attack the victims – for example, the email servers from which phishing emails originate or the web servers on which phishing pages are hosted. Very often, these email and web servers are hosted on legitimate systems that have been compromised and are subsequently used for phishing campaigns.

Botnets, which are potentially large networks of compromised systems that are being illicitly remote controlled, are commonly used for phishing campaigns. Using compromised systems for phishing campaign infrastructure reduces the costs for attackers, protects their identities, and helps them achieve a scale they likely could not by any other means. The availability of phishing kits makes it easy for almost anyone to wage a phishing attack.

Let's take a closer look at where phishing sites are hosted and where their victims are. First, it's important to realize the scale of this problem. By volume, phishing, along with Trojans (as I discussed in *Chapter 4, The Evolution of Malware*), are the tactics attackers use most. Just how many phishing websites are there?

Good sources of data for phishing sites are internet search engines and web browsers. After all, Google and Bing are constantly indexing billions of webpages on the internet so that searches can result in fast, accurate results. Additionally, many millions of people use Google Chrome and Microsoft web browsers to surf the internet. Browsers allow users to report sites that are suspicious or outright unsafe. Google and Microsoft employ capabilities in their browsers and search engines to look for phishing sites, malware-hosting sites, and other types of malicious websites. Then they help users of their products and services avoid the malicious sites they find by integrating continuously updated lists of malicious URLs and IP addresses into their products and services. Both browsers and search engines, among other services, can warn users when they attempt to visit a known malicious website, such as a phishing site. This generates data on malicious websites that both Google and Microsoft periodically publish.

For example, Google's technology that looks for malicious websites is called Safe Browsing. This is how Google describes it:

> *Approximately four billion devices benefit from Google Safe Browsing technology. When our systems have identified a site as potentially harmful, Safe Browsing triggers a warning to users. These warnings are designed to prevent users from visiting harmful sites and help them stay safe online."*
>
> — *Google, n.d.*

In 2019, Google's Safe Browsing detected 32,677 new phishing sites per week, on average. This volume is reflected in *Figure 5.1*. Factors that likely influence the volume of new phishing sites include the number of people employing social engineering tactics, the availability of phishing kits and other automation (such as botnets) that help facilitate attacks, continued low operating costs, and acceptable success rates.

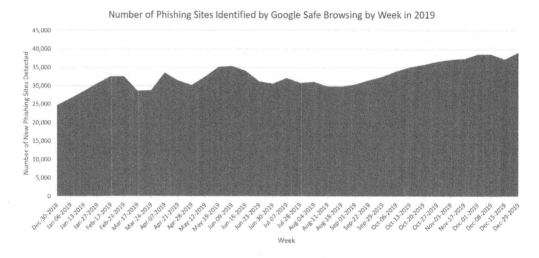

Figure 5.1: The number of phishing websites detected by Google Safe Browsing by week in 2019 (Google, 2020)

The **Anti-Phishing Working Group (APWG)** publishes APWG Phishing Activity Trends Reports on a quarterly basis. Aggregating data from the four APWG quarterly reports published for 2021, *Figure 5.2* reveals that the number of unique phishing sites continued to grow throughout the year, accelerating rapidly in the second half of the year (APWG, n.d.).

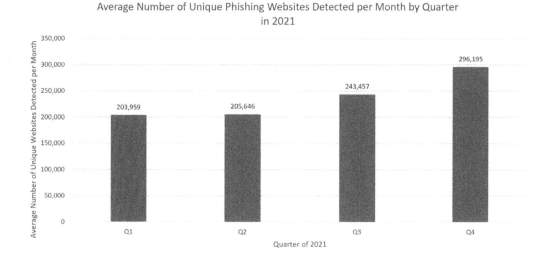

Figure 5.2: The average number of unique phishing websites detected by APWG members each month in 2021, by quarter (APWG, n.d.)

The APWG commented on this trend in the APWG Phishing Activity Trends Report for the fourth quarter of 2021:

> *APWG saw 316,747 attacks in December 2021, which was the highest monthly total in APWG's reporting history. The number of recent phishing attacks has more than tripled since early 2020, when APWG was observing between 68,000 and 94,000 attacks per month." – APWG Feb 23, 2022*

We can also get some insight into the scale of phishing by looking at how many people attempted to visit phishing sites using their web browsers. Google publishes the number of warnings they provide to users of various browsers (including Google Chrome) that leverage Google Safe Browsing.

Figure 5.3 illustrates the average number of browser warnings per week in each quarter in the three years spanning 2019 and 2021. The average number of weekly browser warnings for all of 2021 was 4,128,779.

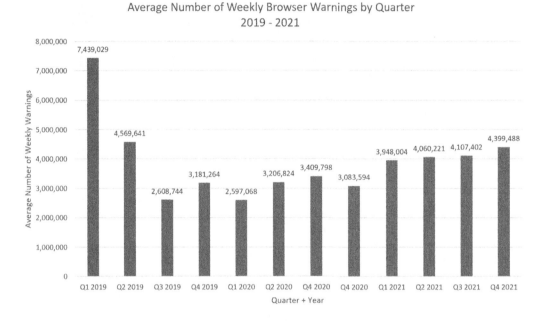

Figure 5.3: The average number of browser warnings provided to users by Google Safe Browsing each week, by quarter, between 2019 and 2021 (Google, n.d.)

The number of warnings was relatively low during 2020 and 2021 compared to previous years. Notable spikes in browser warnings occurred the week of July 15th, 2012 (64,165,701 warnings), the week of Sept 21, 2014 (33,059,895 warnings), and the week of July 31st, 2016 (60,953,154 warnings). The period in 2020 and 2021 had the lowest volume of weekly browser warnings going back to at least October of 2010.

Google, Microsoft, and many other organizations have tried to make it easy for consumers and enterprises to report phishing sites. When phishing sites are reported or detected, legal and technical processes are employed to take down these malicious sites. For example, Microsoft actioned more than 168,000 phishing site take-downs in 2021 (Microsoft Corporation, October 2021). In August of 2022 they announced that they took down "more than 531,000 unique phishing URLs and 5,400 phish kits between July 2021 and June 2022, leading to the identification and closure of over 1,400 malicious email accounts used to collect stolen customer credentials" (Microsoft Corporation, August 2022).

According to Microsoft, "91 percent of all cyberattacks start with email" (Ganacharya, March 2020). The volume of phishing emails has increased over time. A great source of data on phishing emails are massive email services, like Microsoft Office 365 (now called Microsoft 365) and Google Gmail, among others, that receive and filter phishing requests for enterprise customers around the world. Microsoft reported a huge increase in phishing emails going to recipients using Office 365 in 2018:

> *Microsoft analyzes and scans in Office 365 more than 470 billion email messages every month for phishing and malware, which provides analysts with considerable insight into attacker trends and techniques. The share of inbound emails that were phishing messages increased 250 percent between January and December 2018."*
>
> — *Microsoft Corporation, 2019*

Microsoft indicated that the peak month for phishing emails in 2018 was November, where 0.55% of total inbound emails were phishing emails; that is the equivalent of 2,585,000,000 phishing emails in one month (Microsoft Corporation, 2019).

July 2019 appears to be the month with the highest levels in the 2018/2019 time period, with 0.85% of phishing emails detected out of the total volume of emails analyzed by Microsoft worldwide. Assuming the same 470 billion email message volume per month, this is equivalent to 3,995,000,000 phishing email messages in one month. Of course, there are many other on-premises and online email services that receive significant volumes of phishing emails that are not captured in these figures. For example, in August 2019, Google revealed that it was blocking 100 million phishing emails every day:

> *The roughly 100 million phishing emails Google blocks every day fall into three main categories: highly targeted but low-volume spear phishing aimed at distinct individuals, 'boutique phishing' that targets only a few dozen people, and automated bulk phishing directed at thousands or hundreds of thousands of people."*
>
> — *Pegoraro, 2019*

That's approximately 3 billion phishing emails per month on average, in the same ballpark as Microsoft at that time. In 2021, the volume of phishing emails continued to trend upwards. In the first half of 2021, the number of phishing emails observed in Microsoft Exchange global mail flow, per month, was between 620 million and 820 million (Microsoft Corporation, 2021). November appears to be one of attackers' favorite months for phishing campaigns. After that noteworthy spike in November of 2018, another spike occurred in November of 2020 when Microsoft measured volumes almost reaching 1.2 trillion phishing emails (Microsoft Corporation, 2021).

The volumes of phishing emails and the number of active phishing sites make phishing attackers' most widely used tactic. Most phishing emails include a hyperlink to a phishing website. "More than 75% of phishing mails include malicious URLs to phishing sites." (Microsoft Corporation, 2018). Phishing emails typically attempt to take advantage of popular sports and social events, crisis situations, strife, the offer of sales and opportunities, as well as claims of overdue bills, bank account issues, and package shipping glitches, to play on the emotions of their victims and create a sense of urgency. Phishers will use any topic to grab potential victims' attention and compel them to take action that ultimately leads to poor trust decisions and information disclosure.

Frequent targets for phishing attacks include online services, financial sites, social networking sites, e-commerce sites, and so on. The APWG Phishing Activity Trends Report for the fourth quarter of 2021 indicates that Financial Institutions (23.2%), SaaS/Webmail (19.5%), and eCommerce/Retail (17.3%) were the most frequently targeted sectors for phishing attacks during the quarter (APWG Feb 23, 2022).

You might be wondering where the most phishing sites are hosted. In the fourth quarter of 2021, the APWG found that the **generic (gTLD)** and **country code top-level domains (ccTLD)** with the most phishing sites included .com (the most sites by a large margin), .xyz, .org, .net, .buzz, and .br (Brazil) (APWG Feb 23, 2022). The APWG Phishing Activity Trends Report for the second quarter of 2021 included a list of TLDs that had the most unique second-level domains used for phishing during Q2. The ccTLDs included on that list were for the United Kingdom, Montenegro, Tokelau, Mali, Australia, and the Central African Republic.

According to the phishing trend data for 2021 released in May of 2022 by JPCERT/CC, the ccTLDs that hosted the most phishing sites included .cn (China with 69%), .cc (Cocos (Keeling) Islands with 7%), and .jp (Japan with 4%) (JPCERT/CC, 2022).

In the past, I've hypothesized whether there's a connection between a country's malware infection rate and how many phishing sites are hosted in that country's ccTLD. The theory was that phishers use compromised systems to host phishing attacks.

Subsequently, the countries with the highest malware infection rates should also have elevated levels of phishing sites. My conclusion from a non-scientific examination of the historical data I have is that it doesn't appear that phishers rely on the availability of large numbers of compromised systems to set up relatively large numbers of phishing sites. However, I think more rigorous study is required to draw any real conclusions.

Regardless of where attackers host their phishing operations, organizations want to mitigate these attacks. Next, let's discuss some of the mitigations that enterprises can employ to manage phishing attacks.

Mitigating phishing

Phishing websites used to be easier for users to identify than they are today. If a webpage was asking you for credentials or confidential information, but was not protecting that data in transit using HTTPS (the lack of the legitimate lock icon in the web browser indicates this), then why would you type anything into that page? But this is no longer an effective way to identify phishing sites, as the APWG found in their research. As of the third quarter of 2020, 80% or more of phishing sites were found to be using TLS certificates (APWG, September 22, 2021).

Mitigating phishing attacks is both easy and hard. For example, phishing attacks that seek to steal credentials can largely be mitigated by enforcing the requirement to use **multi-factor authentication (MFA)**. According to studies conducted by Microsoft:

> *Your password doesn't matter, but MFA does! Based on our studies, your account is more than 99.9% less likely to be compromised if you use MFA."*
>
> *— Weinert, 2019*

Requiring a second factor for authentication largely mitigates the risks associated with weak, leaked, and stolen passwords. If an attacker successfully tricks a user into disclosing their credentials in a phishing attack, but access to the account requires another factor, such as physical access to a token, landline, or mobile phone, then the credentials by themselves won't give attackers access to the account. Of course, that doesn't stop attackers from trying to use those stolen credentials on hundreds of online financial and e-commerce sites, betting on the chance that the user used the same credentials multiple times; their scripts do this within seconds of obtaining leaked and stolen credentials. Reusing the same password across accounts is still too common but can be largely mitigated by leveraging MFA everywhere.

But as I mentioned in an earlier chapter, MFA isn't available everywhere, especially in enterprise environments with decades of legacy applications. Even when MFA is available, a surprisingly low percentage of consumers and enterprises seem to embrace it. CISOs and security teams should be huge advocates of MFA everywhere because it can be so effective.

Also remember that at a minimum, senior executives should all use MFA everywhere and are the last people that should be exempt from MFA policies; after all, they are the primary targets of Business Email Compromise and other social engineering attacks. Making executives' lives easier by giving them exceptions for the very security policies and controls that mitigate attacks against them specifically isn't prudent and is very literally a gift to attackers.

One effective tool I've seen used in cases where executives demand exceptions for security policies is risk acceptance letters. A risk acceptance letter or risk acknowledgment letter documents that the risks associated with the security policy exception have been explained to the executive, they understand these risks, and accept them on behalf of their entire organization.

Periodically, these risk acceptance letters should be reviewed by the CISO, senior executives, and potentially the Board of Directors, to ensure that systemic, long-term risk has not been inappropriately accepted. When confronted with one of these letters, executives who want security policy exceptions typically pause at the last minute once they have time to reflect on the potential consequences to their organizations and their own careers. In the end, many such executives prudently decide not to demand security policy exceptions.

Of course, phishing isn't limited to credential theft. Attackers use phishing in their attempts to trick people into disclosing information that they otherwise would not share. MFA doesn't mitigate these types of attacks. In these cases, the best mitigation is education. Training information workers to recognize potential phishing attacks and other social engineering tactics isn't foolproof but can be very effective. Some organizations simply refuse to approve phishing exercises designed to train their information workers to recognize phishing attacks. The management of these organizations do their employees a disservice with such decisions.

One of the tools that CISOs have, when faced with management teams that do not support this type of training, is risk management. In my experience, CISOs that quantify risk for their management teams have a better chance of success; it helps put their efforts into context, even when nothing bad happens. Remember that risk is the combination of probability and impact. The fact that most of the largest and highest-profile data breaches in history started with phishing emails can help communicate the risk. So can the volume of phishing emails and the number of phishing sites that I provided in this chapter.

The data tells us that a minimum of 100 million phishing emails are sent every day, and the total number is likely a multiple of this. Additionally, tens of thousands of new active phishing websites come online every week (at a minimum). Combine this with phishing data from your own organization to quantify the probability that information workers receive phishing emails and visit compromised websites, how many, and how often.

Then develop some quantitative impact estimates, ranging from no impact because phishing emails were filtered before they made it to information workers, to a successful compromise that involved data exfiltration and subsequent reputational damage and legal liability for the organization. Such figures can help make the decision to train people to recognize social engineering attacks less abstract and easier to compare to the other risks that management teams already manage.

Also consider whether your organization's information workers really require unfettered access to the internet. Do they really need to visit websites located in the places that host the most phishing sites? Is there really a legitimate business need to allow everyone in an organization to go everywhere on the internet? The .com domain typically has more phishing sites than any other generic top-level domain – isn't this enough risk without enabling everyone in an organization to visit any site in the ccTLDs that typically have two or three times the number of phishing sites than the worldwide average? Allow information workers access to ccTLDs where they have legitimate business purposes in these domains and block connections to other sites from corporate managed assets; this seems like it could reduce the chances of visiting a phishing site hosted in a country code top-level domain, as well as other internet-based threats I discuss in this chapter. Employing actively managed web filtering solutions can make this mitigation relatively easy.

Now let's look at the second tactic the attackers used in our example of a typical attack, a drive-by download attack.

Drive-by download attacks

While phishing attacks are at the intersection of social engineering and weak, leaked, and stolen passwords, drive-by download attacks are at the intersection of social engineering and unpatched vulnerabilities. Drive-by attacks are typically performed by attackers using social engineering to trick users into visiting a malicious website. They can do this several ways, including via email, online ads, putting links to malicious sites in the comments sections of webpages and social network posts, and many other tactics. Sometimes, attackers compromise a legitimate website and use it to host drive-by download attacks; the more popular the website, the better for the attackers as it increases their chances of successfully compromising as many systems as possible.

Getting potential victims to malicious websites under the control of attackers is the first step in the attack. The next step is to exploit unpatched vulnerabilities on the victims' systems. To do this, attackers will attempt to run scripts that have embedded URLs or they will use an inline frame (IFrame) to load another HTML document page unbeknownst to the user. IFrames have legitimate uses, making it complicated to distinguish between good ones and malicious ones. Attackers will place IFrames the size of a pixel on their malicious webpages so that users cannot see them. When these HTML documents load, they can, among other things, run scripts that detect the victim's operating system and browser versions, select and download corresponding exploits for common vulnerabilities for these versions, and ultimately download and install other malware that gives attackers illicit control of the compromised system. Such malicious IFrames can be placed on webpages of legitimate websites that have been compromised. This means that visiting a trusted website with a system that is not fully patched can result in a compromised system that attackers can control remotely, cripple with ransomware, and so on.

Figure 5.4 reveals for the period between July 2012 and January 2020, the highest number of drive-by download pages discovered on the internet was in 2013, where more than one drive-by download page was found per 1,000 URLs indexed by Microsoft's Bing search engine. However, more recently, the worldwide average was 0.09 and 0.08 of these malicious sites per 1,000 URLs indexed in 2018 and 2019, respectively. That means the number of drive-by download sites in 2013 was 14 times higher than the number in 2019. The data in *Figure 5.4* has been collated from Microsoft's Security Intelligence Report and the Interactive Microsoft Security Intelligence Reports. Microsoft appears to have stopped publishing this data regularly.

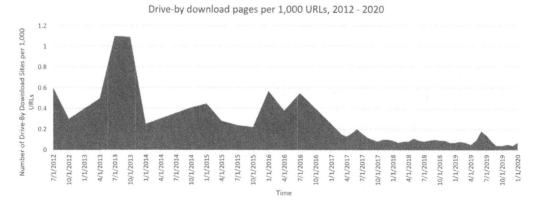

Figure 5.4: Drive-by download pages per 1,000 URLs indexed by Microsoft's Bing search engine between 2012-2020 as published in the Microsoft Security Intelligence Report Volumes 14–21 (Microsoft Corporation, 2012–2017) and Interactive Microsoft Security Intelligence Reports (Microsoft Corporation, May 2020)

The components used in drive-by download attacks can be distributed, with several different remote systems hosting them. The scripts that run can be hosted on different "redirector" servers, the exploits used to exploit unpatched vulnerabilities can be hosted on separate exploit servers, and the malware that ultimately gets downloaded to the victims' systems can be hosted on separate malware-hosting servers. Distributing components of drive-by download attacks this way provides several advantages to attackers. It allows attackers to be more agile, enabling them to adjust their attacks quickly. This helps them optimize their attacks and makes it harder to find and dismantle all the components attackers use.

Subsequently, the infrastructure used to host the components of drive-by download attacks are distributed all over the world. *Table 5.1* provides the locations with the highest number of drive-by download URLs per 1,000 URLs indexed by Microsoft's Bing search engine in 2019 (Microsoft Corporation, 2020). I'm sharing data from this specific time period with you because it is especially interesting – note the top entry in the table.

Location	Number of drive-by download URLs per 1,000 URLs
Oman	687.3
French Polynesia	2.22
Gambia	1.89
Afghanistan	1.85
Saint Lucia	1.57
Myanmar	1.16
Libya	1.09
Colombia	0.48
Russia	0.45
El Salvador	0.43
Worldwide Average	0.08

Table 5.1: Locations with the highest number of drive-by download sites in 2019 (Microsoft Corporation, 2020)

The number of drive-by download pages per 1,000 URLs in Oman in 2019 isn't a typo. According to data published by Microsoft, there were 687.3 drive-by download URLs for every 1,000 URLs in Oman, averaged across the twelve months of 2019 (Microsoft Corporation, 2020). That's 8,591.25 times higher than the worldwide average. In November of 2019, Microsoft reports that there were 1,251.94 drive-by download URLs for every 1,000 URLs found by Bing in Oman (Microsoft Corporation, 2020). That suggests a very high concentration of drive-by download URLs in this ccTLD at the time.

Although this could be a simple error in the data, there could be another, less banal explanation. The ccTLD for Oman is .om. Attackers could be registering and using domain names in this ccTLD to catch web browser users that type .om instead of .com. This hypothesis seems plausible given how often people could make the trivial mistake of typing google.om instead of google.com, apple.om instead of apple.com, and so on. How many people would make mistakes like this every day? It seems like it could be enough to get the attention of attackers leveraging drive-by download sites. This is what some cybersecurity researchers were reporting back in 2016. Could this tactic still have been in widespread use almost three years later in the last quarter of 2019?

> *According to Endgame security researchers, the top level domain for Middle Eastern country Oman (.om) is being exploited by typosquatters who have registered more than 300 domain names with the .om suffix for U.S. companies and services such as Citibank, Dell, Macys, and Gmail. Endgame made the discovery last week and reports that several groups are behind the typosquatter campaigns.*
>
> *— Spring, 2016*

Mitigating drive-by download attacks

These attacks tend to rely on unpatched vulnerabilities to be successful. Attackers have exploit libraries that they leverage for their drive-by download attacks. Studies have shown that attackers have used between one and over twenty exploits on a single drive-by URL. If the underlying vulnerabilities that these exploits try to take advantage of are patched, these attacks won't be successful. Therefore, a well-run vulnerability management program will mitigate drive-by download attacks.

Additionally, preventing exposure to malicious websites like drive-by download sites can be helpful. Consider whether allowing information workers and system administrators unfettered access to the internet is required and worth the risk. Why do they need access to the .om ccTLD, for example, or any of the other ccTLD domains where there likely aren't legitimate business reasons to visit? Leveraging actively managed web filtering services can be helpful; blocking access to parts of the internet from corporate assets that don't have a clear business purpose can also be helpful.

Don't allow system administrators to visit the internet using web browsers from servers that process anything, or from systems that are important. Secure Access Workstations or Privileged Access Workstations should be used for server administration to limit risk to important systems.

Browsing to sites on the public internet should be strictly forbidden on such systems and prevented with technical controls. In environments where this simply isn't possible, strict URL filtering on outbound internet connections should be enforced to enable access to approved websites while preventing unfettered access to the internet.

Running up-to-date anti-malware software from a trusted anti-malware vendor can also be an effective mitigation. Drive-by download attacks typically result in malware being downloaded to the victim's system. If anti-malware software detects the exploit attempt and blocks the download and installation of such malware, a potential disaster is averted.

I mentioned that attackers typically distribute components of drive-by download attacks across separate infrastructure located in different places around the world. Let's now take a closer look at malware distribution sites, which can be used as part of drive-by download attacks or used to deliver malware employing other tactics to victims.

Malware-hosting sites

We've seen that a great source of data for malicious websites, like phishing sites and drive-by download sites, are internet search engines and popular web browsers. These data sources can also give us a glimpse into malware-hosting sites on the internet. I say a glimpse, because things can change very quickly as many attackers have become adept at covering their tracks and making it hard to find the infrastructure they use for their attacks. Remember, no one is omniscient. We have a bunch of data snapshots that we can stitch together over time to provide us with a glimpse of the threat landscape. Frequently, the landscape changes before researchers can collect, analyze, understand, and act on such data.

This is where the promise of **Machine Learning (ML)** and **Artificial Intelligence (AI)** is helping – churning through massive amounts of complicated datasets much faster than humans can do this job manually. And, of course, attackers have also been busy trying to find ways to defeat systems that leverage ML and AI (Microsoft Defender ATP Research Team, 2018).

But let's start by looking at some data that Google has published on malware-hosting sites. They have a unique view of malware-hosting sites as they operate the world's most popular internet search engine.

Google publishes data on the malware-hosting sites they find via their Safe Browsing service. They describe this as the following:

> *Malware can hide in many places, and it can be hard even for experts to figure out if their website is infected. To find compromised sites, we scan the web and use virtual machines to analyze sites where we've found signals that indicate a site has been compromised."*
>
> — *Google, 2020*

Over time, Google's "Autonomous system scan history" tool provided data on "attack sites" from January 2007 up until recently when they stopped publishing this data. From the data they did publish, it appears the most attack sites hosting malware that they found was in November 2012. The week of November 11, 2012, Google's Safe Browsing service identified 6,192 attack sites on the internet (Google, 2020). Another notable peak was the week starting September 15, 2013, when 5,282 attack sites were identified (Google, 2020). These relatively huge numbers have dwindled in more recent times. Between 2018 and 2019, the highest number of attack sites identified by Safe Browsing was 379, and between January and April 2020, 30 attack sites appears to be the maximum identified in any single week (Google, 2020). Like drive-by download sites, the number of malware-hosting sites appears to have dwindled over time.

Another source of data on malware distribution sites is URLhaus (`https://urlhaus.abuse.ch/statistics/`). URLhaus collects URLs for malware-hosting sites and shares them with Google Safe Browsing, among others. Their purpose, according to their website, is as follows:

> *URLhaus is a project operated by abuse.ch. The purpose of the project is to collect, track and share malware URLs, helping network administrators and security analysts to protect their network and customers from cyber threats."*
>
> — *URLhaus, 2022*

According to data published by URLhaus, between July 25, 2022, and August 21, 2022, there were between 3,290 and 7,000 active malware distribution sites online every day (URLhaus, 2022).

Hosting networks in the United States and China appear most often in their lists of top malware-hosting networks (URLhaus, 2022).

Mitigating malware distribution

Legitimate websites that are compromised and then used to distribute malware can lead to many poor outcomes for consumers and organizations alike. For this reason, it is important that organizations that operate websites understand and focus on the cybersecurity fundamentals. Recall your introduction to the Cybersecurity Usual Suspects in *Chapter 1*. The Cybersecurity Usual Suspects include unpatched vulnerabilities, security misconfigurations, weak, leaked, and stolen credentials, insider threats, and social engineering. Managing the cybersecurity fundamentals is critical to prevent websites from becoming malware distribution sites. Everyone setting up a website on the internet must accept this responsibility.

The vendors and organizations that scour the internet looking for malware distribution sites will typically contact the webmasters of sites that they find distributing malware. According to data that Google published on their notification activities between 2006 and 2022, the lowest average webmaster response time to a notification their site was infected with malware was 15 days (Google, 2022). 90 days was a much more common average response time. Google also tracked whether infected websites were reinfected after webmasters were notified and had disinfected them. Average website reinfection rates ranged between 2% and 40% between 2006 and 2022. The data suggests that this isn't an issue of inattentive webmasters from the distant past, as website reinfection rates remain higher than you'd expect even in recent times. For example, the week of January 2, 2022, the reinfection rate was 37% – near the top end of the reinfection rate range for the 16-year period (Google, 2022). The week of May 15, 2022, the reinfection rate had dropped to 14%. Again, if the underlying Cybersecurity Usual Suspects are not addressed continuously, this enables attackers to compromise IT environments repeatedly and sell access to others.

Given this data, the call to action is clear. If your organization operates a website on the internet, it's your organization's responsibility to pay attention to abuse reports. Reviewing abuse reports for corporate assets isn't something that IT staff should do in their spare time; it should be part of every enterprise's governance processes.

The table stakes for operating a website on the internet are actively managing the cybersecurity fundamentals and monitoring and acting on abuse reports in a responsible period of time. If an organization isn't willing to do these things, it should do everyone a favor and shut its websites down.

Running current anti-malware solutions, from a trusted vendor, on internet-connected systems can also be an effective mitigation. But remember that attackers will often seek to subvert anti-malware solutions once they successfully initially compromise a system. The anti-malware vendors know this and make it harder for attackers to do this. But once an attacker has System or Administrator access to a system, they own that system, making it much harder to prevent the compromise of system security defenses. A great example is a rootkit hiding from the operating system and the security software that relies on it. For this reason, I like performing periodic offline anti-virus scans. For example, Microsoft offers Windows Defender Offline, which will scan the system without using the active operating system's kernel. Windows Defender Offline is baked into Windows 10 and Windows 11 and is available for older versions of Windows via a download that can be run from a DVD or USB drive (Microsoft Corporation, 2020). **Endpoint Detection and Response (EDR)** and **Extended Detection and Response (XDR)** tools promise to help as well.

Of course, organizations using the cloud can simply shut down systems every couple of hours and automatically rebuild them from known good instances. Short-lived systems like this provide very little time for attackers to make use of compromised systems. However, even in short-lived environments, a well-run vulnerability management program and anti-malware solutions can be useful. I'll discuss this further in *Chapter 12, Modern Approaches to Security and Compliance*.

But now, let's look at the final stage of the typical attack pattern we started this chapter with, some of the typical post-compromise activities.

Post compromise — botnets and DDoS attacks

Once systems have been initially compromised via one of the Cybersecurity Usual Suspects, like unpatched vulnerabilities and/or social engineering as we discussed in this chapter, any information of value is siphoned from victims' systems to be sold or traded. At this point, attackers have full control of the systems they have compromised. Many times, victims' systems are enlisted into botnets and used to perform whatever illicit projects their operators desire, including DDoS attacks.

There's a lot that can be written about botnets, how they operate, and the projects they are typically employed on. In fact, entire books have been dedicated to botnets. I won't try to duplicate those here. But I do want to briefly mention a few things on this topic.

It goes without saying that botnets have garnered a lot of attention over the years. When I worked at Microsoft, the Microsoft **Digital Crimes Unit (DCU)** worked with law enforcement and industry experts to disrupt some of the largest botnets in operation. This work helped to dramatically reduce spam on the internet and degrade the attack power these botnets provided to their operators.

Some of these botnets were composed of hundreds of thousands or millions of compromised systems and were capable of sending tens of billions of spam and phishing email messages per day. Rustock and Waledac are two examples of such botnets. To do this, the DCU had to approach the problem as a novel legal challenge in which they sought and were given legal control over the domains and physical infrastructure these botnets used (Jones, 2011).

Attackers will drain anything of value from the systems they have complete control over, including cached credentials. Massive lists of leaked and stolen credentials have been found on the internet over the years (Solomon, 2017). If the compromised systems or accounts have authenticated and authorized access to other systems in the environment, attackers will potentially have access and control over them as well, exacerbating the damage to the organization.

Accelerating detection and recovery activities can reduce the amount of time attackers control these assets, thus potentially reducing the damage they do to other victims and the costs associated with the recovery and restoration of normal operations. Threat intelligence can help organizations identify systems communicating with known botnet command-and-control infrastructures. Attackers know this and have been hosting some of their infrastructures in public web hosting and cloud environments in an effort to hide their operations among legitimate network traffic.

One of the illicit purposes that botnets have been used for over the years has been **Distributed Denial of Service (DDoS)** attacks. Modern DDoS attacks use sophisticated techniques to overwhelm their targets with network traffic, thus depriving legitimate use of the services hosted by the victim.

How large can DDoS attacks get? In February 2018, attackers launched an attack on GitHub. This DDoS attack is said to have peaked at 1.35 Tbps, which is the equivalent of more than 126 million packets per second (Kottler, 2018). This attack used a novel approach, by abusing memcached instances that were not secure. This approach enabled attackers to amplify their attack by a factor of 51,000; put another way, for every 1 byte of network traffic that attackers sent, up to 51,000 bytes (51 KB) were sent to their target. This allowed attackers to overwhelm GitHub's network capacity with a massive amount of UDP traffic that interrupted network connectivity to the site for almost 10 minutes.

More recently, in January 2022, Microsoft mitigated another record-breaking volumetric DDoS attack that threw 3.47 Tbps at their network, sending approximately 340 million packets per second.

The attack Microsoft mitigated came from about 10,000 sources and from countries that include the United States, China, South Korea, Russia, Thailand, India, Vietnam, Iran, Indonesia, and Taiwan. Attack vectors were floods of User Datagram Protocol packets reflected over port 80 using SSDP, CLDAP, NTP, and Domain Name System servers." — Dan Goodin, January 2022

On June 1st, 2022, Google reportedly prevented the largest HTTPS DDoS attack ever from denying service to one of their customer's internet services hosted in Google's cloud. This 69-minute attack peaked at 46 million requests per second using HTTPS-based requests. According to the Google product manager that was interviewed after the attack, it was like "receiving all the daily requests to Wikipedia (one of the top 10 trafficked websites in the world) in just 10 seconds" (Kan, August 18, 2022). A botnet was suspected of generating the attacks.

Perhaps a less sophisticated but more interesting DDoS attack from the history books was the attack on critical infrastructure in Estonia in 2007. Some attributed this attack to Russia (Anderson, 2007). The reason this is interesting is that it perhaps gave us a preview of what to expect in future cyberwar conflicts – simultaneous kinetic and online attacks that overwhelm the ability to wage warfare physically and logistically. A modern version of this playbook was reportedly used just prior to Russia's military invasion of Ukraine, 15 years later in 2022. In mid-February of that year, DDoS attacks targeted military and financial institutions in Ukraine. Eight days later , Russia crossed the border and started its invasion of Ukraine. These DDoS attacks were not record-setting but could have been much more disruptive had they not been effectively mitigated.

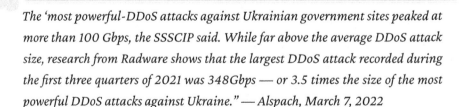

The 'most powerful-DDoS attacks against Ukrainian government sites peaked at more than 100 Gbps, the SSSCIP said. While far above the average DDoS attack size, research from Radware shows that the largest DDoS attack recorded during the first three quarters of 2021 was 348Gbps — or 3.5 times the size of the most powerful DDoS attacks against Ukraine." — Alspach, March 7, 2022

The attack playbook used against Ukraine before and during the invasion is of high interest to many people including other governments and DDoS mitigation vendors themselves.

Of course, not all DDoS attacks need to be that large or innovative to be disruptive. However, organizations have options to help them mitigate such attacks. There are many vendors that offer DDoS protection services, some of which include AWS Shield, Amazon CloudFront, Google Cloud Armor, Microsoft Azure DDoS Protection, Cloudflare, Akamai, and many others. In addition to protection services, the cloud offers techniques that can be used to scale infrastructure automatically as needed during DDoS attacks (Amazon Web Services, June 2015).

To summarize, the key is to focus on the cybersecurity fundamentals, so your systems do not end up being part of a botnet and used to attack countless other organizations and consumers. As I discuss in *Chapter 9*, *Cybersecurity Strategies*, investing in detection and response capabilities will help organizations minimize the damage and costs associated with botnets and the grief they bring with them to the internet.

Summary

This chapter focused on internet-based threats. We examined phishing attacks, drive-by download attacks, and malware distribution sites. So many attacks leverage social engineering that CISOs and security teams must spend time and resources to mitigate it. For example, every week, tens of thousands of new phishing sites are connected to the internet, and every month, billions of phishing emails are sent to prospective victims.

Most phishing emails include a link to a phishing site (Microsoft Corporation, 2018) and most phishing sites leverage HTTPS (TLS certificates) (APWG, September 22, 2021). Accounts are nearly 100% less likely to be compromised when MFA is enabled (Weinert, 2019). Anti-social engineering training for information workers can also be an effective mitigation.

Drive-by download attacks leverage unpatched vulnerabilities to install malware unbeknownst to the user. The number of drive-by URLs has been dramatically reduced from the peak in 2013. According to data released by Microsoft, Oman's ccTLD hosted 8,591 times more drive-by download sites than the worldwide average in 2019 (Microsoft Corporation, 2020). This could indicate that attackers are using the .om domain to attack users that mistype URLs in the .com domain. A well-run vulnerability management program and running up-to-date anti-malware from a trusted vendor can be effective mitigations for drive-by downloads.

The number of malware-hosting sites, drive-by download sites, and phishing sites changes over time, sometimes dramatically. Subsequently, a cybersecurity strategy that doesn't include mitigations for all these types of internet-based threats could have high-risk gaps.

Systems compromised by phishing attacks, drive-by downloads, and other malicious websites can end up being enlisted into botnets and used to attack other organizations and consumers, including participating in DDoS attacks.

That wraps up our look at internet-based threats. I've exposed you to a lot of data, graphs, and tables in the last three chapters in an effort to provide a data-driven view of some of the threats that CISOs and security teams face every day. I'm going to elevate this conversation about threats in the next few chapters and explore why so many of the CISOs and security teams I've met with over the past decade view governments as threats to their organization. This topic area is less about malicious programs and more about the public policy and foreign policy objectives of national governments. We'll examine the roles that governments play in cybersecurity as well as the topic that 99% of all enterprise customers outside of the United States wanted to discuss with me when we met, the threat of government access to data. When we finally discuss cybersecurity strategies later in this book, you should have a rounded understanding of most of the threats you need to mitigate with your strategies.

References

- Amazon Web Services (June, 2015). "AWS Best Practices for DDoS Resiliency". *Amazon Web Services*. Retrieved from: `https://d1.awsstatic.com/whitepapers/Security/DDoS_White_Paper.pdf` Latest ed: September 21, 2021

- Anderson, N. (May 14, 2007). "Massive DDoS attacks target Estonia; Russia accused". *Ars Technica*. Retrieved from: `https://arstechnica.com/information-technology/2007/05/massive-ddos-attacks-target-estonia-russia-accused/`

- Google (n.d.). "Google Transparency Report. Google Safe Browsing." *Google*. Retrieved from `https://transparencyreport.google.com/safe-browsing/overview?unsafe=dataset:0;series:malware,phishing;start:1148194800000;end:1587279600000&lu=unsafe`

- Google (May, 2020). "Safe Browsing site status." *Google Transparency Report*. Retrieved from: `https://transparencyreport.google.com/safe-browsing/search?hl=en`

- Google (August, 2022). "Safe Browsing." *Google Transparency Report*. Retrieved from: `https://transparencyreport.google.com/safe-browsing/search?hl=en`

- Google (May 9, 2020). "Where malware originates." *Google Transparency Report*. Retrieved from: `https://transparencyreport.google.com/archive/safe-browsing/malware?autonomous_scan_history=systemId:18779;dataset:0&lu=global_malware&global_malware=time:q`

- Jones, J. (March 17, 2011). "Microsoft Takedown of Rustock Botnet." *Microsoft*. Retrieved from: `https://www.microsoft.com/security/blog/2011/03/17/microsoft-takedown-of-rustock-botnet/`

- Kottler, S. (March 1, 2018). "February 28th DDoS Incident Report." *The GitHub Blog*. Retrieved from: `https://github.blog/2018-03-01-ddos-incident-report/`

- Microsoft Corporation (2012-2017). *Microsoft Security Intelligence Report*. Redmond: Microsoft Corporation

- Microsoft Corporation (2012-2017). *Microsoft Security Intelligence Report Volumes 14–21*. Redmond: Microsoft Corporation.

- Microsoft Corporation (2015-2017). *Microsoft Security Intelligence Report Volumes 19–23*. Redmond: Microsoft Corporation. Retrieved from: `www.microsoft.com/sir`

- Microsoft Corporation (2016). *Microsoft Security Intelligence Report Volume 21*. Redmond: Microsoft Corporation. Retrieved from: `https://query.prod.cms.rt.microsoft.com/cms/api/am/binary/RE2GQwi`

- Microsoft Corporation (2018). *Microsoft Security Intelligence Report Volume 23*. Redmond: Microsoft Corporation. Retrieved from: `https://query.prod.cms.rt.microsoft.com/cms/api/am/binary/RWt530`

- Microsoft Corporation (2019). *Microsoft Security Intelligence Report Volume 24*. Redmond: Microsoft Corporation. Retrieved from: `https://info.microsoft.com/ww-landing-M365-SIR-v24-Report-eBook.html?lcid=en-us`

- Microsoft Corporation (May 8, 2020). "Drive-by download pages." *Microsoft Corporation*. Retrieved from: `https://www.microsoft.com/securityinsights/Driveby` in April 2020

- Microsoft Corporation (May 15, 2020). "Help protect my PC with Microsoft Defender Offline." *Microsoft Corporation*. Retrieved from `https://support.microsoft.com/en-us/windows/help-protect-my-pc-with-microsoft-defender-offline-9306d528-64bf-4668-5b80-ff533f183d6c`

- Microsoft Corporation (May 8, 2020). "Malware encounter rates." *Microsoft Corporation*. Retrieved from: `https://www.microsoft.com/securityinsights/Malware` in April 2020

- Microsoft Defender ATP Research Team (August 9, 2018). "Protecting the protector: Hardening machine learning defenses against adversarial attacks." *Microsoft Corporation*. Retrieved from: `https://www.microsoft.com/en-us/security/blog/2018/08/09/protecting-the-protector-hardening-machine-learning-defenses-against-adversarial-attacks/`

- Pegoraro, R. (August 9, 2019). "We keep falling for phishing emails, and Google just revealed why."*Fast Company*. Retrieved from: `https://www.fastcompany.com/90387855/we-keep-falling-for-phishing-emails-and-google-just-revealed-why`.

- Solomon, H. (December 11, 2017). "Searchable database of 1.4 billion stolen credentials found on dark web." *IT World Canada*. Retrieved from: `https://www.itworldcanada.com/article/searchable-database-of-1-4-billion-stolen-credentials-found-on-dark-web/399810`

- Spring, T. (March 14, 2016). "Typosquatters Target Mac Users With New '.om' Domain Scam." *Threatpost*. Retrieved from: `https://threatpost.com/typosquatters-target-apple-mac-users-with-new-om-domain-scam/116768/`

- URLhaus (May 9, 2020). "About." *URLhaus*. Retrieved from: `https://urlhaus.abuse.ch/about/`

- URLhaus (August 24, 2022). "Statistics." *URLhaus*. Retrieved from: `https://urlhaus.abuse.ch/statistics/`

- Weinert, A. (July 9, 2019). "Your Pa$$word doesn't matter." *Microsoft Corporation*. Retrieved from: `https://techcommunity.microsoft.com/t5/azure-active-directory-identity/your-pa-word-doesn-tmatter/ba-p/731984#`

- APWG (Anti-Phishing Working Group) (n.d.). "APWG Phishing Activity Trends Reports for various quarters." *APWG*. Retrieved from `https://apwg.org/trendsreports/`

- APWG (Anti-Phishing Working Group). (February 23, 2022). "APWG Phishing Activity Trends Reports 4th Quarter 2021." *APWG*. Retrieved from `https://apwg.org/trendsreports/`

- APWG (Anti-Phishing Working Group). (September 22, 2021). "APWG Phishing Activity Trends Reports 2nd Quarter 2021." *APWG*. Retrieved from `https://apwg.org/trendsreports/`

- Microsoft Corporation. (October, 2021). "Microsoft Digital Defense Report." *Microsoft*. Retrieved from `https://query.prod.cms.rt.microsoft.com/cms/api/am/binary/RWMFIi`

- Ganacharya, Tanmay. (March 20, 2020). "Protecting against coronavirus themed phishing attacks." *Microsoft Security Blog*. Retrieved from: `https://www.microsoft.com/security/blog/2020/03/20/protecting-against-coronavirus-themed-phishing-attacks/`

- JPCERT/CC (May 25, 2022). "Trends of Reported Phishing Sites and Compromised Domains in 2021." *JPCERT/CC Eyes*. Retrieved from: `https://blogs.jpcert.or.jp/en/2022/05/phishing2021.html`

- Microsoft Corporation. (August 2022). "Cyber Signals August 2022." *Microsoft Corporation*. Retrieved from `https://query.prod.cms.rt.microsoft.com/cms/api/am/binary/RE54L7v`

- Kan, Michael. (August 18, 2022). "Google Fends Off Record-Breaking DDoS Attack." *PCMag*. Retrieved from: `https://www.pcmag.com/news/google-fends-off-record-breaking-ddos-attack`

- Goodin, Dan. (January 28, 2022). "Microsoft fends off record-breaking 3.47Tbps DDoS attack." *Ars Technica*. Retrieved from: `https://arstechnica.com/information-technology/2022/01/microsoft-fends-off-record-breaking-3-47-tbps-ddos-attack/`

- Alspach, Kyle. (March 7, 2022). "Ukraine: We've repelled 'nonstop' DDoS attacks from Russia." *Venture Beat*. Retrieved from: `https://venturebeat.com/security/ukraine-weve-repelled-nonstop-ddos-attacks-from-russia/`

Join our community on Discord

Join our community's Discord space for discussions with the author and other readers:

`https://packt.link/SecNet`

6

The Roles Governments Play in Cybersecurity

When I was 17 years old, I started working on a 4-year Bachelor of Arts degree, majoring in political science. I was very interested in several facets of political science, including federalism, division of powers in government, how and why elections work, the theory of authorization, international relations, and political philosophy. Later, I also studied computer science and completed an MBA. When my career took me deeper and deeper into cybersecurity, I had no idea that studying political science would turn out to be so valuable in this field. Back then, reading works by Plato, René Descartes, Thomas Hobbes, David Hume, Karl Marx, and George Orwell hardly seemed applicable to computers or the security of them. But as I'd come to realize a decade or two later, the cybersecurity field would evolve into the intersection of technology, security, privacy, regulations, public safety, foreign policy, and national security.

In my career, among other experiences, I was fortunate enough to work as one of the most senior cybersecurity advisors at both Microsoft and **Amazon Web Services (AWS)**. I led teams of cybersecurity advisors at both of these companies. In these roles, I met with many of the organizations that I refer to in this chapter. I learned so much in these discussions - I want to share some of this knowledge with you.

When I worked as Microsoft's Global Chief Security Advisor, I traveled the world meeting with CISOs and security teams to give threat intelligence briefings and discuss how we could help their cybersecurity programs. I would spend weeks at a time in Europe, Africa, Asia, and South America. I also hosted the CISOs of Microsoft's biggest accounts at Microsoft headquarters in Redmond, Washington.

I learned so much from spending time with these people and listening to how they thought about threats, risk, mitigations, and cybersecurity. Many of the things I learned from them inform how I think about cybersecurity. The collective wisdom of these CISOs was incredible.

Initially, I spent most of my time with private sector customers who were focused on protecting company data, assets and ultimately their shareholders' value. Then I started meeting more and more public sector organizations and learned that their challenges were a lot bigger and arguably more important than developing products and services for markets, creating meaningful brands, maximizing profit, and driving growth.

When I joined AWS as their Worldwide Public Sector Security and Compliance Leader for **Europe, the Middle East, and Africa (EMEA)**, my family and I moved to London in the United Kingdom. In this role, my full-time job was advising federal and provincial/state governments, pan-European institutions, national security agencies, healthcare and educational institutions, non-profit organizations, federal banks, and other public sector verticals across EMEA. Over the next two and a half years, I traveled to two or three cities a week in EMEA to meet with public sector organizations to discuss cybersecurity. I spent a lot of time in cities that were the centers of government for their countries or regions, such as London, Paris, Brussels, the Hague, Berlin, Stockholm, Helsinki, Bern, and many others. It might sound glamorous, but the amount of travel I did was extreme! The number of planes, trains, buses, and taxis that I took every week was dizzying.

In this job, representing a large well known American company in EMEA, I learned a lot about the European perspective on privacy. Privacy expectations permeate the public and private sectors in western Europe. I've seen American business executives struggle with this European perspective – chafing against what they viewed simply as a restrictive business environment created by "socialist" governments. But as I learned from my many discussions with customers and co-workers in Germany specifically, the events of the 1930s in Germany and subsequently World War II deeply influenced the imperative for privacy in Germany and across the rest of Europe. The Holocaust irrevocably changed Europe and privacy is viewed as a key tool to prevent anything like that from occurring there again. From this perspective, the right to privacy for citizens is far more important than optimizing regulatory environments for successful business outcomes. When American companies do not understand and pay attention to this perspective, it creates an obvious tension between their business objectives and the kind of society Europeans want to live in. This is reflected in regulations such as the **General Data Protection Regulation (GDPR)**.

After working in EMEA for almost three years, my family and I relocated back to Seattle where I worked as AWS' Global Security and Compliance Lead for Worldwide Public Sector. In this role I worked with teams of cybersecurity advisors around the world supporting AWS field sales teams in the U.S., Canada, across South America, Asia, and in EMEA. In these roles, I grew professionally and personally a great deal. I also came away with a deep understanding of the unique challenges that public sector organizations have with regulatory compliance, privacy, and cybersecurity.

When it comes to cybersecurity, many of the CISOs I've advised rely on governments to help them achieve their objectives by setting and regulating industry security standards, while others look to governments as a source of threat intelligence, guidance, and protection; while yet other CISOs view governments as threats to their organizations. What role do governments really play in cybersecurity? After thousands of conversations with private and public sector organizations around the world about cybersecurity, I thought I'd share some insights that might help answer this question. Let's explore this next.

The pursuit of happiness

Before we dive into the roles that governments play in cybersecurity and why they play those roles, I think it's helpful context to review the reasons governments exist in the first place. Without this context, I've seen some cybersecurity professionals struggle to understand what *government* means to their security programs and to the industry more broadly.

Political philosophers have pontificated on the purpose of government for centuries and I certainly won't try to duplicate their work here. Social contract theory helps set the stage for the direction I want to take you. Thomas Hobbes' book *Leviathan*, first published in 1651, describes a time before governments and the rights they bestow existed as a "state of nature" where every person had a natural right to everything. That is, there was no private property - property was yours as long as you could prevent others from taking it away from you. Subsequently, there was perpetual war and violence. The result was that life was "solitary, poor, nasty, brutish, and short" (Hobbes, 2008).

However, if each person was willing to give up their natural right to everything via a social contract with each other, political order and security would ensue to improve everyone's lives. In other words, because each of us has given up our natural right to everything and instead allowed a government to reign over us, we benefit from a civil society with security.

This same state of nature exists between countries. Subsequently, countries need militaries to protect their national interests and international law and international relations are used to try to manage tensions between countries so that war is less frequent.

Of course, I'm glossing over a lot of detail here and not mentioning equally interesting works by John Locke, Jean-Jacques Rousseau, and many others, but this is supposed to be a book about cybersecurity, right? Hobbes' *Leviathan* lays out a "theory of authorization" – the "how" and "why" governments exist.

Fast forward about 125 years and the following statement was included in the newly written United States Declaration of Independence, concerning rights given to people by their Creator and that government should protect:

> *We hold these truths to be self-evident, that all men are created equal, that they are endowed by their Creator with certain unalienable Rights, that among these are Life, Liberty, and the pursuit of Happiness." – (The United States Declaration of Independence, 1776).*

Of course, the U.S. isn't the only country where political discourse on the rights of citizens and the role of government was had; there are several similar concepts used by other countries. Some examples include the Canadian Charter of Rights and Freedoms containing "life, liberty, security of the person" (Canadian Charter of Rights and Freedoms, s 7, Part 2 of the Constitution Act, 1982) and the national motto of France, "liberty, equality, fraternity" (Embassy of France in the U.S., 2013).

If governments exist to provide their citizens such benefits, how do they manage to do this? The simple modern-day answer is that they establish ministries, departments, and/or agencies to perform specific functions and divide the work of serving citizens among them. Let me give you some examples:

- The U.S. Department of Defense whose mission is to "provide the military forces needed to deter war and ensure our nation's security" (U.S. Department of Defense, 2022).
- Global Affairs Canada who "define, shape and advance Canada's interest and values in a complex global environment. We manage diplomatic relations, promote international trade, and provide consular assistance. We lead international development, humanitarian, and peace and security assistance efforts. We also contribute to national security and the development of international law" (Government of Canada, 2022).
- The role of the **Australian Federal Police** (**AFP**) is to "enforce Commonwealth criminal law, contribute to combating complex, transnational, serious and organized crime impacting Australia's national security, and to protect Commonwealth interests from criminal activity in Australia and overseas" (Australian Federal Police, 2022).

- In the UK, the Ministry of Justice has three priorities that include, "protect the public from serious offenders and improve the safety and security of our prisons, reduce reoffending, deliver swift access to justice" (UK Government, 2022).

- In Germany, the Federal Office of Information Security (known as the BSI) has the stated objective of "preventively promote information and cyber security to enable the and advance the secure use of information and communication technology in society" (Germany Federal Office of Information Security, 2022).

The examples in this list are from different countries, but most large, developed countries have ministries, departments, or agencies that play all the roles seen in the list as well as many more. Ideally, the sum of the parts of a country's government should support the overall objectives of government, such as citizens' pursuit of happiness, for example. I realize I've simplified a lot of concepts along the way, and I haven't even touched on the differences between national, provincial/state, regional, and local government. I also haven't discussed different political philosophies or systems of government, such as communism, and how governments' objectives might be different when grounded in different political philosophies. I had the opportunity to visit China and Russia in my career to meet with both public and private sector organizations, to speak at cybersecurity events, and to do press interviews. Cybersecurity professionals in these countries definitely operate in different political, economic, cultural, and social environments. However, like western democracies, they also have well-resourced adversaries and subsequently they must also rely on their governments to play critical roles in cybersecurity for their nations, the regions and municipalities within their borders, and their individual organizations. They might organize themselves differently, but I think you'll see very similar cybersecurity roles and functions across different large, developed governments around the world.

I think I've provided enough high-level context to tackle the central question - what roles do governments play in providing their citizens with cybersecurity?

In my conversations with CISOs, I'd often heard them use the term "government" in a way that suggests it is one thing. For example, "the government should do this" or "the government took the wrong action." But as I've already discussed, governments are typically organized into many different parts. It is also important to be aware that some parts of government might pursue their agendas in ways that potentially conflict with other parts of the same government. For example, an agency with some responsibility for public safety might participate in industry efforts to reduce vulnerabilities in software and drive awareness among consumers to keep their systems up to date.

Driving down the number of vulnerabilities in the products that consumers use and keeping consumers' systems patched means less criminal exploitation of citizens, less crime for law enforcement to manage, fewer criminal cases in the courts, less associated costs to society, and so on. But in another part of the same government that has some responsibility for national security, they are proactively trying to discover new vulnerabilities and buy new vulnerabilities from other security researchers. Instead of reporting vulnerabilities to the vendors that can fix them, like the public safety agency and the industry recommends, they secretly stockpile vulnerabilities so that they can be used to attack adversaries in a national security context. It is important to recognize that both of these contrasting agendas are important and support citizens' pursuit of happiness.

Although it might seem innocuous, referring to a government as a simple, single entity instead of a group of individual departments or ministries with different, sometimes conflicting charters, often leads to some overly simplistic conclusions in a cybersecurity context. In my experience, this tended to be especially true of statements made about the U.S. government by security professionals outside the U.S. Once they deemed "the U.S. government" to be a threat to their organization, that simplistic thinking meant that every government department and every private sector firm doing business with the government was suspect at best. Guilt by association – software, hardware, cloud services, and encryption technologies all suddenly become untrustworthy simply because the entire U.S. government was labeled as untrustworthy and a threat. I had this conversation with so many CISOs in EMEA that I dedicated an entire chapter of this book to this topic – *Chapter 7, Government Access to Data*.

Now let's take a closer look at some of the roles that governments play in cybersecurity.

Governments as cybersecurity market participants

Governments participate in all sorts of markets. They license intellectual property, lease, buy, and sell assets such as real estate, securities, energy, advertising, goods, and services. Governments procure and manage fleets of automobiles, ships, and aircraft. Governments are also very active in labor markets where they are typically major employers that hire and fire employees, contract workers, agencies, and other outside parties. The economies of most countries rely on governments as major sources of spending and employment.

The scope and scale of national governments typically dwarf even the largest private sector enterprises within their borders. Remember that national governments typically have numerous departments or ministries that represent arms of the military, national police, national courts, national intelligence capabilities, national banks, healthcare institutions, education institutions, energy, and many other functions.

To operate at such a large scale, abundant resources are required. For example, the projected budget spend for the U.S. federal government in 2022 was $7.2 trillion (USASpending.gov, 2022).

Governments also require information technology and cybersecurity. All government departments and agencies must have the people, processes, and technologies required to forward their charters and to protect, detect, respond to, and recover from modern day threats. To do this they must procure a lot of the same technologies as companies operating in the private sector, such as clients, servers, operating systems, endpoint protection, IDS/IPS, **Security Information and Event Management systems (SIEMs)**, backup/restore capabilities, cloud services, managed security services, and others. The combination of these factors typically gives governments immense purchasing power.

To take advantage of this, most large technology companies have sales, professional services, and support groups dedicated to public sector accounts in each country where they do business. I worked with dedicated public sector groups at both Microsoft and AWS. These dedicated teams tend to understand and cater to public sector customers much better than simply treating them like they are commercial sector customers. Most public sector customers are not motivated by profit the way private sector customers tend to be. Supporting citizens and their pursuit of happiness tends to be the motivating force for public sector customers. Understanding how governments procure technologies and services is key to competing for their business.

While governments procure lots of technologies and cybersecurity capabilities, they also require the technical expertise to develop, deploy and operate IT and cybersecurity capabilities. However, governments must compete for technical talent with the private sector. Generally speaking, large, profitable, private sector ventures are typically able to afford top industry talent, while most government departments typically can't. Technology companies use stock, stock options, and/or large annual cash bonuses as key parts of their total compensation packages to attract and retain top talent. Meanwhile, most governments are perpetually trying to constrain or reduce their IT budgets and do more with fewer resources, leveraging offshoring, as well as using managed cloud services and managed security services. That doesn't mean that governments won't attract and retain very talented people – it's common to see some government department booths at cybersecurity industry events focused on recruiting the same groups of attendees that commercial sector organizations are.

Governments' purchasing power is so great that they typically require their supply chain partners to comply with specific standards. Let's examine governments' role as standards bodies next.

Governments as standards bodies

The term "standards" is an overloaded term in cybersecurity. It means different things to different people. For example, popular guidance is often referred to as a standard. In this context, guidance is a set of recommendations for solving a problem, while standards are specifications on how things must be done and they are used in comparative evaluations. In this section, I'm using it with a broad meaning, not strictly limited to what formal standards developing organizations produce.

Because governments procure so many goods and services, it is important that they set and maintain standards to ensure measurable minimum levels of functionality and quality in the things they procure. This is also true of cybersecurity capabilities. This is how the **National Institute of Standards and Technology (NIST)** describes cybersecurity standards.

> *The goal of cyber security standards is to improve the security of information technology (IT) systems, networks, and critical infrastructures. A cyber security standard defines both functional and assurance requirements within a product, system, process, or technology environment. Well-developed cyber security standards enable consistency among product developers and serve as a reliable metric for purchasing security products." (Scarfone, K., Benigni, D. and Grance, T., 2009)*

NIST is part of the U.S. Department of Commerce. Its mission is to "promote U.S. innovation and industrial competitiveness by advancing measurement science, standards, and technology in ways that enhance economic security and improve our quality of life" (NIST, n.d.). NIST's vision statement is, "NIST will be the world's leader in creating critical measurement solutions and promoting equitable standards. Our efforts stimulate innovation, foster industrial competitiveness, and improve the quality of life" (NIST, n.d.).

Most of the CISOs I advised over the years typically used NIST cybersecurity standards in at least three ways. First, if their organization did business with the U.S. federal government or aspired to, they would select one or more NIST standards that were applicable to the product or service they wanted to sell, and work to comply with the requirements of those standards.

A second way many CISOs leveraged NIST standards was to ensure their control sets were complete. They would compare the controls implemented in their IT estates and their settings to NIST standards to ensure they didn't have obvious gaps. Some organizations take this one step further and use compliance with standards as their enterprise cybersecurity strategy. I'll discuss this strategy, which I call "Compliance as a Security Strategy," in detail in *Chapter 9, Cybersecurity Strategies*.

The third way I saw many CISOs use NIST standards was to prove they were managing their security programs in a way that complied with stringent U.S. government cybersecurity standards, whether they did business with the U.S. government or not. If these CISOs had a data breach on their watch, they could point to their NIST standards compliance as evidence that they weren't an outlier and that they were managing their cybersecurity program responsibly and in alignment with others in the industry. This could help blunt the potential negative reputational and financial damage and regulatory outcomes that accompany data breaches so often today.

The NIST standards I encountered most often in these three contexts included NIST SP 800-53 and NIST SP 800-171. I spent months helping customers in different countries plan and implement compliance with NIST SP 800-53 in their AWS environments. If you haven't seen NIST SP 800-53, it's not a simple checklist for IT teams to follow. Revision 5 has 492 pages that include 357 pages of controls. When faced with so much complexity, repeatable processes and automation become your best friends. I'll discuss this in more detail in *Chapter 12, Modern Approaches to Security and Compliance*.

Besides cybersecurity standards, NIST also runs programs and publishes a plethora of helpful frameworks and great information. Some of the resources that I used heavily with customers include:

- NIST **Cryptographic Module Validation Program (CMVP)**: provides U.S. federal agencies with a "security metric to use in procuring equipment containing validated cryptographic modules" (NIST, n.d.). Many security teams demand that encryption modules in the hardware they procure and the operating systems' kernels they use are validated as conforming to FIPS 140-2 or more recently FIPS 140-3. The CMVP provides a searchable database of vendors and their products that have been validated.

- The NIST **Cybersecurity Framework (CSF)**: provides helpful guidance to organizations that are starting a cybersecurity program or want to improve their existing program. The CSF includes five key Functions for security teams to focus on, including Identify, Protect, Detect, Respond, Recover. You can find more information in NIST Special Publication 1271 (NIST, August 2021).

Of course, the U.S. government isn't the only organization that publishes cybersecurity standards. This is a good place to insert a joke for geeks: "The good thing about standards is that there are so many to choose from" (Tanenbaum, Andrew S. n.d.). In fact, the other major standards body for cybersecurity is a non-government organization. Many of the customers I met outside the U.S., that didn't do business with the U.S. government, choose to baseline on standards from the **International Organization for Standardization (ISO)** instead of NIST.

To them, NIST was too U.S. government-centric, and ISO was viewed as more internationally recognized. The CISOs I worked with would typically pick one or the other and baseline their operations and internal audit on it. That is, they were either a "NIST shop" or an "ISO shop." However, some of the CISOs I met had embraced standards from both NIST and ISO for various reasons – the most common being the customers they sold their products to were global, not just located in the U.S. Subsequently they tried to comply with standards from both organizations to attract as many customers around the world as possible.

ISO is based in Geneva, Switzerland. You might wonder why the acronym for the International Organization for Standardization is ISO instead of IOS. You can imagine this question is asked a lot – so the ISO publishes the answer on their website.

> *Because 'International Organization for Standardization' would have different acronyms in different languages (IOS in English, OIN in French for Organisation internationale de normalisation), our founders decided to give it the short form ISO. ISO is derived from the Greek 'isos', meaning equal. Whatever the country, whatever the language, we are always ISO." (ISO, n.d.)*

Notice the emphasis on "being equal." This is because the ISO is composed of members from different countries, all of which have influence over the consensus-based standards the ISO publishes. ISO describes themselves this way,

> *ISO is an independent, non-governmental international organization with a membership of 167 national standards bodies. Through its members, it brings together experts to share knowledge and develop voluntary, consensus-based, market relevant International Standards that support innovation and provide solutions to global challenges." (ISO, n.d.)*

Currently ISO has 24,481 standards, 167 members each representing one country, and 808 technical committees and subcommittees for managing standards development (ISO, n.d.). The ISO standards I encountered most often when talking with CISOs included the ISO/IEC 27000 family of standards, that include among others, ISO/IEC 27001 a standard on information security management and ISO/IEC 27018, "Information technology — Security techniques — Code of practice for protection of personally identifiable information (PII) in public clouds acting as PII processors" (ISO, 2019).

Another example of a non-governmental organization that develops standards is the **Internet Engineering Task Force (IETF)**.

> *The Internet Engineering Task Force (IETF) is a large open international community of network designers, operators, vendors, and researchers concerned with the evolution of the Internet architecture and the smooth operation of the Internet."*
> *(Internet Engineering Task Force, n.d.)*

You can learn about the IETF's mission at: `https://www.ietf.org/about/mission/`.

But let's get back to governments acting as standards bodies. Governments in other countries, besides the U.S., also have standards bodies that publish cybersecurity standards for organizations in their regions and their supply chain partners. A great example is the **Federal Office of Information Security** (known as the **BSI**) in Germany. I had the opportunity to meet with representatives of the BSI a few times over the years. Germany is the single largest market in the **European Union (EU)**. This means that the standards published by BSI are very influential in Germany and in the EU. Subsequently, big global technology providers like Microsoft and AWS, among others, as well as technology providers based in Western Europe, pay close attention to the guidance and standards that the BSI publishes. The BSI describes their mission this way,

> *"We assume responsibility for all issues related to information security. We protect the federal administration from cyber attacks and monitor the current cyber security situation nationally and internationally, investigate and assess existing security risks and anticipate the impact of new developments. Based on this knowledge, we support citizens, companies and authorities at federal, state and municipality level with services in the core areas of information, consulting, operational protection and development, including standardisation [sic] and certification." (BSI, 2022)*

The BSI offers standards and certifications in numerous areas, including:

- BSI minimum standards for the Federal Administration's IT
- eHealth
- RFID
- Electronic Identities
- Smart Metering
- Electronic payment transactions

- Cryptographic specifications
- Others

Most large, developed countries have some office or agency responsible for developing cybersecurity standards for their national government's use or more broadly across industries within their borders. However, in many cases I've found that they are similar to NIST SP 800-53. This is another reason so many of the CISOs I know adopt NIST SP 800-53 as the standard they try to conform to.

Next, let's examine governments' role as enforcers.

Governments as enforcers

Governments provide at least two different functions in their role as enforcers, in a cybersecurity context – regulators and law enforcement. Let's quickly look at both functions.

Regulators

We just discussed governments as standards bodies. As we discussed, standards are important not only for government procurement purposes, but also for the broader markets. However, just because a standards body publishes some standards, doesn't necessarily mean that private and public sector organizations will spend the time, effort, or budget to conform with those standards. Typically, there must be some sort of clear benefit or incentive for organizations to change the way they operate.

Sometimes, markets or industries are too slow to change by themselves and a "market failure" results. In cases like this, governments use the tools they have in their toolboxes; in the case of cybersecurity this includes regulation. Regulations typically implement restrictions that industries must conform with. Examples of regulated standards for cybersecurity purposes include the California Consumer Privacy Act, the **Federal Information Security Modernization Act (FISMA)** in the U.S., and the **General Data Protection Regulation (GDPR)** in the EU and the **European Economic Area (EEA)**. To give you a sense for the teeth that the European Parliament put into the GDPR, failure to comply with it could result in a fine up to €20 million or up to 4% of annual worldwide revenue, whichever is larger. There have been more than 900 administrative fines handed out related to GDPR non-compliance, the largest of which were given to large high-tech companies like Amazon ($877 million), WhatsApp ($255 million), Google Ireland ($102 million), Facebook ($68 million), and many others (Tessian, May 5, 2022). Avoiding these administrative fines is the incentive for private and public sector organizations to comply with this regulated standard.

As they say, a rising tide raises all boats. The extra-territorial scope of GDPR has helped improve data protection standards and practices around the world. Most of the compliance teams I talked with were focusing on complying with the strictest data protection standard, which is GDPR, that then makes complying with other less stringent standards generally much easier and less expensive.

Ransomware is another area where regulation is changing market behavior. In the wake of the Colonial Pipeline Company ransomware attack that shut down a pipeline system in the Eastern U.S. for several days in May of 2021, calls for new regulation resulted. Here are some examples of regulatory related activity resulting from this one cyber-attack:

- The U.S. **Federal Energy Regulatory Commission (FERC)** renewed calls for calls for mandatory cybersecurity standards for the United States' pipeline infrastructure (Federal Energy Regulatory Commission, 2021).

- The U.S. **Environmental Protection Agency (EPA)** issued a second emergency fuel waiver meant to further alleviate fuel shortages in U.S. states impacted by the pipeline shutdown (U.S. Environmental Protection Agency, 2021). This waived requirements for low volatility conventional gasoline and **Reformulated Gasoline (RFG)** in a dozen states.

- The Department of Homeland Security approved a temporary Jones Act Waiver to ease oil supply constraints in targeted parts of the U.S. eastern seaboard (U.S. Department of Homeland Security, 2021). This waiver enabled the transport of oil products between the Gulf Coast and East Coast of the U.S.

- The U.S. **Department of Transportation (DOT)** allowed states to use Interstate highways to transport overweight loads of gasoline and other fuels, to help address shortages (U.S. Department of Transportation, 2021).

- The President of the United States signed an *Executive Order on Improving the Nation's Cybersecurity* (The White House, 2021). This executive order had a profound effect on how the U.S. federal government was expected to manage cybersecurity moving forward including all of its suppliers in its supply chain. The high-level pillars or focus areas of the executive order included (The White House, 2021):

  - Remove Barriers to Threat Information Sharing Between Government and the Private Sector.

  - Modernize and Implement Stronger Cybersecurity Standards in the Federal Government.

- Improve Software Supply Chain Security.

- Establish a Cybersecurity Safety Review Board.

- Create a Standard Playbook for Responding to Cyber Incidents.

- Improve Detection of Cybersecurity Incidents on Federal Government Networks.

- Improve Investigative and Remediation Capabilities.

Typically, a cyber-attack on a U.S. based company would not result in so much regulatory related activity. But in this case, the convergence of yet another high-profile ransomware attack, a multi-million-dollar ransom demand that was paid potentially in violation of U.S. Department of the Treasury's **Office of Foreign Assets Control (OFAC)** regulations, an attack on a company in an industry that was deemed U.S. critical infrastructure, the interruption of nearly half the gas supply in the Eastern seaboard of the U.S., and the attackers' location in Russia contributed to this crescendo of government activity. At the core of all this activity was the uncertainty around the attackers' motivation – was it simply profit or was it a state sponsored attack? Even after the attack was attributed to attackers in Russia using DarkSide ransomware, their motivations were still suspect. As I mentioned in *Chapter 4*, *The Evolution of Malware*, the attackers issued a statement to try to make their motivations clear and deescalate the situation.

Notice how some of the regulatory related activity that resulted from this ransomware attack were unintended consequences, easing or waiving regulatory restrictions to blunt the effects of the attack. What if the opposite was also possible? What if attackers could use regulations to attack their victims? For example, in a completely hypothetical scenario, a criminal noticed that a large multi-national company was recording personal information of their customers, which included residents of the EU, in an immutable blockchain ledger. Although the company could have completely legitimate business reasons for doing this, the immutable property of the database they chose to use makes it impossible for the company to delete customer information if an EU-based customer requested it. Realizing that this misstep likely violates GDPR, and it could cost the company tens of millions of dollars in administrative fines, the criminal issues a ransom demand to the company in exchange for their promise not to file a privacy complaint with a Data Protection Authority in the EU. Interesting conundrum!

Law enforcement

The other function that governments perform in their role as enforcers is law enforcement. Law enforcement is supposed to be a deterrent to crime. That is, the consequences of serious crime are arrest and prosecution - things that most people want to avoid. However, in the same way the internet levels the playing field for individuals and small businesses to compete with big businesses, it enables crime on a scale never imagined before. The internet enables individuals or small groups to simultaneously attack vast numbers of people, businesses, and institutions. This is the first time in human history where relatively small numbers of attackers have a level playing field that enables them to attack much larger organizations in much larger numbers. An individual can perpetrate a large DDoS attack or a drive-by download attack against very well-resourced organizations and be successful.

There are at least a few reasons why this is the case. First, the internet is a global network that allows attacks to perpetrate their attacks from almost anywhere in the world against victims located almost anywhere. Criminals have used borders to evade arrest and prosecution for centuries and the internet enables this on a vast scale. For example, given the current situation with Russia invading Ukraine and all the sanctions placed on it, it is highly unlikely that Russia will prioritize investigating cybercrimes against organizations in western countries. The same can be said for the Democratic People's Republic of Korea (also known as North Korea) and China.

The second reason law enforcement isn't a deterrent to serious cybercrime is the challenge of strong attribution that I discussed earlier in this book. If victims don't know who is attacking them, how can they determine what a proportional response is? Which government (national, regional, municipal) should help with the response and which specific ministry, department, or agency should lead? Is the attack a matter of national security or a criminal matter? If it is a criminal matter, which law enforcement agencies should be involved – national police (such as the FBI in the U.S.), regional (state/provincial) police, or municipal police? Which jurisdiction should lead the investigation – where the victims are located, where the attack originated from, or where it is suspected that the attackers are based?

Still, if law enforcement doesn't make a serious effort to investigate, arrest and prosecute cybercriminals, then there really is no deterrent at all. Of course, law enforcement in most major countries take cybercrimes very seriously because of the consequences to victims, their communities, industries, economies, and to society.

In the U.S., several federal agencies have authority to bring cybercrime related law enforcement actions including the **Federal Bureau of Investigation (FBI)**, the **Securities and Exchange Commission (SEC)**, the Secret Service, the U.S. Attorney's Office, the **Internal Revenue Service (IRS)**, the **Federal Trade Commission (FTC)**, and **U.S. Immigration and Customs Enforcement (ICE)**. Because of the scale of the problem, none of these organizations can investigate all cybercrimes where U.S. citizens are victimized. The FBI published some guidelines for the voluntary sharing of cyber-incident information between **state, local, tribal, and territorial (SLTT)** law enforcement organizations and the U.S. federal government; these guidelines provide an insight into the types of incidents that the FBI are willing to engage on.

> *In particular, a cyber incident should be reported if it:*
>
> *May impact national security, economic security, or public health and safety.*
>
> *Affects core government or critical infrastructure functions.*
>
> *Results in a significant loss of data, system availability, or control of systems.*
>
> *Involves a large number of victims.*
>
> *Indicates unauthorized access to, or malicious software present on, critical information technology systems.*
>
> *Violates federal or SLTT law." (US Federal Bureau of Investigation, n.d.)*

The FBI's guidelines further note that, "no matter which "door" SLTT law enforcement uses, information is shared within the federal government to provide an appropriate response while protecting citizens' privacy and civil liberties under the law" (U.S. Federal Bureau of Investigation, n.d.).

In 2020, the FBI discussed a new strategy to fight cybercrime, that will "impose risk and consequences on cyber adversaries" (Wray, Christopher. 2020). He further stated,

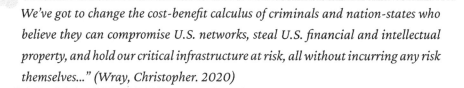

> *We've got to change the cost-benefit calculus of criminals and nation-states who believe they can compromise U.S. networks, steal U.S. financial and intellectual property, and hold our critical infrastructure at risk, all without incurring any risk themselves..." (Wray, Christopher. 2020)*

The pillars of this strategy include (U.S. Federal Bureau of Investigation, 2020):

- Unique Authorities: leverage both criminal and counterintelligence authorities to fight cyber-criminals and foreign threat actors who compromise U.S. networks.

- World-Class Capabilities: adapt to cyber-threats by leveraging new innovative investigative techniques, developing new tools, and recruiting a world-class workforce.

- Enduring Partnerships: leverage the FBI's strengths to enable their partners to defend systems, perform attribution, impose sanctions on threat actors, and pursue adversaries overseas.

Of course, other major countries also have ministries, departments, and agencies involved in law enforcement action resulting from cybercrimes. Most of the governments I advised had multiple agencies that shared the responsibility to investigate and respond to cybercrimes. Cybercrime, in the annals of crime, is relatively new and still evolving. Consequently, the way in which governments organize themselves to fight it is also new and evolving. In my experience, it was rare to find a federal or regional law enforcement organization or regulatory authority that wasn't trying to position itself to be more relevant in the fight against cybercrime, especially when new government agencies were being created for this specific purpose. An open question in many of these cases seemed to be, were new agencies needed because the old institutions weren't effective at fighting cybercrime? Did new approaches to crime require new approaches to law enforcement? The answer to these questions is likely to continue to play out well into the future.

I realize I barely scratched the surface of this subject, and I didn't discuss law enforcement as a potential cyber-threat. However, I have dedicated an entire chapter that focuses on law enforcement and cybersecurity in *Chapter 7, Government Access to Data*. If you view governments as a cyber-threat and law enforcement more specifically as a threat, this chapter should be of high interest to you.

Next, let's look at governments as defenders.

Governments as defenders

Law enforcement is largely reactive. That is, someone commits a crime and then law enforcement swings into action. Governments can also invest in proactive cybersecurity capabilities. That is, things that can help mitigate or blunt attacks against institutions, firms, and citizens. There are at least three functions that governments provide when playing the role of defender in a cybersecurity context: public safety, national security, and military.

Public safety

First, most major national governments have a department or ministry that is responsible for public safety. Sometimes public safety is a subset of the work a government department does. Over the past dozen years, I've seen more and more countries create new national cybersecurity centers that include public safety, among other things, in their charters. Examples include the **National Cyber Security Centre (NCSC)** in the UK, the **National Cyber Security Centre of Ireland (NCSC)**, **The French National Cybersecurity Agency (ANSSI)**, the Canadian Centre for Cyber Security, the **Cyber Security Agency (CSA)** in Singapore, the Australian Cyber Security Centre, and the **Cybersecurity and Infrastructure Security Agency (CISA)** in the U.S. All these government organizations are at least in part, responsible for driving awareness about cybercrime and related threats among government departments, industry, and citizens. Some of them also provide cybersecurity advisory services to government departments, protect critical infrastructure, manage incident response processes, and manage **Cyber Threat Intelligence (CTI)** programs. Some of these centers were created by merging parts of **National Computer Emergency Response Teams (CERTs)**, large government departments with cybersecurity charters, law enforcement, and intelligence agencies together. The combination of the capabilities that these stakeholder organizations bring together is much greater than any of them could develop themselves. Typically, the one function they lack within their departments is enforcement, which they partner with law enforcement agencies to perform.

Most of these cybersecurity centers offer educational opportunities to public and private sector organizations, and to citizens. The concept here is that a better educated society will be able to recognize cyber-attacks more readily, report them, and hopefully help mitigate them. I had the opportunity to attend some of these events, such as the UK NCSC's CyberUK security event.

National security

Another function governments provide in their role as defenders is national security. I've found this to be a loaded term that means different things to different people. Governments have been gathering intelligence and practicing military espionage to understand their adversaries' military capabilities as long as governments have existed. Today, this includes both cyber-offensive and cybersecurity capabilities.

Gathering intelligence is typically a function that national security organizations perform. Since military secrets are highly classified, they are typically protected using encryption and key management technologies and processes. Therefore, intelligence agencies also have deep expertise in signals intelligence (gathering intelligence by intercepting signals between systems) and cryptography, so that they might intercept and access classified information that they otherwise would not have access to, as well as protect their own governments' information more effectively.

Here's how the **U.S. National Security Agency** (**NSA**) describes their charter,

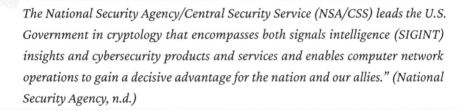

> *The National Security Agency/Central Security Service (NSA/CSS) leads the U.S. Government in cryptology that encompasses both signals intelligence (SIGINT) insights and cybersecurity products and services and enables computer network operations to gain a decisive advantage for the nation and our allies." (National Security Agency, n.d.)*

The NSA also provides combat support for the U.S. military and its allies. We discussed governments as standards bodies earlier in the chapter. The NSA is another example of this, as they "set common protocols and standards so that our military can securely share information with our allies, NATO and coalition forces around the world. Interoperability is a key to successful joint operations and exercises" (National Security Agency, n.d.).

The NSA also focuses on cybersecurity.

> *NSA Cybersecurity prevents and eradicates threats to U.S. national security systems, with an initial focus on the Defense Industrial Base (DIB) and the improvement of the nation's weapons' security. At its core, NSA Cybersecurity aims to defeat the adversary through the seven core missions and functions:*
>
> *- Provide intelligence to warn of malicious cyber threats and information U.S. Government (USG) policy*
>
> *- Develop integrated Nuclear Command & Control Systems threat, vulnerability, risk, and cryptographic products & services*
>
> *- Release integrated threat, assessment, and mitigation/protection products for the Department of Defense (DoD) and USG customers*
>
> *- Execute high-assurance cryptography and security engineering*
>
> *- Offer combined defense/offence operations with key government partners*
>
> *- Enable the defense of the agency's networks in coordination with NSA's Chief Information Officer*
>
> *- Promote information sharing to support the agency's cybersecurity mission*
>
> *(National Security Agency, n.d.).*

Of course, other countries have organizations dedicated to national security as well. In the UK, domestic intelligence and foreign intelligence services are provided by **Military Intelligence, Section 5 (MI5)** and **Military Intelligence, Section 6 (MI6)** respectively. There are numerous other stakeholders and participants including **Government Communications Headquarters (GCHQ)**, the National Cyber Security Centre, the Home Office, and many others.

In Canada, national security organizations include the **Canadian Security Intelligence Service (CSIS)**, the **Royal Canadian Mounted Police (RCMP)**, the **Communications Security Establishment (CSE)**, and the Canadian Centre for Cyber Security, among others.

The Israeli Intelligence Corps has Unit 8200. This is said to have a similar charter as the NSA in the U.S., specializing in **signals intelligence (SIGINT)**. Many former Unit 8200 members have gone on to establish successful cybersecurity company startups and to lead major companies.

There are also international partnerships that focus on the national security of partner countries. A great example of this type of organization is the Five Eyes. This is an alliance between Australia, Canada, New Zealand, the United Kingdom, and the United States, focusing on intelligence sharing (Office of the Director of National Intelligence, n.d.). The concept here is sharing intelligence across five countries provides these governments with better visibility of potential threats.

Many of the CISOs and security teams I advised considered the aforementioned intelligence agencies as threats to their organizations. I discuss intelligence gathering, such as SIGINT, as cyber-threats in *Chapter 7, Government Access to Data*.

One of the reasons governments have national security intelligence programs is to provide their military forces with information needed to deter war and defend their borders and their allies. Let's discuss this function next.

Military

The **Department of Defense (DoD)** is the largest agency in the U.S. government and the largest employer in the world, employing over 2.9 million people in more than 4,800 sites located in over 160 countries (U.S. Department of Defense, 2022). The DoD has a budget of $752.9 billion. The armed forces of the U.S. include the Army, Marine Corps, Navy, Air Force, Space Force, and Coast Guard. There are two reserve components - the Army National Guard and the Air National Guard. As I mentioned earlier, the stated mission of the DoD is to "provide the military forces needed to deter war and ensure our nation's security." This includes both offensive and defensive aspects of cybersecurity.

With so many people, DoD performs a myriad of cybersecurity functions. I'm sure an entire book could be dedicated to describing what the DoD does and the cybersecurity functions it provides. In this section I'll simply provide an introduction into one of the ways the DoD is leveraging the military for cybersecurity purposes. I think **United States Cyber Command (USCYBERCOM)** is a good starting point as it provides insight into the DoD's cybersecurity strategy and how the military is being leveraged as part of that strategy.

USCYBERCOM is a unified **combatant command (CCMD)** of the DoD. The DoD has eleven of these unified combatant commands organized around geographic locations or around specific functions. Cyber is one of those functions. USCYBERCOM is called a "joint command" because it is composed of several parts of the armed forces including the Army, Navy, Air Force, and the Marines. The NSA is also a partner in this joint command. The DoD's vision for USCYBERCOM is,

> *Achieve and maintain superiority in the cyberspace domain to influence adversary behavior, deliver strategic and operational advantages for the Joint Force, and defend and advance our national interests." – (United States Cyber Command, April 2018)*

USCYBERCOM's strategy paper, "Achieve and Maintain Cyberspace Superiority Command - Vision for U.S. Cyber Command," really is a great read. It is very well written and describes the cybersecurity challenge through a military lens. I think the following two excepts from this paper summarize their strategy. The first excerpt describes USCYBERCOM's view of the challenge that adversaries pose.

> *The security of the United States and our allies depends on international stability and global prosperity. The spread of technology and communications has enabled new means of influence and coercion. Adversaries continuously operate against us below the threshold of armed conflict. In this "new normal," our adversaries are extending their influence without resorting to physical aggression. They provoke and intimidate our citizens and enterprises without fear of legal or military consequences. They understand the constraints under which the United States chooses to operate in cyberspace, including our traditionally high threshold for response to adversary activity. They use this insight to exploit our dependencies and vulnerabilities in cyberspace and use our systems, processes, and values against us to weaken our democratic institutions and gain economic, diplomatic, and military advantages...Aggressive non-state actors like terrorists, criminals, and hacktivists pose lesser threats than states but can still damage our military capabilities and critical infrastructure, as well as endanger American lives." - (United States Cyber Command, April 2018)*

This second excerpt from the paper focuses on how USCYBERCOM operates to address these cyber threats to the U.S.

Superiority through persistence seizes and maintains the initiative in cyberspace by continuously engaging and contesting adversaries and causing them uncertainty wherever they maneuver. It describes how we operate—maneuvering seamlessly between defense and offense across the interconnected battlespace. It describes where we operate—globally, as close as possible to adversaries and their operations. It describes when we operate—continuously, shaping the battlespace. It describes why we operate—to create operational advantage for us while denying the same to our adversaries...Through persistent action and competing more effectively below the level of armed conflict, we can influence the calculations of our adversaries, deter aggression, and clarify the distinction between acceptable and unacceptable behavior in cyberspace. Our goal is to improve the security and stability of cyberspace. This approach will complement the efforts of other agencies to preserve our interests and protect our values. We measure success by our ability to increase options for decision makers and by the reduction of adversary aggression." - (United States Cyber Command, April 2018)

Of course, the U.S. isn't the only military force in the world that has been developing offensive and defensive capabilities. In 2013, the cybersecurity firm Mandiant published a report revealing that a military unit in China was allegedly responsible for hundreds of cyber-attacks on U.S. companies (CBS News, 2013). Mandiant identified Unit 61398 of the **People's Liberation Army** (**PLA**) as the source of these attacks and had tracked them to an office building in Shanghai (CBS News, 2013). In 2014, the U.S. Department of Justice indicted five members of Unit 61398 on charges related to intellectual property theft. John Carlin, assistant attorney general for national security discussed these charges at a Brookings Institution event at the time.

...we follow the facts and evidence where they lead. Sometimes, the facts and evidence lead us to a lone hacker in a basement in the U.S., or an organized crime syndicate in Russia. And sometimes, they lead us to a uniformed member of the Chinese military." – (Brookings, May 22, 2014)

Unit 61398 is believed to be just one of many such PLA groups in China that focus on cybersecurity capabilities. Military units of various other countries allegedly conducting cyber operations have popped up in news feeds ever since. Democratic People's Republic of Korea (North Korea) and Iran are two such examples.

I hope that provides a little insight into some of the ways that some countries are leveraging their military forces for cybersecurity purposes. When viewed through this lens, it becomes obvious that governments have developed and are using offensive cyber capabilities as part of their national defense strategies. Does this mean that governments are threats? I don't think there is a single answer to this question because, as we've discussed in this chapter, governments play many different roles. If you or your organization are criminal in nature or an adversary of a country's intelligence or military agencies, then the answer is more straightforward. However, I've had so many public and private sector security teams, who aren't in any way involved in criminal enterprises, or economic or military espionage, state that the U.S. government is a direct threat to them, that this deserves a deeper examination.

Do these government agencies and major companies really believe they are targets of U.S. military operations? Or do they think they are under investigation by the U.S. Department of Justice or some law enforcement agency? Why would they deem the U.S. government as a threat and by association their U.S.-based supply chain partners?

Now that we've discussed the roles governments play, this makes conversations about governments as threats potentially much more productive. I've found that when security teams can articulate specific threats, only then can specific mitigations be developed with confidence. A cyber-attack by the U.S. military is quite a different risk than a law enforcement agency serving an organization with a search warrant. Getting specific about the threats and risks you really need to be concerned with helps you better prioritize resources and avoid investing in mitigating risks that are ridiculously vague or improbable. This is the discussion that the next chapter in this book, *Chapter 7, Government Access to Data*, is dedicated to. In this chapter, we will also examine why so many security teams around the world view the U.S. government as a threat and whether this is a rational perspective.

Summary

Governments typically pledge to provide their citizens with national security, law enforcement, judicial systems, and other essential functions that provide security and support citizens' pursuit of happiness. To do this, governments organize themselves into different departments, ministries, and agencies. In this chapter we explored the different roles governments play in providing cybersecurity for their citizens and some real-world examples of how they do this.

The roles governments play in cybersecurity include market participants, standards bodies, enforcers, and defenders. We examined each of these roles in this chapter.

Governments are market participants in that they have purchasing power in markets for cybersecurity products, services, and professional services. They also compete for cybersecurity talent with the private sector.

In their role as standards bodies, governments work with industry stakeholders to develop and set cybersecurity standards. NIST in the U.S. and the BSI in Germany are great examples. Non-government-organizations such as ISO and IETF also set standards.

Governments act as enforcers typically providing regulatory and law enforcement functions. Cybersecurity regulations typically seek to set a minimum standard that public and private sector organizations must meet. Some organizations use compliance with regulated standards as cybersecurity strategies – a strategy I discuss in a later chapter. Governments use law enforcement to deter crime, including cybercrime. The FBI is a great example of a law enforcement agency that fights cybercrime.

Governments also play the role of defender for their citizens. This includes parts of governments that provide public safety, national security, and military forces. We examined how each of these functions is leveraged for cybersecurity purposes. National security and military functions can leverage both defensive and offensive cybersecurity capabilities to support their charters.

References

- Hobbes, T. (2008). *Leviathan* (J. C. A. Gaskin, Ed.). Oxford University Press.
- Canadian Charter of Rights and Freedoms, *s 7, Part 2 of the Constitution Act, 1982, being Schedule B to the Canada Act 1982 (UK), 1982, c 11*. Retrieved from https://justice.gc.ca/eng/csj-sjc/rfc-dlc/ccrf-ccdl/check/art7.html

- Embassy of France in the U.S. (December 20, 2013). *Liberty, Equality, Fraternity*. Retrieved from https://web.archive.org/web/20141018141249/http://www.ambafrance-us.org/spip.php?article620

- U.S. Department of Defense. (2022). *About U.S. Department of Defense*. Retrieved from https://www.defense.gov/About

- Government of Canada. (2022). *Global Affairs Canada*. Retrieved from https://www.international.gc.ca/global-affairs-affaires-mondiales/home-accueil.aspx?lang=eng

- Australian Federal Police. (2022). *Our Organization*. Retrieved from https://www.afp.gov.au/about-us/our-organisation

- UK Government. (2022). *Ministry of Justice About Us*. Retrieved from https://www.gov.uk/government/organisations/ministry-of-justice/about

- Germany Federal Office of Information Security. (2022). *What are the functions of the BSI?* Retrieved from https://www.bsi.bund.de/EN/Home/home_node.html

- USASpending.gov. 2022. FY 2022 *spending by Budget Function*. Retrieved from https://www.usaspending.gov/explorer/budget_function

- Scarfone, K., Benigni, D. and Grance, T. (2009), *Cyber Security Standards*, Wiley Handbook of Science and Technology for Homeland Security, John Wiley & Sons, Inc., Hoboken, NJ, [online], https://tsapps.nist.gov/publication/get_pdf.cfm?pub_id=152153 (Accessed September 8, 2022)

- NIST. (n.d.). *About NIST*. Retrieved from https://www.nist.gov/about-nist

- NIST. (n.d.). *Cryptographic Module Validation Program*. Retrieved from https://csrc.nist.gov/projects/cryptographic-module-validation-program

- NIST. (August, 2021). NIST Special Publication 1271, *Getting Started with the NIST Cybersecurity Framework: A Quick Start Guide*. Retrieved from https://nvlpubs.nist.gov/nistpubs/SpecialPublications/NIST.SP.1271.pdf

- The Internet Engineering Task Force. (n.d.). *Who we are*. Retrieved from https://www.ietf.org/about/who/

- ISO. (n.d.). *About us*. Retrieved from https://www.iso.org/about-us.html

- ISO. (2019). ISO/IEC 27018:2019, *Information technology — Security techniques — Code of practice for protection of personally identifiable information (PII) in public clouds acting as PII processors*. Retrieved from https://www.iso.org/standard/76559.html?browse=tc

- Tessian. (May 5, 2022). *30 Biggest GDPR Fines So Far* (2020, 2021, 2022). Retrieved from https://www.tessian.com/blog/biggest-gdpr-fines-2020/

- U.S. Federal Bureau of Investigation. (n.d.). *Law Enforcement Cyber Incident Reporting, A Unified Message for State, Local, Tribal, and Territorial Law Enforcement.* Retrieved from https://www.fbi.gov/file-repository/law-enforcement-cyber-incident-reporting.pdf/view

- Wray, Christopher. (September 2020). *FBI Strategy Addresses Evolving Cyber Threat, Director Wray Emphasizes Closer Partnerships to Combat Cyber Threats and Impose Greater Costs to Cyber Actors.* Retrieved from https://www.fbi.gov/news/stories/wray-announces-fbi-cyber-strategy-at-cisa-summit-091620

- U.S. Federal Bureau of Investigation. (2020). *FBI Cyber Strategy.* Retrieved from https://www.ic3.gov/Media/PDF/Y2020/PSA201008.pdf

- Federal Energy Regulatory Commission. (May 10, 2021). *Statement from FERC Chairman Richard Glick: Chairman Glick and Commissioner Clements Call for Examination of Mandatory Pipeline Cyber Standards in Wake of Colonial Pipeline Ransomware Incident.* Retrieved from https://www.ferc.gov/news-events/news/statement-ferc-chairman-richard-glick-chairman-glick-and-commissioner-clements

- U.S. Environmental Protection Agency. (May 11, 2021). *EPA Issues Fuel Waiver for Twelve States and the District of Columbia Impacted by Colonial Pipeline Shutdown.* Retrieved from https://www.epa.gov/newsreleases/epa-issues-fuel-waiver-twelve-states-and-district-columbia-impacted-colonial-pipeline

- U.S. Department of Homeland Security. (May 12, 2021). *Statement by Secretary Mayorkas on the Approval of a Jones Act Waiver in Response to Eastern Seaboard Oil Supply Constraints.* Retrieved from https://www.dhs.gov/news/2021/05/12/statement-secretary-mayorkas-approval-jones-act-waiver-response-eastern-seaboard-oil

- U.S. Department of Transportation. (May 11, 2021). *USDOT Announces Additional Measures to Help States in Areas Affected by the Colonial Pipeline Incident.* Retrieved from https://www.transportation.gov/briefing-room/usdot-announces-additional-measures-help-states-areas-affected-colonial-pipeline

- The White House. (May 12, 2021). *Executive Order on Improving the Nation's Cybersecurity.* Retrieved from https://www.whitehouse.gov/briefing-room/presidential-actions/2021/05/12/executive-order-on-improving-the-nations-cybersecurity/

- The White House. (May 12, 2021). *FACT SHEET: President Signs Executive Order Charting New Course to Improve the Nation's Cybersecurity and Protect Federal Government Networks.* Retrieved from https://www.whitehouse.gov/briefing-room/statements-releases/2021/05/12/fact-sheet-president-signs-executive-order-charting-new-course-to-improve-the-nations-cybersecurity-and-protect-federal-government-networks/

- National Security Agency. (n.d.). *Mission & Combat Support.* Retrieved from `https://www.nsa.gov/About/Mission-Combat-Support/`

- Office of the Director of National Intelligence. (n.d.). *Five Eyes Intelligence Oversight and Review Council (FIORC).* Retrieved from `https://www.dni.gov/index.php/who-we-are/organizations/enterprise-capacity/chco/chco-related-menus/chco-related-links/recruitment-and-outreach/217-about/organization/icig-pages/2660-icig-fiorc`

- National Security Agency. (n.d.). *National Security Agency/Central Security Service.* Retrieved from `https://www.nsa.gov/Cybersecurity/Overview/`

- United States Cyber Command. (April, 2018). *Achieve and Maintain Cyberspace Superiority Command, Vision for U.S. Cyber Command.* Retrieved from `https://www.cybercom.mil/Portals/56/Documents/USCYBERCOM%20Vision%20April%202018.pdf?ver=2018-06-14-152556-010`

- CBS News. (February 19, 2013). *China military unit behind many hacking attacks on U.S., cybersecurity firm says.* Retrieved from `https://www.cbsnews.com/news/china-military-unit-behind-many-hacking-attacks-on-us-cybersecurity-firm-says/`

- Brookings. (May 22, 2014). *Unit 61398 Indictment Exposes Real Faces and Names Behind Shanghai Keyboards Used To Steal from U.S. Businesses.* Retrieved from `https://www.brookings.edu/blog/brookings-now/2014/05/22/unit-61398-indictment-exposes-real-faces-and-names-behind-shanghai-keyboards-used-to-steal-from-u-s-businesses/`

Join our community on Discord

Join our community's Discord space for discussions with the author and other readers:

`https://packt.link/SecNet`

7

Government Access to Data

In previous chapters of this book, we discussed several types of threats in detail, including the exploitation of vulnerabilities, different categories of malware, ransomware (targeted attacks with extortion), and internet-based threats like phishing, drive-by download attacks, and DDoS attacks. In this chapter we'll explore another potential threat that concerns many CISOs and security teams – governments. Note that I'll be discussing legal concepts and mechanisms, regulations, and laws in this chapter. I'm not an attorney and I'm not offering legal advice. I recommend that you consult a qualified attorney for advice on the topics you read in this chapter. Additionally, what is written in this chapter and in the entire book are my own personal opinions and not those of my current employer or any former employers. With that said, let's get started!

Things changed dramatically in June 2013. At the time, I worked at Microsoft as the Director of Trustworthy Computing. In those days, customers typically wanted threat intelligence briefings from me, and to discuss threats to their Windows system networks, but that all changed in June 2013. That's when Edward Snowden gave a trove of classified documents to journalists that revealed details about some of the United States government's intelligence-gathering programs. After the first news stories were published, a global news cycle ensued. Predictably, numerous large international public and private sector organizations were suddenly interested in whether their data was safe in the hands of technology companies that were based in the United States. At that time, the underlying question from international organizations was whether US-based companies were obligated to give US intelligence agencies whatever data they wanted. Since then, many other details of US intelligence agencies' activities have come to light, and questions about the role of US-based technology firms in these activities haven't stopped coming.

Fast-forward 4 years to 2017 and I am working for another large US-based technology company, and I'm based in London in the United Kingdom. My job was to advise public sector organizations on how to modernize their cybersecurity strategies and show them how cloud computing can help. One topic that public sector organizations across Europe and the Middle East wanted to talk about was government access to data, more specifically, US government access to data. This was especially true in Germany, Belgium, France, Switzerland, the UK, and Scandinavia.

Meanwhile, when I'd go back to the US and talk to customers and colleagues there, they were largely unaware of the debate that had been going on in Europe about the trustworthiness of US technology providers. They simply didn't think that the United States' closest allies in Europe would be concerned about using the products and services provided by US-based technology companies. After all, the US's position as the dominant technology innovation leader in the world meant that they would follow **World Trade Organization (WTO)** trade rules and never steal intellectual property from other countries in the way that China was accused of doing. If they crossed that line, they would have more to lose than any other country in the world. What was the big deal? I must admit, although I had traveled to Europe to visit customers a couple of times per year over the previous decade, until I lived in London and talked to European-based companies and public sector organizations every day, I too hadn't fully realized the extent to which the trustworthiness of the United States had been severely tarnished, but as I came to learn, there is a collective consciousness among Western Europeans. This collective consciousness has been permeated by the cumulative impact of a series of revelations about US intelligence agencies' operations in Europe. Let me give you some examples:

- Classified documents leaked by Edward Snowden triggered a series of news cycles revealing the scope and scale of some US intelligence gathering programs. The White House initially defends these programs, but later apologizes for their overreach. (Gidda, 2013)
- Documents leaked by Edward Snowden suggested that the **National Security Agency (NSA)** monitored the phone conversations of 35 world leaders. (Ball, 2013)
- WikiLeaks published a series of classified reports they called "Espionnage Élysée." The reports alleged that the NSA had intercepted the communications of three different French Presidents, cabinet ministers, and the French ambassador to the US (James Regan, 2015). WikiLeaks also asserts that "the US has had a decade-long policy of economic espionage against France, including the interception of all French corporate contracts and negotiations valued at more than $200 million." (WikiLeaks, 2015)

- WikiLeaks published a series of classified documents they called "Euro Intercepts", that alleged that the NSA had intercepted the communications of senior German government officials, including German Chancellor Angela Merkel, her senior staff, as well as staff of former chancellors going back almost 2 decades. According to WikiLeaks, "WikiLeaks so far shows the NSA explicitly targeted for long-term surveillance 125 phone numbers for top German officials and did so for political and economic reasons, according to its own designations." (WikiLeaks, 2015)

These revelations, and others, have damaged the relationship the US had with their European allies. Unfortunately, this is not limited to Europe – Brazil (WikiLeaks, 2015) and Japan (WikiLeaks, 2015) are two other examples. For US technology companies caught in the middle, this developed into a quagmire of distrust. Every time I walked into a meeting with a company or a public sector organization in Western Europe, I knew this collective consciousness would be generating serious headwinds. Just how strong were those headwinds? During some of the public events I spoke at, I'd survey audiences with a question like this:

Which one of these threats is your organization most concerned about? Select only one answer.

1. Attackers from China
2. Attackers from Russia
3. US government access to data using a valid warrant or subpoena
4. Other

In Western Europe, between 2017 and 2020, typically 80%-90% of the people I surveyed selected answer 'C'. If this surprises you, you probably live in the United States. If you live in Germany, France, or another location in the **European Union (EU)** or the **European Economic Area (EEA)**, this likely will not surprise you at all.

The good news for CISOs, their security teams, compliance and risk management professionals, and other executives, is that these dramatic revelations have led to levels of transparency that can help them quantify and manage the risk associated with government access to data. I'll explain how to do this, but first, we need to unpack this issue a bit more because typically there are a lot of assumptions, generalizations, and misconceptions about it. In fact, there are a few different scenarios that are typically conflated in conversations about government access to data; these scenarios do not have the same risk (probability and impact) for every organization. In this chapter, I will share some of the things I've learned after having thousands of conversations with organizations around the world about this topic, and hopefully, take some of the emotion out of your risk calculations.

Understanding government access to data

As I discussed in *Chapter 6, The Roles Governments Play in Cybersecurity*, oftentimes, the term "government" is used in a way that suggests it is one homogeneous thing. In reality, governments can be organized into many different parts. In the context of government access to data, it's important to recognize that specific parts of governments want to use data in ways that support their specific agendas. Narrowing the conversation to focus on these scenarios makes it possible to better understand the risks they might pose to your organization and possible mitigations against them. The more specifically we can define a threat, the clearer it becomes as to whether we can mitigate, transfer, or accept the risk it poses to our organization. Thinking about the US government as a single entity with a single agenda isn't accurate and isn't helpful to CISOs, security teams, and executives that are serious about understanding and mitigating risks to their organizations. In the thousands of conversations I've had about government access to data, many CISOs, security teams, and executives tended to conflate three different scenarios. Let's look at each of them.

The signals intelligence scenario

The signals intelligence scenario is where government agencies gather intelligence by intercepting and analyzing communications and electronic signals, potentially employing cryptanalysis on encrypted communications. Signals intelligence programs were the focus of many of those dramatic WikiLeaks announcements. The reality is this type of intelligence gathering is employed by many major governments around the world. (Wikipedia, n.d.) The US uses this type of intelligence gathering to get visibility into its adversaries' evolving military capabilities. (National Security Agency Central Security Service, n.d.) Keep in mind that the US shares intelligence with the other members of NATO and the "Five Eyes" signals intelligence sharing alliance. (National Security Agency Central Security Service, n.d.)

Many of the executives I met expressed concern about the information leaked by WikiLeaks because it suggests that some of the targets of signals intelligence have been world leaders, their staffs, and the public at large via mass data collection programs. Getting them to put their personal outrage aside and articulate how they plan to manage the risk that such programs pose to their organizations was sometimes challenging. Many executives told me that simply not using US-based technology providers was the way they planned to mitigate this threat.

Since these US intelligence programs, their objectives, their targets, and their capabilities are all classified, managing such risks with so little information can be challenging – but choosing not to use US-based technology providers would not mitigate the threat that these programs posed, in any way, because signals intelligence doesn't depend on its targets using technology that is designed, manufactured, or operated by US-based technology firms.

The unlawful government access to data scenario

The unlawful government access to data scenario is where a government agency steals data from an organization or a vendor in its supply chain, as opposed to obtaining a valid court order to compel it. Military espionage and economic espionage are the motivations that tend to be associated with this scenario. The US has admitted to performing acts of military espionage; the Stuxnet attack on Iran would be an example of this type of activity. China has often been accused of economic espionage – allegedly stealing intellectual property from organizations in the West and giving it to organizations in China to give them a competitive and economic advantage. Of course, there are examples of other countries performing acts of espionage as well; examples include France (Ewing, 2014), the United Arab Emirates (Christhopher Bing, 2019), Saudi Arabia (Mark Mazzetti, 2019), Israel (Mehul Srivastava, 2019), Russia (Wikipedia, n.d.) and many others.

How do CISOs manage the risks associated with adversaries that have massive or unlimited budgets, can sequester any technical expertise they need, and infiltrate their organizations from within? Again, trying to mitigate this type of threat by refusing to use US technology providers' products and services is not effective. This might be emotionally satisfying for executives that want to take a stand against economic espionage, but it's completely ineffective mitigation and akin to accepting the risk.

For organizations that are serious about managing this type of risk, there are both legal and technical mitigations available to them. An example of legal mitigation is the United States Constitution. If a US law enforcement agency or US intelligence agency simply steals data that is stored inside the United States, if caught, they are subject to the laws of the United States, including potential prosecution and prison time for those involved in the crime – but if the same data is stored outside the United States, in the heart of Bavaria, Germany for example, there is no United States Constitution protecting it there. Non-US organizations that really are serious about managing the risk of unlawful US government access to data actually circumvent the legal mitigations against this threat by demanding that their data stay resident in their countries.

This is counterintuitive for many of the executives I've talked to, but if executives can remove the emotions that have permeated the collective consciousness of Western Europeans, they can devise risk management strategies that are much more effective.

In the case of unlawful government access to data, most private and public sector organizations have higher priority risks to manage, but others, such as intelligence agencies, militaries, witness protection programs, and commercial organizations with high-value intellectual property that is seriously at risk from acts of espionage, unlawful government access to data or espionage is a priority risk that they will invest considerable resources into mitigating. Strong encryption and effective key management are crucial technical controls in this scenario that I'll discuss later in this chapter, as well as in *Chapter 9*, *Cybersecurity Strategies*.

The lawful government access to data scenario

Lawful government access to data is a scenario where a law enforcement or intelligence agency gets a valid court order compelling an organization or a vendor in its supply chain to provide specific evidence that is in their possession, for use in a criminal investigation.

For most of the large private and public sector organizations that I have advised in relation to government access to data, the risk they fear isn't that they might receive a subpoena or warrant that compels them to produce evidence in a criminal matter. After all, most of these organizations have General Counsels and legal departments that already manage such legal requests. Over time, some of these legal departments have developed processes to manage such requests and surface the risks they pose to senior management, oversight committees, and their Boards of Directors. This allows them to manage the potential domestic legal risks posed by such law enforcement requests. It also helps them manage potential international legal consequences where obeying local laws could compel them to potentially break international laws or regulations like the **General Data Protection Regulation** (**GDPR**). It also allows them to manage other risks like the reputational risk to their organization.

The risk that these organizations are actually worried about is that one of their partners or a vendor in their supply chain would receive a court order for evidence in a criminal matter and they wouldn't be notified. If they don't know that law enforcement is trying to compel the production of data that they are responsible for, then they can't employ their own attorneys and their own internal legal processes to manage the request; that is, a risk to their organization exists that they don't know about and subsequently they can't manage.

You might wonder how often a scenario like this happens. In the United States, gag orders that prevented recipients of court orders from telling the target of investigations about the order were a matter of course – but Microsoft filed a lawsuit against the US Department of Justice in April 2016 to stop the practice. As Brad Smith, Microsoft's General Counsel and President, explained, "When we filed our case, we explained that in an 18-month period, 2,576 of the legal demands we received from the US government included an obligation of secrecy, and 68 percent of these appeared to be indefinite demands for secrecy. In short, we were prevented from ever telling a large number of customers that the government had sought to access their data." (Smith, 2017) As a result of this lawsuit, the US Department of Justice changed its practices so that such gag orders are the exception to the rule, not the norm.

There is far more transparency and data available on the risk of lawful government access to data than the previous two scenarios I have discussed. This makes it easier for CISOs and other executives to understand the risk and whether their organization should invest resources to mitigate it, transfer it, or accept it. I'll focus the bulk of the rest of this chapter on discussing the risk of lawful government access to data and provide some insights to help you manage it.

Lawful government access to data

Law enforcement agencies all over the world seek evidence for use in criminal cases. This is core to the function they play in government and in society. Sometimes, the investigative trail they follow leads them to potential evidence that is located overseas. The challenge for law enforcement in these cases is that they need a way to compel the production of evidence from people who are not subject to their local legal jurisdiction. Put another way, the domestic legal mechanisms that law enforcement agencies use to collect evidence in their country won't be sufficient by themselves to enable investigators to collect evidence that is located in other countries. This challenge for law enforcement isn't a new one. Criminals have sought to cover their tracks and subvert legal processes by crossing jurisdictional boundaries for centuries. This challenge is exacerbated in a world where data can be transmitted across international legal boundaries in a fraction of a second and stored in almost any country in the world, using consumer-grade commodity technologies available to hundreds of millions of people, in many cases, for free. How are law enforcement agencies supposed to successfully conduct investigations into terrorism, espionage, child exploitation, and other serious crimes, if they lack the legal tools to request evidence that is stored outside of their country?

To help address this challenge, one of the legal mechanisms that many governments have put in place is **Mutual Legal Assistance Treaties (MLATs)**. The last time I counted, the US had signed approximately 65 MLATs for use in criminal matters with countries around the world. (US Department of Justice, n.d.) Most of these are bilateral treaties, and a few are multilateral, such as with the EU. MLATs have been in place for many years. For example, the current MLAT between the United States and Germany has been in place since 2004. Similarly, the current MLAT between the US and France was signed in 1998, the MLAT between the US and the EU was signed in 2003, and the MLAT between Sweden and the US was signed in 2001. These MLATs have been put in place with the stated purpose of enabling cooperation in criminal investigations, as you can see in the "letter of transmittal" included within each MLAT.

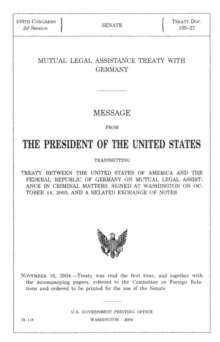

LETTER OF TRANSMITTAL

THE WHITE HOUSE, *November 16, 2004.*
To the Senate of the United States:

With a view to receiving the advice and consent of the Senate to ratification, I transmit herewith the Treaty Between the United States of America and the Federal Republic of Germany on Mutual Legal Assistance in Criminal Matters, signed at Washington on October 14, 2003, and a related exchange of notes. I transmit also, for the information of the Senate, the report of the Department of State with respect to the Treaty.

The Treaty is one of a series of modern mutual legal assistance treaties being negotiated by the United States in order to counter criminal activities more effectively. The Treaty should be an effective tool to assist in the prosecution of a wide variety of crimes. The Treaty is self-executing.

The Treaty provides for a broad range of cooperation in criminal matters. Mutual assistance available under the Treaty includes: taking the testimony or statements of persons; providing documents, records, and articles of evidence; locating or identifying persons; serving documents; transferring persons in custody for testimony or other purposes; executing requests for searches and seizures; undertaking telecommunications surveillance, undercover investigations, and controlled deliveries; assisting in proceedings related to immobilization and forfeiture of assets, restitution to the victims of crime and collection of fines; and any other form of assistance not prohibited by the laws of the State from whom the assistance is requested.

I recommend that the Senate give early and favorable consideration to the Treaty, and give its advice and consent to ratification.

GEORGE W. BUSH.

Figure 7.1: Left: the MLAT between the United States and Germany signed in 2003 (U.S. Government printing office, 2004); Right: the "Letter of Transmittal" on page 3 of the MLAT between the United States and Germany that explains the purpose of the MLAT (U.S. Government printing office, 2004)

| 109TH CONGRESS
2d Session | SENATE | TREATY DOC.
109–13 |

MUTUAL LEGAL ASSISTANCE AGREEMENT WITH THE
EUROPEAN UNION

MESSAGE

FROM

THE PRESIDENT OF THE UNITED STATES

TRANSMITTING

AGREEMENT ON MUTUAL LEGAL ASSISTANCE BETWEEN THE
UNITED STATES OF AMERICA AND THE EUROPEAN UNION (EU),
SIGNED ON JUNE 25, 2003 AT WASHINGTON, TOGETHER WITH
TWENTY-FIVE BILATERAL INSTRUMENTS WHICH SUBSEQUENTLY
WERE SIGNED BETWEEN THE UNITED STATES AND EACH EURO-
PEAN UNION MEMBER STATE IN ORDER TO IMPLEMENT THE
AGREEMENT WITH THE EU, WITH EXPLANATORY NOTE

SEPTEMBER 28, 2006.—Agreement was read the first time, and together
with the accompanying papers, referred to the Committee on Foreign
Relations and ordered to be printed for the use of the Senate

★ (Star Print)

LETTER OF TRANSMITTAL

THE WHITE HOUSE, *September 28, 2006.*
To the Senate of the United States:

With a view to receiving the advice and consent of the Senate to ratification, I transmit herewith the Agreement on Mutual Legal Assistance between the United States of America and the European Union (EU), signed on June 25, 2003, at Washington, together with 25 bilateral instruments that subsequently were signed between the United States and each European Union Member State in order to implement the Agreement with the EU, and an explanatory note that is an integral part of the Agreement. I also transmit, for the information of the Senate, the report of the Department of State with respect to the Agreement and bilateral instruments.

A parallel agreement with the European Union on extradition, together with bilateral instruments, will be transmitted to the Senate separately. These two agreements are the first law enforcement agreements concluded between the United States and the European Union. Together they serve to modernize and expand in important respects the law enforcement relationships between the United States and the 25 EU Member States, as well as formalize and strengthen the institutional framework for law enforcement relations between the United States and the European Union itself.

The U.S.-EU Mutual Legal Assistance Agreement contains several innovations that should prove of value to U.S. prosecutors and investigators, including in counterterrorism cases. The Agreement creates an improved mechanism for obtaining bank information from an EU Member State, elaborates legal frameworks for the use of new techniques such as joint investigative teams, and establishes a comprehensive and uniform framework for limitations on the use of personal and other data. The Agreement includes a nonderogation provision making clear that it is without prejudice to the ability of the United States or an EU Member State to refuse assistance where doing so would prejudice its sovereignty, security, public, or other essential interests.

I recommend that the Senate give early and favorable consideration to the Agreement and bilateral instruments.

GEORGE W. BUSH.

Figure 7.2: Left: the multilateral MLAT between the United States and the EU signed in 2003 (U.S. GOVERNMENT PRINTING OFFICE, 2006); Right: the "Letter of Transmittal" on page 3 of the MLAT between the United States and the EU that explains the purpose of the MLAT (U.S. GOVERNMENT PRINTING OFFICE, 2006)

MLATs between the US and other countries provide a way for law enforcement in participating countries to request evidence located in the US and vice versa. An important aspect of how these MLATs work is the legal standard applied to search and seizure requests. To understand this, we need to go back to the founding documents of the United States and look at the initial amendments to the Constitution of the United States, otherwise known as the Bill of Rights (National Archives, n.d.). This is where civil rights and liberties are defined for citizens of the United States.

The Fourth Amendment to the United States Constitution prohibits unreasonable search and seizure, as follows:

> "[t]he right of the people to be secure in their persons, houses, papers, and effects, against unreasonable searches and seizures, shall not be violated, and no Warrants shall issue, but upon probable cause, supported by Oath or affirmation, and particularly describing the place to be searched, and the persons or things to be seized." (Cornell Law School, n.d.)

The concept of "probable cause" has been the focus of much legal debate and numerous court cases since at least the late 1780s when the Bill of Rights was proposed. One definition of probable cause is as follows:

> "Probable cause is a requirement found in the Fourth Amendment that must usually be met before police make an arrest, conduct a search, or receive a warrant. Courts usually find probable cause when there is a reasonable basis for believing that a crime may have been committed (for an arrest) or when evidence of the crime is present in the place to be searched (for a search)." (Cornell Law School, n.d.)

Whether it's a US law enforcement agency or a law enforcement agency in another MLAT country using an MLAT to request data, the standard applied to the request is the US legal standard of probable cause. Put another way, the US will not make an MLAT request or service an MLAT request unless it meets the probable cause standard; this means that MLAT requests must meet the highest legal standard in the world for search and seizure.

This nuance provides additional protection for people under investigation in countries where the legal bar for search and seizure is lower than in the United States.

You might be wondering how these MLATs work. Let me provide an example scenario to illustrate how they work. In this scenario, a burglary in the capital city of France has been committed. Some super important and valuable technical specifications were physically stolen from a safe in a building in Paris, but the perpetrator was caught in the act by the police. From all indications, this was an act of industrial espionage, as the perpetrator was stealing intellectual property that he could sell to the competitors of the victim company. In this scenario, the crime is 100% French: it happened in France, the perpetrator is a French citizen, the victim is a French company, French law enforcement is investigating, and French courts will decide the verdict and any potential punishment for the crime.

As the French law enforcement officers interrogate the burglar, they discern that a buyer of the stolen intellectual property is waiting for word that the crime has been successful, but the burglar will not identify the buyer to the police. The police suspect that the burglar has been communicating with the buyer via email. If they could get access to the burglar's email inbox, they might be able to identify the buyer and prosecute them for the crime as well. The burglar will not give the investigators access to his email or any details about his account. After searching the burglar's residence in Paris, with his permission, and inspecting his personal computer, the police believe they have identified the email provider the burglar has an email account with. The investigators contact the email provider to get the burglar's account details but discover that the email provider is a US-based company located in California. An attorney for the email provider told the investigators that the email provider would not cooperate in their investigation without a valid court order from a court in the United States.

After consulting the French Ministry of Justice, the police officers determine that if they want potential email evidence that is stored in the US, they will have to use the MLAT on Mutual Legal Assistance in Criminal Matters that France has signed with the United States.

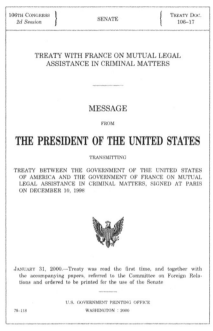

LETTER OF TRANSMITTAL

THE WHITE HOUSE, *January 31, 2000.*
To the Senate of the United States:

With a view to receiving the advice and consent of the Senate to ratification, I transmit herewith the Treaty Between the Government of the United States of America and the Government of France on Mutual Legal Assistance in Criminal Matters, signed at Paris on December 10, 1998. I transmit also, for the Senate's information, an explanatory note agreed between the Parties regarding the application of certain provisions. The report of the Department of State with respect to the Treaty is enclosed.

The Treaty is one of a series of modern mutual legal assistance treaties being negotiated by the United States in order to counter criminal activities more effectively. The Treaty should be an effective tool to assist in the prosecution of a wide variety of crimes, including terrorism and drug trafficking offenses. The Treaty is self-executing.

The Treaty provides for a broad range of cooperation in criminal matters. Mutual assistance available under the Treaty includes: obtaining the testimony or statements of persons; providing documents, records, and items of evidence; locating or identifying persons or items; serving documents; transferring persons in custody for testimony or other purposes; executing requests for searches and seizures; assisting in proceedings related to immobilization and forfeiture of assets, restitution, and collection of fines; and rendering any other form of assistance not prohibited by the laws of the Requested State.

I recommend that the Senate give early and favorable consideration to the Treaty and give its advice and consent to ratification.

WILLIAM J. CLINTON.

Figure 7.3: Left: the multilateral MLAT between the United States and France signed in 1998 (U.S. GOVERNMENT PRINTING OFFICE, 2000); Right: the "Letter of Transmittal" on page three of the MLAT between the United States and France that explains the purpose of the MLAT (U.S. GOVERNMENT PRINTING OFFICE, 2000)

The French investigators are not 100% positive that the burglar has an account with this specific US-based email provider, nor are they certain that emails from the buyer really exist, but this is one line of inquiry they are pursuing. The first thing they must ascertain is whether the burglar has an email account with the email provider. They fill out the MLAT request paperwork and request confirmation that the burglar has an email account with the email provider. When the French investigators submit their MLAT request to the US, it gets evaluated several times.

Internationally recognized legal expert and law professor, Peter Swire, describes the process this way:

> *"Each successful request is evaluated by the DOJ's* **Office of International Affairs (OIA)***, a US Attorney's office, a federal magistrate judge, and then again by the* **Federal Bureau of Investigation (FBI)** *and the OIA. The OIA, US Attorney's office, and magistrate judge each review to ensure that enough evidence exists for the type of information sought—a probable cause warrant for content, and a 2703(d) order showing a reasonable and articulable suspicion for much non-content data. After the magistrate judge approves the request, and the company produces the records, the FBI and OIA review the records so that only data responsive to the request is returned to France, and that no data is included that may violate the US First Amendment, such as prosecution of a political or speech crime." (Peter Swire, 2016)*

All these reviews and evaluations take time. According to White House legal experts, incoming valid MLAT requests to the US take, on average, *ten months* to fulfill, "with some requests taking considerably longer." (Richard A. Clarke, 2013) In our French burglary scenario, 10 months after the French investigators submitted their MLAT request to find out if the burglar had an email account, the answer comes back affirmative and includes some account information such as the name and address on the account, when it was opened, and the email address.

During the 10 months that the MLAT was being processed, the French investigators continued several other lines of inquiry related to the burglary. They learned from an associate of the burglar that an email from the buyer does exist, and it could help identify and prosecute the buyer. If the French investigators now want to request a copy of a specific email they have knowledge of in the inbox of the burglar's account, they will need to submit another MLAT request. This new request will likely take another 10 months to process. After nearly 2 years, the French investigators finally receive a copy of the email that they hoped would identify the buyer. The contents of the email do incriminate the buyer but do not provide any details as to their identity other than their email address. The email provider that the buyer used to send the email to the burglar is located in the United States. The French investigators will now have to make another MLAT request to the US to get account information from the buyer's email provider that might help them reveal the identity of the buyer. The French investigators are optimistic that after nearly 3 years of waiting for MLAT request responses, they will know the identity of the buyer of the stolen technical specifications. Their lines of inquiry continue.

The moral of this story is do not become a French investigator. Of course, I'm joking – but I do hope my example scenario provides you with some insight into why law enforcement agencies around the world are demanding more modern legal mechanisms to expedite the production of evidence that is located overseas. In their view, the MLATs are simply too slow. I'm sure this is a view shared by the victims of serious crimes as well.

This is the problem that the **Clarifying Lawful Overseas Use of Data (CLOUD)** Act tries to solve. Let's examine this next.

The CLOUD Act and the PATRIOT Act

Unfortunately, this poorly chosen acronym has caused a lot of confusion in both the public and private sectors. The CLOUD Act does not just apply to **Cloud Service Providers (CSPs)**. It applies to a variety of service providers, including email providers, telephone companies, social media sites, and other types of organizations – but the acronym itself has led many of the executives that I've talked to, to believe that the CLOUD Act was specifically designed to give the US government unfettered access to data when it's in a US-based service provider's cloud service. This isn't true – but, in my experience, I've seen many foreign competitors of US-based CSPs try to use this confusion to their advantage, despite the fact that the CLOUD Act applies to many, if not all, of them as well.

2201

1   **DIVISION V—CLOUD ACT**

2   **SEC. 101. SHORT TITLE.**

3   This division may be cited as the "Clarifying Lawful

4   Overseas Use of Data Act" or the "CLOUD Act".

5   **SEC. 102. CONGRESSIONAL FINDINGS.**

6   Congress finds the following:

7   (1) Timely access to electronic data held by

8   communications-service providers is an essential

9   component of government efforts to protect public

10   safety and combat serious crime, including ter-

11   rorism.

Figure 7.4: The CLOUD Act (United States Congress, 2018)

The CLOUD Act was signed into law on March 23, 2018. Many of the executives that I've talked to since the CLOUD Act was passed describe the CLOUD Act as the "USA PATRIOT Act 2.0." This is another misconception that non-US-based technology companies like to play up. However, the 32-page CLOUD Act isn't an amendment or extension of the 10 titles of the Uniting and Strengthening America by **Providing Appropriate Tools Required to Intercept and Obstruct Terrorism (PATRIOT)** Act that was enacted in October of 2001 in the wake of the 9/11 terrorist attacks. Both the PATRIOT Act and the CLOUD act amend the Stored Communications Act in different ways for different purposes. Title II of the PATRIOT Act focused on enhanced surveillance procedures; it expanded the scope of wiretapping and surveillance orders and enabled the surveillance of packet-switched networks.

This is different from the CLOUD Act, which provides an international legal framework to expedite law enforcement agencies' lawful access to evidence stored overseas. This is referred to as the "production of evidence" in legal parlance, but it is easy to understand why some executives would jump to the conclusion that these acts are somehow related, especially if they live in Germany, France, Brazil, Japan, or other places where US intelligence has allegedly intercepted their government leaders' communications. I've seen some non-US-based managed service providers using the PATRIOT Act to convince organizations to buy their services instead of those from US-based providers. These arguments make little sense in this context, as most public sector and private sector organizations are not involved in terrorism or money laundering to support terrorism. Additionally, all 10 titles of the PATRIOT Act have expired (Electronic Frontier Foundation, 2020).

Among many of the executives and cybersecurity teams that I have met outside the US, there is no doubt that the PATRIOT Act is reviled. The information leaked by Edward Snowden and WikiLeaks did nothing to improve the United States' reputation internationally – but CISOs and vendors aren't helping their organizations by perpetuating outdated arguments about ethereal risks; procuring non-US products and services doesn't mitigate the perceived risks. CISOs need to get specific about the risks that their organizations really need to manage so that they can decide how to apply the limited resources they have to specific mitigations for those risks.

The CLOUD Act amends the Stored Communications Act, which was passed in 1986. The Stored Communications Act enables US law enforcement to include electronic communications in their investigations, but the Stored Communications Act didn't cover Internet-related scenarios because the Internet was nascent when it was written. Subsequently, it didn't contemplate scenarios like Internet-based storage or global cloud services.

The CLOUD Act modernizes some of the tools given to US law enforcement in the Stored Communications Act and makes it clear that organizations doing business in the United States (whether they are US-based or based elsewhere) can be legally compelled to provide data for criminal investigations regardless of where it's stored.

There are several key things the CLOUD Act did not change. The CLOUD Act did not increase the scope of warrants issued under US law. The collection of bulk data is still not permitted. Foreign governments still have sovereign immunity; meaning, in layman's terms, if a government decided they did not want to participate in such a law enforcement request for data that they controlled, they wouldn't put themselves in jail. Law enforcement must still have a valid court order for the specific evidence they want to collect; this means the CLOUD Act does not enable law enforcement to go on "fishing expeditions." There are no provisions in the CLOUD Act that force service providers to provide a back door or unfettered access to data. Critically, the CLOUD Act does not require service providers to decrypt data that their customers have encrypted or attempt to break the encryption that is protecting their data. This has become a hot topic over the past several years with calls from the US, UK, and Australian governments for service providers to give law enforcement an "encryption backdoor" that gives them the ability to decrypt encrypted data for law enforcement investigations (Paul, 2019). Major technology companies have pushed back on the technical viability of this idea, as attackers could potentially use such a backdoor to compromise systems and data. Needless to say, this will be an area of privacy law that will continue to evolve in the future.

Like the PATRIOT Act, I've seen some non-US-based vendors sow fear, uncertainty, and doubt in the minds of their customers using the CLOUD Act. I've also seen public and private sector organizations based in Europe assert this themselves. The argument that these people make is that using a US-based cloud provider makes it easier for the US government to get access to data because of the CLOUD Act, but this characterization does not provide a complete picture because it conveniently omits a few key facts.

It is true that US-based telephone companies, email providers, social media companies, CSPs, and other such companies are required to follow the letter of the law in the United States including the CLOUD Act – but US jurisdiction is not limited to US-based companies. The US has jurisdiction over any company that has "minimum contacts" with it. This includes a range of scenarios. For example, a foreign-owned, foreign-based company that has a physical presence in the US, such as a branch office or US headquarters, is subject to US law. If the company has personnel or customers in the US, it's likely subject to US law.

US courts have ruled in the past that simply having a non-US website that US customers visit can bring an organization under US legal jurisdiction. For organizations that are really trying to understand and manage the risks associated with being subject to US legal jurisdiction, they'll need to examine all the vendors they already have in their supply chains. For enterprises and federal government departments, chances are, those "local" IT vendors, consulting firms, and service providers that they have been using for decades also have a physical presence in the US and/or revenue from US customers that make them subject to US law, potentially including the CLOUD Act. It doesn't matter if these local vendors have data centers in the heart of Bavaria, Paris, or Stockholm. If they are subject to US jurisdiction because they have minimum contacts with the US, they can be legally compelled to turn over data stored in these data centers for US law enforcement investigations. When their executives face jail time and their US business interests are threatened because of a failure to comply with valid court orders, businesses tend to cooperate. Not many businesses would abandon their investments in the US market simply to defy a valid court order in a criminal investigation, especially when the legal bar being applied for the search and seizure exceeds their own countries' legal standard.

An example of this is the arrest of Huawei's Chief Financial Officer as she flew from Hong Kong to Mexico connecting in Vancouver, Canada, at the request of US authorities (Julie Gordon, 2018). Huawei appeared to be willing to cooperate with the US law enforcement's investigation – given their CFO was in custody, they had a presence in the US, and they had future ambitions for the US market. At the time of writing, this CFO is still in Vancouver where she has negotiated a deferred prosecution deal with the US authorities that's in effect until December 2022 (Reuters, 2021).

Simply put, organizations that want access to US markets are required to follow the letter of US law whether the data they have is in the US or not. We haven't seen a mass exodus of German, French, Swiss, or Swedish companies from the US, so European customers of these companies need to accept that the data residency protection arguments forwarded by such companies are largely hollow – but this reality isn't necessarily a bad thing, since data residency does not equate to better data security. After all, the physical location of data does not mitigate any of the Cyber-security Usual Suspects that I discussed at length in *Chapter 1*. Nearly 100% of attacks happen over a network. Whether the data is in a data center in Berlin, Bern, Beijing, or Boston makes no difference to attackers who will likely never have physical access to the infrastructure. Strong encryption and effective key management, supported by other technologies and processes, mitigate unauthorized access to data, not data residency. I will discuss encryption and key management in more depth later in this chapter.

Another key fact that's rarely mentioned by non-US service providers is that the CLOUD Act enables the US to request data for investigations of US citizens and residents of the United States.
It's not intended to enable the US to collect data on European citizens, Brazilian citizens, Japanese
citizens, and so on that aren't related to the crime being investigated. The staunchest anti-US
CLOUD Act audiences that I've encountered in Europe would get very quiet when I'd show them
this excerpt from Section 3, Preservation of Records; Comity Analysis of Legal Process, of the
CLOUD Act.

> *''(2) MOTIONS TO QUASH OR MODIFY.—(A) A provider of electronic commu-*
> *nication service to the public or remote computing service, including a foreign elec-*
> *tronic communication service or remote computing service, that is being required to*
> *disclose pursuant to legal process issued under this section the contents of a wire or*
> *electronic communication of a subscriber or customer, may file a motion to modify*
> *or quash the legal process where the provider reasonably believes—*
>
> *(i) that the customer or subscriber is not a United States person and does not reside*
> *in the United States; and*
>
> *(ii) that the required disclosure would create a material risk that the provider would*
> *violate the laws of a qualifying foreign government..."*

This doesn't mean that service providers will always be able to move to quash court orders because they won't always know who their customers are, or what their citizenship or residency
status is. Additionally, courts have some discretion and might disagree with a provider's move to
quash – but I think this excerpt communicates the intent of the CLOUD Act in a way that effectively counters the conflated notions some audiences have about signals intelligence, unlawful
access to data, and lawful access to data. In order for a service provider based in a non-US country
to get a "procedural opportunity," such as a motion to quash an order, the provider's country
needs to sign a CLOUD Act executive agreement with the US. CLOUD Act executive agreements
can be used to define the scope, terms, and conditions of overseas evidence production orders
between the parties in the agreement. The UK government was the first government in the world
to sign a CLOUD Act executive agreement with the US. They released the details of this executive
agreement in October 2019 (United States Department of Justice, 2019). Some of the key terms
and conditions included:

- **They agreed on some definitions, including a definition of "serious crime" that the CLOUD Act applies to:** "Serious Crime means an offense that is punishable by a maximum term of imprisonment of at least three years." (United States Department of Justice, 2019)

- **Reciprocity:** The US may not target the data of persons within the UK and vice versa.

- **Some use limits are defined:** The UK can decide not to provide evidence in cases in which the death penalty is sought by the US. The US can decide not to provide evidence in cases where there are concerns about free speech.

- **Orders must be certified as legitimate:** "Each Order subject to this Agreement must include a written certification by the Issuing Party's Designated Authority that the Order is lawful and complies with the Agreement, including the Issuing Party's substantive standards for Orders subject to this Agreement." (United States Department of Justice, 2019)

- **Third-country notification:** If the target of the investigation is not in the US or the UK, authorities in the third country should be notified unless specific extenuating conditions are present.

As you can see from this example, a CLOUD Act executive agreement can provide more specificity so that organizations can better understand the scope and limits of the CLOUD Act. Also, in October 2019, the US and Australia jointly announced that they started negotiating a bilateral CLOUD Act executive agreement (United States Department of Justice, 2019). That executive agreement was signed by Australia's Minister for Home Affairs in December 2021 (Department of Home Affairs, Australia Government, 2021).

The EU has also expressed the intent to make cross-border electronic evidence (e-evidence) requests faster and easier with their proposed e-evidence regulation (European Commission, 2019):

> **Create a European Production Order:** *this will allow a judicial authority in one Member State to obtain electronic evidence (such as emails, text, or messages in apps, as well as information to identify a perpetrator as a first step) directly from a service provider or its legal representative in another Member State, which will be obliged to respond within* **10 days**, *and within* **6 hours** *in cases of emergency (compared to up to 120 days for the existing European Investigation Order or an average of 10 months for a Mutual Legal Assistance procedure);"* (European Commission, 2019)

Of course, not everyone agrees that accelerating the production of evidence in criminal investigations by streamlining checks and balances is a good idea – but, for CISOs and security teams, they need to put their personal feelings aside and determine if these developments pose an incremental risk that their organizations should invest in mitigating.

Managing the risk of government access to data

With so many governments around the world working to find ways to facilitate and expedite the cross-border production of data for law enforcement purposes, what should CISOs do? First, it's important to recognize that not every organization needs to be concerned about government access to data, MLATs, and the CLOUD Act. Most of the executives I've advised had not previously parsed the specific threats that are often lumped into the risk of government access to data. For some of them, once they recognized that signals intelligence, unlawful access to data, and lawful access to data are different threats, they adopted a less emotional, more pragmatic approach – but, for others, they still wanted more clarity on the risks that these threats pose. Since the industry has very little authoritative data to inform risk calculations for communications being intercepted by signals intelligence and data being stolen in unlawful access to data scenarios, these risks are harder to quantify. Let's put them aside for the moment. Let's focus on lawful government access to data, as there is a lot of data available that will inform our risk calculations for this threat. Note that the scenario is quite different if an organization is being investigated itself for criminal acts versus being asked to produce data they control for an investigation not related to them. I'll focus on the latter scenario, as I'm not qualified to offer advice on the former. The question we want to try to answer is, in the context of government access to data, what is the incremental risk of adding a particular vendor or vendor's service to our supply chain or IT portfolio? Put another way, since there already is a risk that law enforcement will ask organizations directly for access to data that they control, we want to figure out what the increased risk is of adding a service provider's product(s) to their IT portfolio.

Remember that risk is the combination of probability and impact; that is, the probability of a specific threat being realized and the impact on the organization if it is realized. There are several different ways to calculate risk. Some of the organizations I've discussed risk management with use a quantitative approach to calculate risk where they try to assign numeric values to the probability and impact sides of the risk equation. Other organizations I've talked to use a qualitative approach to calculate risk in a way that doesn't assign numeric values to probability and impact; they use risk categories instead, such as low, medium, and high.

Some organizations use a combination of qualitative and quantitative approaches. Whatever approach your organization uses, it is likely going to be better than not using a risk-based approach at all. You might have to iterate to find which approach works best for your organization if it hasn't already adopted one. Ultimately, these approaches help determine which risks have the highest combined probability and impact on the organization.

Determining the potential impact of a court order demanding the production of specific data that an organization controls, related to a criminal investigation, will likely require the expertise of the organization's General Counsel and legal team. For an enterprise-sized public or private sector organization, chances are their legal team has already managed such requests in the past and this risk isn't new to them, even if it's the first time the CISO has contemplated it. I have found that legal teams rarely copy CISOs into such matters unless there is some compelling reason to do so. This is why most CISOs are unaware that their organization already processes law enforcement requests for information. Many of the CISOs I've advised had no idea their legal departments had received such requests in the past and were operating on the assumption that this was a new risk to the organization, but senior management teams have been managing all sorts of risks since the day the company or agency was formed. Even if the organization has never received a request for information from a law enforcement agency, the legal team is typically the team that will manage such requests and has the best insights into the potential impact on the organization. The legal team is the best place to start when determining the potential impact of a warrant or subpoena. Depending on the type of organization, the business that they are in, and the nature of the request, it might also be prudent to get the advice of Public relations experts as well, if there could be a potential impact on the reputation or brand of the company. Only your organization can really evaluate and understand the impact that these requests could have.

On the probability side of the risk equation, this is where industry transparency reports and information request reports are valuable. Most top-tier technology companies publish reports that give their customers visibility into the volume of warrants, subpoenas, national security letters, and other court orders that they receive. They do this because it helps their customers understand the risk of lawful government access to data associated with using their products and services. Here is a list of some of the transparency reports published by major vendors.

- Adobe Law Enforcement Requests: `https://www.adobe.com/legal/lawenforcementrequests/transparency.html`
- Amazon Information Request Reports: `https://aws.amazon.com/compliance/amazon-information-requests/`

- Apple Transparency Report: `https://www.apple.com/legal/transparency/`
- Cisco Transparency and Law Enforcement Requests for Customer Data: `https://www.cisco.com/c/en/us/about/trust-center/transparency.html`
- Meta (Facebook) Transparency Report: `https://transparency.facebook.com/government-data-requests`
- Google Requests for User Information: `https://transparencyreport.google.com/user-data/overview`
- Microsoft Law Enforcement Requests Report: `https://www.microsoft.com/en-us/corporate-responsibility/law-enforcement-requests-report`

These vendors should be commended for listening to their customers and for their transparency. Google has published an interesting "history of transparency" on their website: `https://transparencyreport.google.com/about`.

For vendors that don't publish this data, it is difficult to estimate the probability side of the risk equation related to using their products; it can be difficult to manage something you cannot measure. If your organization is using managed service providers, have they been providing you with similar reports on the volume of court orders they have been receiving? Remember, many of these managed service providers, especially the big providers that have been in the industry for decades, are likely subject to US jurisdiction just like the US-based hyper-scale CSPs are. If lawful access to data is a risk that your organization is interested in understanding, you should ask all the vendors in your supply chain for data that helps you understand and manage it.

Before I dive into some of the data in these reports, you'll need some definitions so that you can understand what the data in these reports means. There are no industry standards about the kind of data to publish and how it should be reported, but many of these reports include data that is similar.

First, there are the concepts of "content" and "non-content." In this context, content means the contents of a file that is created and/or owned by the vendor's customer. Some examples include the content of an e-mail, a picture, a spreadsheet, a document, and so on. Law enforcement might request the contents of a specific email as I described earlier in the chapter. They might request a specific document or picture. It's the contents of the file that they are interested in for their investigation. This is typically referred to as "data," "content," or "user content" in these industry transparency reports.

Many times, law enforcement investigators don't know that a specific file even exists or that a suspect even has an account for a particular online service. Since they aren't omniscient and they can't lawfully request unfettered access to an online service to check if the suspect has an account, they must submit a request via a warrant, subpoena, or court order with the service provider. The answer to this type of request doesn't involve user content. The request is limited to account details such as when the account was opened, the name and address associated with the account, billing information, and other account details. This is typically referred to as "non-content" or "meta-data" in industry reports. Note that some information you might think should be considered content is categorized by the law as meta-data. For example, the "to" and "from" fields in an email are considered non-content. This information is contained in the header of an email, like the envelope that a physical letter is posted in, and isn't considered confidential information. After all, it's on the outside of the envelope where anyone that can see the envelope can see addresses printed on it.

Many of these reports provide aggregate numbers such as the total number of law enforcement requests they received in a specified period of time, typically a half year or quarter, and the number of times or percentage of cases where this content was provided to law enforcement. The number of requests received and the number of accounts those requests impacted can be different. For this reason, some of these reports also contain the number of accounts that were impacted. Some of these reports also provide a breakdown of the number of requests that were rejected or only partially fulfilled. Some of the vendors provide a breakdown of the number of warrants, subpoenas, **National Security Letters (NSLs)**, preservation requests, and other court orders they have received.

In these reports, you might see references to national security requests or similar labels; there are generally two types of orders that get lumped into this category, NSLs and **Foreign Intelligence Surveillance Act (FISA)** orders. The US FISA of 1978 and its various amendments are focused on providing law enforcement and intelligence agencies with a mechanism to request court orders to support covert investigations into espionage and terrorism. Since the investigations are covert, court orders that support these investigations require a court that is not open to the public but still has appropriate oversight. The **Foreign Intelligence Surveillance Court (FISC)** reviews applications and the **Foreign Intelligence Surveillance Court of Review (FISCR)** handles appeals (Congressional Research Service, 2021). These courts provide oversight to ensure that the FISA is observed in the collection of intelligence. There is an ongoing debate about the nature of the FISA and the oversight it requires.

The other type of national security order you might see in some industry reports is called an NSL. The FBI and the Executive Branch of the US government can use NSLs to request some limited subscriber data (non-content) as part of national security investigations. Google has published a breakdown of the FISA orders and NSLs it has received, including copies of some lightly redacted NSLs they have received. If you are interested in seeing what an NSL looks like, visit `https://transparencyreport.google.com/user-data/us-national-security`. Microsoft also breaks out FISA orders and NSLs into separate reports from the normal law enforcement requests they receive. You can see this data here: `https://www.microsoft.com/en-us/corporate-responsibility/us-national-security-orders-report`. US authorities do not permit vendors to publish the exact number of FISA orders or NSLs that they receive; they can only publish ranges such as 0-499 or 500-999. There is a mandatory 6-month delay, after which the newest data can be published. Presumably, they take these precautions so that foreign purveyors of espionage or terrorist organizations are not able to reverse engineer how many court orders are issued or get any clues about investigations.

The volume of law enforcement requests

It is helpful to understand how many law enforcement requests vendors receive in order to calculate the probability side of the risk equation. *Figure 7.5* provides the total number of law enforcement requests from around the world submitted to each vendor, not including NSLs, FISA orders, or non-account related requests such as requests for information on mobile devices. The period covered is the first half of 2018 (1H18) to the first half of 2021 (1H21). The sources of data for this table are the transparency reports, law enforcement requests reports, and so on that each vendor has published on their public website (Apple, n.d.; Amazon, n.d.; Google, n.d.; Meta, n.d.; Microsoft, n.d.).

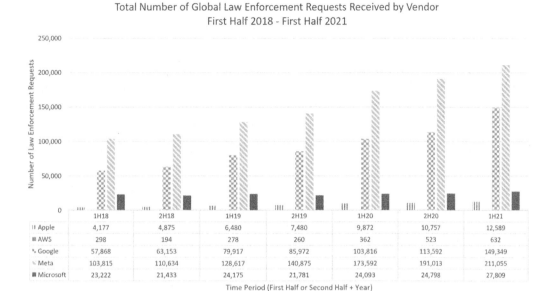

Total Number of Global Law Enforcement Requests Received by Vendor
First Half 2018 - First Half 2021

	1H18	2H18	1H19	2H19	1H20	2H20	1H21
Apple	4,177	4,875	6,480	7,480	9,872	10,757	12,589
AWS	298	194	278	260	362	523	632
Google	57,868	63,153	79,917	85,972	103,816	113,592	149,349
Meta	103,815	110,634	128,617	140,875	173,592	191,013	211,055
Microsoft	23,222	21,433	24,175	21,781	24,093	24,798	27,809

Time Period (First Half or Second Half + Year)

Apple AWS Google Meta Microsoft

Figure 7.5: Total number of law enforcement requests from around the world each vendor
reported receiving in each 6-month period between the first half of 2018 (1H18) and the first
half of 2021 (1H21) (Apple, n.d.; Amazon, n.d.; Google, n.d.; (Meta n.d.); Microsoft, n.d.)

There are some big differences in the number of requests that each of these vendors received. Vendors that operate popular consumer communications systems, like email, chat, and social media, appear to have received more law enforcement requests on average. This could be because two-way communications mechanisms like these enable law enforcement to connect victims and perpetrators, and criminals with other criminals, during their investigations.

As you can see from this data, with a few exceptions, the volume of law enforcement requests increased over time. I think this trend was predictable. I expect the number of law enforcement information requests submitted to service providers, not just US-based providers, to continue to increase over time. People and organizations are becoming more reliant on online services. More people are using these services and they are using a greater number of services for a growing number of purposes – a trend that will likely continue. At the same time, more and more law enforcement agencies around the world are learning that suspects in their criminal investigations are using online services more and they might contain evidence when crimes are committed. As I mentioned earlier, many governments around the world have been working on ways to make it easier for law enforcement to get lawful access to data regardless of where it is stored. All these factors lead me to believe that the volume of requests from law enforcement across the industry will likely continue to increase over time. This simply reflects that everywhere around the world, societies are moving online, and criminals are coming with them.

We are kind of comparing apples and oranges in *Figure 7.5*. Although it is helpful to understand the total volume of law enforcement requests that each vendor receives, counting requests for data in consumer services isn't the same as requests for enterprise data. This contrast is clear when comparing the volume of requests that a consumer service company like Meta receives with that of AWS, which serves the private and public sectors almost exclusively. In the first half of 2021, AWS received 0.3% of the volume of requests that Meta received. Remember, CISOs are concerned about law enforcement requests for their organizations' data, which is not the same as requests for pictures, emails, and texts for criminal investigations focused on crimes that consumers are involved in. Put another way, we want to understand the probability that one of these vendors receives a request for enterprise data. To do this more precisely, we shouldn't count requests for consumer data as part of that probability calculation.

I've seen European-based vendors weaponize these numbers in an effort to compete with the big US-based technology companies. They'll point at the relatively large volume of law enforcement requests that Meta receives and paint the entire US technology industry with that brush. Listening to their pitch, you could believe that every company in Silicon Valley provided the US government with unfettered access to data. Of course, this is not true. However, it is easier for Western European executives to buy into this view because of the erosion of trust in the US that I discussed earlier. If it was suddenly revealed that the head of your country's government was spied on for years by one of your closest allies, how would you feel? However, executives, CISOs, and security team members need to ask themselves whether they really need to be concerned with US-based consumer services as part of their own risk calculations.

Do they plan to store their enterprise data on Facebook? They need to get specific about the threats and risks to their organization's data and not be distracted by claims that the entire high-tech industry in the US is somehow corrupted. This polarized view isn't helpful in managing risk for private or public sector organizations.

Breaking the data down to provide the number of requests submitted on a country-by-country basis is another pivot that some vendors offer in their transparency reports. The more detail they provide in their reports, the more accurate risk estimates can be. For example, many of the CISOs I have talked to don't care if their own country sends their vendors requests for information – it's really only the US requests they are concerned about.

Additionally, many CISOs aren't overly concerned about non-content data because they consider such data as publicly available or easily discoverable, like an email address, for example. If they can determine the number of requests made by US law enforcement where content was produced, that gives them a good insight into the specific threat that they are concerned about.

The probability of US law enforcement accessing data in the cloud

At this point, let's look at how we can use this data to understand the probability side of the risk equation. Let's use a real-world example. In this example, a CIO of a company based in Germany wants to understand the risk of adding US-based hyper-scale CSPs' services to their current portfolio of on-premises IT. The CIO is worried that using US-based service providers will make it easier for the US government to get access to their data. Let's help this CIO get a better idea of the probability side of the risk equation. Since the CIO is adamant that they are only concerned about requests from the US, we'll only include those requests in our calculation. The CIO isn't planning to use consumer-grade services to process, store, or transmit their organization's data, so we'll only focus on hyper-scale CSPs that provide services for enterprise customers. These CSPs include AWS, Google, and Microsoft.

Let's start with the global total number of requests received by the three CSPs this CIO is interested in. Again, these numbers do not include national security orders like NSLs or FISA orders. The number of law enforcement requests received by Google was significantly larger than the other CSPs. Presumably, many of these requests focused on potential evidence stored in Google's Gmail email service and Google search results, both of which are used heavily by consumers.

Microsoft also provides the Outlook consumer email service and Bing for internet searches.

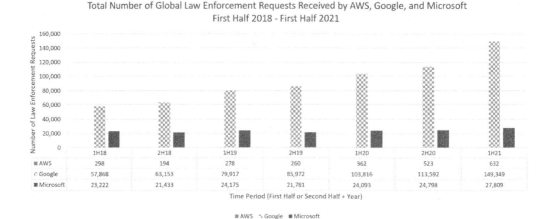

Figure 7.6: Total number of law enforcement requests from around the world submitted to select US-based CSPs between the first half of 2018 (1H18) and the first half of 2021 (1H21) from law enforcement agencies around the world (Amazon, n.d.; Google, n.d.; Microsoft, n.d.)

Now, let's remove the requests made by law enforcement agencies outside of the US. *Figure 7.7* reflects all the requests made by US law enforcement during the same time scales. Notice how much smaller the graph's scale and these numbers are compared to the previous figure. This reveals that there is a significant volume of requests that come from law enforcement agencies outside the US. Many executives I advised believed that the US was the only country that made such requests.

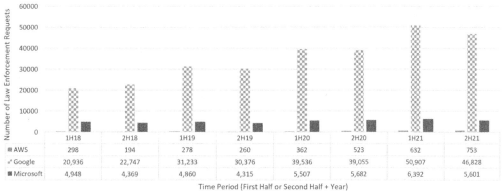

Figure 7.7: Total number of US law enforcement requests submitted to AWS, Google, and Microsoft between the first half of 2018 (1H18) and the second half of 2021 (2H21) (Amazon, n.d.; Google, n.d.; Microsoft, n.d.)

Now, let's only include the requests where content was potentially provided to the requesting law enforcement agency. I removed the requests that were non-content-related, rejected or invalid, or where no data was found. This takes a little analysis because these vendors report this data in different ways. This gives us an estimate of the raw number of requests from US law enforcement agencies where content was requested using a valid warrant or court order, and some content was provided.

Notice again that the scale of the graph is smaller than previous graphs and the volumes of requests are lower.

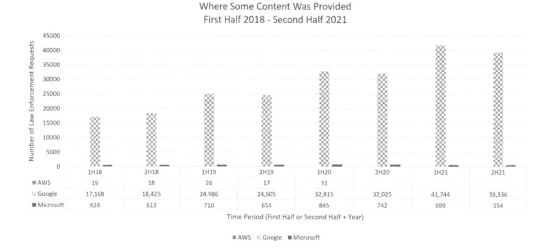

Figure 7.8: Total number of US law enforcement requests submitted to AWS, Google, and Microsoft where some content was provided between the first half of 2018 (1H18) and the second half of 2021 (2H21) (Amazon, n.d.; Google, n.d.; Microsoft, n.d.)

Figure 7.8 shows us the volume of US law enforcement requests received by these CSPs where content was disclosed to authorities. As a percentage of all US requests sent to Microsoft during this period, 10% to 15% resulted in content disclosures. Google reported that the percentage of requests they received during this period where some information was disclosed ranged from 80% to 84%.

The AWS request counts in *Figure 7.8* are based on data published in the Amazon Information Request Reports for periods including 2018, 2019, and the first half of 2020. In these reports, Amazon provides definitions for different types of law enforcement demands they receive, including search warrants.

> *"Search warrants may be issued by local, state, or federal courts upon a showing of probable cause and must specifically identify the place to be searched and the items to be seized. We may produce non-content and content information in response to valid and binding search warrants. Amazon objects to overbroad or otherwise inappropriate search warrants as a matter of course." (Amazon, 2018)*

The request counts in *Figure 7.8* are based on "full response" and "partial response" counts for search warrants received from local, state, and federal courts in the US as published by Amazon. Using these figures, we can get an estimate of the number of times content was disclosed to law enforcement. These figures might include cases where AWS was asked for content, but instead only provided non-content (meta-data). The Amazon Information Request reports published between 2018 and the first half of 2020 don't provide enough detail to get more specific than that. During the 5 6-month periods between 2018 and the first half of 2020, these cases represented between 7% and 10% of all US requests AWS received. Amazon changed the format of its reports in the second half of 2020 and newly published reports no longer include these figures, as reflected in *Figure 7.8*. However, for the second half of 2020 and both halves of 2021, they do include the total number of all law enforcement requests (globally) that resulted in the "disclosure of content information" (Amazon, 2021). Although it's not specific to US law enforcement like the Google and Microsoft data is, this data still provides some insight into the frequency that content is disclosed to law enforcement. The number of cases where content was disclosed as a result of a valid law enforcement request was between 2% and 3% of all requests (3% in 2H20, 2% in 1H21, and 2.4% in 2H21) (Amazon, n.d.).

We can continue to analyze this law enforcement request and disclosure data in at least a couple of different ways in order to get even more precise probability estimates for our risk calculations. For example, where the data is available, we can focus on the number of law enforcement requests that these CSPs received for enterprise customers only. This might provide the CIO in our scenario with the best estimate of the probability that these CSPs will receive a request for their enterprise data.

Google started publishing data specifically on law enforcement requests for enterprise customers in 2019 as part of their transparency report on a web page called "Enterprise cloud requests for customer information" (Google, n.d.). *Figure 7.9* provides the number of requests from US law enforcement that involved Google enterprise cloud customers only. The figure also provides the percentage of these requests that resulted in some content being disclosed.

Like Microsoft, Google reports the number of national security requests separately – so they aren't included in these figures.

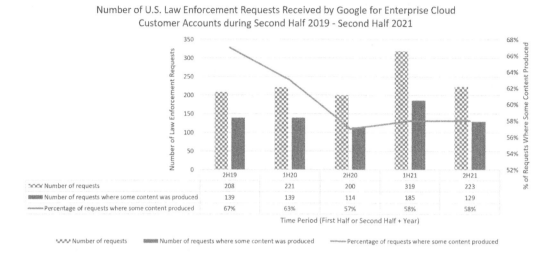

Figure 7.9: *The number of US law enforcement requests that involve only Google enterprise cloud customers and the percentage of requests where enterprise cloud customer information was disclosed (Google, n.d.)*

Figure 7.9 reveals much smaller volumes of requests once all the law enforcement requests for Google consumer accounts are removed and only Google enterprise cloud customer requests are visible. For example, in the second half of 2021, there were a total of 46,828 US law enforcement requests, which resulted in data being shared in 84% of those requests (Google, n.d.). Of these requests, only 223 involved Google enterprise cloud customers, resulting in content being disclosed 58% of the time (Google, n.d.).

Microsoft and AWS do not appear to publish the same information as Google in their respective transparency reports. However, in the case of AWS, the vast majority of its customers are enterprises. They focus on providing cloud services to private and public sector organizations, not consumers. Presumably, the majority of the volume of requests they receive involve enterprise customers, although AWS does not state what types of customers law enforcement requests involve in the Amazon Information Request Reports covering the period between 2018 and the first half of 2020 (Amazon, n.d.). *Figure 7.10* is based on data from these reports and shows us the number of requests from US law enforcement that AWS received, along with the percentage of cases where a partial or full response was provided. Again, the number of cases where content was potentially disclosed is estimated using the "partial response" and "full response" figures published by AWS. The actual numbers could be smaller.

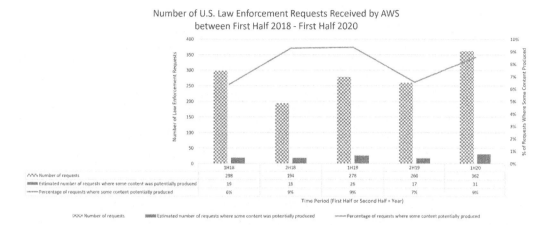

Figure 7.10: The number of US law enforcement requests that AWS received and the percentage of requests where a partial or full response was provided, for the period between 2018 and the first half of 2020 (Amazon, n.d.)

What about the volume of US law enforcement requests that Microsoft receives, where they were compelled to disclose enterprise customer content? Microsoft answers this question in the FAQ section of their Law Enforcement Requests Report.

> *"In the second half of 2021, Microsoft received 120 requests from law enforcement around the world for accounts associated with enterprise cloud customers. In 65 cases, these requests were rejected, withdrawn, no data, or law enforcement was successfully redirected to the customer. In 55 cases, Microsoft was compelled to provide responsive information: 29 of these cases required the disclosure of some customer content and in 26 of the cases we were compelled to disclose non-content information only. Of the 29 instances that required disclosure of content data, 26 of those requests were associated with US law enforcement." (Microsoft, n.d.)*

Based on this information and other information in the same report, 25,182 requests were made by law enforcement agencies around the world in the second half of 2021. Of these, only 120 requests (0.5%) were associated with enterprise cloud customers. Microsoft was compelled to disclose enterprise customer content to US authorities in 26 of these cases. This means that enterprise customer content was disclosed to US authorities in 0.1% of all the requests Microsoft received in the second half of 2021.

There is one more piece of information that could help the CIO of the German-based company understand the probability of US government access to data. The CIO doesn't really care how many requests US law enforcement makes for content that US-based companies hold because it's clear that US-based companies are under the jurisdiction of US law enforcement agencies. This CIO would like to understand the number of requests US law enforcement makes for data held outside the US in Germany, the EU, and the EEA, where some customer content is disclosed. These figures could be one of the best inputs for their risk calculations associated with adding a US-based CSP to their existing IT operations. Fortunately for the CIO, AWS and Microsoft provide data that answers this question.

AWS started publishing the following question in the **Frequently Asked Questions (FAQs)** section of their Amazon Information Request Reports in the second half of 2020 when their report format was updated. "How many requests resulted in the disclosure to the U.S. government of enterprise content data located outside the United States?" (Amazon, 2021) *Figure 7.11* provides the answers that AWS specified for each 6-month period between the second half of 2020 and the first half of 2022. To summarize, AWS did not disclose enterprise content data located outside the US to the US government during the 24 months between the second half of 2020 (2H20) and the first half of 2022 (1H22).

Time Period	Answer
1H22	"None"
2H21	"None"
1H21	"None"
2H20	"None"

Figure 7.11: AWS's answer to the question "How many requests resulted in the disclosure to the US government of enterprise content data located outside the United States?" for each 6-month period between the second half of 2020 and the first half of 2022 (Amazon, n.d.)

Microsoft published the following item in the FAQ section of their Law Enforcement Requests Report, "Number of warrants from U.S. law enforcement resulting in disclosure of enterprise content data stored outside the United States." (Microsoft, n.d.) *Figure 7.12* provides the associated data from these reports for each 6-month period between the first half of 2020 and the second half of 2021. These figures represent between 0.02% and 0.05% of the total number of US law enforcement requests during these periods.

Time Period	Answer	Total US Requests	% of Total
2H21	3	5,601	0.05
1H21	2	6,392	0.03
2H20	1	5,682	0.02
1H20	2	5,507	0.04

Figure 7.12: Microsoft's answer to the question "Number of warrants from US law enforcement resulting in disclosure of enterprise content data stored outside the United States" for each 6-month period between the first half of 2020 (1H20) and the second half of 2021 (2H21), includes the percentage of the total number of requests each answer represents (Microsoft, n.d.)

Also, in the FAQ section of their Law Enforcement Requests Report, Microsoft provides some context on the volume of CLOUD Act requests they received, which presumably is already reflected in *Figure 7.12*.

> *"In the second half of 2021, Microsoft received 5,601 legal demands for consumer data from law enforcement in the United States. Of those, 136 warrants sought content data which was stored outside of the United States.*
>
> *In the same time frame, Microsoft received 90 legal demands from law enforcement in the United States for commercial enterprise customers who purchased more than 50 seats. Of those demands, 3 warrants resulted in disclosure of content data related to a non-US enterprise customer whose data was stored outside of the United States." (Microsoft, n.d.)*

This data will give the CIO of the German company some confidence that the frequency at which US law enforcement targets foreign companies and public sector organizations with warrants and court orders is truly anomalous. This data will help inform the probability side of their risk calculations related to leveraging US-based CSPs. Additionally, this data enables the CIO to recognize vendors who try to spread fear, uncertainty, and doubt about US law enforcement accessing data in the cloud. Now that we have some insight into the volume of law enforcement requests, the CIO still wants to understand the volume of US intelligence agencies' national security orders that these three US-based CSPs receive. Let's examine this next.

The GDPR, FISA Section 702, and Schrems II

If you live in the US, you might wonder why the CIO of a highly regarded company in Germany would be concerned about US NSLs and FISA orders. After all, if the CIO's firm isn't involved in terrorism, money laundering to fund terrorism, or espionage, why would they be concerned with US laws established to surveil such activities?

The answer to this question is a bit complicated, but I'll try to summarize the situation which means I'll be glossing over a lot of detail. The GDPR regulates the cross-border transfer of personal information outside of the EU and the EEA. I've heard many American executives state that the GDPR doesn't apply to them because they don't do business in the EU or EEA. However, the GDPR is extra-territorial, meaning it doesn't just regulate data transfer between EU member states – it applies worldwide. It applies to both the commercial sector and the public sector. Subsequently, many countries have enacted their own similar local versions of the GDPR to ensure their industries comply with it.

It is important to understand the purpose of the GDPR is to enable cross-border commerce while protecting people's personal information. Some of the security professionals in the US I've discussed the GDPR with assume it tries to prevent the transfer of data, but its purpose is to regulate the transfer of data.

> "Directive 95/46/EC of the European Parliament and of the Council seeks to harmonise the protection of fundamental rights and freedoms of natural persons in respect of processing activities and to ensure the free flow of personal data between Member States." (The European Parliament and The Council Of The European Union, 2016)

Under the GDPR, the transfer of the personal data of EU data subjects to countries outside the EEA (called third countries) is not permitted, unless specific requirements are met, or the third country has a GDPR "adequacy decision." Data can be transferred between the EEA and the third country without any extra safeguards when the third country has an adequacy decision. The adequacy decision indicates that the third country has levels of data protection and privacy that meet the EU's standards. Currently, only 15 countries in the world have one of these adequacy decisions. You can see the list of countries with adequacy decisions on the European Commission's website: https://ec.europa.eu/info/law/law-topic/data-protection/international-dimension-data-protection/adequacy-decisions_en/.

The other two ways that EU data subject personal information could be transferred out of the EEA were **Standard Contractual Clauses (SCCs)** and the EU-US Privacy Shield. Failure to comply with the GDPR could lead to administrative fines of up to €20 million or 4% of the organization's annual worldwide revenue from the previous year, whichever of these is larger; this gives this regulation enough potential bite to garner a lot of attention. Subsequently, every private sector and public sector customer I advised in Europe after May 2018, when enforcement of the GDPR started, wanted to discuss the best practices for complying with the GDPR. Since then, there have been hundreds of GDPR administrative fines imposed. So far, the largest GDPR administrative fine was an estimated $887,000,000 (Business Insider, 2021). American big tech companies including Amazon, Instagram, WhatsApp, Google, and Facebook were levied some of the largest fines – tens of millions of dollars and, in some cases, hundreds of millions (Cohen, 2022).

In July 2020, the **Court of Justice of the European Union (CJEU)** invalidated the adequacy decision that under-pinned the EU-US Privacy Shield. Until that time, the Privacy Shield was used as a legal framework to facilitate cross-border data transfers of EU data subject personal data for commercial uses between the EU and the US. By following the Privacy Shield program's data protection requirements, program participants' data transfers would be deemed compliant with EU law. The CJEU's legal decision to invalidate the Privacy Shield is referred to as Schrems II, named after the Austrian lawyer who filed the complaint against Facebook that led to the court's ruling, known as Data Protection Commissioner v. Facebook Ireland Limited, Maximillian Schrems. The CJEU's ruling found,

> "...Privacy Shield inadequate in part because it does not restrain U.S. intelligence authorities' data collection activities. According to the CJEU, U.S. law allows intelligence agencies to collect and use the personal data transferred under the Privacy Shield framework in a manner that is inconsistent with rights guaranteed under EU law. The CJEU focused on Section 702 of the Foreign Intelligence Surveillance Act, Executive Order 12333, and Presidential Policy Directive 28, which govern how the U.S. government may conduct surveillance of non-U.S. persons located outside of the United States." (Congressional Research Service, 2021)

The court's finding directly referenced FISA Section 702 and Executive Order 12333. You might be wondering what these have to do with the GDPR and data transfers. The NSA describes FISA Section 702 this way,

"In general, Section 702 authorizes the Attorney General and Director of National Intelligence to make and submit to the FISA Court written certifications for the purpose of acquiring foreign intelligence information. Upon the issuance of an order by the FISA Court approving such a certification and the use of targeting and minimization procedures, the Attorney General and Director of National Intelligence may jointly authorize for up to one year the targeting of non-United States persons reasonably believed to be located overseas to acquire foreign intelligence information." (National Security Agency/Central Security Service, n.d.)

One issue that the CJEU cited was, "Section 702's limitations on judicial remedies for EU citizens as falling short of the GDPR's requirements" (Congressional Research Service, 2021). That is, in some circumstances, FISA Section 702 could permit secret surveillance with no opportunity for judicial review for EU citizens. For example, if US authorities decided to use the evidence collected from FISA Section 702 surveillance to prosecute a non-US person for a crime, that person and their attorneys would, at some point, be given notice that this surveillance took place and be confronted with the evidence collected (Congressional Research Service, 2021). The court could then review the surveillance and its lawfulness – but if the authorities decided not to prosecute the target of the surveillance for a related crime, the target would likely never know they had been under surveillance and would not have an opportunity to request judicial review of the surveillance and the personal information collected. The CJEU also found that EU citizens did not have enforceable rights under Executive Order 12333 and that it didn't include sufficient protections to limit surveillance to a reasonable scope (Congressional Research Service, 2021).

With the EU-US Privacy Shield invalidated and no adequacy decision for the US, only SCCs remain to protect organizations that transfer the personal data of EEA data subjects outside the EEA. SCCs are contractual clauses that include EU pre-approved clauses that impose data protection standards on the organizations that use them. However, the technical implementation of the rather vague data protection standards and requirements in SCCs leaves their legal efficacy open to interpretation. This uncertainty leaves some organizations uncomfortable with using SCCs as the legal means to transfer the personal data of EEA data subjects outside the EEA. Keep in mind, for many of these organizations, the decision to use SCCs represents up to €20 million or 4% of their annual worldwide revenue in potential GDPR administrative fines.

This is one reason the CIO of the German company in our scenario, and so many others, are concerned about the risk that US national security orders pose to their organizations. Under the CJEU's current interpretation, FISA Section 702 and Executive Order 12333 do not offer EU data subjects the same rights as US citizens where US intelligence surveillance is concerned. One of the risks envisioned is that if US authorities intercept an EU organization's cross-border data transfers, there is no legal protection for the EU data subjects impacted and it could be a violation of the GDPR for the organization doing the transfer. With the potential of tens of millions of Euros in fines and a ruined reputation across the EEA, many organizations are concerned and paying close attention as the legal landscape shifts around them, subsequently slowing down their adoption of new technologies.

The Edward Snowden and WikiLeaks revelations about US intelligence programs have largely polarized the collective consciousness among Western Europeans. The massive benefits of cross-border commerce with one of the largest commercial markets in the world and intelligence sharing with one of the world's biggest intelligence apparatuses no longer offset the risks the EU perceives in US intelligence data gathering. They also seem to be willing to forgo the undeniable benefits the US-based hyper-scale CSPs' services offer, along with other modern technologies that the US can provide, that can help bring both the European public and private sectors into the future.

This context provides a better understanding of the impact side of the risk equation that organizations face if the aforementioned scenario were realized – a maximum of €20 million or 4% of their annual worldwide revenue and a ruined reputation – but, in this scenario, what does the probability side of the risk equation look like for organizations that add a US-based CSP's services to their existing IT estate? Let's examine this next to help the German CIO we are advising understand both sides of the risk equation.

The Probability of US Intelligence Accessing Data in the Cloud

You might recall that national security orders include NSLs and FISA orders that are lumped into ranges such as 0-499. Let's look at the volume of these requests that Microsoft, Google, and AWS receive.

Microsoft provides some context for why they are only permitted to publish the volume of FISA orders and NSLs in ranges.

> *"Prior to 2014, US technology providers were not allowed to report any information regarding US national security demands. As a result of litigation that Microsoft and other technology companies filed against the US government in 2014, the government agreed for the first time to permit technology companies to publish data about FISA orders. While there remain some constraints on what we can publish, this report presents the most comprehensive, legally permissible picture of the types of requests that we receive from the US government pursuant to national security authorities." (Microsoft, 2021)*

Note that both Microsoft and Google make it clear in their respective reports that NSLs cannot be used to request customer content. Microsoft states,

> *"National Security Letters may require the disclosure of basic subscriber information such as the name, address and length of service of a customer who has subscribed to one of our services. NSLs may not be used to require the disclosure of the content of a customer's communications or data. NSLs may only be used to request basic subscriber information that is relevant to U.S. national security and cannot be used for criminal, civil, or administrative investigations." (Microsoft, 2021)*

Google's description of how NSLs are used, published in their Google Transparency Report, is consistent with Microsoft's. Google described their use this way:

> *"Using a NSL, the FBI can seek "the name, address, length of service, and local and long distance toll billing records" of a subscriber to a wire or electronic communications service. The FBI can't use NSLs to obtain anything else from Google, such as Gmail content, search queries, YouTube videos or user IP addresses." (Google, n.d.)*

Given this, I'll focus this examination on the volume of FISA orders that resulted in the disclosure of some content. Both Microsoft and Google provide the volume of national security requests under the FISA for both content and non-content requests. Let's look at the FISA order content request volumes.

Based on the data published by Microsoft, for each 6-month period starting with the second half of 2011 to the end of the first half of 2014, Microsoft received between 0 and 999 FISA orders seeking disclosure of content. In the 6.5 years between 2015 and the first 6 months of 2021 (the most recent period published), they received between 0 and 499 of these content-seeking orders in each 6-month period (Microsoft, 2021).

Google publishes national security order data in a section of its Transparency Report called "United States national security requests for user information" (Google, n.d.). For the 8 years between 2011 and 2018, Google reports the number of FISA requests for content that they received in each half-year period was between 500 and 999 (Google, n.d.). More recently, in the 2 years between 2019 and the end of 2021, they received between 0 and 499 such requests in each reporting period (Google, n.d.).

AWS publishes the range of the national security requests they receive. In each 6-month period in the 3.5 years between 2018 and the end of the first half of 2022, they reported that AWS received between 0 and 250 requests. They've published the same statement in several of their recent Amazon Information Request Reports: "the reporting range is 0-249 for all national security requests made to Amazon (including AWS)" (Amazon, 2021).

Given these reported figures, it is possible that none of the three US-based CSPs have received a FISA order in recent years. However, because US authorities prohibit vendors from releasing the exact number of FISA orders they receive, we are left with a choice of which figure to use for our risk calculation, whether to use zero or the maximum number in the range. We could simply use the maximum number in each reported range to ensure we don't underestimate the probability.

To calculate the probabilities, let's divide the number of requests by the number of active customers that use these services. It is likely that we won't be able to find exact numbers or even estimates of the number of customers that were actively using each CSP's services during each time period, but since these are some of the biggest high-tech companies in the world, we know anecdotally that they have millions of active enterprise customers each. It is likely that AWS, Google, and Microsoft have many millions of enterprise customers worldwide, but let's purposely use a low number. If we just use 2 million enterprise customers as the base of our division calculation, this will render a higher probability than if we use a larger, more accurate customer base number. This will make it less likely that we underestimate the probabilities.

Figure 7.13 contains the estimated percentages of AWS's enterprise customers impacted by the FISA orders received by AWS in each 6-month period between the first half of 2018 (1H18) and the first half of 2022 (1H22), based on the data published in numerous Amazon Information Request Reports.

The number of enterprise customers used as the base is just an estimate – the actual number could be higher.

Time Period	Max number of FISA orders / number of enterprise customers	Percentage
1H22	249 / 2,000,000	0.0125%
2H21	249 / 2,000,000	0.0125%
1H21	249 / 2,000,000	0.0125%
2H20	249 / 2,000,000	0.0125%
1H20	249 / 2,000,000	0.0125%
2H19	249 / 2,000,000	0.0125%
1H19	249 / 2,000,000	0.0125%
2H18	249 / 2,000,000	0.0125%
1H18	249 / 2,000,000	0.0125%

Figure 7.13: The volume of FISA orders, as reported in the Amazon Information Request Reports from 2018 to the first half of 2022, divided by an estimated base of 2 million enterprise customers, converted into a percentage (Amazon, n.d.)

Figure 7.14 leverages data published in Google's Transparency Report for the period between 2018 and the first half of 2022. The FISA orders in the figure are those that were seeking content. The calculation, using 2 million customers as a base, provides an estimated percentage of those Google customers potentially impacted by FISA orders seeking content. The actual number of Google customers is likely much higher.

Time Period	Max number of FISA orders / number of enterprise customers	Percentage
1H22	499 / 2,000,000	0.025%
2H21	499 / 2,000,000	0.025%
1H21	499 / 2,000,000	0.025%
2H20	499 / 2,000,000	0.025%
1H20	499 / 2,000,000	0.025%
2H19	499 / 2,000,000	0.025%
1H19	499 / 2,000,000	0.025%
2H18	999 / 2,000,000	0.050%
1H18	999 / 2,000,000	0.050%

Figure 7.14 The volume of FISA orders seeking content, as reported in the Google Transparency Report from the first half of 2018 (1H18) to the first half of 2022 (1H22), divided by an estimated base of 2 million customers, converted into a percentage (Google, n.d.)

The percentages of an estimated 2 million Microsoft customers who were potentially impacted by FISA orders between 2018 and the end of the first half of 2021 are provided in *Figure 7.15*. The number of customers is a purposely low estimate, while the FISA order data is provided by Microsoft's US National Security Orders Report (Microsoft, 2021).

Time Period	Max number of FISA orders / number of enterprise customers	Percentage
1H21	499 / 2,000,000	0.025%
2H20	499 / 2,000,000	0.025%
1H20	499 / 2,000,000	0.025%
2H19	499 / 2,000,000	0.025%
1H19	499 / 2,000,000	0.025%
2H18	499 / 2,000,000	0.025%
1H18	499 / 2,000,000	0.025%

Figure 7.15: The volume of FISA orders seeking content, as reported in Microsoft's National Se-curity Orders Report, between the first half of 2018 (1H18) to the first half of 2021 (1H21), divided by an estimated base of 2 million customers, converted into a percentage (Microsoft, 2021)

As the data in these three figures illustrates, in the most recent time periods for which we have data, the estimated probability of realizing the threat of US authorities using FISA orders to get access to content from the three US-based hyper-scale CSPs is between 0.0125% and 0.05%. If we had an accurate number of active users, these percentages would likely be even smaller. For example, at one point Microsoft disclosed that they had 20 million users actively using their Teams service (Spataro, 2019). If we used this user base as the denominator in our calculation, the percentages of the Microsoft customers impacted would be much smaller (0.002495%). If we made similar tweaks to Google's and AWS's user bases in our calculations, their respective probability percentages would be lower than my estimates.

You might be wondering if these probabilities are good or bad. What do we tell the CIO of the German company we are advising? The answer really depends on two things. First, since the risk is the combination of probability and impact, the CIO needs to discuss the potential impact with their General Counsel and legal team. Remember that some threats can be super-low-probability, but if they are realized, the impact can be high. Although the probability of both US law enforcement requests and FISA orders is very low, the CIO really needs to understand the potential impact on their organization. A 0.0125% probability of a potential maximum fine equivalent to €20 million or 4% of annual revenue might still be too high of a risk for organizations that are extremely risk-averse. Some of the executives I met in Western Europe told me that *any chance* that their organizations' reputations could be tarnished was too high. Put another way, if the probability wasn't zero, it was unacceptable to them. Of course, risk decisions need to be made on an organization-by-organization basis.

Keep in mind that voluntarily putting dramatic restrictions on the ability of organizations, industries, or groups of countries to compete or fulfill their charter effectively also has associated risks and consequences.

There are opportunity costs for not taking risks in life. In the case of the EEA and cloud computing, instead of being at the forefront of new technologies as they have been for decades, they are at risk of being left behind. These tiny probabilities related to FISA orders are slowing the adoption of new technologies and subsequently slowing progress everywhere new technologies could be leveraged.

The second factor to consider when interpreting these probability figures is that risks are relative. Most organizations have limited resources, so they must prioritize their investments. This applies to managing risk too. The CIO of the German company should stack rank US law enforcement requests and FISA order risks with all the other risks that their organization has identified. These risks likely include financial risks, economic risks, legal risks, HR risks, other cybersecurity risks like ransomware, and many others. Stack ranking each threat by its probability and impact on the organization will help the CIO identify which risks the organization needs to prioritize. Some organizations use limits or thresholds (anything above a specified risk score) to determine which risks will be mitigated and which risks are accepted. If the risk of lawful government access to data is a priority risk for the organization, then the CISO, security team, and legal team should identify a list of possible mitigations and their costs to the organization. The company's risk management stakeholder community or board can then decide whether to mitigate the risk, try to transfer it somehow, or accept it. This risk management decision should be revisited periodically to determine if any changes are prudent based on new information or changing circumstances.

There are some organizations that are legally required to prevent all forms of unauthorized access to their data, including requests from law enforcement and intelligence agency requests. These organizations typically have sovereign immunity. These include law enforcement agencies, intelligence agencies, national security agencies, arms of the military, and organizations responsible for the economies of nations like federal reserves, judiciaries, and so on. There are also commercial sector companies that must protect their most sensitive intellectual property, trade secrets, and customer information, or they face extinction. However, the vast majority of private and public sector organizations I've talked to over the years won't spend extra time or resources trying to mitigate government access to data because they have higher priority risks to mitigate using the resources they have. Most organizations simply accept the risk of government access to data because it's much lower than other risks that they face. After all, you rarely see news reports that a company went out of business after receiving a request for specific data in their possession for a criminal investigation unrelated to the company itself – but you do see headlines nearly every week about ransomware crippling organizations and costing them millions.

Despite the near-zero probabilities associated with lawful access to data, it is a risk that some organizations still choose to mitigate. Let's look at what this entails.

Mitigating government access to data

The security controls used to mitigate lawful government access to data might or might not also be effective in mitigating unlawful government access to data and signals intelligence threat scenarios; it's difficult to determine with so little insight and publicly available data on these activities. However, from a cybersecurity strategy perspective, all three of these scenarios essentially represent the same type of threat – the threat of unauthorized access to data. For security professionals, this is a simple but powerful construct. Many of the same controls they are already familiar with will help mitigate unauthorized access to data regardless of who is trying to access it.

The CIO of the German company we have been advising in this chapter now understands how low the probability of US government access to data is. The CIO is surprised that the probability estimates are so low, given all the negative press and concern this topic garners in the EU. However, in an abundance of caution, the company wants to take extra measures to reduce this probability even further. Next, we'll step through some high-level guidance that will help the CIO's company further mitigate the risk of US government access to data when they leverage US-based CSPs' services.

Setting and understanding the scope

Getting specific about the data you are trying to protect is crucial. Trying to protect *some* data or *all* data is a theoretical or academic exercise. I have discussed this with so many CISOs and executives who initially refused to pivot from their emotional, theoretical objections to real-world solutions. Walking them through the data from transparency reports and the associated probability calculations typically helped take the emotion out of these conversations. If you *really* want to protect data from unauthorized access, identifying the specific data that needs to be protected is a crucial first step. The smaller the scope, the better chance you have of success. However, developing a repeatable pattern from this exercise that can be applied to other larger datasets is a best practice.

Identify how this target data flows through your organization, including through its supply chain. This involves identifying where and how the target data is transmitted, stored, and processed on your network and third-party networks that your organization leverages. Understanding these data flows enables you to apply people, processes, and technologies to protect against and detect unauthorized access attempts and respond as quickly and efficiently as possible.

Typically, this is a challenging task with complicated legacy solutions running in large complex IT environments, but protecting the target data effectively isn't possible without first understanding how it flows. Again, get as specific as possible when identifying all storage, networks, databases, and compute resources that are involved in the target data flows. Once target data flows are well understood, you can develop a plan to address any gaps where the target data is not appropriately protected.

For organizations that already have effective security development practices, this work might have already been completed as part of the application development process. A very effective early step in a security development life cycle is the development of a threat model. A former Microsoft co-worker of mine, Adam Shostack, wrote an excellent book on this topic that I recommend reading: *Threat Modeling: Designing for Security* (Shostack, 2014).

Setting realistic objectives

An important part of planning is to set objectives. In this case, the CIO has set a realistic objective for mitigating government access to data: ensure all access to the target data is first approved by the company's own access request processes. For governments potentially seeking access to the target data, this means ensuring the only course of action they have is to come through the company's front doors in the light of day with a valid court order so that the company's General Counsel and legal team can manage their requests. Remember, your organization's legal team and outside counsel are the best mitigations against lawful requests for data. Your legal team should ensure court orders are valid and binding, and challenge orders that are overbroad.

However, they can't manage target data access requests that they aren't aware of. If government requests go to an organization's supply chain partners instead of directly to them, the government could get access to the target data without giving the organization any opportunity to oppose that action. This is the reason so many CISOs outside the US are concerned with US law enforcement requests that have gag orders attached and FISA orders issued by a secret court.

Still, CISOs and executives that attempt to mitigate a risk with a probability of 0.025% (or lower) by simply refusing to use US-based CSP services pay severely disproportionate opportunity costs because their organizations give up using cloud services that are likely 5 to 10 years ahead of what they can possibly accomplish in their legacy on-premises IT environments. I'll discuss this in more depth in *Chapter 12, Modern Approaches to Security and Compliance*.

Security professionals can't prevent governments from making lawful requests for their target data, but they can do their best to ensure such requests must go directly to their organizations instead of their supply chain partners.

In other words, securing the target data so supply chain partners cannot access it to fulfill government demands they might receive will force governments seeking data to request it directly from its owner/controller. This should be the primary objective of mitigating the risk of government access to data.

One important consideration is whether all the vendors in their supply chain are willing and able to challenge legal requests for data. The US-based hyper-scale CSPs have all publicly stated that their attorneys review the requests they receive and ensure that they follow the letter of the law and are not overreaching. Their cloud businesses depend on trust. For them, losing their customers' trust means losing their share of a rapidly growing *trillion-dollar* industry in its nascent years. Therefore, they are willing to defend their customers' privacy by challenging requests when it is appropriate to do so – but it's likely that not every technology provider in an organization's supply chain will be willing and able to resist these legal requests. If this is a risk an organization is serious about, then it should choose its vendors with this in mind.

Planning data protection controls

Now that we have identified the target data we want to protect, we understand how it flows through our organization's systems and those of our supply chain partners, and we have a clear objective, we can design processes and technologies, managed by people and systems, to restrict access to the target data. There are numerous legal, administrative, and technical controls that could be employed to do this. I won't reprint NIST SP 800-53 here. The rest of this book is dedicated to examining security strategies and some of them can be used to protect data. However, I will draw your attention to one capability that I consider to be the ultimate control for preventing unauthorized access to data in the public cloud: client-side encryption. Regardless of where my advisory conversations with CISOs and executives started, they would almost always end with discussions about encryption and key management options. Together with some supporting controls, client-side encryption can protect your target data in the cloud from attackers, CSPs, supply chain partners, and governments alike. However, it does have its own limitations and opportunity costs that I'll discuss.

Client-side encryption

Encryption can help maintain the confidentiality and integrity of your data. Depending on the requirements, encryption can also help organizations meet some of their compliance obligations. If encryption really can help with all these things, then why haven't organizations been encrypting everything everywhere? Historically, encryption and key management introduced friction into the operationalization of data.

Put another way, there has been a tension between the security benefits that encryption and key management provide and the operational requirements most organizations have for their data. Given this, most organizations that employ encryption do so relatively sparingly, attempting to balance security risks with operational risks like costs, lack of expertise, and business consequences.

The CIO of the German company we are advising is interested in protecting their target data in the cloud from unauthorized access, including unauthorized access attempts by the CSPs themselves. AWS, Google, and Microsoft have all developed impressive encryption and key management capabilities for use with their cloud services. They want to help their customers protect data that is in transit and at rest. They have taken slightly different approaches to these challenges, but the common denominator is that they have tried to make using encryption and key management as frictionless as possible. They have designed systems that can perform lightning-fast encryption and decryption operations that help protect millions of customers' data at massive scales.

For protecting data at rest, there are two general options these CSPs offer: server-side encryption and client-side encryption. Server-side encryption is managed by the CSP after the customer has transferred their data to the service. For example, when a customer saves new data to a cloud storage service, it is protected by **Transport Layer Security (TLS)** as it is moved from its origin to the cloud storage service. Once it gets into the cloud storage service, server-side encryption can be employed to protect it. The cloud storage service is responsible for properly implementing the encryption and decryption algorithms used and for managing the keys. The customer brings the data and the CSP services encrypt it and then decrypt it as customers access it. The complexity of the encryption, decryption, and key management is abstracted from the customer. Put another way, the customer has delegated the responsibility for encryption and key management to the CSP.

The CIO of the German company we are advising is quick to point out that when server-side encryption is used, the CSPs have access to the keys used for encryption and decryption processes because they are managing them. This is accurate – but the CSPs have designed and implemented key management services that are backed by **Hardware Security Modules (HSMs)**. HSMs are designed to make it hard or impossible to remove key material from them, even by their system administrators. These HSMs are typically tamper-evident, meaning if someone tried to physically break into one of them, it would be obvious to anyone inspecting the HSM. Given how HSMs are designed, physical access would not enable easy access to key material. By doing this, the CSPs mitigate the risk of insider threats to the key material and earn the trust of their customers. However, the German CIO does not want to use server-side encryption and let their CSP manage keys on their behalf.

Remember, they are trying to mitigate an already tiny risk – they want mitigation options that result in a near-zero risk of unauthorized access to their target data.

This is a scenario where client-side encryption can help. Using this approach, before data is transmitted anywhere, it is first encrypted by the client application handling the data. The client application running in the customer's on-premises IT environment handles encryption and decryption operations, as well as retrieving and using keys for these purposes. This means that the developer of the application, in this case, the CSP's customer, is responsible for implementing encryption algorithms, managing keys, and performing encryption and decryption operations. Leveraging client-side encryption means the customer, not the CSP, is responsible for encryption and key management.

Because the customer can decide where and how their keys will be used, and they perform all the encryption and decryption operations themselves, they can choose to never share their keys or cleartext data with their CSP. Let me provide an example scenario. A customer has an application running in their own on-premises data center that processes data and then stores it. The customer wants to take advantage of the many benefits of cloud storage services but does not want the CSP to get access to the data they store in the cloud. They can use client-side encryption to accomplish this. After the application processes the data, it needs to prepare it for storage. The application can generate encryption keys or retrieve them from the customer's own on-premises key management infrastructure, such as an HSM. The application uses these keys to encrypt the data it is going to store in the cloud. Once the data has been encrypted in the customer's own on-premises data center, the application transfers the encrypted data to the CSP's storage service. Now, an encrypted copy of the original data is in the cloud storage service. The cleartext data and the encryption keys were never transferred outside the customer's own on-premises data center. Because the CSP doesn't have access to the original cleartext data or the keys, there is no risk that they can access the data using the encrypted copy stored in their cloud storage service.

There are a few different ways client-side encryption can be leveraged in a storage scenario like this one. Here are some of the options the customer has in this example scenario. Note that this is not an exhaustive list of options:

- Instead of running the application performing the encryption in the on-premises data center, it could be run on a **virtual machine** (**VM**) running in the cloud. When the application needs to, it can reach back into the on-premises data center via a VPN connection or dedicated connection to retrieve keys to perform encryption and decryption operations, after which it destroys the keys in the memory of the VM. The CSP still does not have access to cleartext data or keys.

- Instead of running the key infrastructure in the on-premises data center, it can be run on VMs in the cloud. These VMs can be managed by the customer or a trusted third party, like a vendor or non-commercial agency, that provides key infrastructure services. The CSP still does not have access to cleartext data or keys.

- Instead of leveraging a key management infrastructure themselves, the customer can delegate some of this responsibility to the CSP. For example, AWS CloudHSM is a service that enables customers to provision their own single-tenant HSM instance in the cloud that is FIPS-validated. The CSP manages the hardware, and the customer is responsible for managing most other aspects of this infrastructure themselves, including backups. The customer gets the benefits of using an HSM without the costs and complexity of buying and maintaining their own hardware. The CSP cannot access the key material in the HSM because it is specifically designed to prevent this.

- Instead of provisioning and managing key infrastructure themselves, the customer can delegate this entirely to the CSP. All the CSPs offer fully managed key vault solutions that are backed by HSMs. These key management services are integrated into many of the CSPs' other services to enable seamless encryption and decryption operations at scale in the cloud as data moves from service to service. The CSP secures and manages the keys. There are some options that allow customers to import key material from their own key management infrastructures to the CSP's managed key services, giving the customer more control over the durability and lifetime of the keys.

All these options provide customers with some flexibility in how they mitigate the risk of unauthorized access to data. However, client-side encryption is not a panacea – it does have some limitations that need to be carefully considered. The confidentiality and integrity that client-side encryption provides come at a cost. Organizations that adopt this approach must have the technical expertise to manage their own encryption and decryption operations at the application level, in addition to managing their own key infrastructures. This isn't as much fun as it sounds; I've never met anyone involved in managing HSMs that looked forward to doing so. There's also the integrity of the data to be concerned with – if there's a mistake in the client-side encryption code or in managing the keys, the organization's data could be lost forever. It's a huge responsibility for organizations that choose to manage all the details themselves. Organizations should acquire validated cryptography libraries and modules instead of developing their own. Additionally, client-side encryption typically introduces higher costs. Moving data between on-premises data centers and the cloud for encryption and decryption operations typically has transfer costs associated with it. HSMs are not inexpensive to procure or manage either.

In the storage scenario I described, client-side encryption is relatively straightforward. Client-side encryption can also be used with databases that support it, but this is much more complex than a simple storage scenario. Encrypting data at the field level to prevent unauthorized access to sensitive data while preserving database indexing and search functionality requires planning and expertise.

Moreover, client-side encryption can't be used with all cloud services. For example, leveraging fully managed services in the cloud typically means the CSP needs to process cleartext data and subsequently cannot process encrypted data without access to the keys. Until homomorphic encryption or other solutions that enable the processing of encrypted data are widely adopted, client-side encryption isn't going to be a helpful option for all scenarios.

Some of the organizations I advised, who had very stringent data protection requirements, started their journey to the cloud leveraging client-side encryption. Initially, they viewed it as the best option to mitigate the risk of unauthorized access to data in the cloud – but over a period of years, as they became more comfortable with how cloud services were designed and operated, with the identity and access management capabilities in the cloud, and with the monitoring and audit capabilities, they started using HSMs provided by their CSP and in some cases, the CSP's fully managed key vault solutions. Many of these customers concluded that using partially managed or fully managed HSMs in the cloud mitigated the same risks as client-side encryption, but without the added complexity and costs.

This concludes this brief introduction to client-side encryption. If you are interested in a deeper dive into client-side encryption and server-side encryption, please watch this video I recorded on the topic, *AWS Security Webinar: The Key to Effective Cloud Encryption*, available at `https://www.youtube.com/watch?v=78qFK-r7WBI`.

One final note about encryption and key management. Did you know it can help meet data residency requirements? Encryption and effective key management can help reduce an organization's attack surface. Instead, reduce the challenge of protecting all the organization's data wherever it is, for decades, to just protecting the keys used to encrypt and decrypt it. It is typically much easier to protect keys because the attack surface and the size of keys are both much smaller than protecting all the cleartext data itself. This reduced attack surface can also help your organization meet data residency requirements. The process of employing properly implemented strong encryption transforms data into something that resembles random noise. This means encrypted data is not the original cleartext data any longer and it never will be again without the decryption keys.

Given this, shouldn't the encrypted version of the data, resembling random noise, be permitted to be transmitted and stored anywhere? If the encryption/decryption keys never leave their origin country or region, neither does the original cleartext data, regardless of where the encrypted data travels, right? So many security professionals that I discussed data residency with struggled with this concept. Many of them clung to the notion that the physical location of their data somehow made it more secure. That's one of the cool things about math – it works the same everywhere in the world. Arguments about nascent quantum computing capabilities aside, if properly implemented strong encryption protects the confidentiality and integrity of data in Germany, it also protects it when it goes across borders to the United States. Keep this in mind when thinking through your organization's data residency requirements so that you don't pay an excessive opportunity cost for a mitigation, like data residency, that has little or no security value.

At this point, the CIO of the German company we have been advising now better understands the probability and impact of US lawful government access to data and some of the ways it can be mitigated. The company now has better information to make better decisions.

Conclusion

For many of the executives I talk to about government access to data, once they understand some of the nuances and the risks associated with it, they are far more comfortable using US-based service providers and technology companies. They are also better prepared to ask the non-US-based vendors in their current supply chains if they are subject to US jurisdiction, the same way US providers are. This exercise helps them understand the current risks of government access to data that they've likely been accepting for years or decades. Some of the executives that I have advised still want to mitigate this risk to ensure that their own legal teams and processes are used to manage requests from law enforcement. Encryption and key management can be very effective at mitigating unauthorized access to data, whether it's attackers or governments trying to gain access to it. Of course, there are many other possible mitigations as well. These are topics I'll discuss in other chapters.

The topic of government access to data has been evolving, especially in Western Europe. The narrative there has evolved from demands for data residency to the need for data sovereignty to the imperative for digital sovereignty. Many governments' demands for data residency have been met with US-based providers building data centers in numerous countries around the world.

Some of the countries that now have data centers operated by US-based providers within their borders, that meet those countries' stringent security and compliance requirements, started making a different argument; data is more valuable than oil and their country cannot cede control of this critical resource to the US. They view this as a threat to the economic sovereignty of their country, and therefore, they argue, they must build their own national cloud services to counter this threat. The uncertainty that the Schrems II legal decision has introduced, combined with the potential for large GDPR fines, has resulted in a lot of friction for organizations in the EEA contemplating the adoption of new technologies.

For many executives, CISOs, and security teams that are responsible for protecting the data of public sector or private sector organizations, this evolving narrative can be distracting, but they cannot ignore it because other executives in their organization that read these headlines will question their organization's cybersecurity strategy using this lens. This is another great reason to have a well-thought-out cybersecurity strategy. With it, CISOs will be able to answer questions about how they are managing the risk of government access to data, using mitigations that actually work versus investing in data residency and other politicized mechanisms that are tantamount to security theater.

This concludes our in-depth examination of government access to data. We've spent most of the first half of this book examining threats. Now, we'll shift our focus to cybersecurity strategies. In the next chapter of this book, we will explore the ingredients for a successful cybersecurity strategy.

Summary

I hope this chapter helps put government access to data into a useful perspective. Nearly all the organizations outside the US that I have advised over the years wanted to discuss this topic before they were willing to discuss anything else with a US-based technology provider, but once we discussed some of the nuances that I shared in this chapter, they were far more comfortable with their organization's ability to manage the associated risks. Remember, getting specific about threats is the key to managing risk.

- There are three different scenarios related to government access to data that often get conflated:

    - **The signals intelligence scenario**: Government agencies gather intelligence by intercepting and analyzing communications and electronic signals, potentially employing cryptanalysis.

- **The unlawful government access to data scenario**: A government agency steals data from an organization or a vendor in their supply chain, as opposed to getting a valid court order to compel it; military espionage and economic espionage are typical motivations.

- **The lawful government access to data scenario**: A law enforcement or intelligence agency gets a valid court order compelling an organization or a vendor in their supply chain to provide specific evidence that is in their possession, for a criminal investigation.

- The various transparency reports, law enforcement requests reports, and national security requests reports provided by vendors provide us insight into the risk posed by lawful government access to data. There is very little current, authoritative information available on the other two scenarios.

- Encryption and effective key management are important controls for mitigating all three of these threats and other types of unauthorized access to data. Client-side encryption enables organizations to encrypt sensitive data before they put it in the cloud, keeping the cleartext data and keys on-premises. Without the keys, no one can access the data stored in the cloud.

- The CLOUD Act is not an updated version of the PATRIOT Act. The PATRIOT Act has expired.

- Many countries in the world have MLATs with the United States for the purpose of cooperation in criminal matters, including the search and seizure of evidence stored in their country. France, Germany, Sweden, the EU, and many other countries have signed these treaties with the US over the past two decades. These reciprocal agreements have been the primary mechanism for law enforcement requests for data stored overseas. The average time for an MLAT request to be completed was reported to be 10 months.

- The purpose of the CLOUD Act is to speed up the production of overseas evidence in criminal investigations. It does not expand the scope of law enforcement requests or permit bulk data collection. It provides additional safeguards over MLATs for countries that sign CLOUD Act Executive Agreements with the US, as the UK has.

- Risk is the combination of the probability and impact of a specific threat. Many General Counsels and legal teams for enterprises and public sector organizations already process some volume of law enforcement requests and should be consulted in terms of their impact.

- In July 2020, the CJEU invalidated the GDPR adequacy decision that underpinned the EU-US Privacy Shield. The CJEU expressed concerns about the FISA, specifically Section 702, in their decision.

- Using available data from the transparency reports published by major US-based vendors, the probability of a US government request for data in the cloud is typically a fraction of 1%. Stack ranking this risk with the other risks that organizations manage can help determine whether any resources should be invested to mitigate this threat.

References

- Amazon. (2018). *Amazon Information Request Report*. Amazon. Retrieved from `https:// d1.awsstatic.com/certifications/Information_Request_Report_June_2018.pdf`

- Amazon. (2021). *Amazon Information Request Report*. Amazon. Retrieved from `https:// d1.awsstatic.com/Information_Request_Report_December_2021_bia.pdf`

- Amazon. (n.d.). *Law Enforcement Information Requests*. Retrieved from Amazon: `https:// www.amazon.com/gp/help/customer/display.html?nodeId=GYSDRGWQ2C2CRYEF`

- Apple. (n.d.). *Privacy Account Requests*. Retrieved from Apple: `https://www.apple.com/ legal/transparency/account.html`

- Ball, J. (2013, 10 25). *NSA monitored calls of 35 world leaders after US official handed over contacts*. Retrieved from The Guardian: `https://www.theguardian.com/world/2013/ oct/24/nsa-surveillance-world-leaders-calls`

- Business Insider. (2021, July 30). *Amazon has been fined a record $887 million for violating data privacy rules in Europe*. Retrieved from Insider: `https://www.businessinsider.com/ amazon-eu-fine-data-privacy-gdpr-luxembourg-european-union-2021-7`

- CHRISTOPHER BING, J. S. (2019, 01 30). *Inside the UAE's Secret Hacking Team of American Mercenaries*. Retrieved from Reuters: `https://www.reuters.com/investigates/special- report/usa-spying-raven/`

- Cohen, J. (2022, September 9). *Record-Setting GDPR Fines Are Drops in the Bucket for Big Tech*. Retrieved from PCMag: `https://uk.pcmag.com/social-media/142547/record- setting-gdpr-fines-are-drops-in-the-bucket-for-big-tech?amp=1`

- Congressional Research Service. (2021). *EU Data Transfer Requirements and U.S. Intelligence Laws: Understanding Schrems II and Its Impact on the EU-U.S. Privacy Shield*. Congressional Research Service.

- Congressional Research Service. (2021). *Foreign Intelligence Surveillance Act (FISA): An Overview*. Congressional Research Service.

- Cornell Law School. (n.d.). *Fourth Amendment*. Retrieved from Legal Information Institute: `https://www.law.cornell.edu/wex/fourth_amendment`

- Cornell Law School. (n.d.). *Probable Cause.* Retrieved from Legal Information Institute: https://www.law.cornell.edu/wex/probable_cause

- Department of Home Affairs, Australia Government. (2021, 12 15). *Australia-US CLOUD Act Agreement.* Retrieved from Australia Government Department of Home Affairs: https://www.homeaffairs.gov.au/about-us/our-portfolios/national-security/lawful-access-telecommunications/australia-united-states-cloud-act-agreement

- European Commission. (2019, 02 05). *E-evidence - cross-border access to electronic evidence.* Retrieved from European Commission: https://ec.europa.eu/info/policies/justice-and-fundamental-rights/criminal-justice/e-evidence-cross-border-access-electronic-evidence_en

- EWING, P. (2014, 05 22). *Gates: French cyber spies target U.S.* Retrieved from Politico: https://www.politico.com/story/2014/05/france-intellectual-property-theft-107020

- Gidda, M. (2013, 08 21). *Edward Snowden and the NSA files – timeline.* Retrieved from The Guardian: https://www.theguardian.com/world/2013/jun/23/edward-snowden-nsa-files-timeline

- Google. (n.d.). *Google Transparency Report.* Retrieved from Google: https://transparencyreport.google.com/user-data/overview

- James Regan, M. J. (2015, 06 23). *NSA spied on French presidents: WikiLeaks.* Retrieved from Reuters: https://www.reuters.com/article/us-france-wikileaks/nsa-spied-on-french-presidents-wikileaks-idUSKBN0P32EM20150623

- Julie Gordon, S. S. (2018, 12 07). *U.S. accuses Huawei CFO of Iran sanctions cover-up; hearing adjourned.* Retrieved from Reuters: https://www.reuters.com/article/us-usa-china-huawei/u-s-accuses-huawei-cfo-of-iran-sanctions-cover-up-hearing-adjourned-idUSKBN1O60FY

- Mark Mazzetti, A. G. (2019, 03 21). *A New Age of Warfare: How Internet Mercenaries Do Battle for Authoritarian Governments.* Retrieved from New York Times: https://www.nytimes.com/2019/03/21/us/politics/government-hackers-nso-darkmatter.html

- Mehul Srivastava, R. S. (2019, 05 14). *Israel's NSO: the business of spying on your iPhone.* Retrieved from Financial Times: https://www.ft.com/content/7f2f39b2-733e-11e9-bf5c-6eeb837566c5

- Meta. (n.d.). *Meta Transparency Center.* Retrieved from Meta: https://transparency.fb.com/data/government-data-requests/?source=https%3A%2F%2Ftransparency.facebook.com%2Fgovernment-data-requests

- Microsoft. (2021). *US National Security Orders Report*. Microsoft.

- Microsoft. (n.d.). *Law Enforcement Requests Report*. Retrieved from Microsoft: https://www.microsoft.com/en-us/corporate-responsibility/law-enforcement-requests-report

- National Archives. (n.d.). *The Bill of Rights: What Does it Say?* Retrieved from National Archives: https://www.archives.gov/founding-docs/bill-of-rights/what-does-it-say

- National Security Agency Central Security Service. (n.d.). *Signals Intelligence*. Retrieved from National Security Agency Central Security Service: https://www.nsa.gov/Signals-Intelligence/

- National Security Agency Central Security Service. (n.d.). *UKUSA Agreement Release*. Retrieved from National Security Agency Central Security Service: https://www.nsa.gov/news-features/declassified-documents/ukusa/

- National Security Agency/Central Security Service. (n.d.). *Foreign Intelligence Surveillance Act of 1978 (FISA)*. Retrieved from National Security Agency/Central Security Service: https://www.nsa.gov/Signals-Intelligence/FISA/

- Paul, K. (2019, 12 10). *U.S. senators threaten Facebook, Apple with encryption regulation*. Retrieved from Reuters: https://uk.reuters.com/article/us-usa-encryption-facebook/u-s-senators-threaten-facebook-apple-with-encryption-regulation-idUKKBN1YE2CK

- Peter Swire, J. D. (2016, 11 15). *A Mutual Legal Assistance Case Study: The United States and France*. Retrieved from Peterswire.net: http://peterswire.net/wp-content/uploads/mutual-legal-assistance-case-study-US-France.pdf

- Reuters. (2021, 09 24). *Huawei CFO, U.S. reach agreement on charges*. Retrieved from YouTube: https://www.youtube.com/watch?v=LbxekyZWx1o

- Richard A. Clarke, M. J. (2013, 12 12). *LIBERTY AND SECURITY IN A CHANGING WORLD*. Retrieved from Obamawhitehouse.archives.gov: https://obamawhitehouse.archives.gov/sites/default/files/docs/2013-12-12_rg_final_report.pdf

- Rubin, G. T. (2019, 11 22). *Punt on Patriot Act Sets Up New Push by Opponents*. Retrieved from Wall Street Journal: https://www.wsj.com/articles/punt-on-patriot-act-sets-up-new-push-by-opponents-11574418600

- Shostack, A. (2014). *Threat Modeling: Designing for Security*. Wiley.

- Smith, B. (2017, 10 23). *DOJ acts to curb the overuse of secrecy orders. Now it's Congress' turn*. Retrieved from Microsoft On the Issues: https://blogs.microsoft.com/on-the-issues/2017/10/23/doj-acts-curb-overuse-secrecy-orders-now-congress-turn/

- Spataro, J. (2019, 11 19). *5 attributes of successful teams*. Retrieved from Microsoft 365: https://www.microsoft.com/en-us/microsoft-365/blog/2019/11/19/5-attributes-successful-teams/

- The European Parliament and The Council Of The European Union. (2016, 04 27). *REGULATION (EU) 2016/679 OF THE EUROPEAN PARLIAMENT AND OF THE COUNCIL*. Retrieved from EUR-Lex: https://eur-lex.europa.eu/legal-content/EN/TXT/PDF/?uri=CELEX:32016R0679&from=EN

- U.S. GOVERNMENT PRINTING OFFICE. (2000). *TREATY WITH FRANCE ON MUTUAL LEGAL ASSISTANCE IN CRIMINAL MATTERS*. Retrieved from United States Congress: https://www.congress.gov/106/cdoc/tdoc17/CDOC-106tdoc17.pdf

- U.S. GOVERNMENT PRINTING OFFICE. (2004). *MUTUAL LEGAL ASSISTANCE TREATY WITH GERMANY*. Retrieved from United States Congress: https://www.congress.gov/108/cdoc/tdoc27/CDOC-108tdoc27.pdf

- U.S. GOVERNMENT PRINTING OFFICE. (2006, 10 28). *MUTUAL LEGAL ASSISTANCE AGREEMENT WITH THE EUROPEAN UNION*. Retrieved from United States Congress: https://www.congress.gov/109/cdoc/tdoc13/CDOC-109tdoc13.pdf

- United States Congress. (2018, 03 21). *DIVISION V—CLOUD ACT*. Retrieved from Justice.gov: https://www.justice.gov/criminal-oia/cloud-act-resources

- United States Department of Justice. (2019, 10 03). *Agreement between the Government of the United States of America and the Government of the United Kingdom of Great Britain and Northern Ireland on Access to Electronic Data for the Purpose of Countering Serious Crime*. Retrieved from United States Department of Justice: https://www.justice.gov/ag/page/file/1207496/download#Agreement%20between%20the%20Government%20of%20the%20United%20States%20of%20America%20and%20the%20Government%20of%20the%20United%20Kingdom%20of%20Great%20Britain%20and%20Northern%20Ireland%20on%20Access

- United States Department of Justice. (2019, 10 07). *Joint Statement Announcing United States and Australian Negotiation of a CLOUD Act Agreement by U.S. Attorney General William Barr and Minister for Home Affairs Peter Dutton*. Retrieved from United States Department of Justice: https://www.justice.gov/opa/pr/joint-statement-announcing-united-states-and-australian-negotiation-cloud-act-agreement-us

- United States Department of Justice. (2019, 10 03). *U.S. And UK Sign Landmark Cross-Border Data Access Agreement to Combat Criminals and Terrorists Online.* Retrieved from United States Department of Justice: https://www.justice.gov/opa/pr/us-and-uk-sign-landmark-cross-border-data-access-agreement-combat-criminals-and-terrorists

- US Department of Justice. (n.d.). *Mutual Legal Assistance in Criminal Matters.* Retrieved from US Department of Justice: https://findit.state.gov/search?utf8=%E2%9C%93&affiliate=dos_stategov&sort_by=&query=%22Mutual+Legal+Assistance+in+Criminal+Matters%22

- USA GOV. (n.d.). *A-Z Index of U.S. Government Departments and Agencies.* Retrieved from USA GOV: https://www.usa.gov/federal-agencies

- WikiLeaks. (2015, 07 08). *All the Chancellor's Men.* Retrieved from WikiLeaks: https://wikileaks.org/nsa-germany/

- WikiLeaks. (2015, 07 04). *Bugging Brazil.* Retrieved from WikiLeaks: https://wikileaks.org/nsa-brazil/

- WikiLeaks. (2015, 06 29). *Espionnage Élysée.* Retrieved from WikiLeaks: https://wikileaks.org/nsa-france/

- WikiLeaks. (2015, 07 31). *Target Tokyo.* Retrieved from WikiLeaks: https://wikileaks.org/nsa-japan/

- Wikipedia. (n.d.). *Illegals Program.* Retrieved from Wikipedia: https://en.wikipedia.org/wiki/Illegals_Program

- Wikipedia. (n.d.). *Signals intelligence by alliances, nations and industries.* Retrieved from Wikipedia: https://en.wikipedia.org/wiki/Signals_intelligence_by_alliances,_nations_and_industries

Join our community on Discord

Join our community's Discord space for discussions with the author and other readers:

`https://packt.link/SecNet`

8

Ingredients for a Successful Cybersecurity Strategy

There's no doubt that enterprises today, more than ever, need effective cybersecurity strategies. However, a sound strategy is not in and of itself a guarantee of success. There are several ingredients that are necessary for a cybersecurity program to be successful. This chapter will describe what a cybersecurity strategy looks like and each of the necessary ingredients for success in detail.

Let's begin with a fundamental question that we'll need to answer before discussing cybersecurity strategies in any detail: what do we actually mean when we say "cybersecurity strategy"?

What is a cybersecurity strategy?

Organizations that have a super-strong security culture essentially have cybersecurity baked into them. For everyone else, there's strategy. In my experience, the terms "strategy" and "tactics" are poorly understood in the business world. One person's strategy is another person's tactics. I once worked with a Corporate Vice President who would tell me that I was talking about tactics when I was explaining our strategy. Throughout my career, I've been in meetings where people have talked past each other because one person is discussing strategies and the other is discussing tactics.

Additionally, security and compliance professionals sometimes use the term "strategy" when they are referring to frameworks, models, or standards. There are lots of these in the industry and many organizations use them, for example, ISO standards, NIST standards, OWASP Top 10, CIS Benchmarks, STRIDE, risk management frameworks, SOC 2, PCI, HIPAA, the Cloud Security Alliance Cloud Controls Matrix, the AWS Cloud Adoption Framework Security Perspective, the AWS Well-Architected Framework Security Pillar, and many more.

All of these can be helpful tools for organizations seeking to improve their security postures, comply with regulations, and demonstrate that they meet industry standards.

I'm not proposing a new dictionary definition of the term "strategy," but I do want to explain what I mean when I'm discussing cybersecurity strategies in this book. In my view, there are at least two critical inputs to a cybersecurity strategy:

- Each organization's high-value assets.

- The specific requirements, threats, and risks that apply to each organization, informed by the industry they are in, the place(s) in the world where they do business, and the people associated with each organization.

High-Value Assets (HVAs) are also known as "crown jewels." There are many definitions for these terms. But when I use them, I mean the organization will fail or be severely disrupted if the asset's confidentiality, integrity, or availability is compromised. HVAs are rarely the computers that the organization's information workers use. Yet I've seen so many organizations focus on the security of desktop systems as if they were HVAs. Given the importance of HVAs, it would be easy to focus on them to the exclusion of lower-value assets. But keep in mind that attackers often use lower-value assets as an entry point to attack HVAs. For example, those old development and test environments that were never decommissioned properly typically aren't HVAs. But they are often found to be a source of compromise.

One of the first things a CISO needs to do when they get the job is to identify the organization's HVAs. This might be more challenging than it sounds as the crown jewels might not be obvious to people that don't possess expertise specifically related to the business they are supporting. Interviewing members of the C-suite and members of the board of directors can help to identify assets that would truly cause the business to fail or be severely disrupted.

Working backward from the organization's objectives can also help identify its HVAs. As security teams do this analysis, they should be prepared for some nuances that weren't initially obvious. For example, could the business still meet its objectives without power, water, heating, air conditioning, and life-safety systems? Depending on the business and the type of building(s) it uses, if elevators aren't available, is there any point letting employees and customers through the front door? Customers might be willing to walk up a few flights of stairs, but would they be willing to walk up 40 flights of stairs if that was necessary? Probably not.

If this disruption was sustained for days, weeks, or months, how long could the business survive? Where are the control systems for these functions? And when was the last time the security posture of these systems was assessed? Identifying an organization's HVAs doesn't mean that CISOs can ignore everything else. Understanding which assets are truly HVAs and which aren't helps CISOs prioritize their limited resources and focus on avoiding extinction events for the organization.

Once the CISO has identified their organization's crown jewels, the next step is to ensure that the internal stakeholder community (IT, legal, procurement, and others), the C-suite, and the board of directors understand and agree with that list. This clarity will be very helpful when the time comes to request more resources or different resources than the organization has leveraged in the past. When the organization needs to make hard decisions about reductions in resources, clarity around HVAs will help with risk-based decisions. The time and effort spent getting the senior stakeholder community on the same page will make the CISO's life easier moving forward. Getting buy-in on the list of crown jewels might be easy in some organizations, but CISOs need to be prepared to defend their list. Some stakeholders will want their assets on the list even when they aren't deemed crown jewels, while others will want their assets removed from the list to avoid potential extra scrutiny and work. Using a structured methodology, or at least defining principles or a scoring system that is used to determine what is and what is not a crown jewel, is strongly recommended.

The second critical input to a cybersecurity strategy is the specific requirements, threats, and risks that apply to the organization, informed by the industry they are in, the place(s) in the world where they do business, and the people associated with it. This input helps further scope the requirements of the cybersecurity program. For example, the industry and/or location where they do business might have regulatory compliance requirements that they need to observe, or they could face stiff fines or get their business license revoked. Keep in mind that most organizations can't identify all possible threats and risks to them. That would require omniscience and is a natural limitation of a risk-based approach.

After publishing thousands of pages of threat intelligence when I worked at Microsoft (Microsoft Corporation, 2007-2016), I can tell you that there are global threats that have the potential to impact everyone, but there are also industry-specific threats and regional threats. Using credible threat intelligence to inform the strategy will help CISOs prioritize capabilities and controls, which is especially helpful if their resources are limited. Trying to protect everything as if it's of the same value to the organization is a recipe for failure. CISOs must make trade-offs, and it's better if they do this knowing the specific threats that apply to the industry and region of the world where they do business.

This doesn't mean CISOs can ignore all other threats, but identifying the highest-risk threats to their organization's crown jewels will help them focus resources in the most important places.

Most of the first half of this book is dedicated to helping you understand the threat landscape and how it has evolved over the last couple of decades. I've provided deep dives into vulnerability disclosure trends, the evolution of malware, including ransomware, and insights into internet-based threats like phishing, drive-by download attacks, and DDoS attacks. I've also provided insights into governments as threats with an examination of government access to data. CISOs and security teams need credible sources of threat intelligence to keep them abreast of the latest tactics, techniques, and procedures attackers use.

Without the two inputs I've described here, CISOs are left implementing best practices and industry standards that are based on someone else's threat model. These can be helpful in moving organizations in the right direction, but they typically aren't based on the HVAs of individual organizations and the specific threats they need to care about. Using best practices and industry standards that aren't informed by these two inputs will make it more likely that there will be critical gaps.

At this point, you might be wondering what a cybersecurity strategy looks like. *Figure 8.1* presents a cybersecurity strategy:

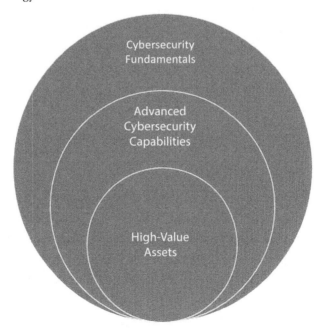

Figure 8.1: An illustrative example of a cybersecurity strategy

HVAs are central and are supported by the other parts of the strategy. The cybersecurity fundamentals include the foundational capabilities that support a successful security program, such as vulnerability management and identity management, among others. You might recall that I discussed the importance of cybersecurity fundamentals in *Chapter 1*. Do you remember the Cybersecurity Usual Suspects? Let me provide a brief refresher here because we will use these concepts to evaluate the cybersecurity strategies we examine in the next chapter.

The cybersecurity fundamentals are the parts of a strategy that focuses on mitigating the Cybersecurity Usual Suspects, or the five ways enterprises get initially compromised. The Cybersecurity Usual Suspects are:

- Unpatched vulnerabilities
- Security misconfigurations
- Weak, leaked, and stolen credentials
- Social engineering
- Insider threats

Cybersecurity strategies must be informed by the Cybersecurity Usual Suspects and be effective at mitigating them – this is what the Cybersecurity Fundamentals do. I consider these concepts to be critical ingredients of effective cybersecurity strategies. Strategies that do not focus on the fundamentals and therefore do not address the Cybersecurity Usual Suspects need to be complemented by other strategies that do, or the approach will have gaps that attackers can take advantage of.

Advanced cybersecurity capabilities are investments that organizations should make as they become very proficient at the fundamentals. If your organization isn't *really* good at the fundamentals, then that's the place they should invest in first before investing in advanced cybersecurity capabilities. Investing in the cybersecurity fundamentals will provide the best return on investment for most organizations.

For organizations that are really good at the cybersecurity fundamentals, advanced capabilities are the second line of defense. It is likely that no matter how good they are at vulnerability management, identity management, and cybersecurity training for their staff, they won't be able to keep up with the volume of threats or prevent credential leakage, or they'll simply make a mistake somewhere along the way. This is where advanced capabilities can help. Designed properly, they can help prevent initial compromise or detect it quickly enough for automated and manual response processes to disrupt or stop the attack. Advanced capabilities can help reduce attackers' dwell times in their victims' environments, thus reducing potential damage and the cost of recovery.

Other ingredients for a successful strategy

There is a bunch of management-related work that needs to be done to ensure the CISO, the security team, and the rest of the organization can effectively execute a cybersecurity strategy. This section outlines some of the ingredients that give a strategy the best chance of success.

For example, CISOs that tell the businesses they support, "no, you can't do that," are no longer in high demand. Security teams must align with their organizations' business objectives, or they won't be successful. Let's take a closer look at this ingredient.

Business objective alignment

I've met many CISOs that were struggling in their roles. Some of them simply weren't properly supported by their organizations. It's easy to find groups of executives that think cybersecurity threats are overblown and everything their CISO does is a tax on what they are trying to accomplish. To these folks, cybersecurity is just another initiative that should stand in line behind them for resources. After all, the company won't get to that next big revenue milestone via a cost center, right?

Working with executives that don't understand the cybersecurity threats their organization faces and really don't have the time to pay attention isn't uncommon. Most CISOs must work with other executives to get things done, even if those executives don't realize they have a shared destiny with the CISO; when the CISO fails, they all fail. But the best CISOs I've met tend to thrive in such environments.

Whether a CISO works in an environment like the one I described, or they are lucky enough to work with people that care if they are successful, to be successful, CISOs need to align with the business they support. CISOs that don't understand and embrace the objectives of the organizations they support generate friction. There is only so much friction senior leaders are willing to tolerate before they demand change. Deeply understanding the business and how it works gives enlightened CISOs the knowledge and credibility required to truly support their organizations. Put another way, "purist" CISOs that try to protect data in isolation of the people, business processes, and technologies that their organization relies on to succeed are only doing part of the job they were hired to do.

A cybersecurity strategy will only be successful if it truly supports the business. Developing a strategy that helps mitigate the risks that the security team cares most about might give the team the satisfaction that they have a buttoned-up plan that will make it difficult for attackers to be successful.

But if that strategy also makes it difficult for the business to be competitive and agile, then the security team must do better.

The best way to prove to your C-suite peers that you are there to help them is to learn about the parts of the business they manage, what their priorities are, and earn their trust. None of this is going to happen in your **Security Operations Center (SOC)**, so you are going to have to spend time in their world, whether that's on a factory floor, in a warehouse, on a truck, or in an office. Walk a mile in their shoes and they'll have an easier time following your counsel and advocating for you when it's important.

Lastly, remember it's the CISO's job to discover, communicate, manage, and mitigate risk to the business, not to decide what the organization's risk appetite is. The board of directors and senior management have been managing risk for the organization since it was founded. They've been managing all sorts of risks, including financial risks, economic risks, HR risks, legal risks, and many others. Cybersecurity risks might be the newest type of risk they've been forced to manage, but if the CISO can learn to communicate cybersecurity risks in the same way that the other parts of the business do, the business will do the right thing for their customers and shareholders or they will pay the price – but that's the business's decision, not the CISO's.

That said, accountability, liability, and empowerment go hand in hand. Many CISOs face the harsh reality that they are made accountable for mitigating risks accepted by the business but are not empowered to make the necessary changes or implement countermeasures. Simply put, a CISO's job is a hard one. This might help explain why CISO tenures are typically so short compared to those of other executives.

Having a clear and shared vision of where cybersecurity fits into an organization's wider business strategy is not only important within the upper echelons of an organization; the organization as a whole should have a clear stance on its vision, mission, and imperatives for its cybersecurity program. We'll take a look at this next.

Cybersecurity vision, mission, and imperatives

Taking the time to develop and document a vision, mission statement, and imperatives for the cybersecurity program can be helpful to CISOs. A shared vision that communicates what the future optimal state looks like for the organization from a cybersecurity perspective can be a powerful tool to develop a supportive corporate culture. It can inspire confidence in the cybersecurity team and the future of the organization. It can also generate excitement and good will toward the security team that will be helpful in the course of their work.

Similarly, a well-written mission statement can become a positive cultural mantra for organizations. A good mission statement can communicate what the security team is trying to accomplish while simultaneously demonstrating how the security team is aligned with the business, its customers, and shareholders. The mission statement will help communicate the security team's objectives as it meets and works with other parts of the organization.

Finally, business imperatives are the major goals that the cybersecurity team will undertake over a 2- or 3-year period. These goals should be ambitious enough that they can't be achieved in a single fiscal year. Imperatives support the strategy and are aligned with the broader business objectives. When the strategy isn't aligned with broader business objectives, this can show up as an imperative that is out of place – a square peg in a round hole. Why would the business support a big multi-year goal that isn't aligned with its objectives? This should be a message to the CISO to realign the strategy and rethink the imperatives. These multi-year goals become the basis for the projects that the cybersecurity group embarks on. An imperative might be accomplished by a single project or might require multiple projects. Remember a project has a defined start date, end date, and budget.

Don't confuse this with a program that doesn't necessarily have an end date and could be funded perpetually. Programs can and should contribute to the group's imperatives.

Developing a vision, mission statement, and imperatives for the cybersecurity program isn't always easy or straightforward. The vision cannot be actioned without the support of stakeholders outside of the cybersecurity group, and convincing them of the value of the program can be time-consuming. The future rewards from this work, for the CISO and the cybersecurity group as a whole, typically make the effort worthwhile. We'll briefly discuss securing this support next, as one of the important ingredients of a successful cybersecurity strategy.

Senior executive and board support

Ensuring that the senior executives and the board of directors understand and support the organization's cybersecurity strategy is an important step for a successful security program. If the senior executives understand the strategy and had a hand in developing and approving it, they should show more ownership and support for it moving forward. But if they don't have a connection to the strategy, then the activities that are executed to support it will be potentially disruptive and unwelcome. They won't understand why changes are being made or why the governance model behaves the way it does.

Two of the important questions CISOs should ask when they are interviewing for a new CISO job are who the role reports to and how often the CISO will be meeting with the board of directors or the Board Audit Committee. If the CISO isn't meeting with the board quarterly or twice per year, that's a red flag. It might be that the role that the CISO reports to meets with the board instead. But unless that role is steeped in the strategy and the daily operations, they should be sharing or delegating the job of meeting with the board to the CISO. This gives the CISO firsthand experience of discussing priorities with the board. It also allows board members to get their updates directly from the CISO and ask them their questions directly. I'd be very hesitant to take a CISO job where the role didn't meet directly with the board at least a couple of times per year.

This experience is important and demonstrates that the CISO is a legitimate member of the organization's C-suite. If the CISO doesn't have the opportunity to ask the board for help with their peers, including the CEO, that's one more reason their peers don't really need to support them. Adding a management layer between the CISO and the board can be a tactic that senior management uses to delay, influence, or deter the CISO from making progress with their security program. It can also provide shelter to CISOs that don't have the business acumen or corporate maturity to interact directly with the board.

But if the executive management team is truly supportive of the CISO and the cybersecurity strategy, they should welcome the opportunity for the CISO to get the help they need as quickly as possible without instituting more bureaucracy. Besides, the executive team should already know what the CISO is going to tell the board if they are taking their responsibilities seriously. Of course, history has taught us that this is not always the case where cybersecurity is concerned.

If the CISO is successful at getting directional approval from the Board of Directors on the cybersecurity strategy, this will make it easier for the board to understand why the security team is doing what they are doing. It will also make it easier for the CISO to elicit help when needed and report results against the strategy. I don't claim this is an easy thing to do. The first couple of times I met with boards of directors was like meeting the characters in an Agatha Christie novel or from the game of Clue. The board members I've met have all been very accomplished professionally. Some are humble about their accomplishments, while others assert their accomplishments to influence others. There always seems to be at least one board member who claims to have cybersecurity experience, who wants to ask tough questions and give the CISO advice on cybersecurity. But if the CISO can effectively communicate a data-driven view of results against the cybersecurity strategy, the same strategy that the board approved, these conversations can be very helpful for all stakeholders. Additionally, results from internal and external audits typically provide boards with some confidence that the CISO is doing their job effectively.

After talking with executives at literally thousands of organizations around the world about cybersecurity, I can tell you that there are real differences in how much risk organizations are willing to accept. In addition to gaining support from senior executives and the board, it is important to have a good understanding of their appetite for risk, as we'll discuss next, since this could significantly impact cybersecurity strategy.

Understand the risk appetite

Some organizations are in hypercompetitive industries where innovation, speed, and agility are top priorities; these organizations tend to be willing to accept more risk when faced with security and compliance decisions that will potentially slow them down or otherwise impede their ability to compete. For these companies, if they don't take calculated risks, they won't be in business long enough to make decisions in the future.

Other organizations I've talked to are very risk averse. That doesn't mean they necessarily move slowly, but they demand more certainty when making decisions. They are willing to take the time to really understand factors and nuances in risk-based decisions in an effort to make the best possible decision for their organization. Of course, there are also organizations in the spectrum between these two examples.

CISOs that understand the risk appetite of the senior management in their organizations can help them make faster, better decisions. I've seen many CISOs over the years decide to play the role of "the adult in the room" and try to dictate how much risk the organization should accept. In most cases, this isn't the CISO's job. Providing context and data to help the business make informed risk-based decisions is a function CISOs should provide. Sometimes, they also have to educate executives and board members who do not understand cybersecurity risks. But I find it useful to always keep in mind that, in established organizations, executive suites were managing many types of risks for the organization long before cybersecurity risks became relevant to them. Note, this could be different for start-ups or in organizations where the CISO also has deep expertise in the business they support; in these scenarios, the CISO might be expected to make risk decisions for the organization more directly. But in all cases, understanding how much risk the organization is willing to accept in the normal course of business is important for CISOs.

The organization's appetite for risk will show up in its governance model and governance practices. In many cases, organizations that accept more risk in order to move faster will streamline their governance practices to minimize friction and blockages. Organizations that want to take a meticulous approach to decision-making will typically implement more governance controls to ensure decisions travel fully through the appropriate processes.

For this reason, it's important that CISOs validate their understanding of their organization's risk appetite instead of making assumptions about it. This is where their knowledge of the business and their peers' priorities will help.

In addition to a knowledge of business priorities, it's important to have a realistic idea of the organization's current capabilities and technical talent. We'll discuss that next.

Realistic view of current cybersecurity capabilities and technical talent

Many of the CISOs I know aspire to have a world-class cybersecurity team designing, implementing, and operating sophisticated and effective controls. However, being honest with themselves about their current state of affairs is the best starting point.

The entire industry has been suffering from an acute shortage of cybersecurity talent for over a decade. This problem is getting worse as more and more organizations come to the realization that they need to take cybersecurity seriously or suffer potential non-compliance penalties and negative reputational consequences. Recent high-profile ransomware attacks reinforce this reality. Assessing the talent that a security team currently has helps CISOs, as well as CIOs, identify critical gaps in expertise. For example, if a security team is understaffed in a critical area such as vulnerability management or incident response, CIOs and CISOs need to know this sooner rather than later. If you have people that are untrained on some of the hardware, software, or processes that they are responsible for or are expected to use, identifying those gaps is the first step in addressing them. It also helps CIOs and CISOs identify professional growth areas for the people on the security team and spot potential future leaders. Cross-pollinating staff across teams or functions will help develop them in ways that will potentially be useful in the future.

The key is for CIOs and CISOs to be as realistic in their assessments as they can be so that they have a grounded view of the talent in the organization. Don't let aspirations of greatness paint an inaccurate picture of the talent the organization has. This will make it easier to prioritize the type of talent required and give the organization's recruiters a better chance of attracting the right new talent.

Cartography, or doing an inventory of your current cybersecurity capabilities, is another important exercise. The results will inform the development of the cybersecurity imperatives that I discussed earlier, as well as helping to identify critical gaps in capabilities. It can also help identify over-investment in capabilities. For example, it's discovered that the organization procured three identity management systems and only one of them is actually deployed.

This is occurring while the organization doesn't have enough vulnerability scanners to do a competent job of scanning and patching the infrastructure in a reasonable amount of time.

In most big, complex IT environments, this won't be an easy task. It might turn out to be relatively easy to get a list of entitlements from the procurement department or a deployed software inventory from IT. But knowing that a particular appliance, piece of software, or suite of capabilities has been deployed only answers part of the question the CISO needs answered. Really understanding the maturity of the deployment and operation of those capabilities is just as important but is typically much harder to determine. Just because an identity management product is in production doesn't mean all of its capabilities have been implemented or enabled, the product is being actively managed, and the data it produces is being consumed by anyone.

Discovering these details can be challenging, and measuring their impact on your strategy might be too difficult to realistically contemplate. But without these details, you might not be able to accurately identify gaps in protection, detection, and response capabilities, and areas where over-investment has occurred.

If CIOs and CISOs can get an accurate view of the current cybersecurity talent and capabilities they have, it makes it much easier and less expensive for them to effectively manage cybersecurity programs for their organizations.

In my experience, there can be a lot of conflict and friction in organizations when cybersecurity teams and compliance teams do not work well together. Let's explore this dynamic next.

Compliance program and control framework alignment

I've seen cybersecurity and compliance teams in conflict with one another over control frameworks and configurations. When this happens, there tends to be a disconnect between the cybersecurity strategy and the compliance strategy within the organization. For example, the CISO might decide that the cybersecurity team is going to embrace NIST 800-53 as a control framework that they measure themselves against. If the compliance team is measuring compliance with ISO/IEC 27001, this can result in conversation after conversation about control frameworks and configurations. Some organizations work out these differences quickly and efficiently, while other organizations struggle to harmonize these efforts.

A common area for misalignment between cybersecurity and compliance teams is when controls in an internal standard and an industry standard differ. Internal standards are typically informed by the specific risks and controls that are most applicable to each organization.

But differences between an internal standard and an industry standard can happen when the internal standard is newer than the industry standard or vice versa. For example, the industry standard states that an account lockout policy must be set to a maximum of five incorrect password entries. The cybersecurity team knows that this control is "security theatre" in an environment that enforces a strong password policy and especially on systems that have MFA enabled. But in order to meet the industry standard, they might be forced to turn on the account lockout policy, thus enabling attackers to lock accounts out any time they want to with a denial-of-service attack.

I've seen compliance professionals argue with CISOs on the efficacy of such dated control standards, who are simply trying to successfully comply with an industry standard without considering that they are actually increasing risk for the entire organization. I've even seen some of these compliance professionals, in the course of their work, claim that they can accept risk on behalf of the entire organization where such decisions are concerned – which is rarely, if ever, the case.

The reality is that industry and regulated standards typically take years to be developed, refined, approved, and published. Subsequently, they're often going to be behind the times in terms of risks and risk mitigation.

It should be recognized and acknowledged that both compliance and security are important to organizations. Compliance is driven by the regulation of liability, and security is driven by prevention, detection, and response. CISOs should foster normalization and the alignment of applied frameworks for security and compliance. Compliance professionals need to recognize that any organization that places compliance as a priority will eventually be compromised because industry and regulated standards are almost always based on someone else's threat model.

The cybersecurity group and the compliance group should work together to find ways to meet standards while also protecting, detecting, and responding to modern-day threats. These different, but overlapping, disciplines should be coordinated with the common goal of helping to manage risk for the organization. As I mentioned earlier, the cybersecurity strategy should be informed by the organization's HVAs and the specific risks they care about. The compliance team is the second line of defense designed to ensure the cybersecurity team is doing their job effectively by comparing their controls against internal, industry, and/or regulated standards. But they need to be prepared to assess the efficacy of controls where there are differences or where they conflict, instead of blindly demanding a standard be adhered to.

Typically, the decision to accept more risk by meeting a dated industry standard, for example, should be made by a risk management board or the broader internal stakeholder community instead of by a single individual or group.

Internal and external audit teams are the third line of defense that helps to keep both the cybersecurity team and the compliance team honest by auditing the results of their work. No one wins when these teams fight over control frameworks and standards, especially when the frameworks or standards in question are based on someone else's threat model, as is almost always the case with industry and regulated standards. Some organizations try to solve this problem by moving the CISO to report to the compliance organization. This might work for some organizations that are in heavily regulated industries.

However, simply put, cybersecurity and compliance are different disciplines. Compliance focuses on demonstrating that the organization is successfully meeting internal, industry, and/or regulated standards. Cybersecurity focuses on protecting, detecting, and responding to modern-day cybersecurity threats. Together, they help the organization manage risk. I'm going to discuss compliance as a cybersecurity strategy in detail in *Chapter 9, Cybersecurity Strategies*.

Next, we'll talk about the importance of cybersecurity and IT maintaining a happy and productive relationship with one another.

An effective relationship between cybersecurity and IT

In my experience, CISOs that have a good working relationship with their business's IT organizations are typically happier and more effective in their job. An ineffective relationship with IT can make a CISO's life miserable. It's also true that CISOs can make the jobs of CIOs and VPs of IT disciplines frustrating. I've met so many CISOs that have suboptimal working relationships with their organization's IT departments. I've seen many cybersecurity groups and IT organizations interact like oil and water, when the only way to be successful is to work together. After all, they have a shared destiny. So, what's the problem? Well, simply put, in many cases, change is hard. It is easy for CIOs to interpret the rise of CISOs as a by-product of their own shortcomings, whether this is accurate or not. CISOs represent change, and many of them are change leaders.

Moreover, I think this dynamic can develop for at least a few reasons. The way that these groups are organized can be one of them. The two most common ways I've seen cybersecurity groups integrated, which are typically much newer than IT departments in large, mature organizations, are as follows:

- The CISO reports to the CIO or CTO in IT and shares IT resources to get work done.
- The CISO reports outside of IT to the CEO, the board of directors, legal, compliance, the CFO, or a "transformation" office. There are two flavors of this model:

- The CISO has their own cybersecurity resources but needs IT resources to get work done.
- The CISO has their own cybersecurity and IT resources and can get work done independently of IT.

The scenario where the CISO reports to the IT organization, historically, has been very common. But this reporting line has been evolving over time. Estimates vary, but I think less than 50% of the CISOs I recently met report to IT. One of the reasons for this change in reporting lines is that all too often, CIOs prioritize IT priorities over cybersecurity.

In many cases, cybersecurity is treated like any other IT project in that it must queue up with other IT projects and compete with them for resources to get things done. Frustrated CISOs would either be successful in convincing their boss that cybersecurity wasn't just another IT project, or they were forced to escalate. There are no winners with such escalations, least of all the CISO. In many cases, the CISO gets left with a CIO that resents them and sees them as a tax on the IT organization.

It took years for many CIOs to realize that every IT project has security requirements. Deprioritizing or slowing down cybersecurity initiatives means that every IT project that has a dependency on cybersecurity capabilities will either be delayed or will need an exception to sidestep these requirements. The latter tends to be much more common than the former. When CEOs and other executives began losing their jobs and directors on boards were being held accountable because of data breaches, many organizations were counseled by outside consultants to have their CISOs report to the CEO or directly to the board of directors. This way, cybersecurity would not be deprioritized without the most senior people being involved in making those risk decisions.

A new challenge is introduced when the CISO reports outside of IT to the CEO, the board of directors, or another part of the company. Where is the CISO going to get the IT staff required to get things done? When the CISO reported to IT, it was likely easier to get access to IT resources, even if they had to queue up. CISOs that sit outside the IT organization only have a few options. They can get resources from IT and become their customer, or they must hire their own IT resources. Becoming a customer of IT sounds like it could make things easier for CISOs, but only when they have a good relationship with IT that leads to positive results. Otherwise, it might not be sufficiently different from the model where the CISO reports to IT.

As expedient as hiring their own resources sounds, there are challenges with this approach. For example, change control can become more complex because IT isn't the only group of people that can make changes in the environment. Many times, this results in IT engineers watching cybersecurity engineers making changes in their shared environment and vice versa.

Using twice as many resources to ensure things get done in a timely manner is one way to approach this problem. But most organizations can find better uses for their resources.

I've seen a better approach in action. When CISOs, CIOs, and CTOs have mutual respect for each other's charters and sincerely support each other, the work is easier, things get done more efficiently, and top talent is easier to attract and retain for all of them. Instead of a relationship defined by resource contention or assertions of authority, CISOs need to have good, effective working relationships with their IT departments to ensure they can do their jobs. Building such relationships isn't always easy, or even possible, but I believe this is a critical ingredient for a successful cybersecurity strategy. Ideally, these relationships blossom into a security culture that the entire organization benefits from.

On the topic of culture, the last ingredient for a successful cybersecurity strategy that I'll discuss in this chapter is a strong security culture. This culture involves everybody in the organization understanding their role in helping to maintain a good security posture to protect the organization from compromise. Let's talk about it in a little more detail in the next and final section of this chapter.

Security culture

Management consultant and writer Peter Drucker famously said that, "Culture eats strategy for breakfast." I agree wholeheartedly. Organizations that are successful at integrating security into their corporate cultures are in a much better position to protect, detect, and respond to modern-day threats. For example, when everyone in the organization understands what a social engineering attack looks like and is on the lookout for such attacks, it makes the cybersecurity team's job much easier and gives them a greater chance of success. Contrast this with work environments where employees are constantly getting successfully phished and vulnerabilities are constantly being exploited because employees are double-clicking on attachments in emails from unknown senders. In these environments, the cybersecurity team is spending a lot of their time and effort reacting to threats that have been realized. A strong security culture helps reduce exposure to threats, decrease detection and response times, and thus reduce the associated damage and costs.

Culture transcends training. It's one thing for employees to receive one-time or annual security training for compliance purposes, but it is quite another thing for the concepts and calls to action that employees learn in training to be constantly sustained and reinforced by all employees and the work environment itself. This shouldn't be limited to front-line information workers. Developers, operations staff, and IT infrastructure staff all benefit from a culture where security is included.

A security culture can help employees make better decisions in the absence of governance or clear guidance.

One note on the gamification of cybersecurity training: I've seen good results when organizations shift some of their cybersecurity training away from reading and videos to more interactive experiences. For example, I've facilitated "game days" and "executive security simulations" focused on helping organizations learn about threat modeling and cloud security. I've seen many groups of executives and security teams embrace these sessions and provide glowing feedback.

CISOs have a better chance of success when everyone in their organizations helps them. I encourage CISOs, with the help of other executives, to invest some of their time and resources in fostering a security culture, as it will most certainly pay dividends.

Summary

In this chapter, we discussed what a cybersecurity strategy is and some of the ingredients that give a strategy the best chance of success. We briefly reviewed the cybersecurity fundamentals and the Cybersecurity Usual Suspects in this chapter. I also introduced **High-Value Assets (HVAs)** and other concepts that I refer to frequently throughout the rest of this book.

There are at least two critical inputs to a cybersecurity strategy: your organization's HVAs and the specific requirements, threats, and risks that apply to your organization, informed by the industry you are in, the place(s) in the world where you do business, and the people associated with the organization. If an HVA's confidentiality, integrity, or availability is compromised, the organization will fail or be severely disrupted. Therefore, identifying HVAs and prioritizing protection, detection, and response for them is critical. This does not give security teams permission to completely ignore other assets. Clarity on HVAs helps security teams to prioritize and to avoid extinction events for their organizations.

There are five ways that organizations get *initially* compromised; I call them the Cybersecurity Usual Suspects. They are unpatched vulnerabilities, security misconfigurations, weak, leaked, and stolen credentials, social engineering, and insider threats. Whether the attacker is a purveyor of commodity malware or a nation-state, the ways they will try to initially compromise their victims' IT environments are limited to the Cybersecurity Usual Suspects. Being very proficient at the cybersecurity fundamentals that mitigate the Cybersecurity Usual Suspects makes it much harder for attackers, whether they are a nation-state trying to steal intellectual property or an extortionist.

A cybersecurity strategy is required for success, but it is not sufficient by itself. Ingredients for a successful strategy include:

- Business objective alignment
- Cybersecurity vision, mission, and imperatives
- Senior executive and board support
- Understanding of the organization's risk appetite
- A realistic view of current cybersecurity capabilities and technical talent
- Compliance program and control framework alignment
- An effective relationship between cybersecurity and IT
- Security culture

We've spent the first eight chapters of this book discussing threats, background information, and context that will help us examine some popular cybersecurity strategies. In the next three chapters, we will examine numerous different strategies, dive into an implementation example of one of them, and discuss how to measure the effectiveness of cybersecurity strategies.

References

- Microsoft Corporation. (2007-2016). "Microsoft Security Intelligence Report." *Microsoft Corporation*. Retrieved from www.microsoft.com/sir.

Join our community on Discord

Join our community's Discord space for discussions with the author and other readers:

https://packt.link/SecNet

Cybersecurity Strategies

Every enterprise should have a cybersecurity strategy, and the CISO of each organization should be able to articulate it. Whether your organization has a strategy or not, I hope this chapter provokes some thought and provides some tools that are helpful. In this chapter, we'll cover a sampling of cybersecurity strategies that have been employed over the past two decades, including:

- Protect and Recover Strategy
- Endpoint Protection Strategy
- Physical Control and Security Clearances Strategy
- Compliance as a Security Strategy
- Application-Centric Strategy
- Identity-Centric Strategy
- Data-Centric Strategy
- Attack-Centric strategies
- Zero Trust
- A brief look at DevOps

Let's begin by discussing which strategy is the right approach for your organization.

Introduction

I discussed some of the ingredients for a successful cybersecurity strategy in *Chapter 8, Ingredients for a Successful Cybersecurity Strategy*. These include what I consider to be a critical ingredient, the Cybersecurity Usual Suspects, that is, the five ways that organizations get initially compromised.

I have spent most of the preceding chapters in this book discussing the most common threats that CISOs and security teams are typically concerned about, including vulnerabilities, exploits, malware, ransomware, internet-based threats like phishing attacks, and government access to data. In this chapter, I will combine all these concepts into an examination of some of the cybersecurity strategies that I have seen employed in the industry over the past couple of decades. You have probably seen some of these before and perhaps have used some of them. My objective for this chapter isn't to show you a bunch of strategies so that you can select one to use. My objective is to provide you with a framework for determining the efficacy of cybersecurity strategies, including strategies that I won't discuss in this chapter but that you might encounter in your career. In other words, I hope to teach you how to fish instead of giving you a one-size-fits-all strategy that I know will only help a fraction of organizations that use it.

The right strategy for your organization is the one that helps mitigate the most important risks to your organization. Risk is relative; therefore, no one strategy can be a silver bullet for all organizations. I'll resist the temptation to simply tell you to use the NIST Cybersecurity Framework (NIST, n.d.), ISO/IEC 27001 (ISO, n.d.), or any of the other great frameworks that are available. Your organization has likely already embraced one or more of these frameworks, which is unavoidable for enterprise-scale organizations from a **Governance, Risk, and Compliance (GRC)** perspective; that is, your organization must prove it's doing what the rest of the industry is doing, or it will be seen as an outlier. GRC frameworks are typically designed to help insulate organizations from liability after an incident, and subsequently, many organizations prioritize them. However, the pace of data breaches hasn't slowed down, despite the number of great frameworks available. For example, the **European Data Protection Board (EDPB)** published a report on the results of the **General Data Protection Regulation (GDPR)** after the first nine months that GDPR was enforceable. Almost 65,000 data breach notifications were filed with the EDPB in those first nine months.

The vast majority of these organizations were likely compliant with their own security policies, thus illustrating the difference between cybersecurity and compliance. This is likely the tip of the iceberg, but it gives us some indication that organizations, both large and small, need help with cybersecurity strategy.

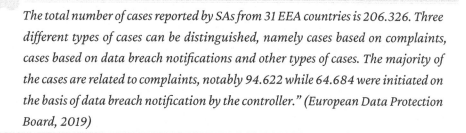

The total number of cases reported by SAs from 31 EEA countries is 206.326. Three different types of cases can be distinguished, namely cases based on complaints, cases based on data breach notifications and other types of cases. The majority of the cases are related to complaints, notably 94.622 while 64.684 were initiated on the basis of data breach notification by the controller." (European Data Protection Board, 2019)

In this chapter, I'll give you a slightly contrarian view that is meant to be food for thought. If your organization already has a cybersecurity strategy and it uses industry frameworks, this chapter will give you some questions to ask yourself about the effectiveness of your current strategy. If your organization doesn't have a cybersecurity strategy that you can articulate, this chapter will give you some ideas about some of the strategies that other organizations have used, their advantages and disadvantages, and a way to measure their potential effectiveness.

As you saw in *Chapter 8, Ingredients for a Successful Cybersecurity Strategy*, where I described what a cybersecurity strategy is, I'm purposely simplifying the descriptions of these strategies. I have talked to some CISOs that had incredibly dense cybersecurity strategies that few people in their organization could fully comprehend or repeat. Keeping the strategy simple to understand makes it easier for the stakeholder community and the people doing the work to understand the strategy and explain it to their teams (repeat it). If the strategy requires a secret decoder ring or knowledge of a specific technical industry standard to understand, it is unlikely that senior stakeholders who don't have cybersecurity backgrounds will understand it and really have confidence in it. It's likely that there are only a few teams within IT and the cybersecurity group that are responsible for understanding and executing the full strategy. You can reserve the super complicated version of the strategy, with overlays for GRC, product development, recruiting, supporting local cybersecurity educational programs, succession planning, and other components, for stakeholders that need and appreciate all that detail and ambition.

Regardless of how sophisticated a cybersecurity strategy is, its success relies on the ingredients I described in *Chapter 8* and crucially, how well it addresses the cybersecurity fundamentals. Measuring how a strategy performs over time is important so that adjustments can be made to improve it. Let's look at measuring efficacy next.

Measuring the efficacy of cybersecurity strategies

Let me reacquaint you with two concepts that I introduced in *Chapter 1* and mentioned again in *Chapter 8*. We are going to use these two concepts to measure the potential efficacy of the strategies that we examine.

Remember that the five ways that organizations get initially compromised, called the Cybersecurity Usual Suspects, are:

- Unpatched vulnerabilities
- Security misconfigurations
- Weak, leaked, or stolen credentials
- Social engineering
- Insider threats

Once an IT environment has been initially compromised, there are many, many **tactics, techniques, and procedures (TTPs)** that attackers can use to move laterally, steal credentials, compromise infrastructure, remain persistent, steal information, destroy data and infrastructure, and so on. Most of these TTPs have been around for years. Occasionally, the industry will see attackers employing novel approaches. Mitigating the Cybersecurity Usual Suspects is what I call the cybersecurity fundamentals. Organizations that focus on getting really good at the cybersecurity fundamentals make it much harder for attackers to be successful. Focusing on the things that all attackers do to initially compromise environments, the Cybersecurity Usual Suspects, is a hard requirement for any strategy or combination of strategies that organizations employ.

Put another way, if an organization's cybersecurity strategy doesn't include being excellent at the cybersecurity fundamentals, it is setting itself up for failure. Why? We know that 99.9% of successful compromises start with the Cybersecurity Usual Suspects. If that's true, why would your organization use a strategy that doesn't at least mitigate these attack vectors? Why would you use a strategy that you know has gaps in it, which attackers have used for decades to attack other organizations? Remember the submarine analogy that I used in the preface section of this book. Why would you set sail in a submarine that you know has flaws in its hull? Would you be confident enough to dive hundreds of feet under the surface of the ocean in that submarine, and allow immense pressure to build on every square millimeter of that hull? That sounds foolhardy, right? Still, there will be some organizations that will be willing to take large risks so that they can compete in fast-moving, competitive industries.

This is where some of the executives I've met felt like they must make a choice between cybersecurity and moving fast. But moving fast and cybersecurity are not mutually exclusive; this isn't a choice that they have to make, as they can get both cybersecurity efficacy AND business speed, agility, and scalability if they have a strategy that enables them to do so. Investing in approaches that willfully fail to address the most common ways organizations get compromised is a fool's errand. Additionally, if an environment is already compromised, the organization still needs to focus on the cybersecurity fundamentals in order to prevent even more attackers from getting a foothold, thereby preventing the attackers already inhabiting the environment from getting back into it, if they can ever be driven from it. Whatever strategy an organization employs, it needs to incorporate the cybersecurity fundamentals.

Once an organization hones its ability to manage the cybersecurity fundamentals and establishes a foundation that it can build on, then it makes sense to invest in advanced cybersecurity capabilities – capabilities that will help the organization when it fails to manage the cybersecurity fundamentals perfectly over time. Your strategy needs a solid foundation, even if it has advanced cybersecurity capabilities, because the platforms these advanced capabilities rely on for information and their own security can be undermined by unpatched vulnerabilities, security misconfigurations, social engineering, insider threats, and weak, leaked, and stolen passwords.

Being excellent at addressing all the cybersecurity fundamentals in both Production and Development/Test environments is a requirement for successfully deploying and operating advanced cybersecurity capabilities in your IT environment. For example, if an organization doesn't have a plan to find and correct security vulnerabilities and misconfigurations in the hardware and software they deploy as part of their advanced cybersecurity capabilities, they shouldn't bother deploying them because, over time, they will just increase the organization's attack surface.

You might be wondering why you must invest in advanced cybersecurity capabilities at all if your organization is really good at the cybersecurity fundamentals. Because you have to plan for failure. You have to assume that the organization will be breached – it's not a matter of *if*, only a matter of *when* and *how often* it will happen. This "assume breach" philosophy is important for at least two reasons. First, history has taught us that planning to achieve 100% perfect protection for large on-premises IT environments for a sustained period of time is a wildly optimistic ambition. People in your organization and supply chain will make mistakes, and some of these will be security-related.

For example, your applications, whether development is done in-house or through vendors, will have bugs in them. Some of these bugs will be security vulnerabilities. Some of these vulnerabilities will be exploitable. You need to plan for this eventuality. You need to plan for the mistakes that administrators make that lead to security misconfigurations. You need to plan for the scenario where the trusted vendors in your supply chain get compromised or turn malevolent. This is an area where Red Teams can ground strategy in reality as they specialize in taking advantage of unrealistic assumptions.

The second reason organizations need to adopt an "assume breach" philosophy is that it gives their security teams permission to think about some key questions that security teams who believe they can achieve 100% effective protection, forever, never ask themselves. For example, how would they know when they have been compromised? What will they do when they get compromised? These are questions that many security teams never ask themselves because they will not, or cannot, adopt an "assume breach" philosophy.

Some corporate cultures will not tolerate failure, so the idea that they plan for failure makes no sense to them; it's like admitting that they aren't good enough to do their jobs. In other organizations, senior executives will not support a plan for failure. I've met many executives that do not understand that they are in a submarine under immense pressure, surrounded by badness. Some of the executives I've talked to believe they are in a winnable battle. They believe that if they are smart enough, hire the right people, and buy the right protection capabilities, they will win the battle. But cybersecurity is a journey, not a destination. It doesn't have a beginning and an ending the way a battle does. It's constant, like pressure on the hull of a submarine. Planning for failure is the antithesis of their world view, so they refuse to support CISOs that know they need to embrace a more modern approach to cybersecurity. This is one reason why, when I worked as a cybersecurity advisor, I always tried to spend time with cybersecurity strategy stakeholders other than the CISO and the security team. Very often, the security team understands everything I've written here, but one or two executives or board members have uninformed views.

Advanced cybersecurity capabilities are the part of your strategy that will help you identify, protect, detect, respond and recover (NIST, n.d.). This is the part of your strategy that helps augment and identify shortcomings in the cybersecurity fundamentals. You need them both for the strategy to be successful. The **High-Value Assets** (**HVAs**) component of the strategy acknowledges the importance of HVAs. As I mentioned in *Chapter 8*, if the confidentiality, integrity, or availability of an HVA is compromised, this typically means the organization itself will fail.

The sustained compromise of an HVA could be an extinction event for a company (Ashford, 2016) and drive public sector organizations back to using pencils, paper, and the processes they used before they invested in IT.

Planning and investing in security specifically focused on HVAs, in addition to the cybersecurity fundamentals and advanced cybersecurity capabilities, will help organizations manage the risk to their most important assets.

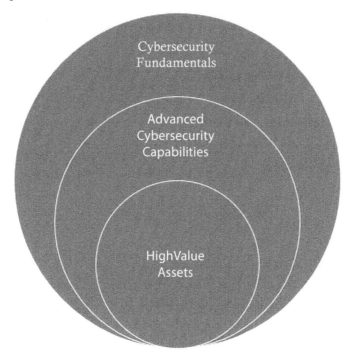

Figure 9.1: An illustration of a cybersecurity strategy

Regardless of organizations' HVAs and which advanced cybersecurity capacities they decide to invest in (which is highly variable between organizations), the entire strategy model I've outlined here relies on the foundation that the cybersecurity fundamentals provide. Without a solid foundation, a strategy will fail over time. Any cybersecurity strategy that an enterprise pursues needs to focus on the cybersecurity fundamentals at a minimum. Given this, I'm going to introduce a simple method to help determine a strategy's potential efficacy by estimating how well it incorporates the cybersecurity fundamentals and mitigates the Cybersecurity Usual Suspects.

I will estimate the potential efficacy of the cybersecurity strategies we examine by using a simple scoring system. I call this system the **cybersecurity fundamentals scoring system (CFSS)**. This system assigns a score between 0 and 10 for each of the Cybersecurity Usual Suspects, based on how well the strategy mitigates the risk. Higher scores mean that the strategy is more effective at mitigating each particular Cybersecurity Usual Suspect. For example, a score of 20 means the strategy fully mitigates the risk associated with a specific Cybersecurity Usual Suspect. A low score, such as a score of 1, for example, means that the strategy's ability to mitigate the risk is relatively low. The CFSS includes a separate score for each of the five Cybersecurity Usual Suspects, as shown in *Table 9.1*:

Cybersecurity Usual Suspect	Score
Unpatched vulnerabilities	0-20
Security misconfigurations	0-20
Weak, leaked, stolen credentials	0-20
Social engineering	0-20
Insider threat	0-20

Table 9.1 CFSS summary

The total of all five of the scores is the CFSS total score for the strategy. The lowest possible CFSS total score for a strategy is 0, while the highest is 100. For example, as shown in *Table 9.2*, let's say we have a strategy called "XYZ" and we estimate scores for the five measures in the CFSS. When we add up the individual scores, we get a CFSS total score of 23 out of a possible 100 points:

XYZ Strategy Example	Score
Unpatched vulnerabilities	10
Security misconfigurations	10
Weak, leaked, stolen credentials	2
Social engineering	0
Insider threat	1

Table 9.2: An example of the CFSS

The goal is to find a strategy that gives us a perfect 100 score, although this is likely more aspirational than probable. But this type of scoring system gives us a way to estimate a strategy's ability to mitigate all five ways organizations get initially compromised, as well as a way to compare strategies across the cybersecurity fundamentals.

Potentially, this approach can help us identify a combination of strategies that gives us a perfect score, or a high score, across the Cybersecurity Usual Suspects if no single strategy does this. Finally, it can also help us determine where the gaps are in a strategy that's currently in use by an organization. If you know where the weaknesses or gaps are, then you can develop a plan to address these inadequacies.

Before we start measuring strategies using this framework, I want to point out a couple of hidden risks using this type of rating. Like most risk-based approaches, it is based on the assumption that CISOs and security teams will be able to accurately estimate the level of risk and identify effective mitigations. In my experience, I have seen some CISOs overestimate their capabilities and their ability to effectively mitigate risks, all while simultaneously underestimating the risks themselves and the effectiveness of the cybersecurity fundamentals. A second risk is that this approach assumes all five of the Cybersecurity Usual Suspects are equally important to the organization. However, it's important to recognize that since each organization is different, mitigations can have different values for different organizations.

Now that we have a cybersecurity strategy concept in mind and a scoring system to help us determine the relative efficacy of different approaches, let's examine numerous cybersecurity strategies in more detail.

Cybersecurity strategies

As I mentioned in *Chapter 8, Ingredients for a Successful Cybersecurity Strategy*, some of the cybersecurity professionals I have met with have a negative reaction when the term "strategy" is used in a cybersecurity context. This is a word that can be used in at least a few different ways. Security and compliance professionals sometimes use the term "strategy" when they are referring to frameworks, models, or standards. I explained what I mean when I use this term, in detail, in *Chapter 8, Ingredients for a Successful Cybersecurity Strategy*. If you haven't read that chapter already, I recommend that you read it because it provides a lot of context that I won't repeat here. You'll see me use the terms **framework**, **approach**, and **model**, interchangeably throughout all the chapters. Please feel free to associate whatever term makes the most sense to you when I use any of these terms.

The following list contains many of the strategies that I have seen in use over the last two decades in the industry. I'm going to examine each of these strategies in detail and provide an estimated CFSS score for each one. The CFSS scores that I provide are my own subjective opinions and are subject to my own assumptions and biases. I provide you with some context on why each Cybersecurity Usual Suspect was scored the way it was so that you can understand my approach and agree or disagree with it.

I invite you to think through your own CFSS score estimate for each of these strategies:

- Protect and Recover Strategy
- Endpoint Protection Strategy
- Physical control and security clearances as a strategy
- Compliance as a Security Strategy
- Application-Centric Strategy
- Identity-Centric Strategy
- Data-Centric Strategy
- Attack-Centric Strategy
- Zero Trust strategy

As we review these strategies, even if your organization doesn't use any of them, please ask yourself if your supply chain vendors use any of them. If you don't know about the strategies they are using to manage the risk to their organizations and to their customers, then you might want to ask them how they are mitigating the Cybersecurity Usual Suspects. This is the minimum they should be doing for themselves and for their customers. Many enterprises already use security questionnaires, some of which have hundreds of questions, to get a better idea of whether potential vendors' security policies meet their standards. In these cases, it could be valuable to add a few questions about the strategy to these questionnaires to gauge the security maturity of the vendor.

Finally, let's examine some cybersecurity strategies!

Protect and Recover Strategy

Let's start with a relatively old strategy that I call the *Protect and Recover Strategy*. It's also known as the *perimeter security* strategy. As the cliché goes, it's typically described as having a hard outer shell and a soft, sometimes gooey, center. This analogy is often used because once an organization's perimeter defenses get penetrated, little or nothing impedes attackers from moving laterally in the environment and staying persistent indefinitely. The organization is left trying to recover the original data and IT environment, usually with mixed success. It is considered an old-fashioned strategy by today's standards, but I find a surprising number of organizations still cling to it.

As the name suggests, the focus of this strategy is to prevent attackers from being successful by investing in protection technologies such as firewalls, **Demilitarized Zones (DMZs)**, proxy servers, and micro-segmentation. Let's go back to 2003 for a great example of why this strategy became so popular.

By 2003, there had already been successful mass worm attacks on the internet, such as Code Red and Nimda. The risk of such attacks was no longer theoretical, as many people had argued it was at the time. The industry was just starting to understand that software had vulnerabilities and that some of these were exploitable. At that time, I was working on Microsoft's customer-facing Security Incident Response Team. Many of the organizations I helped blamed Microsoft for not doing more to protect Windows from such attacks.

There was a widespread belief among enterprise customers that if they replaced Microsoft Windows with another operating system, then they'd be secure. They were the manufacturer of the world's most widely used operating system, and subsequently, garnered a lot of attention from legitimate security researchers and attackers alike. Of course, now, all these years later, I think everyone understands that all vendors have vulnerabilities in their software and hardware. If you still have any doubts about this, please go back and re-read *Chapter 3, Using Vulnerability Trends to Reduce Risk and Costs.* In 2003, the mitigation for the risk that unpatched vulnerabilities posed was the firewall. When Microsoft turned on Windows Firewall by default in Windows XP Service Pack 2, it was hoped that this would prevent the exploitation of vulnerabilities in Windows services and applications listening on the network.

Windows Firewall, together with several other security mitigations, including automatic updates, successfully blunted the mass worm attacks of the era. Many enterprise-scale organizations already had corporate firewalls in place at the perimeter of their networks in 2003. But most of them had exceptions for all traffic going to and from ports 80 and 443 so that HTTP and HTTPS traffic could flow freely; these are the so-called "universal firewall bypass ports." For the next few years, enterprises that didn't already have DMZs put them in place to enforce better control on network traffic coming from and going to the internet.

This evolution in security strategy was an important and effective step for the industry. But somewhere along the way, the original benefits of perimeter security were distorted. Ultimately, perimeter security was supposed to provide organizations with two things. First, it protected resources that were supposed to be private from public access. Second, blocking anonymous inbound network traffic to vulnerable services listening on the network gave organizations more time to test and deploy security updates. But the idea that firewalls, DMZs, and network segmentation could somehow provide a long-term solution to vulnerability management or the other four Cybersecurity Usual Suspects, 5 to 10 years before application layer capabilities were built into some of these products, was misguided.

The underlying assumption of the *Protect and Recover Strategy* is that the organization will be able to deploy and operate adequate protection technologies and processes. If these fail, then recovery is their plan. Because the organization will be so good at protection, it doesn't really need to invest in detection and response capabilities. Most of the organizations that embraced this approach also invested in backup and recovery capabilities, but not necessarily for security purposes; rather, these capabilities mitigated the risk of data loss. When their protection strategy ultimately failed, their backup and recovery capabilities were their backstop. So, although these two components weren't necessarily meant to be parts of a coherent cybersecurity strategy, they have been so commonly deployed in enterprise environments that they complement each other very well. If the assumption that the organization can effectively protect itself 100% of the time, forever, turns out to be untrue, then they can restore from backup.

This approach is characterized by investments primarily in perimeter and network protection, as well as backup and recovery. Professionals with networking expertise could extend their expertise into the security domain. This made a lot of sense since nearly 100% of attacks happened using networks. For many enterprises, their networking groups extended the scope of their charters to include network security, DMZs, and managing firewalls.

The *Protect and Recover Strategy* has some advantages. Technologies and disciplines like TCP/IP, routing and switching, firewall configuration, and operations are areas that have a trained workforce compared to other security disciplines such as application security, malware reverse engineering, or red and blue teaming. Because it's a relatively mature strategy, there is a very well-developed vendor and consulting ecosystem that has decades of experience supporting it. A trained workforce, and this ecosystem, make this strategy a natural choice for organizations that constrain themselves to primarily using IT staff and vendors they already have commercial contracts with, for cybersecurity.

Of course, this strategy also has some disadvantages. History has shown this to be a poor cybersecurity strategy. Some of you might disagree with my description of this strategy, but you can't disagree that in literally every major breach that made headlines in the last 20 years, the victim organization had been using this approach in some way. The reason this approach has failed time and again is that its underlying assumption is deeply flawed. The assumption that the organization will never be compromised because it will be 100% successful at protecting itself is wildly optimistic. Today, enterprises that don't invest in detection and response capabilities, in addition to protection and recovery capabilities, could be considered negligent.

Reducing the time between compromise and detection is seen as a modern cybersecurity mantra that the *Protect and Recover Strategy* was not designed to embrace. Subsequently, organizations that use this strategy can have very long periods between initial compromise and detection, sometimes hundreds of days or spanning years. This strategy doesn't recognize that attackers have a disproportionate advantage over defenders; defenders need to be perfect 100% of the time, which is an unrealistic aspiration, while attackers only need to be good or lucky once.

This strategy relies on developers, administrators, vendors, partners, and users not making any mistakes or poor trust decisions that could lead to compromise. But as we've seen for decades, users will unwittingly bring threats through layers of perimeter defenses themselves. Without detection and response capabilities, once an organization is penetrated, attackers can typically persist indefinitely, making recovery aspirational and expensive.

The good news is that many of the organizations that used the *Protect and Recover Strategy* in the past have matured their approach over time. They still employ this strategy but use it in combination with other strategies. They've also upgraded the technologies and products they rely on. Today, next-generation firewalls go far beyond filtering TCP and UDP ports and can perform deep packet inspection. But a question these organizations still need to consider is whether their business partners and supply chain partners still employ this old strategy. For many years, attackers have been targeting small, less mature partners and suppliers in order to get access to their large customers' infrastructures and data. Small legal firms, marketing, and advertising firms, and even heating and air conditioning vendors, have been targeted for this purpose. Many small firms like these, in countries around the world, still use the *Protect and Recover Strategy*. In many cases, they have not invested in relatively expensive cybersecurity expertise that could help them modernize their approaches.

CFSS score

How well does the *Protect and Recover Strategy* mitigate the Cybersecurity Usual Suspects? *Table 9.3* contains my CFSS score estimates:

Cybersecurity fundamentals	Score (0-20)
Unpatched vulnerabilities	10
Security misconfigurations	10
Weak, leaked, stolen credentials	0
Social engineering	5
Insider threat	0

CFSS Total Score (max=100)	25

Table 9.3: The CFSS score estimate for the Protect and Recover Strategy

As you might have gleaned from my description of this strategy, although it has some benefits, it doesn't address the cybersecurity fundamentals very well.

For unpatched vulnerabilities, I gave this strategy 10/20. This score reflects that firewalls and segmentation can make it harder for attackers and malware to access exploitable vulnerabilities listening on network ports. If network traffic can't make it to the vulnerable service's port, then the vulnerability can't be exploited. But this mitigation isn't a permanent condition for an exploitable vulnerability. As soon as an administrator changes the rule for the firewall filter blocking the port, then the vulnerability could potentially become instantly exploitable, unbeknownst to the administrator. Typically, filters will block unsolicited inbound traffic to a port, but they will allow inbound traffic resulting from legitimate outbound traffic on the same port. Under the right conditions, the service or application could be enticed to make an outbound connection to a destination under the control of attackers. Firewalls only provide temporary mitigation to unpatched vulnerabilities, thus giving vulnerability management teams more time to find and patch vulnerabilities. The vulnerable software needs to be uninstalled from the system (which can't be easily done for most operating system components) or it needs to be patched. The *Protect and Recover Strategy* doesn't focus on vulnerability management. The same is true for security misconfigurations. This strategy doesn't help us fully mitigate these two Cybersecurity Usual Suspects – the best it can do is delay exploitation. For this reason, I gave it partial marks in these two areas.

This strategy does nothing to address weak, leaked, or stolen credentials or insider threat. Therefore, both received a score of zero.

Finally, I gave this strategy's ability to mitigate social engineering partial marks. Firewalls and DMZs can filter connections based on URLs and IP addresses. They can prevent users who are tricked into clicking on malicious links from connecting to known malicious servers and unauthorized sites. Outbound traffic can be blocked and flagged, as well as inbound replies to such outbound traffic. The challenge has been keeping up with attackers who use compromised systems all over the world to host complex multicomponent attacks, and constantly changing sources and destinations for attacks. History has taught us that this approach does not mitigate social engineering attacks very effectively.

This is because it still relies on users and administrators to make sound trust decisions, which has always been challenging. Nonetheless, I gave it partial marks for social engineering for what it can do.

With a CFSS total score of 25 out of a possible 100, clearly, this strategy must be used in combination with other strategies in order to really address the cybersecurity fundamentals, as well as provide a foundation that an enterprise can build on. Many organizations have already come to this conclusion and have evolved their approaches. But some of the smaller organizations in their supply chain likely still use this strategy because they lack the expertise and resources to evolve. How many small businesses and independent consultants still rely on the firewalls built into their wireless access points for protection?

Protect and Recover Strategy summary

The CFSS total score for this strategy is 25/100. It must be used in combination with other strategies.

Advantages:

- Large vendor ecosystem to help organizations implement and operate
- Relatively large, trained workforce with years of experience

Disadvantages:

- History has shown this to be a poor strategy; failing to invest in detection and recovery capabilities gives attackers an unnecessary advantage
- Attackers have a disproportionate advantage over defenders because defenders must be perfect
- It relies on developers, administrators, and users not making mistakes or poor trust decisions that lead to compromise – individuals bring threats through the perimeter and host-based defenses themselves
- Once penetrated, attackers can persist indefinitely, making recovery aspirational because of a lack of investment in detection and response capabilities

Now, let's examine a strategy that doesn't focus on the network perimeter.

Endpoint Protection Strategy

Next, I'll discuss another relatively old strategy, the *Endpoint Protection* Strategy. This is what I call a "proxy" strategy. The idea here is that endpoints, such as personal computers, mobile devices, some types of IoT devices, and so on, are used to process, store, and transmit data.

Therefore, if we protect these endpoints, we are, by proxy, protecting the data, which is the whole point of data protection. Stated another way, the data will be compromised if the endpoints/devices are compromised, so the endpoints must be protected. Once upon a time, many organizations used this strategy by itself to protect their assets. The underlying assumption is that protecting endpoints and devices is an effective proxy for protecting the organization's data.

The *Endpoint Protection Strategy* is characterized by investments in host protection technologies like asset inventorying and vulnerability management solutions, anti-malware solutions, file integrity monitoring, host-based firewalls, application whitelisting, web browser protections, mobile device management, enterprise configuration management, endpoint hardening, IoT device management, **Endpoint Detection and Response (EDR)**, and **Extended Detection and Response (XDR)**, among many others. Many of these capabilities are already built into Windows and Linux operating systems, but that doesn't stop endpoint protection vendors from offering better implementations of these features that typically have integrated management and reporting capabilities.

What's an endpoint? It turns out there are a lot of possible definitions. First, it's important to understand that different operating system manufacturers allow different levels of system access to third-party **Independent Software Vendors (ISVs)**, which can have a big impact on what their solutions are capable of. Vendors that sell endpoint protection solutions have their own definitions that support their specific value propositions. This used to be a short list of major antivirus vendors, but in recent years, the list has grown, and the vendors have become far more diverse. Currently, I count more than 20 different vendors that are actively marketing endpoint protection platform solutions. These include (in alphabetical order): BitDefender, BlackBerry Cylance, Check Point, Cisco, CrowdStrike, Cybereason, ESET, Fortinet, F-Secure, Kaspersky, Malwarebytes, Microsoft, Palo Alto Networks, Panda Security, SentinelOne, Sophos, Symantec, Trellix, Trend Micro, VMware Carbon Black, and Webroot. There are a bunch of other vendors in this space, including regional vendors in China, among others.

Some of these vendors have antivirus labs with decades of experience, while others are leveraging security company acquisitions and innovations from other areas to try to disrupt the endpoint protection market. Many vendors include analytics, response, and cloud capabilities as part of their solutions.

Having worked in an anti-malware lab and on a security incident response team, I have an appreciation for this approach. Endpoints are where most of the action happens during a data breach. No matter how good firewall and IDS vendors' products get, they simply do not have the same vantage point as the endpoint device typically has itself.

You can see the fish a lot better when you are in the fishbowl versus watching from outside of it. Solutions installed directly on the endpoints enable continuous monitoring and a range of automated actions when triggers are hit. Endpoint protection scanning engines are some of the most impressive feats of programming in the world. These engines are designed to unpack numerous file compression and obfuscation formats that can be nested by attackers, in virtual computing environments that simulate real operating systems, in order to determine if files are malicious in near real time.

Threats can be file-based, macros, scripts, polymorphic viruses, boot viruses, rootkits, and so on, across different operating systems and filesystems. Of course, they have a lot more functionality like heuristics, behavioral analysis, browser protections, malicious IP address filtering, and much, much more. When you dig into the functionality of some of these endpoint protection solutions and consider how hard it is to develop them and keep them current, they are super impressive.

However, engineering alone is not enough. These solutions are only as good as the research and response labs that care for and feed them. Maintaining critical masses of great researchers, analysts, and supporting staff is an important function that these vendors provide. The combination of impressive engineering and a world-class research and response lab is the key to selecting an effective endpoint protection vendor. The large vendor ecosystem that I described earlier is very positive. This is because it creates healthy competition and these vendors keep each other honest by supporting third-party testing (av-test.org and av-comparatives.org, among others) and industry conferences (annual Virus Bulletin International Conference (Virus Bulletin, n.d.)) where they discuss how to govern their industry, among other things.

But of course, this approach also has challenges. History has taught us that the *Endpoint Protection Strategy*, by itself, is insufficient. Have any of the victims in massive data breaches that have hit the headlines in the last 10 years not been running endpoint protection solutions? First, relying on a patient to diagnose and cure itself is an optimistic approach. Once the trusted computing base of a system has been compromised, how can endpoint protection solutions reliably use it to detect threats on the system and clean them? Endpoint protection solutions have been targets for attackers and their malware for decades. One of the first things many families of malware do after they initially compromise a system is to disable or subvert the endpoint protection solution. This is where remote attestation services can help, but in my experience, few organizations use such services because of their complexity. Some vendors use virtualization and other techniques to protect their solutions from attackers. But rest assured that attackers will continue to research ways to subvert endpoint protection solutions.

The playing field is never level in this game. Attackers can buy all the endpoint solutions available on the market and test their malware and tools, prior to attacking with them, to ensure no solution can detect or clean them. The endpoint protection vendors don't have that same advantage. But more fundamentally, can the patient really be trusted to cure itself? Some organizations will clean compromised systems with endpoint solutions and allow them to continue running in production, while others have policies to flatten and rebuild any system that has been compromised. Virtualization has made this easier and the cloud, as I'll discuss in detail later, makes this even easier and more effective. But the key to this approach is still accurate threat detection. Keep in mind that although the aspirational goal for all these solutions is to detect, block, and, if necessary, clean 100% of threats, this isn't realistic. The internal goals of research and response labs are typically more realistic and attainable. For example, detection for 100% of threats in the "zoo" (their private malware library) is likely a common goal among these vendors. But detection goals for emerging threats might be 80%. After all, it takes time for research and response labs to get samples of threats, process them, and deploy appropriate protections to their customers, especially when attackers are using mass automation to generate millions of them constantly.

Would you set sail in a submarine that had the goal of keeping 80% of the water outside the hull? Probably not. But as I wrote in *Chapter 4, The Evolution of Malware*, if you don't use endpoint protection because it doesn't protect the endpoint from 100% of threats, then you aren't protecting the endpoints from the millions of threats that endpoint protection solutions do protect against.

CFSS score

Let's look at how the *Endpoint Protection Strategy* helps organizations address the cybersecurity fundamentals. *Table 9.4* contains my CFSS score estimates. Remember that these are just estimates based on my experience and they don't reflect the state of the art in endpoint protection.

Please feel free to develop your own estimates if you think I'm way off base with mine:

Cybersecurity fundamentals	Score (0-20)
Unpatched vulnerabilities	20
Security misconfigurations	20
Weak, leaked, stolen credentials	15
Social engineering	10
Insider threat	10
CFSS Total Score (max=100)	75

Table 9.4: The CFFS score estimate for the Endpoint Protection Strategy

I gave this strategy full marks for mitigating unpatched vulnerabilities and security misconfigurations. The combination of inventorying, scanning, updating, hardening, and monitoring can be very effective. For weak, leaked, and stolen credentials, I estimated endpoint protection mitigating 15/20. Organizations that use Secure Access Workstations or Privileged Access Workstations (endpoints hardened for attacks specifically looking for cached administrator credentials) as part of their endpoint strategy can mitigate this type of threat to a large extent, but not completely. Endpoint protection solutions can also help partially mitigate social engineering, as well as insider threat, by making it harder for users and administrators to make some of the common mistakes and poor trust choices that lead to compromise, but they won't fully mitigate malicious insiders.

Although the *Endpoint Protection Strategy* is insufficient by itself, it would be hard to imagine a successful enterprise cybersecurity strategy that didn't use it in combination with other strategies. It seems like the industry agrees with this assessment as more and more organizations I have talked to have adopted or plan to adopt **Security Orchestration, Automation, and Response (SOAR)** solutions. Some vendors describe SOAR as an evolutionary step in endpoint protection in that it combines functionality from a stack of different capabilities, including endpoint protection and response.

Endpoint Protection Strategy summary

The CFSS total score for this strategy is 75/100. It must be used in combination with other strategies.

Advantages:

- Superior visibility and control running on the endpoint

- Large vendor ecosystem to help with decades of experience

- Constant threat research, response, and evolving technologies to stay ahead of attackers

Disadvantages:

- History has shown this to be a poor strategy by itself as it didn't prevent many of the major data breaches that have been in the headlines.

- Users resist systems that are too restrictive or impact productivity; individuals bring threats through defenses themselves in many cases. This approach can only partially mitigate the mistakes or poor trust decisions that developers, administrators, and users make that lead to compromise.

- Speed is a factor. Relatively slow and complicated vulnerability management processes give attackers an advantage. Organizations that have a good endpoint strategy but deploy security updates and other protections relatively slowly accept more risk.

- Endpoint protection suites have inconsistent performance histories and aspirational performance goals. Organizations that don't understand the internal goals of the endpoint protection vendors might not fully understand the associated risks.

- Managing endpoint security relies on accurate and timely asset inventorying and management capabilities. This has been notoriously hard in on-premises environments. I will discuss how the cloud makes this easier later.

- Many organizations allow employees to use personal unmanaged or partially managed laptops, desktops, and mobile devices, known as the **Bring Your Own Device** (**BYOD**) strategy. Subsequently, the risk associated with the transmission, storage, and processing of corporate data on these devices might not be fully understood.

- Routing, switching, storage, IoT, and other hardware devices might not be integrated into an organization's *Endpoint Protection Strategy*, but should be.

That's the *Endpoint Protection Strategy*. Now, let's move on to security strategies involving physical control and security clearances.

Physical control and security clearances as a security strategy

I see this next strategy in widespread use, especially by public sector organizations. I call this strategy the *Physical Control and Security Clearances* Strategy. As you can probably tell from the name, it relies on having physical control of the infrastructure used to transmit, store, and process data, as well as data classification and associated security clearances. The idea behind this strategy is that not all data has the same relative value to the organization that controls it. By classifying the data into different categories that reflect the relative value of the data, we can ensure the most valuable data is protected in ways that are commensurate with that value.

There are many different data classification schemes in use in the public and private sectors; many organizations have developed their own data classification schemes. We don't have to look any further than the US federal government to see a great example of a data classification scheme that has been deployed on a massive scale. Executive Order 13526 (United States Government Publishing Office, 2009) defines a three-tier system for classifying national security information. It defines those three tiers as Top secret, Secret, and Confidential. Another similar example is the UK government's security classification for third-party suppliers (U.K. Cabinet Office, 2013). It also defines three classifications that indicate the sensitivity of information. These categories include Top secret, Secret, and Official. There are many other examples of data classification schemes.

Data classification policies such as these can dictate the people, processes, and technologies that must be employed to handle data in each category. As such, the number and nature of the categories in the data classification schemes that organizations adopt can have a huge effect on organizations' cultures, recruiting practices, IT investments, and budgets, among other things.

This is where security clearances can become a factor. For some organizations, in order for personnel to be granted access to information that has been classified into a specific category, that personnel must have a current security clearance that permits access to information in that category. For example, if someone doesn't have a clearance that permits access to data that has been classified as secret, then they should not be granted access to information that has been classified as secret. In order to get a security clearance, there can be background checks involved, some of which are much deeper and more involved than others.

For example, some security clearances require a criminal history check. Other, deeper, background checks require a criminal history check, an employment background check, and a financial credit score check, in addition to the applicant providing personal references, who will be interviewed as part of the background check process. Some security clearances have specific citizenship requirements. Some clearances have a one-time process that applicants go through, while other clearances need to be periodically renewed. Some technology vendors give their customers insight into the background checks they subject their employees to. Microsoft is an example; they've published a personnel management overview (Microsoft Corporation, 2023).

You might be wondering why employers simply don't perform all these checks periodically as a matter of course. Different countries and jurisdictions have local labor laws and statutory regulations that protect the privacy and the rights of employees. For example, in the US, too many credit checks can lower an individual's credit score. Allowing employers to institute administrative procedures that potentially negatively impact current or potential employees is not cool. Note that many data classification schemes don't require security clearances, because they are designed to simply provide a way for the staff handling the data to understand how it should be handled.

From a security perspective, organizations that are serious about this approach are essentially trying to create a closed system for their data that has a high level of security assurance. People that handle data, especially sensitive data, will be vetted to minimize the likelihood that they have malicious intent or could be easily bribed or blackmailed to break their organization's policies. This concept of assurance also extends to their processes and technology. For example, some organizations have policies that dictate that data will only be transmitted, stored, and processed by hardware and software that has gone through their certification processes. All other electronics are never allowed into their on-premises environments. This includes anything that has a power cord or a battery.

The business processes that these vetted employees use to operate their certified systems are carefully engineered to ensure auditability and ensure that multiple people participate, to keep each other honest. The underlying assumptions that make this closed system work are that the organization has end-to-end control of its entire infrastructure and that its supply chain is subject to security clearances and certification processes. Numerous trusted IT suppliers participate in these types of supply chains in countries all over the world.

The essence of this strategy can be traced back decades, if not centuries, when it's been heavily employed by militaries and national security organizations throughout the world. Of course, there have been national security failures throughout history, which tells us this approach isn't foolproof. In modern times, this model has been evolving.

It works well on a small scale, but it gets incrementally harder to manage as it scales up. As their operations scaled, it became harder for these organizations to manage all their IT in-house. The types of organizations that use this model face the same IT resource and recruiting challenges as other industries.

Subsequently, many of them have outsourced much of their IT to cope with these challenges. In many cases, this means that the contractors they use to manage their IT have physical access to the data centers and servers processing their data.

More specifically, in the course of their work, these contractors have access to the operating systems and hypervisors running on those servers, the virtualized workloads, and the data in those workloads. But the organization that owns the data must maintain its closed system to protect the data – that's its strategy. Because the contractors potentially have access to classified data, they require the same security clearances as the organization's regular personnel. The contractor's datacenters and the IT infrastructure in them also must go through the organization's certification processes. Since this is all complicated and very expensive to accomplish, to make it economically viable, the contracts between these organizations and qualified contractors tend to be very long-term, sometimes 10, 20, or even 30 years in duration. This managed service provider model is the way that IT has been outsourced to these organizations for the last 20+ years. Of course, there are a bunch of advantages and disadvantages to using managed service providers; I'll touch on a few of these later.

To recap, the focus of the *Physical Control and Security Clearances Strategy* is the security assurance of hardware and software, and periodic background checks of datacenter staff and administrators. It is characterized by investments in people, processes, and technologies that help maintain physical security, assurance, and confidence in the character of datacenter staff and administrators. Data classification also typically plays a critical role in helping protect the most important data. This approach has numerous benefits. Some governments literally have hundreds of years of practice using this type of strategy. However, it can help partially mitigate insider threats by identifying potentially risky job candidates and personnel that could have access to sensitive data. Third-party verification or attestation of the trustworthiness of hardware and software contributes to security assurance and helps demonstrate due diligence. There is a large vendor ecosystem to help organizations that want to pursue this type of strategy.

Of course, this strategy also has some important disadvantages and limitations. First, data classification is challenging for most organizations. Using data classification can be very helpful for organizations that want to ensure that their most sensitive data is protected appropriately.

Treating all data as if it has the same relative value to the organization is the most expensive way to manage data. But data classification schemes are notoriously difficult to successfully institute in large organizations. In my experience, the organizations that have the most success with data classifications are those organizations where security is deeply embedded in the culture. Military and paramilitary organizations, law enforcement agencies, national defense departments, and intelligence agencies are some examples of organizations where data classification is deeply engrained into the culture, people, processes, and supporting technologies. For these organizations, typically there literally is risk to human life if data classification is not administered correctly.

Many commercial organizations have tried and failed – some, multiple times – to institute data classification schemes. The typical challenge for these organizations is finding a way to classify data that doesn't make it hard or impossible for information workers to get work done. Organizations that allow the same people who create the data to classify the data usually end up with large amounts of data that have been over-classified or under-classified, depending on the consequences to employees. For example, in military organizations, under-classifying data could lead to severe consequences such as loss of life and/or criminal charges. Data in these organizations tends to get over-classified because workers are better safe than sorry; they'll rarely get into trouble for over-classifying data, despite the immense extra costs when everyone in a large organization does this habitually.

In organizations where there aren't life or death consequences or national security concerns, data can be under-classified more easily, making it easier for information workers to get their work done. Executives in some of these organizations believe the rules don't apply to them and demand ad hoc access to whatever data they need, regardless of how it is classified or why. This is one reason they are often the targets of Business Email Compromise schemes and other social engineering attacks. They can get access to any data and often, they are exempt from the inconvenient security controls that mitigate such attacks. A recipe for disaster that is often realized.

Of course, in neither of these scenarios, where data is under- or over-classified, does data classification fulfill its promise. Some commercial and public sector organizations decide not to institute data classification schemes because their past attempts to do so have all failed or have not achieved their desired objectives. Instead, these organizations have concluded that data classification is too complex and expensive to be worthwhile. For them, it's easier and more effective to treat all their data as if it's the same value. Some of them will employ less formal, very simple data classification schemes by marking some documents and data as confidential or internal only. But the data protection requirements are the same for all their data.

Keep in mind that in many organizations, the one system that typically stores, processes, and transmits the data of all classifications is email. It's relatively rare for organizations to have two separate email systems – one email system for unclassified data and one for classified data. Subsequently, data of all classifications can end up in emails, which can become a source of data leakage.

Data residency is often a requirement for organizations that embrace this security strategy. That is, they require that all datacenters that process and store their data must be located in a specific country or jurisdiction. For example, all the data for a federal government department must stay within the national borders of the country. There are a few different reasons for data residency requirements, but the most common one cited is that data residency provides better security for the data and that the organization requires data sovereignty, which they likely will not have within the borders of another country. In order to maintain their closed system, they cannot risk putting a datacenter in a location that another government has sovereign control over.

Data residency doesn't mitigate any of the Cybersecurity Usual Suspects. This is because 99% of the attacks happen remotely over the network, regardless of the physical location of the datacenter. Attackers don't care where the datacenter is physically located because that is not an effective mitigation for the vast majority of attacks.

This is why many organizations that embrace the *Physical Control and Security Clearances Strategy* put "air gaps" into their networks. Put another way, their networks are not directly connected to the internet. I've seen organizations try to accomplish air gaps in a few ways. Some simply don't procure internet connectivity from an ISP. Some use data diodes that are certified to only allow network traffic flow in one direction. Some organizations call a network "air-gapped" when it's behind a DMZ with very specific firewall rules. To truly air-gap a network can be incredibly difficult to accomplish and maintain over time. The ubiquity of mobile devices, IoT devices, and common office equipment, like copiers that want to phone home with inventory and service information, makes it challenging to keep a disconnected network, disconnected. Some organizations maintain two networks, one for classified information and the other for non-classified information. Information workers in these environments typically have two computers on their desks, one connected to each of these networks. Some of the organizations that use air-gapped networks require all mobile devices, laptops, and electronics to be kept in lockers at the front door of their facilities. I've visited many of these types of facilities around the world over the years, advising public sector customers.

Organizations that achieve and maintain air-gapped networks can make it much harder for attackers to leverage the Cybersecurity Usual Suspects to initially compromise their networks. However, as the Stuxnet attack and so many other attacks on air-gapped networks over the years have proven, it's not an insurmountable challenge. Moreover, data residency is far less effective than other available controls that help mitigate the risks that these organizations have in mind with their data residency requirements. Encryption and effective key management are primary among these controls, as I discussed in *Chapter 7, Government Access to Data*. Leveraging modern encryption and key management technologies, organizations can achieve very strong data protection while operationalizing data so that it can help them make better decisions faster.

Perhaps the biggest challenge for the *Physical Control and Security Clearances Strategy* is that the world has changed in some key ways, all of which will make this strategy harder to pursue and less effective as time goes on. Organizations that currently use strategies like this one are being challenged in several ways.

For example, most organizations today want to take advantage of machine learning and artificial intelligence. They'll be challenged to do this in a scalable way in their accredited on-premises, air-gapped IT environments or via their traditional managed service providers' datacenters. In order to keep up with their adversaries, many of which aren't encumbered by the same certification and accreditation processes, organizations are going to have to change the way they procure and operate IT services. To do this, they will have to give up some of the end-to-end control they have had for decades. Their closed systems will have to evolve. For some of these organizations, this kind of change is super hard because initially it's uncomfortably different from how they've done governance, risk, and compliance for the last few decades. This doesn't mean they have to settle for a less secure IT environment, but they do have to re-evaluate how to mitigate the risks they care about in a world where they don't own the infrastructure end-to-end. Rising on-premises IT costs to maintain the status quo, in the face of tsunami after tsunami of innovation in the cloud, means that organizations that employ this type of strategy will either successfully evolve or become increasingly irrelevant.

CFSS score

Let's look at *Table 9.5* – how well does the *Physical Control and Security Clearances Strategy* help address the cybersecurity fundamentals? I'll estimate scores for two flavors of this strategy, one with an air-gapped network and one without an air-gapped network. As you'll see, this makes a big difference in terms of the scores.

Cybersecurity fundamentals	Score (0-20)
Unpatched vulnerabilities	10
Security misconfigurations	10
Weak, leaked, stolen credentials	15
Social engineering	10
Insider threat	10
CFSS Total Score (max=100)	55

Table 9.5: The CFSS score estimate for the Physical Control and Security Clearances Strategy with an air-gapped network

None of this strategy's attributes, such as data classification, security clearances, or end-to-end control of certified hardware help to fully mitigate unpatched vulnerabilities, security misconfigurations, and weak, leaked, or stolen passwords. Like the *Protect and Recover Strategy*, an air-gapped network can give security teams more time to address these Cybersecurity Usual Suspects, but they still must be addressed. Weak, leaked, and stolen credentials are harder to use if there is no remote network access to the target network. If the principle of least privilege is applied accurately and consistently, this can make it harder to achieve unauthorized access to sensitive data.

As I discussed earlier in this chapter, data classification and security clearances can help mitigate insider threat, particularly malicious insiders. But it doesn't fully mitigate users and administrators that make mistakes or poor trust decisions that lead to compromise. Because of this, I gave it partial marks for insider threat and social engineering. This approach seems to be optimized to mitigate unlawful government access to data, such as military and economic espionage. For many of the organizations that I have advised who use this strategy, this is definitely a real risk for them – perhaps their highest priority risk. But clearly, this isn't the only high-priority risk they need to mitigate.

I've seen organizations use this strategy without implementing an air-gapped network. Without the air-gapped network, relying on data classification, security clearances, and end-to-end certified hardware is far less effective at addressing the cybersecurity fundamentals:

Cybersecurity fundamentals	Score (0-20)
Unpatched vulnerabilities	0
Security misconfigurations	0

Weak, leaked, stolen credentials	0
Social engineering	10
Insider threat	10
CFSS Total Score (max=100)	20

Table 9.6: The CFSS score estimate for the Physical Control and Security Clearances Strategy without an air-gapped network

To really mitigate the Cybersecurity Usual Suspects, whether an air-gapped network is used or not, this approach needs to be used in combination with other cybersecurity strategies. I've met with many organizations that already know this and have been pursuing complementary strategies for years. But the cultures of many of these organizations make it difficult for them to adopt new approaches and technologies; to coin a phrase, they have a glacial approach in an era of unmitigated global warming. The internet and the cloud have democratized IT, giving everyone capabilities that they didn't have before. The challenge for organizations that have used this strategy for years or decades is adapting their current approach quickly enough, all to enable them to mitigate a larger number of well-resourced adversaries than they've ever had in the past.

Physical Control and Security Clearances Strategy summary

The CFSS total estimated score for this strategy, using air-gapped networks, is 55/100. For organizations that use this strategy, but without an effective air-gapped network, my estimate of the CFSS total score is 20/100. My conclusion is that this strategy must be used in conjunction with other cybersecurity strategies in order to fully address the cybersecurity fundamentals.

Advantages:

- Militaries and governments have hundreds of years of practice using similar approaches
- Air-gapped networks can help partially mitigate some of the Cybersecurity Usual Suspects
- Helps partially mitigate insider threat, including unlawful government access to data, by making it harder for malicious insiders to succeed
- Third-party verification/attestation of hardware contributes to security assurance and helps demonstrate due diligence
- Has a large vendor ecosystem to help organizations that pursue this approach

Disadvantages:

- Enormous costs are usually associated with the type of certified infrastructure typically leveraged with this approach

- The underlying assumption that data residency provides better security is not valid

- Since most attacks are perpetrated remotely without physical access to hardware and regardless of the physical location of data, the success of this approach depends heavily on network air gaps to partially mitigate the Cybersecurity Usual Suspects

- Data in highly restrictive, air-gapped environments can be harder to operationalize

- Doesn't fully mitigate insider threat because it focuses on mitigating malicious insiders, which does not include the mistakes that non-malicious insiders make that lead to poor security outcomes

- Gives attackers an advantage because they can use new technologies faster than defenders

Now, let's move on and consider how some organizations use *Compliance as a Security Strategy*.

Compliance as a Security Strategy

Compliance and cybersecurity are two different, slightly overlapping disciplines. Compliance typically focuses on proving that an organization meets requirements defined in regulated, industry, and/or internal standards. Compliance can be helpful in numerous ways, chief among them would be for cybersecurity insurance purposes and demonstrating due diligence to limit liability. This is different from cybersecurity, which focuses on identifying, protecting, detecting, responding, and recovering (NIST, n.d.). But I have seen many organizations conflate these different disciplines because they overlap each other, as I've illustrated in *Figure 9.2*. I've seen similar illustrations where compliance is a subset of cybersecurity or vice versa. I think arguments can be made for all of these approaches. The approach that some organizations I have discussed this with have taken is to rotate the two circles in *Figure 9.2* on top of each other and pretend that they are the same thing.

That's not to say that organizations can't align their efforts in order to pursue both compliance and cybersecurity. This is what most organizations need to do, but many fail to do so.

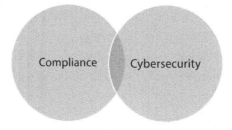

Figure 9.2: Compliance and security disciplines overlap but are different

I've discovered that there are a variety of reasons that organizations conflate compliance and cybersecurity. First, some regulated standards have non-compliance penalties or fines associated with them. This provides an incentive for organizations to prove that they are meeting these standards and invest in compliance programs. But since most organizations have resource constraints, many of them believe they are forced to decide whether to use their resources on compliance or cybersecurity. In some cases, organizations end up using this strategy because their well-resourced, well-intentioned compliance organization over-functions. That is, they extend their efforts beyond proving they meet applicable standards, to performing functions that you'd typically see a security team perform. There's nothing wrong with this per se, but we need to recognize that their area of expertise and the center of gravity for their program is compliance. Some of the organizations that I have seen using this strategy do so simply because their compliance program is older and more mature than their cybersecurity program; they've had compliance obligations for years or decades in their industry, and cybersecurity is a relatively new investment for them.

The underlying assumption of this strategy is that meeting compliance obligations is sufficient for protecting the organization's data. Subsequently, the focus is on meeting the organization's regulatory, industry, and internal compliance obligations, and demonstrating this in audits.

These could include standards like PCI, HIPAA, GDPR, NIST standards, ISO standards, or an organization's own internal IT security standards, among others. This strategy is characterized by investments in people, processes, and technologies that help organizations meet their compliance obligations. This typically manifests itself as well-defined control sets and repeatable processes that are periodically audited.

This strategy can be very advantageous, healthy, and positive for organizations that do not have a cybersecurity strategy or mature governance practices. Most of the regulated security-related standards that have been instituted in industries provide a minimum set of requirements that organizations should work to achieve. The steps that organizations typically need to take to get their IT governance, infrastructure, and operations in shape to be audited for the first time against an industry standard can dramatically improve their security posture and their overall cybersecurity program. Organizations should not underestimate the effort and potential change related to complying with regulated standards and industry standards. This effort is typically rewarded with much better security than where they started, as well as a foundation they can potentially extend and continue to build on.

The challenge for many organizations is to recognize that most regulated security-related standards are minimum requirements, not some sort of certification that means they can't be compromised.

Although regulatory compliance is required for many organizations, it's insufficient to protect their systems and data from modern-day threats. This is where *Compliance as a Security Strategy* tends to fall short. History has taught us that this is a poor strategy. There is no shortage of examples of large, well-funded organizations that met regulated standards but were breached all the same. Think about all the financial institutions, retailers, and restaurants that met their industries' regulated standards, but were breached anyway. Think about all the organizations in the healthcare industry around the world that worked hard to comply with stringent regulated industry data protection standards, and lost control of patient data to attackers. My own personal data has been compromised multiple times in data breaches in all of these industries over the past 15 years. This doesn't mean that regulated security-related standards are worthless. As I mentioned, they are very positive for many, many organizations. I'd rather use my credit card in a restaurant that tries to comply with PCI DSS than one that doesn't.

Regulated security-related standards are insufficient by themselves. There are at least a couple of reasons for this. First, standards like these typically have a defined scope, such as credit card holder information or patient information. The control sets to support these standards are designed for the infrastructure and data that are in the defined scope. But what about the other HVAs that organizations have? If the organization uses its limited resources to only address the scope that's audited and subject to penalties, it is likely not paying enough attention to other HVAs and its broader infrastructure. The second reason regulated standards are insufficient is that they rarely keep pace with the threat landscape or advances in technology. This has more to do with how slowly standards can be adopted in industries and their economic impact than with the standards bodies themselves. Deploying updated security-related standards requirements to millions of retailers and restaurants around the world takes years. Subsequently, organizations typically need a broader cybersecurity strategy that embraces compliance but supplements its shortcomings in material ways. Simply put, enterprises need to do both.

CFSS score

My CFSS score estimates for *Compliance as a Security Strategy* reveals that this strategy can partially mitigate all the Cybersecurity Usual Suspects. Remember, the goal is to find a strategy or combination of strategies that give us a perfect 100/100 CFSS total score. Subsequently, this strategy will need to be used in combination with other strategies to fully address the Cybersecurity Usual Suspects:

Cybersecurity fundamentals	Score (0-20)
Unpatched vulnerabilities	10

Security misconfigurations	10
Weak, leaked, stolen credentials	10
Social engineering	10
Insider threat	10
CFSS Total Score (max=100)	50

Table 9.7: The CFSS score estimate for Compliance as a Security Strategy

I gave this strategy partial marks across the board because it can help organizations mitigate all these threats, but it's typically used with limited scope and is slow to adapt to changes in the threat landscape. This strategy can and does create a foundation, albeit incomplete, that many organizations can build on with complementary approaches.

Compliance as a Security Strategy summary

The CFSS total estimated score for this strategy is 50/100. This strategy can be very beneficial for organizations as a starting point for a broader cybersecurity strategy. Organizations that integrate their compliance requirements into a more holistic cybersecurity strategy can potentially reduce complexity and costs and achieve better security.

Advantages:

- Can be very positive for organizations that do not have a security strategy or have immature governance practices
- Third-party verification/attestation by auditors is valuable to demonstrate due diligence.
- Large vendor and audit firm ecosystem to help
- Can reduce complexity and costs, and achieve better security when integrated with cybersecurity efforts
- Complying with some regulated standards, like GDPR, for example, can help organizations achieve better data protection

Disadvantages:

- History has shown this to be a poor strategy as many organizations that complied with standards were breached anyway.
- Typically relies on compliance and audit teams, as well as third-party auditors, to arbitrate the organization's security posture.

- Focuses on implementing control sets specified in regulated standards with a specific scope that typically does not include all HVAs.

- Only attains minimum requirements specified by regulations when they were last published; rarely reflects modern-day risks and mitigations.

- Attackers have a disproportionate advantage over defenders. This is because they can have complete visibility into the control sets required to comply, and those control sets rarely keep pace with changes in the threat landscape.

- In some cases, regulatory compliance uses resources that could otherwise be used for more effective cybersecurity.

Now, let's look at the *Application-Centric Strategy*.

Application-Centric Strategy

This is another proxy strategy. Applications process, store, and transmit data. If we protect the application, then by proxy, we are protecting the data. This approach focuses on protecting applications by reducing the number of vulnerabilities in them and the severity of those vulnerabilities. It also endeavors to make the vulnerabilities that are inevitably left in applications *really* difficult, if not impossible, to exploit. These are the same principles that underpin the vulnerability improvement framework that I introduced in *Chapter 3, Using Vulnerability Trends to Reduce Risk and Costs.* An underlying assumption of this approach is that it is much less expensive to fix bugs and mitigate vulnerabilities before an application is released into production. This involves investments in people, processes, and technologies, which can include threat modeling, security development life cycles, static and dynamic code analysis tools, penetration testing, mobile device management, mobile application management, bug bounties, and others.

I'm a big believer in this strategy; after all, would you set sail in a submarine where someone is drilling holes in the hull from the inside? This continues to be an underestimated risk, as many enterprises still don't seem to select vendors or solutions based on their security development practices.

I led marketing communications for Microsoft's **Security Development Lifecycle (SDL)** (Microsoft Corporation, n.d.) for several years and saw how it could help development teams first-hand. However, you don't have to have a massive development organization like Microsoft to benefit from this strategy.

As the saying goes, a rising tide lifts all boats. CISOs, security teams, compliance professionals, and development organizations can all help raise the security tide mark for their organization over time by implementing security development education, policies, and processes that are supported by tools and automation, to help improve the quality of the software both developed in-house and procured from third parties. For example, requiring that every in-house-developed application requires a threat model, prior to developers writing any code, can help improve the design and mitigate potential vulnerabilities. Similarly, requiring static code analysis at specific milestones in development can help reduce the number and severity of vulnerabilities that make it into production. Organizations that don't enforce security requirements in every phase of the development process typically pay a higher price for this decision, after their applications have been deployed.

But like all the other strategies, this one has drawbacks and limitations as well. The same operating system features, tools, IDEs, development libraries, and frameworks (C++, the JRE, .NET, and so on) that are used to protect applications can also be a persistent source of vulnerabilities. The **Java Runtime Environment (JRE)** was a perennial example for many years. It saves development teams lots of time and expense, but the opportunity cost is that their application could inherit vulnerabilities that need to be patched in the JRE itself. The time between vulnerabilities being discovered in these frameworks and being fixed represents a risk to the users of their applications.

Another drawback of this strategy that I've seen organizations grapple with numerous times is that although fewer vulnerabilities and lower severity vulnerabilities are measurable metrics, they are hard to translate into business value. Arguing that attacks didn't happen because of the investment in application security can be tough arguments for CISOs and development organization leaders to make and other executives to understand. What seems like common sense to CISOs and vulnerability management teams can remain nebulous for other stakeholders.

As I wrote in *Chapter 3, Using Vulnerability Trends to Reduce Risk and Costs,* using data from your vulnerability management program to provide visibility on the state of the environment can help you make the case for application security. Trying to drive the number of unpatched vulnerabilities to zero and using data to help other executives understand the progress against this goal and the associated costs, can help them understand why it is important to prevent new vulnerabilities from being introduced into the environment via third-party and in-house applications.

CFSS score

All that said, let's see how the *Application-Centric Strategy* scores in the CFSS:

Cybersecurity fundamentals	Score (0-20)
Unpatched vulnerabilities	20
Security misconfigurations	20
Weak, leaked, stolen credentials	10
Social engineering	10
Insider threat	10
CFSS Total Score (max=100)	70

Table 9.8: The CFSS score estimate for the Application-Centric Strategy

I gave this strategy full marks for its ability to mitigate unpatched vulnerabilities and security misconfigurations. I realize this is a little optimistic for most organizations, but there are some scenarios where this could be possible. I gave this strategy partial marks for its ability to mitigate insider threat, social engineering, and weak, leaked, or stolen credentials. For example, designing applications that require MFA and provide rich logging and audit capabilities can help partially mitigate these threats.

Application-Centric Strategy summary

All organizations can benefit from this approach. However, by itself, its CFSS total estimated score is 70/100. I recommend that organizations embrace this strategy and subsidize it with other approaches that will help fully address all the cybersecurity fundamentals.

Advantages:

- Can reduce the number and severity of vulnerabilities in software that the organization procures and develops in-house.
- Can lower maintenance costs, minimize business disruptions, and measurably improve application security.
- Leverages mitigations built into operating systems, IDEs, development libraries and frameworks (C++, the JRE, .NET, and so on), and containers. This reduces complexity, costs, and effort for development teams while potentially improving security.
- Large existing vendor ecosystem to help.

Disadvantages:

- Relies on developers to produce vulnerability-free source code or make it impossible for vulnerabilities to be exploited; history teaches us this is optimistic
- Subject to vulnerabilities in the operating systems, IDEs, development libraries, frameworks, and containers, among other technologies
- Business ROI can be challenging to communicate effectively

Onward now, to the *Identity-Centric Strategy*.

Identity-Centric Strategy

You'll remember that one of the Cybersecurity Usual Suspects is weak, leaked, and stolen credentials. Credentials and the assets that they protect have been a currency for attackers for decades. Many people reuse passwords across applications, systems, and services. When one of those is compromised and the credentials are stolen, attackers immediately try those credentials on other systems and services across the internet, such as major online banking portals, e-commerce sites, social networks, and so on. The industry has long wanted to deprecate passwords in favor of better authentication methods and use data from authentication and authorization systems to make better resource access decisions. These concepts are central to the *Identity-Centric* Strategy.

Although the concept of identity and proving your identity is ancient, the *Identity-Centric Strategy* is a relatively new strategy that gained popularity rapidly. The idea behind this strategy is that during most successful data breaches, at some point, attackers will use legitimate credentials. There's a saying in the cybersecurity industry, "attackers don't break in – they log in." How can we use this to our advantage to protect, detect, and respond to attacks? Well, authentication and authorization processes can potentially generate some useful metadata. For example, if we can ascertain the approximate location that an authentication or authorization request is coming from, we might be able to calculate a level of confidence in its legitimacy. Similarly, if we can compare some key attributes of the request to characteristics of past requests from the same account, this too might help provide us with some level of confidence that the request was legitimate. There's a bunch of metadata like this that can help organizations protect, detect, and respond to attacks. Here's a partial list of such data:

- Strength of the credential used for the request (old protocols versus new protocols)
- Location and temporal data:
    - Origin location of request

- Time of day of request
- Time between requests from different locations – is it impossible to travel between those locations in the time between the requests?

- Trustworthiness of the device the request is coming from:

  - Does it have a valid digital certificate installed by the organization?
  - Is it a corporate-managed device or an unmanaged personal device?
  - Is the latest operating system version installed on the device?
  - Does the hardware or operating system version have known unpatched vulnerabilities?

- User behavior:

  - How many times did the user enter incorrect credentials?
  - When was the last time the user was prompted for **Multi-Factor Authentication (MFA)** and what was the result?

The underlying assumption of this strategy is that organizations can better protect data, detect compromises, and respond faster by better protecting the identities used to access data, and by using identity metadata to look for indicators of compromise. The focus of this approach is protecting the credentials used to access the organization's data, especially the credentials of privileged accounts, such as administrators. Incident Response teams, forensics experts, as well as Red and Blue teams, all know that privileged account credentials are like gold to attackers. When I worked on Microsoft's customer-facing **Computer Incident Response Team (CIRT)**, attackers' modus operandi was very consistent; once the attackers initially compromised an IT environment using one of the Cybersecurity Usual Suspects, within seconds, their scripts were running, trying to harvest cached credentials on the compromised system. They would use those credentials to move laterally through the environment if they could, looking for more cached credentials along the way. Finding cached credentials for privileged accounts made it much easier for attackers to penetrate the environment even deeper, and then get access to more resources and data. If attackers were able to exfiltrate a copy of the victim's Microsoft Active Directory, they would perform an offline attack, using rainbow tables and/or other tools to get access to more credentials relatively quickly (Wikipedia, n.d.). Once attackers got to this stage, recovery was aspirational. I met numerous organizations over the years that found themselves in this scenario. Some of them decided to "share" their IT environment with attackers because recovery was too expensive and resource intensive.

Others decided to rebuild their infrastructure from scratch or used the compromise as the impetus to start fresh in the cloud. Since attackers try to harvest credentials as a matter of course, many organizations focus on protecting credentials and use identity metadata to accelerate detection.

The *Identity-Centric Strategy* is characterized by investments in MFA, enforcing the principle of least privilege, identity management technologies, credential vaulting and hygiene practices, and detecting credentials that are being misused (Pass-the-Hash and Golden Ticket attacks are examples). For example, to counter attacks on Microsoft Active Directory, Microsoft has taken numerous steps to make it harder for attackers to succeed. In addition to engineering improvements in their products, they have published guidance on how to harden Active Directory (Microsoft Corporation, 2021).

They also published a lot of content on what is referred to as a "Red Forest" or **Enhanced Security Administrative Environment** (**ESAE**), which has recently been replaced with a newer Privileged Access Strategy (Microsoft Corporation, 2022). These types of architectures help protect privileged account credentials and make it much harder for attackers to get access to them. But these advanced architectures and configurations are not for the faint of heart. Meeting and maintaining the requirements of these environments can be challenging. Using **Privileged Access Workstations** (**PAWs**) in conjunction with privileged access accounts and interfaces requires administrative self-discipline to govern and operate IT in such a strictly controlled environment. However, protecting credentials in an on-premises distributed environment has never been easy.

The identity space has exploded over the past couple of decades. There are vendors that specialize in access management, privileged access, identity governance, and several other areas. Some vendors that sell technologies that support an *Identity-Centric Strategy* call identity the "new perimeter" to highlight the importance of protecting credentials and credential hygiene. It's also important to note that identity plays a central role in cloud computing as well as *Zero Trust* strategies where many of the same concepts are leveraged. I'll discuss this type of strategy later in the chapter. There are several vendors in the identity space that can help make protecting credentials easier and provide access to valuable metadata to accelerate anomaly detection. Some of the vendors that I have seen organizations leverage include BeyondTrust, CyberArk, Google, Microsoft, Okta, Ping Identity, and others.

CFSS score

How does the *Identity-Centric Strategy* score in the CFSS? It doesn't fully address any of the cybersecurity fundamentals:

Cybersecurity fundamentals	Score (0-20)
Unpatched vulnerabilities	5
Security misconfigurations	5
Weak, leaked, stolen credentials	15
Social engineering	10
Insider threat	10
CFSS Total Score (max=100)	45

Table 9.9: The CFSS score estimate for the Identity-Centric Strategy

This strategy doesn't mitigate unpatched vulnerabilities or security misconfigurations. But some vulnerabilities and security misconfigurations require authenticated access in order to be exploited. Organizations that focus on enforcing the principle of least privilege and practice good credential hygiene can make reliable exploitation of vulnerabilities and misconfigurations much more difficult and "limit the blast radius." Subsequently, I gave this strategy partial marks for these two cybersecurity fundamentals. I couldn't give it full marks for mitigating weak, leaked, and stolen credentials because legacy applications tend to fall through the cracks with this strategy; MFA typically can't be deployed everywhere, and metadata isn't always going to be available. Similarly, this approach can help partially mitigate insider threat by implementing **Just-in-Time** (**JIT**) and **Just-Enough-Administration** (**JEA**) models, credential vaulting, and other mitigations. Social engineering can be partially mitigated with MFA and least privilege, among other controls, but can't be completely mitigated. I'm sure some readers would give this strategy a higher score than I did – please use your own estimates where warranted.

Identity-Centric Strategy summary

This strategy needs to be used in combination with other strategies to fully mitigate the Cybersecurity Usual Suspects. Although it didn't score particularly high, it's certainly a valuable, modern, complementary approach to improving protection, detection, and containment capabilities. However, that might be understating the importance of identity in a modern cybersecurity strategy.

Identity will remain central to an effective cybersecurity strategy, helping to address the cybersecurity fundamentals and providing advanced capabilities. Investments in this area can pay big dividends for CISOs.

Advantages:

- Focuses on improving governance and technologies with a historically poor track record
- A large vendor ecosystem to help
- Can help manage risk related to weak, leaked, and stolen passwords
- MFA is becoming ubiquitous
- The strength of a credential, the location of a login attempt, the trustworthiness of the device, and MFA controls can all help build confidence in the legitimacy of authentication requests
- Can quickly identify authentication/authorization anomalies
- Can add friction to the authentication/authorization processes, which makes it harder for attackers to infiltrate
- Can bolster containment efforts and make it harder for attackers to move laterally and contain the "blast radius" of some attacks

Disadvantages:

- Traditionally, federated identity systems have been complex, expensive, and hard to govern and manage; simply put, identity has always been a challenge in large enterprise IT environments.
- Legacy applications can be challenging to govern and secure using a modern *Identity-Centric Strategy*. There are typically far more legacy applications than modern applications in large, complex, mature enterprise IT environments.
- MFA is typically not implemented everywhere, leaving gaps and opportunities for attackers.
- Can be complicated, time-consuming, and expensive to fully implement in enterprise on-premises environments.

Next, let's look at a strategy that has had a resurgence in popularity – the *Data-Centric Strategy*.

Data-Centric Strategy

The *Data-Centric Strategy* has been growing in popularity for several reasons, including numerous high-profile data breaches, revelations about government data collection programs, the dramatically increased frequency of ransomware attacks, and the increasing risk of intellectual property theft.

There are also increasing regulatory demands that aim to help protect consumer privacy and have significant noncompliance fines associated with them, such as GDPR, for example. In addition, because of the challenges we discussed with the *Protect and Recover Strategy*, the *Endpoint Protection Strategy*, the *Application-Centric Strategy*, the popularity of BYOD, IT environments, and the emergence of IoT, some organizations have decided to stop using strategies that solely rely on proxies to protect their data. Instead of relying on the security provided by firewalls, endpoints, and applications, their strategy is to protect the data, no matter where it is.

Whether their data is inside their perimeter, accessed from a managed device, or processed by an application that meets their security development requirements, the data still needs to be protected. Some CISOs make the assumptions that endpoints cannot be fully trusted, and that data can move in unexpected ways without their knowledge. They want to ensure that even in scenarios where they are not in control of their data, it's still protected.

This is where the *Data-Centric Strategy* can help. There are several underlying assumptions for this approach. First, data, not the systems that process it, transmit it, or store it, is the HVA. Instead of focusing on the security of hardware and software that handles data, the focus should be on the data itself. Another assumption is that data will move without the organization's approval or knowledge, and therefore it must be protected, regardless of where it is. Some CISOs go so far as to assume that some of the systems that process their data are compromised and that the data must be protected in a compromised environment. Finally, organizations still require that their data can be shared appropriately within their organization and with authorized partners, such as outside manufacturing, marketing, PR, and law firms. That is, although the data must be secure, it still must be accessible and usable internally and externally. The focus of this strategy is to protect data wherever it is transmitted, processed, and stored, preferably forever, but for a reasonably long period of time. This approach is characterized by investments in encryption and key management technologies, **Data Loss Prevention (DLP)**, and potentially, data classification.

A simplified example of this is encrypted PDF files, which can be read by authorized users, but the content cannot be copied and pasted. A more complicated example is the extreme data-centric solutions offered by blockchain platforms that implement data protection mechanisms as part of the data itself.

The heart of this strategy is encryption and key management; if data is encrypted everywhere all the time, the attack surface area can be dramatically reduced. For example, instead of trying to protect all files, everywhere they currently are and will be in the future, forever, encryption can help make this more manageable.

Encryption and key management can help maintain the confidentiality and integrity of the data it protects. Encrypting large numbers of files reduces the attack surface by shifting the focus from protecting all these files to potentially protecting a much smaller number of encryption keys. If strong, properly implemented encryption is employed, the primary focus can shift from the security of the encrypted files to managing the keys that are used to encrypt and decrypt them. Of course, if the owner of the data doesn't have access to the encrypted files, they can't decrypt them, and the data is lost—for example, when encrypted files are encrypted again during a ransomware attack. This means we shouldn't be cavalier with our data just because it's encrypted. However, the mathematical properties of properly implemented strong encryption can help reduce risk.

Besides reducing the attack surface, encryption buys organizations time. That is, properly encrypted data looks the same as random noise, and without the keys to decrypt the data, it will likely take many years of effort for attackers to decrypt a portion of the data. The confidentiality and integrity of the data are preserved during that time. But it is still prudent to assume that encrypted data has a finite lifespan. Periodically rotating keys and re-encrypting data can help extend this lifespan, but at some point, the algorithms or key lengths used will no longer provide adequate protection in the face of new technologies and advances in cryptanalysis. For example, for several years, there have been industry-wide efforts to develop post-quantum or quantum-safe encryption algorithms that can be used to preserve the confidentiality and integrity of data after quantum computers become a reality. A thoughtful approach to managing encryption, decryption, and keys is required; this is not a "set it and forget it" solution to data protection.

You might be wondering, given that various types of encryption have been around for millennia, if encryption and key management are so powerful, then why haven't organizations always been encrypting everything, everywhere? Why have there been so many data breaches involving unencrypted data? Traditionally, there's been a tension between securing information and operationalizing information. Let me give you an example of this tension. I'll use a completely fictional scenario, where there are life and death consequences for unauthorized access to information – a witness protection program.

In this fictional scenario, the list of witnesses that the program is protecting is handwritten on paper. The list hasn't been digitized in any way; it only exists on paper. No one person has ever seen the entire list, as parts of the list are managed by separate program managers and are physically compartmentalized. The list is put into a fireproof filing cabinet that has a combination lock and steel bars locked across its drawers. The keys to these locks are given to separate program officers, requiring all of them to be present to open the filing cabinet.

The filing cabinet is in a vault, in a secured area in the middle of police headquarters, surrounded by on-duty police officers, with armed guards at the one fortified entrance to the building 24 hours a day. Of course, the building has an extensive security system, including video surveillance, mantraps, and card key access points. The vault can only be opened by following a specific protocol that requires the participation of two additional senior law enforcement officials, under specific conditions.

I hope you agree that the list in this scenario has been secured in a way that mitigates many potential risks and that unauthorized access to the list would require extraordinary measures. Ethan Hunt from Mission Impossible might be able to breach all these controls, but I'm sure you'll agree that it would be difficult for most other people. However, an additional consequence of these controls is that legitimate, authorized access to the list has been encumbered, making it a complicated and slow process. In this scenario, since there can be life-and-death consequences to unauthorized access, access is purposely designed to be slow, cumbersome, and meticulous. However, if there was an emergency or some other need for quick access or repetitive access to the list, this process would frustrate those needs.

In another fictional scenario, a company that specializes in providing real-time advice on trading stocks has a different challenge. This company will go out of business if it can't access information, process it, and provide valuable advice to its large customer base in near real time. The information it has typically loses its value within minutes. Security controls are important to the company as it has very aggressive competitors and regulators that would like to understand what its secret to success is. However, if security controls encumber the near real-time distribution of information inside the company or to its customers, the company will fail to keep its promises to its customers and go out of business in a hyper-competitive market. This company purposely prioritizes speed and agility over security. If it doesn't, it won't be in business very long.

These two scenarios demonstrate the tension between the need for data security and the need to operationalize information, which has traditionally challenged organizations. Combine this tension with the fact that encryption and key management have traditionally required specific, relatively hard-to-find, and expensive expertise, and this begins to explain why organizations haven't simply encrypted all their data, all the time.

Because of this tension and the traditional challenges associated with encryption, many organizations decide to encrypt only their most sensitive data. This reduces complexity and costs, while still ensuring their most valuable data is protected. To do this, many organizations have adopted data classification schemes in order to identify and more effectively protect high-value data.

But as I mentioned earlier in this chapter, data classification policies are notoriously difficult for organizations to implement and adhere to. Many of the organizations I have talked to, particularly those that tried to implement data classification policies and failed, have concluded that it is more efficient to treat all data as if it's the same value. For them, this approach is less complicated and less expensive than trying to consistently identify the relative value of individual datasets and applying different security control sets based on that value. But these organizations are still faced with the challenge of managing encryption and key management.

Wouldn't it be cool if CISOs didn't have to make these trade-offs? That is, they could have it all – uncompromising data security, the operational capabilities that enable organizations to move fast, the ability to share data when needed, and better visibility and control. Who wouldn't want that? This is what the *Data-Centric Strategy* seeks to enable. Instead of just managing the security of the hardware and software that handles data, secure the data itself using encryption, key management, authentication, and authorization. In a world where data breaches have become common, this strategy can provide an effective line of defense when most other protection mechanisms fail. In addition, if encryption and decryption functions require authentication and authorization, the metadata generated from these activities can provide useful information on where the data is and who is trying to access it.

From a high level, the technologies used to support these capabilities include client-side or server-side encryption libraries or applications, **Public Key Infrastructures (PKIs)**, federated identity systems with authorization capabilities, as well as logging and reporting capabilities. A good example of a service that combines all these components is **Azure Rights Management (Azure RMS)** (Microsoft Corporation, 2022). Let me give you an example of how this service works, from a high level.

A company needs to protect confidential information from falling into the wrong hands but needs to share it with its outside law firm in a way that still protects the confidentiality and integrity of the data. They encrypt the file using Azure RMS and assign a policy to it that defines who is authorized to open and decrypt the file. They send the file to the law firm via email using Microsoft 365. When the staff at the law firm try to open the file, they get prompted to enter their Azure Active Directory credentials. Because they are also a Microsoft 365 corporate user and have an identity federation configured with the company's account, when they enter their credentials, Azure Active Directory authenticates them and reads the policy to determine what type of actions they are permitted to do with the file. The policy allows the law firm to open the file, decrypt it, and read it. If the file is forwarded to someone that doesn't have those permissions, they won't be able to open it or decrypt it.

Meanwhile, the company can track where in the world authentication requests to open the file have come from, which credentials were used in authentication requests, failed and successful attempts to open the file, and so on. Pretty cool. I'll discuss other cool capabilities that the cloud provides in *Chapter 12, Modern Approaches to Security and Compliance.*

You might have noticed that the one critical component that enables the example scenario I described is identity. An identity strategy, like the *Identity-Centric Strategy* I described earlier in this chapter, is required for this *Data-Centric Strategy* to be successful. Without authentication and authorization capabilities, the *Data-Centric Strategy* isn't scalable.

DLP can also be employed in a *Data-Centric Strategy*. DLP can be a powerful tool to help prevent data from leaving an organization in an unauthorized way, including malicious and non-malicious data theft and leakage. DLP can monitor data that moves via the network, email, USB drives, and other removable media. But increasingly ubiquitous encryption can make it more difficult for DLP to achieve complete visibility. Additionally, DLP policy violations rarely result in consequences for the employees and executives that break them; this provides little incentive to pay attention to DLP-related policies. Finally, DLP can only slow down malicious insiders as they steal information, not stop them completely. They will almost always find a way to smuggle information out of an IT environment, like using the camera on their mobile phone to take a picture of it right off the screen of a secure workstation, for example. However, DLP combined with the *Physical Control and Security Clearances Strategy* – an air-gapped network in a facility that enforces a policy prohibiting all outside electronics including mobile phones, has physically removed USB and peripheral ports on computers in the facility, and searches employees as they enter and leave the facility – has a much better chance of preventing data theft. But few organizations outside those responsible for national security impose these types of controls

CFSS score

Perhaps unexpectedly, the *Data-Centric Strategy* does not earn a great CFSS score by itself. After all, if the underlying infrastructure used for encryption, key management, authentication, authorization, logging, DLP, and other functions is compromised using one or more of the Cybersecurity Usual Suspects, then attackers can potentially get access to the data before it gets encrypted, or they could get access to credentials or decryption keys.

Protecting the data is a powerful mitigation, but it requires that the components that make it possible are also protected:

Cybersecurity fundamentals	Score (0-20)
Unpatched vulnerabilities	5
Security misconfigurations	5
Weak, leaked, stolen credentials	0
Social engineering	15
Insider threat	15
CFSS Total Score (max=100)	40

Table 9.10: The CFSS score estimate for the Data-Centric Strategy

I gave this approach partial marks for unpatched vulnerabilities and security misconfigurations because it can protect the confidentiality and integrity of the data, while vulnerability management teams scan and update systems; like the *Protect and Recover Strategy*, this approach can give vulnerability management teams more time to get this done.

It can also protect data for a period of time after the exploitation of vulnerabilities and misconfigurations. But it doesn't prevent the attackers from destroying the data or encrypting it themselves using ransomware. Crucially, it doesn't prevent attackers from exploiting vulnerabilities in the infrastructure, moving laterally, collecting credentials, persisting, and collecting data before it gets encrypted in web browsers and email clients, and so on. Of course, most credentials in Microsoft Active Directory and other modern directory services are encrypted, but that's not the focus of the *Data-Centric Strategy*. It offers nothing new to protect passwords, as it relies on identity systems and federated identities. Subsequently, I gave it 0 out of 20 for weak, leaked, and stolen passwords.

This strategy can mitigate some forms of social engineering when used with the principle of least privilege and a meaningful separation of duties. This is also true of insider threats. Encrypted data can remain confidential, even when administrators make mistakes that lead to poor security outcomes, but there are limits. Malicious insiders will potentially have a harder time with a meaningful separation of duties that limits their access to key material. Thus, I gave both social engineering and insider threat partial marks.

Data-Centric Strategy summary

Despite its relatively low CFSS score, I am a fan of the *Data-Centric Strategy*. Although it doesn't mitigate the Cybersecurity Usual Suspects by itself, it does act as an advanced capability, providing an important extra layer of protection and detection. Authenticated, authorized encryption and decryption operations can be very effective for protecting data. Using the metadata that I described can also be very helpful to security teams. For CISOs who try to protect everything as if it's the same value to the organization (which can be a recipe for disaster), dramatically reducing the attack surface area that they must focus on can be very helpful.

For many organizations, data classification can help determine which datasets they need to focus on protecting. But data classification is notoriously hard to implement and adhere to. Modern approaches to encryption and key management make it much easier and less expensive to encrypt everything all the time, especially in the cloud.

Advantages:

- Potentially reduces the surface area to protect by focusing on data on the endpoint, email, network, proxy servers, and in the cloud.

- Can help protect data, detect data breaches, and respond to incidents quicker than traditionally possible.

- Modern, properly implemented encryption can effectively protect data from unauthorized access for relatively long periods. This time can be helpful as security teams can then focus on the cybersecurity fundamentals and other advanced capabilities with more confidence.

- Encryption can help make data destruction easier; destroying the keys effectively destroys the data they protect.

- DLP can be a powerful tool to help prevent data from leaving an organization and to help detect data leakage.

Disadvantages:

- Many organizations find data classification policies and technologies hard to implement and use consistently over time. Subsequently, many organizations have tried and failed to do data classification in a meaningful way.

- Key management can be challenging for some organizations. An on-premises PKI is not for the faint of heart and requires technical expertise. A failed PKI can have disastrous implications; the cloud makes this much easier.

- Many organizations terminate encrypted communications to inspect data and apply DLP policies as it moves. Increasing the use of encryption for data in transit and at rest has made it more challenging for DLP to be effective.

- Enforcing DLP policy violations can be challenging for some CISOs; how often is a senior executive reprimanded for breaking DLP policies? Many organizations do not adequately enforce policy violations when they're flagged by DLP.

- Relies on a sound identity strategy and federated identity implementation, which can be challenging to architect, implement, operate, and govern.

Moving on to the next cybersecurity strategy that I will discuss, the *Attack-Centric Strategy*.

Attack-Centric Strategy

The idea behind the *Attack-Centric Strategy* is that the ways security teams protect systems, detect compromises, and respond to attackers should be informed by the TTPs that attackers actually use. Put another way, understanding how attackers operate and planning defenses around that makes those defenses more effective. The underlying assumption of this approach is that forcing attackers to be successful multiple times during intrusion attempts makes it much harder for them and decreases detection and recovery times. The focus of this approach is understanding how attackers operate and making each tactic and each technique they use ineffective. Lowering attackers' return on investment by increasing the time, effort, and costs associated with their attack will force attackers to rethink or abandon their attack. This approach is characterized by investments in numerous areas to block or impede attackers at each stage of their attack.

Two consummate examples of this approach are Lockheed Martin's Intrusion Kill Chain (Eric M. Hutchins, Michael J. Cloppert, and Rohan M. Amin, Ph.D.) and MITRE ATT&CK® (MITRE). Both of these complementary approaches are informed by the steps attackers take to attack their victims and the specific tactics, techniques, and procedures they use. For example, the Intrusion Kill Chain Approach defines seven phases or stages during an attack: Reconnaissance, Weaponization, Delivery, Exploitation, Installation, Command and Control, and Actions on Objectives (Eric M. Hutchins, Michael J. Cloppert, and Rohan M. Amin, Ph.D). Attackers could use some or all of these phases in their attacks. Knowing this, organizations can layer their defenses to detect, deny, disrupt, degrade, deceive, and destroy at every stage of the attack (Eric M. Hutchins, Michael J. Cloppert, and Rohan M. Amin, Ph.D.). This will make it much harder for attackers to succeed because they must potentially defeat multiple layers of defenses, specifically designed around their modus operandi.

Similarly, MITRE ATT&CK® is designed to be a knowledge base of attackers' TTPs. Over the past decade, this framework has been evolving. MITRE described it this way in a 2020 whitepaper,

> *ATT&CK focuses on how external adversaries compromise and operate within computer information networks. It originated out of a project to document and categorize post-compromise adversary tactics, techniques and procedures (TTPs) against Microsoft Windows systems to improve detection of malicious behavior. It has since grown to include Linux and macOS, and has expanded to cover behavior leading up to the compromise of an environment, as well as technology-focused domains like mobile devices, cloud-based systems, and industrial control systems."*
> *(Strom, Applebaum, Miller, Nickels, Pennington, and Thomas, 2020).*

Today, ATT&CK can be used in several different ways, including the following (Strom, Applebaum, Miller, Nickels, Pennington, and Thomas, 2020):

- Emulating adversaries
- Red team/Blue team exercises
- Developing behavioral analytics
- Identifying gaps in defensive capabilities
- **Security Operations Center** (**SOC**) maturity assessments
- Enriching **Cyber Threat Intelligence** (**CTI**)

Like the Intrusion Kill Chain, ATT&CK seeks to define the tactics (unordered steps or goals) attackers can take or want to achieve in their attacks, and the specific actions (techniques and sub-techniques) they use to accomplish each tactic. The tactics in this framework include Reconnaissance, Resource Development, Initial Access, Execution, Persistence, Privilege Escalation, Defense Evasion, Credential Access, Discovery, Lateral Movement, Collection, Command and Control, Exfiltration, and Impact.

This framework provides a list of the specific techniques attackers are known to have used in each of the defined tactics. For example, in the Reconnaissance tactic, the step in an attack where attackers are researching their target(s), the framework currently provides 10 techniques that attackers use to perform this research. One of those 10 techniques is "Gather Victim Org Information."

This technique currently has 4 sub-techniques associated with it, such as "Business Relationships" for example. This sub-technique indicates that attackers can gather information about business relationships that their targets have, to evaluate whether these relationships can be leveraged in their attacks in some way. The framework also provides examples of procedures attackers can use in each sub-technique, along with mitigation and detection advice.

Let me give you another example. Let's say an attacker has accomplished the initial compromise of a network and now wants to move laterally. Of course, defenders want to make that hard or impossible. According to ATT&CK, the Lateral Movement tactic has 9 techniques. For defenders, knowing there are 9 techniques is helpful because they can try to put mitigations for each one in place. One of those techniques is Internal Spearphishing; attackers could decide to use spearphishing leveraging the victim organization's own email system, to trick targeted information workers into disclosing information and credentials that will enable the attacker to move laterally. ATT&CK provides examples of procedures that specific attackers have used in the past to do this, as well as mitigation and detection recommendations. This particular technique does not have any sub-techniques associated with it.

Understanding the tactics, each technique, and each sub-technique helps defenders design and implement layers of capabilities that make accomplishing each tactic much harder or impossible. The number of tactics, techniques, and sub-techniques can potentially change over time when new ones are discovered. Subsequently, ATT&CK is a living framework that will continue to be updated. According to the FAQ on their website, they plan to update it bi-annually (MITRE ATT&CK®, n.d.).

You might have noticed that the tactics defined in ATT&CK are similar to the steps defined in the Intrusion Kill Chain approach, but a little more granular. MITRE includes the following question and answer in the FAQ on their website:

> *"What is the relationship between ATT&CK and the Lockheed Martin Cyber Kill Chain®?*
>
> *ATT&CK and the Cyber Kill Chain are complementary. ATT&CK sits at a lower level of definition to describe adversary behavior than the Cyber Kill Chain. ATT&CK Tactics are unordered and may not all occur in a single intrusion because adversary tactical goals change throughout an operation, whereas the Cyber Kill Chain uses ordered phases to describe high level adversary objectives." (MITRE ATT&CK®, n.d.)*

Naturally, there have been efforts to combine these two frameworks. One example is The Unified Kill Chain that "…extends and combines existing models, such as Lockheed Martins' Cyber Kill Chain® and MITRE's ATT&CK™ for Enterprise" (Pols, 2022).

As ATT&CK has evolved, it has become a very popular approach for cybersecurity teams. This approach makes a lot of sense to me because it can be used to mitigate the Cybersecurity Usual Suspects and provide advanced capabilities as well. The cybersecurity industry has coalesced around this framework, with numerous vendors offering products, services, and professional services offerings to support organizations that want to embrace it.

Let's see how the *Attack-Centric Strategy* scores using the CFSS.

CFSS score

The *Attack-Centric Strategy* has the highest CFSS score of any of the individual strategies I've examined in this chapter. In fact, my estimates of how capable it is of addressing all the cybersecurity fundamentals give it a near-perfect score, as shown in *Table 9.11*:

Cybersecurity fundamentals	Score (0-20)
Unpatched vulnerabilities	20
Security misconfigurations	20
Weak, leaked, stolen credentials	20
Social engineering	15
Insider threat	20
CFSS Total Score (max=100)	95

Table 9.11: The CFSS score estimate for the Attack-Centric Strategy

The reason this approach scores so well is that it focuses on the ways that attackers initially compromise IT environments and the methods and tools they use post initial compromise. That is, it covers all the bases. The reason I didn't give it a perfect 100/100 is that social engineering is nearly impossible to completely mitigate in enterprises. Sooner or later, someone will make a mistake or a poor trust decision that leads to a suboptimal security outcome.

Despite the industry's best efforts to educate information workers, executives, and IT administrators, and design software and hardware to make it harder for social engineering attacks to be successful, the data suggests that attackers are relying on it as much as they ever have. In an environment where mitigations for the Cybersecurity Usual Suspects are well managed, attackers are forced to turn to the one tactic they know has the best chance of succeeding: social engineering. They will continue to rely on humans to make mistakes and poor trust decisions, as the research I provided in *Chapter 4, The Evolution of Malware* suggests.

Attack-Centric Strategy summary

The *Attack-Centric Strategy* garnered a very high CFSS score. It can help CISOs and their teams focus on the cybersecurity fundamentals. This strategy is also capable of helping security teams go beyond the fundamentals and thoughtfully implement advanced cybersecurity capabilities and help protect their HVAs. That said, for most organizations that have limited resources, it isn't easy or inexpensive to design, procure, implement, operate, and support layers and layers of cybersecurity capabilities. Many organizations that aspire to use this approach realize they don't have the technical expertise or budget to truly embrace it in the long term.

Depending on the previous strategy or strategies that an organization has leveraged, they might have only invested in protection, but not necessarily detection and response. Subsequently, if they start using the *Attack-Centric Strategy*, they will likely increase investment in detection and response capabilities.

Advantages:

- Potentially levels the playing field between attackers and defenders as they both understand attackers' TTPs
- Forces attackers to be successful multiple times instead of just once or twice, which is how many of the other cybersecurity strategies are designed
- Designed to help detect intrusions as early in the attack as possible, in order to reduce remediation and recovery time and costs
- A vast ecosystem of vendors to help

Disadvantages:

- This approach requires most organizations to increase investments in detection and response capabilities, thus typically increasing complexity and costs.
- Typically relies on technology from multiple vendors to work in concert to protect, detect, and respond to threats. This could require technical expertise across multiple vendors' technologies, which might not be a realistic requirement for many organizations with limited resources and technical talent.
- Because of all the layers that this approach requires, it can be challenging to architect, deploy, and operate.
- This can be a relatively expensive strategy to pursue.

Next, let's look at a strategy that is currently extremely popular in the industry, *Zero Trust*.

Zero Trust

One of the underlying assumptions of all the strategies I've discussed in this chapter is that once a user or system has authenticated access to the IT environment, then it is trusted. The popularity of this convenient capability is evidenced by the ubiquity of **Single Sign-On (SSO)** requirements among enterprises. It's interesting that this assumption is as old as the oldest strategies I have examined. This assumption hasn't changed much since enterprises started procuring their first PCs. Some will argue that this assumption is one reason the industry has seen so many data breaches over the decades. I think it's fair to say that champions of the *Zero Trust* model would agree with this. Although this approach is regarded by many as new, it was first conceived almost 20 years ago by a group of CISOs, according to industry lore.

The concept behind this approach is that all resources, including those inside the perimeter, should be untrusted. This makes a lot of sense in a world where less and less IT infrastructure and fewer and fewer information workers are behind corporate firewalls. For example, the ongoing explosion of IoT devices should easily outnumber the number of desk-bound PCs and servers in datacenters, the same way that mobile devices have dramatically eclipsed them over the past 15 years. Additionally, as I discussed in my examination of the *Protect and Recover Strategy*, history has taught us that the old-school perimeter security approach, by itself, is a failure because its underlying assumptions have been proven to be wildly optimistic. You'll remember that one of those assumptions was that security teams could achieve perfect protection, forever, and they didn't require investments in detection and response capabilities.

If we assume that all network traffic, systems, devices, and users cannot be trusted, regardless of whether they are behind an enterprise perimeter, this could potentially change a security team's approach in a substantial way. Authenticating and authorizing applications, network connections, devices, and users for each operation they attempt, instead of just at the time of first access, can make it harder for attackers to initially compromise an environment, move laterally, stay persistent, and get access to sensitive data. Don't trust and always verify.

However, by itself, applying a design principle that requires near-constant authentication and authorization for users, systems, and devices doesn't address unpatched vulnerabilities, security misconfigurations, social engineering, or non-malicious insider threat. Remember the cliché, "attackers don't break in, they log in". If an attacker has valid credentials, what does authenticating them every time they try to access a resource actually help mitigate? This approach requires strong identity verification and for the principle of least privilege to be religiously enforced, just like some of the other strategies I have discussed.

Consequently, *Zero Trust* needs a bunch of other elements to evolve into a full-blown cybersecurity strategy.

Marry the rigor of near-constant authentication and authorization with the capabilities of the *Identity-Centric Strategy* that I discussed earlier, and this approach can help make better authentication and authorization decisions in real time. This approach might also benefit from many of the capabilities of the *Endpoint Protection Strategy* to provide the visibility and control needed on endpoints. Some vendors are resurrecting and integrating **Network Access Control (NAC)** and **Network Access Protection (NAP)** type capabilities into their *Zero Trust* product offerings to ensure endpoints meet corporate policies, such as being fully patched and running up-to-date anti-malware protection, among other requirements. Put another way, these capabilities enable the enterprise to treat its own endpoints as untrusted, keeping them disconnected from the internal corporate network until they prove they should be trusted by meeting security standards.

In fact, *Zero Trust* could borrow something from all the strategies I discussed in this chapter in order to address all the cybersecurity fundamentals and add advanced capabilities. This is in fact what's been happening. Almost every cybersecurity vendor today offers some sort of *Zero Trust* product or product line to support organizations that want to embrace the concept of treating everything as if it is untrusted. Googling "Zero Trust security" resulted in 334,000,000 results. Given there's so much interest in the concept, but the concept itself can be implemented in a myriad of ways, vendors and other interested parties, such as governments, provide their own visions of what *Zero Trust* means and how it should be implemented. Here are some examples.

Amazon Web Services (`https://aws.amazon.com/security/zero-trust/`):

> *Zero Trust is a security model centered on the idea that access to data should not be solely made based on network location. It requires users and systems to strongly prove their identities and trustworthiness, and enforces fine-grained identity-based authorization rules before allowing them to access applications, data, and other systems. With Zero Trust, these identities often operate within highly flexible identity-aware networks that further reduce surface area, eliminate unneeded pathways to data, and provide straightforward outer security guardrails." (Amazon Web Services, 2022).*

Cisco (`https://www.cisco.com/c/en/us/solutions/collateral/enterprise/design-zone-security/zt-frameworks.html`):

> *Security is not a one-size-fits-all and Zero Trust is more than network segmentation. To help understand the architecture, Cisco has broken it down into three pillars:*
>
> - *User and Device Security: making sure users and devices can be trusted as they access systems, regardless of location*
>
> - *Network and Cloud Security: protect all network resources on-prem and in the cloud, and ensure secure access for all connecting users*
>
> - *Application and Data Security: preventing unauthorized access within application environments irrespective of where they are hosted" (Cisco, 2022)*

Google (`https://storage.googleapis.com/pub-tools-public-publication-data/pdf/43231.pdf`):

> *Google's BeyondCorp initiative is moving to a new model that dispenses with a privileged corporate network. Instead, access depends solely on device and user credentials, regardless of a user's network location—be it an enterprise location, a home network, or a hotel or coffee shop. All access to enterprise resources is fully authenticated, fully authorized, and fully encrypted based upon device state and user credentials. We can enforce fine-grained access to different parts of enterprise resources. As a result, all Google employees can work successfully from any network, and without the need for a traditional VPN connection into the privileged network. The user experience between local and remote access to enterprise resources is effectively identical, apart from potential differences in latency." (Ward, R., Beyer, B., 2014).*

Microsoft (`https://www.microsoft.com/en-us/security/business/zero-trust`):

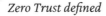

> *Zero Trust defined*
>
> *Instead of assuming everything behind the corporate firewall is safe, the Zero Trust model assumes breach and verifies each request as though it originates from an open network. Regardless of where the request originates or what resource it accesses, Zero Trust teaches us to "never trust, always verify." Every access request is fully authenticated, authorized, and encrypted before granting access. Microsegmentation and least privileged access principles are applied to minimize lateral movement. Rich intelligence and analytics are utilized to detect and respond to anomalies in real time." (Microsoft Corporation, 2022).*

The White House – Executive Order on Improving the Nation's Cybersecurity (`https://www.whitehouse.gov/briefing-room/presidential-actions/2021/05/12/executive-order-on-improving-the-nations-cybersecurity/`):

...the term "Zero Trust Architecture" means a security model, a set of system design principles, and a coordinated cybersecurity and system management strategy based on an acknowledgment that threats exist both inside and outside traditional network boundaries. The Zero Trust security model eliminates implicit trust in any one element, node, or service and instead requires continuous verification of the operational picture via real-time information from multiple sources to determine access and other system responses. In essence, a Zero Trust Architecture allows users full access but only to the bare minimum they need to perform their jobs. If a device is compromised, Zero Trust can ensure that the damage is contained. The Zero Trust Architecture security model assumes that a breach is inevitable or has likely already occurred, so it constantly limits access to only what is needed and looks for anomalous or malicious activity. Zero Trust Architecture embeds comprehensive security monitoring; granular risk-based access controls; and system security automation in a coordinated manner throughout all aspects of the infrastructure in order to focus on protecting data in real time within a dynamic threat environment. This data-centric security model allows the concept of least-privileged access to be applied for every access decision, where the answers to the questions of who, what, when, where, and how are critical for appropriately allowing or denying access to resources based on the combination of sever [sic]."

The last definition I provided from Executive Order 14028 published by the White House has a real-world impact. *Zero Trust* is mentioned eleven times in that Executive Order, instructing branches of the US government to implement *Zero Trust* to improve their cybersecurity. By doing this, this Executive Order also instructed every IT and cybersecurity vendor in the world that already sells products and services to the US government, or aspires to, to support this definition of *Zero Trust* or elements of it. As I mentioned in *Chapter 6, The Roles Governments Play in Cybersecurity*, when the largest standards body and IT consumer in the world sets requirements, the entire industry pays attention as they all want their share of that business. However, many questions remain about how to implement such an architecture, especially at massive scales suggested by Executive Order 14028.

How do we score *Zero Trust* using the CFSS?

CFSS score

Given the number of descriptions and definitions of *Zero Trust*, I'm not sure I can give it a single CFSS score. It seems like the score is a function of the specific implementation used. For example, how does this approach address unpatched vulnerabilities? Simply increasing the frequency of authentication and authorization events for a user, system, or device does nothing to mitigate this Cybersecurity Usual Suspect. However, if you extend this principle to endpoints, treat them like they are untrusted, and force them to be fully patched before getting access to any corporate resources, then you could almost completely mitigate the threat that unpatched vulnerabilities pose. This approach could also dramatically reduce the scale and scope of your vulnerability management program because endpoints would have to scan themselves for missing security updates and install them before getting access to the network. Getting the endpoints to do that work instead of a centralized vulnerability management program can help reduce the pressure on the program while reducing risk to the enterprise. The Vulnerability Management team could reduce the frequency of scanning systems that do their own patching, to perhaps weekly or monthly to identify systems that aren't being updated as expected.

Of course, trusting endpoints to prove their own integrity is riddled with challenges. Are the endpoints untrusted or not? Do we trust them just enough to tell us if they are secure enough to connect to the corporate network? Wouldn't *Zero Trust* mean that some sort of remote attestation service running on separate hardware from the endpoints is required to determine if the endpoints meet security standards? Where do we draw the line? It appears the answer to this question is left to each individual organization and vendor. If we are honest with each other, *Zero Trust* still requires organizations to trust a bunch of technologies in order to test whether other technologies should be trusted. So, in this case, "zero" doesn't mean none.

Google offers an interesting point of view here:

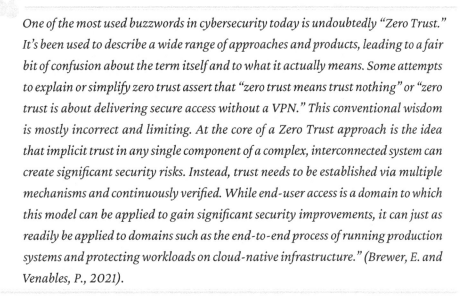

> *One of the most used buzzwords in cybersecurity today is undoubtedly "Zero Trust." It's been used to describe a wide range of approaches and products, leading to a fair bit of confusion about the term itself and to what it actually means. Some attempts to explain or simplify zero trust assert that "zero trust means trust nothing" or "zero trust is about delivering secure access without a VPN." This conventional wisdom is mostly incorrect and limiting. At the core of a Zero Trust approach is the idea that implicit trust in any single component of a complex, interconnected system can create significant security risks. Instead, trust needs to be established via multiple mechanisms and continuously verified. While end-user access is a domain to which this model can be applied to gain significant security improvements, it can just as readily be applied to domains such as the end-to-end process of running production systems and protecting workloads on cloud-native infrastructure." (Brewer, E. and Venables, P., 2021).*

My conclusion is that I can't provide a CFSS score for *Zero Trust*. It's not a cybersecurity strategy, it's a design principle or philosophy that can be applied as prudently as necessary. It could be applied to the mechanisms used to mitigate all the Cybersecurity Usual Suspects or not at all.

Looking for implicit trust assumptions in threat models can lead to positive improvements in many organizations' security postures. I don't think there's any doubt about that. For example, it might challenge some developers to try to design e-commerce applications capable of doing transactions on systems that are assumed to be compromised. The result should be better than assuming the system will never be compromised, right?

However, the success of this approach will depend on its implementation. For example, I mentioned that some vendors are using NAC/NAP in their *Zero Trust* solutions. The reason NAC/NAP failed the first time they became popular in the industry is because of the horrible user experience they imposed on users. All VPN users that connected to their office, where NAC/NAP were implemented, had the same dreaded experience at one time or another; they just wanted to check their emails, download a presentation, or quickly get access to some information, only to be quarantined and forced to slowly download and install security updates, antivirus signatures, endure reboots, and so on. Despite the positive advantages of ensuring systems were patched before connecting to the corporate network, it degraded the user experience so much that users would avoid connecting to the network for as long as they could. When they finally had to connect to the network, the user experience was even worse because of the backlog of updates the system required. This had the opposite effect on security than what was intended. Those vendors that offer *Zero Trust* solutions that leverage this same approach are doomed to the same fate. Users will only deal with so much overhead in their daily work before they actively try to avoid it or work around it.

The user experience shouldn't be worse in environments with *Zero Trust* implementations – it needs to be better. This one factor will likely decide the effectiveness and fate of *Zero Trust*.

We have covered quite a bit of ground! Let's conclude our review of cybersecurity strategies by summarizing what we've been discussing.

Cybersecurity strategies summary

We have reviewed several popular cybersecurity strategies. These strategies include:

- Protect and Recover Strategy
- Endpoint Protection Strategy
- Physical Control and Security Clearances Strategy
- Compliance as a Cybersecurity Strategy
- Application-Centric Strategy
- Identity-Centric Strategy
- Data-Centric Strategy
- Attack-Centric Strategy

We also discussed *Zero Trust*, which I concluded wasn't a strategy in the same way as the others on the list are.

A summary of my CFSS score estimates for these strategies is provided in *Table 9.12*. As you can see, I gave the *Attack-Centric Strategy* the highest estimated CFSS score. In my view, it is the only strategy that has the greatest potential to help organizations address the cybersecurity fundamentals, mitigate the Cybersecurity Usual Suspects, and potentially help implement advanced capabilities:

Cybersecurity Strategy	Unpatched vulnerabilities	Security misconfigurations	Weak, leaked, stolen credentials	Social engineering	Insider threat	Total Score
Protect and Recover Strategy	10	10	0	5	0	25
Endpoint Protection Strategy	20	20	15	10	10	75
Physical Control and Security Clearances Strategy	10	10	15	10	10	55
Compliance as a Cybersecurity Strategy	10	10	10	10	10	50
Application-Centric Strategy	20	20	10	10	10	70
Identity-Centric Strategy	5	5	15	10	10	45
Data-Centric Strategy	5	5	0	15	15	40
Attack-Centric Strategy	20	20	20	15	20	95

Table 9.12: CFSS score estimate summary

The reality is most organizations that I have met with use a combination of some of these strategies. For example, it would be bold for an enterprise not to have both a perimeter security strategy and an endpoint security strategy, even as the industry offers newer, shinier technologies. Many organizations have some regulatory compliance requirements that they must pay attention to. It can be helpful for those organizations that already use some of these approaches to deliberately and thoughtfully reconcile where there has been over-investment and under-investment, and where gaps currently exist. This is another advantage that the *Attack-Centric Strategy* has over these other strategies and combinations of them – investment and gap analysis is built right into it. I will discuss this in more detail in *Chapter 11, Measuring Performance and Effectiveness*.

You might disagree with my CFSS score estimates for some or all of these strategies. That's good. I encourage you to use the CFSS to perform your own scoring estimates for all the approaches I examined in this chapter and others I didn't cover. Security professionals all have different experiences, which could lead them to score one or more of these strategies higher or lower than I have. Frankly, this is to be expected as I've never met a security professional that didn't have an opinion. Despite this, most organizations do not have a cybersecurity strategy that their CISOs or other executives can articulate. My objective for this chapter is to provoke critical thought about the ways that organizations have been approaching cybersecurity and perhaps hold a mirror for CISOs and security teams to look into.

Now, let's look at a potentially helpful approach that is different, in some important ways, from the more classical approaches discussed in this chapter.

DevOps and DevSecOps

DevOps represents a change in the way that organizations have traditionally approached application development and deployment. Traditionally, developers and operations staff were managed as separate disciplines that rarely worked together. Developers would write code to specifications and when they wanted to deploy it, they "threw it over the fence" to the operations team. Sometimes, the operations team encountered issues deploying the application, so they would send it back to the development team with the issues that were preventing successful deployment. Developers and operations would iterate on this process, typically at a slow and frustrating pace. Because these groups only communicated with each other periodically, the developers often lacked the operational and environmental context that would help them develop applications that could be deployed and operated in a real IT environment. Similarly, the operations teams often didn't have the technical details on the application to help them perform successful deployments.

The feedback loop between teams was slow, leading to milestone delays, slow development cycles, and quality issues.

DevOps tries to address these challenges by tightly integrating developers and operations staff. They can give each other feedback more efficiently and faster when they work with each other day in and day out. Operations staff can inform the design and functionality choices that the developers make while they are developing the application. The developers can get constant feedback on the viability and supportability of their ideas from the operations staff. This can lead to faster development and deployment cycles, better quality applications, less rework, and happier teams.

DevOps typically includes concepts like continuous testing, **Continuous Integration (CI)**, **Continuous Delivery (CD)**, continuous deployment, and continuous performance monitoring. This goes beyond the technologies, services, and products that support these concepts because most organizations must make significant changes to their development philosophies, cultures, and processes to embrace DevOps.

DevSecOps is DevOps with the explicit acknowledgment that security must be embedded in the philosophies, cultures, processes, and supporting technologies for this approach to be successful. Some argue that the "Sec" in DevSecOps is gratuitous because DevOps cannot be done properly without embedding security in it. I agree wholeheartedly. If your organization is currently doing DevOps and has decided that it'll evolve into a DevSecOps approach later, then you are likely already doing DevOps wrong. Remember, someone recently said that "culture eats strategy for breakfast." This is why DevOps is potentially so powerful and transformational for IT organizations.

The value of DevOps is extended when it is used together with containers and/or cloud computing. For example, since infrastructure is code in the cloud, infrastructure is deployed, configured, and supported using code. This means that provisioning and managing infrastructure in the cloud can benefit from the virtues of DevOps. Developers can specify the hardware, software, and configuration for infrastructure in the code they write, informed by the requirements and continuous feedback provided by operations teams. This approach enables organizations to provision infrastructure faster than traditional approaches and at virtually any scale desired.

From a security perspective, DevOps offers a powerful model for building and deploying applications and infrastructure. This is where the concept of a CI/CD pipeline is useful. The pipeline typically handles functions like checking code into a repository, automated building, automated testing, and deploying the tested code into production. The pipeline itself can be composed of a combination of tools, products, and services from one or multiple vendors. Some organizations that have embraced DevOps deploy all applications and all infrastructure via a CI/CD pipeline.

Put another way, nothing gets into their production environments unless it goes through a pipeline. Enforcing pipeline policies like this can offer organizations at least a few advantages versus legacy approaches. For example, when applications and infrastructure are required to go through a pipeline and the pipeline has automated checks to ensure regulatory, industry, and internal security standards are met, then everything that makes it into production is in this known good state.

This assurance makes short-lived environments possible by enabling infrastructure to be discarded and redeployed in a known good state, every few hours. If that infrastructure gets compromised, attackers will only have control of that asset for a relatively short time before it gets blown away and replaced. This can make it harder for attackers to get a foothold in an environment and remain persistent. It can also help dramatically reduce the amount of work for vulnerability management teams. Instead of constantly performing inventories of systems, scanning them for security vulnerabilities, patching, and rebooting them, they can scan and patch the relatively small number of "gold images" used for infrastructure deployments. When a short-lived infrastructure is discarded and replaced, the new infrastructure is based on the up-to-date gold image. Verifying the patch status of a short-lived infrastructure is less work for vulnerability management teams, and less disruptive to the business. There are similar advantages for compliance teams, as well as internal and external auditors.

Of course, DevOps isn't a panacea. DevOps and CI/CD pipelines done poorly can be a bad thing for organizations. To date, most of the organizations I've discussed DevOps with only use it in parts of their IT environment, and the rest of the organization is still chained to legacy models. Developers can become enamored with CI/CD pipelines. For example, developers that embrace CI/CD pipelines can end up spending more of their time developing tools and automation for their pipelines than working on applications and infrastructure. Organizations can also end up with too many CI/CD pipelines. Predictably, some attackers see potential victims shifting to DevOps and using CI/CD pipelines, so they target the pipeline infrastructure itself; CI/CD pipelines could end up becoming HVAs for some organizations and require more security rigor than they were initially prepared for.

I think the security and non-security advantages of DevOps and CI/CD pipelines outweigh any challenges they present. This is the reason the entire industry has been moving to this model and will continue to do so for many years to come.

Summary

CISOs and security teams should select their organization's cybersecurity strategy based on how well it addresses the cybersecurity fundamentals, as the minimum bar. Without examining how their strategy mitigates all the Cybersecurity Usual Suspects, they could be lulling themselves into a false sense of security. The CFSS can help security teams determine how well their current or future strategies address the cybersecurity fundamentals.

Of the strategies examined in this chapter, the *Attack-Centric Strategy*, was deemed as the strategy most capable of mitigating the Cybersecurity Usual Suspects and enabling advanced cybersecurity capabilities. The *Endpoint Protection Strategy* and the *Application-Centric Strategy* rounded out the top three strategies in this evaluation but will need to be used in combination with other strategies to fully address the cybersecurity fundamentals.

The *Zero Trust* approach holds the potential to raise the security waterline for the entire industry. But how this approach is implemented and the user experience it imposes will determine its effectiveness and its fate.

DevOps is a holistic approach that leads to changes in development philosophies, cultures, and processes for the organizations that embrace it. This is the destination that many organizations aspire to get to. This approach might not be as beneficial for legacy IT environments, where the more traditional cybersecurity strategies that I examined might be used during the transition to modern architectures, like the cloud.

That completes my examination of cybersecurity strategies. In the next chapter, we will dive deep into an implementation example of the strategy that had the highest CFSS estimated total score, the *Attack-Centric Strategy*.

References

- Amazon Web Services. (2022). *Zero Trust on AWS*. Retrieved from: `https://aws.amazon.com/security/zero-trust/`
- Ashford, W. (August 3, 2016). *One in five businesses hit by ransomware are forced to close, study shows*. Retrieved from ComputerWeekly: `https://www.computerweekly.com/news/450301845/One-in-five-businesses-hit-by-ransomware-are-forced-to-close-study-shows`

- Brewer, E., Venables, P. (August 25, 2021). *A unified and proven Zero Trust system with BeyondCorp and BeyondProd*. Retrieved from: `https://cloud.google.com/blog/products/identity-security/applying-zero-trust-to-user-access-and-production-services`

- Cisco. (June 27, 2022). *Zero Trust Frameworks Architecture Guide*. Retrieved from: `https://www.cisco.com/c/en/us/solutions/collateral/enterprise/design-zone-security/zt-frameworks.html`

- Hutchins, E.M., Cloppert, M.J., Amin, R.M. Ph.D. (n.d.). *Intelligence-Driven Computer Network Defense Informed by Analysis of Adversary Campaigns and Intrusion Kill Chains*. Retrieved from Lockheed Martin: `https://lockheedmartin.com/content/dam/lockheed-martin/rms/documents/cyber/LM-White-Paper-Intel-Driven-Defense.pdf`

- European Data Protection Board. (2019). *First overview on the implementation of the GDPR and the roles and means of the national supervisory authorities*. Brussels: European Data Protection Board.

- Microsoft Corporation. (September 2, 2022). *Privileged access: Strategy*. Retrieved from Microsoft: `https://learn.microsoft.com/en-us/security/compass/privileged-access-strategy`

- Microsoft Corporation. (n.d.). *Microsoft Security Engineering*. Retrieved from Microsoft Corporation: `https://www.microsoft.com/en-us/securityengineering/sdl/`

- Microsoft Corporation. (2022). *Embrace proactive security with Zero Trust*. Retrieved from Microsoft Corporation: `https://www.microsoft.com/en-us/security/business/zero-trust/`

- MITRE ATT&CK®. (n.d.). *MITRE ATT&CK Frequently Asked Questions*. Retrieved from MITRE ATT&CK®: `https://attack.mitre.org/resources/faq/`

- MITRE. (n.d.). *MITRE ATT&CK*. Retrieved from MITRE ATT&CK®: `https://attack.mitre.org/`

- Strom, B.E., Applebaum, A., Miller, D.P., Nickels, K.C., Pennington, A.G., & Thomas, C.B. (2020). *MITRE ATT&CK®: Design and Philosophy*. MITRE Corporation

- NIST. (n.d.). *Cybersecurity Framework*. Retrieved from NIST: `https://csrc.nist.gov/Projects/cybersecurity-framework/nist-cybersecurity-framework-a-quick-start-guide`

- NIST. (n.d.). *Cybersecurity Framework*. Retrieved from NIST: `https://www.nist.gov/cyberframework`

- PA Consulting. (n.d.). *Oak Door Data Diode*. Retrieved from PA Consulting: `https://www.paconsulting.com/services/build-brands-products-and-services`

- Pols, Paul. (October 2022). *The Unified Kill Chain*. Retrieved from: `https://www.unifiedkillchain.com/assets/The-Unified-Kill-Chain.pdf`

- The White House. (May 2021). *Executive Order on Improving the Nation's Cybersecurity*. Retrieved from: `https://www.whitehouse.gov/briefing-room/presidential-actions/2021/05/12/executive-order-on-improving-the-nations-cybersecurity/`

- U.K. Cabinet Office. (May 2018). *Government Security Classifications*. Retrieved from GOV.UK: `https://assets.publishing.service.gov.uk/government/uploads/system/uploads/attachment_data/file/715778/May-2018_Government-Security-Classifications-2.pdf`

- United States Government Publishing Office. (December 29, 2009). *Executive Order 13526 of December 29, 2009*. Retrieved from GovInfo: `https://www.govinfo.gov/content/pkg/DCPD-200901022/pdf/DCPD-200901022.pdf`

- Virus Bulletin. (n.d.). *Virus Bulletin*. Retrieved from Virus Bulletin: `https://www.virusbulletin.com/`

- Ward, R., Beyer, B., (December 2014). *BeyondCorp, A New Approach to Enterprise Security*. Retrieved from: `https://storage.googleapis.com/pub-tools-public-publication-data/pdf/43231.pdf`

- Wikipedia. (n.d.). *Rainbow table*. Retrieved from Wikipedia: `https://en.wikipedia.org/wiki/Rainbow_table`

- Microsoft Corporation. (Jan 6, 2023). *Personnel management overview*. Retrieved from Microsoft Corporation: `https://learn.microsoft.com/en-us/compliance/assurance/assurance-human-resources?view=o365-worldwide`

- Microsoft Corporation. (May 31, 2017). *Best Practices for Securing Active Directory*. Retrieved from Microsoft: `https://learn.microsoft.com/en-us/windows-server/identity/ad-ds/plan/security-best-practices/best-practices-for-securing-active-directory`

Join our community on Discord

Join our community's Discord space for discussions with the author and other readers:

`https://packt.link/SecNet`

10

Strategy Implementation

In the previous chapter, I discussed numerous cybersecurity strategies. In this chapter, I'll take one of those strategies and illustrate how it can be implemented in a real IT environment. The objective is to take the theoretical and make it a little more real for you. I'll provide some tips and tricks I've learned in my career along the way.

In this chapter we will cover the following:

- What is the Intrusion Kill Chain?
- Some ways that the traditional Kill Chain model can be modernized
- Factors to consider when planning and implementing this model
- Designing security control sets to support this model

Since the MITRE ATT&CK® framework is also popular, very useful, and complementary to the Intrusion Kill Chain, I'll point out some of the areas where it is helpful.

Introduction

You might recall from the last chapter, the Attack-Centric Strategy had the highest **Cybersecurity Fundamentals Scoring System (CFSS)** estimated total score. It earned nearly a perfect score with 95 points out of a possible 100. It earned such a high score because it almost fully addresses all the cybersecurity fundamentals, with the exception of social engineering, which can't really be fully mitigated.

Two popular examples of Attack-Centric frameworks used by security professionals in the industry include the Intrusion Kill Chain (Hutchins, Cloppert, Amin, n.d.) and the MITRE ATT&CK® model (MITRE, n.d.).

In this chapter, I'll provide an example of how an Attack-Centric Strategy can be implemented. The model I will focus on is the Intrusion Kill Chain framework first pioneered by Lockheed Martin. I have found that security professionals either love or hate this model. I've actually had the opportunity to do a couple of big budget implementations of it, so I have some first-hand experience with it. As I contemplated these implementations, I realized an Intrusion Kill Chain could probably be implemented in several different ways. I'll describe one way this framework can be implemented, fully recognizing that there are other ways it can be implemented, and that mine might not be the best way.

The Intrusion Kill Chain framework is based on Lockheed Martin's paper *Intelligence-Driven Computer Network Defense Informed by Analysis of Adversary Campaigns and Intrusion Kill Chains* (Hutchins, Cloppert, Amin, n.d.). In my opinion, this paper is required reading for all cybersecurity professionals. Some of the concepts in this paper might seem mainstream or even dated now, but when it was first published, it introduced concepts and ideas that changed the cybersecurity industry. Some might argue that this model has seen its best days and that there are now better approaches available, like the MITRE ATT&CK model. This isn't quite true as ATT&CK is meant to be complementary to the Intrusion Kill Chain approach. According to MITRE:

> *What is the relationship between ATT&CK and the Lockheed Martin Cyber Kill Chain®?*
>
> *ATT&CK and the Cyber Kill Chain are complementary. ATT&CK sits at a lower level of definition to describe adversary behavior than the Cyber Kill Chain. ATT&CK Tactics are unordered and may not all occur in a single intrusion because adversary tactical goals change throughout an operation, whereas the Cyber Kill Chain uses ordered phases to describe high level adversary objectives." (MITRE, n.d.)*

Also, keep in mind that the CFSS score suggests that the Attack-Centric Strategy can nearly fully mitigate the Cybersecurity Usual Suspects. Regardless of what this approach's champions or its detractors say about it, *Chapter 9, Cybersecurity Strategies,* gave you the CFSS method to decide its potential efficacy for yourself. I recommend making use of this tool when faced with disparate opinions about cybersecurity strategies. Additionally, keep in mind that this approach can be used in on-premises IT environments, in cloud environments, and in hybrid environments. Another strength of this approach is that it is technology neutral, meaning it isn't limited to a specific technology or vendor. This means it can be used by most organizations now and into the future as they evolve their IT strategies.

However, I do believe there is a better, more modern cybersecurity strategy for cloud environments. I'll discuss this in *Chapter 12, Modern Approaches to Security and Compliance.*

What is an Intrusion Kill Chain?

An Intrusion Kill Chain is the stages or phases that can be used in attacks by attackers. The phases provided in Lockheed Martin's paper include:

- Reconnaissance
- Weaponization
- Delivery
- Exploitation
- Installation
- Command and Control (C2)
- Actions on Objectives

Although you can probably tell from the name of each of these phases what they encompass, let me quickly summarize them for you. Note that this is based on my own interpretation of Lockheed Martin's paper, and other interpretations are possible.

Attackers select their target in the Reconnaissance phase (Hutchins, Cloppert, Amin, n.d.). Certainly, many attackers select targets opportunistically, many times by coincidence, as evidenced by all the commodity malware present on the internet.

So-called **Advanced Persistent Threat (APT)** attackers spend time and effort researching who they should target based on their motivations for the attack. They will likely spend time in this phase discovering the IP address space their target uses, the hardware and software they use, the types of systems they have, how the business or organization works, which vendors are in their supply chain, and who works there. They can use a range of tools to conduct this research, including technical tools to do DNS name lookups, IP address range scans, the websites where the organization advertises job openings that typically include technical qualifications based on the hardware and software they use, among many others.

Once attackers have selected their target and have some understanding of where they are on the internet and the technologies they use, then they figure out how they are going to attack the victim. This phase is called Weaponization (Hutchins, Cloppert, Amin, n.d.). For example, based on their research on the target, they see that they use Adobe products.

So, they plan to try to initially compromise the environment by exploiting potentially unpatched vulnerabilities for Acrobat Reader, for example. To do this, they construct a malformed .pdf file that is capable of exploiting a particular vulnerability (CVE ID) when a victim opens it. Of course, this attack will only work if the vulnerability they are using has not been patched in the target's environment.

Now that the attackers have decided how they are going to try to initially compromise the target's environment, and they've built a weapon to do this, next they have to decide how they will deliver their weapon to the target. In the Delivery phase, they decide if they are going to send the malformed .pdf file as an email attachment, use it as part of a watering hole attack, put it on USB drives and throw it into the organization's parking lot, and so on.

Once the weapon has been delivered to a potential victim, attackers need a way to activate the weapon. In our malicious .pdf example, the attacker hopes that the victim tries to open the malformed file so that their exploit runs on the victim's system. This phase is aptly called the Exploitation phase (Hutchins, Cloppert, Amin, n.d.). If the victim's system isn't patched for the specific vulnerability that the exploit is designed to take advantage of, then the attacker's exploit will successfully execute.

When the attacker's exploit executes, it could download more malware to the victim's system or unpack malware from within itself. Typically, this will give the attacker remote access to the victim's system. This phase is called Installation (Hutchins, Cloppert, Amin, n.d.).

Once the attackers have successfully installed their tools on the victim's system, they can send commands to their tools or to the system itself. The attackers now control the system fully or partially, and they can potentially run arbitrary code of their choice on the victim's system. This phase of the attack is the **Command and Control (C2)** phase (Hutchins, Cloppert, Amin, n.d.). They might try to further penetrate the environment by attempting to compromise more systems.

Actions on Objectives is the final phase of the Intrusion Kill Chain. Now that attackers control one or more compromised systems, they pursue their objectives. As I discussed in *Chapter 1, Introduction* their motivations could include profit, economic espionage, military espionage, notoriety, revenge, and many others. Now, they are in a position to achieve the specific objectives to satisfy their motivation. They might steal intellectual property, stay persistent to collect information, attempt a kinetic attack to physically damage their victim's operations, destroy systems, and so on.

> *Note that I have written that these are phases in an attack that attackers can use in attacks. I didn't write that each of the phases is always used in attacks. This is a nuance that some of the detractors of this framework typically miss. They often argue that attackers don't have to use all seven phases that are listed in Lockheed Martin's paper. They only use the phases they have to use. Therefore, the model is flawed and shouldn't be used. I will admit that I have never understood this argument, but I hear it often when discussing this framework. It's helpful to keep the intended purpose of this framework in mind—to make it harder for attackers to succeed. Also, remember the tip I gave you in Chapter 4, The Evolution of Malware, about claims of omniscience? This argument relies on omniscience. We will never know what all attackers do. Because we don't know what attackers will do in the present or the future, we must be prepared to protect, detect, and respond to whatever they choose to do. That is, we need to be grounded in the reality that attackers can use any of these phases."*

For example, some environments are already compromised, making it easier for attackers in the present and potentially in the future to penetrate the victim's environment without going through the first three or four phases. That doesn't mean that an attacker didn't already successfully go through these phases in a previous attack, and it doesn't mean attackers won't use them in the future. We don't know what the future holds and we don't control attackers. We aren't omniscient or omnipotent. We do know attackers will always use at least one of these phases—they have to. Subsequently, defenders must be prepared, regardless of which phases attackers use.

This is a difference between the Intrusion Kill Chain framework and the ATT&CK framework that is often pointed out. ATT&CK provides tactics that attackers might or might not use. These tactics are different from the ordered steps or stages in the Intrusion Kill Chain. Despite this difference, they both have the same limitation in that they cannot be used to predict the future. They provide ways to visualize the steps attackers could take in their attacks and organize defenses around them. The number and order of those steps cannot be predicted because of the large number of combinations and permutations of the states of IT environments and the choices attackers can make. Spirited discussions among security team members as to which approach to use is likely a good use of time.

However, those that argue that neither of these approaches should be used without offering a viable cybersecurity strategy themselves aren't being helpful. The key to using either of these approaches is to measure the performance of the cybersecurity capability investments you choose to make and make changes where prudent. Using either of these approaches or both of them together still requires that you measure the efficacy of your particular implementation. This is the topic of *Chapter 11, Measuring Performance and Effectiveness*.

Knowing what the attacker's full Intrusion Kill Chain could look like can help defenders make it much harder for attackers to be successful. By significantly increasing the effort required for attackers to be successful, we reduce their return on investment, and potentially their determination. To do this, the authors of the Intrusion Kill Chain paper suggest that defenders use a Courses of Action Matrix (Hutchins, Cloppert, Amin, n.d.). This matrix allows defenders to map out how they plan to detect, deny, disrupt, degrade, deceive, and destroy the attacker's efforts in each of the seven phases of their Intrusion Kill Chain. An example of this is illustrated in *Figure 10.1*.

Kill Chain Phase	Detect	Deny	Disrupt	Degrade	Deceive	Destroy
Reconnaissance						
Weaponization						
Delivery						
Exploitation						
Installation						
Command and Control (C2)						
Actions on Objectives						

Figure 10.1: A Courses of Action Matrix (Hutchins, Cloppert, Amin, n.d.)

By layering controls into this matrix, the objective is to make it much harder, or impossible, for attackers to progress through their Intrusion Kill Chain. Multiple complementary capabilities can be included in each of the cells in the matrix. Stopping attackers as early in their Intrusion Kill Chain as possible reduces the potential damage and associated recovery time and costs. Instead of attackers being successful after they defeat a firewall or a single set of controls, they must overcome the layered defenses in the Courses of Action Matrix for each step in their attack.

Modernizing the Kill Chain

One consideration before implementing this framework is whether defenders should use the original Intrusion Kill Chain framework or use an updated version of it. There are several ways this framework can be modernized. The ATT&CK framework is an example of a modernized Intrusion Kill Chain. At the time of writing, the current version (ATT&CK version 12.0) provides 14 tactics instead of the 7 stages provided by the original Intrusion Kill Chain framework.

Although tactics and stages are slightly different, the concept is the same – understanding how attackers initially compromise and penetrate enterprise IT environments enables defenders to better protect, detect, and respond to those attacks.

I'll give you some ideas how the original Intrusion Kill Chain can be modernized in this section. However, don't be afraid to embrace the notion of iterative improvement based on your organizations' experiences with this framework or others.

Mapping the Cybersecurity Usual Suspects

I hope I have imparted the importance of mitigating the five ways that organizations are initially compromised. The Intrusion Kill Chain framework can be modified or reorganized around the Cybersecurity Usual Suspects to ensure that they are mitigated and make it easier to identify gaps in an organization's security posture. This can be done in a couple of different ways. First, they can be integrated into the original Intrusion Kill Chain framework. That is, the controls used to mitigate the Cybersecurity Usual Suspects are spread across the Courses of Action Matrix like all the other controls are. The challenge with this approach is that it can make it difficult to identify over-investment, under-investment, and gaps in those specific areas, especially if your matrix is large. To compensate for this, a column could be added to the matrix where the Cybersecurity Usual Suspects that each control mitigates is tracked. Some rows won't have an entry in this column because many controls will be advanced cybersecurity capabilities, not necessarily focused on the Cybersecurity Usual Suspects.

Another way to make it easier to ensure the Cybersecurity Usual Suspects are fully mitigated is to use two separate lists. Inventory the controls that mitigate the Cybersecurity Usual Suspects in one list and everything else in a separate Courses of Action Matrix. This way, you'll have complete, unobscured visibility into the controls implemented to mitigate the Cybersecurity Usual Suspects, and all other controls as well. This might mean that there is some duplication of controls in these lists that makes it more complicated to track changes over time.

I prefer the second approach, that is, using two separate lists. I like clear visibility into the controls that mitigate the Cybersecurity Usual Suspects. Put another way, one list for controls focused on protecting, detecting, and responding to attempts to initially compromise an IT environment and another list for post-compromise controls. This approach makes it easier to keep track of the controls that represent the foundation of the strategy. However, feel free to use either approach or a different one that works best for your organization. This is the approach I will use in the example provided in this chapter. I've already discussed the Cybersecurity Usual Suspects and the Cybersecurity Fundamentals extensively in other chapters. The example I'll provide here will focus on the advanced cybersecurity capabilities component of the strategy.

Updating the matrix

Another modification to this approach worth considering is whether to update the phases and the actions in the Courses of Action Matrix. For example, the Reconnaissance phase of the Intrusion Kill Chain can be split into two separate phases. This separation recognizes that there are potentially two different times in an intrusion attempt when attackers typically perform reconnaissance. Prior to the attack, attackers might spend time selecting their target and researching ways that they could be attacked. After one of the Cybersecurity Usual Suspects is used to initially compromise the victim, then the attackers might perform some reconnaissance again to map out the victim's network and where the **High-Value Assets (HVAs)** are. The reason why separating these two phases can be helpful is that the tools, techniques, tactics, and procedures used by attackers can be different before and after initial compromise. Updating the matrix by replacing the Reconnaissance phase with the **Reconnaissance I and Reconnaissance II** phases will enable security teams to map different controls to stop attackers in each of these phases. Keep in mind that, in both of these cases, attackers might use non-intrusive reconnaissance tactics or choose to use intrusive reconnaissance tactics.

This same type of modification has been implemented in the ATT&CK framework where they have **Reconnaissance and Discovery** tactics. The former focuses on informing targeting while the latter focuses on learning about the compromised environment.

Another potential update to the phases is dropping the **Weaponization** phase. That might seem like a significant change to the original framework, but in my experience, it doesn't change the controls defenders typically use. This phase of an attack is where the attackers, who have now decided how they are going to attack the victim, plan to reuse old weapons or build and/or buy new weapons to use in their attack. Most of this activity happens out of the view of defenders. Subsequently, very few of the attacker's activities in this phase can be influenced by controls available to defenders. If attackers are cavalier about the sources they procure weapons from, threat intelligence vendors or law enforcement could get tipped off about their activities and perhaps their intentions. This could be helpful if the weapon is a zero-day vulnerability that the intended victim could deploy workarounds to mitigate, but frankly, focusing on the other attack phases will likely have a much higher return on investment for defenders as they potentially have more visibility and control. The Weaponization phase is too opaque for most organizations to realistically influence. Put another way, CISOs typically do not have very effective controls for protection and detection prior to the Delivery phase; prioritizing investments in mitigations that have a clear, measurable value is important.

This is reflected in the ATT&CK framework as well. In ATT&CK parlance, this weaponization concept is called **Resource Development**. It has fewer techniques (7) associated with it than any of the other tactics in the framework. The mitigation ATT&CK offers for many of these techniques is "This technique cannot be easily mitigated with preventive controls since it is based on behaviors performed outside of the scope of enterprise defenses and controls" (MITRE, n.d.).

The Courses of Action Matrix can be updated to include some different actions. For example, Destroy could be dropped in favor of some more realistic actions, such as **Limit and Recover**. Using Limit as an action recognizes that defenders want to make it hard or impossible for attackers to move freely during their attack. For example, limiting the delivery options available to attackers, and limiting the scope of the infrastructure that attackers can control, both make it harder for attackers to be successful. Using a Restore action helps organizations plan their recovery if all the other mitigations layered in the model fail to perform as expected. For both Limit and Restore, not every cell in the matrix will necessarily have controls in them. For example, there likely is no control that will help Recover during the Reconnaissance I phase because the environment hasn't been attacked yet. There will potentially be several cells in the matrix without entries—this is to be expected. An example of the updated Courses of Action Matrix is illustrated in *Figure 10.2*:

Kill Chain Phase	Detect	Deny	Disrupt	Degrade	Deceive	Limit	Restore
Reconnaissance I							
Delivery							
Exploitation							
Installation							
Command and Control (C2)							
Reconnaissance II							
Actions on Objectives							

Figure 10.2: An example of an updated Courses of Action Matrix (Hutchins, Cloppert, Amin, n.d.)

Of course, these updates are completely optional. Implementing the original Intrusion Kill Chain model can be an effective way for many organizations to improve their security posture. I suggest that before CISOs get serious about implementing this model, they spend some time thinking through whether any modifications to the original model will be advantageous. Then, they should update the Courses of Action Matrix before moving forward with this model as this will save time, expense, and potentially frustrating rework.

Intrusion Kill Chain or ATT&CK?

Another decision to make is whether to use the Intrusion Kill Chain framework or the ATT&CK framework, or a combination of these approaches. In my experience, the relatively small number of high-level stages that the Intrusion Kill Chain offers makes it easier for Strategy and Architecture teams to visualize attacks and design and implement layer defenses for them.

Besides being a simpler model, I find this approach to be aligned with how cybersecurity vendors tend to market and sell their products and services. This makes it easier for the teams that negotiate deals with cybersecurity vendors, such as Procurement and Legal teams, to do their work. For example, an anti-malware vendor might highlight the various benefits of their product such as high detection rates, low false positive detection rates, and advanced heuristics. In ATT&CK parlance, the same vendor would highlight that they have the best lsass.exe injection detection in the industry. Notice how the altitude of these benefits is different?

Lastly, I've found that the Intrusion Kill Chain framework is easier for senior stakeholders to understand. This includes IT leadership, **Senior Leadership Teams (SLT)** and Board of Directors members. Remember one piece of advice I provided in *Chapter 8, Ingredients for a Successful Cybersecurity Strategy*: getting support from these stakeholders can be critical to the success of your strategy. If they can't understand the strategy, they might not get fully behind it. I've found the ATT&CK taxonomy with tactics, techniques, sub-techniques, mitigations, detections, and so on, is harder for SLT and Board of Directors members to understand. This is another reason I have found the Intrusion Kill Chain framework valuable – it can be easier to get support for.

Where I have found the ATT&CK framework to be more helpful than the Intrusion Kill Chain is in doing security control validation and testing, designing and testing enterprise detection strategies, attack simulations – any place where knowledge of the granular techniques attackers might use could be helpful. The knowledgebase aspect of ATT&CK is really helpful in these scenarios, but the Intrusion Kill Chain largely leaves it up to Strategy and Architecture teams to figure these things out for themselves.

Subsequently, leveraging a combination of these approaches can make sense. Using the Intrusion Kill Chain framework to make things more straightforward for Strategy, Architecture, Procurement, Legal, and other stakeholders, such as SLT and members of Boards, and using ATT&CK to inform the details for security teams, can be a powerful combination for some organizations.

Of course, some organizations simply standardize on the ATT&CK framework and try to use it consistently everywhere – this is also a great approach. Whichever route your organization goes down, remember that the best approach is the one that is going to be most successful for your organization, not someone else's. Remember, best practices are based on someone else's threat model.

I'll mention one caveat here. Both of these approaches can be used in the cloud. The question for CISOs is, can your organization manage two separate cybersecurity strategies – one for the cloud and one for on-premises? Or should you use the same strategy in both environments to make things simpler and more consistent? In my role as a cybersecurity advisor, I found a surprising number of CISOs that expressed a preference to operate separate strategies for the cloud and their on-premises environments. I'll discuss this more in *Chapter 12, Modern Approaches to Security and Compliance*.

Getting started

Existing IT environments, especially those already under the management of a CISO, will likely have some cybersecurity controls already deployed in them. If an Attack-Centric Strategy and the Intrusion Kill Chain approach is new to an organization, chances are that the existing controls were deployed in a way that isn't necessarily consistent with the Courses of Action Matrix. Mapping currently deployed cybersecurity controls to the Courses of Action Matrix will help determine where potential gaps exist between currently deployed cybersecurity capabilities and a fully implemented Courses of Action Matrix. It can also help identify areas of over-investment and under-investment. For example, after mapping their current cybersecurity capabilities to this matrix, the security team realizes that they have invested heavily in capabilities that deny the delivery of the attacker's weapons but have not invested anything that helps detect delivery attempts; in fact, they now realize they have underinvested in detection capabilities across the entire Kill Chain. This mapping exercise can help expose optimistic assumptions about organizations' security capabilities. Some security professionals call this type of exercise cartography.

This exercise can be illuminating, but also challenging to perform, especially in large complex environments. Most organizations I've advised didn't have a complete, up-to-date list of tools, products, services, and configurations that are useful in an exercise like this one. Even organizations that have asset inventories and configuration management databases often find their data to be incomplete, out of date, and inaccurate. I've seen industry estimates suggesting that the average on-premises IT environment has 20% undocumented assets and services, and even higher estimates in some industries, like healthcare. Experience tells me these estimates are low.

Some organizations try to use procurement artifacts to determine what their IT department bought, but this is usually different than what was actually deployed. Faced with the challenge of getting an accurate, up-to-date inventory of the cybersecurity capabilities they have running in their environment, most organizations start with the data they have, and manually verify what has been implemented. This isn't necessarily a bad thing because it can provide a view that is accurate and current, but also includes qualitative insights that can't be rendered from an asset inventory database.

Maturity of current cybersecurity capabilities

I have had the opportunity to do this mapping exercise in some large, complicated IT environments. Let me share some of the things I've learned, to save you some time if you are faced with the same challenge.

As you map current cybersecurity capabilities to the Courses of Action Matrix, one factor to be aware of is the maturity of the implementation of each control or capability. That is, an item on a software inventory list might not offer any clue as to whether the control is fully implemented or partially implemented. Understanding the maturity of each control's implementation is key to really understanding where gaps exist, and where under - and over-investment has occurred.

For example, an organization procures a suite of cybersecurity capabilities from a top-tier industry vendor. This suite is capable of providing several important functions including file integrity monitoring, anti-malware scanning, and data loss prevention for desktops and servers. When mapping capabilities to the Courses of Action Matrix, it is easy to look at the capabilities the suite can provide and include all of them in the inventory of the organization's current capabilities. However, the question is, how many of the suite's capabilities have actually been deployed? A related question is, who is responsible for operating and maintaining these controls? These can be difficult questions to answer in large, complicated IT environments. However, without uncovering the truth about the maturity of the current implementation, the confidence of the mapping and the potential efficacy of the strategy can be undermined. Remember the submarine analogy I've used throughout this book; would you really be keen to set sail in a submarine if you didn't really know if all the critical systems were fully operational? Probably not.

Many organizations aspire to have a world-class cybersecurity team. To support this aspiration, a principle some of them use when evaluating and procuring cybersecurity capabilities is that they only want best-of-breed technologies. That is, they only want the best products and won't settle for less than that. For most organizations, this is highly ambitious because attracting and retaining cybersecurity talent is a challenge for the entire industry.

Adopting a "best-of-breed" procurement philosophy makes this acute talent challenge even harder. This is because it potentially narrows the number of people that have experience with these expensive and relatively rare "best-of-breed-only" implementations. This approach can also be dangerous for organizations that are cash rich and believe they can simply buy effective cybersecurity instead of developing a culture where everyone participates. Most of the organizations that I've seen with this philosophy end up buying a Ferrari and using its ashtray. They simply do not have the wherewithal to architect, deploy, operate, and maintain only the best of breed, so they only use a fraction of the available capabilities. In some cases, organizations that find themselves in this scenario over-invest in an area by procuring the same or similar capabilities, but they do this by procuring products they can successfully deploy and operate. Performing this mapping exercise in organizations that have found themselves in this scenario can be especially hard. This is because it uncovers hard truths about overly optimistic ambitions and assumptions, as well as cybersecurity investments with marginal returns. However, this process can be a necessary evil for organizations with the courage to look in the mirror and the willingness to make positive, incremental changes to their current security posture. There's nothing wrong with being ambitious and aiming high if those ambitions are realistically attainable by the organization.

It can be challenging to quantify how much of a cybersecurity suite or set of capabilities has been successfully deployed. One approach I've tried, with mixed results, is to break out the functionality of the set of capabilities into its constituent categories and use a maturity index to quantify how mature the deployment is using a scale between 1 and 5, where 5 is most mature. This can help determine whether more investment is required in a particular area. In large, complex environments, this is easier said than done, and some might wonder if it's worth the time and effort as they struggle through it. However, the more detail security teams have about the current state of their affairs, the more confidence they'll have moving forward with this strategy.

Pervasiveness of current cybersecurity capabilities

Another data point to consider collecting as you map current cybersecurity capabilities to the Courses of Action Matrix is the pervasiveness of the implementation of each control or capability. For example, a server operations team procures a tool that helps them detect and block exploitation of vulnerabilities on the servers it's installed on. How many servers is this tool actually installed and running on? Is it installed on all servers running Windows and different flavors of Linux? In some IT environments it is not safe to assume the tool is running on all servers. Determining the percentage of servers the tool is actually running on will help you get a more accurate picture of existing cybersecurity capabilities.

In some environments, different teams manage IT and make decisions independently. In scenarios like this one, the pervasiveness of cybersecurity capabilities might be limited to specific networks or specific parts of the organization. For example, while the company might have a total inventory of 100 security tools, only 20% of them are deployed in any one IT environment. This is important to understand for accurate cybersecurity capability inventories. Including a pervasiveness percentage estimate in your spreadsheet for each capability can be very helpful for some organizations.

Who consumes the data?

One principle I have found helpful in mapping the current security capabilities of an IT environment to the Courses of Action Matrix is that the data generated by every control set needs someone or something to consume it. For example, a security team performing this mapping discovers that the network management team implemented potentially powerful IDS/IPS capabilities that were included with a network appliance they procured last fiscal year. Although these capabilities are enabled, they discover that no one in the network management team is actively monitoring or reviewing alerts from this system and that the organization's **Security Operations Center (SOC)** wasn't even aware that they existed. The net result of these capabilities is equivalent to not having them at all, since no one is consuming the data they generate. A human doesn't necessarily have to consume this data; orchestration and automation systems can also take actions based on such data. However, if neither a human nor a system is consuming this data, then security teams can't really include these capabilities in their mappings of currently implemented controls, unless those deficiencies are addressed.

As security teams perform this mapping, for each control they identify, they should also record who or what consumes the data it generates. Recording the name of the person that is the point of contact for the consumption of this data will pay dividends to security teams. A point of contact might be a manager in the SOC or in the **Network Operations Center (NOC)**, an Incident Response team member, a Managed Service Provider, or a vendor. This information is valuable in building confidence in the organization's true cybersecurity capabilities. However, it is also very valuable in measuring the efficacy of your strategy, which I will discuss in detail in *Chapter 11, Measuring Performance and Effectiveness*.

Kill Chain Phase	Detect	Detect Maturity Index (1-5)	Detect Data Consumer	Detect Consumer PoC	Deny	Deny Maturity Index (1-5)	Deny Data Consumer	Deny Consumer PoC
Reconnaissance I								
Delivery								
Exploitation								
Installation								
Command and Control (C2)								
Reconnaissance II								
Actions on Objectives								

Figure 10.3: An example of a partial Courses of Action Matrix (Hutchins, Cloppert, Amin, n.d.), which includes a maturity index, who or what is going to consume data from each control, and a point of contact (PoC)

As shown in *Figure 10.3*, as the Courses of Action Matrix is updated, it expands quickly. I have used a spreadsheet to do this mapping in the past. I'll admit that this isn't the most elegant way to perform such mappings. One mapping I did was over 120 pages of controls in a spreadsheet; navigating that spreadsheet wasn't much fun. Additionally, using a spreadsheet is not the most scalable tool and reporting capabilities are limited. If you have a better tool, use it! If you don't have a better tool, rest assured that the mapping exercise can be done using a spreadsheet or a document. However, the bigger and more complex the environment is, the more challenging using these tools becomes.

Cybersecurity license renewals

Most software and hardware that is procured from vendors have licensing terms that include a date when the licenses expire. When a license expires, it must be renewed, or the product must be decommissioned. Another update to the Courses of Action Matrix to consider, which can be very helpful, is to add a column to track the contract renewal date for each capability listed. If you are taking the time to inventory the software and hardware used for cybersecurity, also record the expiry/renewal date for each item. This will give you an idea of the time each item on the list has before its license expires and renewal is required. Embedding this information into the control mapping itself will give you visibility of the potential remaining lifetime for each capability and can help remind the security team when to start reevaluating each product's effectiveness and whether to renew or replace existing capabilities.

Another similar date that can be helpful to track is the end of life/support dates for products; typically, after this date, manufacturers deprecate products and no longer offer security updates for them. Over time, these products increase the attack surface in IT environments as vulnerabilities in them continue to be disclosed publicly, even after their end of support dates. Tracking these dates can help us avoid surprises. Tracking these dates as part of a modified Courses of Action Matrix is optional.

CISOs and security teams shouldn't rely on their Procurement departments to flag renewal dates for them; it should work the other way around. Many of the CISOs I've talked to want to have visibility of this "horizon list," how it impacts their budgets, and key milestone dates when decisions need to be made. What CISO wouldn't want some advanced notice that their network IDS/IPS was going to be turned off because their license was about to lapse? The more lead time these decisions have, the fewer last-minute surprises security teams will have. Additionally, when I discuss measuring the efficacy of this strategy in the next chapter, you'll see that having this information at your fingertips can be helpful.

Of course, this update to the matrix is optional. Renewal dates can be tracked in a separate document or database. However, being able to cross - reference the renewal dates and the cybersecurity capabilities in your mapping should be something CISOs can do easily. They need to have sufficient lead time to determine whether they want to keep the products and services they already have in production or replace them.

Kill Chain Phase	Detect	Detect Maturity Index (1-5)	Detect Data Consumer	Detect Consumer PoC	Detect Renewal Date	Deny	Deny Maturity Index (1-5)	Deny Data Consumer	Deny Consumer PoC	Deny Renewal Date
Reconnaissance I										
Delivery										
Exploitation										
Installation										
Command and Control (C2)										
Reconnaissance II										
Actions on Objectives										

Figure 10.4: An example of a partial Courses of Action Matrix (Hutchins, Cloppert, Amin, n.d.), which includes a maturity index, who or what is going to consume data, a point of contact (PoC), and the renewal date for each control

Implementing this strategy

By the end of the mapping process, CISOs and security teams should have a much better inventory of the cybersecurity capabilities and controls that have been deployed, as well as how the data from these are being consumed by the organization. This is a great starting point for implementing the Intrusion Kill Chain framework. However, do not underestimate how challenging it can be for organizations with large, complex IT environments to accomplish this.

For some organizations, it will be easier to divide mapping work into smaller, more achievable projects focused on parts of their environment, than trying to map their entire environment. Moving forward with this strategy without an accurate, current mapping can easily lead to overinvestments, under-investments, and gaps in security capabilities. Although these can be corrected over time, it will likely make it more expensive and time-consuming than it needs to be.

Kill Chain Phase	Detect	Detect Description	Detect Maturity Index (1-5)	Detect Data Consumer	Detect Consumer PoC	Detect Renewal Date	Deny	Deny Description	Deny Maturity Index (1-5)	Deny Data Consumer	Deny Consumer PoC	Deny Renewal Date
Reconnaissance I												
Delivery	control_name	Network IDS/IPS	3	SOC	Leonard Nimoy	09/15/24	control_name	email spam filter	2	eMail Administrator	Will Smith	01/01/24
Delivery	control_name	System image agent	1	IR Team	Bruce Dern	06/03/22	control_name	USB disable policy	2	Server Support	Bruno Mars	n/a
Exploitation	control_name	Windows Error Reporting	1	No one	No one	n/a	control_name	Anti-virus suite	4	SOC	Leonard Nimoy	04/15/21
Exploitation	control_name	System Integrity Monitor	2	SOC	Leonard Nimoy	09/09/22	control_name	File Integrity Monitoring	2	SOC	Leonard Nimoy	06/15/22
Exploitation	control_name	Anti-virus suite	4	Desktop Support	Kathy Bates	04/15/21	control_name	ASLR	5	Desktop Support	Kathy Bates	n/a
Installation	control_name	File Integrity Monitoring	2	Desktop Support	Kathy Bates	06/15/22	control_name	Anti-virus suite	4	Desktop Support	Kathy Bates	04/13/21
Installation	control_name	File Integrity Monitoring	2	Server Support	Bruno Mars	06/15/22	control_name	Anti-virus suite	4	Server Support	Bruno Mars	04/15/21
Installation	control_name	Anti-virus suite	4	SOC	Leonard Nimoy	04/15/21						
Installation	control_name	Anti-virus suite	4	IR Team	Bruce Dern	04/15/21						
Command and Control (C2)	control_name	Network IDS/IPS	3	NOC	Keanu Reeves	09/15/24	control_name	Network IDS/IPS	3	NOC	Keanu Reeves	09/15/24
Command and Control (C2)	control_name	Network IDS/IPS	3	SOC	Leonard Nimoy	09/15/24						
Reconnaissance II	control_name	Network IDS/IPS	3	NOC	Keanu Reeves	09/15/24	control_name	Network IDS/IPS	3	NOC	Keanu Reeves	09/15/24
Reconnaissance II	control_name	Network IDS/IPS	3	SOC	Leonard Nimoy	09/15/24						
Actions on Objectives	control_name	File Integrity Monitoring	2	Server Support	Bruno Mars	06/15/22	control_name	File Integrity Monitoring	2	Server Support	Bruno Mars	06/15/22
Actions on Objectives	control_name	File Integrity Monitoring	2	Desktop Support	Kathy Bates	06/15/22	control_name	File Integrity Monitoring	2	Desktop Support	Kathy Bates	06/15/22
Actions on Objectives	control_name	Deception technology	2	SOC	Leonard Nimoy	05/31/25						

Figure 10.5: An example of a part of an updated Courses of Action Matrix (Hutchins, Cloppert, Amin, n.d.) that contains a mapping of an organization's current cybersecurity capabilities

I've provided an example of what the first two actions across an updated set of phases looks like in *Figure 10.5*. An actual mapping for a large organization could potentially be much larger, but I want to give you an idea of what a mapping looks like. In an actual mapping, `control_name` will be the names of the specific products, services, features, or functionality that detect, deny, disrupt, and so on for each phase of an attack. The **Description** field is meant to be a short description of what each control does. I suggest providing more detail in this field than I have here so that it's clear what each control's function and scope is.

There is a Maturity Index for each control, ranging from 1 to 5, with 5 indicating that the implementation is as full and functional as possible. A maturity index of 1 or 2 indicates that while the product or feature has a lot of functionality, relatively little of it has been deployed or is being operated. This index will help inform our assumptions about how effective each control currently is versus its potential. This helps avoid the trap of assuming a control is operating at peak efficiency when in reality it isn't fully deployed, or it's not being actively operated or monitored. Color - coding this field or entire line items based on this field can make it even easier to understand the maturity of each control.

I have not included a "Pervasiveness" column in *Figure 10.5*, but had I, it would contain a percentage representing the estimated amount of the environment each control is installed and running on. Alternatively, I could have included two columns for Pervasiveness, one representing the low end of the estimated percentage range, and a second one for the high end of the range.

For example, 30% in the low column and 50% in the high column indicates that the control is installed and running on between 30% and 50% of the environment in scope. Having two columns will allow you to filter the data in potentially more interesting ways later when you are analyzing the data and rationalizing the Courses of Action Matrix.

The Data Consumer for each action is the specific group or department in the organization that is using data from the control to detect, deny, disrupt, degrade, and so on. The **Consumer PoC** column contains the names of each point of contact in the group or department that is consuming the data from each control. This can make it easier to periodically verify that the data from each control is still being consumed as planned. After all, there's no point deploying mitigations if no one is actually paying any attention to them. The time, effort, and budget spent on such controls can likely be used more effectively somewhere else in the organization.

Finally, the **Renewal Date** column for each action provides visibility into the potential expiry date of each control. It does this to help minimize potential unexpected lapses in the operational status of each control. This helps avoid the revelation that a mitigation you thought was fully operational has actually been partially or entirely disabled because of a lapse in licensing or a product going out of support; these surprises can burn CISOs and security teams.

Rationalizing the matrix — gaps, under-investments, and over-investments

Without a mapping of current cybersecurity capabilities to the Courses of Action Matrix, it can be very easy to over-invest or under-invest in cybersecurity products and have gaps in protection, detection, and response capabilities. What exactly do I mean by over-investments, under-investments, and gaps? Performing a mapping of existing cybersecurity capabilities and controls to an Intrusion Kill Chain framework can be a lot of work. However, for some CISOs, it can result in an epiphany.

Identifying gaps

Performed correctly, this mapping can reveal key areas where organizations haven't invested at all—a gap. For example, in *Figure 10.5*, the Reconnaissance I row doesn't have any entries in it; this can be a clear indication that the organization has a gap in their control set, which could make this phase of the attacker's Intrusion Kill Chain easier for them. It isn't uncommon for organizations to fail to invest in this area. A gap like this is a clear opportunity for improvement.

Identifying areas of under-investment

Under-investments in an area can be more subtle in the Courses of Action Matrix. An under-investment can appear as a relatively small number of entries for an activity or phase in the matrix. This where the maturity index, pervasiveness percentage, and descriptions can help.

A single entry in the matrix with a maturity index of 5 might be all the investment that is needed for that action. But an entry with a maturity index of 5 and a pervasiveness percentage of 10% might be a different story. The combination of the maturity index, pervasiveness percentage, and the description should help make this determination. However, the entry's description should be verbose enough for the security team to understand if the functionality and scope of the capability will really break attackers' Kill Chains or if more investment is warranted in that area of the matrix. The right control might be deployed, but if it's only partially implemented or partially operational, it might not be sufficient to break a Kill Chain or be effective in all scenarios. Further investment into maturing that control or expanding where it operates might be solutions to this problem. Another possible solution is investing in a different control to supplement the current mitigation. From this perspective, the Courses of Action Matrix becomes an important document to help during an incident and is central to negotiations over budgets and resources with non-technical executives.

Identifying areas of over-investment

Over-investing in areas is a common problem that I've seen both public and private sector organizations suffer from. It can occur slowly over time or quickly in the wake of a data breach. In the Courses of Action Matrix, an over-investment can appear as a lot of entries in one or two areas that perform the same or similar functions. For example, I've seen organizations procure multiple **Identity and Access Management (IAM)** products and fully deploy none of them. This can happen for a range of reasons. For example, they may have been unrealistic about their ability to attract and retain the talent required to deploy these products.

Another example is that in the wake of a successful intrusion, it's not uncommon for a victimized organization to decide that it's time to make a big investment in cybersecurity. With a newfound sense of urgency and exuberance, they don't take the time to get an inventory of current capabilities and their maturity before they go on a shopping spree.

Mergers and acquisitions can also leave organizations with over-investments in some areas of the matrix. Suddenly, after a merger, the organization has twice as many cybersecurity tools as it had before the merger. Performing cybersecurity capability inventories can be especially challenging after a recent merger or acquisition.

Finally, simply put, some salespeople are really good at their jobs. I've seen entire industries and geographical areas where everyone has literally procured the same SIEM or endpoint solution during the same 1 or 2 fiscal years. There's nothing wrong with this, but it's unlikely they all started with the same environments, comparable cybersecurity talent, and the same licensing renewal dates for their current products. When a good salesperson is exceedingly successful, this can sometimes lead to over-investments in areas.

For organizations that haven't performed a cybersecurity capabilities inventory using a Courses of Action Matrix before, one area that seems to almost always be over-invested in is the intersection of Deny and Exploitation in the Courses of Action Matrix. There's good reason for this – stopping attackers before they get past this point in their Kill Chain can limit their scope of control and minimize damage and recovery costs. This is the stage in attacks that many security professionals refer to as "left of boom." In other words, stop them before they successfully complete the Exploitation phase of their attack and move to the Installation phase. Subsequently, it is not uncommon to see big over-investments in this one area in enterprise IT environments.

In recent years, the intersection of Detect and Exploitation in the Courses of Action Matrix has also become crowded as the industry really pivoted around deploying detection capabilities instead of just relying on protective capabilities. Don't panic if the first time you complete a Courses of Action Matrix for an organization, the entire matrix is relatively empty except for Detect and Deny for Exploitation. It can be rewarding to see an over-confident CISO's expression change when they see their organization's Courses of Action Matrix for the first time and realize they have been over-investing in the same two areas for years. This is fairly typical the first time this Attack-Centric Strategy is embraced. It also means there's lots of opportunity for improvement.

Planning your implementation

It's important to identify gaps, under-invested areas, and areas of over-investment as these will inform the implementation plan. Hopefully, many of the areas that the organization has already invested in won't require changes. This will allow the security and IT teams to focus on addressing gaps and shortcomings in their current security posture. At the point where these teams have a current mapping and have identified gaps, areas of under-investment, and areas of over-investment, they can start planning the rest of their implementation.

What part of the Courses of Action Matrix should security teams work on first? For some organizations, focusing on addressing existing gaps will offer the highest potential ROI. However, there are some factors to consider, including the availability of budgets and cybersecurity talent. The overarching goal is to break attackers' Kill Chains.

However, remember that there are some efficiencies to doing this as early in the Kill Chain as possible. Stopping an attack before Exploitation and Installation can help minimize costs and damage. However, as I discussed in regard to the Protect and Recover Strategy, the assumption that security teams will be able to do this 100% of the time is overly optimistic and will likely set the organization up for failure. Subsequently, some of the CISOs I've discussed this with decided to invest a little bit in every part of the matrix. However, sufficient budget and resource availability can be limiting factors for this approach.

Most CISOs I've talked to have limited budgets. For those that don't, they are typically still limited by their ability to architect, deploy, and operate new capabilities quickly; the cybersecurity talent shortage is industry wide. The renewal date for each item in the matrix can help inform a time-line used to address gaps and investment issues. Choosing not to renew licenses for less effective products in areas of over-investment might help free up some of the budget that can be used to address gaps and areas of underinvestment. Not every organization has over-investments, and many are chronically under-invested across the matrix. For organizations in this category, taking advantage of as many of the "free" controls in operating systems and integrated development environments as possible can be helpful.

For example, **Address Space Layout Randomization (ASLR)** and **Data Execution Prevention (DEP)** can help make the Exploitation phase of an attack harder to accomplish and inconsistent. ASLR is a memory safety feature that can make exploiting vulnerabilities harder for attackers by randomizing address space locations. This makes it harder for attackers to consistently predict the memory locations of vulnerabilities they wish to exploit. ASLR should typically be used in combination with DEP (Matt Miller, 2010). DEP is another memory safety feature that stops attackers from using memory pages meant for data to execute their code (Matt Miller, 2010).

These features are built into most modern operating systems from major vendors today, although not all applications take advantage of them. Still, thoughtfully using such free or low-cost controls can help organizations with limited budgets pursue this strategy.

Another way I've seen CISOs plan their implementation is to use results from Red Team and Blue Team exercises and penetration tests. Penetration tests typically focus on confirming the effectiveness of security controls that have been implemented, where the Red Team exercises focus on outrunning and outsmarting defenders. This is a direct way of testing the effectiveness of the people, processes, and technologies that are part of your current implementation. Just as important as identifying gaps, these exercises can identify controls and mitigations that are not performing as expected.

These exercises can also help inform the maturity indexes in your mapping and help prioritize items in your implementation plan in a practical, less theoretical way. The ATT&CK framework can also be very helpful in planning attack simulations that reveal areas for improvement and subsequent investment.

Finally, one other way I've seen CISOs decide to implement frameworks like this one is to invest in high ROI areas first. They do this by identifying where they get the biggest bang for their investment. This is done by identifying controls that provide mitigations in multiple parts of the matrix. For example, if the same control potentially helps break the attacker's Kill Chains in the Delivery, Exploitation, and Command and Control phases, they'll prioritize that one over controls that only potentially break one phase of an attack (Hutchins, Cloppert, Amin, n.d.). Put another way, they look for areas where they can use two or three mitigations for the price of one. The more detailed their matrix is, the more of these opportunities they can identify.

I will revisit many of the factors that I discussed in this section in *Chapter 11, Measuring Performance and Effectiveness*.

Designing control sets

With a current control set mapping, identified gaps, areas of under-investment, areas of over-investment, and a plan for which of these areas will be addressed, security teams can start designing control sets. This part of the process can be challenging, but a lot of fun as well.

After all, designing controls to make it as hard as possible for attackers to succeed is fun! For some people, spending money is fun too, and there is an opportunity to lay the groundwork to do that in this exercise.

There are more combinations and permutations of possible control sets than I can cover in this book. This section is meant to provide you with more detail on each part of the updated Courses of Action Matrix that I outlined and provoke some thought about ways that security teams could design control sets for their organization. This isn't a blueprint that should be followed; it's really just a high-level example. I didn't receive any promotional payments for any products or companies I mentioned in this section, and I don't endorse them or make any claims or warranties about them or their products. Please use whatever companies, products, services, and features meet your requirements. If you'd like professional recommendations, I recommend consuming the reports and services of industry analyst firms such as Forrester and Gartner, among others. This is where CISO councils, professional societies, and gated social networks can be very helpful. Getting first-hand accounts of the efficacy of strategies, products, and services directly from other CISOs can be very helpful.

Analyst firms can't be too publicly critical of a company or its products, but I haven't met many CISOs that weren't willing to be candid in private conversations behind closed doors.

Additionally, this is another place where the ATT&CK framework can help. The mitigations listed for each technique and sub-technique under the equivalent tactic or tactics in the ATT&CK framework can provide many ideas for effective controls. Using ATT&CK for this purpose can save security teams a lot of time designing control sets. ATT&CK can also inform testing for these control sets and attack simulations to ensure they all work as expected.

Reminder: the stages and actions in the modified Courses of Action Matrix that I'll cover in this section are illustrated in *Figure 10.6*. In other words, I'll be giving you ideas about the cybersecurity capabilities that can be used to populate the cells in *Figure 10.6*.

Kill Chain Phase	Detect	Deny	Disrupt	Degrade	Deceive	Limit	Restore
Reconnaissance I							
Delivery							
Exploitation							
Installation							
Command and Control (C2)							
Reconnaissance II							
Actions on Objectives							

Figure 10.6: Modified Courses of Action Matrix

Attack phase – Reconnaissance I

In this phase of an attack, attackers are selecting their targets, performing research, mapping and probing their target's online presence, and doing the same for the organizations in their intended victim's supply chain. Attackers are seeking answers to the basic questions of what, why, when, and how. Their research isn't limited to IP addresses and open TCP/UDP ports; people, processes, and technologies are all potential pawns in their attacks.

The challenge for defenders in this stage of the attack is that these types of reconnaissance activities blend in with legitimate network traffic, emails, telephone calls, employees, and so on. It can be very difficult to identify the attacker's reconnaissance activities when they aren't anomalous. Still, it can be worthwhile to invest in cybersecurity capabilities in this stage because, as I mentioned earlier, breaking the attacker's Kill Chains as early as possible typically has the highest ROI.

Categorizing reconnaissance activities into passive and active groups (Sanghvi, Dahiya, 2013) can help security teams decide where investments are practical. For example, it might be prohibitively expensive to try to identify attackers performing passive research by reading an organization's job postings website just to identify the types of hardware and software it uses.

However, it might be practical to detect and block IP addresses of systems that are actively scanning for vulnerabilities on corporate firewalls. Many passive reconnaissance activities can be conducted out of the sight of defenders and subsequently won't generate log entries or alerts that defenders can use. However, many threat intelligence vendors offer services to their customers that scrape social media sites and illicit marketplaces, all to look for chatter on the dark web about their IP address ranges, domains, known vulnerabilities, credentials for sale, and imminent attacks. Active reconnaissance activities tend to interact directly with the victims and their supply chains, potentially providing defenders with a more direct glimpse of them.

Figure 10.7: Reconnaissance activity categories

Some cybersecurity capabilities that can help in this phase of an attack include:

- **Threat intelligence services** can help detect passive reconnaissance activities, potentially giving defenders notice of known vulnerabilities in their defensive posture and imminent attacks. Ideally, this can give them some time to address these known vulnerabilities and better prepare themselves for an attack. Some examples of threat intelligence vendors that currently offer such services include:

  - Digital Shadows
  - FireEye
  - Kroll
  - MarkMonitor
  - Proofpoint
  - Many, many others, including smaller, boutique firms

- **Web Application Firewalls (WAF)** can detect application layer attacks like SQL injection, cross-site scripting, and so on. A WAF can help detect, deny, disrupt, and degrade application layer attacks. Some examples of WAFs include:

  - Amazon Web Services
  - Barracuda
  - Cloudflare

- F5
- Imperva
- Microsoft
- Oracle
- Many, many others

- **Firewalls** – there are at least a few different flavors of firewalls. Firewalls can detect, deny, disrupt, and degrade some active network reconnaissance activities. There are too many examples of vendors that offer firewall products to list, but some examples include:

  - Barracuda
  - Cisco
  - Check Point Software Technologies
  - Juniper Networks Palo Alto Networks
  - SonicWall
  - Many, many others

- **Deception technologies** can be employed to deceive attackers performing active reconnaissance. Deception technology systems present systems as the legitimate infrastructure of the intended target or vendors in their supply chain. Attackers spend time and resources performing reconnaissance on these systems instead of production infrastructure and systems. Examples of deception technology vendors include:

  - Attivo Networks
  - Illusive Networks
  - PacketViper
  - TrapX Security
  - Many, many others

- **Automation** can be combined with threat intelligence and detection capabilities to enable dynamic responses to reconnaissance activities. For example, if a WAF or firewall detects probes from known malicious IP addresses, automation could be triggered to dynamically adjust the lists of blocked IP addresses for some period of time, or automation could try to degrade reconnaissance and waste the attacker's time by allowing ICMP network traffic from malicious IP addresses and blocking TCP traffic to ports 80, 443, and other open ports.

This would allow attackers to see systems were online, but not connect to services running on them. This type of automation might be harder to accomplish in legacy on-premises environments, but it's baked into the cloud by default and relatively easy to configure. I'll discuss cloud capabilities in more detail in *Chapter 12, Modern Approaches to Security and Compliance*.

This is what the Courses of Action Matrix for the Reconnaissance I phase looks like based on the capabilities I discussed in this section. Of course, this is just scratching the surface of what's possible in this phase, but it provides you with some ideas of what some actions might look like for this first stage in an attack.

You'll notice that I didn't include any entries for the Restore action. Since reconnaissance typically doesn't result in damage or compromise, there's nothing in this stage of an attack to recover.

As I mentioned, creating a Courses of Action Matrix using Excel isn't ideal, but it works. However, the tables this exercise creates are too large to print here, in a book, and still be readable. Subsequently, I'm going to provide lists of example controls for each section of an example matrix. I don't include controls for phases, like Restore for example, unless there are items in it. To simplify things further, I don't include any of the modifications I discussed earlier because they are unique to each organization. This list isn't meant to be exhaustive; it provides examples of basic controls that you can use as a starting point to develop your own Courses of Action Matrix. As you'll see, some of the items are repeated multiple times in the Courses of Action Matrix because those controls can perform multiple roles in the matrix.

Example controls for Reconnaissance I

The following are examples of controls that can be used in the Reconnaissance I phase:

- **Deception Technology**: Can help detect the attacker's reconnaissance activities and trick attackers into spending time performing recon on fake assets instead of real ones.
- **Web Application Firewall (WAF)**: Can detect application layer attacks like SQL injection, cross-site scripting, and so on.
- **Firewalls**: Can detect network probes and some reconnaissance activity.
- **Threat intelligence reconnaissance services**: Can help detect passive reconnaissance activities, giving defenders notice of known vulnerabilities in their defensive posture and imminent attacks.

- **Automation**: Use automation when reconnaissance activities are detected, to adjust firewall rules and other controls in ways that can deny, disrupt, degrade, or limit the activities.

	Detect	Deny	Disrupt	Degrade	Deceive	Limit	Restore
Deception Technology	X				X		
WAF	X		X	X			
Firewalls	X		X	X			
Threat intelligence reconnaissance services	X						
Automation		X	X	X		X	

Figure 10.8: A summary of control ideas for the Reconnaissance I phase

Insights from ATT&CK

ATT&CK can be very helpful in identifying specific types of reconnaissance techniques attackers have been using and potential mitigations and detection methods for them. Under the Reconnaissance tactic in the current version of ATT&CK (v12.0) there are 10 techniques (MITRE, 2020):

- Active scanning
- Gather victim host information
- Gather victim identity information
- Gather victim network information
- Gather victim organization information
- Phishing for information
- Search closed sources
- Search open technical databases
- Search open websites/domains
- Search victim-owned websites

The first 9 of the listed techniques have multiple sub-techniques associated with them. For example, active scanning is a technique that has 3 sub-techniques associated with it. These include scanning IP blocks, vulnerability scanning, and wordlist scanning (MITRE, 2020). The only mitigation listed for many of the techniques and sub-techniques is, "this technique cannot be easily mitigated with preventive controls since it is based on behaviors performed outside of the scope of enterprise defenses and controls. Efforts should focus on minimizing the amount and sensitivity of data available to external parties" (MITRE, 2020).

Full details on this ATT&CK tactic are available at: https://attack.mitre.org/tactics/TA0043/

Attack phase – Delivery

At this point in an attack, the attackers have already decided which organization to target, done some research to help them execute their attack, and potentially done some active reconnaissance scanning and probed the intended victim's internet presence. Based on this information, they've also gone through some Weaponization stage or process where they procured and/or built weapons that will help them initially compromise their targets and enable their illicit activities afterwards. This Weaponization process typically happens out of the sight of defenders. However, as I mentioned in the Reconnaissance I phase, some threat intelligence vendors' services can sometimes get an insight into these activities.

The attacker's weapons can include people, processes, and technologies. With all this in hand, attackers must deliver these weapons to their targets; this is the objective of the Delivery phase. Attackers have a range of options to deliver their weapons to their targets and the vendors in their supply chains. Some examples of delivery mechanisms include malicious email attachments, malicious URLs in emails, malicious websites that attract the victims' attention, malicious insiders, self-propagating malware such as worms, leaving malicious USB drives in victims' premises, and many others.

Some investments that can help in this phase of an attack include:

- **Education/training**: Recall the threat intelligence research I provided in *Chapter 4*, *The Evolution of Malware*. It's clear that different types of malware go in and out of vogue with attackers, but their mainstay approach has always been social engineering. Therefore, educating information workers and training them to spot common social engineering attacks can be very helpful in detecting the delivery of the attacker's weapons. The challenge is that social engineering training isn't a one-time activity, it's an ongoing investment. When training stops, current employees start to forget these lessons and new employees don't get trained. Note that the training itself needs to be kept up to date in order to continue being effective. The combination of training and simulations, such as phishing simulations, can be an effective way to help information workers spot and report social engineering when they see it.

  Some organizations simply don't have a culture that supports social engineering training that includes simulated phishing campaigns and other social engineering attacks against employees. However, organizations that don't do this type of training miss the opportunity to let their employees learn from experience and from failure.

A culture where everyone tries to help the CISO is much more powerful than those where the security team is always reacting to uninformed, poor trust decisions that untrained information workers will make every day. Sometimes, senior executives or their direct reports simply don't want to be embarrassed if they make a poor choice in a phishing simulation. These executives need to check their egos and their pride at the door when they come to work, in order to give their organizations the best chance at spotting and stopping attackers' favorite tactics. Besides, they are the very targets for **Business Email Compromise (BEC)**, which has become a popular and profitable endeavor among attackers. They are the last people that should get exceptions or avoid such training.

- **Microsoft Defender for Office 365**: Email is a major vector for social engineering attacks. The volume of email-based attacks is relatively huge in any period of time. Offering information workers email inboxes without effective protection is setting the organization up for failure. Cloud-based services like Microsoft Defender for Office 365 help inoculate all their users by blocking threats that any of their users get exposed to. Services this large can easily identify the IP addresses that botnets and attackers use for spam, phishing, and other email-based attacks, and block them for all their users.

  There are numerous third-party solutions that can be used as alternatives to Microsoft Defender for Office 365 or complement it, including:

  - Abnormal Security
  - Barracuda
  - Check Point Software Technologies
  - Mimecast
  - Proofpoint
  - Many others

- **Deception technology**: I'm a big fan of deception technology. This technology goes beyond honeypots and honey-nets, offering full-blown environments that attract attackers, signal their presence, and waste their time, driving down their return on investment. Using deception technology to present vulnerable systems to attackers, systems that are critical infrastructure, or systems that store or have access to potentially valuable data can divert their efforts from legitimate systems. Deception technology can also be effective at detecting malicious insiders that are attracted by the bait they offer.

- **Anti-malware and endpoint security suites**: Anti-malware software and other types of endpoint security software can detect and block the attempted delivery of different types of cyber weapons. As I discussed in *Chapter 4, The Evolution of Malware*, anti-malware software isn't optional in a world where the number of malicious files outnumbers legitimate files. Some of the anti-malware and endpoint security vendors that offer products include:

    - Blackberry Cylance
    - CrowdStrike
    - Carbon Black
    - F-Secure
    - Kaspersky
    - McAfee
    - Microsoft
    - Trellix
    - Trend Micro
    - Many others

- **Web browser protection technologies**: Blocking access to known bad websites and insecure content, as well as scanning content before the browser downloads it, can help prevent exposure to drive-by download attacks, phishing attacks, malware hosting sites, and other malicious web-based attacks.

- **File Integrity Monitoring (FIM)**: FIM can help detect, block, disrupt, and degrade the delivery phase by maintaining the integrity of operating system and application files.

- **IDS/IPS**: Several vendors offer IDS/IPS systems including Cisco, Juniper Networks, and many others.

- **Short-lived environments**: Systems that only live for a few hours can disrupt and degrade the attacker's ability to deliver their weapons, especially more complicated multi-stage delivery scenarios. The cloud can make leveraging short-lived environments relatively easy; I'll discuss this concept more in *Chapter 12, Modern Approaches to Security and Compliance*.

- **Restore**: I've met with many organizations over the years that rely on blocking mechanisms like anti-malware software to detect and block delivery, but will rebuild systems if there is any chance they were compromised. If delivery is successful, even if exploitation and installation is blocked, some organizations want to flatten and rebuild systems or restore data from backups to ensure that everything is in a known good state.

Next, we'll look at what the Courses of Action Matrix for the Delivery phase looks like based on the capabilities I discussed in this section.

Example controls for Delivery

The following are examples of controls that can be used in the Delivery phase:

- **Education/training**: Information worker education and training to spot social engineering attacks.

- **Microsoft Defender for Office 365**: Detects and blocks delivery of malicious email and files.

- **Deception Technology**: Can attract attackers and detect weapon delivery to deception assets.

- **Anti-malware suites**: Can detect and block delivery of malicious content from storage media, the network, and via web browsers.

- **FIM**: Can detect and block attempts to replace system files.

- **IDS/IPS**: Can detect and potentially disrupt or stop delivery of malicious content delivered via the network.

- **USB drive prohibit policy**: Blocking USB and removable media from mounting on systems can prevent delivery of malware and other malicious content. This can also help block data exfiltration.

- **Web browser protection technologies**: Some browsers can block their users from visiting known malicious web sites, thus preventing them from being exposed to phishing, exploits, malware, and other internet-based attacks.

- **Short-lived environments**: Systems that are replaced every few hours can make the Delivery phase harder for attackers.

- **IAM technologies**: Enforcing the principle of least privilege and meaningful separation of duties can help limit weapon delivery in an IT environment.

- **Backups**: Restore from backups as needed when weapon delivery could not be stopped.

- **Images and containers**: Rebuild infrastructure as needed when weapon delivery could not be stopped.

Note that the same control ideas in the list can apply to Disrupt and Degrade in the Delivery attack phase.

	Detect	Deny	Disrupt	Degrade	Deceive	Limit	Restore
Education/training	▓						
Microsoft Defender for Office 365	▓	▓					
Deception Technology	▓				▓		
Anti-malware suites	▓	▓	▓	▓			
FIM	▓	▓	▓	▓			
IDS/IPS	▓	▓	▓	▓			
USB drive prohibit policy		▓					
Web browser protection technologies		▓					
Short-lived environments			▓	▓			
IAM technologies					▓	▓	
Backups							▓
Images and containers							▓

Figure 10.9: A summary of control ideas for the Delivery phase

The examples I have provided here are simple, but I hope they give security teams some ideas. Layering capabilities into the mix that break the Delivery phase, regardless of the delivery vector, is key.

Insights from ATT&CK

The Initial Access tactic in the ATT&CK framework provides 9 techniques with 10 sub-techniques that attackers have been using to "gain their initial foothold within a network" (MITRE, 2019):

- Drive-by compromise
- Exploit public-facing application
- External remote services
- Hardware additions
- Phishing:
  - Sub-technique: Spearphishing attachment
  - Sub-technique: Spearphishing link
  - Sub-technique: Spearphishing via service
- Replication through removable media
- Supply chain compromise:
  - Sub-technique: Compromise software dependencies and development tools
  - Sub-technique: Compromise software supply chain

- Sub-technique: Compromise hardware supply chain

- Trusted relationship

- Valid accounts:

    - Sub-technique: Default accounts

    - Sub-technique: Domain accounts

    - Sub-technique: Local accounts

    - Sub-technique: Cloud accounts

ATT&CK suggests numerous mitigation and detection capabilities to make these techniques harder or impossible for attackers to rely on. For example, for the exploit public-facing application technique, mitigations include application isolation, WAF, network segmentation, Privileged account management, updating software regularly, and vulnerability scanning (MITRE, 2019).

Full details on this ATT&CK tactic are available at: `https://attack.mitre.org/tactics/TA0001/`

Attack phase – Exploitation

After attackers have successfully delivered their weapons to their targets, the weapons must be activated. Sometimes, the Delivery and Exploitation phases occur in immediate succession, such as a drive-by download attack. In this scenario, a user is typically tricked into going to a malicious website via a URL in an email or online content. When they click the link and their web browser performs name resolution and loads the page, scripts on the malicious page will detect the operating system and browser and then try to deliver exploits for that software. If the software isn't patched for the vulnerabilities those exploits are designed for, then attackers will typically download more malware to the system, install tools, and continue with their Kill Chain. The Delivery and Exploitation phases happen at almost the same time in this type of attack. In other attacks, like email-based attacks, delivery can happen minutes, hours, days, weeks, or even months before the user opens the email and clicks on a malicious attachment or URL to a malicious website. In this scenario, the Delivery and Exploitation phases are distinct (Hutchins, Cloppert, Amin, n.d.). Some attackers seek instant gratification, while others prefer the "low and slow" method.

Defenders must be prepared for attacks across this spectrum. They cannot assume that the Delivery and Exploitation phases will always occur at nearly the same time, but they must be prepared for such scenarios. Breaking the Exploitation phase of the attacker's Kill Chain is critical, because if they successfully complete this phase of their attack, they could potentially have a foothold in the environment from which they can further penetrate it.

After this phase in an attack, managing defenses can become harder for defenders. Because many attacks are automated, post-Exploitation phase activities can happen very quickly. Breaking the attacker's Kill Chains "left of boom," as the saying goes, is a prudent goal for security teams.

The best way to prevent exploitation of unpatched vulnerabilities and security misconfigurations (two of the Cybersecurity Usual Suspects) is to scan everything every day. Scanning all IT assets every day helps identify where unpatched vulnerabilities and security misconfigurations exist in the environment, thus surfacing the residual risk so that it can be mitigated, transferred, or accepted consciously. This helps security and remediation teams understand whether they are exceeding remediation **Service Level Agreements (SLAs)** and accepting more risk than the organization planned to. When a system with an unpatched Log4j vulnerability magically appears in the environment, scanning everything every day means it is spotted within 24 hours of appearing and can be remediated appropriately. In addition to scanning everything every day, the following list provides you with some example controls that can be used to break attacker activities in the Exploitation phase of an attack. Hopefully, this will give you some ideas on how to make the Exploitation phase much more challenging for attackers:

- **Containerization and supporting security tools**: Using container technologies such as Docker and Kubernetes has many advantages, not least in helping to reduce the attack surface area of systems and applications. Of course, containers are software too and subsequently have vulnerabilities of their own. There are vendors that offer tools to help detect and prevent exploitation in environments that leverage containers. Some examples include:

    - Aqua Security
    - CloudPassage
    - Illumio
    - Tenable
    - Twistlock
    - Others

- **IAM controls**: Strictly following the principle of least privilege can make vulnerability exploitation harder. Sometimes, the attacker's code runs under the account context of the user that executed it, instead of under elevated privileges. Limiting user privileges can make it harder for exploitation to succeed or have the intended effect.
- **Short-lived environments**: Systems that only live for a few hours and are replaced with fully patched systems can make it much harder for exploitation to succeed.

Example controls for Exploitation

The following are examples of controls that can be used in the Exploitation phase:

- **Anti-malware suites**: Anti-malware can detect and block the exploitation of vulnerabilities.
- **Containerization and supporting security tools**: Containers can reduce the attack surface area and supporting security tools can help detect and prevent exploitation.
- **FIM**: Can detect some exploitation attempts.
- **Log reviews**: Reviewing various system logs can reveal indicators of exploitation.
- **ASLR**: Operating systems' ASLR can make exploitation inconsistent or impossible.
- **DEP**: Operating systems' DEP can make exploitation inconsistent or impossible.
- **IAM controls**: Strictly following the principle of least privilege can deny exploitation in some scenarios.
- **Microsoft Defender Application Guard**: This opens untrusted web sites and files in isolated Hyper-V-enabled containers that are separate from the host operating system, to prevent malicious websites and files from damaging the system or stealing credentials.
- **Short-lived environments**: Systems that are replaced every few hours can make exploitation harder.
- **Deception technology**: Can attract attackers and deceive them into attacking fake environments.
- **Honeypots**: Can attract attackers and can expose the exploits they use.
- **Backups**: Restore from backups as necessary when exploitation cannot be stopped.
- **Images and containers**: Rebuild infrastructure as necessary when exploitation cannot be stopped.

A summary illustration of the example controls for the Exploitation phase is provided in *Figure 10.10*.

	Detect	Deny	Disrupt	Degrade	Deceive	Limit	Restore
Anti-malware suites	▓		▓				
Containerization and supporting security tools	▓		▓				
FIM	▓						
Log reviews	▓						
ASLR		▓				▓	
DEP		▓	▓			▓	
IAM controls		▓	▓				
Microsoft Defender Application Guard		▓	▓				
Short-lived environments				▓			
Deception technology					▓		
Honeypots					▓		
Backups							▓
Images and containers							▓

Figure 10.10: A summary of control ideas for the Exploitation phase

Spending time carefully layering controls to break the Exploitation phase of an attacker's Kill Chain is time well spent. An entire chapter in this book could be devoted to exploitation; I have only scratched the surface here, but I encourage CISOs and security teams to spend more time researching and considering how to implement this particular phase of this framework in their environments.

Insights from ATT&CK

The Execution tactic in the ATT&CK framework "consists of techniques that result in adversary-controlled code running on a local or remote system" (MITRE, 2019). This tactic has 13 techniques with 21 sub-techniques associated with it (MITRE, 2019):

- Command and scripting interpreter:

  - Sub-technique: PowerShell

  - Sub-technique: AppleScript

  - Sub-technique: Windows Command Shell

  - Sub-technique: Unix Shell

  - Sub-technique: Visual Basic

  - Sub-technique: Python

  - Sub-technique: JavaScript

  - Sub-technique: Network Device CLI

- Container administration command
- Deploy container
- Exploitation for client execution
- Inter-process communication:

    - Sub-technique: Component Object Model
    - Sub-technique: Dynamic Data Exchange
    - Sub-technique: XPC Services

- Native API
- Scheduled task/job:

    - Sub-technique: At
    - Sub-technique: Cron
    - Sub-technique: Scheduled Task
    - Sub-technique: Systemd Timers
    - Sub-technique: Container Orchestration Job

- Serverless execution
- Shared modules
- Software deployment tools
- System services:

    - Sub-technique: Launchctl
    - Sub-technique: Service Execution

- User execution:

    - Sub-technique: Malicious link
    - Sub-technique: Malicious file
    - Sub-technique: Malicious image

- Windows Management Instrumentation

ATT&CK offers 82 mitigations for these techniques and sub-techniques. Some of these mitigations apply to a single technique and some are used to mitigate multiple techniques. The top five mitigations that appear most often and therefore potentially have the biggest return on investment include (MITRE, 2019):

- **Mitigation ID M1038**: Execution Prevention, "Use application control where appropriate." (15/82 = 18%)

- **Mitigation ID M1040**: Behavior Prevention on Endpoint, "On Windows 10, enable Attack Surface Reduction (ASR) rules to prevent..." (11/82 = 13%)

- **Mitigation ID M1026**: Privileged Account Management (9/82 = 11%)

- **Mitigation ID M1018**: Disable or Remove Feature or Program (6/82 = 7%)

- **Mitigation ID M1042**: User Account Management (6/82 = 7%)

Details associated with these Mitigation IDs, along with full details on the ATT&CK Execution tactic are available at: `https://attack.mitre.org/tactics/TA0002/`

Attack phase – Installation

Simply successfully exploiting a vulnerability isn't the goal for most modern-day attackers, as it was back in 2003. Notoriety has been replaced by much more serious and sinister motivations. Once attackers successfully deliver their weapons and exploitation is successful, they typically seek to expand their scope of control in their victims' environments.

To do this, they have a range of options available to them, such as unpacking malware or remote-control tools from within the weapon itself or downloading them from another system under their control.

More recently, "living off the land" has regained popularity with attackers that seek to use tools, scripts, libraries, and binaries that are native and pre-installed with operating systems and applications. This tactic allows them to further penetrate compromised environments, all while evading defenders that focus on detecting the presence of specific files associated with malware and exploitation. Be aware that "living off the land" tactics can be used in several phases of an attacker's Kill Chain, not just in the Installation phase. Also, note that although it has been modernized somewhat, this tactic is as old as I am and relies on the knowledge of past defenders being lost in time.

When I worked on Microsoft's Incident Response team in 2003, every attacker "lived off the land." We saw a lot of creative tactics being used by attackers in those days. One lesson I learned was that removing all the built-in support tools in the operating system, such as ping.exe, tracert.exe, and many others that attackers relied on, forced attackers to bring more of their own tools. Finding any of those tools on systems in the supported IT environment was an indicator of compromise. In the meantime, Desktop and Server Support personnel could download their own tools from a network share for troubleshooting purposes and remove them when they were done. Today, attackers are more sophisticated, using system binaries and libraries that can't really be removed without potentially damaging the operating system. However, leaving attackers with as little land to live off as possible can help defenders in multiple phases of an attack.

Attackers also relied on a lot of tricks to stay hidden on a system. For example, they would run components of their remote-control or surveillance software on a victim's system by naming it the same as a system file that administrators would expect to be running on the system but running it from a slightly different directory. The file and the process looked normal, and most administrators wouldn't notice it was running from the system directory instead of the system32 directory. This tactic was so common that I developed some popular support tools for Windows that could help detect such shenanigans, including Port Reporter, Port Reporter Parser, and PortQry (Microsoft Corporation, n.d.).

These tools are still available on the Microsoft Download Center for free download, although I doubt that they will run properly on Windows 11-based systems today as many Windows APIs have changed since I developed these tools. Of course, I had to have some fun when I developed these tools; my name appears in the Port Reporter log files and when the hidden /dev switch is run with Portqry.

Figure 10.11: Easter egg fun with Portqry version 2.0

Some of the capabilities that will help break the Installation phase of attacks include:

- **Anti-malware suites**: Anti-malware software can detect and block the attempted installation of different types of weapons. Keep anti-malware suites up to date; otherwise, they can increase the attack surface themselves.

- **FIM**: I'm a fan of FIM. When it works properly, it can help detect installation attempts and, ideally, stop them. It can also help meet compliance obligations that many organizations have. FIM capabilities are built into many endpoint protection suites and can be integrated with SIEMs. Some of the FIM vendors/products I've seen in use include:

  - McAfee
  - Qualys
  - Tripwire
  - Many others

- **IAM controls**: Adhering to the principle of least privilege can make it harder for installation to succeed.

- **Windows Device Guard**: This can lock down Windows 10 systems to prevent unauthorized programs from running (Microsoft Corporation, 2017). This can help prevent exploitation and installation during an attack.

- **Mandatory Access Control, Role-Based Access Control on Linux systems**: These controls help enforce the principle of least privilege and control access to files and processes, which can make installation much harder or impossible.

Example controls for Installation

The following are examples of controls that can be used in the Installation phase:

- **Anti-malware suites**: Anti-malware can detect and block installation.

- **FIM**: Can detect and prevent changes to systems and application files.

- **Log reviews**: Reviewing various system logs can reveal indicators of installation.

- **Short-lived environments**: Systems that are replaced every few hours can make installation harder.

- **Windows Device Guard**: Can make it harder for unauthorized programs to run.

- **Mandatory Access Control, Role-Based Access Control (RBAC), Attribute-Based Access Control (ABAC)**: These controls can make it harder for unauthorized programs to run.

- **IAM controls**: Strictly following the principle of least privilege can make installation much harder or impossible.

- **Deception technology**: Can attract attackers and deceive them into attacking fake environments.

- **Backups**: Restore from backups as necessary when installation cannot be stopped.

- **Images and containers**: Rebuild infrastructure as necessary when installation cannot be stopped.

Note that many of the same control ideas in the list can apply to Deny, Disrupt, and Degrade in the Installation attack phase.

	Detect	Deny	Disrupt	Degrade	Deceive	Limit	Restore
Anti-malware suites	▓	▓	▓	▓			
FIM	▓					▓	
Log reviews	▓						
Short-lived environments		▓	▓	▓			
Windows Device Guard		▓	▓	▓		▓	
Mandatory Access Control, Role-Based Access Control (RBAC), Attribute-Based Access Control (ABAC)		▓	▓	▓			
IAM controls		▓				▓	
Deception technology					▓		
Backups							▓
Images and containers							▓

Figure 10.12: A summary of control ideas for the Installation phase

There are lots of other controls that can help detect, deny, disrupt, degrade, deceive, and limit attackers during the Installation phase of their attack. If attackers are successful in this phase, most organizations will not rely on anti-malware or host-based restore points to recover; they will format the system and rebuild it from scratch, using images or backups. The cloud makes this much easier, as I discussed earlier, with short-lived environments, autoscaling, and other capabilities.

Insights from ATT&CK

There are three tactics in the ATT&CK framework that could potentially be included in the Installation stage of attackers' Kill Chains, depending how security teams want to categorize them. These tactics are Persistence, Privilege Escalation, and Defense Evasion. Let's take a closer look at two of them.

Persistence is a tactic where "the adversary is trying to maintain their foothold" (MITRE, 2019). The Privilege Escalation tactic is where the "adversary is trying to gain higher-level permissions" (MITRE, 2021). Between the two of these tactics, there are 71 techniques and sub-techniques, and 151 mitigations.

There are 19 techniques and 19 sub-techniques associated with Persistence (MITRE, 2019):

- Account Manipulation:

    - Sub-technique: Additional Cloud Credentials

    - Sub-technique: Additional Cloud Roles

    - Sub-technique: Additional Email Delegate Permissions

    - Sub-technique: Device Registration

    - Sub-technique: SSH Authorized Keys

- BITS Jobs

- Boot or Logon Autostart Execution:

    - Sub-technique: Registry Run Keys / Startup Folder

    - Sub-technique: Authentication Package

    - Sub-technique: Time Providers

    - Sub-technique: Winlogon Helper DLL

    - Sub-technique: Security Support Provider

    - Sub-technique: Kernel Modules and Extensions

    - Sub-technique: Re-opened Applications

    - Sub-technique: LSASS Driver

    - Sub-technique: Shortcut Modification

    - Sub-technique: Port Monitors

    - Sub-technique: Print Processors

    - Sub-technique: XDG Autostart Entries

    - Sub-technique: Active Setup

    - Sub-technique: Login Items

- Boot or Logon Initialization Scripts:

    - Sub-technique: Logon Script (Windows)

    - Sub-technique: Logon Hook

    - Sub-technique: Network Logon Script

    - Sub-technique: RC Scripts

    - Sub-technique: Startup Items

- Browser Extensions
- Compromise Client Software Binary
- Create Account:
    - Sub-technique: Cloud Account
    - Sub-technique: Domain Account
    - Sub-technique: Local Account
- Create or Modify System Process:
    - Sub-technique: Launch Agent
    - Sub-technique: Systemd Service
    - Sub-technique: Windows Service
    - Sub-technique: Launch Daemon
- Event-Triggered Execution:
    - Sub-technique: Change Default File Association
    - Sub-technique: Screensaver
    - Sub-technique: Windows Management Instrumentation Event Subscription
    - Sub-technique: Unix Shell Configuration Modification
    - Sub-technique: Trap
    - Sub-technique: LC_LOAD_DYLIB Addition
    - Sub-technique: Netsh Helper DLL
    - Sub-technique: Accessibility Features
    - Sub-technique: AppCert DLLs
    - Sub-technique: AppInit DLLs
    - Sub-technique: Application Shimming
    - Sub-technique: Image File Execution Options Injection
    - Sub-technique: PowerShell Profile
    - Sub-technique: Emond
    - Sub-technique: Component Object Model Hijacking
    - Sub-technique: Installer Packages
- External Remote Services

- Hijack Execution Flow:

  - Sub-technique: DLL Search Order Hijacking

  - Sub-technique: DLL Side-Loading

  - Sub-technique: Dylib Hijacking

  - Sub-technique: Executable Installer Filer Permissions Weakness

  - Sub-technique: Dynamic Linker Hijacking

  - Sub-technique: Path Interception by PATH Environment Variable

  - Sub-technique: Path Interception by Search Order Hijacking

  - Sub-technique: Path Interception by Unquoted Path

  - Sub-technique: Service Filer Permissions Weakness

  - Sub-technique: Services Registry Permissions Weakness

  - Sub-technique: COR_PROFILER

  - Sub-technique: KernelCallback TableImplant Internal Image

- Modify Authentication Process:

  - Sub-technique: Domain Controller Authentication

  - Sub-technique: Password Filter DLL

  - Sub-technique: Pluggable Authentication Modules

  - Sub-technique: Network Device Authentication

  - Sub-technique: Reversible Encryption

  - Sub-technique: Multi-Factor Authentication

  - Sub-technique: Hybrid Identity

- Office Application Startup:

  - Sub-technique: Add-ins

  - Sub-technique: Office Template Macros

  - Sub-technique: Office Test

  - Sub-technique: Outlook Forms

  - Sub-technique: Outlook Home Page

  - Sub-technique: Outlook Rules

- Pre-OS Boot:

    - Sub-technique: System Firmware

    - Sub-technique: Component Firmware

    - Sub-technique: Bootkit

    - Sub-technique: ROMMONkit

    - Sub-technique: TFTP Boot

- Scheduled Task/Job:

    - Sub-technique: At

    - Sub-technique: Cron

    - Sub-technique: Scheduled Task

    - Sub-technique: Systemd Timers

    - Sub-technique: Container Orchestration Job

- Server Software Component:

    - Sub-technique: IIS Components

    - Sub-technique: SQL Stored Procedures

    - Sub-technique: Terminal Services DLL

    - Sub-technique: Transport Agent

    - Sub-technique: Web Shell

- Traffic Signaling:

    - Sub-technique: Port Knocking

    - Sub-technique: Socket Filters

- Valid Accounts:

    - Sub-technique: Default Accounts

    - Sub-technique: Domain Accounts

    - Sub-technique: Local Accounts

    - Sub-technique: Cloud Accounts

ATT&CK offers 76 mitigations for techniques and sub-techniques associated with the Persistence tactic. Some of these mitigations apply to a single technique and some are used to mitigate multiple techniques. Details associated with these mitigations, along with full details on the ATT&CK Persistence tactic are available at: `https://attack.mitre.org/tactics/TA0003/`

The Privilege Escalation tactic has 13 techniques and 52 mitigations associated with it. Details associated with its techniques, sub-techniques, and mitigations are available at `https://attack.mitre.org/tactics/TA0004/`. The techniques and sub-techniques include:

- Abuse elevation control mechanisms:

    - Sub-technique: Setuid and Setgid

    - Sub-technique: Bypass User Account Control

    - Sub-technique: Sudo and Sudo Caching

    - Sub-technique: Elevated Execution with Prompt

- Access token manipulation:

    - Sub-technique: Token Impersonation/Theft

    - Sub-technique: Create Process with Token

    - Sub-technique: Make and Impersonate Token

    - Sub-technique: Parent PID Spoofing

    - Sub-technique: SID-History Injection

- Boot or logon autostart execution:

    - Sub-technique: Registry Run Keys / Startup Folder

    - Sub-technique: Authentication Package

    - Sub-technique: Time Providers

    - Sub-technique: Winlogon Helper DLL

    - Sub-technique: Security Support Provider

    - Sub-technique: Kernel Modules and Extensions

    - Sub-technique: Re-opened Applications

    - Sub-technique: LSASS Driver

    - Sub-technique: Shortcut Modification

    - Sub-technique: Port Monitors

    - Sub-technique: Print Processors

- Sub-technique: XDG Autostart Entries
- Sub-technique: Active Setup
- Sub-technique: Login Items

- Boot or login initialization scripts:

    - Sub-technique: Logon Script (Windows)
    - Sub-technique: Login Hook
    - Sub-technique: Network Logon Script
    - Sub-technique: RC Scripts
    - Sub-technique: Startup Items

- Create or modify system process:

    - Sub-technique: Launch Agent
    - Sub-technique: Systemd Service
    - Sub-technique: Windows Service
    - Sub-technique: Launch Daemon

- Domain policy modification:

    - Sub-technique: Group Policy Modification
    - Sub-technique: Domain Trust Modification

- Escape to host
- Event-triggered execution:

    - Sub-technique: Change Default File Association
    - Sub-technique: Screensaver
    - Sub-technique: Windows Management Instrumentation Event Subscription
    - Sub-technique: Unix Shell Configuration Modification
    - Sub-technique: Trap
    - Sub-technique: LC_LOAD_DYLIB Addition
    - Sub-technique: Netsh Helper DLL
    - Sub-technique: Accessibility Features
    - Sub-technique: AppCert DLLs
    - Sub-technique: AppInit DLLs

- Sub-technique: Application Shimming
- Sub-technique: Image File Execution Options Injection
- Sub-technique: PowerShell Profile
- Sub-technique: Emond
- Sub-technique: Component Object Model Hijacking
- Sub-technique: Installer Packages

- Exploitation for privilege escalation
- Hijack execution flow:

  - Sub-technique: DLL Search Order Hijacking
  - Sub-technique: DLL Side-Loading
  - Sub-technique: Dylib Hijacking
  - Sub-technique: Executable Installer File Permissions Weakness
  - Sub-technique: Dynamic Linker Hijacking
  - Sub-technique: Path Interception by PATH Environment Variable
  - Sub-technique: Path Interception by Search Order Hijacking
  - Sub-technique: Path Interception by Unquoted Path
  - Sub-technique: Services File Permissions Weakness
  - Sub-technique: Services Registry Permissions Weakness
  - Sub-technique: COR_PROFILER
  - Sub-technique: KernelCallbackTable

- Process injection:

  - Sub-technique: Dynamic-link Library Injection
  - Sub-technique: Portable Executable Injection
  - Sub-technique: Thread Execution Hijacking
  - Sub-technique: Asynchronous Procedure Call
  - Sub-technique: Thread Local Storage
  - Sub-technique: Ptrace System Calls
  - Sub-technique: Proc Memory
  - Sub-technique: Extra Window Memory Injection
  - Sub-technique: Process Hollowing

- Sub-technique: Process Doppelgänging
- Sub-technique: VDSO Hijacking
- Sub-technique: ListPlanting

- Scheduled task/job:

  - Sub-technique: At
  - Sub-technique: Cron
  - Sub-technique: Scheduled Task
  - Sub-technique: Systemd Timers
  - Sub-technique: Container Orchestration Job

- Valid accounts:

  - Sub-technique: Default Accounts
  - Sub-technique: Domain Accounts
  - Sub-technique: Local Accounts
  - Sub-technique: Cloud Accounts

The most frequently referenced mitigations between the Persistence and Privilege Escalation tactics include (MITRE, 2021):

- **Mitigation ID M1026**: Privileged Account Management (17/151 = 11%)
- **Mitigation ID M1018**: User Account Management (16/151 = 11%)
- **Mitigation ID M1022**: Restrict File and Directory Permissions (13/151 = 9%)
- **Mitigation ID M1038**: Execution Prevention (11/151 = 7%)
- **Mitigation ID M1040**: Behavior Prevention on Endpoint (10/151 = 7%)

Attack phase – Command and Control (C2)

If attackers are successful in the Installation phase of their attack, typically they seek to establish communications channels with the compromised systems. These communications channels enable attackers to send commands to the systems that they compromised, enabling them to take a range of actions in the next phases of their attacks. A botnet is a great illustrative example. Once attackers have compromised systems and installed their C2 software on them, they can use those "zombie" systems for a plethora of illicit purposes including identity theft, intellectual property theft, DDoS attacks, and so on.

There are numerous techniques that attackers can employ for C2 communications. Some are more innovative and interesting than others. Communicating across the network is the most straightforward approach and attackers have developed many different methods and protocols to facilitate C2 communications; these range from simply listening on a predefined TCP or UDP port number for commands to using more elaborate protocols like RPC and DNS, custom-built protocols, and employing proxies to further obfuscate their communications.

All these techniques can potentially help attackers remotely control compromised environments while evading detection. They want their network traffic to blend in with other legitimate network traffic. Some attackers have developed impressive domain generation algorithms that allow attackers to dynamically change IP addresses used for C2 communications. Conficker was the first big worm attack to use this method, more than 15 years ago. Some attackers have developed obfuscated and encrypted protocols that make it harder for defenders to detect and stop the attacker's commands.

By detecting, denying, disrupting, degrading, deceiving, and limiting C2 communications, defenders can minimize damage and expense to their organizations and accelerate recovery, all while increasing the expense to attackers. This is an area where vendors that have extensive networking expertise and capabilities, married with threat intelligence, can really add value. Some of the ways that defenders can do this include:

- IDS/IPS: These systems can detect and block C2 communications in several places on networks. Many organizations run IDS/IPS in their DMZs and inside their corporate networks. Many vendors offer IDS/ IPS systems, including:

    - Cisco
    - FireEye
    - HP
    - IBM
    - Juniper
    - McAfee
    - Others

- Network micro-segmentation: This can provide granular control by enabling organizations to apply policies to individual workloads. This can make it harder for attackers to use compromised systems for C2 communications.

- Log reviews: Analyzing logs, NetFlow data, and DNS queries in an environment can help detect C2 communications. Since there can be too much data for humans to do this manually, many organizations now employ artificial intelligence and/or machine learning to do this for them. Of course, the cloud makes this much easier than trying to do this on-premises.

Example controls for C2

The following are examples of controls that can be used in the C2 phase.

- **IDS/IPS**: Can detect and stop attackers' communications.
- **Firewalls and proxy servers**: Communication with remote networks can be detected and blocked by firewalls and proxy servers.
- **Log reviews**: Reviewing various system logs, including DNS queries, can reveal indicators of C2 communications.
- **Short-lived environments**: Systems that are replaced every few hours can make C2 communications harder to achieve and inconsistent.
- **IAM controls**: Strictly following the principle of least privilege can make some C2 communications techniques much more difficult.
- **Network micro-segmentation**: Enforcing rules that restrict communications can make C2 communications more difficult.
- **Deception technology**: Attackers communicating with fake environments waste their time and energy.

Note that the same control ideas in the list above can apply to Disrupt, Degrade, and Limit in the C2 attack phase.

	Detect	Deny	Disrupt	Degrade	Deceive	Limit	Restore
IDS/IPS	▓	▓				▓	
Firewalls and proxy servers	▓	▓					
Log reviews	▓					▓	
Short-lived environments		▓	▓	▓		▓	
IAM controls		▓	▓	▓		▓	
Network micro-segmentation			▓	▓		▓	
Deception technology					▓	▓	

Figure 10.13: A summary of control ideas for the C2 phase

A critical aspect of detecting and preventing C2 communications is threat intelligence. Keep the tips I provided in *Chapter 2, What to Know about Threat Intelligence*, on how to identify credible threat intelligence, in mind while evaluating vendors to help in this phase of the framework. Providing old intelligence, commodity intelligence, and false positives is rarely helpful but seems to be a common challenge many vendors have. I've also found that unless C2 communications or other malicious network traffic can be traced back to a specific identity context in the compromised environment, it can be less actionable. Subsequently, C2 detection and prevention systems that are integrated with identity systems seem to have an advantage over those that do not have such integrations. The value of these systems seems to be a function of the time and effort spent fine-tuning them, especially to minimize false positives.

Insights from ATT&CK

The ATT&CK framework provides a great list of techniques attackers use for C2 communications (MITRE, 2019). This is another good example of how the ATT&CK framework and the Intrusion Kill Chain framework complement each other. The ATT&CK Command and Control tactic is where "the adversary is trying to communicate with compromised systems to control them" (MITRE, 2019). This tactic has 16 techniques and 23 sub-techniques (MITRE, 2019):

- Application Layer Protocol:
    - Sub-technique: DNS
    - Sub-technique: File Transfer Protocols
    - Sub-technique: Mail Protocols
    - Sub-technique: Web Protocols
- Communication Through Removable Media
- Data Encoding:
    - Sub-technique: Non-Standard Encoding
    - Sub-technique: Standard Encoding
- Data Obfuscation:
    - Sub-technique: Junk Data
    - Sub-technique: Protocol Impersonation
    - Sub-technique: Steganography

- Dynamic Resolution:

    - Sub-technique: DNS Calculation

    - Sub-technique: Domain Generation Algorithms

    - Sub-technique: Fast Flux DNS

- Encrypted Channel:

    - Sub-technique: Asymmetric Cryptography

    - Sub-technique: Symmetric Cryptography

- Fallback Channels

- Ingress Tool Transfer

- Multi-Stage Channels

- Non-Application Layer Protocol

- Non-Standard Port

- Protocol Tunneling

- Proxy:

    - Sub-technique: Domain Fronting

    - Sub-technique: External Proxy

    - Sub-technique: Internal Proxy

    - Sub-technique: Multi-hop Proxy

- Remote Access Software

- Traffic Signaling:

    - Sub-technique: Port Knocking

    - Sub-technique: Socket Filters

- Web Service:

    - Sub-technique: Bidirectional Communication

    - Sub-technique: Dead Drop Resolver

    - Sub-technique: One-Way Communication

ATT&CK provides 52 mitigations for these techniques and sub-techniques. Some of these mitigations address a single technique and some are used to mitigate multiple techniques. The mitigations that appear most often and therefore potentially have the biggest return on investment include (MITRE, 2019):

1. **Mitigation ID M1031**: Network Intrusion Prevention (31/52 = 60%)

2. **Mitigation ID M1037**: Filter Network Traffic (6/52 = 12%)

3. **Mitigation ID M1021**: Restrict Web-Based Content (6/52 = 12%)

4. **Mitigation ID M1020**: SSL/TLS Inspection (4/52 = 8%)

5. **Mitigation ID M1042**: User Account Management (6/82 = 7%)

Details associated with these Mitigation IDs, along with full details on the ATT&CK Command and Control tactic are available at: `https://attack.mitre.org/tactics/TA0011/`

Attack phase – Reconnaissance II

One of the things that attackers often command the compromised systems that they control to do is help them map out their victim's network. Attackers often want to explore networks to look for valuable data, valuable intellectual property, and high-value assets that they can steal, damage, or demand a ransom for their return. They also look for information, accounts, infrastructure, and anything else that might help them gain access to the aforementioned list of valuables. Again, they are trying to blend their reconnaissance activities into the common, legitimate network traffic, authentication, and authorization processes that occur on their victims' networks. This helps them evade detection and stay persistent on the network for longer periods.

Detecting reconnaissance activities can help defenders discover compromised systems in their environment. Additionally, making this type of reconnaissance difficult or impossible for attackers to perform might help limit the damage and expense associated with a compromise. This can be easier said than done, especially in legacy environments with lots of homegrown applications and older applications whose behavior can be surprising and unpredictable in many cases. Many a SOC analyst have spotted a sequential port scan on their network, only to find some homegrown application using the noisiest possible way to communicate on the network. This behavior can usually be traced back to a developer trying to solve a problem while making their life easier. The world is full of applications like this, which make detecting true anomalies more work.

This is another phase where attackers routinely "live off the land." Whether they are running scripts to perform reconnaissance or doing it manually, when defenders leave most of the tools attackers need installed by default on systems, it makes the attackers' jobs easier.

Removing or restricting the use of these common tools everywhere possible inconveniences attackers and will make it easier to detect when these tools, or others like them, are used in the environment. However, it's unlikely that security teams will be able to remove all the binaries and libraries that attackers can use from their environments.

Some of the other capabilities included in the control lists above include:

- **Deception technology**: Whether the party performing reconnaissance inside the network is an attacker or an insider, deception technology can be helpful in detecting their presence. When someone starts poking at assets that no one in the organization has any legitimate business touching, this can be a red flag. Additionally, if attackers take the bait offered by deception technologies, like stealing credentials, for example, and they use those credentials somewhere else in the environment, that's a very good indication of reconnaissance activities.

- **User Behavior Analytics (UBA)**: UBA, or Entity Behavioral Analytics, can help identify when users and other entities access resources out of the norm. This can indicate an insider threat or stolen credentials being used by attackers and uncover reconnaissance activities. There are many vendors that provide products that do this type of detection, including:

  - Exabeam
  - ForcePoint
  - LogRhythm
  - Microsoft
  - RSA
  - Splunk
  - Many others

- **SAW/PAW: Secure administrator workstations (SAWs)** or **privileged access workstations (PAWs)** will make it much harder for attackers to steal and use credentials for administrator accounts and other accounts with elevated privileges. Monitored and audited SAWs/PAWs help detect unusual use of privileged credentials.

- **Active Directory hardening**: Makes it harder for attackers to access and steal credentials.

- **Encryption everywhere**: Protecting data while it travels across the network and everywhere it rests can be a powerful control for preventing effective reconnaissance.

Example controls for Reconnaissance II

The following are examples of controls that can be used in the Reconnaissance II phase:

- **Deception technology**: Deception technologies can help detect the attacker's reconnaissance activities and can trick attackers into spending time performing reconnaissance on fake environments instead of real ones.

- **Log reviews**: Reviewing various system logs, including DNS queries, can reveal indicators of compromise.

- **UBA**: This can detect anomalous behavior.

- **SAW/PAW**: Monitored and audited SAWs/PAWs help detect unusual use of privileged credentials. This can make it much harder for attackers to steal and use credentials for administrator accounts and other accounts with elevated privileges.

- **Network micro-segmentation**: Enforcing rules that restrict network traffic can make reconnaissance more difficult.

- **IAM controls**: Strictly following the principle of least privilege can make it harder to perform reconnaissance.

- **Encryption everywhere**: Encrypting data in transit and at rest can protect data from attackers.

- **Active Directory hardening**: This makes it harder for attackers to access and steal credentials.

Note that the same control ideas in the list above can apply to Deny, Disrupt, Degrade, and Limit in the Reconnaissance II attack phase.

	Detect	Deny	Disrupt	Degrade	Deceive	Limit	Restore
Deception technology	▓				▓		
Log reviews	▓						
UBA	▓						
SAW/PAW	▓	▓	▓	▓		▓	
Network micro-segmentation		▓	▓	▓		▓	
IAM controls		▓	▓	▓		▓	
Encryption everywhere		▓	▓	▓		▓	
Active Directory hardening		▓	▓	▓		▓	

Figure 10.14: A summary of control ideas for the Reconnaissance II phase

There are many more ways to detect and make reconnaissance harder for attackers, however, it seems like only after a successful compromise, during the response, are the tell-tale signs of reconnaissance spotted. Investments in this phase of the framework can have big returns for security teams.

Insights from ATT&CK

This is another good example of an integration point between the ATT&CK framework and the Intrusion Kill Chain framework. ATT&CK provides at least two tactics that could be used by attackers in the Reconnaissance II stage of their attacks. These tactics are Discovery and Credential Access (MITRE, n.d.). However, other tactics could also be used while attackers move around their victims' environments, such as Defense Evasion, Lateral Movement, Collection (MITRE, n.d.). This is one of the characteristics that makes ATT&CK powerful; it doesn't assume attacks are sequential discrete steps – attackers can choose to do many things and iterate between tactics as needed. Let's take a closer look at the Discovery tactic.

Discovery has 30 techniques and 13 sub-techniques (MITRE, 2019):

- Account Discovery:

    - Sub-technique: Cloud Account

    - Sub-technique: Domain Account

    - Sub-technique: Email Account

    - Sub-technique: Local Account

- Application Window Discovery
- Browser Bookmark Discovery
- Cloud Infrastructure Discovery
- Cloud Service Dashboard
- Cloud Service Discovery
- Cloud Storage Object Discovery
- Container and Resource Discovery
- Debugger Evasion
- Domain Trust Discovery
- File and Directory Discovery
- Group Policy Discovery
- Network Service Discovery
- Network Share Discovery
- Network Sniffing
- Password Policy Discovery

- Peripheral Device Discovery
- Permission Groups Discovery:
    - Sub-technique: Cloud Groups
    - Sub-technique: Domain Groups
    - Sub-technique: Local Groups
- Process Discovery
- Query Registry
- Remote System Discovery
- Software Discovery:
    - Sub-technique: Security Software Discovery
- System Information Discovery
- System Location Discovery:
    - Sub-technique: System Language Discovery
- System Network Configuration Discovery:
    - Sub-technique: Internet Connection Discovery
- System Network Connections Discovery
- System Owner/User Discovery
- System Service Discovery
- System Time Discovery
- Virtualization/Sandbox Evasion:
    - Sub-technique: System Checks
    - Sub-technique: User Activity Based Checks
    - Sub-technique: Time Based Evasion

For these 43 techniques and sub-techniques, ATT&CK offers 18 mitigations. Some are unique and some are used multiple times across techniques and sub-techniques. The most frequently cited mitigations include the following:

1. "This type of attack technique cannot be easily mitigated with preventive controls since it is based on the abuse of system features" (MITRE, 2019) (58% of techniques and sub-techniques cited this lack of mitigation)

2. **Mitigation ID M1018**: User Account Management (5/18 = 28%)

3. **Mitigation ID M1028**: Operating System Configuration (4/18 = 22%)

Information on all the techniques, sub-techniques, and mitigations is available at https://attack. mitre.org/tactics/TA0007/.

Attack phase – Actions on Objectives

Remember that there are many possible motivations for attacks, including notoriety, profit, military espionage, economic espionage, revenge, anarchy, and many others. Once attackers make it to this phase in their attack, their objectives are potentially within their reach. In this phase, they might lock administrators out of systems, exfiltrate data, compromise the integrity of data, encrypt data, damage infrastructure, make systems unbootable, or simply just stay persistent to watch their victims and collect data. What attackers do in the Actions on Objectives stage of their attacks depends on their motivations.

In some cases, this is the defender's last chance to detect and stop attackers before recovery becomes more expensive and potentially aspirational. However, the fact that attackers made it to this phase in their Kill Chain does not automatically mean they have access to all resources and are in full control of the IT environment; their objective might be much more tightly scoped, or the security controls that have been deployed to impede their progress might have had the intended effect. This could mean that many of the controls used to break other phases of the Kill Chain can still be helpful in this phase. If attackers were able to defeat or bypass controls in earlier phases of their attack, this doesn't mean they can do so everywhere in the IT environment, anytime. Detecting and denying attackers is ideal, but disrupting, degrading, deceiving, and limiting their attacks is highly preferable to recovering from them.

Some of the controls to consider when mitigating this phase of an attack include:

- **Data backups**: If attackers choose to destroy data by damaging storage media or firmware, wiping storage media, encrypting data, or otherwise tampering with the integrity of data, backups can be very helpful. Offline backups are highly recommended as attackers will happily encrypt online backups if they can with their ransomware or cryptoware.

- **SAW/PAW**: SAW or PAW can make it much harder for attackers to use privileged accounts to lock administrators out of the systems they manage.

- **Encryption everywhere**: Remember that encryption not only provides confidentiality, but it can also safeguard the integrity of data; encryption can help detect that data has been altered.

- **IAM controls:** Identity is central to security. If attackers already own the Active Directory instance in the environment, then it's going to be very hard or impossible to expel them. However, if they only have access to some accounts, IAM controls can still help limit the scope of their attack.

Example controls for Actions on Objectives

The following are examples of controls that can be used in the Actions on Objectives phase:

- **Anti-malware suites:** Anti-malware can detect and block malware.
- **FIM:** Can detect and prevent changes to systems and application files.
- **Log reviews:** Reviewing various system logs can reveal indicators of compromise.
- **User Behavior Analytics:** Can detect anomalous behavior.
- **Deception technology:** Deception technologies can detect the attacker's actions on assets and deceive them into attacking fake environments.
- **SAW/PAW:** Monitored and audited SAWs/PAWs help detect unusual use of privileged credentials.
- **Short-lived environments:** Systems that are replaced every few hours can make it harder for attackers to persist in compromised IT environments.
- **Windows Device Guard:** Can make it harder for unauthorized programs to run.
- **Mandatory Access Control, Role-Based Access Control (RBAC), Attribute-Based Access Control (ABAC):** Can make it harder for unauthorized programs to run.
- **IAM controls:** Strictly following the principle of least privilege can make it harder for the attacker's actions on objectives.
- **Encryption everywhere:** Encrypting data in transit and at rest can protect data from attackers.
- **Backups:** Restore from backups as necessary.
- **Images and containers:** Rebuild infrastructure as necessary.
- **Disaster recovery processes and technologies:** Recover IT systems efficiently to minimize downtime and data loss.

Note that the same control ideas in the list above can apply to Deny, Disrupt, Degrade, and there are very similar controls for Limit in the Actions on Objectives attack phase.

	Detect	Deny	Disrupt	Degrade	Deceive	Limit	Restore
Anti-malware suites	▓	▓	▓	▓		▓	
FIM	▓	▓	▓	▓		▓	
Log reviews	▓						
User Behavior Analytics	▓						
Deception technology	▓				▓		
SAW/PAW	▓						
Short-lived environments		▓	▓	▓		▓	
Windows Device Guard		▓	▓	▓		▓	
Mandatory Access Control, Role-Based Access Control (RBAC), Attribute-Based Access Control (ABAC)		▓	▓	▓	▓	▓	
IAM controls		▓	▓	▓	▓	▓	
Encryption everywhere		▓	▓	▓	▓	▓	
Backups							▓
Images and containers							▓
Disaster recovery processes and technologies							▓

Figure 10.15: A summary of control ideas for the Actions on Objectives phase

Insights from ATT&CK

Actions on Objectives is another phase where there's great potential integration between the Intrusion Kill Chain model and the ATT&CK framework. There are at least two ATT&CK tactics that can be used by attackers in the Action on Objectives stage of their attacks, Exfiltration and Impact (MITRE, n.d.). Let's take a quick look at both of these tactics.

The ATT&CK Exfiltration tactic "consists of techniques that adversaries may use to steal data from your network" (MITRE, 2019). This tactic has 9 techniques and 8 sub-techniques (MITRE, 2019):

- Automated Exfiltration:
    - Sub-technique: Traffic Duplication
- Data Transfer Size Limits
- Exfiltration Over Alternative Protocol:
    - Sub-technique: Exfiltration Over Asymmetric Encrypted Non-C2 Protocol
    - Sub-technique: Exfiltration Over Symmetric Encrypted Non-C2 Protocol
    - Sub-technique: Exfiltration Over Unencrypted Non-C2 Protocol
- Exfiltration Over C2 Channel
- Exfiltration Over Other Network Medium:
    - Sub-technique: Exfiltration Over Bluetooth

- Exfiltration Over Physical Medium:

  - Sub-technique: Exfiltration over USB

- Exfiltration Over Web Service:

  - Sub-technique: Exfiltration to Cloud Storage

  - Sub-technique: Exfiltration to Code Repository

- Scheduled Transfer

- Transfer Data to Cloud Account

For these 17 techniques and sub-techniques, ATT&CK offers 36 mitigations. Some are unique and some are used multiple times across techniques and sub-techniques. The most frequently cited mitigations include the following:

1. **Mitigation ID M1057**: Data Loss Prevention (7/36 = 19%)

2. **Mitigation ID M1031**: Network Intrusion Prevention (7/36 = 19%)

3. **Mitigation ID M1037**: Filter Network Traffic (5/36 = 14%)

Information on all the techniques, sub-techniques, and mitigations for the Exfiltration tactic is available at https://attack.mitre.org/tactics/TA0010/.

The ATT&CK Impact tactic is where "the adversary is trying to manipulate, interrupt, or destroy your systems and data." (MITRE, 2019). This tactic has a total of 26 techniques and sub-techniques. These include (MITRE, 2019):

- Account Access Removal

- Data Destruction

- Data Encrypted for Impact

- Data Manipulation:

  - Sub-technique: Runtime Data Manipulation

  - Sub-technique: Stored Data Manipulation

  - Sub-technique: Transmitted Data Manipulation

- Defacement:

  - Sub-technique: External Defacement

  - Sub-technique: Internal Defacement

- Disk Wipe:

    - Sub-technique: Disk Content Wipe

    - Sub-technique: Disk Structure Wipe

- Endpoint Denial of Service:

    - Sub-technique: Application Exhaustion Flood

    - Sub-technique: Application or System Exploitation

    - Sub-technique: OS Exhaustion Flood

    - Sub-technique: Service Exhaustion Flood

- Firmware Corruption

- Inhibit System Recovery

- Network Denial of Service:

    - Sub-technique: Direct Network Flood

    - Sub-technique: Reflection Amplification

- Resource Hijacking

- Service Stop

- System Shutdown/Reboot

For these 13 techniques and 13 sub-techniques, ATT&CK offers 36 mitigations. Some of these mitigations address a single technique and some are used to mitigate multiple techniques. The most frequently cited mitigations include the following:

1. **Mitigation ID M1053**: Data Backup (9/36 = 25%)

2. **Mitigation ID M1037**: Filter Network Traffic (8/36 = 22%)

3. **Mitigation ID M1022**: Restrict File and Directory Permissions (4/36 = 11%)

4. **Mitigation ID M1041**: Encrypt Sensitive Information (3/36 = 8%)

Information on all the techniques, sub-techniques, and mitigations for the Impact tactic is available at https://attack.mitre.org/tactics/TA0040/.

At this point, we've covered all the phases in our modified Intrusion Kill Chain. We've discussed numerous ideas for effective controls for each phase and complemented these ideas with insights from the ATT&CK framework. Note that we didn't include every tactic that is included in the ATT&CK Matrix for Enterprise in our Kill Chain design; there are many more tactics, techniques, and mitigations to inform your Intrusion Kill Chain control set design.

You can get a complete, up-to-date list of tactics at `https://attack.mitre.org/tactics/enterprise/`.

The complete list of techniques and sub-techniques is available at `https://attack.mitre.org/techniques/enterprise/`.

The complete list of all the mitigations is available at `https://attack.mitre.org/mitigations/enterprise/`.

Conclusion

That's one way to implement the Intrusion Kill Chain framework. Obviously, there are other possible interpretations and approaches to implementing this model. I've seen some very well thought out and sophisticated approaches to this framework at conferences and documented on the internet, but the best way is the one that addresses the specific HVAs and risks that your organization is concerned about.

Remember that best practices are based on the threats and assets that someone else has in mind, not necessarily yours.

This might be obvious, but the Intrusion Kill Chain framework can help CISOs and security teams take a structured approach to managing intrusions. Arguably, intrusions are the most serious threats for most organizations because of their potential impact, but there are other threats that CISOs need to address. DDoS attacks, for example, typically don't involve intrusion attempts or require a Kill Chain framework to address them.

Additionally, the Intrusion Kill Chain approach has become a little dated in a world where the cloud has disrupted and improved upon traditional approaches to IT and cybersecurity. Although this approach still has the potential to be highly effective in on-premises and hybrid environments, a framework designed to break Intrusion Kill Chains and stop so-called advanced persistent threat (APT) actors isn't as relevant in the cloud. Used effectively, CI/CD pipelines, short-lived environments, autoscaling, and other capabilities the cloud offers simply leave no place for APT actors or other attackers to get a foothold in order to move laterally and remain persistent. Simply put, the cloud gives CISOs the opportunity to change the playing field dramatically. I'll discuss the cybersecurity benefits the cloud offers in more detail in *Chapter 12, Modern Approaches to Security and Compliance*.

Given that the industry will continue to transition from the old-fashioned on-premises IT world to the cloud over the next decade, the Intrusion Kill Chain framework still seems well poised to help organizations as a transitional Attack-Centric cybersecurity strategy.

It can help organizations on-premises and in the cloud as they modernize their workforces to take advantage of DevOps, as well as Zero Trust methods, as they come to fruition.

It can also help CISOs who want to leverage a single cybersecurity strategy across their entire IT estate, including legacy on-premises and cloud environments. I have provided a head-start on developing a Kill Chain approach for on-premises environments in this chapter. Additionally, I co-authored a whitepaper when I worked at AWS that will give security teams a big head-start on implementing an Intrusion Kill Chain in AWS. This paper is titled, "Classic intrusion analysis frameworks for AWS environments" (Rains, et al. 2022), and at the time of writing it is still available for public download on the AWS website. This paper contains 70 pages of AWS services and security controls mapped to the Intrusion Kill Chain framework. This will potentially save security teams weeks or months of work trying to do this mapping themselves.

Finally, employing this strategy is potentially far superior to not having a cybersecurity strategy or using many of the other strategies I examined in *Chapter 9, Cybersecurity Strategies*. If your organization doesn't have a cybersecurity strategy or it does but no one can articulate it, you could likely do far worse than to embrace the Intrusion Kill Chain strategy. To do so, in many cases, you'll have to get far more detailed and specific than the high-level example that I have provided here. However, I think I have provided you with a head-start on the best-scoring cybersecurity strategy. This is not a bad thing to have!

Summary

CISOs and security teams have numerous cybersecurity strategies, models, frameworks, and standards to choose from when developing their approach to protecting, detecting, and responding to modern-day threats. One Attack-Centric Strategy that we examined in *Chapter 9, Cybersecurity Strategies*, the Intrusion Kill Chain, deserves serious consideration as it garnered the highest CFSS estimated total score. It earned nearly a perfect score with 95 points out of a possible 100. This chapter sought to provide you with an example of one way this model can be implemented.

The Intrusion Kill Chain model was pioneered by Lockheed Martin; the Kill Chain phases provided in Lockheed Martin's paper on this topic include Reconnaissance, Weaponization, Delivery, Exploitation, Installation, **Command and Control** (**C2**), and Actions on Objectives (Hutchins, Cloppert, Amin, n.d.). One consideration before implementing this framework is whether defenders should use the original Intrusion Kill Chain framework or update it.

There are several ways this framework can be modernized. It can be modified or reorganized around the Cybersecurity Usual Suspects to ensure that they are mitigated and make it easier to identify gaps in an organization's security posture.

Split the Reconnaissance phase into two phases instead of one; one attackers can use before initial compromise and one after compromise. The Weaponization phase can be dropped as CISOs typically do not have very effective controls for protection and detection prior to the Delivery phase. The Destroy phase can be replaced with more pragmatic phases such as Limit and Restore. Adding a maturity index, to capture and communicate how much or how well each cybersecurity capability mitigates threats, can help identify areas of under-investment and potential gaps in defenses. Including an estimate of how pervasively a control has been deployed can also be helpful. Adding a point of contact for each mitigation, to make it clear who is consuming the data generated by cybersecurity capabilities, will help ensure there are no unmanaged mitigations in the environment. Tracking cybersecurity license renewals and support deadlines will help prevent lapses in capabilities.

The Intrusion Kill Chain approach can be complemented with the ATT&CK framework, published by MITRE. ATT&CK has many uses. For example, the tactics, techniques, and sub-techniques provided by ATT&CK can be leveraged to inform the control set design and testing for your Kill Chain.

Rationalizing mitigations can help identify gaps and areas of under - investment and over-investment. Where to start with an implementation can be informed by many factors, including budget, resources, gaps, and areas of under-investment and over-investment. Implementing controls that help break attackers' Kill Chains in multiple places might offer security teams higher ROIs.

That concludes my example of how a cybersecurity strategy can be implemented. I hope the tips and tricks I have provided are helpful to you. In the next chapter, I'll examine how CISOs and security teams can measure whether the implementation of their strategy is effective. This can be an important, yet elusive goal for security teams.

References

- Hutchins, E.M., Cloppert, M.J., Amin, R.M. Ph.D. (n.d.). *Intelligence-Driven Computer Network Defense Informed by Analysis of Adversary Campaigns and Intrusion Kill Chains*. Retrieved from Lockheed Martin: https://lockheedmartin.com/content/dam/lockheed-martin/rms/documents/cyber/LM-White-Paper-Intel-Driven-Defense.pdf
- Sanghvi, H. P., Dahiya, M. S. (2013). *Cyber Reconnaissance: An Alarm before Cyber Attack*. International Journal of Computer Applications (0975 – 8887), Volume 63– No.6, pages 2-3. Retrieved from https://research.ijcaonline.org/volume63/number6/pxc3885202.pdf
- Matt Miller, M. (December 8, 2010). *On the effectiveness of DEP and ASLR*. Retrieved from Microsoft Security Response Center: https://msrc-blog.microsoft.com/2010/12/08/on-the-effectiveness-of-dep-and-aslr/

- Microsoft Corporation. (October 13, 2017). *Control the health of Windows 10-based devices*. Retrieved from Microsoft Docs: `https://docs.microsoft.com/en-us/windows/security/threat-protection/protect-high-value-assets-by-controlling-the-health-of-windows-10-based-devices`

- Microsoft Corporation. (n.d.). *PortQry Command Line Port Scanner Version 2.0*. Retrieved from Microsoft Download Center: `https://www.microsoft.com/en-us/download/details.aspx?id=17148`

- MITRE. (n.d.). *MITRE ATT&CK®*. Retrieved from MITRE ATT&CK®: `https://attack.mitre.org/`

- MITRE. (n.d.). *MITRE ATT&CK® FAQ*. Retrieved from MITRE ATT&CK®: `https://attack.mitre.org/resources/faq/`

- MITRE. (October 18, 2020). *Reconnaissance*. Retrieved from MITRE ATT&CK®: `https://attack.mitre.org/tactics/TA0043/`

- MITRE. (July 19, 2019). *Initial Access*. Retrieved from MITRE ATT&CK®: `https://attack.mitre.org/tactics/TA0001/`

- MITRE. (July 19, 2019). *Execution*. Retrieved from MITRE ATT&CK®: `https://attack.mitre.org/tactics/TA0002/`

- MITRE. (July 19, 2019). *Persistence*. Retrieved from MITRE ATT&CK®: `https://attack.mitre.org/tactics/TA0003/`

- MITRE. (January 6, 2021). *Privilege Escalation*. Retrieved from MITRE ATT&CK®: `https://attack.mitre.org/tactics/TA0004/`

- MITRE. (July 19, 2019). *Command and Control*. Retrieved from MITRE ATT&CK®: `https://attack.mitre.org/tactics/TA0011/`

- MITRE. (July 19, 2019). *Discovery*. Retrieved from MITRE ATT&CK®: `https://attack.mitre.org/tactics/TA0007/`

- MITRE. (July 19, 2019). *Exfiltration*. Retrieved from MITRE ATT&CK®: `https://attack.mitre.org/tactics/TA0010/`

- MITRE. (July 19, 2019). *Impact*. Retrieved from MITRE ATT&CK®: `https://attack.mitre.org/tactics/TA0040/`

- Rains, Walker, Ryland, Scott-Cowley, Evans, Lyle, Samuel, Hodges, Alexander, Gera, & Vyas. (2022). *Classic Intrusion Analysis Frameworks for AWS Environments: Application and Enhancement*. Retrieved from `https://docs.aws.amazon.com/whitepapers/latest/classic-intrusion-analysis-frameworks-for-aws-environments/classic-intrusion-analysis-frameworks-for-aws-environments.html`

Join our community on Discord

Join our community's Discord space for discussions with the author and other readers:

`https://packt.link/SecNet`

11

Measuring Performance and Effectiveness

How do we know if the cybersecurity strategy we've employed is working as planned? How do we know if the CISO and the security team are being effective? This chapter will focus on measuring the effectiveness of cybersecurity strategies.

Throughout this chapter, we'll cover the following topics:

- Using vulnerability management data
- Measuring the performance and efficacy of cybersecurity strategies
- Examining an Attack-Centric Cybersecurity Strategy as an example
- Using intrusion reconstruction results
- Leveraging MITRE ATT&CK®

Let's begin this chapter with a question. Why do CISOs need to measure anything?

Introduction

There are many reasons why cybersecurity teams need to measure things. Compliance with regulatory standards, industry standards, and their own internal security standards are usually chief among them.

There are hundreds of metrics related to governance, risk, and compliance that organizations can choose to measure themselves against. Anyone who has studied for the **Certified Information Systems Security Professional (CISSP)** certification knows that there are numerous security domains, including **Security and Risk Management, Asset Security, Security Architecture and Engineering, Communication and Network Security, Identity and Access Management (IAM)**, and a few others (ISC2, 2021). The performance and efficacy of the people, processes, and technologies in each of these domains can be measured in many ways. In fact, the number of metrics and the ways they can be measured is dizzying. If you are interested in learning about the range of metrics available, I recommend reading Debra S. Herrmann's 848-page leviathan of a book on the topic, *Complete Guide to Security and Privacy Metrics: Measuring Regulatory Compliance, Operational Resilience, and ROI* (Herrmann, 2007).

Besides measuring things for compliance reasons, cybersecurity teams also try to find meaningful metrics to help prove they are adding value to the businesses they support. This can be challenging and a little unfair for CISOs. **Key Performance Indicators (KPIs)** and **Objectives and Key Results (OKRs)** typically measure performance against targets or objectives. For security teams, it's failing to achieve an objective that tends to do the damage. It can be tough to find meaningful data that helps prove that the investments and efforts of the CISO and cybersecurity team are the reasons why the organization's IT infrastructure hasn't been compromised or had a data breach. Was it their work that prevented attackers from being successful? Or did the organization simply "fly under the radar" of attackers, as I've heard so many non-security executives suggest? This is where that submarine analogy that I introduced in the preface can be helpful. There is no flying under the radar on the internet where cybersecurity is concerned; there's only constant pressure from all directions. Besides, hope is not a strategy; it's the abdication of responsibility.

Nevertheless, CISOs need to be able to prove to their peers, the businesses or citizens they support, and shareholders that the results they've produced aren't a byproduct of luck or the fulfillment of hope. They need to show that their results are the product of successfully executing their cybersecurity strategy.

I've seen many CISOs try to do this through opinion and anecdotal evidence. But without data to support opinions and anecdotes, these CISOs tend to have a more difficult time defending the success of their strategy and cybersecurity program. It's only a matter of time before an auditor or consultant offers a different opinion that challenges the CISO's description of the current state of affairs.

Data is key to measuring the performance and efficacy of a cybersecurity strategy. Data helps CISOs manage their cybersecurity programs and investments and helps them prove that their cybersecurity program has been effective and constantly improving. In this chapter, I'll provide suggestions to CISOs and security teams on how they can measure the effectiveness of their cybersecurity strategy. To do this, I'll use the best scoring strategy I examined in *Chapter 9, Cybersecurity Strategies*, and *Chapter 10, Strategy Implementation*, the Attack-Centric Strategy, as an example. I'll also draw on concepts and insights that I provided in the preceding chapters of this book. I will not cover measuring things for compliance or other purposes here as there are many books, papers, and standards that already do this. Let's start by looking at the potential value of vulnerability management data.

Using vulnerability management data

For organizations that are just bootstrapping a cybersecurity program or for CISOs that have assumed leadership of a program that has been struggling to get traction in their organization, vulnerability management data can be a powerful tool. Even for well-established cybersecurity programs, vulnerability management data can help illustrate how the security team has been effectively managing risk for their organization and improving over time. Despite this, surprisingly, I've met some CISOs of large, well-established enterprises who do not aggregate and analyze or, otherwise, use data from their vulnerability management programs. This surprises me when I come across it, because this data represents one of the most straightforward ways available for CISOs to communicate the effectiveness of their cybersecurity programs.

A challenge for CISOs and IT executives is to develop a performance overview based on data that aligns with the way business executives measure and communicate performance. The impact of such data can also be entirely different for CISOs.

For example, when a product production site is behind target, additional resources and action plans will kick in to help compensate. But for CISOs, additional resources are rarely the result of being behind target; for the most part, security programs are supposed to be like a utility – there when you need it, but out of sight until then.

As I discussed at length in earlier chapters, unpatched vulnerabilities and security misconfigurations are two of the five Cybersecurity Usual Suspects that are managed via a vulnerability management program. Subsequently, a well-run vulnerability management program is not optional. As I discussed in *Chapter 8, Ingredients for a Successful Cybersecurity Strategy*, asset inventories that are complete and up to date are critical to the success of vulnerability management programs and cybersecurity programs overall. After all, it's difficult for security teams to manage assets that they do not know exist.

Vulnerability management teams should scan everything in their inventories every single day for vulnerabilities and misconfigurations. This can help minimize the amount of time that unmitigated critical and high-severity vulnerabilities and misconfigurations are present and exploitable in their environments. Remember that vulnerabilities and misconfigurations can be introduced into IT environments in multiple ways: newly disclosed vulnerabilities (on average, 69 per day in 2022), software and systems built from old images or restored from backup, legacy software and systems that go out of support, and orphaned assets that become unmanaged over time, among other ways.

Every day that a vulnerability management team scans all their assets, they will have a new snapshot of the current state of the environment that they can stitch together with all the previous days' snapshots. Over time, this data can be used in multiple ways by the cybersecurity team. Let me give you some examples of how this data can be used.

Assets under management versus total assets

The number of assets scanned by a vulnerability management team versus the total number of assets that an organization owns and operates can be an interesting data point for some organizations. The difference between these two numbers potentially represents risk, especially if there are assets that are not actively managed for vulnerabilities and misconfigurations by anyone. I've seen big differences between these two numbers in organizations where IT has been chronically understaffed for long periods, and there isn't enough documentation or tribal knowledge to inform accurate asset inventories. Subsequently, there can be large swaths of IT assets that are not inventoried and are not actively managed as part of a vulnerability management program.

I've also seen big differences in these numbers when CISOs do not have good relationships with IT leadership; in cases like this, inaccurate IT inventories seem common and represent a real risk to an organization. In some of the cases I've seen, IT knows where all or most of the assets are but won't proactively work with the CISO to ensure they are all inventoried and patched. As I wrote in *Chapter 8, Ingredients for a Successful Cybersecurity Strategy*, CISOs must work to have good relationships with their stakeholder communities, especially with their IT organizations. CIOs and CTOs also need to realize that their roles have a shared destiny with the CISO; when the vulnerability management program fails, they all fail and should share the "glory." The days when the CISO is the sole scapegoat for IT security failures are largely in the past – regulators, boards, and shareholders know better after decades of data breaches. CISOs that find themselves in this scenario should work to improve their relationship with their IT partners. In some cases, this is easier said than done.

In the example scenario illustrated in *Figure 11.1*, the vulnerability management program continues to manage vulnerabilities and misconfigurations for the same number of IT assets throughout the year. They are blissfully unaware that there are subnets with IT assets they are not scanning for vulnerabilities and misconfigurations. They are also not scanning the new IT assets that have been introduced into the environment during the year. The space between the two lines in the graph represents the risk to the organization.

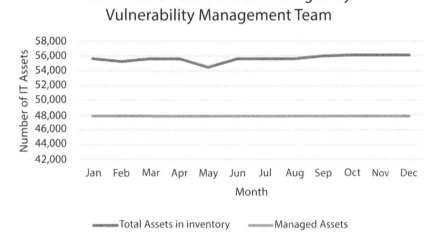

Figure 11.1: An example of trend data illustrating the difference between the total number of IT assets in inventory and the number of assets enrolled in the vulnerability management program

The total number of IT assets and the total number of assets that are scanned for vulnerabilities and misconfigurations every day should be identical to minimize risk. However, there might be good reasons, in large complex environments, for there to be exceptions to this rule. But exceptions still need to be known, understood, and tracked by the teams responsible for managing vulnerabilities; otherwise, the risk to the organization does not get surfaced at the right management level in the organization. Put another way, if the organization is going to have unpatched systems, the decision to do this and for how long needs to be accepted by the highest appropriate management layer and revisited periodically.

The appropriate management layer for decisions like this might not be in IT at all – it depends on the organization and the governance model it has adopted. Remember, a decision to allow an unpatched system to run in the environment is a decision to accept risk on behalf of the entire organization, not just the owner or manager of that asset.

I've seen project managers all too enthusiastic to accept all manner of risks on behalf of their entire organization in order to meet the schedule, budget, and quality goals of their projects. This is despite the fact that the scope of their role is limited to the projects they work on. If a risk is never escalated to the proper management level, it could remain unknown and potentially unmanaged forever. Risk registers should be employed to track risk and periodically revisit risk acceptance and transference decisions.

In environments where the total number of IT assets and the total number of assets that are actively managed for vulnerabilities are meaningfully different, this is an opportunity for CISOs and vulnerability program managers to show how they are working to close that gap and thus reduce risk for the organization. They can use this data to educate IT leadership and their Board of Directors on the risks posed to their organizations. To do this, they can use partial and inaccurate asset inventories and talk about the presence of unmanaged assets. CISOs can provide stakeholders with regular updates on how the difference between the number of assets under the remit of the vulnerability management team and the total number of assets that the organization owns and operates trends over time, as IT and their cybersecurity team work together to reduce and minimize it. This data point represents a real risk to an organization, and the trend data illustrates how the CISO and their vulnerability management team have managed it over time. If this number trends in the wrong direction, it is the responsibility of senior leadership and the management board to recognize this and to help address it.

Figure 11.2 illustrates that the CISO and vulnerability management team have been working with their IT partners to reduce the risk posed by systems that have not been enrolled in their vulnerability management program.

This is a positive trend that the CISO can use to communicate the value of the cybersecurity program.

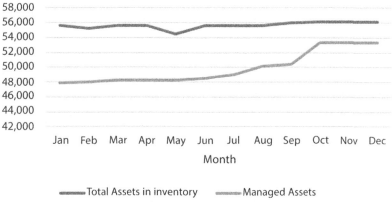

Figure 11.2: An example of trend data illustrating an improving difference between the total number of IT assets in the inventory and the number of assets enrolled in the vulnerability management program

Known unpatched vulnerabilities

Another key data point from vulnerability management programs is the number of known unpatched vulnerabilities that are present in an environment. Remember that there are many reasons why some organizations have unpatched systems in their IT asset inventories. To be perfectly frank, the most frequently cited reason I have heard for this is a lack of investment in vulnerability management programs; understaffed and under-resourced programs simply cannot manage the volume of new vulnerabilities in their environments. Testing security updates and deploying them requires trained people, effective processes, and supporting technologies, in addition to time.

Regardless of the reasons, it is still important to understand which systems are unpatched, the severity of the unpatched vulnerabilities, and the mitigation plan for them. Regularly sharing how the number of unpatched vulnerabilities is reduced over time can help communicate how the CISO and cybersecurity team are contributing to the success of the business. One nuance for rapidly changing environments to consider is how the number of vulnerabilities was reduced, despite material changes to infrastructure or increases in the number of IT assets. To communicate this effectively, CISOs might have to educate some of their stakeholder community on the basics and nuances of vulnerability management metrics, as well as their significance to the overall risk of the organization. There are typically only one or two members on a Board of Directors that have a background in cybersecurity, and even fewer executives with that experience in the typical C-suite. In my experience, educating these stakeholders is time well spent and will help everyone understand the value that the cybersecurity team is providing. In cases where the vulnerability management team is under-resourced, this data can help build the business case for increased investment in an easy-to-understand way.

Figure 11.3 illustrates a scenario where a vulnerability management team was successfully minimizing increases in unpatched vulnerabilities in their environment, despite modest increases in the number of IT assets enrolled in their program. However, an acquisition of a smaller firm that closed in October introduced a large number of new IT assets that the vulnerability management team was expected to manage. This was somewhat disruptive to the program for a short period and led to a dramatic increase in the number of unpatched vulnerabilities, which the team was able to reduce to more typical levels by the end of the quarter.

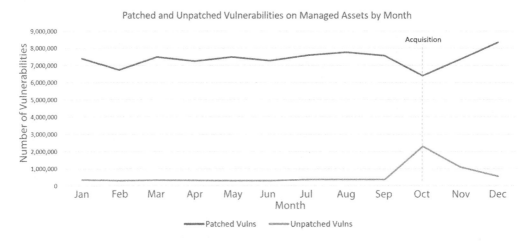

Figure 11.3: An example of trend data illustrating the number of patched vulnerabilities and the number of unpatched vulnerabilities on assets enrolled in an organization's vulnerability management program

With data like this, the CISO and cybersecurity team look like heroes. Without data like this, it would be much harder to describe the scope of the challenge that the acquisition brought with it for the vulnerability management team, the subsequent increased workload, and the positive results. It's not all positive news, though, as this organization has a significant number of unpatched vulnerabilities in its environment, and with a larger number of assets to manage, it will be challenged to keep unpatched vulnerability counts low over time. The CISO should be able to articulate the plan to reduce the number of unpatched vulnerabilities to as close to zero as possible, using this same data to ask for more resources to accelerate that effort. Note that the figures I used in this example are completely fictional; actual data can vary wildly, depending on the number of assets, hardware, software, applications, remediation policies, governance practices, and so on.

But reducing the number of unpatched vulnerabilities can be easier said than done for some organizations. Some known vulnerabilities simply can't be patched. There are numerous reasons for this. For example, many vendors will not offer security updates for software that goes out of support. Some vendors go out of business and, subsequently, security updates for the products their customers have deployed will never be offered. Another common example is legacy applications that have compatibility issues with specific security updates for operating systems or web browsers. In cases like this, often there are workarounds that can be implemented to make exploitation of specific vulnerabilities unlikely or impossible, even without installing the security updates that fix them. Typically, workarounds are meant to be short-term solutions until the security update that fixes the vulnerabilities can be deployed. However, in many environments, workarounds become permanent tenants. Reporting how known unpatched vulnerabilities are being mitigated using workarounds, instead of security updates, can help communicate risk and how it's being managed. Providing categories such as workarounds in progress, workarounds deployed, and no workaround available can help business sponsors see where decisions need to be made. The number of systems with workarounds deployed on them, as well as the severity of the underlying vulnerabilities that they mitigate, provides a nuanced view of risk in the environment. Marry this data with the long-term mitigation plan for the underlying vulnerabilities and CISOs have a risk management story they can share with stakeholders.

Unpatched vulnerabilities by severity

Another potentially powerful data point is the number of vulnerabilities unpatched in an environment, categorized by severity. As I discussed at length in *Chapter 3, Using Vulnerability Trends to Reduce Risk and Costs*, critical and high-severity vulnerabilities that are known to be actively exploited on the internet represent the highest risk because of the probability and impact of their exploitation.

Understanding how many of these vulnerabilities are present in the environment at any time, how long they have been present, and the time to remediation are all important data points to help articulate the risk they pose. Longer-term, this data can help CISOs understand how quickly these risks are being mitigated and uncover the factors that lead to relatively long lifetimes in their environments. This data can help vulnerability management program managers and CISOs build the business case for more resources and better processes and technologies. This data can also be one of the most powerful indicators of the value of cybersecurity and remediation teams and how effectively they have been managing risk for the organization, because the risk these vulnerabilities pose is among the most serious and is easy to articulate to executives and boards.

Don't discount the value of medium-severity vulnerabilities in IT environments for attackers. Because of the monetary value of critical and high-rated vulnerabilities, attackers have been finding ways to use a combination of medium-severity vulnerabilities to compromise systems. CISOs and vulnerability management teams need to manage these vulnerabilities aggressively to minimize risk to their environments. This is another opportunity to show value to the businesses they support and communicate progress by patching these vulnerabilities constantly.

Vulnerabilities by product type

Another potentially useful dataset is vulnerabilities categorized by product type. Let's face it – most of the action occurs on user desktops because they bring threats through perimeter defenses into IT environments. Just as eyes are the windows to the souls of people, so too are browsers to operating systems. Attackers are constantly trying to find and exploit vulnerabilities in web browsers and operating systems.

The data explored in *Figure 11.4* is also touched upon in *Chapter 3, Using Vulnerability Trends to Reduce Risk and Costs*:

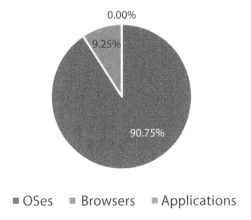

Top 25 Product Vulnerability Distribution
1999 - 2022 (Jan - Jul)

0.00%

9.25%

90.75%

■ OSes ■ Browsers ■ Applications

Figure 11.4: Vulnerabilities in the 25 products with the most CVEs categorized by product type
(1999–2022) (CVE Details, 2022)

Vulnerability management teams can develop similar views for their environments to illustrate the challenge they have and their competence and progress in managing it. Data like this, combined with the previous data points I discussed, can help illustrate where the risk is for an organization and help optimize its treatment. The number of unpatched, critical-, high-, and medium-severity vulnerabilities in operating systems, web browsers, and applications in an environment, along with the number of systems not managed by a vulnerability management program, can help CISOs and their stakeholders understand the risk in their IT environment. Of course, depending on the environment, data pertaining to cloud-based assets, mobile devices, hardware, firmware, appliances, routing and switch equipment, and other technologies that are in use in each IT environment will provide a more complete view. The mix of these technologies and their underlying vulnerabilities is unique to each organization.

Providing executive management teams and board members with quantitative data like this helps them understand reality versus opinion. Without this type of data, it can be much more difficult to make compelling business cases and communicate progress against goals for cybersecurity programs. This data will also make it easier when random executives and other interested parties, such as overly aggressive vendors, ask cybersecurity program stakeholders about the "vulnerability du jour" that makes it into the news headlines. If senior stakeholders know that their CISO, vulnerability management team, and remediation teams are managing vulnerabilities and misconfigurations in their environment competently and diligently, a lot of noise that could otherwise be distracting to CISOs can be filtered out.

This reporting might sound complicated and intimidating to some. The good news is that there are asset management and vulnerability management products available that provide rich analytics and reporting capabilities. CISOs aren't limited to the ideas I've provided in this chapter, as asset management and vulnerability management vendors have lots of great ways to help measure and communicate progress. The key is to use analysis and reporting mechanisms to effectively show stakeholders how your vulnerability management program is reducing risk for the organization and to ask for resources when they are needed.

Although data from vulnerability management programs can be very helpful for CISOs, it only helps them manage two of the five cybersecurity usual suspects. There is potentially much more data that can help CISOs understand and manage the performance and efficacy of their cybersecurity strategies. Let's explore this next using the example I discussed at length in *Chapter 10, Strategy Implementation*, an Attack-Centric Strategy known as the Intrusion Kill Chain framework (Hutchins, E.M., Cloppert, M.J., Amin, R.M., n.d.).

Measuring the performance and efficacy of an Attack-Centric Strategy

As I mentioned in *Chapter 9, Cybersecurity Strategies,* and *Chapter 10, Strategy Implementation*, the Intrusion Kill Chain framework has many attributes that make it an attractive cybersecurity strategy. First, it earned the highest **Cybersecurity Fundamentals Scoring System (CFSS)** estimated total score in *Chapter 9, Cybersecurity Strategies.*

This means it has the greatest potential to fully mitigate the Cybersecurity Usual Suspects. Additionally, this approach can be used in on-premises environments and hybrid and cloud environments. Perhaps the thing I like most about this framework is that its performance and efficacy can be measured in a relatively straightforward way. Let's examine this in detail.

Performing intrusion reconstructions

This will likely seem odd when you read it, but when it comes to measuring the performance and efficacy of a cybersecurity strategy, intrusion attempts are gifts from attackers to defenders. They are gifts because they test the implementation and operation of defenders' cybersecurity strategies. But in order to derive value from intrusion attempts, every successful, partially successful, and failed intrusion attempt must be decomposed and studied. In doing this, there are two key questions to be answered. First, how far did attackers get with their Intrusion Kill Chain before they were detected and ultimately stopped? Second, how did attackers defeat or bypass the layers of mitigating controls that the cybersecurity team deployed to break their Intrusion Kill Chain? Put another way, if attackers made it to phase four of their Intrusion Kill Chain, how did they get past all the mitigations layered in phases one, two, and three?

These are the central questions that intrusion reconstructions (Hutchins, E.M., Cloppert, M.J., Amin, R.M., n.d.) should help answer. In seeking the answers to these two questions, intrusion reconstructions should also answer many other questions that will help measure the performance and efficacy of each implementation of this approach. As you'll see as I describe this process, the underlying theme of these questions is whether the people, processes, and technologies that are working to break attackers' Intrusion Kill Chains are effective. We want to uncover if any changes are required in each phase of our Attack-Centric Strategy. Let's get started.

The concept of intrusion reconstructions is discussed in Lockheed Martin's paper on Intrusion Kill Chains (Hutchins, E.M., Cloppert, M.J., Amin, R.M., n.d.). Again, I recommend reading this paper. The approach I'll describe in this chapter is slightly different from the approach described in Lockheed Martin's paper. There are at least a few ways intrusion reconstructions can be done; I'll describe one way that I've used with some success in the past.

This approach assumes that defenders will not be able to perform attribution with any confidence, so it doesn't rely on attribution the way that other approaches might. I consider this an advantage, as strong attribution is aspirational and is less likely as attackers become more sophisticated. The goal of this approach to intrusion reconstructions is to identify areas where the implementation of the Intrusion Kill Chain framework can be improved, not identify attackers and take military or legal action against them.

Let me offer some advice on when to do intrusion reconstructions. Do not perform reconstructions while incident response activities are underway. Using valuable resources and expertise that have a role in your organization's incident response process, during an active incident, is an unnecessary distraction.

The reconstruction can wait until periods of crisis have passed. Ideally, reconstructions can be done while the details are still fresh in participants' minds in the days or weeks after the incident has passed. However, if your organization is always in crisis mode, then ignore this advice and get access to people and information when you can. Maybe you can help break the crisis cycle by identifying what deficiencies are contributing to it.

To perform an intrusion reconstruction, I strongly suggest that you have at least one representative from all the teams that are responsible for cybersecurity strategy, architecture, protection, detection, response, and recovery. In really large environments, this can be scoped to the relevant teams that were responsible for the areas involved in the intrusion attempt. Once the organization gets good at doing reconstructions, the number of participants can likely be reduced even more. But you need the expertise and visibility that each team has to reconstruct what happened during each failed, partially successful, and fully successful intrusion attempt. Remember that one of the modifications we made to the Courses of Action Matrix (Hutchins, E.M., Cloppert, M.J., Amin, R.M., n.d.) in *Chapter 10*, *Strategy Implementation*, was adding a "data consumer point of contact" for each mitigation. This information can be helpful in identifying the right people from different teams to participate in reconstructions.

A decision should be made regarding whether to invite vendors to participate in these meetings. I have found it helpful to have trusted representatives from some of the cybersecurity vendors we used participating in intrusion reconstructions.

There are at least a couple of benefits to this approach. First, vendors should be able to bring expertise about their products and services and provide insights that might otherwise be missed. Second, it's important to share the "gifts" that attackers give you with the vendors that you've selected to help you defend against them. These exercises can inform your vendors' efforts to make better products, which your organization and others can benefit from. But it also gives you the opportunity to see how helpful your vendors really are willing to be, and whether they are willing to be held accountable for their shortcomings. I found that some of the vendors I used, who I thought would have my back during security incidents, folded up like a circus tent and left town when I really needed them. During intrusion reconstructions, these same vendors had the courage to participate, but typically blamed their customers for their products' failure to perform as expected. If you do enough reconstruction exercises with vendors, you'll likely be able to determine whether they really have the desire and capability to help your organization in the way you thought they would. This knowledge comes in handy later when their product license renewal dates approach. I'll discuss this more later in this chapter.

All that said, inviting vendors to participate in reconstructions also has risk associated with it. Simply put, some vendors are really poor at keeping confidential information confidential. My advice is to discuss including vendors in these meetings, on a case-by-case basis, with the stakeholders that participate in the reconstruction exercises. If a vendor adds enough value and is trustworthy, then there is a case for including them in these exercises. Discussing this idea with senior leadership for their counsel is also a prudent step prior to finalizing a decision to include vendors in these exercises.

If your organization has a forensics team or uses a vendor for forensics, these experts can be incredibly helpful for intrusion reconstruction exercises. The tools and skills they have can help determine if systems in the reconstruction have been compromised, when, and likely how. In my experience, I've come across two flavors of forensics teams.

The first is the traditional forensics team, which has certified forensics examiners who follow strict procedures to maintain the integrity of the evidence they collect. In my experience with organizations that have this type of forensics team, they have the need for a full-time team of experts that can preserve evidence, maintain the chain of custody, and potentially testify in court in the criminal matters they help investigate. More often, organizations outsource this type of work.

The other flavor of forensics team, which I see much more often, performs a different function and is sometimes simply referred to as Incident Responders. They too seek to determine if systems have been compromised. But these teams typically do not have certified forensics professionals, do not maintain the integrity of evidence, and do not plan to testify in a court of law. In fact, many times, their efforts to determine if a system has been compromised result in destroying what would be considered evidence in a criminal proceeding. This is where I've encountered interesting and sometimes provincial attitudes among certified forensics experts, as many of them wouldn't call these efforts forensics at all because they destroy evidence rather than properly preserve it. But these folks need to keep in mind that many engineers that wear pinky rings (Order of the Engineer, n.d.) resent IT engineers using "engineer" in their titles; architects that design buildings don't like IT architects using their title either, and the title "security researcher" makes many academic researchers cringe. But I digress. The reality is, not every organization wants to spend time and effort tracking down attackers and trying to prosecute them in a court of law. Organizations need to decide which flavor of forensics professionals they need and can afford. Both types of forensics experts can be worth their weight in gold when they help determine if systems have been compromised and participate in intrusion reconstruction exercises.

Who should lead reconstruction exercises? I recommend that the individual or group responsible for the cybersecurity strategy leads these exercises. This individual or group is ultimately responsible for the performance and efficacy of the overall strategy. They are also likely responsible for making adjustments as needed to ensure the success of the strategy. An alternative to the strategy group is the **Incident Response (IR)** team. The IR team should have most, if not all, of the details required to lead an intrusion reconstruction. If they don't, you've just identified the first area for improvement.

The IR team manages incidents, so they really should have most of the information related to partially and fully successful intrusion attempts at their fingertips. But they might not be involved in failed attempts that don't qualify as incidents. In these cases, SOC personnel, operations personnel, and architects likely have key information for the reconstruction.

Keep in mind that the goal isn't to triage every port scan that happens on the organization's internet-facing firewalls. I suggest getting agreement among the groups that will participate in reconstruction exercises most often on a principle that is used to determine the types of intrusions that reconstructions should be performed on. That is, define the characteristics of intrusion attempts that determine whether a formal reconstruction is performed. As shown in *Figure 11.5*, using our updated Courses of Action Matrix from *Chapter 10, Strategy Implementation*, an effective principle could be that any intrusion that makes it further than the Deny action in the Delivery phase should be reconstructed. A much less aggressive principle could be that any intrusion attempt that results in a Restore action should be reconstructed. There are numerous other options between these two examples.

The goal of such a principle is to impose consistency that helps appropriately balance risk and the valuable time of reconstruction participants. This principle doesn't need to be chiseled into stone-it can change over time. When an organization first starts performing reconstructions, it can have a relatively aggressive principle that enables it to learn quickly. Then, once lessons from reconstructions have "normalized" somewhat, a less aggressive principle can be adopted. But getting agreement among the stakeholders in these reconstruction exercises on the principle used to initiate them is important for their long-term success and, therefore, the success of the cybersecurity strategy. Too few reconstructions relative to intrusion attempts could mean the organization isn't paying enough attention to the gifts it's being given by attackers and is potentially adjusting too slowly to attacks. Too many reconstructions can be disruptive and counterproductive. The agreed-upon principle should strike the right balance for the stakeholder community over time.

Kill Chain Phase	Detect	Deny	Disrupt	Degrade	Deceive	Limit	Restore
Reconnaissance I							
Delivery							
Exploitation							
Installation							
Command and Control (C2)							
Reconnaissance II							
Actions on Objectives							

Figure 11.5: An example of an updated Courses of Action Matrix (Hutchins, E.M., Cloppert, M.J., Amin, R.M., n.d.)

Once the appropriate participants, or their delegates, have been identified, and an intrusion reconstruction leader is ready to facilitate, a reconstruction meeting can be scheduled. Providing participants with enough lead time and guidance to gather the appropriate data for reconstruction will help save time and frustration. In my experience, some reconstruction exercises are straightforward because the intrusion attempt was detected and stopped in an early phase. In these cases, the number of participants and the amount of data they need to reconstruct the intrusion attempt can be relatively minor. Subsequently, the amount of time typically needed for this exercise is relatively short, such as 45 minutes or an hour, for example. If you are just starting to do reconstructions in your organization, you'll naturally need a little more time than you'll need after becoming accustomed to them. For more complicated intrusion attempts, especially when attackers make it to the later stages of their Kill Chain, more participants with more data might be required, increasing the amount of time needed for reconstruction exercises.

Many of the organizations I've worked with label security incidents with code names. All subsequent communications about an incident use its code name. This way, if an email or other communications are seen by someone who has not been read into the incident, its context and significance are not obvious. Communications about, and invitations to, intrusion reconstructions should use incident code names when organizations label incidents with them. If you decide to use incident code names, be thoughtful about the names you use, avoiding labels that are potentially offensive. This includes names in languages other than English.

Consider the potential impact on the reputation of an organization if the code name ever became public knowledge. Stay away from themes that are inconsistent with the organization's brand or the brand it aspires to build in the minds of its customers. There really is no compelling business reason to use anything but benign codenames. These are boring but effective on multiple levels.

Now we have a code name for our reconstruction exercise, participants that are going to bring relevant data, potentially some trustworthy vendors that will participate, and a leader to facilitate the exercise.

The point of the exercise is to reconstruct the steps that attackers took in each phase of their Kill Chain. It might not be possible to do this with complete certainty, and some assumptions about their tactics and techniques might be necessary. But the more detail the reconstruction can include, the easier it will be to identify areas where people, processes, and technologies performed as expected or underperformed. Be prepared to take detailed notes during these exercises. A product of intrusion reconstruction exercises should be a report that contains the details of the intrusion attempt, as well as the performance of the defenses that the cybersecurity team had in place. These artifacts will potentially have value for many years as they will provide helpful continuity of knowledge about past attacks, even when key staff leave the organization. Put another way, when the lessons learned from these intrusion attempts are documented, they are available for current and future personnel to learn from. This is another reason I call intrusion attempts "gifts."

Our updated Kill Chain framework has seven phases. Where should a reconstruction exercise start? In the first phase, or perhaps the last phase? The answer to this question is, it depends. Sometimes, an intrusion is straightforward and can be charted from beginning to end in sequential order. However, with complicated intrusions or intrusions that started months or years earlier, it might not be prudent or possible to approach a reconstruction that way. Start with the phase that you have the best information on and the most certainty about. This could be late in the Kill Chain. From your starting point, build a timeline in both directions, using the data and insights that the reconstruction participants can offer. It might not be possible to build the entire timeline because of a lack of data, or because of uncertainty.

The more details the reconstruction uncovers, the better, as this will help identify opportunities for improvement, gaps, and failures in defenses. In my example, I will simply start at the first phase and work forward through the Kill Chain. But just be aware that this might not be possible to do for every intrusion. Let's start with the Reconnaissance I phase.

It might not be possible to attribute any particular threat actor's activities in the Reconnaissance I phase, prior to their attack. With so much network traffic constantly bombarding all internet-connected devices, it is typically challenging to pick out specific probes and reconnaissance activities conducted by specific attackers. But it's not impossible. This is an area where the combination of **Artificial Intelligence (AI)**, **Machine Learning (ML)**, good threat intelligence, and granular logs is very promising. Using AI/ML systems to churn through massive amounts of log data, such as network flow data, DNS logs, authentication and authorization logs, API activity logs, and others, in near real time to find specific attackers' activities is no longer science fiction. Cloud services can do this today at scale. The icing on the cake is that you can get security findings read to your SOC analysts by Amazon Alexa (Worrell, 2018)!

These are the types of capabilities that, until recently, were only possible in science fiction. But now, anyone with a credit card and a little time can achieve this with the capabilities that cloud computing provides. Truly amazing! I'll discuss cloud computing more in the next chapter.

Collecting data and insights from the Delivery phase of an attack is obviously super-important. The key question is, how did the attackers defeat or bypass the layers of mitigations that the cybersecurity team deployed to break this phase of their Kill Chain? How did they successfully deliver their weapon and what people, processes, and technologies were involved?

To answer these questions, I have found it useful to draw system flow charts on a whiteboard during the reconstruction exercise with the participants' help. Start by drawing the infrastructure that was involved with as much detail as possible, including perimeter defenses, servers, clients, applications, system names, IP addresses, and so on. Draw a map of the infrastructure involved and chart how data is supposed to flow in this infrastructure, the protocols used, authentication and authorization boundaries, the identities involved, storage, and so on. Then, draw how the attackers delivered the weapon during their intrusion attempt and what happened during delivery.

This is another place where the MITRE ATT&CK framework can be super helpful. Its Initial Access tactic contains a myriad of ways attackers can deliver their weapons. Use this knowledge base to help identify the specific techniques attackers used, and accelerate intrusion reconstructions in the process.

What enabled the attacker's success in this phase? The answer to this question involves asking and answering numerous other questions. Let me give you some examples. A useful data point in an intrusion reconstruction is how long it took for the attack to be detected. Building an attack timeline can be a useful tool to help determine how an attack was executed. In the context of the Delivery phase, was the delivery of the weapon detected, and what control detected it? If delivery wasn't detected, document which controls were supposed to detect it. If there is a clear gap here in your implementation of the Kill Chain framework, document that. This information will be very useful later when you remediate deficiencies in the implementation of the strategy.

Were there any controls that should have detected delivery, but failed to do so? Why did these controls fail to operate as expected? Did they fail because they simply did not do what the vendor said they would do? Did they fail because of integrations or automation between controls, or systems not working as intended? This is where log data and other sources of data from systems in the reconstruction flow chart can be very helpful. Try to piece together how the weapon was delivered, step by step, through data in logs of various systems in the flow chart.

Does it look like all these systems performed as expected? If not, identify anomalies and weak links. In some cases, log data might not be available because logging wasn't turned on or aggressive data retention controls deleted the log data. Is there a good justification for not enabling logging on these systems and storing logs to help in the future? Again, ATT&CK might be able to provide a list of mitigations that you can check in your reconstruction, to ensure its comprehensive.

Was there enough data to determine how the weapon was delivered? Sometimes, it's simply not possible to determine how the weapon was delivered with the data that is available. Some IR teams refer to the first system that was compromised in an intrusion as "patient zero." In some intrusions, the attacker's entry point is very obvious and can be tracked back to an email, a visit to a malicious website, a USB drive, malware, and so on. In other cases, if the initial compromise was achieved weeks, months, or years earlier, and attackers were adept at covering their tracks, finding patient zero is aspirational, and simply might not be possible. Think about what would have helped you in this scenario. Would increasing the verbosity of logging have helped? Would archiving logs for longer periods or shipping logs offsite have helped? Is there some capability that you don't currently have that would have helped fill this gap?

Did the data consumers for the Delivery phase mitigations get the data they needed to detect and break this phase? For example, did the SOC get the data it needed to detect intrusion? Did the data consumers identified in the updated Courses of Action Matrix receive or have access to the data as intended? If not, what went wrong? Did the data delivery mechanism fail, or was the required data filtered out at the destination for some reason? There could have been multiple failures in the collection, delivery, and analysis of the data. Dig into this to identify the things that did not work as planned and document them.

Did the controls, automation, and integrations work as expected but people or processes were the sources of the failure? This scenario happens more than you might think. The architecture was sound, the systems worked as expected, the technologies performed as expected, the weapon was detected, but no one was paying attention, or the alert was noticed but was dismissed. Unfortunately, people and process failures are as common, if not more common, than technical control failures. Failures in SOC processes, poor decision-making, vendors that make mistakes, and sometimes just laziness among key personnel can lead to failures to detect and break attacks.

Did attackers and/or defenders get lucky anywhere in this phase of the attack? Some security professionals I've met have told me they don't believe in luck. But I attribute this belief to naivety. I've seen attacks succeed because of a comedy of errors that likely could not be repeated or duplicated.

Combinations of people, processes, technologies, and circumstances can lead to attack scenarios as likely as winning a lottery. Don't discount the role that luck can play. Remember that not all risks can truly be identified; "black swan" events can happen (Taleb, 2007).

Once the reconstruction team understands how the Delivery phase of the attack was accomplished and this has been documented, we can move on to the next phase of the attack, the Exploitation phase (Hutchins, E.M., Cloppert, M.J., Amin, R.M., n.d.). Here, the reconstruction team will repeat the process, using data to try to determine if exploitation was attempted, detected, and stopped. The same questions we asked for the Delivery phase apply in this phase as well. What controls failed to prevent and detect exploitation? Use the techniques and sub-techniques in ATT&CK's Execution tactic as a source of questions to ask here. Which techniques in the Execution tactic did the attacker use? Did you have any mitigations deployed that should have stopped or detected this technique? Where did gaps in protection and detection controls contribute to attacker success in this phase of their attack?

Did vendors' cybersecurity mitigations work as advertised? Did data consumers get the data they required to detect and break this phase? Did the IR process start and work as planned? What can we learn from attackers' success in this phase to make such success harder or impossible in the future? Document your findings.

Continue to perform this investigation for all the phases of the Kill Chain. There might be phases where nothing occurred because attackers were stopped prior to those phases. Note where and when the attack was successfully detected and successfully broken. If the attack had not been broken in the phase it was, would the mitigations layered in later phases have successfully detected and stopped the attack? Continue to make full use of ATT&CK as a knowledge base of specific techniques and mitigations in your reconstruction, as a source of questions to ask. Which techniques in ATT&CK did the attacker use, did your organization have any of the mitigations ATT&CK suggests for those techniques deployed and did they work as expected? This can help ensure your intrusion reconstructions are comprehensive and accelerate them. Be as candid with yourselves as possible in this assessment; platitudes, optimism, and plans in the undefined future may not be enough to break the next attacker's Intrusion Kill Chain. However, sober determination to make it as difficult as possible for attackers can be helpful. Remember to document these thoughts.

Now the reconstruction is complete, and you have asked and answered as many questions as needed to uncover what happened, ideally in every step of the attack. Next, let me provide some examples of the specific actionable things the reconstruction should have identified in the wake of failed, partially successful, and fully successful attacks.

Using intrusion reconstruction results

First, recall the discussion on identifying gaps and areas of over- and under-investment in *Chapter 10, Strategy Implementation*. An intrusion reconstruction can confirm some of the analysis on gaps and under-investments that were done while planning the implementation of this strategy. For example, if a gap in detection in the Delivery phase was identified during planning and later intrusion reconstruction data also illustrates this same gap, this is strangely reassuring news. Now, the CISO has more data to help build the business case for investment to mitigate this gap. It's one thing for a CISO to say they need to invest in detection capabilities or bad things can happen. But such requests are much more powerful when CISOs can show senior executives and the Board of Directors that attackers have been actively using known gaps.

It counters any notion that the risk is theoretical when CISOs can provide evidence that the risk is real. It also helps build a sense of urgency where there was none before. If the intrusion attempt led to unplanned expenses related to response and recovery activities, this will help illustrate the current and potential future costs related to the gap. This data can inform both the probability and the impact sides of the risk equation, making it easier to compare to other risks. Using data like this, CISOs can give their management boards updates on gaps and under-investment areas at every cybersecurity program review meeting until they are mitigated.

When reconstruction exercises uncover previously unknown gaps or areas of under-investment, this truly is a gift from attackers. In doing so, attackers provide CISOs valuable insights into deficiencies in the implementations of their strategies, as well as a clear call to action to implement new mitigations or improve existing ones. Intrusion reconstruction data can also help to inform cybersecurity investment roadmaps. Remember that stopping attackers as early in the Intrusion Kill Chain as possible is highly preferable to stopping them in later phases. Reconstruction data can help cybersecurity teams identify and prioritize mitigations that will help make it harder or impossible for attackers to make it to later phases of their attack. Helping cybersecurity teams understand deficiencies and areas for improvement in the Delivery and Exploitation phases is a key outcome of intrusion reconstruction exercises. This data can then be used to plan the investment roadmap that charts the people, processes, and technologies an organization plans to deploy and when. Since most organizations have resource constraints, reconstruction data and the investment roadmaps they inform can become central to a cybersecurity team's planning processes.

Remember those cybersecurity imperatives and their supporting projects I discussed in *Chapter 8, Ingredients for a Successful Cybersecurity Strategy*? An imperative is a big, audacious, multi-year goal, ideally aligned with an organization's business objectives.

Upgrading to a much-needed modern identity system or finally getting rid of VPNs in favor of modern remote access solutions for thousands of Information Workers are two examples. Reconstruction data can help provide supporting data for cybersecurity imperatives and provide a shared sense of purpose for the staff that work on them. Conversely, reconstruction data might not always support the notion that planned imperatives are the right direction for the organization.

There's no expectation that these will necessarily align, especially in large organizations with complex environments and multiple imperatives. But when lightning strikes and intrusion reconstruction data suggests that an imperative is critical to the organization, it can supercharge the project teams that are working on it. This type of positive momentum can be beneficial by helping to maintain project timelines and getting projects across their finish lines.

Identifying lame controls

Another potential action area stemming from an intrusion reconstruction is correcting mitigations that failed to perform as expected. These are controls that have been deployed and are actively managed, but did not protect, detect, or help respond to the intrusion attempt as designed. To state the obvious, CISOs and security teams can't rely on controls that don't work the way they should. There is a range of possible root causes for controls that fail.

A common root cause for failure is that the control doesn't actually perform the function that the security team thought it did. Mismatches between security controls' functions and security teams' expectations are, unfortunately, very common. Some controls are designed to mitigate very specific threats under specific circumstances. But such nuances can get lost in vendors' marketing materials and sales motions. This is a critical function that architects play on many cybersecurity teams: to really understand the threats that each control mitigates and how controls need to be orchestrated to protect, detect, and respond to threats to their organizations. They should be thoughtfully performing the cybersecurity capabilities inventories I discussed in *Chapter 10, Strategy Implementation*, and making changes to those inventories to minimize gaps and areas of under-investment. But, as I previously mentioned, the maturity of the controls' implementation is an important factor, as is the consumption of the data generated by controls. This is something architects can have a hand in, that is, inventorying and planning, but data consumers, operations personnel, and SOC engineers, among others, need to help complete this picture. Otherwise, mismatches between control functions and expectations can burn the cybersecurity team.

Another common cause for mitigations failing to perform as expected is they simply don't work the way vendors say they work. I know this is a shocking revelation for a few people, and it's an all-too-common challenge for security teams.

If vendors kept all their promises, then there wouldn't be a global cybersecurity challenge, nor would there be a multi-billion-dollar cybersecurity industry. This is one reason it is prudent to have layers of defenses, so that when one control fails, other controls can help mitigate the threat. This is an area where CISOs can share and learn a lot from other CISOs. Professional experience with specific vendors and specific products is often the best reference to have.

Another common reason for mitigations failing to protect, detect, or respond is that the trusted computing base that they rely on has been compromised. That is, attackers have undermined the mitigations by compromising the hardware and/or software they depend on to run. For example, one of the first things many attackers do once they use one or more of the Cybersecurity Usual Suspects to compromise a system is disable the anti-malware software running on it. A less obviously visible tactic is to add directories to the anti-malware engine's exceptions list so that the attacker's tools do not get scanned or detected. Once attackers or malware initially compromise systems, it is common for them to undermine the controls that have been deployed to protect systems and detect attackers. Therefore, becoming excellent at cybersecurity fundamentals is a prerequisite to deploying advanced cybersecurity capabilities. Don't bother deploying that expensive attacker detection system that uses AI to perform behavioral analysis unless you are also dedicated to managing the cybersecurity fundamentals for that system. Attackers will undermine those advanced cybersecurity capabilities if unpatched vulnerabilities, security misconfigurations, and weak, leaked, or stolen credentials enable them to access the systems they run on. I discussed this at length in earlier chapters, but I'll reiterate it here again. No cybersecurity strategy, not even a high-scoring strategy like the Intrusion Kill Chain framework, will be effective if the cybersecurity fundamentals are not managed effectively.

Additionally, it's important that the cybersecurity products themselves are effectively managed with the cybersecurity fundamentals in mind. Anti-malware engines and other common mitigations have been sources of exploitable vulnerabilities and security misconfigurations in the past. They too must be effectively managed so that they don't increase the attack surface area instead of decreasing it.

Another action item, related to failed controls, that can emerge from intrusion reconstruction exercises is addressing control integrations that failed. For example, an intrusion attempt wasn't detected until relatively late in an attacker's Kill Chain because, although a control successfully detected it in an earlier phase, that data never made it to the SIEM. Broken and degraded integrations like this example are common in large, complex IT environments and can be difficult to detect.

It would be ideal if cybersecurity teams could simply rely on data consumers to identify anomalies in data reporting from cybersecurity controls, but in many cases, the absence of data isn't an anomaly. Technical debt in many organizations can make it challenging to identify and remediate poor integrations. Many times, such integrations are performed by vendors or professional services organizations who have limited knowledge of their customers' IT environments. This is where SOC engineers can be valuable; they can help ensure integrations are working as expected and improve them over time.

Learning from failure

In addition to identifying gaps and suboptimal controls and integrations, intrusion reconstructions can help CISOs and cybersecurity teams confirm that they have the right investment priorities. Data from reconstructions can help re-prioritize investments so that the most critical areas are addressed first. Not only can this data help rationalize investment decisions, but it can also help CISOs justify their investment decisions, especially in the face of criticism from CIOs and CTOs who have different opinions and possibly differing agendas. Investing in areas that break attackers' efforts instead of new capabilities that IT has dependencies on, might not be a popular choice among IT leadership. But using intrusion reconstruction data to defend such decisions will make it harder for others to disagree.

Besides identifying technologies that didn't work as expected, intrusion reconstructions can provide an opportunity to improve people and processes that performed below expectations. For example, in cases where lapses in governance led to poor security outcomes, this can be good data to help drive positive changes in governance processes and associated training. If complying with an internal standard or an industry standard wasn't helpful in protecting, detecting, or responding to an attack, Intrusion reconstruction might be an impetus for change.

Allowing people in an organization to learn from failure is important. After spending time and effort to understand and recover from failures, organizations can increase their return on these investments by disseminating lessons from failures to the people in the organization who will benefit the most from them. Reconstruction data can help build a case for social engineering training for executives or the entire organization, for example.

Identifying helpful vendors

Vendors are important partners for organizations as they typically provide technologies, services, people, and processes that their customers rely on. Intrusion reconstruction data can help identify vendors that are performing at or above expectations. It can also help identify vendors that are failing to perform as expected.

This includes how vendors participate in intrusion reconstruction exercises themselves. Reconstruction exercises can help reveal those vendors who tend to blame their customers for failures in their products' and services' performance, which is rarely helpful. This, along with data on how vendors' products and services performed, can help inform vendor product license renewal negotiations. Once security teams get a taste of how the vendors' products really perform and how helpful they are willing to be during intrusions, they might be willing to pay much less for them in the future, or not willing to use them at all. If your organization doesn't already do this, I suggest maintaining a license renewal and end-of-life "horizon list" that shows you when key dates related to renewals and products' end of life are approaching.

Ensure your organization gives itself enough prior notice so it can spend a reasonable amount of time to re-evaluating whether better mitigations exist. After deploying and operating vendors' products, the organization likely has much more data of better quality on its current vendors' performance to inform product evaluations than it did when it originally procured them.

Reward the vendors who are helpful and consider replacing vendors that don't understand their core value is supposed to be customer service. Looking at all the vendors I mentioned in *Chapter 10, Strategy Implementation*, in addition to all the vendors I didn't mention, there is no shortage of companies competing for your organization's business. Don't settle for vendors that blame your organization for their failures. Even if it is true, they should be helping you overcome these challenges instead of playing the blame game. Intrusion reconstruction exercises are their opportunity to prove they are invested in your success, instead of being an uninterested third party on the sidelines, waiting for the next license renewal date. If they have been trying to help your organization get more value out of its products but your organization hasn't been receptive, then this should be reconciled prior to making rash decisions. Replacing good vendors that have been constantly swimming upstream to help your organization doesn't help you and could set your cybersecurity program back months, or even years. But their products either work as advertised and they are willing to help you get them into that state in a reasonable period of time, or they should be replaced. Otherwise, they just increase the attack surface area while using resources that could be used elsewhere to better protect, detect, and respond to threats.

Intrusion reconstruction data is likely the best data you'll have to truly gauge your cybersecurity vendors' performance. Use it in license renewal negotiations to counter marketing fluff and sales executives' promises that the latest version or the next version solves all your challenges, including their inability to provide essential levels of customer service. Sometimes, desperate vendors, sensing they are going to lose business, decide to "end-run" the CISO and cybersecurity team by appealing directly to other executives or the Board of Directors. This can turn out to be suboptimal for CISOs that get saddled with products that don't help them.

But it's harder for executives and the board to award more business to such vendors when the CISO has been briefing them on intrusion reconstruction results, as well as showing them how helpful or unhelpful some of their vendors have been. If executives still decide to award more business to vendors who, the data indicates, have not been performing to expectations, they have decided to accept risk on behalf of the entire organization. CISOs get stuck managing this type of risk all the time. But as the data continues to mount, it will become harder for everyone to simply accept the status quo. Data, instead of opinion alone, should help organizations make better decisions about the cybersecurity capabilities they invest in.

Informing internal assessments

The last potential action item area stemming from the results of intrusion reconstructions that I'll discuss is penetration testing and Red/Blue and Purple Team exercises. Many organizations invest in penetration testing and Red/Blue and Purple Teams so that they can simulate attacks in a more structured and controlled way. Lessons from intrusion reconstruction exercises can inform penetration testing and Red Team/Purple Team exercises. If reconstruction exercises have uncovered weaknesses or seams that attackers can use in an implementation of a cybersecurity strategy, these should be further tested until they are adequately addressed. When professional penetration testers and Red Teams are provided with intrusion reconstruction results, it can help them devise tests that will ensure these weaknesses have been properly mitigated. Ideally, penetration testers and Red/Blue and Purple Teams find implementation deficiencies before attackers get the chance to.

Adversary emulations leveraging ATT&CK

Making the most of all the "gifts" that attackers give your security team by testing your defenses is important. However, the objective is to break their Kill Chains as early as possible. To do this, it is prudent for security teams to test and assess the implementation of their cybersecurity strategies on an ongoing basis. Large, complex enterprise IT environments are constantly changing, sometimes in unexpected ways. At the same time, attackers are evolving their attacks and potentially becoming more effective. Don't wait for attackers to show you where underperforming controls and gaps are – find them, before they do, to minimize potential damage and costs.

You might recall in *Chapter 9, Cybersecurity Strategies*, that I mentioned several different ways that the ATT&CK framework can be used. ATT&CK can be leveraged for Cyber Threat Intelligence purposes, threat detection, assessments, and emulating attackers. Subsequently, ATT&CK can be an invaluable tool for testing and assessing how strategy implementations are working.

Fortunately, MITRE published a series of blog posts that provide guidance on how to get started using ATT&CK for each of these purposes. If you are planning to use ATT&CK for any of these purposes, these blog posts are recommended reading. They provide a security team maturity model (just starting, mid-level, and advanced) and guidance for teams at each level in the model:

- Getting Started with ATT&CK: Threat Intelligence (`https://medium.com/mitre-attack/getting-started-with-attack-cti-4eb205be4b2f`)

- Getting Started with ATT&CK: Detection and Analytics (`https://medium.com/mitre-attack/getting-started-with-attack-detection-a8e49e4960d0`)

- Getting Started with ATT&CK: Adversary Emulation and Red Teaming (`https://medium.com/mitre-attack/getting-started-with-attack-red-29f074ccf7e3`)

- Getting Started with ATT&CK: Assessments and Engineering (`https://medium.com/mitre-attack/getting-started-with-attack-assessment-cc0b01769cb4`)

For example, the blog post on adversary emulation and Red Teaming provides a helpful definition as a starting point, followed by step-by-step guidance on how to leverage ATT&CK in this context, for each of the three security team maturity levels.

> *"For those unfamiliar with it, adversary emulation is a type of red team engagement that mimics a known threat to an organization by blending in threat intelligence to define what actions and behaviors the red team uses. This is what makes adversary emulation different from penetration testing and other forms of red teaming. Adversary emulators construct a scenario to test certain aspects of an adversary's* **tactics, techniques, and procedures** *(TTPs). The red team then follows the scenario while operating on a target network in order to test how defenses might fare against the emulated adversary" (Blake Strom, Tim Schulz, and Katie Nickels, 2019).*

These blog posts reference numerous ATT&CK resources that you should be aware of. In the context of emulating attackers, MITRE provides "adversary emulation plans." The purpose of these plans is to "allow defenders to more effectively test their networks and defenses by enabling red teams to more actively model adversary behavior, as described by ATT&CK" (MITRE, n.d.). You can find these adversary emulation plans here: `https://attack.mitre.org/resources/adversary-emulation-plans/`.

This concludes our discussion on measuring the performance and effectiveness of cybersecurity strategies.

Summary

Cybersecurity teams need to measure many different things for a range of purposes, including complying with regulatory, industry, and internal standards. However, this chapter focused on how CISOs and cybersecurity teams can measure the performance and efficacy of the implementation of their cybersecurity strategy, using an Attack-Centric Strategy as an example.

Data helps CISOs manage their cybersecurity programs and investments and helps them prove that their cybersecurity program has been effective and constantly improving; it can also help illustrate the effectiveness of corrective actions after issues are detected. A well-run vulnerability management program is not optional; leveraging data from it represents one of the easiest ways for CISOs to communicate effectiveness and progress. Vulnerability management teams should scan everything in their inventories every single day for vulnerabilities and misconfigurations. This can help minimize the amount of time that unmitigated vulnerabilities and misconfigurations are present and exploitable. Valuable trend data can emerge from vulnerability management scanning data over time. Some examples of valuable data include:

- The number of assets under the remit of the vulnerability management team versus the total number of assets that the organization owns and operates.
- The number of vulnerabilities unpatched in the environment by vulnerability severity.
- Vulnerabilities by product type can help illustrate where the most risk exists in an environment; the number of unpatched, critical-, high-, and medium-severity vulnerabilities in operating systems, web browsers, and applications in an environment, along with the number of unmanaged systems, can help CISOs and their stakeholders understand the risk in their IT environment.

Attack-Centric strategies, like the Intrusion Kill Chain, make it relatively easy to measure performance and efficacy; to do this, intrusion reconstructions are used. Intrusion reconstruction results can help CISOs in many different ways, not least by identifying mitigations that failed to perform as expected. To derive value from intrusion attempts, every successful, partially successful, and failed intrusion attempt must be decomposed and studied to answer two key questions:

1. How far did attackers get with their Intrusion Kill Chain before they were detected and ultimately stopped?

2. How did attackers defeat or bypass all the layers of mitigating controls that the cybersecurity team deployed to break their Intrusion Kill Chain before they were stopped?

Organizations that have the resources should test and assess the effectiveness of their strategy implementation on an ongoing basis. This can help security teams discover and address shortcomings before attackers have a chance to.

In the next and final chapter, we'll explore some modern approaches to cybersecurity and compliance.

References

- Order of the Engineer (n.d.). Retrieved from Order of the Engineer: `https://order-of-the-engineer.org/`

- CVE Details (2022). *Top 50 Products By Total Number Of "Distinct" Vulnerabilities*. Retrieved from CVE Details: `https://www.cvedetails.com/top-50-products.php`

- Hutchins, E.M., Cloppert, M.J., Amin, R.M. Ph.D. (n.d.). *Intelligence-Driven Computer Network Defense Informed by Analysis of Adversary Campaigns and Intrusion Kill Chains*. Retrieved from Lockheed Martin: `https://lockheedmartin.com/content/dam/lockheed-martin/rms/documents/cyber/LM-White-Paper-Intel-Driven-Defense.pdf`

- Herrmann, D. S. (2007). *Complete Guide to Security and Privacy Metrics: Measuring Regulatory Compliance, Operational Resilience, and ROI*. Auerbach Publications.

- ISC2 (2021). *CISSP Domain Refresh*. Retrieved from ISC2 Certifications: `https://www.isc2.org/-/media/ISC2/Certifications/Domain-Refresh/CISSP-Domain-Refresh.ashx`

- Taleb, N. N. (2007). *The Black Swan: The Impact of the Highly Improbable*. Penguin Books

- Worrell, C. (April 3, 2018). *How to Use Amazon Alexa to Get Amazon GuardDuty Statistics and Findings*. Retrieved from AWS Security Blog: `https://aws.amazon.com/blogs/security/how-to-use-amazon-alexa-to-get-amazon-guardduty-statistics-and-findings/`

- Strom, B., Schulz, T., Nickels, K. (July 17, 2019). *Getting Started with ATT&CK: Adversary Emulation and Red Teaming*. Retrieved from `https://medium.com/mitre-attack/getting-started-with-attack-red-29f074ccf7e3`

- MITRE. (n.d.). *Adversary Emulation Plans*. Retrieved from MITRE ATT&CK®: `https://attack.mitre.org/resources/adversary-emulation-plans/`

Join our community on Discord

Join our community's Discord space for discussions with the author and other readers:

https://packt.link/SecNet

12

Modern Approaches to Security and Compliance

In the previous chapters of this book, I introduced you to the Cybersecurity Usual Suspects, and we discussed **Cybersecurity Threat Intelligence (CTI)**, vulnerability disclosures, threats such as malware and internet-based threats, the roles governments can play in cybersecurity, and government access to data. We also discussed ingredients that can help support a successful cybersecurity strategy, evaluated some cybersecurity strategies, took a close look at how the best scoring strategy could be implemented, and discussed how to measure the performance of that strategy.

Now we are going to take a closer look at how newer, more modern technologies, such as cloud computing, can help security and compliance teams modernize their methods. This was my full-time job between 2012 and 2022. During this period, I discussed the security and compliance advantages of the cloud with thousands of private and public sector enterprise customers in my roles at Microsoft and **Amazon Web Services (AWS)** – two of the three preeminent **Cloud Service Providers (CSPs)** in the world. At Microsoft, I worked as the Global Chief Security Advisor, among other roles, and at AWS, I was the Global Security and Compliance Lead for Public Sector. Often, I was the very first person customers would talk to about the cloud once they decided to seriously evaluate it. I feel so fortunate to have had the opportunity to work with so many brilliant people at these CSPs, and to have helped so many enterprise customers around the world modernize their IT and improve their security and compliance programs. I'll share some of the things I learned along the way and some key insights in this chapter. Please note that all the views and opinions written in this chapter, as well as the rest of this book, are my own personal opinions and not those of any of my past or present employers.

This chapter will introduce some concepts that will help put the cloud into context for CISOs and security and compliance professionals who haven't fully embraced it yet. It will also provide security and compliance teams that have experience in the cloud with some food for thought on effective approaches to cybersecurity and compliance in cloud environments that they might not be leveraging.

In this chapter, we'll cover the following topics:

- The power of **Application Programming Interfaces (APIs)**
- The advantages of automation to help mitigate the Cybersecurity Usual Suspects
- Cybersecurity strategies in the cloud
- Encryption and key management

Let's begin by looking at how the cloud is different from what IT and security teams have been doing in on-premises IT environments.

Introduction

The emergence of commercial cloud computing in 2006 led to a lot of debate among some organizations as to whether the cloud could be trusted, as well as whether it is as secure as on-premises IT environments. However, for many organizations, the cloud represents much more than new technology. Simply put, the cloud represents change. Let's face it, change is easy for some organizations, like startups, while it can be more difficult for large, well-established, and highly regulated organizations, such as financial services institutions and some verticals in the public sector.

Very often, it's the CISO in these organizations who is change averse, operating as if the ideal outcome is a stalemate with attackers, in IT environments where CISOs have some control over change. As long as nothing changes, they can maintain this state of relative success and continue to improve. However, of course, things are constantly changing; it just takes time for us busy humans to notice it. Businesses that don't keep pace with technological advancements can fall behind their competitors and fall prey to the startups seeking to disrupt their industry – the wolf is always at the door. CISOs can't be faulted for hoping to maintain the status quo when they have been successful. However, CISOs that don't spend some of their time pretending to be a CTO can do their organizations a disservice by slowing them down too much and hampering innovation.

This doesn't mean that CISOs can, or should, advocate for the adoption of every new technology that appears on the horizon. However, after more than a decade of being debated, the verdict is clear – the cloud is a game changer for security and compliance professionals. The cloud is a great cybersecurity talent amplifier that can help organizations execute on their current cybersecurity strategy or embrace a more modern approach to security and compliance.

Let's start this discussion with a quick introduction to cloud computing. I've found that level setting everyone, even IT, security, and compliance professionals who have been using the cloud, on what the cloud is and what it is not, can help provide a shared understanding that we can build upon. Otherwise, common misconceptions and inaccurate information tend to hinder meaningful conversations about security and compliance in the cloud.

How is cloud computing different?

The three most popular CSPs in the world are AWS, Microsoft and Google. These CSPs are often referred to as hyperscale CSPs because their cloud offerings are available all over the globe and at previously unimagined scales.

When organizations first contemplate leveraging services offered by CSPs, the first topics most of them want to explore are security and compliance. They need to understand how CSPs can provide the IT capabilities they need, while meeting or exceeding industry security standards, regulated standards and their own internal security standards. I've heard a lot of myths about cloud computing, and I've seen the cloud help organizations achieve things they couldn't possibly achieve in their own on-premises IT environments.

Although cloud computing is being adopted by industries all over the world, this has happened unevenly and more slowly in some regions of the world. As cloud computing started to get traction with enterprises, service model descriptions made it easy to educate people on what the cloud is and what it isn't. Three cloud computing service models became popular: **Infrastructure as a Service (IaaS)**, **Platform as a Service (PaaS)** and **Software as a Service (SaaS)**. These service model descriptions made it easier for everyone to understand the types of cloud services available and where they might fit into each organization's IT portfolio. For example, organizations could run their own virtual servers in a CSP's IaaS offering, such as **Amazon Elastic Compute Cloud (Amazon EC2)**, Microsoft Azure Virtual Machines, or Google Compute Engine.

CSPs offer services based on massive physical IT infrastructures that they've built around the world. Over time, the physical infrastructure model that CSPs have roughly coalesced around is based on the model that AWS pioneered: the concept of Regions and Availability Zones. In AWS parlance, an Availability Zone is a cluster of datacenters, and a Region is a cluster of Availability Zones. There are meaningful differences in the size and scope of CSPs' infrastructures and how they leverage components of this model. You can learn about each CSP's infrastructure on their respective websites:

- AWS: `https://aws.amazon.com/about-aws/global-infrastructure/`

- Google: https://cloud.google.com/compute/docs/regions-zones/
- Microsoft: https://azure.microsoft.com/explore/global-infrastructure/

Although the terms IaaS, PaaS and SaaS are still in widespread use today, they are slowly becoming obsolete. Back when they were first coined, CSPs only had a handful of services and these service models helped describe how each service was deployed. However, this has been changing rapidly. At the time of writing, the three aforementioned hyperscale CSPs offered hundreds of cloud services. Subsequently, newer acronyms like **Containers as a Service (CaaS)**, **Identity as a Service (IDaaS)** and **Function as a Service (FaaS)** have cropped up. This proliferation of services has been accelerating because the developers of new services can use existing services as building blocks. For example, if a CSP is developing a new cloud service and they need storage for it, instead of building a new storage infrastructure from scratch, they can simply use one of the existing cloud storage services that meets their requirements. Not only does this approach help accelerate the development of new cloud services, but it means services could have IaaS, PaaS and/or SaaS components, blurring the lines between these old service model descriptions. In other words, solutions to specific problems are becoming more important than maintaining service model definitions. As this cloud services proliferation continues, enterprises will be able to procure solutions for the specific problems that they want to solve, and the old service models will become less and less important.

One important distinction when it comes to service models is the difference between the services that hyperscale CSPs provide and those of traditional **Managed Service Providers (MSPs)**. Many organizations around the world have leveraged MSPs for decades. Governments, for example, tend to sign very long-term agreements with MSPs to manage their datacenters and provide IT services to them. MSPs have played an important role for such organizations, for at least a couple of reasons. First, MSPs have successfully maintained a critical mass of IT talent that would otherwise be challenging for enterprises to attract and retain themselves. Second, MSPs became intimately familiar with the IT environments of their customers because they managed them; this tribal knowledge provided the continuity that enterprises needed in order to minimize potential disruptions when key staff turned over. Of course, MSPs offer other benefits to their customers as well.

More and more organizations want to move from a **Capital Expenditures (CAPEX)** model to an **Operational Expenditures (OPEX)** model. CAPEX typically requires organizations to make large IT investments up front and record these costs in accounting records over a period of years based on depreciation or amortization schedules.

Because they pay up front for under this CAPEX model, they have to estimate their capacity and utilization needs and hope these estimates are correct, otherwise they end up paying up front for capacity they might never use. Studies on actual IT server utilization in enterprise datacenters, suggest that actual server utilization is almost always a fraction of what was estimated and procured. An OPEX model is attractive to some organizations that cannot afford to pay up front for IT equipment. The cloud allows them to pay as they go, paying for just the specific resources that they use. MSPs and CSPs can help their customers with this shift. However, MSPs tend to have an outsourcing-based business model, while CSPs offer a self-service model for transformation instead of replication of existing processes.

Cloud Service Providers versus Managed Service Providers

One mistake that is easy to make for enterprises that contemplate using the cloud for the first time is the assumption that CSPs are just another flavor of MSP. They aren't. Hyperscale CSPs offer an extremely scalable and agile self-service IT model where their customers only pay for what they use, measured in compute seconds and the amount of data they store or transfer across networks. Anyone with a credit card can open an account and get access to hundreds of services that would be prohibitively expensive to build in on-premises or MSP IT environments. When customers are finished using their CSP's services, they can typically walk away from them with no obligations whatsoever.

Conversely, MSPs manage datacenters and systems on behalf of their customers. Because of the up-front investments required to physically build datacenters and the systems that run in them, the MSP model typically requires long-term contracts that ensure MSPs can derive appropriate returns on their investments. This model puts MSPs and their customers at a disadvantage. CSPs spread their expenses across millions of customers around the world, where MSPs tend to have a much smaller set of customers to service, who must pay for everything themselves. Some MSPs have built their customers their own private clouds, which seek to mimic the elasticity and the other characteristics of cloud computing. However, in my experience, the term private cloud is a euphemism for limited scale, limited services, and slow to change. In some cases, a private cloud is simply just an outsourced datacenter. Comparing these to the range of services that hyperscale CSPs offer isn't really an apples-to-apples comparison. Subsequently, many MSPs have evolved their products and services to run on top of CSP services. This makes a lot of sense, as they too can benefit from the economies of scale that the hyperscale CSPs provide.

They do this by dramatically reducing capital expenses, getting virtually unlimited scale for their products and enabling them to embrace an incredible pace of innovation that they could not likely achieve themselves. There is a huge opportunity for MSPs to design, build and manage systems for their customers. However, instead of focusing on IT infrastructure administration, they can focus more on innovation. They can also achieve better security for their customers. I'll discuss some of the ways the cloud can provide better security and compliance in this chapter.

The failure to understand the difference between CSPs and MSPs can slow organizations down when they evaluate the security and compliance of the cloud. Many organizations spend an inordinate amount of time trying to understand how they maintain the status quo if they choose to leverage the cloud. However, as I mentioned earlier, the cloud represents change; reconciling these two things is one of the first things organizations are confronted with when they first contemplate using the cloud. This reconciliation can manifest itself several different ways. Let me give you a couple of examples.

Migrating to the cloud

As I mentioned earlier, as a group, hyperscale CSPs offer hundreds of services to their customers. Despite this, many enterprises still choose to lift and shift applications into the cloud. This typically means that they take an application they have been running on servers in their on-premises IT environment and run it on servers hosted in the cloud. This type of transition to the cloud allows them to maintain the people, processes, and technologies that they have been using for years, while moving from CAPEX to OPEX. For many organizations, this is completely natural as they have deep expertise building and managing these systems in their on-premises IT environment, and they can continue to leverage this expertise when they move those same systems into the cloud. In the cloud, they can leverage the same or similar hardware and software that they have been using on-premises. Subsequently, this type of transition can be relatively easy and quick.

The challenge with lifting and shifting applications is that complexity, inefficiencies, and technical debt also get shifted into the cloud with the applications. Still, for some organizations, this type of transition can be a starting point for bigger and better things. Typically, once organizations start using the cloud, develop some expertise with it and explore its broader set of capabilities, they make broader use of it in the future. Instead of lifting and shifting more applications, they re-platform applications, repurchase applications, or refactor applications using cloud-native capabilities. Over time, they stop managing the cloud like they managed on-premises IT and real innovation begins to flourish. However, for some organizations, this transition and evolution can take time.

To speed things up, some organizations decide to make big, bold moves. Instead of lifting and shifting legacy applications to the cloud, they decide to migrate a mission-critical application to the cloud. Their logic is that since the application is critical to the business, it will get done right the first time and the things they learn in the process can be applied to all the other less critical applications that follow it to the cloud; this approach will accelerate their digital transformations and help them to potentially leapfrog their waffling competitors.

Cybersecurity assessment questionnaires

Some CISOs grapple with the change that the cloud represents and seek to maintain the status quo. This is because they have successfully managed their cybersecurity program in their organizations' current IT environment. Change can represent risk for some organizations. The place I've seen this illustrated most often is with the security assessments that enterprise security teams use to determine if new solutions meet their security standards and requirements. Such assessments seek to determine if a minimum set of controls are in place to protect the organization's data while it's being processed, stored, and transmitted by new solutions. For example, one assessment question could determine whether the new solution protects data in-transit with the newest version of the **Transport Layer Security (TLS)** protocol. Another assessment question could determine if data at rest in the solution is encrypted using a specific algorithm. Another assessment question could be whether the vendor has a specific third-party security attestation or certification, like ISO 27001, for example.

In some organizations, when new cloud-based solutions come to the security team for a security assessment, they apply the same assessment process they have been using to assess new solutions in their on-premises IT environment. This seems reasonable; after all, the assessment checks whether solutions meet the organization's security standards.

Some of the security assessment questionnaires that I've seen over the years have been elaborate and include hundreds of questions. Many of these questionnaires were developed over a period of many years and have been customized to reflect the specific IT environments and compliance requirements of the organizations that employ them.

However, many of the questions in such assessment questionnaires are based on some key underlying assumptions; for example, an assumption that the assessors will have physical access to the hardware in order to answer their questions. Another similar example is that the assessors will be assessing systems that the organization manages themselves. Another popular assumption I've seen is that the technology used by a solution will never deviate from current commercially available technologies.

For example, the hypervisor that a solution's virtualized workloads run on runs exactly the same way as the hypervisors they have been running in their on-premises IT environments. One last example is the assumption that the vendor providing the solution only has one solution and not a huge suite or stack of technologies that can be combined in different ways to solve problems. When any of these assumptions or others are not true, the assessments that are based on them cannot be fully completed. When this happens, some security teams simply reject a solution because they couldn't determine if it met their standards using their tried-and-true security assessment questionnaire. However, the glaring flaw in their assessment process is that it didn't check if the solution met the organization's security standards; it checked whether the questions in their questionnaire could be answered as written. This is a subtle but important difference.

Let me use an exaggerated analogy to illustrate what I mean. For the past few decades, car owners have been able to take their cars to professionally managed garages to have multi-point inspections completed. In some cases, these inspections are mandated by law, like emissions inspections, for example. However, what happened to the owner of the first fully electric car when they took their car for the legally mandated emissions inspection? Was the garage able to process the assessment that is required by law? Did the car have an exhaust pipe or catalytic converter for the garage to test? After all, every car must have these technologies, right?

Given that the garage couldn't test this car the same way they had been testing cars for decades, should they fail to certify the car, even though it exceeds car emissions standards in a way that legacy internal combustion engines could never achieve? Some security teams reject cloud-based solutions because they cannot assess them the same way they've always assessed solutions.

Few security teams spontaneously question the assumptions that their years' old assessment processes are based on. Their security requirements don't necessarily have to change. However, they need to evolve and modernize their assessment processes to determine if new technologies can meet or exceed those requirements. The goal of security assessments is to ensure new solutions meet organizations' security requirements, not to ensure their security assessment questions never have to change. Enterprises need to question their assumptions occasionally to check if they are still accurate and relevant.

Let's jump right into it! Next, I'll share why I think the cloud is a game changer for security and compliance professionals.

Security and compliance game changers

There are numerous ways that the cloud can tilt the playing field in favor of defenders. In this section, I'll cover two security and compliance game changers.

The power of APIs

Application Programming Interfaces (APIs) provide a powerful mechanism for systems to interact with humans and other systems. There are different kinds of APIs, but generally, APIs define the specific inputs a system is willing to accept and the outputs it will provide. The details of how the system processes inputs and provides outputs can be abstracted from view, thus simplifying the system for humans and other systems that want to use it. In other words, I don't need to know how the system works internally in order to use it. I just need to know about its APIs. I can call an API and pass it the information it requires and then wait for the output, while the magic of software happens.

Magic here is a euphemism for all the smart engineers' and developers' work on the hardware, firmware, operating systems, and software that make up the stack of technologies that the API and its system rely on.

APIs can be programming language-specific and thus included as part of **Software Development Kits (SDKs)**. This makes it easy for developers that know C++, Java, or other newer, popular programming languages to leverage APIs. Although APIs were once primarily used by developers to help them develop applications, operations roles now also make use of APIs to deploy and operate IT infrastructure, thus helping to herald the DevOps era.

In the context of cloud computing, APIs can be called from within an application, from a command line, or from the web console provided by the CSP. Let me give you some examples.

Let's say we wanted to provision and launch five virtual machines in Amazon EC2, in one of the three currently available Availability Zones in the London Region. We could use the RunInstances API (AWS, 2020):

```
https://ec2.amazonaws.com/?Action=RunInstances
&ImageId= ami-0c5300e833c2b32f3
&InstanceType=t2.micro
&MaxCount=5
&MinCount=1
&KeyName=my-key-pair
&Placement.AvailabilityZone=eu-west-2a
&AUTHPARAMS
```

If we used the AWS Console to do the same thing, the Launch Instance wizard would collect all the configuration information for the virtual machines and make the same type of API call on our behalf.

We could also use the AWS **Command-Line Interface (CLI)** to launch these virtual machines, specifying the same parameters, and the CLI would make the same type of API call for us:

```
aws ec2 run-instances --image-id ami-0c5300e833c2b32f3 --count 5
--instance-type t2.micro --key-name my-key-pair
```

Under the covers of the system that this AWS CLI command is run from, it will send this type of request to Amazon EC2 using the HTTPS protocol on TCP port 443 (AWS, 2020).

One important thing to keep in mind is that API calls require authentication, authorization, integrity and confidentiality mechanisms. I won't get into all these details here, but the CSPs offer documentation that will help you understand the mechanisms they've implemented, or not implemented, to provide these things for their APIs. For example, you can read about security for AWS CLI at this URL: https://docs.aws.amazon.com/cli/latest/userguide/security.html.

Of course, like AWS, Google Cloud and Microsoft Azure have similar APIs and support a range of programming and scripting languages, as well as CLIs. This is an example from the CLI SDK from Google, first creating a virtual machine and then starting it (Google, n.d.)

```
gcloud compute instances create example-instance --image-family=rhel-8
--image-project=rhel-cloud --zone=us-central1-a
gcloud compute instances start example-instance --zone=us-central1-a
```

A similar example can be seen here regarding the creation of a virtual machine in Microsoft Azure using **Representational State Transfer (REST)** APIs (Microsoft Corporation, 2020). Once the virtual machine has been created, another API call will start it. This can also be done using the Azure CLI, Azure PowerShell, and the Azure portal:

```
PUT https://management.azure.com/subscriptions/{subscription-
id}/resourceGroups/myResourceGroup/providers/Microsoft.Compute/
virtualMachines/{vm-name}?api-version=2022-08-01
{
    "location": "westus",
    "properties": {
        "hardwareProfile": {
            "vmSize": "Standard_D1_v2"
    },
    "storageProfile": {
        "osDisk": {
            "name": "myVMosdisk",
        "image": {
```

```
        "uri": "http://{existing-storage-account-name}.blob.core. windows.
net/{existing-container-name}/{existing-generalized-os-image-blob-name}.
vhd"
    },
    "osType": "Windows",
    "createOption": "FromImage",
    "caching": "ReadWrite",
    "vhd": {
        "uri": "http://{existing-storage-account-name}.blob.core. windows.
net/{existing-container-name}/myDisk.vhd"
    }
    }
},
"osProfile": {
    "adminUsername": "{your-username}",
    "computerName": "myVM",
    "adminPassword": "{your-password}"
},
"networkProfile": {
    "networkInterfaces": [
    {
        "id": "/subscriptions/{subscription-id}/resourceGroups/
myResourceGroup/providers/Microsoft.Network/networkInterfaces/ {existing-
nic-name}",
        "properties": {
            "primary": true
                }
            }
        ]
    }
}
}
```

As you've seen, using APIs enables the users of these services to deploy infrastructure, such as servers, firewalls, network load balancers and third-party appliances. However, it also allows us to configure that infrastructure exactly the way we want it to be configured. For example, when deploying servers, we can specify the operating systems, IP addresses, network security configurations, routing tables, and so on.

This is extremely powerful. With a single command, we can start one virtual machine or a hundred thousand virtual machines, all configured exactly the way we want them configured. Because we know exactly how our systems should be configured, we can compare the current configurations of the systems that are running in production to our standard configuration and determine if there are any differences. We can do this constantly in order to detect changes that could be indicators of compromise.

In on-premises IT environments, this would typically involve deploying agents or management software on the servers that will monitor configuration changes.

One challenge that many organizations have is deploying and managing multiple agents and management suites from different vendors. Each agent requires some level of management and security updates to ensure it doesn't increase the attack surface area. Typically, CISOs and CIOs look for ways to reduce the number of agents running on systems and resist the idea of deploying more of them in their environments. Meanwhile, the sources of system configuration changes can include all sorts of things – administrators, management software, users, malware, restoring from backups, and so on. This can make it challenging to detect changes and determine if changes to systems are indicators of compromise.

In the cloud, since everything happens via APIs, the APIs provide the perfect choke point for visibility and control. If organizations can monitor their API calls and take action based on what's happening, they will have great visibility and control. In this environment, deploying agents and management software to hundreds or thousands of systems is optional because the APIs are baked into the cloud. If an organization has regulatory compliance requirements that dictate specific control configurations, they can monitor those controls to ensure that they are always in compliance.

In practice, API calls are logged to API logging services for this purpose. For example, AWS CloudTrail is an API logging service that logs the API calls in AWS accounts (AWS, 2020). Earlier, when we ran the command that started five virtual machines in AWS EC2, if AWS CloudTrail was enabled, it would have logged an event that captured the details of that API call. This event contains an incredible amount of detail, including which account was used, the principal that made the call, some authentication and authorization details, the time, the Region, the source IP address the call came from, details on the virtual machine and some details regarding its configuration. These logs can be combined with other logging data, aggregated, and analyzed by humans and data analytics systems, imported into SIEMs in the cloud and/or downloaded to systems in on-premises IT environments. These logs are also essential for incident response investigations.

Google offers Cloud Audit Logs (Google, 2020), while Microsoft provides Azure Monitor (Microsoft Corporation, October 7, 2019), in addition to other logging mechanisms, for similar purposes.

Here is a truncated example of an event logged by AWS CloudTrail:

```
{
    "eventVersion": "1.05",
    "userIdentity": {
        "type": "AssumedRole",
        "principalId": "Example:user123",
        "arn": "arn:aws:sts::Example:assumed-role/Admin/user123",
        "accountId": "Example-ID",
        "accessKeyId": "Example-access-key",
        "sessionContext": {
            "sessionIssuer": {
                "type": "Role",
                "principalId": "Example-principle",
                "arn": "arn:aws:iam::Example:role/Admin",
                "accountId": "Example-ID",
                "userName": "Admin"
            },
            "webIdFederationData": {},
            "attributes": {
                "mfaAuthenticated": "false",
                "creationDate": "2020-04-01T05:09:15Z"
            }
        }
    },
    "eventTime": "2020-04-01T05:09:26Z",
    "eventSource": "ec2.amazonaws.com",
    "eventName": "RunInstances",
    "awsRegion": "eu-west-2",
    "sourceIPAddress": "169.254.35.31",
    "userAgent": "aws-cli/1.3.23 Python/2.7.6 Linux/2.6.18-164.el5 ",
    "requestParameters": {
        "instancesSet": {
            "items": [
```

```
            {
            "imageId": " i-030322d35173f3725",
            "minCount": 1,
            "maxCount": 5,
            "keyName": "my-key-pair"
            }
        ]
    },
    "instanceType": "t2.micro"
```

To recap, every interaction with the cloud happens via an API call. This model has numerous benefits, including security and compliance benefits. Because of this, the visibility and control that the cloud offers are superior to that of most on-premises IT environments, not to mention the simplicity and cost benefits of this approach. Plus, it enables new approaches to IT and security operations. For example, we know that every system that we deploy is configured to meet our security and compliance standards, because that's how it has been defined in the code that we use to deploy them. Since storage and networking are decoupled from compute services, nothing prevents us from simply shutting down systems and deploying new systems to replace them every few hours. It just takes a few lines of code in a script or application to do this, as we saw earlier. If systems are short-lived, it makes it harder for administrators and management software to introduce security misconfigurations over time that attackers can use to get a foothold in the environment.

APIs are powerful, but they too must be properly implemented so that they do not create a porous attack surface. Of course, the CSPs know this and employ expertise, processes, and technology in the development of their APIs to minimize risk. Layer in authentication and authorization mechanisms, protection, monitoring, detection, response, and audit capabilities, and APIs rock!

I've discussed one scenario here, which is using APIs to configure and start virtual machines. Now, imagine if you could use APIs to control hundreds of cloud services that perform all sorts of functions, such as compute, storage, networking, databases, containers, serverless computing, artificial intelligence, machine learning, IoT, and security, to name just a few. Imagine having programmatic control over all of that, at virtually any scale, anywhere in the world – truly amazing. This is the power of APIs! They really are a game changer for security and compliance professionals. The power of APIs is not only available for large organizations with large IT budgets; anyone with a credit card can open an account with a CSP and get the power of these APIs. Next, let's look at another game changer, automation.

The advantages of automation

As we've seen, the power of APIs enables us to configure and control most things in the cloud using code, even infrastructure. To take full advantage of the power of APIs, the cloud offers high levels of automation. In addition to running CLI commands, you can automate complex workflows using scripts, templates, applications, and cloud services.

CSPs offer rich automation capabilities. These capabilities are spread across different cloud services, just like the APIs they leverage. Some examples of services that help automate functions include Microsoft Azure Automation (Microsoft Corporation, October 18, 2018), Google Cloud Composer (Google, 2020) and AWS CloudFormation (AWS, 2020). There are also automation solutions available from third parties, such as Chef (Chef, 2020), Puppet (Puppet, 2020), Ansible (Ansible, 2020), Terraform (Hashicorp, 2020), and many others.

For security and compliance professionals, all these automation capabilities and tools can help provision, configure, manage, monitor, re-configure and deprovision infrastructure and other cloud services. In addition, these rich automation capabilities can help to protect, detect, respond, and recover, while maintaining compliance to regulated standards, industry standards, and internal security standards. In many cases, all of this can happen in near real time because automation, not humans, is performing these operations.

In fact, reducing human participation in these operations has many advantages. Recall the Cybersecurity Usual Suspects that I discussed at length in *Chapter 1, Introduction*; let's look at some examples of how automation can help us mitigate some of these. Let's start by looking at insider threat and social engineering.

Mitigating insider threat and social engineering

Remember the two types of insider threats that I defined earlier: malicious insiders who abuse their privileged access to resources and non-malicious insiders who make mistakes that lead to poor security outcomes. Automation can help mitigate both types of threats. For example, the more automation we develop, test, and implement, the fewer chances administrators will have to make mistakes that have security consequences.

Using automation to complete repeatable processes can lead to more consistent and quicker outcomes that are less prone to human error.

Automating administrative processes will also result in fewer opportunities for malicious insiders to act. This is where the concepts of just-in-time administration and just-enough administration can be helpful.

With high levels of automation in place, administrators will require less access to systems, thus reducing the opportunities they have to steal data or damage infrastructure. Highly automated environments also make it easier to detect when administrators access systems because such occasions will be exceptions to the rules. When malicious insiders know there is increased visibility and scrutiny on them when they directly access data and systems, the frequency that they will attempt to access resources without legitimate reasons is reduced.

Automation can help minimize the amount of access administrators have. For example, instead of allowing administrators full access to systems they connect to, only allowing them to run pre-tested and approved scripts and automation on those systems will reduce the opportunities they have to run arbitrary commands. With enough automation, the only time administrators have legitimate cause to run arbitrary commands is in "break-glass" scenarios where existing automation cannot fix a problem. These cases can be monitored and audited to reduce the chances that a malicious insider will act. During such scenarios, employing quorum-based administration procedures with two or more participants can also help mitigate insider threats. Adding more automation over time to cover more support scenarios can dramatically reduce the opportunities that administrators have to run arbitrary commands.

There are also privacy benefits to using automation. If humans don't have access to sensitive data, then they can't be exposed to **Personally Identifiable Information (PII)** or **Protected Health Information (PHI)**, or sensitive financial information. Using automation to interact with data, instead of humans, helps organizations fulfill the privacy promises they make to their customers or citizens.

Sounds great, right? Maybe too good to be true? Can't we already do this in on-premises IT environments by using bastion hosts and **Secure Shell (SSH)** sessions? Great questions. Let's look at a real-world example.

The security team's requirements in this example specify that administrators cannot directly access the systems they are managing. This means using SSH to access systems directly isn't going to meet requirements. If they did use SSH to access these systems, then they might be able to run arbitrary commands on these systems, which is something the security team wants to avoid.

The security team in this scenario also wants to limit the use of bastion hosts in their environment. They have been burned using bastion hosts in the past. Bastion hosts typically span a higher security zone and a lower security zone, allowing administrators to get access to systems in the higher security zone from the lower security zone; subsequently, bastion hosts need to be managed as if they are part of the higher security zone.

It turns out that this can be harder than it sounds and lapses in this fictional organization's processes led to a system compromise in their environment. Having been burned once, they want to minimize the number of bastion hosts in their environment.

One way to meet these requirements using AWS, for example, is to use the AWS Systems Manager service to run commands on virtual machines running in the Amazon EC2 service. To do this, the Systems Manager Agent will be installed on those virtual machines. This is easy to do using automation. As each virtual machine is provisioned in EC2 using code, the Systems Manager Agent will also be installed on them. Once that agent is properly configured, administrators can run tested and approved scripts from the AWS Systems Manager console that will execute on those virtual machines via the Systems Manager Agent (AWS, 2020).

There are a few cool advantages to this approach. First, administrators do not need to have administrator credentials for the virtual machines they are managing. Since they are running scripts from the AWS Systems Manager service in the cloud, they don't need local credentials to access individual systems. If administrators don't know the usernames and passwords for those systems, they can't log directly into them. They are limited to running the tested and approved scripts from the cloud. This helps to mitigate the risk of insider threat for those systems.

This approach also mitigates the some of the risk associated with social engineering on these systems. Administrators can't be tricked into giving up credentials for those systems because they don't know them. Since the only way administrators interact with these systems is by remotely running pre-approved scripts on them, they can't be tricked into running arbitrary commands or installing new software, which can undermine the security of these systems and lead to bad security outcomes. Of course, given how insidious social engineering is, this approach must be married with some other mitigations to fully mitigate it; for example, **Multi-Factor Authentication** (MFA) for the AWS accounts themselves. However, I hope you can see the potential advantages of this approach when it comes to mitigating typical social engineering attacks against administrators. When administrators only have access when they need it and that access is tightly scoped and controlled, there's less opportunity for typical social engineering tactics to be successful.

Remember that one of the big advantages of using the cloud is scalability. If we install the Systems Manager Agent on every virtual machine that we deploy, using automation, of course, we will have the ability to use this administration method on as many systems as required – the scale is virtually unlimited. Using automation, we can manage three systems or three thousand systems with the same technique and amount of effort.

As the number of systems that we manage increases or decreases, there is no additional work required by administrators because they run the same scripts regardless of the number of systems they manage; managing more systems doesn't mean administrators have more access.

If we are logging the API calls that are generated by the administrators' interactions with the AWS Systems Manager service in AWS CloudTrail, then their activities can be monitored and audited in near real time (AWS, 2020). We can also monitor and audit any interaction administrators have with the virtual machines themselves to ensure administrators only access these systems in break-glass events.

Of course, other CSPs have rich automation capabilities as well. For example, Microsoft offers a range of services and capabilities to help, including Azure Automation, Azure PowerShell, Azure Monitor, and others. Google offers several services as well, including Cloud Monitoring, Cloud Functions, and Cloud Asset Inventory, among others.

Automation allows us to design systems that don't require direct human interaction very often. This makes it easier to detect when those incidents happen and better mitigate insider threat and social engineering. Next, let's look at how another one of the Cybersecurity Usual Suspects, unpatched vulnerabilities, can be mitigated in this scenario.

Mitigating unpatched vulnerabilities

Let's look at how we can use automation to help manage vulnerabilities on the virtual machines we use. As we saw in *Chapter 3*, *Using Vulnerability Trends to Reduce Risk and Costs*, to date, Vulnerability Management teams have been faced with as many as 69 new vulnerability disclosures per day across the industry that potentially impact their systems. Automation in the cloud can help reduce the amount of work related to inventorying systems, scanning systems, and patching systems.

For example, recall that I wrote in *Chapter 3* that accurate inventories are critical to vulnerability management teams. In the cloud, because nothing gets provisioned or deprovisioned without using APIs, APIs and automation help provide accurate inventories quickly. Inventorying environments like this doesn't take hours or days – it can be nearly instantaneous.

There are many methods available to scan and patch virtual machines in the cloud. In our AWS example, AWS Systems Manager can be used to patch systems. Also, chances are, the vendors your organization uses for vulnerability management software in your on-premises IT environment also have similar capabilities built for the cloud. This allows your organization to take the expertise it has developed from managing vulnerabilities in its on-premises IT environment and continue to leverage it in the cloud.

You might be wondering how vulnerability management processes are potentially impacted for virtual machines running in the cloud when the number of systems can be scaled up and down completely dynamically to meet load and application availability targets. In this scenario, Amazon EC2 Auto Scaling can be used to accomplish this (AWS, 2016). It can also help keep systems up to date. Instead of scanning and patching every system in a big fleet of systems, Auto Scaling can be used to dramatically reduce this effort. To do this, the Amazon Machine Image used to build the virtual machines is scanned for vulnerabilities, and security updates are installed as needed after testing. This ensures the image is up to date and security updates have been tested. After the Amazon Machine Image has been updated, shut down a virtual machine running in production that is based on the older version of that image. Based on the load and availability rules you set for Auto Scaling, when Auto Scaling decides it's time to launch a new virtual machine, it does so using the image that you just patched and tested. When the new virtual machine starts, it is fully patched. You can use automation to thoughtfully shut down the virtual machines running in production that are based on the old image, and Auto Scaling will restart new, fully patched virtual machines to replace them. No scanning and patching hundreds or thousands of systems. And the pain from reboots is largely mitigated. This is a much easier way to do something that has long been a pain point for large enterprises.

Google and Microsoft also provide tools to make finding and mitigating vulnerabilities efficient. For example, Google offers OS inventory management, OS patch management, and Web Security Scanner, while Microsoft offers Azure Automation and Microsoft Defender for Cloud, among other tools. There are numerous third-party vendors that provide vulnerability management solutions for cloud environments, including Qualys, Tenable, and many others.

Of course, this is just one method to perform patching – there are others. There is also the potential to eliminate patching altogether by using services that the CSPs manage for you. As I mentioned earlier in this chapter, IaaS is but one type of service model in the cloud; there are hundreds of services from CSPs that do not require you to provision, manage, and patch servers at all. If you don't need to manage servers yourself, why bother?

Let the CSPs manage infrastructure for you, and you can spend the time normally relegated to such tasks to reducing technical debt in other areas, project work that never seems to get done, or innovating – imagine that. Imagine spending time figuring out how to use serverless computing, AI, ML, and IoT to better protect, detect, and respond to threats, instead of testing patches and rebooting servers. Using managed services doesn't increase the attack surface that your security team needs to track and manage – the CSPs do that for you.

The net result is potentially dramatically increased IT capabilities without increasing your IT attack surface and the number of systems to patch and manage. For example, using a managed service to increase detection capabilities for your cloud IT estate, without provisioning any additional infrastructure that you need to manage. This will potentially give you more visibility without increasing complexity and technical debt.

The cloud can definitely help mitigate unpatched vulnerabilities and make this much easier than it is in most on-premises environments, something that has plagued enterprises for decades. Now, let's see how automation in the cloud can help mitigate another of the Cybersecurity Usual Suspects, security misconfigurations.

Mitigating security misconfigurations

As I wrote in *Chapter 1, Introduction*, security misconfigurations can be poor default settings in hardware, operating systems, and applications, or can occur over time as systems "skew" out of their organization's standards based on the tweaks administrators or software updates introduce. Additionally, in big IT environments, abandoned technology can quickly become a forgotten risk that isn't actively managed. Because of the constant struggle large enterprises have had with keeping things configured the way they need them, Change Management emerged as a full-blown IT discipline, supported by an entire industry of vendors. This is important, not just for security purposes, but also for compliance purposes. Ensuring systems comply with regulated standards, industry standards, and internal IT standards is important and, in many cases, required.

In our example scenario, organizations can choose to install management software on the servers that they deploy in the cloud. They can continue to measure and remediate configuration changes in much the same way they have been in their on-premises IT environment.

They can also harness the power of APIs and the automation built into the cloud. For example, AWS Config is a cloud service that monitors resources for configuration changes and enables you to take a range of actions based on those changes.

In our example scenario, the security team might decide that one type of change should be automatically remediated; when the change is detected, automation will change the configuration back to its standard setting. Alternatively, just to be safe, automation can be used to shut down the misconfigured system and, if enabled, Auto Scaling will start a new system that meets all of the organization's standards to replace it.

The Security team might deem another type of change to be an indicator of compromise that needs to be investigated by their Incident Response team. In this case, automation can take a snapshot of the virtual machine, create a new **Virtual Private Cloud** (**VPC**) – let's call it IR Clean Room – copy the snapshot into the isolated IR Clean Room, connect the IR team's forensics software to the image, send a message to the IR team to investigate it, and shut down the original virtual machine. If configured, Auto Scaling will start a new, pristine virtual machine that meets all approved standards to take its place. It does this all in near real time. Notice that in these examples, there was no management software or agent on the virtual machine and no SOC analysts performing manual queries looking for indicators of compromise. Since infrastructure is code, we can automate any number of actions to suit the organization's needs.

In a compliance context, this functionality is powerful as it can help keep things configured in a way that complies with standards. When we use automation to detect changes and take appropriate action, we can also use that automation to generate compliance artifacts that will help the organization prove continuous compliance with the specific standards that apply to them. This helps reduce manual audits and manual remediation of misconfigured systems.

Microsoft Azure Automation and Google Cloud Asset Inventory provide similar capabilities for their respective services. There are also third parties that provide automation solutions such as Ansible, Chef, Terraform, and several others.

Next, let's look at how automation in the cloud helps mitigate the last of the Cybersecurity Usual Suspects: weak, leaked, and stolen credentials.

Mitigating weak, leaked and stolen credentials

CSPs and numerous third-party vendors offer identity and access management solutions for the cloud and hybrid environments. For example, Microsoft offers Azure Active Directory and supporting services such as just-in-time privileged access capabilities via Azure Active Directory **Privileged Identity Management** (**PIM**) (Microsoft Corporation, 2022). Third parties such as Centrify, CyberArk, and many others also provide services that can help in several different scenarios. Google Cloud offers Cloud Identity and Access Management, while AWS offers AWS Identity and Access Management.

CSPs offer MFA, which is a highly effective control that mitigates weak, leaked and stolen credentials to a great extent. Leveraging MFA and limiting the amount of time users have access to resources between authentication requests can make it much harder for attackers to use stolen and leaked credentials successfully.

Using a secrets manager to manage access keys, certificates, and credentials that automatically changes and rotates them periodically can also be effective. To do this, Google offers Google Cloud Secret Manager (Google, 2020), Microsoft offers Azure Key Vault (Microsoft Corporation, 2020) and AWS provides AWS Secrets Manager (AWS, 2020). Again, there are many third-party vendors that also offer solutions, including Docker Secrets, SecretHub, and others.

In fact, there are so many capabilities and so much functionality in identity and access management services and solutions, entire books have been dedicated to this topic area. Identity is the key to security. I highly recommend spending some time learning about the powerful identity and access management capabilities that CSPs and other vendors have to offer.

Security and compliance game changers – summary

APIs and automation in the cloud are two game changers for security and compliance professionals. That's not to say that APIs and automation are not available in on-premises IT environments. However, the investment and effort to bring these capabilities on par with those baked into the cloud would be prohibitively expensive and difficult to implement; considering anyone with a credit card and a few minutes to open an account with a CSP gets these capabilities by default, it would be difficult to justify implementing on-premises versions.

We've now seen that the cloud can offer some effective and innovative ways to address all the Cybersecurity Usual Suspects. Put another way, the cloud makes addressing the Cybersecurity Fundamentals easier than mitigating them in on-premises IT environments. We've only really scratched the surface here because the example scenario I used throughout this section was an IaaS example. As I mentioned, CSPs offer hundreds of services that span and blend IaaS, PaaS, SaaS, FaaS, IDaaS, and others. Not to mention, I didn't dive into any of the security services these CSPs offer. Entire books have been dedicated to the topic of cloud security.

Now let's look at how the cloud can support the cybersecurity strategies that we examined in *Chapter 9, Cybersecurity Strategies*.

Using cybersecurity strategies in the cloud

In *Chapter 9, Cybersecurity Strategies*, we examined several cybersecurity strategies that I have seen employed in the industry over the past two decades. We evaluated these strategies using the **Cybersecurity Fundamentals Scoring System (CFSS)**. The CFSS score estimate for each strategy helps us understand how well they address the Cybersecurity Fundamentals. To refresh your memory, a summary of the CFSS scores for each strategy is provided in *Figure 12.1*.

Cybersecurity Strategy	Unpatched vulnerabilities	Security misconfigurations	Weak, leaked, stolen credentials	Social engineering	Insider threat	Total Score
Protect and Recover Strategy	10	10	0	5	0	25
Endpoint Protection Strategy	20	20	15	10	10	75
Physical Control and Security Clearances Strategy	10	10	15	10	10	55
Compliance as a Cybersecurity Strategy	10	10	10	10	10	50
Application-Centric Strategy	20	20	10	10	10	70
Identity-Centric Strategy	5	5	15	10	10	45
Data-Centric Strategy	5	5	0	15	15	40
Attack-Centric Strategy	20	20	20	15	20	95

Figure 12.1: CFSS score estimate summary

Almost any of these strategies can be used in the cloud. Let's look at a few of these strategies in the context of the cloud.

Using the Protect and Recover Strategy in the cloud

CSPs offer granular firewall and network controls that can help organizations adopt and operate the Protect and Recover Strategy. The power of APIs and automation in the cloud enables Network teams and Security teams to provision and operate Web Application Firewalls, as well as network firewalls at the edge of their cloud estates, and build and operate DMZs. They also provide VPCs or Virtual Networks that add another layer of control over network traffic, in addition to network ACLs, routing tables, subnet rules, host-based firewalls, and so on. CSPs typically offer a dizzying array of network controls.

Since all these controls can be provisioned and monitored via code and automation, it's much easier to execute this strategy in the cloud versus on-premises. In the cloud, there is no hardware to order and receive, no racking and stacking in the datacenter, and nothing requiring more rack space, power, or cooling. You just run code and the CSPs do everything else. If you need to scale your infrastructure up or down, it's just more code and automation. You only pay for what you use and can shut it down any time your organization decides to. The Protect and Recover Strategy is a poor scoring strategy, as we discussed in *Chapter 9, Cybersecurity Strategies*. It can be used in combination with other strategies to more fully address the cybersecurity fundamentals. It's easier to extend this strategy in the cloud too, because everything is code. Let's look at a better scoring strategy now.

Compliance as a Cybersecurity Strategy in the cloud

Let's look at another strategy from *Chapter 9, Cybersecurity Strategies*, Compliance as a Cybersecurity Strategy. Earlier in this chapter, we looked at how APIs and automation in the cloud help mitigate security misconfigurations. Those same capabilities can help organizations continuously comply with security standards, whether they are regulated, industry, or internal standards. I've already discussed how APIs and automation can ensure that systems are properly configured and continuously monitored for configuration changes. However, there's one important nuance to executing this strategy to be aware of.

Many security teams and compliance teams that contemplate using the cloud for the first time wonder how they can prove that they are complying to standards, that is, when they don't own the datacenters their infrastructures are running in and subsequently can't get their auditors access to these facilities. Regardless of who owns the datacenters, many organizations still must prove to their auditors and regulators that they are complying with required standards.

In most cases, this is another advantage of leveraging hyperscale CSPs. AWS, Google, and Microsoft all have numerous certifications and attestations across their cloud services. For example, ISO 27001 is table stakes for any CSP today – they all must have this certification to satisfy requirements for their enterprise customers. There are two certifications that are most valuable to many CISOs.

The first is the American Institute of CPAs' **System and Organization Controls (SOC)**, in particular the SOC2 Type II certification (AICPA, n.d.). There are at least a couple of things that make this certification valuable to CISOs, Security teams, and Compliance teams. First, the scope of controls that are audited in a SOC2 Type II typically answer most of the questions that enterprises have about security. Second, this isn't a "point in time" snapshot of control settings or architectural design; it takes organizations that pursue the SOC2 Type II 6 months of continuous audit to achieve it. The steps that organizations take to get ready for this type of audit can dramatically improve their security posture. Then, to achieve this certification and maintain it over time and continuously prove that services are being operated the way they are described can be a big challenge. Many enterprises would never even attempt to get this certification because it's hard to do and can be expensive. However, the hyperscale CSPs achieve and maintain this certification across many of their services in order to keep their security standards among the highest in the industry.

CSPs will typically share their SOC2 Type II audit reports with their customers. For Security teams and Compliance teams, it is worth downloading these reports and reviewing them to ensure the solution(s) they are evaluating meet or exceed their standards. Questions not answered by the SOC2 Type II audit report can be directed to the CSPs themselves, who are typically happy to answer them.

Another attestation that many CISOs and security teams find valuable is the **Cloud Computing Compliance Controls Catalog (C5)**, designed by the **Federal Office for Information Security (BSI)**, a federal government office in Germany (The BSI, 2018). The C5 is an in-depth security assurance attestation. It has criteria for many domains, including policies, personnel, physical security, identity and access management, encryption, and others. Again, the scope and complexity of this attestation can make it a challenge to achieve and maintain. Like the SOC2 Type II, for CISOs, this attestation contains answers to many of the questions they have about CSPs' security control sets.

SOC2 Type II and the C5 are like treasure troves of security information for CISOs, Security teams, Compliance teams, and auditors. CSPs typically combine these with numerous other certifications and attestations to help their customers prove they are meeting their compliance requirements. However, customers of CSPs have a role to play in this as well. Remember that CSPs are different from **Managed Service Providers (MSPs)**. CSPs offer self-service clouds. Their customers and **Independent Software Vendors (ISVs)** can build on top of those clouds to create solutions. However, the CSPs' certifications' and attestations' scopes do not cover the portion of solutions that are architected and operated by their customers; unlike MSPs, CSPs typically don't have the visibility, or the access, required to do this.

This arrangement means that CSPs and their customers both bear responsibility for their respective portions of the solutions they architect and operate. Google, Microsoft, and AWS all refer to this arrangement as a shared responsibility. Both CSPs and their customers provide the appropriate certifications and attestations to prove that their respective portions of their solutions meet the requirements of the standards they are bound to. This arrangement typically saves CSPs' customers time and money. This is because the portion of their solutions that they must attest to can be dramatically reduced in almost all cases. For example, since CSPs' customers don't own the datacenters that their infrastructures are running in, they have essentially delegated the responsibility to audit and certify those datacenters to their CSPs. Put another way, they no longer have to deal with the complexity and cost of physical datacenters, as the CSPs do this for them. It's a win for CSPs' customers because they can meet or exceed the security standards they are responsible for while reducing the amount of effort and cost to them.

Information on the compliance programs that CSPs operate on can be found on their respective websites, but the auditors' reports themselves are typically reserved for CSPs' customers; here are the locations that contain compliance program information for AWS, Google, and Microsoft:

- AWS: `https://aws.amazon.com/compliance/programs/`

- Goggle: `https://cloud.google.com/security/compliance/`
- Microsoft: `https://www.microsoft.com/en-us/trust-center/compliance/compliance-overview`

The combination of APIs, automation, and the certifications and attestations provided by CSPs can help organizations that want to pursue Compliance as a Cybersecurity Strategy. For organizations that want to extend this strategy to fully address the Cybersecurity Fundamentals, the cloud typically makes this easier than in on-premises IT environments. This is because of the APIs and automation capabilities we have discussed. Everything is code. Let's look at one more strategy that we examined in *Chapter 9*, *Cybersecurity Strategies*, and see how it can be implemented in the cloud.

Using the Attack-Centric Strategy in the cloud

The best scoring of all the strategies that we examined was the Attack-Centric Strategy. In *Chapter 10*, *Strategy Implementation*, we did a deep dive into this strategy and illustrated one way it could be implemented. In *Chapter 11*, *Measuring Performance and Effectiveness*, we examined one way the efficacy of this strategy can be measured. However, can this strategy be implemented in the cloud?

The short answer to this question is, yes, it can be implemented in the cloud. In fact, I co-authored a whitepaper that will help security teams implement an Intrusion Kill Chain model in AWS. You can read more about this approach and get access to the paper at this URL: `https://aws.amazon.com/blogs/security/whitepaper-available-classic-intrusion-analysis-frameworks-for-aws-environments/`.

In *Chapter 10*, *Strategy Implementation*, we discussed how the MITRE ATT&CK® framework can complement the Intrusion Kill Chain model, which we examined in depth. Both of these frameworks can be used in the cloud. To do this, you'll likely want to scope your efforts to developing a Courses of Action Matrix (Hutchins, E.M., Cloppert, M.J., Amin, R.M., n.d.) like we did in *Chapter 10*, for the solution you are implementing in the cloud. Put another way, since this can be a time-intensive exercise, as you saw, you don't need to build a Courses of Action Matrix for every cloud service that a CSP offers, only the ones you plan to use. If you plan to leverage AWS, this is already done for you in the aforementioned whitepaper that I co-authored. An entire Courses of Action Matrix is already built for you that includes every AWS security service and feature (that was available when we wrote the paper). The appendix in that paper provides 70 pages of service and feature mappings to phases of a modified Intrusion Kill Chain framework. Developing this appendix was months of work for a team of us at AWS and provides security teams with a huge head start. If you are planning to use Google Cloud or Microsoft's cloud services, they might have similar content available, or you'll have to develop your own Courses of Action Matrix.

Building a Courses of Action Matrix for solutions developed for IaaS environments is, in some respects, similar to performing this mapping for on-premises IT environments. This is because much of the hardware and software can be the same or similar. For example, the operating system mitigations identified for a solution running on Linux or Windows will be very similar, regardless of whether that operating system is running in the cloud or on-premises. However, as we discussed earlier, cloud-native controls and third-party solutions can also be layered into the environment, in addition to these operating system mitigations, to implement a set of controls that will make it much harder for attackers to be successful. For example, the same services that help us detect configuration changes will help us detect indicators of compromise in the cloud, in near real time. The same identity and access management capabilities we discussed will make it much harder for attackers to use stolen credentials to move laterally. The techniques we talked about to help keep systems up to date will make it harder for attackers to find and exploit unpatched vulnerabilities.

Note that although the Intrusion Kill Chain approach lends itself well to solutions that are built in IaaS environments, this approach is less helpful for solutions that are built using cloud services higher up the stack, like managed services. In these cases, CSPs are responsible for securing the underlying IT environment, typically leaving less direct access and less direct control of the under-lying IT infrastructure to their customers' security teams. This doesn't mean security teams don't have the visibility and control they require – it's just the opposite, as we've discussed. However, the types of mitigating controls will likely be different than traditional solutions developed for on-premises or IaaS environments.

The controls should be different because some of the threats and risks are certainly different. Subsequently, the Intrusion Kill Chain might not be the best scoring approach for organizations in the cloud, depending on the types of services they use. As enterprises consume more and more services that blur the boundaries between IaaS, PaaS, SaaS, FaaS, IDaaS, and other models, the less relevant the Intrusion Kill Chain approach becomes.

This isn't a bad thing – it's just more change to embrace. Remember, the role of CISOs and security teams isn't to ensure the status quo, it's to protect their organizations' data, even when these organizations decide it's time to evolve the technologies and processes they use in order to stay competitive and/or relevant. The cloud offers the opportunity to modernize not only technolo-gies and processes, but also the cybersecurity strategies that can be employed. Let's explore this concept a little further and look at a more modern approach to cybersecurity that I mentioned in *Chapter 9, Cybersecurity Strategies*, called **DevOps**.

DevOps — A modern approach to security in the cloud

For the lack of a better name, let's simply call this approach DevOps. I've also heard some security professionals refer to it as "immutable short-lived infrastructure" or simply as "re-paving." This strategy represents a more modern approach compared to the other cybersecurity strategies that we've examined. It recognizes that development and IT operations disciplines have been joining forces, partly because, together, these roles are aptly positioned to take advantage of the power of APIs and automation. Because everything is code in the cloud, including infrastructure, teams that understand both development and IT infrastructure operations can take full advantage of all the cloud has to offer. Let's look at some of the ways that a DevOps-driven security strategy can help security teams protect, detect, and respond to modern threats in cloud-based environments.

Remember back to *Chapter 4, The Evolution of Malware*, where I described why the Windows ecosystem has so much more malware than the Apple iOS ecosystem. The key, it would seem, is how software has traditionally been distributed in these ecosystems. Microsoft allowed software developed by anyone to be freely installed by its customers on their Windows-based systems.

Apple, on the other hand, provides a single source for all applications destined for iOS-based devices, their App Store. While Windows customers were left to make their own decisions about the trustworthiness of the software they wanted to run, Apple imposed a security standard for all ISVs to meet before their apps could be distributed to iOS-based devices. This difference in software distribution methods, at least partially, explains why the Apple iOS ecosystem has maintained such a low prevalence of malware.

Let's take this lesson and apply it to our approach to security in the cloud. Leveraging continuous testing, **Continuous Integration (CI)**, and Continuous Delivery or **Continuous Deployment (CD)** can help minimize how much questionable software makes it into the cloud-based environments that CSPs' customers build and operate. In their CI/CD pipelines, they can impose automated (and manual) security and compliance checks. These ensure that any software or infrastructure that gets deployed into production environments through these pipelines meets their organizations' security and compliance requirements.

To do this, each step of the CI/CD pipeline will have the appropriate security and compliance checks automated in it. For example, a DevOps team could develop or procure automation that looks for issues contained in the OWASP Top 10 (OWASP, 2022). Another common example is the requirement to perform static code analysis and/or a specific set of functional security tests. Infrastructure will have to meet the control setting requirements defined by each organization's compliance team, and this will be verified as items go through the pipeline.

Implementing such tests is typically done in code and automation, so the number and types of checks that can be conducted are almost unlimited. Of course, because this can be effective and fun, once some DevOps teams start developing these checks, they'll spend more time on the development of their CI/CD pipelines than they will on applications and infrastructure.

If an application or infrastructure item does not pass one of these checks, the pipeline will stop, the appropriate staff can be alerted, the application or infrastructure will not progress through the rest of the pipeline, and it will not be introduced into the production environment as planned. The deficiency in the application or infrastructure item will have to be addressed in order to pass the check that failed and then go through the entire pipeline again.

This way, only items that pass every security and compliance check in the pipeline will make it into production. This means Security and Compliance teams can have high confidence that everything being introduced into their production environment meets all their security and compliance requirements and that they will not introduce more risks into that environment. To accomplish this, everything must go through a CI/CD pipeline. Put another way, the only way to get an application or infrastructure item into production is through a CI/CD pipeline. For the best chance of success, organizations need to have the discipline, as well as the governance mechanisms, to enforce this requirement. Managing multiple CI/CD pipelines is a predictable and common outcome, especially for large, distributed organizations. The risk for some organizations is that the number of CI/CD pipelines proliferates to levels that begin to compromise the high security and compliance standards that the initial pipelines imposed; too many pipelines can turn into a governance issue.

Also, note that attackers have clued into the fact that more and more organizations are using DevOps and CI/CD pipelines. This makes the CI/CD pipelines themselves a potential target for attackers. Understanding the stack of technologies and automations that your organization uses for its pipelines and taking steps to protect them is important. For some organizations, CI/CD pipelines can become high value assets and warrant special attention, as I discussed in *Chapter 8, Ingredients for a Successful Cybersecurity Strategy*.

Now that security and compliance teams have confidence in their deployments, how do they keep those environments in that pristine condition over time? They can use the services and automation we discussed earlier in this chapter to monitor for configuration changes. When configurations change, they can use automation to bring them back into compliance or impose deeper investigations into how and why they changed.

As we discussed earlier, there is a range of options for vulnerability management in the cloud. Continuing to use the technologies and processes that your organization has used for years in its on-premises environment is likely one possible option.

However, using automation, like the Auto Scaling example I provided earlier, has the potential to simplify and accelerate vulnerability management. Another option is for organizations to evolve from managing servers and applications themselves, to using cloud services higher up the stack and leaving infrastructure patching to the CSPs. Of course, a combination of all of these approaches is also permissible. However, if you are going to modernize processes, technologies, and your strategy, I strongly recommend that you get out of the vulnerability management game as much as you can. After all, the only way to win that game is not to play it. Patch a relatively small number of images, not hundreds or thousands of running VMs, and use managed services where possible to delegate vulnerability management to the CSPs.

One of the reasons that Attack-Centric strategies gained such popularity in the industry is that they can make it hard for "advanced" threat actors to be successful – the so-called **Advanced Persistent Threat** (**APT**). However, this is where the power of APIs and high levels of automation can also be helpful. For example, when organizations thoughtfully shut down subsets of servers running in the cloud every few hours and replace them with new ones that meet all requirements, it can make it harder for attackers to get and maintain a foothold in that environment. Short-lived, relatively immutable systems can leave very little oxygen for attackers to use, unlike systems that remain running for months or years.

The detection capabilities in the cloud are superior to those found in most on-premises environments. Remember the power of APIs and automation in the cloud provides visibility and control that few on-premises environments can achieve. The cloud can make it easy to log API calls, network traffic, authentication and authorization operations, encryption and decryption key operations, and so on. However, one challenge most security teams share, whether they use the cloud or not, is that the vast amount of data in all these logs make it nearly impossible for humans to review it and use it in a timely way. This is where the cloud can also help. **Artificial Intelligence** (**AI**) and **Machine Learning** (**ML**) services can be used to review all of these logs and API activity, instead of security team members, and identify things that really warrant human attention. This is possible because AI/ML services can scale as large as needed to churn through enormous log datasets far, far faster than humans can. As they do this, these services, with the help of automation, can detect and respond to all sorts of attacks, including DDoS, malware, exploitation of vulnerabilities, insider threat, and many more.

Let me summarize the characteristics of this strategy I called DevOps, sometimes referred to as "immutable short-lived infrastructure," and sometimes simply referred to as "repaving":

- Automation is used to provision and configure systems and other infrastructure. Everything that gets released into production cloud accounts/environments must go through a CI/CD pipeline.

- The CI/CD pipeline can employ automated and manual security and compliance checks and tests to ensure everything that makes it into production meets security and compliance standards. If something doesn't meet standards, the pipeline stops, and the deficiencies are remediated.

- Systems are designed to be immutable—that is, designed not to change while running in production. Changes to immutable systems running in production are typically an indicator of compromise. This makes threat detection easier and faster.

- All changes are made on the image(s) that running instances are based on. This includes scanning for and installing security updates. The images are scanned and patched, not the running instances. This dramatically reduces the complexity and time it takes to manage vulnerabilities on large numbers of systems.

- To minimize insider threat opportunities, administrators have no direct approach to cybersecurity access to systems running in production. SSH, RDP, and other remote access software are prohibited from running on production systems. Administrators are limited to running tested and pre-approved scripts on systems running in production, except during break-glass scenarios that are monitored and audited. MFA is used to authenticate administrators to the cloud where they can initiate execution of these scripts.

- Automation is used to thoughtfully shut down production systems every few hours in a way that will not impact the availability of applications. Auto Scaling or other automation will restart systems based on the fully patched image(s) as they are needed. This reduces and limits the amount of time that compromised systems can be used by attackers in the production environment.

- Managed services are used to enhance detection and response capabilities instead of deploying more systems to host security functions. This provides superior detection and response capabilities and does not increase the attack surface or the number of systems to manage.

- Make use of ubiquitous encryption capabilities to protect data in the cloud and protect keys. I'll discuss this later in this chapter.

- Note that although I've focused on using virtual machines in this strategy description, an increasing number of organizations leverage containers and container orchestration software in very similar ways to achieve better security.

Finally, if all these capabilities failed to protect, detect, and respond to attackers, DevOps and the cloud can make recovering production environments much easier than in typical on-premises environments. Since everything is code, rebuilding environments in the cloud can be relatively easy if some planning and thoughtful preparation has been done. Let's take a quick look at some **Disaster Recovery (DR)** capabilities in the cloud.

Disaster Recovery in the cloud

As we discussed in *Chapter 4, The Evolution of Malware*, targeted attacks that involve extortion (also called ransomware attacks) are commonplace today. Ransomware is a man-made disaster. Subsequently, most of the CISOs and security teams I have talked to in the last few years are much more interested in DR than ever before. In addition to the specter of ransomware, fear of an increased frequency of extreme weather events, due to climate change, is also driving interest in DR.

DR is "the process of providing fast, reliable recovery of IT systems to minimize downtime and data loss" (Rains, 2022). The traditional approach to DR has led many organizations to build physical datacenters with specific distances between them. If one datacenter is impacted by a weather event, power disruption, or man-made disaster, the organization plans to resume IT operations in another datacenter. The distance between datacenters is arbitrary in that there is no industry standard – each organization makes their own calculations based on the types of risks they are trying to mitigate. But generally, the larger the distance between the datacenters, the less likely a single weather event, earthquake, fire, or power disruption will impact them.

In the cloud, as I mentioned earlier, Regions and Availability Zones are used to design highly available and resilient cloud infrastructures. The distance between datacenters in an Availability Zone can be large enough to mitigate localized power outages and large-scale weather events. For organizations that want even more assurance, they can use multiple Regions and get the advantages of using even more Availability Zones that have greater distances between them. For example, an organization could use a cloud region located on the West coast of the U.S. and plan to use a Region on the East coast for DR. The chances of a single event disrupting operations on both sides of the country at the same time are very low. Many large multi-national firms use cloud Regions in different countries for various purposes, including for DR purposes.

For example, they leverage a cloud Region on the East coast of the U.S. and another Region in Ireland for DR purposes. Since there are so many Regions and Available Zones available, there are many different options for DR purposes. However, remember that the speed of light is a constant. The further the distance between the datacenters, the more network latency will become a limiting factor.

When I worked at AWS, I wrote a blog post about how they think about distances between their datacenters and Availability Zones for DR purposes. If you are interested in reading it, that blog post is titled "The Goldilocks zone for disaster recovery, business continuity planning, and disaster preparedness." It is available at this URL: `https://aws.amazon.com/blogs/publicsector/goldilocks-zone-disaster-recovery-business-continuity-planning-disaster-preparedness/`.

The cloud offers organizations the ability to leverage all the classic DR architectures, including backup and restore, Pilot Light, Warm Stand-by, and Multi-Site Active/Active. For example, implementing a Pilot Light design is relatively easy because everything is code. Duplicating your production cloud environment, when it's needed, is as simple as using pre-developed and pre-tested code and automation to reprovision and configure all the existing cloud infrastructure in a different Availability Zone or Region. Much of it can be sitting in a cloud account provisioned, but not in a running state. Typically, customers won't pay for this infrastructure until it is in a running state. Once the infrastructure is up and running as expected, perhaps as quickly as a few minutes (depending on complexity), then the appropriate DNS records are changed to point to the new infrastructure. This is a bit of an oversimplification, but it is wildly less complicated and expensive than procuring real estate for datacenters, conducting construction projects to build datacenters, procuring the appropriate power and backup power infrastructures, procuring, implementing and operating all the IT infrastructure, paying real estate taxes every year, etc.

Rest assured, if you want to implement DR as part of a Protect and Recover strategy, an Attack-Centric strategy, a DevOps strategy, or other strategies in the cloud, you have a lot of flexibility and options at your disposal because of the power of APIs and automation in the cloud. The key to choosing which DR architectures to use should be based on the **recovery point objectives (RPOs)** and **recovery time objectives (RTOs)** for each application in scope for your DR plans. Define these, and then design DR architectures that can achieve them for you.

AWS published a good blog post series that can provide more insights called "Disaster Recovery (DR) Architecture on AWS":

- Part 1: https://aws.amazon.com/blogs/architecture/disaster-recovery-dr-architecture-on-aws-part-i-strategies-for-recovery-in-the-cloud/
- Part 2: https://aws.amazon.com/blogs/architecture/disaster-recovery-dr-architecture-on-aws-part-ii-backup-and-restore-with-rapid-recovery/
- Part 3: https://aws.amazon.com/blogs/architecture/disaster-recovery-dr-architecture-on-aws-part-iii-pilot-light-and-warm-standby/
- Part 4: https://aws.amazon.com/blogs/architecture/disaster-recovery-dr-architecture-on-aws-part-iv-multi-site-active-active/

This concludes this section on cybersecurity strategies in the cloud. However, before we come to the end of this chapter and this book, I do want to highlight another important set of capabilities that the cloud provides: encryption and key management.

Encryption and key management

In my experience, most conversations about security in the cloud conclude by discussing encryption and key management. No matter what topics a conversation starts with, such as vulnerabilities, exploits, malware, internet-based threats, or government access to data, they conclude by discussing encryption and key management. This is because encryption is recognized and proven to be a powerful data protection control that helps provide confidentiality and integrity for data whether it's in the cloud, hybrid environments, or on-premises.

No matter which cybersecurity strategy or combination of strategies organizations pursue, when the rubber hits the road, protecting the data is the objective. That's what can be so distracting about the cybersecurity strategies we examined that are proxies for data protection. Security teams get so focused on protecting endpoints or applications that they can lose sight that the underlying objective is to protect data. The proxies I mentioned are important and must be effectively managed, but don't forget about the data!

The CSPs all know this and offer their customers rich sets of encryption and key management capabilities. Their goal is to protect data when it is in transit and at rest. TLS (currently version 1.3) is the de facto internet standard for protecting data in transit. Subsequently, CSPs support TLS, in addition to providing other mechanisms for protecting data in-transit, like VPN connections or directly connecting their cloud infrastructures to their customers' networks, as examples.

As I discussed in *Chapter 7, Government Access to Data*, CSPs offer a range of encryption options to protect data at rest, enabling their customers to encrypt data before they put it in the cloud (in some scenarios) and/or after they put it in the cloud. Recall the difference between client-side encryption and server-side encryption. The current encryption standard that CSPs offer for encrypting data at rest is the **Advanced Encryption Standard (AES)**, typically using 128-bit or 256-bit key lengths.

If an attacker had access to data (access is typically authenticated and authorized) protected by AES256, breaking this type of encryption using brute-force techniques and lots of conventional computing power would likely take far, far more time than the value lifetime of the data.

An important nuance for Security teams to understand is exactly what is being encrypted and which risks that type of encryption mitigates. For example, if the underlying storage media is encrypted, but the data being written to the media is not encrypted prior to being written, then the risks being mitigated are the loss or theft of the storage media. Encrypted storage media helps mitigate attacks where attackers have physical access to the storage media. If someone gets physical access to the encrypted storage media but doesn't possess the keys to mount and decrypt it, the data written on it is protected from unauthorized access. However, if attackers seek to access the data logically instead of physically, over a network, for example, then storage-level encryption will likely not mitigate this risk because the data is decrypted as it is accessed from the network.

It's important to understand the specific risk that needs to be mitigated and the specific mitigations for that particular risk, in order to have confidence that the risk has truly been mitigated. If the desire is to prevent unauthorized access to data at rest, over a network, then encrypting the data itself, instead of just the storage media, will be a more effective mitigation. This might sound obvious, but this is a common mistake Security teams make during application security assessments.

In addition to offering data encryption options, CSPs are really providing authenticated and authorized data encryption. That is, each encryption operation API call is authenticated and must be authorized; encryption and decryption operations will not occur without being authenticated and authorized first. Using Identity and Access services this way provides Security teams with a lot of flexibility. For example, one person or group of people can be authorized to encrypt data, but not authorized to decrypt it. Another group can be given permissions to decrypt data, but not to do both encryption and decryption operations. Authenticated and authorized encryption enables a separation of duties that can be helpful in many scenarios.

For many organizations, one of the most challenging parts of encryption can be key management. The stakes are high because if an organization's keys are damaged, lost, or stolen, it could have a catastrophic impact on them. Generally speaking, CSPs want to make key management easy and safe for their customers. Google offers Cloud Key Management Service (Google, 2020), Microsoft offers Azure Key Vault (Microsoft Corporation, 2020), and AWS provides the AWS Key Management Service (AWS, 2020). Of course, there are third-party vendors that also offer encryption and key management services, such as Thales, Equinix, and others.

The CSPs' key management services can offer an interesting advantage in that they can be integrated into their other cloud services. This means that some cloud services can perform encryption and decryption on behalf of users. The data protection advantage here is that the data can be protected by AES encryption until it's in the physical memory of the servers running the service that is going to process it. Once processing completes, the service can re-encrypt the data again before moving it into storage or other services for more processing. The keys used for encryption and decryption can be protected in transit between the key management services and the services that use them. This means that unencrypted data only sees the light of day in highly controlled environments that are authorized by the data owner. This can help maximize the number of places and the time that the data is protected with encryption. CSPs' key management services tend to be designed for low latency and high availability in order to process billions of requests.

Some organizations want a separation of duties between the vendor they use for compute and storage and the vendors that provide key management services. Third-party vendors that offer key management services can play this role, or CSPs' customers themselves can operate and maintain their own key management infrastructures. The organizations that choose this option should be comfortable managing their own key management infrastructure or allowing a third party to do it for them. However, managing **Hardware Security Modules (HSMs)** and **Public Key Infrastructures (PKIs)** is notoriously difficult. This makes using CSPs' key management services a popular option.

For organizations that need to keep their keys on-premises but still want to get the benefits of the cloud, client-side encryption is a potential solution. Using client-side encryption means that the data owner encrypts the data before they put it into a cloud service. For example, the data owner has their own on-premises key management infrastructure. Prior to putting data into a cloud storage service, they generate a key on-premises and then use an application also running on-premises to encrypt the data using this key. Then, they authenticate and securely transfer the encrypted data to the cloud storage service. In this scenario, their CSP never had access to their unencrypted data or the encryption key, as neither left the on-premises IT environment.

To decrypt this data, the data owner authenticates to the cloud storage service, securely downloads the encrypted data, and uses their on-premises application and on-premises key to decrypt the data. Again, neither the unencrypted data nor the encryption key was ever shared with the CSP.

Client-side encryption isn't limited to storage scenarios; it can be used with other services, like databases, for example. In this scenario, client-side encryption is used to encrypt records or individual fields as they are written to a database service running in the cloud. To do this, an encryption key is retrieved from the on-premises key management system and temporarily used for encryption operations by the application performing the encryption. Once the record is encrypted as it's written to the database, the encryption key can be removed from the memory of the application that performed the encryption operation, thus reducing the time the key is resident on a system outside of the on-premises key management system. The application performing encryption and decryption operations on the database records can run on-premises or in the cloud. Since the CSP's customer has full control of the keys, the CSP cannot get access to the keys unless the customer grants them access. Indexes and database keys are left unencrypted so that indexing and searching the database can still be performed. For this reason, it's important not to put sensitive data into these fields. To decrypt the data, the appropriate records are retrieved and decrypted after the key is provided from the on-premises key management system. After the decryption operation, the key can once again be removed from the memory of the application performing the decryption operation.

There are many different ways to perform client-side encryption and key management. However, this method can be more complicated and expensive to implement than simply using the integrated encryption and key management services that CSPs offer. Some organizations that start off using client-side encryption with keys kept on-premises, over time, conclude that using CSPs' key management services mitigate the risks they are most concerned about and help to simplify their applications. After all, encryption and decryption operations in the cloud are performed using API calls that are authenticated, authorized, monitored, and potentially controlled using automation, as we discussed earlier.

The CSPs want to provide their customers with the confidentiality and integrity that client-side encryption provides, without the extra complexity and costs. After all, moving key material between on-premises IT environments and cloud environments also has risks associated with it and doesn't improve application performance, especially at scale. The CSPs offer sophisticated alternatives to client-side encryption that can also help mitigate insider threats in many scenarios.

The list below contains some examples:

- **The AWS Nitro System**: `https://aws.amazon.com/ec2/nitro/`
- **AWS Nitro Enclaves**: `https://aws.amazon.com/ec2/nitro/nitro-enclaves/`
- **AWS Graviton2 processors feature always-on 256-bit DRAM encryption**: `https://docs.aws.amazon.com/AWSEC2/latest/UserGuide/data-protection.html`
- **Azure encryption overview**: `https://learn.microsoft.com/en-us/azure/security/fundamentals/encryption-overview`
- **Azure Confidential Computing**: `https://azure.microsoft.com/en-us/solutions/confidential-compute/#overview`
- **Google Cloud Data Encryption**: `https://cloud.google.com/security/encryption`
- **Google Confidential Computing**: `https://cloud.google.com/blog/products/identity-security/introducing-google-cloud-confidential-computing-with-confidential-vms`

Combining properly implemented encryption and effective key management, along with the power of APIs and automation in the cloud, helps protect data in ways that would be more complex to duplicate in on-premises IT environments. Encryption and key management help to protect data from many of the threats we discussed throughout this book; they are powerful data protection controls that should be part of whichever cybersecurity strategies your organization pursues.

Conclusion

For organizations that haven't adopted the cloud yet, or won't in favor of their on-premises IT environments, a quote comes to my mind:

> *The future is already here – it's just not evenly distributed."*
>
> — *(Gibson, 2003)*

The opportunity to leverage the power of APIs and cloud automation on a scale not imagined before is waiting for every organization. Not only do these game changers make provisioning, configuring, operating, and deprovisioning applications and IT infrastructure much easier, but they provide security and compliance professionals the visibility and control they likely haven't had in the past. I encourage CISOs and security teams to embrace the cloud as a way to do more with less and offset the industry's perpetual cybersecurity talent shortage.

Summary

This chapter introduced some of the security and compliance benefits of cloud computing. I focused my discussion on the world's most popular CSPs' basic capabilities, that is, of Amazon Web Services, Google, and Microsoft.

The physical infrastructure model that hyperscale CSPs have roughly coalesced around is based on the concept of Regions and Availability Zones. This concept is that an Availability Zone is a cluster of datacenters and a Region is a cluster of Availability Zones. There are meaningful differences in the size and scope of CSPs' infrastructures and how they leverage components of this model. Although the terms IaaS, PaaS, and SaaS are still in widespread use today, they are slowly becoming obsolete. Newer services that solve specific problems can blur the lines between IaaS, PaaS, and SaaS service models, making them less important.

CSPs are different from traditional **Managed Service Providers (MSPs)** in some key ways. It is important that executives recognize this when they first contemplate using the cloud in order to avoid confusion that will slow them down. MSPs that build on top of CSPs' offerings continue to play important roles for their customers and the industry.

In this chapter, I discussed two security and compliance game changers that the cloud provides:

- The power of **Application Programming Interfaces (APIs)**
- The advantages of automation

Every interaction with the cloud via administration consoles, CLIs, and applications happens using APIs. APIs provide the perfect choke point for visibility and control. If organizations can monitor their API calls and take action based on what's happening, they will have greater visibility and control. To take full advantage of the power of APIs, the cloud offers high levels of automation. In addition to running CLI commands, you can automate complex workflows using scripts, templates, applications, and cloud services. Automation in the cloud can help address the Cybersecurity Fundamentals in ways that are potentially more efficient than in traditional IT environments.

The cloud is flexible enough to support almost any of the cybersecurity strategies that we discussed in *Chapter 9, Cybersecurity Strategies*. DevOps offers a more modern approach compared to the other cybersecurity strategies that we examined. Because everything is code in the cloud, including infrastructure, teams that understand both development and IT infrastructure operations can take full advantage of all the cloud has to offer.

Continuous Integration (**CI**), Continuous Delivery, and **Continuous Deployment** (**CD**) pipelines can have the appropriate security and compliance checks automated in them; for example, the OWASP Top 10 (OWASP, 2020).

I hope you found this second edition of my book helpful. In this book, I tried to cover the topics that CISOs and security teams wanted to discuss with me most often, in my role as a cybersecurity advisor at two of the world's leading technology companies. I tried to pack this book with data, useful frameworks, and insights that will potentially help CISOs, aspiring CISOs, and other cybersecurity professionals better understand some key aspects of cybersecurity and help them make better decisions. Of course, the threat landscape will continue to evolve, and I hope some of what I have written here will help organizations as they try to navigate it.

Bon voyage!

References

- AICPA. (n.d.). *SOC 2® - SOC for Service Organizations: Trust Services Criteria*. Retrieved from AICPA: `https://www.aicpa.org/interestareas/frc/assuranceadvisoryservices/aicpasoc2report.html`

- Amazon Web Services. (March 2020). *Cloud Computing with AWS*. Retrieved from AWS: `https://aws.amazon.com/what-is-aws`

- Ansible. (April 2020). *Red Hat Ansible*. Retrieved from Red Hat Ansible: `https://www.ansible.com/`

- AWS. (October 20, 2016). *Fleet Management Made Easy with Auto Scaling*. Retrieved from AWS Compute Blog: `https://aws.amazon.com/blogs/compute/fleet-management-made-easy-with-auto-scaling/`

- AWS. (April 2020). *Amazon Elastic Compute Cloud API Reference*. Retrieved from AWS: `https://docs.aws.amazon.com/AWSEC2/latest/APIReference/API_RunInstances.html`

- AWS. (April 2020). *AWS CloudFormation*. Retrieved from AWS: `https://aws.amazon.com/cloudformation/`

- AWS. (April 2020). *AWS CloudTrail*. Retrieved from AWS: `https://aws.amazon.com/cloudtrail/`

- AWS. (April 2020). *AWS Key Management Service (KMS)*. Retrieved from AWS: `https://aws.amazon.com/kms/`

- AWS. (April 2020). *AWS Secrets Manager*. Retrieved from AWS: `https://aws.amazon.com/secrets-manager/`

- AWS. (April 2020). *Logging AWS Systems Manager API calls with AWS CloudTrail*. Retrieved from AWS: https://docs.aws.amazon.com/systems-manager/latest/userguide/monitoring-cloudtrail-logs.html

- AWS. (April 2020). *Remotely Run Commands on an EC2 Instance*. Retrieved from AWS: https://aws.amazon.com/getting-started/hands-on/remotely-run-commands-ec2-instance-systems-manager/

- AWS. (April 2020). *Using the AWS CLI*. Retrieved from AWS: https://docs.aws.amazon.com/cli/latest/userguide/cli-chapusing.html

- Chef. (April 2020). *Chef*. Retrieved from Chef: https://www.chef.io/products/chef-infra/

- Hutchins, E.M., Cloppert, M.J., Amin, R.M. (n.d.). *Intelligence-Driven Computer Network Defense Informed by Analysis of Adversary Campaigns and Intrusion Kill Chains*. Retrieved from Lockheed Martin: https://lockheedmartin.com/content/dam/lockheed-martin/rms/documents/cyber/LM-White-Paper-Intel-Driven-Defense.pdf

- Gibson, W. (December 4, 2003). Books of the Year. *The Economist*.

- Google. (April 2020). *Cloud Audit Logs*. Retrieved from Google Cloud: https://cloud.google.com/logging/docs/audit

- Google. (April 2020). *Cloud Key Management Service*. Retrieved from Google Cloud: https://cloud.google.com/kms/

- Google. (April 2020). *Cloud Composer*. Retrieved from Google Cloud: https://cloud.google.com/composer

- Google. (January 22, 2020). *Introducing Google Cloud's Secret Manager*. Retrieved from Google Cloud Blog: https://cloud.google.com/blog/products/identity-security/introducing-google-clouds-secret-manager

- Google. (n.d.). *gcloud compute instance create*. Retrieved from Google: https://cloud.google.com/sdk/gcloud/reference/compute/instances/create

- Hashicorp. (April 2020). *Terraform*. Retrieved from Terraform by Hashicorp: https://www.terraform.io/

- Microsoft Corporation. (October 18, 2018). *An introduction to Azure Automation*. Retrieved from Microsoft Azure: https://docs.microsoft.com/en-us/azure/automation/automation-intro

- Microsoft Corporation. (October 7, 2019). *Azure Monitor overview*. Retrieved from Microsoft Azure: https://docs.microsoft.com/en-us/azure/azure-monitor/overview

- Microsoft Corporation. (March 2020). *Azure Products.* Retrieved from Microsoft Azure: `https://azure.microsoft.com/en-us/services/`

- Microsoft Corporation. (April 2020). *Key Vault.* Retrieved from Microsoft Azure: `https://azure.microsoft.com/en-us/services/key-vault/`

- Microsoft Corporation. (April 2020). *Manage secrets in your server apps with Azure Key Vault.* Retrieved from Microsoft Learn: `https://docs.microsoft.com/en-us/learn/modules/manage-secrets-with-azure-key-vault/`

- Microsoft Corporation. (April 2020). *Virtual Machines - Start.* Retrieved from Microsoft Corporation: `https://docs.microsoft.com/en-us/rest/api/compute/virtualmachines/start`

- Microsoft Corporation. (November 4, 2022). *What is Azure AD Privileged Identity Management?* Retrieved from Microsoft Azure: `https://docs.microsoft.com/en-us/azure/active-directory/privileged-identity-management/pim-configure`

- MITRE. (October 9, 2019). *Cloud Matrix.* Retrieved from MITRE ATT&CK®: `https://attack.mitre.org/matrices/enterprise/cloud/`

- OWASP. (2022). *Top 10 Web Application Security Risks.* Retrieved from OWASP: `https://owasp.org/www-project-top-ten/`

- Puppet. (April 2020). *Puppet Enterprise.* Retrieved from Puppet: `https://puppet.com/products/puppet-enterprise/`

- The BSI. (January 25, 2018). *Cloud Computing Compliance Controls Catalogue.* Retrieved from Federal Office for Information Security: `https://www.bsi.bund.de/SharedDocs/Downloads/EN/BSI/Publications/CloudComputing/ComplianceControlsCatalogue-Cloud_Computing-C5.html`

- Rains, T. (January 31, 2022). *The Goldilocks zone for disaster recovery, business continuity planning, and disaster preparedness.* Retrieved from the AWS Public Sector Blog: `https://aws.amazon.com/blogs/publicsector/goldilocks-zone-disaster-recovery-business-continuity-planning-disaster-preparedness/`

Join our community on Discord

Join our community's Discord space for discussions with the author and other readers:

`https://packt.link/SecNet`

packt.com

Subscribe to our online digital library for full access to over 7,000 books and videos, as well as industry leading tools to help you plan your personal development and advance your career. For more information, please visit our website.

Why subscribe?

- Spend less time learning and more time coding with practical eBooks and Videos from over 4,000 industry professionals

- Improve your learning with Skill Plans built especially for you

- Get a free eBook or video every month

- Fully searchable for easy access to vital information

- Copy and paste, print, and bookmark content

At www.packt.com, you can also read a collection of free technical articles, sign up for a range of free newsletters, and receive exclusive discounts and offers on Packt books and eBooks.

Other Books You May Enjoy

If you enjoyed this book, you may be interested in these other books by Packt:

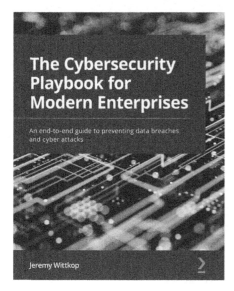

The Cybersecurity Playbook for Modern Enterprises

Jeremy Wittkop

ISBN: 9781803248639

- Understand the macro-implications of cyber attacks
- Identify malicious users and prevent harm to your organization
- Find out how ransomware attacks take place
- Work with emerging techniques for improving security profiles
- Explore identity and access management and endpoint security
- Get to grips with building advanced automation models
- Build effective training programs to protect against hacking techniques
- Discover best practices to help you and your family stay safe online

Cybersecurity and Privacy Law Handbook

Walter Rocchi

ISBN: 9781803242415

- Strengthen the cybersecurity posture throughout your organization
- Use both ISO27001 and NIST to make a better security framework
- Understand privacy laws such as GDPR, PCI CSS, HIPAA, and FTC
- Discover how to implement training to raise cybersecurity awareness
- Find out how to comply with cloud privacy regulations
- Examine the complex privacy laws in the US

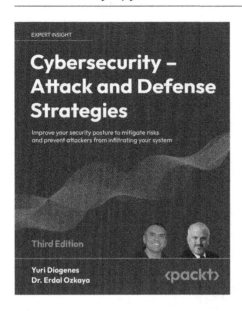

Cybersecurity – Attack and Defense Strategies, Third Edition

Yuri Diogenes

Dr. Erdal Ozkaya

ISBN: 9781803248776

- Learn to mitigate, recover from, and prevent future cybersecurity events
- Understand security hygiene and value of prioritizing protection of your workloads
- Explore physical and virtual network segmentation, cloud network visibility, and Zero Trust considerations
- Adopt new methods to gather cyber intelligence, identify risk, and demonstrate impact with Red/Blue Team strategies
- Explore legendary tools such as Nmap and Metasploit to supercharge your Red Team
- Discover identity security and how to perform policy enforcement
- Integrate threat detection systems into your SIEM solutions
- Discover the MITRE ATT&CK Framework and open-source tools to gather intelligence

Packt is searching for authors like you

If you're interested in becoming an author for Packt, please visit authors.packtpub.com and apply today. We have worked with thousands of developers and tech professionals, just like you, to help them share their insight with the global tech community. You can make a general application, apply for a specific hot topic that we are recruiting an author for, or submit your own idea.

Share your thoughts

Now you've finished *Cybersecurity Threats, Malware Trends, and Strategies, Second Edition*, we'd love to hear your thoughts! Scan the QR code below to go straight to the Amazon review page for this book and share your feedback or leave a review on the site that you purchased it from.

https://packt.link/r/1804613673

Your review is important to us and the tech community and will help us make sure we're delivering excellent quality content.

Index

H

I

Download a free PDF copy of this book

Thanks for purchasing this book!

Do you like to read on the go but are unable to carry your print books everywhere? Is your eBook purchase not compatible with the device of your choice?

Don't worry, now with every Packt book you get a DRM-free PDF version of that book at no cost.

Read anywhere, any place, on any device. Search, copy, and paste code from your favorite technical books directly into your application.

The perks don't stop there, you can get exclusive access to discounts, newsletters, and great free content in your inbox daily

Follow these simple steps to get the benefits:

1. Scan the QR code or visit the link below

https://packt.link/free-ebook/9781804613672

2. Submit your proof of purchase
3. That's it! We'll send your free PDF and other benefits to your email directly

Made in United States
North Haven, CT
25 May 2023

36964406R00320